Shirt-Sleeve Diplomat

for my old chief and new colleague.
Josephus Daniels—with my affectionate regards
Franklin D Roosevelt
march 31 st 1933

THE GOOD NEIGHBOR

"In the field of world policy I would dedicate this nation to the policy of the Good Neighbor—the neighbor who resolutely respects himself and, because he does so, respects the rights of others—the neighbor who respects his obligations and respects the sanctity of his agreements in and with a world of neighbors."—From the Inaugural Address (March 4, 1933) of Franklin D. Roosevelt.

JOSEPHUS DANIELS, AMBASSADOR TO MEXICO, 1933-1942

From a painting by Armando Drechsler, 1941, Mexico, D. F.

"I think I can surely say that the only yardstick by which I measured every problem which arose in the nearly nine years I was Ambassador to Mexico was, 'Will it promote the Good Neighbor goal?' "—Josephus Daniels upon leaving Mexico.

Shirt-Sleeve Diplomat

BY JOSEPHUS DANIELS

AMBASSADOR TO MEXICO, 1933-1942

"These things I saw and part of them I was."
—Virgil

CHAPEL HILL: *The University of North Carolina Press*

1947

IN LOVING MEMORY OF

MY WIFE, MY BEST COUNSELLOR

ADDIE WORTH BAGLEY DANIELS
1869–1943

"The truest and tenderest and purest wife ever man was blessed with. To have such a love is the one blessing, in comparison of which all earthly joy is of no value; and to think of her is to praise God."

FOREWORD

"But now, how trowe ye? Such a fantasye
Fell me to mynd, that ay me thought the bell
Said to me, 'Tell on, man quhat the befell.'"
—THE KINGIS QUAIR

IN THIS VOLUME, the fifth of my autobiography, there is compressed what "me befell" in the years 1933-1942, when I was Ambassador from the United States to the Republic of Mexico. I essay no history of the two countries during that period, in which the practice of the Roosevelt Good Neighbor doctrine cemented the friendliest relations on both sides of the Rio Grande. I tell of the things I saw and of the people with whom I was in contact in both countries, with chief emphasis upon what was happening around me in Mexico in relation to officials, fellow diplomats, the Mexican people, and the American colony. It is a newspaperman's story, interlarded with incidents of an official mission to Europe, yearly visits to the United States, and trips into nearly every State in the Mexican Republic. Inevitably it also includes something of the workings of the New Deal in the United States.

In those years I sent copies of my diary weekly to my sons at home, and wrote frequent letters in response to President Roosevelt's request: "Write me often of all that goes on with you in Mexico." From these letters, written when occurrences were fresh, I have drawn freely. In fact, if the volume has any merit, it is in revealing what I reported at the time, together with the recollection of events grave and gay photographed on my memory, and stories of the great and near-great in a changing era. The reader will be given pen pictures of men and things rather than formal history. I try to present a panorama, as seen from the American Embassy, with sidelights on stirring events in a country remarkable for its contrasts and for its charm.

It would lack verity and color if, along with notes about official doings and actions, there was lacking the social atmosphere of an old national capital, particularly as it touched the American Embassy and

vii

the families of the diplomats, drawn from every part of the world.

In the years of which I write, the American Embassy may truly be said to have kept open house. To the many Americans—visitors and members of the colony—welcomed to formal and informal gatherings, the word was, "This is your house. You have the right to be here." My wife and I truly felt ourselves tenants for the time being. We were happy when Mexicans and others who honored us said, "It has the air of old-time Southern hospitality without protocol formality." As its presiding genius, my wife, who to her charm and graciousness added love of people, both the humble and the great, irradiated welcome that all callers knew was genuine and came from the heart.

If the book has the personal touch—even the intimate—readers should remember that its only purpose is to tell what I saw officially and unofficially. And if I tell the story in a light that puts me in the right in various controversies and actions, it should be remembered that I am not only telling my story, but letting the reader understand that I was acting sincerely according to my lights and to my conception of my duties and responsibilities.

If I may be permitted to suggest here such value as the volume may have, I should say that I have undertaken to make a faithful presentation of the shifting scenes in a country, never static, in a period when a radical change took place in the relations between the United States and Mexico. These neighbors have not always seen eye to eye. I found suspicion of "The Colossus of the North" on the part of Mexicans who remembered old antagonisms. The Big Stick and the Dollar Diplomacy of the United States had kept apart the nearest neighbors, both needing the closest coöperation for their countries' good.

On the day of his inauguration Franklin Roosevelt enunciated a doctrine that thrilled all Pan America when he said:

"In the field of world policy, I would dedicate this nation to the policy of the Good Neighbor—the neighbor who resolutely respects himself and, because he does so, respects the rights of others."

That was no mere declamation. It was an expression of Roosevelt's heart's desire, in which I shared, for World Brotherhood, beginning in the Western Hemisphere. He knew that the Good Neighbor policy had to be incarnated in men of good will who were to represent his country in the diplomatic service as well as in the governmental departments. He sought to send abroad men who shared his dreams of friendliness, who would personify, in daily walk and conversation as well as by official acts, the Good Neighbor doctrine. President Roosevelt, through close association in the direction of the Navy in the Wilson administration for nearly eight years, knowing of our common faith in democracy and the new international intercourse, did me the honor to ask me to go to Mexico in the first days of his administration as a living Good Neighbor. That was my only mission. My commission was to show by acts that the Good Neighbor policy would work. No other ambition interested me in the nearly nine years that I walked with love among the hospitable people of Mexico. This volume shows how this happy task was undertaken. I laid down the robes of office with the satisfaction that Roosevelt's ambition for good neighborliness had become an accomplished achievement in the Republic of Mexico. Its acceptance and practice laid the foundation for the perfect coöperation which made the Western Hemisphere the arsenal of united neighbors which at last helped to save the world from the threat of totalitarianism.

Josephus Daniels

Raleigh, North Carolina

CONTENTS

FOREWORD   vii

PART ONE

Mission to Mexico

I. "You Can't Go to Mexico"   3
II. The New Deal Begins   15
III. From Roosevelt to Rodríguez   25
IV. The American Embassy   29

PART TWO

Presidents and Diplomats

V. El Presidente   37
VI. Abelardo Rodríguez   47
VII. Lázaro Cárdenas   56
VIII. Camacho and the Election of 1940   79
IX. Alemán and Vera Cruz   88
X. The Shrine of Madero   93
XI. Foreign Ministers   98

PART THREE

First Settlement of Claims

XII. "Jarndyce vs. Jarndyce"   115

PART FOUR

Education and Religion

XIII. LIGHT FOR DARKNESS   127

XIV. THE CHURCH AFTER THE REVOLUTION   142

XV. AFTER THE CALM, THE STORM   177

PART FIVE

The Six-Year Plan

XVI. "THE LAND BELONGS TO THOSE WHO WORK IT"   199

XVII. LABOR GETS ITS MAGNA CARTA   206

PART SIX

Liquid Gold

XVIII. "CHAPOPOTE" TO PETROLEUM   211

XIX. PRELUDE TO EXPROPRIATION   217

XX. BOLT FROM THE BLUE   227

XXI. MEXICAN REACTION   246

XXII. AMERICAN PROPAGANDA   255

XXIII. RICHBERG LOSES; HURLEY WINS   263

XXIV. DAY OF DELIVERANCE   266

PART SEVEN

The Banker and the Cowboy

XXV. A BANKER DIPLOMAT   271

XXVI. TWENTIETH-CENTURY UNCLE SAM   278

XXVII. ARE DIPLOMATS "SACRED" PERSONS?   282

PART EIGHT

Indians as Good Neighbors

XXVIII. OLDEST AMERICANS   297

PART NINE

Tragedy and Brotherhood

XXIX. KINDNESS IN TRAGEDY AT CANONITAS   315
XXX. A MEXICAN EAGLE FALLS   318

PART TEN

Haven of the Exiled

XXXI. MEXICAN SYMPATHY WITH LIBERALS EVERYWHERE   323
XXXII. THE SCATTERED NATION   334
XXXIII. CONFEDERATES IN MEXICO   338

PART ELEVEN

Visitors to Mexico

XXXIV. THE GOOD NEIGHBOR IN PERSON   347
XXXV. THE AMERICAN EMBASSY A MECCA   351
XXXVI. THE CHANCERY A CLEARING HOUSE   367

PART TWELVE

Friends in Mexico

XXXVII. THE AMERICAN COLONY   379
XXXVIII. THE BRITISH COLONY   390
XXXIX. THE FOURTH ESTATE   398

XL.   TIME OUT FOR STORIES   414

XLI.   THE PLAY'S THE THING   434

PART THIRTEEN

Travels

XLII.   KEEPING IN TOUCH   453

XLIII.   BATTLE MONUMENTS   469

XLIV.   THE LAREDO ROAD OPENING   480

XLV.   DIPLOMATS TOUR MEXICO   485

PART FOURTEEN

The Approach of War; Last Days

XLVI.   OUTPOST OF AMERICAN DEFENSE   497

XLVII.   A NEIGHBOR GOES HOME   507

APPENDIX

Hail and Farewell

FIRST ADDRESS BY AMBASSADOR DANIELS IN MEXICO   519

RESPONSE BY PRESIDENT RODRÍGUEZ   521

ADDRESS BY FOREIGN MINISTER EZEQUIEL PADILLA   522

LAST ADDRESS BY AMBASSADOR DANIELS IN MEXICO   525

INDEX   533

ILLUSTRATIONS

The Good Neighbor—Franklin Delano Roosevelt   *Recto frontispiece*

Josephus Daniels. From a portrait by the Mexican artist, Armando
 Drechsler   *Verso frontispiece*

FACING PAGE

Ambassador Daniels presenting his credentials   28

President Rodríguez, Ambassador Daniels, and Dr. Puig Casauranc, Minister of Foreign Relations   28

"Well Come, Mr. Daniels." From a cartoon by Manuel Aguiles
 Caderes   between 28 and 29

The Embassy Staff on the steps of the American
 Embassy   between 28 and 29

Reception Room in the American Embassy   29

Table set for the first diplomatic dinner given by Ambassador and
 Mrs. Daniels   29

Mrs. Daniels, Señora de Cárdenas, wife of the President of Mexico,
 and Señora de Hay, wife of the Minister of Foreign Relations   46

Ambassador and Mrs. Daniels celebrating their golden wedding at
 the Embassy   46

Ambassador and Mrs. Daniels receive guests at the American
 Embassy   47

General Federico Montes making Ambassador Daniels honorary
 Chief of Police of Mexico City   47

President Cárdenas reviewing a military parade   58

Emilio Portes Gil, President of Mexico and Foreign Minister under
 Cárdenas   59

Pascual Ortiz Rubio, first civilian to be elected President   59

J. Ángel Ceniceros, Acting Minister of Foreign Relations, Ambassador to Cuba   59

FACING PAGE

Eduardo Suárez, Minister of *Hacienda,* financial leader of the administrations of Cárdenas and Camacho   59

President Cárdenas and Ambassador Daniels   80

President Cárdenas congratulating his successor, President Ávila Camacho   80

President Ávila Camacho speaking from the balcony of the National Palace   81

Ambassador Daniels congratulating Señora de Ávila Camacho   81

Miguel Alemán at his inauguration as Governor of Vera Cruz   88

Retable painted by the artist Pancho to commemorate Ambassador Daniels' narrow escape from death   88

Conference on the Claims question: General Eduardo Hay, Ambassador Daniels, Lawrence Lawson, and Gustavo P. Serrano   89

General Hay handing Ambassador Daniels a check for initial payment on agrarian claims   89

Ambassador Daniels delivering an address at the Summer School of the National University of Mexico   140

Ambassador Daniels discussing agrarian problems with Arthur Constantine and Rex Tugwell   140

Amada Morán de Constantine, teacher of Spanish literature in the Summer School and director of the Pan American Round Table of Mexico City   141

Katherine Knox, of the Embassy Staff, carries the United States flag in a Pan American parade of flags   141

School children gathered at the statue of George Washington   141

Monsignor Pascual Díaz Boreto, former Archbishop of Mexico   156

The Reverend James A. Magner, of the Catholic University of America   156

The Reverend John J. Burke   156

Ambassador Daniels with His Excellency, Luis Martínez, Archbishop of Mexico, and the Honorable Michael Francis Doyle, American member of the World Court   156

The heart of Mexico City, with the Cathedral of Mexico on the left and the National Palace on the right   157

Hospital de Jesús, oldest hospital in the Western Hemisphere   157

FACING PAGE

Miss Sallie McKinnon; the Reverend and Mrs. Charles McKean; and one of the Townsend groups.   192

General Board of Religious Education of the Methodist Church in Mexico   193

"The Land Is Now Yours." General Gilardo Magaña reads the announcement delivering the properties to the peons   200

Alejandro Carrillo, secretary of the Confederation of Mexican Labor, and Vicente Lombardo Toledano, president of the Confederation   201

Inauguration of the Workers University, session of 1944   201

Discussing problems following expropriation: General Hay, Foreign Minister, and Vicente Cortez Herrera, Director of Petroleum   256

Señora de Cárdenas, leading the women's movement to contribute jewels to support the expropriation of oil   256

An oil well near Tampico   257

One of the oil fields in Mexico's "Golden Lane"   257

Cover page of *The Atlantic Monthly,* favoring oil propagandists   264

Titles of articles in *The Atlantic Monthly*'s issue of propaganda against Mexico   265

W. R. Davis, the "Man of Mystery," conferring with Prieto Souza and Fritz Flanby on expropriation of oil lands   272

Donald Richberg, representing expropriated oil companies   272

Patrick Hurley, who, as representative of the Sinclair Oil Company, reached an understanding with the Mexican government   272

Secretary of State Cordell Hull and Mexican Ambassador Castillo Nájera signing agreement settling oil, agrarian, and other claims, November 9, 1941   273

Ambassador and Mrs. Dwight Morrow, with Charles Lindbergh and their daughter Anne   280

Plutarco Elías Calles, when President of Mexico, and Ambassador Morrow   280

Pueblo Indian delegates to the Inter-American Conference on Indian life are received at the Embassy   281

Ambassador and Mrs. Daniels attend an Indian Congress   281

Will Rogers, Twentieth-Century Uncle Sam   284

FACING PAGE

Skit on the old-time diplomat: Ambassador Daniels, Robert
McGregor, and Stephen Aguirre   285

Manvilio Islas, the Indian who rescued Miss Constantine from a
crashed plane   300

Framed picture of the two aviators killed in the plane crash: Bronson
H. Rumsey and Daniel S. Roosevelt   300

Flier Francisco Sarabia, just before taking off on his non-stop flight
from Vera Cruz to the New York Exposition in June, 1939   301

The American Embassy's floral wreath at Sarabia's funeral   301

President Ávila Camacho and Julio Álvarez del Vayo, former
Spanish Ambassador to Mexico, who headed the Spanish Republic
in Exile   348

Ramón Beteta, Secretary of Hacienda under Alemán Miguel Alemán, President of Mexico   348

Señor Abelardo Roças, Brazilian Ambassador, with Ambassador
Daniels; Señora de Roças and Ambassador Daniels; Mrs. Wallace
is welcomed to Mexico; Ambassador Daniels saying good-bye to
Señora de Ávila Camacho, wife of the President of Mexico   349

Vice-President Wallace congratulating President Ávila Camacho   364

Toasting President Ávila Camacho's health   364

Vice-President and Mrs. Wallace with Ambassador and Mrs. Daniels
at the American Embassy   365

Vice-President and Mrs. Wallace at a party given at the Embassy 365

Ambassador and Mrs. Daniels with Tyrone Power   396

Grace Moore, who was received at the Embassy by Ambassador and
Mrs. Daniels   396

A group of moving picture stars on the steps of the American
Embassy   397

Ambassador Daniels with members of the University of Mexico football team   397

Ralph McGill, editor of the Atlanta Constitution, visiting at the
Embassy   412

William Allen White and Ambassador Daniels   412

President Cárdenas, Betty Kirk (Mrs. Francis Boyer), newspaper
correspondent, and A. Arroya, Ch., of the Committee on Public
Information   413

FACING PAGE

Miguel Lerdo y Texada, director of the *Típica* Orchestra, which gave
many concerts at the Embassy   432

A young lady in costume   432

Cantinflas, Mexican comedian   432

Roberto Soto, comedian of the Mexican theatre in the role of a
pachuco   432

Nacimiento (Nativity) arrangement and figures carried at the head
of the procession of the *Posada* given at the American Embassy
on December 23, 1937   433

Ambassador Daniels in *charro* costume and Mrs. Daniels in a *China
Poblana* costume   440

The *Jarabe*, danced by Don Carlos Rincón Gallardo, Marqués de
Guadalupe, who is in *charro* costume. The young lady is wearing
a *China Poblana* costume   441

Banquet of the Presidential Electors in Washington, June, 1941:
Homer Cummings, Mrs. Franklin D. Roosevelt, Ambassador
Daniels, Vice-President Wallace, and Michael Francis Doyle   460

Reviewing the Fleet from a battleship in New York Harbor; Secretary Swanson, President Roosevelt, and Ambassador Daniels   460

Monument to William Jennings Bryan, and President Roosevelt
making the speech of acceptance   461

War Memorials: Naval Memorial at Brest; Flanders Field Cemetery; Memorial at Thiaucourt; General Pershing and Ambassador
Daniels at dedication of American Monument at Bellicourt   476

Marker erected at the highest point on the Laredo-Mexico City
Highway   477

At the celebration marking the opening of the highway   477

Vargueno presented by the Embassy and Consular Staffs of the
Republic of Mexico to Ambassador and Mrs. Daniels   492

Sarape presented to Ambassador Daniels by President Cárdenas   493

Silver platter presented by the Diplomatic Corps of Mexico to Ambassador Daniels, Dean of the Diplomatic Corps   493

A Shirt-Sleeve Ambassador goes home   508

"Good-Bye, Boy!" Cartoon by Arias Bernal   509

Part One

MISSION TO MEXICO

"YOU CAN'T GO TO MEXICO"

B UT YOU can't go to Mexico."
That is what my wife said as we sat in our home in Raleigh
on the night of March 7, 1933, having only a few days before returned from Washington, where we had attended the inauguration
of Franklin Roosevelt as President of the United States.

"Why can't I go to Mexico?" I asked her.

"Don't you remember Vera Cruz? Have you forgotten that you
sent the fleet to Vera Cruz in 1914 and as a result a number of
Mexicans were killed by the Navy's landing party?"

My answer—at this distance it seems a strange one—was, "I had
forgotten all about the Vera Cruz expedition." It landed April 21,
1914, and resulted in the death of 126 Mexicans and 19 Americans,
and the wounding of 195 Mexicans and 71 Americans. It took place
in pursuance of this cable:

"FLETCHER,
"Vera Cruz, Mexico
"Seize custom house. Do not permit war supplies to be delivered
to Huerta government or to any other party.

DANIELS

"You and Franklin Roosevelt may have forgotten about it, but you
may be sure the Mexicans have not forgotten. They will not receive
you," my wife said.

I had just finished a brief conversation by long distance with
Cordell Hull in Washington.

"If you will accept, the President will send in your nomination as
Ambassador to Mexico," the Secretary of State had said. "We both
hope this assignment will be agreeable to you."

"I will be glad to serve wherever you and Franklin assign me and
I appreciate the confidence shown," I had told him.

The nomination was sent to the Senate March 13; it was promptly
confirmed, and my commission as American Ambassador Extra-

ordinary and Plenipotentiary was signed by Franklin Roosevelt on the 17th day of March, 1933. I took the oath of office in the Supreme Court Chamber in Raleigh on March 18th. It was administered, at the suggestion of Chief Justice Stacy, by my brother, Judge Frank A. Daniels, in the presence of my friends and family, the Governor, and Supreme Court Judges. It was an interesting coincidence that on the same day my nomination was sent to the Senate, the nomination of Robert Worth Bingham was sent as Ambassador to Great Britain. He was a favorite cousin of my wife, both being descended from Dr. David Worth of the Quaker family that moved from Nantucket to North Carolina.

In Washington I found I was not the only former Navy official who had forgotten the Vera Cruz landing. Dining at the White House, my wife said to the President, "Franklin, I was never so surprised in my life as when you asked Mr. Daniels to go as Ambassador to Mexico."

"Why were you surprised?" he asked. "I think it is an excellent appointment and I am happy that he will represent our country with our nearest neighbor to the South and I know he will make a great Ambassador."

"Have you forgotten Vera Cruz?" she asked.

The President was silent for a moment and then said, "I had forgotten all about the Vera Cruz incident. Had the Chief?"

Here was the Secretary of the Navy and the Assistant Secretary of the Navy, charged with the direction of Naval affairs in the Wilson administration, who did not recall an incident which had roused Mexican resentment—the landing at Vera Cruz, which President Huerta falsely said was "making war on Mexico." It was proof that neither of us nor Wilson had entertained any but friendly feeling for Mexico and had believed we were really aiding liberty-loving Mexicans to free themselves from the Huerta reign of absolutism.

But when it was known that the former Secretary of the Navy had been appointed by the former Assistant Secretary of the Navy as Ambassador to Mexico, it greatly disturbed some people—career diplomats and others—in Mexico, in the United States, in the State Department, and in the American Embassy at Mexico City. Vera Cruz was not all. Indeed, I think that in some instances Vera Cruz was only a handle to hit with. I was—and I remained—a shirt-sleeve diplomat. Some people remembered not only that I had sent the fleet to Vera Cruz but that across nearly half a century in American public affairs I had been a Democrat of the most liberal persuasion.

That part of the American press which wished American diplomacy shaped after old British and French patterns desired the President to name only a career man. They wanted Uncle Sam to put the diplomats in uniform—at least enable them to wear the same kind of spats as the British and French. My own costume did not fit the pattern of the career service. However, if the appointee was rich, such critics forgave his lack of diplomatic experience. In the same week that I was appointed, President Roosevelt named my good friend Robert Worth Bingham (a millionaire publisher) as Ambassador to Great Britain, and Jesse Isidor Straus, a rich member of the R. H. Macy firm, as Ambassador to France. Both were strong Roosevelt supporters. None of the three of us possessed diplomatic experience unless my eight years as Secretary of the Navy might be so regarded (as it should have been). A metropolitan journal pointed out that the Southern editor was a novice in diplomacy, but did not say that such lack of experience was a deterrent in the case of the two rich Ambassadors, who later proved as well qualified in the chancelleries of London and Paris as any career diplomats.

In my case one able newspaperman put all the various factors together. Gerald Johnson, a fellow North Carolinian, wrote in the *Baltimore Sun*: "Daniels' appointment gives a slightly ironical twist to history. He is the man under whose orders the navy shot the windows out of the War College at Vera Cruz. If the Mexicans study the man, they will welcome him with genuine satisfaction. If there is any man in the United States who is completely free of suspicion of subservience to big business interests, Daniels is that man." I am not sure that was a recommendation which reassured some interests in the United States who pretended to be most alarmed about the Vera Cruz incident.

UNPRECEDENTED RAPIDITY IN AGRÉMENT

It was on March 7 that Secretary Hull wired to the Embassy in Mexico City that the President wished to name me as Ambassador Extraordinary and Plenipotentiary to Mexico and asked the Chargé d'Affaires, Arthur Bliss Lane, to "ascertain from the Mexican Government whether Mr. Daniels would be acceptable to them and advise by telegraph as soon as possible." Lane, on the evening of March 7, addressed a note to Dr. José M. Puig Casauranc, Minister of Foreign Relations, asking that the Mexican Government grant the *agrément*. At twelve noon, on the 8th, the Minister telephoned that the Mexican Government granted the *agrément* and would confirm it in writing in the afternoon. Mr. Lane telegraphed the Department that "the unprecedented rapidity in granting the agreement is, I think, indicative of the present desire of the Mexican Government to show every consideration to President Roosevelt and to his administration." He quoted the Foreign Minister as saying that his "government granted the agreement as soon as possible in order to demonstrate its desire to forget the Vera Cruz occupation which occurred while Mr. Daniels was Secretary of the Navy." Dr. Puig informed Mr. Lane that the reason he "desired to announce the appointment to the press as soon as possible was in order to prevent embarrassment to Mr. Daniels upon his arrival from a hostile press." The Minister added that he wished "to give it to the press with a helpful explanation."

Both the New Deal and the Good Neighbor policy were just beginning then. Both stirred hopes in Latin America as well as in the United States. An Associated Press dispatch from Mexico City, on March 14, quoted Foreign Minister José M. Puig Casauranc as declaring he was "delighted" with my appointment. Indeed, after a rumor became current that the government of Mexico had withdrawn acceptance of my appointment, Dr. Puig gave out a statement that "the Mexican government is thoroughly acquainted with Mr. Daniels' official record and his political views as well as his personality. The government gave its approval of his appointment and now looks forward to his early arrival."

I remember that in one of our heart-to-heart talks Roosevelt laughed at our failure to remember the Vera Cruz incident until my wife reminded each of us. But he told me that when someone suggested to him that I would not be received he had said, "If the Mexicans cannot deal with Daniels, they can have no dealings with me." Also not long before I left Washington, he handed me several telegrams he had received from Americans living in Mexico saying that my appointment was resented in Mexico and I would not be well received, one or two demanding that another American be appointed to the post. With a twinkle in his eye, he said, "I am showing you these protests so that you will see that you are not popular with everybody." I was not to be under any illusions about that.

"YOU MUST NOT GO BY VERA CRUZ"

I was soon ready to depart for my post, after coaching by State Department officials, especially my fellow North Carolinian, Herschel V. Johnson, Chief of the Mexican Division.

"I wish," I said to him, "that you would ask the transportation office to buy tickets for my wife and myself from New York to Vera Cruz on the Ward Line."

That seemed a simple request and I was not prepared for the effect it had upon Herschel. He looked as shocked as if my request had broken all the rules of protocol.

"You don't propose to go to Mexico City by way of Vera Cruz, do you?"

"Certainly," I said. "My wife and I always prefer to go by sea when it is possible."

"But," he protested, "under no circumstances ought you to go to your post by way of Vera Cruz. There are people who have not forgotten or forgiven that you ordered Naval ships to take Vera Cruz and that as a result Mexicans were killed. It would be inviting trouble for you to go by that route. I strongly urge you to go by rail and thus avoid what might be unpleasant to you and to both countries."

At first I demurred, but finally decided I ought to let the officials select the route seeing that they might know best and that Uncle Sam was paying for the ticket. Later I learned that on March 24, Mr. Johnson wrote to Chargé d'Affaires Arthur Bliss Lane in Mexico City, saying:

"I agree with you that it would be best for Mr. Daniels to make no stop on his way to Mexico City before he presents his letters to the Mexican President, and I shall endeavor to dissuade him from any such idea, at the same time suggesting that Commissioner Lawson meet him in San Antonio and perhaps go as far as Laredo with him. I must add that Mr. Daniels has asked me to write you that he does not desire one of the Secretaries to meet him at the border; that although he appreciates very much your suggestion in that sense, and their readiness to do so, he feels that it is not strictly necessary, and the trip should not be made in the interests of economy."

A PRECEDENT OVERRULED

Chargé D'Affaires Lane pointed out to the Department:

"On account of the feeling which still exists in Mexico as a result of the occupation of Vera Cruz, the present situation should not be treated as a routine matter. As evidences of such feelings I might cite the presentation of medals this year to relatives of the Mexican cadets who lost their lives during the occupation, and also the refusal of the Mexican government to accept Major Cheadle as Military Attaché in 1928 on account of his having served in the Vera Cruz occupation and especially for the reason that the report of such services was transmitted from the United States and published here. In commenting upon the appointment of Mr. Daniels it seems hardly possible that the American press will fail to mention the fact that he was Secretary of the Navy at the time Vera Cruz was occupied. That such comments would be reported in the Mexican press is almost certain. I trust therefore in this case it will be possible for the Department to make an exception and make the announcement as soon as possible, giving advance notice to the Embassy in order that the Minister of Foreign Affairs may be notified in sufficient time to permit him to advise the press."

Fortunately for me, Foreign Minister Puig Casauranc had served as Ambassador in the United States. He was familiar with my liberal views, which made me acceptable to a liberal government, and knew of my standing with organized labor. He promptly called in the press and was able to convince the editors that it would be wise to let sleeping dogs lie. Moreover he told them of my long career as an editor, which was in my favor with the press.

In Washington President Roosevelt directed Acting Secretary of State Phillips to send this telegram (March 13) to the Embassy in Mexico City:

"The Department of States desires you to call on the Minister of Foreign Affairs and request the Minister to convey to President Rodríguez an expression of the appreciation of the Government of the United States, for the courtesy and consideration shown by him in answering so promptly the request for the agrément to Mr. Daniels as Ambassador of the United States, as an indication on the part of the Mexican Government of its desire to forget differences of the past between the two governments. The Department also desires that President Rodríguez be assured that the President has complete confidence in Mr. Daniels, who is an old and trusted friend and that the selection of so distinguished a national personage and close associate of the President is for the purpose of indicating the deep and friendly interest which this administration has in maintaining the present excellent relations which now so happily exist between the two countries."

CRITICS STONED AMERICAN EMBASSY

Not all was quiet below the chief officials in both countries, however. News stories came across the press wires that on the night of March 24, the American Embassy in Mexico City had been stoned and several windows broken, in a protest against my selection. Broken bottles were found containing hand bills, which read as follows:

"OUST DANIELS

"The Yankee Government has appointed Daniels as Ambassador in Mexico who, as Secretary of the Navy in the Government of Wilson, ordered the landing of Marines in Vera Cruz in 1914.

"THE APPOINTMENT OF DANIELS IS A SLAP AT THE MEXICAN PEOPLE AND THE SPITTING UPON THE MEMORY OF THE DEAD WHO DEFENDED VERA CRUZ.

"The Mexican Government, which only two months ago hypocritically decorated the defenders of Vera Cruz, now propose to welcome DANIELS, ASSASSIN OF AZUETA AND URIBE.

"The appointment of Daniels, well versed in navy and war affairs, is just one more proof of the part which the MEXICAN GOVERNMENT will play in the imperialist war, as GENDARME OF YANKEE IMPERIALISM.

"DANIELS WILL BE THE REAL ADMIRAL OF THE SQUADRON OF WAR WHICH THE MEXICAN GOVERNMENT HAS GIVEN TO SPAIN. DANIELS IS COMING TO ORGANIZE THE NAVAL AND MILITARY FORCES OF MEXICO FOR THE ENTRY IN THE WAR.

"Workers! Peasants! Employees! Soldiers! Marines! Students! Anti-imperialists in General!

"OUST DANIELS

"Refuse the affront of Yankee Imperialism.

"Mobilize the masses against Daniels! Organize meetings and demonstrations of protest!

"Down with the Land-Bourgeois Government of Rodríguez-Calles, that prepares to send the Mexican workers to the imperialist death in South America.

"Down with the War in China and South America and the preparations for the new imperialistic World War! Down with the provocations against the Soviet Union!

"FOR THE TRANSFORMATION OF THE IMPERIALIST WAR IN A CIVIL WAR AGAINST THE BOURGEOIS, AGAINST THE LAND OWNERS, AGAINST IMPERIALISM!

Mexico, March 18, 1933.

"PROLETARIATS OF ALL COUNTRIES, UNITE

The Central Committee of the Communist Party of Mexico, International Communist Section."

SOLDIERS AS BODYGUARDS

The demonstration was explained away by Dr. Puig as the work of Communist agitators. But three weeks later when my wife and I set out by train for Mexico City, the President of Mexico, ordered, without my knowledge, special precautions against any possible incidents, General Almada, chief of the garrison in the Valley of Mexico, was directed to choose six of his most trusted officers to be prepared for a detail of a confidential and emergency character. Dr. Puig told me later that while he did not have in mind that these officers should act as a bodyguard for me, nevertheless he wished them to be prepared for any emergency which might arise. At the same time he sent a message to the Secretary of War:

"STRICTLY CONFIDENTIAL AND URGENT.

April 5, 1933,
706

"General Lázaro Cárdenas,
    Secretary of War and Marines,
    (Attention Citizen Chief of Staff)
    City.

"My esteemed and good friend:

"By an official communication addressed to the Ministry of Foreign Relations by our Ambassador in Washington, we have noticed that Mr. Daniels, designated Ambassador of the United States in our country, will cross the frontier at Nuevo Laredo, Tamaulipas, at 2 A.M., on the morning of April 13. I will appreciate it if you will please urgently order that special precautions be taken in order that the train on which the Ambassador is journeying, shall have absolute security.

"Awaiting that you will be good enough to inform me when the orders above referred to have been given, I am pleased to subscribe myself, as ever, your affectionate friend and servant.

"(Signed) Dr. J. M. Puig Casauranc"

The same day that the Minister for Foreign Affairs sent the above communication to General Cárdenas, he telegraphed the Mexican Consul in Laredo, Texas, as follows:

"ON THURSDAY THIRTEENTH AT TWO IN THE MORNING AMBASSADOR DANIELS WILL ENTER MEXICAN TERRITORY THROUGH THAT PORT STOP WITHOUT MOLESTING HIM AT THAT HOUR PRESENT YOURSELF AT STATION AND ACCOMPANY TRAIN UNTIL ITS DEPARTURE FROM LAREDO MEXICO PLACING YOURSELF OPPORTUNELY IN CONTACT WITH OUR CIVIL AND MILITARY AUTHORITIES FOR PERFECT FACILITIES AND SAFETYNESS FOR THE AMBASSADOR.

"RELATIONS."

During this time my wife and I had been moving very pleasantly toward Mexico unaware of the special precautions. The first I heard of them, I think, was when Stanley Hawks, a Secretary in the American Embassy in Mexico City, told me that General Casillas had informed him that he and five other officers and a car full of soldiers had been sent to Nuevo Laredo by the Mexican War Department to meet the train and act as a special guard for me, as there had been rumors that some demonstrations might take place en route to Mexico City. General Casillas stated that he himself did not believe that any demonstrations would take place, for every precaution had been taken to have the route carefully guarded, and at every station along the way orders had been issued that no persons were to be allowed on the station platform who were in any way suspicious. He told Mr. Hawks that I could be assured that every care would be taken; that the trip would pass off calmly and without any untoward incident. General Casillas said that he was in constant touch by telegraph with the War Department in Mexico City and various points along the route, and that everything was quiet.

Several police agents were sent to San Luis Potosí, where it was thought some people would stage a demonstration. When the train stopped, I said to my wife: "There are Americans and others here to greet us. Let us get off."

Mr. Hawks said, "No. Your lives would be endangered from the large crowd on the platform."

I said, "I did not come to Mexico to be a prisoner," and we went out on the platform, were met by Consul George P. Shaw and his wife, Mexican officials, and American and Mexican citizens. A Mexican officer of the Air Service reported that he had been sent over with a squadron of airplanes from Mexico City to act as an escort to the train on its way to the capital. I thanked the young Lieutenant for this courtesy.

WOULD NOT RUN FROM TROUBLE

Writing later to my sons of my feeling and attitude as our train moved on through what had been said was territory unfriendly, I said:

"Our train was running very late. We ought to have arrived at San Luis Potosí early in the evening, but the train was four or five hours late. The members of the Consulate and their wives remained up to a late hour to greet us. We were also welcomed by the representatives of the Government of that State. I left the train there, as I had done at Monterrey and Saltillo, and talked with the members of the Consulate and citizens who had come down to the train to welcome us to their town. When I returned to the train Mr. A. D. Bell, official of the Missouri

Pacific Railroad, said that the Mexican officers and guards, who were there to see that I had a safe journey to Mexico City, were very much troubled because at every place where the Consuls met me, I left the train and walked up and down on the platform shaking hands with the people who came to meet me. They thought it would have been better if I had stayed on the train and let the Consuls and others come in to greet me there.

"I made up my mind from the minute I left San Antonio that if there was any trouble, I would not run away from it, because I have always thought the surest way to invite trouble is to seem to be afraid. I did not think there would be any trouble, but I have lived long enough to know that no public man can run away from it. If the stories of attacks that were to have been made on me had been true, I knew that no military or secret service man could always make a man in public life safe. It did not save Lincoln's life, or Garfield's or McKinley's. It did not save Mayor Cermak's life in Miami. And it would not have saved Roosevelt's life if he had been standing in his automobile when the shot was fired.

"So I made up my mind on the train to go about my regular duties unafraid and without anticipation of being attacked, and that course has proved a wise one.

"Our train pulled into the station at Mexico City late Sunday morning—a characteristic April day in that cloudless and beautiful city. The papers said our train came in under heavy guard, following an attempt to wreck the train, when a section of the rail was removed from the track, fifty miles north of Monterrey. I was sleeping the sleep of—shall I say the just?—and had no knowledge of the attempt until I read it in the papers later in the day.

"More than 350 police were on duty at the railroad station, Sunday morning April 15, a delegation from the American colony, members of the Embassy staff headed by Counsellor Arthur Bliss Lane, General Guillermo Palma, Chief of Police, gave welcome as the representative of the President. He told me that President Rodríguez, who was at Guadalajara, had given orders for extreme precaution. Half a dozen blocks from the station to the Embassy had been blocked off with police and a large guard was on duty at the Embassy. Some of the Embassy staff were nervous and apprehensive, but neither my wife nor I shared such feeling. Welcomed at the Embassy by members of the staff and their wives, we soon gave greeting to representatives of the press. With my fellow journalists I felt at home, told them of the pleasant and uneventful trip, and our happiness to be in Mexico, a country regarded as a near and dear neighbor. They were cordial and printed my first message to the Mexican people. I spoke of the mutual respect and esteem shared by the people of both countries as exemplified by Ambassador Morrow and Ambassador Clark, and my belief that it would be strengthened in the years ahead by the flowering of Roosevelt's Good Neighbor policy. The Mexico City papers next day said, 'Ambassador Daniels turns critics into friends.' "

After lunch, I said to Counsellor Lane that I wished the car ready for a drive over the city that afternoon.

"Don't do it," he said. "I advise you not to go out of the confines of the Embassy, the Chancery and the gardens until you have presented your credentials and been officially received by the President. It may not be safe. You saw what precautions the police took in view of the posters and actions of certain elements."

My answer was, "Mr. Counsellor. I did not come to Mexico to be a prisoner, and as I have no fear I do not intend to let it appear that I do not feel I am among friends."

We took the ride in the afternoon to Chapultepec and the lovely parks, where the people, as was their wont, were making merry in family parties. It was a peaceful, beautiful day. That afternoon it seemed a very happy country. I liked it at first and was to love it as I stayed. Looking back now with deep affection for it, I remember it as the scene of some of the happiest years of my life—in which happiness was compounded of a chance for usefulness to the two republics and their people.

II

THE NEW DEAL BEGINS

M y mission to Mexico began, of course, in Washington, and in exciting Washington times. The depression had moved across the late winter towards its climax in March. I remember now that while I was at the inauguration of Franklin Roosevelt my son had wired me that, though we fortunately had money in the bank, we could not get any of it out to meet the payroll on our paper. Even the most secure were troubled. Not long after the inauguration, Bernard M. Baruch, my old friend and colleague of the Wilson days, spoke to me about Roosevelt's policy of suspending gold payments. Baruch had been wise enough to foresee and save himself in the days before the Hoover panic. He was one of the few rich men who, seeing the storm coming, got rid of his speculative stocks and put the proceeds in gold, which, he thought, would always be the rock of deliverance. When Roosevelt called in the gold, Baruch talked to me in Washington about it. He had millions of dollars safely stored away in gold. He had obtained it when it was the legal and prudent thing to do and when he believed it would increase in value.

"What ought I to do?" he asked. "I bought it in good faith and under the laws of my country."

"You have done nothing wrong," I replied. "It was wise foresight on your part to foresee the approach of the panic and save your fortune when others were plunging in the era of frenzied finance. But now, when your country adopts a new and, as I think, a better policy, you will, of course, obey the laws today as you have always done."

But along with every trouble there was a sense of creative hopefulness among those of us who had had faith in Franklin Roosevelt's courage even before he spoke and acted against our fears. I remember being in such a group in New York, late in February, at a banquet given in honor of Claude Bowers, the distinguished editor who had wielded one of the most effective pens in the Roosevelt campaign and was to become Ambassador to Spain. At that banquet I was surprised, as was everybody else who heard him, when James A. Farley, the Democratic national chairman, paid a tribute to me and announced that I would be named to an important post in the new administration. At that time—I was seventy-one—I had known enough of public life not to be enamored of it. I was seeking no post and I wanted none unless Roosevelt of his own wish asked me to do some service.

TALKED MYSELF OUT OF A JOB

In fact, I talked myself out of a job. The day after the Bowers banquet, I had a long talk with Roosevelt at his New York home, and he spoke freely about the problems he faced. One of the most important and difficult tasks, he thought, was that of transportation, and he asked me to go with him to Washington and make a study of that problem. To begin with, he wished me to become Chairman of the Shipping Board, to reorganize it and put it on a better basis. After that he hoped that I could also deal with plans for rail transportation. The railroads were in a desperate fix, and he believed a way could be found to restore their prosperity and usefulness.

I agreed to go to Washington and make an independent study, first of the Shipping Board, and then tell him what I thought should be done with it before accepting or declining the chairmanship. He said he had been so engrossed with other matters that he had deferred specific plans and would like my suggestions and my administration of them. Also, he asked me to go to Washington on his special train with his family, friends, and some members of his new cabinet. I was glad that we went on a Baltimore and Ohio train because of my old war-time friendship with Daniel Willard, who was so long its president. I was told—but not by Roosevelt—that he chose the Baltimore and Ohio because, in the campaign, certain officers of the Pennsylvania were very antagonistic to him.

Immediately after the inauguration, I got in touch with my former shipmate, Admiral H. I. Cone, then head of the Shipping Board, who had not had a free hand in its operations. In a few days I learned that waste prevailed in the organization, that it was overloaded with political lawyers, that unconscionable sums had been spent in subsidies and for ships, and that it was an inefficient agency.

I so reported to the President and said that, before making any final recommendation, I thought it would be well to confer with Lewis Douglas, Director of the Budget, and Daniel Roper, the new Secretary of Commerce. I laid before them the information I had obtained in a brief survey and told them that the way to reform that board was to end its existence, do away with the members and a large part of the overpaid and inefficient personnel, and make Shipping a bureau in the Department of Commerce. They agreed with me.

I then called at the White House and told the President the conclusions I had reached, which were concurred in by both Douglas and Roper. I advised that not only the independent Shipping Board be abolished but that every similar board be given such treatment that their duties might be performed under a member of his cabinet. I quoted Woodrow Wilson's remark that "all boards are long, wooden and narrow." He agreed, but asked me to look further into the matter and see if he had the power to abolish the Shipping Board. I found he had not and recommended that he let all the members of the Board go except Cone and one other, who could carry on until he could get the needed legislation. The law required a bipartisan board and, as most Naval officers have no party affiliation, it took some time to find a Naval officer who would qualify as a Republican. One of the officers I wished on the Board was from California and it was necessary that he be a Republican member. I asked him his politics and he said he had not voted since he was in the Navy. I then asked him what was the political faith of the Congressman who had appointed him and he told me he was a Republican. Thereupon I said, "That makes you a Republican for the purpose of holding this office." That was the first and only time in my life that I ever induced a man to call himself a Republican.

Having accomplished the task entrusted to me, I said good-bye to the President—I was leaving the next day for home.

"You have talked yourself out of a job," he said.

I answered that my supreme desire was to see his administration succeed and I believed my advice was good and given without regard to myself.

"Good-bye," he said, "but you will not be in Raleigh long; I'll be asking you to come back."

BEST OR WORST ADVICE?

Inevitably, perhaps, as an old-time Democrat and a close friend of Franklin Roosevelt I was involved in the job plans of others. One or two cases may be illustrative. One day before the inauguration I was talking in Democratic National Headquarters in New York with my old comrade, Louis Howe, who had served as Franklin Roosevelt's secretary and trusted adviser when he was Assistant Secretary of the Navy. While we were talking Raymond Moley came in and said to Howe, "I must see you about a very important matter and get your reaction to a paper I have written." Howe answered, "Come right in. The Chief [like President Roosevelt he always called me Chief] is one of the family and he could give us good advice." Moley then proceeded to say that President Roosevelt wished him to go to Washington as Assistant Secretary of State, chiefly so that he could be near the President and help him on various policies outside as well as inside of the State Department.

"But," he added, "I must have my duties specifically defined. I do not wish to go without knowing exactly what I am to do in the State Department and what matters I am to control." He then took out a paper on which he had written a statement which he said he intended to insist that the President give to the press that day. I did not preserve a copy, but my recollection is clear that the following is substantially the first paragraph of the statement he wished the President to give to the press on March 2: "I have asked Mr. Raymond Moley to go to Washington as Assistant Secretary of State and he will be in full charge of all negotiations relating to the war debts due the United States."

Other equally important functions, according to Moley, were to be committed exclusively to him. As he read I was astonished that any Assistant Secretary should demand to have direction of some of the most important policies of the State Department. After he had finished reading and restating that he could not and would not accept the position tendered unless the powers he had outlined were conferred on him and made public by the President, Moley turned to Howe and asked, "Do you not agree that the President owes it to me to do this?"

I thought I saw in Howe's poker face the disapproval I felt. As he and Moley were associate advisers of the President, I saw he did not wish a break. Instead of answering Moley's question, Howe turned to me and said, "Chief, you have had experience in Washington under two administrations; what is your reaction?"

I gave no answer until Moley turned and asked my opinion. I saw that Moley was bent on insisting, if not demanding, that the President accede to his request. Appealed to by both, I ventured, in the quietest manner possible (restraining my sense of the impropriety of the proposal and the attempt to deny to my long-time friend, Cordell Hull, the full powers and dignity of the office of Secretary of State), to try to convince Moley that he was acting against his future efficient service, by wishing any designation of his particular functions.

I explained that if it was announced that he was to perform certain specified acts, he might thereby be excluded from others in which he might be more useful to the administration. He combated that position. I then went on to say that I judged from what he had said that the President wished to draw upon him for assistance in the working out of agricultural and economic policies, apart from the State Department work. He said that this was true. "Then," I went on to say, "part of your time is to be free to render this general assistance to the President, and I have no doubt Mr. Hull will fix your duties in the Department so as to leave you full time to be at the call of the President."

I stressed the importance of that course to him. He was not convinced. The discussion proceeded and I finally said I thought I knew Cordell Hull well enough to know that if the President should issue such a public statement Hull would decline to accept the portfolio of Secretary of State. I added I did not believe that Franklin would comply with such a request and did not think he ought to be asked.

I saw that what I had said had made little impression on Moley. He left us saying that he did not feel that he could go to Washington unless his duties were specifically assigned and made public as set forth in his draft.

After Moley had departed, Howe, who had withdrawn from the discussion, said: "It was a godsend that you were here when Moley called. You gave him sound advice. He knows how Franklin esteems you. Moley does not like your advice but he will take it. He will not ask Franklin to make any statement. If he did, nothing would persuade Franklin to make the desired assignments." Howe could read Roosevelt's mind better than any other of his close associates.

Howe was right. I did not see Moley again until after the in-auguration when I called at his corner-room office looking toward the White House, where he was installed as Assistant Secretary of State. He greeted me with: "You are in the office of a real Democrat. When I assumed my duties here, I found that the most prominent place was given to a portrait of a former anti-Democrat Secretary of State. I had it removed and put in its place the picture of Andrew Jackson." So saying he pointed to an excellent likeness of Old Hickory. I congratulated him upon the change. He said it was significant of the new type of democracy that had come into power. I recalled the militant foreign policy of Andrew Jackson, who com-pelled France to pay a long-standing debt to the government, and we agreed that only Old Hickory diplomacy could have brought the proper respect for the new republic. We then turned to discuss the big problems facing the Roosevelt Administration, calling for advance in labor and agriculture, and the difficult problems in-herited from the depression era. No reference was made to the un-wanted advice I had given him in New York.

Soon I was off to Mexico and did not keep up with his relations with Secretary Hull until the "blow-up" in London, where Moley received the condemnation of Ambassador Bingham, who later told me he was indignant because Moley thought he could use the American Embassy in London as the place to engineer his plans, which were at variance with those of Cordell Hull. This was fol-lowed by Moley's retirement from the State Department. Later he opposed New Deal policies.

In his book, *After Seven Years,* published in 1939, Mr. Moley makes the following reference to the incident:

"I found dear old Josephus Daniels with Louis Howe and, knowing his experience and reputed finesse, I put the problem to them both. I received, I'm sorry to say, the worst political advice I ever got. They both told me to ignore the stories, that publication of the statement F. D. R. had dictated would create more confusion than there was already. Anyhow—this, when I protested—it would be entirely out of order for me to hand it out in F. D. R.'s absence. I must do nothing until he re-turned."

The Moley example is another illustration of the mistake a President makes when he admits as his intimate any other than a seasoned political supporter. Wilson made a like mistake when he gave too great trust and power to Colonel House.

RUTH BRYAN COVETED FATHER'S MANTLE

Another case had happier consequences. Ruth Bryan Owen, daughter of my old friend William Jennings Bryan, came to see me. She wanted my help in making an insistent request to President Roosevelt that he name her an Assistant Secretary of State, saying that it was the only position she would accept. She added that she had kept for many years the desk at which her father sat when he was Secretary of State and she wished to use it as Assistant Secretary. She asked me to see Secretary Hull and President Roosevelt and secure that post for her. I promised to do what I could and conveyed her request. Hull said both he and the President had her in mind for a good post in the diplomatic field, but that as Roosevelt had appointed William Phillips as Undersecretary and Raymond Moley as Assistant Secretary and as neither of them was a lawyer, he could not name anyone to the other post who was not a learned lawyer. I saw the force of his position.

When I reported to Ruth that her desire could not be gratified, she was greatly disappointed. In vain did I argue with her that she should not want a position in Washington as Assistant Secretary, telling her that Mrs. Franklin Roosevelt had once said that the lowest official social position in Washington was to be the wife of an Assistant Secretary. She was so intent upon being Assistant Secretary, however, that she told me unless she was given that position she would retire from politics. She added, "I have been offered a very attractive position in a Florida college and I shall take that and renounce politics forever."

I parried with the remark that a duck must swim in water and no Bryan could be happy out of the political pond. She went away saying that as she was denied the only post she desired, she would accept no other. She seemed adamant in spite of my argument that she would be happier and could serve her country better as the minister to a foreign country than as Assistant Secretary in Washington. She agreed to think it over. She did, and she could not resist the persuasive President when he expressed his belief that she could best serve the administration by going as Minister to Denmark. It was the possession of her father's desk when he was Secretary of State that made her so desirous of the position in the State Department. Except for that desk, I do not think the assistant secretaryship would have been so attractive to her. Women are often moved by sentiment for family pieces of furniture. These appealed strongly to Ruth.

She became our Minister to Denmark, the first American woman to be named to such a position, and her charm and grace and ability and eloquence, made her one of the most popular and useful of Uncle Sam's diplomats.

UPRIGHT AND FORTHRIGHT CORDELL HULL

I had no desk or demands, but when it was suggested that an ambassadorship might be offered me, I was interested. I told my friend Dan Roper, the new Secretary of Commerce, that if Roosevelt and Hull had any such position in mind, I would prefer Mexico to any other country. He conveyed that information to Secretary Hull. Hull and I had been standing together for genuine tariff reform, the income tax, freer trade between nations, the League of Nations, and liberal policies in government. I had headed the North Carolina delegation to the National Convention in 1928, instructed to vote for Hull for President in the year that Al Smith received the nomination. I early took the measure of the upright and forthright statesman who was to win world renown and hold the portfolio—and fill it—longer than any other man in American history.

ALL PROBLEMS NOT SETTLED

When my appointment was announced a friend congratulated me. "You have the best diplomatic post," he said. "Ten years ago I would have commiserated with you upon going to Mexico. But now, since Dwight Morrow settled all the matters that gave Ambassadors trouble, you will have no worries."

I wondered. To be sure I had read Walter Lippmann's paeans of praise of miracle-worker Morrow in Mexico and the description by our military attaché in Mexico, Colonel Alexander J. McNab, of Morrow as virtually Prime Minister under the Calles regency. They conveyed the impression that Morrow had actually directed the Mexican policies as they related to the United States. I hoped the claims, debt, oil, water, and church troubles had been permanently settled. Particularly, I hoped that, as I tried to embody the Good Neighbor policy, I would not be, as I had been in the Wilson administration at Washington, troubled with oil.

I was soon to find—even before reaching Mexico—that all the problems had not been settled and filed away marked "finis." Almost as soon as I had taken the oath and gone to Washington to get instructions I was given a telegram from Mexico's Foreign Minister, Dr. Puig Casauranc, that as soon as I arrived his government wished to take up the matter of Claims in the hope of reaching an *en bloc* settlement for the Special Claims. This showed that all had not been finally adjusted.

The church question, which had flamed since all church property was taken over by Juárez, was certainly not quiescent. I was told in the State Department that, far from being settled, the problem as it then existed "greatly disturbed" Catholic leaders in the United States. Morrow had composed the situation which existed when no priests were officiating in Catholic churches in Mexico, but the settlement was only like a poultice and the cure was far from completed.

I had known Father John J. Burke, who selected Catholic chaplains for the Navy in World War I, and I visited him and found that he was far from being happy about the matter. He told me that the Catholic church was insisting upon the elimination of laws to which it objected. He was then and after a friendly adviser who, more than any other Catholic in America, knew the situation and advised delicate handling towards the full desires of his church. I was to find in the years ahead that no month would pass that this question in one form or another did not threaten friendly relations.

The insistence of the bondholders, headed by Thomas W. Lamont, of the Morgan firm, for diplomatic aid was another matter that remained, Morrow not having secured final settlement. But oil, the water differences in the Rio Grande and the Colorado, and the old Chamizal borderline quarrel—a veritable *Jarndyce* vs. *Jarndyce* case —were mercifully kept from me until they raised their heads, some threateningly, in the nearly nine years of my service in Mexico. I sought to solve or adjust them as they arose. I had one, and only one, yardstick—that of the Good Neighbor policy, based on the Bible doctrine, "Do unto others as ye would they should do unto us." In all negotiations to adjust the problems, some of which threatened friendly relations, I tested them by that rule of just diplomacy.

It was a job to keep a diplomat in his shirt sleeves.

III

FROM ROOSEVELT TO RODRÍGUEZ

SHORTLY after five o'clock on the afternoon of April 24, I was received at the Palace by President Abelardo Rodríguez. It was an occasion for the pageantry of diplomacy. At half past four the Mexican chief of protocol, Señor Licenciado Vicente Veloz González, and four assistants came to take us to the palace. The members of the Embassy staff and my wife accompanied me. When arrangements were being made for the presentation of my credentials at the Palace and my reception by President Rodríguez, I said to the Counsellor, "Arrange for my wife and the wives of the Embassy staff to go to the palace with us."

He replied, "It is not customary in Mexico for ladies to be present on such occasions."

I told him, "Neither is it customary in the United States, but the best thing to do with such archaic customs is to disregard them. I do not go anywhere except with my wife, an equal partner in all things—at the polls and political gatherings as well as in the home or at church." So the ladies accompanied the Embassy staff to the Palace, and the "busting" of protocol added to the dignity and charm of the occasion.

We made a parade. Motorcycle policemen rode in front. Then came a troop of the Tenth Regiment of Cavalry in front of our cars and another troop behind. About us were numerous but less pictorial detectives. The streets were lined with people. We drove down the famous boulevard, Paseo de la Reforma, the same avenue down which Maximilian and Carlota were driven in their royal coach to Chapultepec Castle upon their ill-starred crowning as Emperor and Empress of Mexico. I did not know that afternoon, as I was informed later, that the reason for the military guard and the splendor of the procession was not so much to give honor to the new Ambassador as to make certain that no incident be created by those who had protested my appointment. In diplomacy, as in some other things, it is sometimes difficult to tell the difference between grandeur and a guard.

Arriving at the old and stately Palace, we were received by General Juan Francisco Azcárate, chief of the presidential staff, whom I was to know as a pioneer in Mexican aviation. My wife and the other ladies in our party, who had preceded us to the Palace, had gone into the Salon Verde, which is a magnificent room, hung with green brocade, used for the reception of Ambassadors. There is another enormous room called "The Hall of the Ambassadors," which is used only for large state receptions.

ADDRESSES ON PRESENTATION OF CREDENTIALS

When we entered, President Rodríguez and Dr. Puig, his Foreign Minister, came in together at the other end of the room and seated themselves on chairs which looked like thrones. I advanced and read my little piece and made the bow becoming to the occasion. (I learned later from General Azcárate that formerly when Ambassadors were presented the Aide would take hold of them to make certain that they bowed with the proper genuflection. Since then Ambassadors have learned how to bow—or exactitude in bowing has seemed to become less important—so that they can do it without physical help.)

My address occupied only a few minutes. Much of it, of course, was couched in the elaborate protocol of international greetings and friendship. But I spoke for the new times as well as of the old "indissoluble ties of friendship":

> "In this period when mankind everywhere is moving towards a better social system, it is gratifying that as never before the United States of America and the United Mexican States are facing the necessary changes with no slavish adherence to precedent or tradition. They have rather embarked upon new and well-considered experiments with optimism born of courage. Both are animated by faith that the social order now in the making in both countries will guarantee to all men equality, justice, liberty, and the full enjoyment of the fruits of their labor.
>
> "Your nearest neighbors to the north have deep admiration for your marked advance in social reform, in public education, in agriculture, in transportation, in communications, and in all measures which promote the well-being of your nationals. The

people and officials of my country feel that each Republic has much to learn from the other. It is in this spirit that I have come to Mexico. I trust to be able to interpret to my countrymen the progressive policies you are projecting and achieving, as I bring to Your Excellency the aims and aspirations which dominate the people of the United States. It is my sincere desire to promote the strongest ties of understanding and amity. If I know my supreme ambition, as I enter upon the duties assigned to me, it is to be an Ambassador of Good Will to your country from the country I am privileged for the time being to represent."

Listening beside his Foreign Minister, Rodríguez that day seemed a young and handsome as well as an able man. When I had finished he rose to make his reply. He took notice of the things I had said and used some of the very language of my address. I remember the central paragraphs of what he said:

"The recognition, so frankly and courageously expressed, of the fact that humanity is passing through a period in which it is obliged to seek better social system, is of inestimable worth to this country, which was one of the first, in the new social era which is beginning, to decide to take a new course in meeting vital needs and satisfying the demands of collective justice, without feeling bound by precedent or by tradition.

"Ever since this social movement began in Mexico, her administrations have sought a better understanding of human problems and a closer relation of all their actions with those problems, thus meeting the greatest social need of these new times and fulfilling a duty to which your President, also, has given expression in exactly that form, and which you are now so aptly confirming.

"It is plain that this recognition of the almost universal phenomenon of the abandonment of the traditional social policy, and the movement of humanity towards a better social system —in order to achieve which nations have had and will have to embark on new economic and social experiments with complete resolution and courage—is a guarantee of increasingly intimate relations between our two countries, because it is an unquestionable sign of better understanding, and will be the source of more effective solidarity."

When he had finished he stepped forward, and I walked over to shake his hand. With the President in the middle, he, Dr. Puig, and I sat down in the throne-like chairs. Behind us stood the President's military staff—a dozen or more brilliantly uniformed men—and their bright uniforms against the green walls of the beautifully decorated room gave a spectacular appearance to the scene. The inevitable photographers came forward and took our pictures, as we sat smiling together.

Afterwards we came home in the same grand way we had gone to the Palace. I remember that Mexican and United States protocol officials, soldiers and secret-service men, and a number of newspapermen stayed at the Embassy for tea. The shirt-sleeve diplomat's mission had formally begun.

Above, Ambassador Daniels presenting his credentials. *First row, left to right,* General Juan F. Azcárate, Chief of Presidential Staff, Ambassador Daniels, and Licenciado Vicente Veloz González, Introducer of Ambassadors. Mrs. Daniels is at extreme right. *Below, seated, left to right,* Ambassador Daniels, President Rodríguez, and Dr. Puig Cassauranc, Minister of Foreign Relations.

..Well come Mr. Daniels

From a cartoon by Manuel Aguiles Caderes.

The Embassy Staff on the steps of the garden entrance of the American Embassy. Mrs. Daniels is in the center of the front row, behind her, to the left, is Ambassador Daniels, in *charro* costume and near her are Mr. and Mrs. Josephus Daniels, Jr., **and Edgar Foster Daniels.**

Above, the reception room in the American Embassy. *Below,* the dining room, with the table set for the first diplomatic dinner given by Ambassador and Mrs. Daniels.

IV

THE AMERICAN EMBASSY

"I NEVER felt so grand, not even coming down the stairs in the stately receptions at the White House to the music of the Marine Band, as when we were escorted from the National Palace down the Avenue Reforma and walked over the red velvet carpet into the Embassy residence," said my wife, as I wrote my sons and gave this description:

"It seemed a far cry from Raleigh, when we were shown to our rooms. A very large bedroom, with French windows, some fifteen feet high, is called the Ambassador's room, and the adjoining room is for the wife of the Ambassador. But, seeing that the room that the Ambassador is expected to sleep in seemed very light, and knowing that your mother likes much light and air, and the other room was darker as it has only one window, although a large one, I changed the usual rule of the Embassy and I took the smaller and darker room and gave your mother the room usually occupied by the Ambassador, which is large enough for three bedrooms, has very large windows and a very large bath."

A year later, when an earthquake broke the plastering in the room my wife occupied and I did not feel it, I laughingly said to her, "You thought it good of me to give you the spacious Ambassador's room and take the smaller room for myself—you know now that I was not as generous as it seemed. I gave you the 'Earthquake room.'" My letter home continued:

"The Embassy compound is in the shape of a somewhat irregular triangle, the residence on one street and the chancery on another. The buildings are connected with high walls which extend around the entire grounds. In between lies the garden, and, as I said, a most beautiful garden. Directly between the buildings is a lawn with some large trees and flowering shrubs; at the side are the flower beds, and over the walls and on the large columns of the residence veranda, which faces the garden are vines. These are climbing roses and fuchsia, blue plumbago, pink geraniums, honeysuckle, heliotrope, and a vine that resembles our Virginia creeper. The flower beds are a mass of flowers of all kinds, for apparently the flowers here bloom with utter disregard to seasons as we know them. Iris, roses, gladioli, dahlias, and chrysanthemums all side by side and all in bloom. Flowers play an important part in Mexican life, as the Mexicans are extremely fond of them and there isn't an adobe hut in the poorest quarter that hasn't its flowers—possibly planted in tin cans of all sizes and varieties, but filled with flowering plants. This love of flowers goes back to the early Mexicans, as history shows that in their early religious practices flowers were much used. All of the Aztec rites have flowers connected with them.

"The residence is well arranged and very comfortable. The drawing room, reception room, and dining room are all extremely large and well adapted to entertaining. There are, in addition to these rooms, two small studies, five bedrooms and baths. These are all on the main floor which is up about ten steps from the ground. The first floor, which is a semi-basement, is occupied by the servants' quarters and garage. And there is a large room and bath on the roof which can be used when necessary. It is still called the Lindbergh room.

"The chancery also has a veranda, facing the garden, with tall columns, corresponding to the ones at the residence. So the effect of the two buildings when one is standing in the garden is quite imposing. My office is a large room facing the garden."

The approach to the Embassy from Londres Street is through tall iron gates. These were watched and tended by a Mexican doorkeeper, Patricio Suárez, who opened it only to those known to be welcome. He had lived in the United States long enough to speak some English and had got his name changed to Patrick.

As a school boy, studying geography, I was interested in faraway lands, and no place pictured on the pages of my well-thumbed book intrigued my imagination quite so much as two white-capped volcanoes which look down upon the American Embassy as tall, silent sentinels. Whether this keen interest was caused by the mystery of the extinct craters of Popocatepetl and Iztaccihuatl, or by the presence of eternal snow resting upon their heads and making crystal crowns, or by the fact that snow could survive in the tropics, or by inability to pronounce the names of those lofty peaks—whether one or all these things piqued my curiosity, I cannot say. All I know is that as a boy they beckoned me, though I never dreamed that one day they would become my daily companions.

EDUCATION OF A NEW AMBASSADOR

Within this view of the mountains, my wife and I were even more interested in the history and people of Mexico than I had been as a boy. I reread Prescott's *Conquest of Mexico* as my wife lost herself in the Madame Calderón de la Barca's story of the Mexico of the last century. As long as we lived in the Embassy, my wife often said she saw much in the Mexico of 1933-1941 like the city described by Madame Calderón de la Barca, the gifted Scottish wife of the Spanish Minister. I got my first insight into the land-hungry followers of Zapata as I read *Tempest Over Mexico* by Rosa King. Prescott had caught my imagination when I read his story as a boy, but my wife gave first place to the story of the conquest as told by Bernal Díaz. She often quoted from him: "When I beheld the scenes that were around me, I thought within myself that this was the garden of the World."

Traveling as well as reading, I went over the terrain followed by Cortés from Vera Cruz to Cuernavaca and found that Prescott wrote so truly that a map could be made from his book without other information. I did not know that Prescott was almost blind and had never seen Mexico or Peru, which he described better than any surveyor could have done. I bought every new book on Mexico which came from the presses and our education was supplemented by the choice spirits who showed us the old and the new blended in the glowing city, as we visited the places made famous in history —places of glamour and of tragedy, highlighted later by the talks we had with Bertita Harding, who wrote *Phantom Crown*. We were later to dig into the stories of Hidalgo and the Virgin of Guadalupe and stories on the ever-changing governments, the part the Roman Catholic church had played, from the day the priests burned the creeds of old Mexican faiths to the later problems following the Revolution. We learned and shared the wisdom of ancient Nezapualcoyotl, who spoke a proverb when he said: "That which was yesterday is not today; and let not that which is today live tomorrow."

The whole process constituted what Henry Adams might have called "The Education of an Ambassador." Looking back, however,

I wonder how we found time for so much reading in the midst of hospitality and official duties. The American colony in Mexico received us with cordiality. Both my wife and I enjoyed also the hospitality graciously extended by many Mexican people, officials and others. The Diplomatic Corps contained many charming and stimulating people.

HOSPITALITY WITH A SOUTHERN ACCENT

It was the happiness of my wife and myself to make the Embassy a central gathering place for Americans, Mexicans, old friends and new ones, neighbors and visitors from all parts of the world. As I look back upon this Southern hospitality in the land of the Montezumas (it was, in fact, American with a Southern accent of hot biscuits and Mexican tortillas) and as I recall the riot of decorations of calla lilies, orchids, and other Mexican flowers, and the tables with Mexican and American food in abundance, I wondered in the later days of rationed food and soaring prices where the money came from for the many luncheons and teas, dinners and parties. But a peso would buy much in those days, and "My Lady Bountiful" had the art and genius to make abundant provision without bankrupting the family exchequer. In the latter part of our stay, Uncle Sam aided by a small appropriation for "Entertainment" which met part of the cost.

For nearly nine years, except during our trips home almost every year, the Embassy virtually kept open house. I say "open house" advisedly. There was rarely a week when guests were not invited to lunch, to large formal teas and to formal dinners. To Mexico came visitors by the hundreds, tourists in groups, bearing letters of introduction, and most of them were invited to break bread at the Embassy.

"THE TIRED OLD AMBASSADOR"

It was pleasant, but it also meant moving at a very rapid pace. As soon as I arrived in Mexico I began my mission by calling not only on all important public officials but also by visiting all the daily newspapers and meeting my brother editors. It meant much walking and climbing of stairs. I enjoyed it, but some of the Embassy staff found the new pace exhausting. At the time I wrote home:

"When my appointment was announced the papers carried the information that I was born in 1862 and was beyond the three score and ten span of life. There are some people who think that the only thing for a man of seventy to do is to die or go into retirement.

"These people thought that President Roosevelt was taking a risk in sending an old man to the big job of making the new Good Neighbor policy work in a country which has not always regarded 'The Colossus of the North' as a good neighbor. That New Deal, they felt, should be entrusted to a lusty and athletic youth. One officer in the Embassy told Arthur Bliss Lane, Counsellor, that Washington had given him, and the other career officers, a tough assignment in looking after and carrying on the work of 'an old Ambassador.' And they got ready to carry the main Embassy load!

"The other day a friend called at the Chancery and asked to see Lane. 'You will see him resting on the porch in the rear of the building,' said a secretary.

"And there was Lane, sans coat, collar and cravat, wiping the perspiration from his brow, the very picture of over-exertion. Surprised at Lane's dishevelled condition, the friend asked: 'What is the trouble?'

" 'Oh, nothing,' replied Lane, 'except I am all in after trying to keep up with a tired old Ambassador.' "

NO SMELL OF OIL ON EMBASSY

The years seemed almost a succession of friendly occasions at the Embassy. Both my wife and I were fond of people, our friends from the States and our friends in Mexico, and neither of us liked anything better than seeing them happy together. The Embassy itself was ideally located and designed for such gatherings. And in its time it has welcomed almost every type of human from America and abroad since it was first occupied in 1916. It was purchased in 1922. Across the garden the Chancery, built on three adjoining lots, was given to the government by Mrs. E. L. Doheny, whose husband made millions in oil operations in Mexico. Some of those who attended Embassy parties suggested that Doheny (who figured in the Teapot Dome scandal as the man who gave Secretary of the Interior Fall "a little black bag" with $100,000 in it), gave the Chancery to the Embassy as an evidence of appreciation for helping him get favors and oil concessions in Mexico. There was, however, no smell of oil on the premises.

Part Two

=================

PRESIDENTS AND DIPLOMATS

V

EL PRESIDENTE

All presidents of Mexico must be generals who either die by the hand of an assassin or are expelled from the country," said a friend of mine in Washington as I was going to my new post, and he added, "You will probably be witness to more such departures of Presidents." To this I replied, "With the adoption of the Good Neighbor doctrine these things will end. There will be no more assassinations or expulsions of Presidents."

"You are the prize optimist," he said, as I departed for Mexico.

No President before General Plutarco Elías Calles had completed his full term and peaceably retired to private life in half a century. However, history proved me a prophet.

I came in close association with seven Presidents of Mexico in my stay in that republic and knew at second hand about four others who held the highest station—all since 1910.

DÍAZ HELD LONGEST TENURE

Of the first, General Porfirio Díaz, I heard from a North Carolina friend, General M. W. Ransom, who, while Minister to Mexico, came to entertain high regard for him and told me how Díaz had advanced Mexico by inducing the investment of foreign capital. As both Ransom and Díaz were generals and conservatives, they had two ties. However, though liking Díaz personally, Ransom was never so fulsome in his praise as was Elihu Root, who, on the occasion of the celebration of the twenty-fifth anniversary of the reign (I use the word reign advisedly, for in his long term something like royalty developed), said of Díaz:

"If I were a Poet I would write eulogies. If I were a musician I would compose triumphal marches. If I were a Mexican, I should feel that the steadfast loyalty of a lifetime would not be too much in return for the blessings he had brought to my country. As I am neither poet, musician, nor Mexican, but only an American who loves justice and liberty and hopes to see their reign among mankind progress and strengthen and become perpetual, I look to Porfirio Díaz, the President of Mexico, as one of the great men to be held up for the hero worship of mankind."

IDEALISTIC MADERO MURDERED

My first real interest in Mexico was aroused when the idealistic liberal, Francisco I. Madero, member of one of the wealthiest families in Mexico owning millions of hectares of land, started the revolution to oust the Díaz government. He had been converted to democracy by education in France and the United States, where he was able to compare the lot of the people with that of the masses in Mexico. His revolution drove out Díaz, but Madero himself fell by assassination at the hands of the soldiers of General Victoriano Huerta.

This usurper had seized power shortly before Woodrow Wilson became President in 1913. I became convinced that the murder of Madero could have been prevented by Henry Lane Wilson, the American Ambassador (a Dollar Diplomat), who was deaf to the entreaty of Señora de Madero and the offer of the Cuban Ambassador to provide a ship to take Madero to safety. Woodrow Wilson dismissed Henry Lane Wilson and refused to recognize Huerta, though most other nations (particularly those having large investments in Mexico), gave him recognition. It was to oust Huerta that Wilson adopted "Watchful Waiting," sent Pershing to Northern Mexico and John Lind as special Ambassador to Mexico City, and directed me to send the American Fleet to "take the Custom House at Vera Cruz and prevent ammunition from falling into Huerta's hands."

HUERTA'S SARDONIC HUMOR

Though he was called an assassin, "a drunken Indian," a betrayer of Madero, who had trusted him as Commander in Chief of the Army, Huerta was not without wisdom in certain lines, and he had a sort of humor that was evidenced in these two stories which I wrote home early in 1933:

"I had a call from Robert Hammond Murray, long-time newspaper correspondent and head of George Creel's Public Information in Mexico, who told me two good stories about Huerta. While Wilson was refusing to recognize him the Mexi-

cans felt that the time had come for Huerta to get out, a member
of his cabinet went to see him and advised that he retire.
Huerta seemed to agree, but said his trouble was that he knew
no man qualified to take the reins and carry on with ability or
wisdom. He asked the Minister who advised his retirement if
he knew such a man.

"The Minister replied: 'I do.'

" 'Who is it?' asked Huerta.

" 'Me,' said the Minister.

" 'That is a good idea,' Huerta said, 'and I will consider it and
talk to you about it later.'

"The next night Huerta was the guest of honor at a big
dinner given by this Minister and attended by most of the
Members of the Cabinet and influential people in the government. When Huerta was leaving, he turned to the Minister who
had advised him to get out. 'I wish to say good-bye to you and
your wife before you leave,' he said.

" 'You have already said goodnight to us,' said the Minister.

" 'No,' Huerta said. 'I want to tell you good-bye before you
leave on your long journey.'

" 'We are not going away,' said the Minister.

" 'Oh yes you are,' said Huerta. 'You are leaving tomorrow
night on a very important mission for the government in
Europe, and you may be gone a long time.'

"The Minister protested that he had no idea of going, but
when Huerta told him again that he was going and going the
next night, the Minister pleaded for a longer time to pack and
to get ready.

" 'I will arrange all that,' said Huerta.

"The next morning a wagon drew up at the Minister's residence with new trunks and suitcases and valises to expedite the
packing. Among the bags was a very beautiful and costly one
for the wife of the Minister, and with it was a note to her from
Huerta, saying that he regretted that the exigencies of her husband's mission in Europe compelled her to pack without a
longer time, but he was quite sure she could obtain her ward-
robe in Paris as well as in Mexico, and told her she would find
in the case he had sent her enough money to enable her to
buy all the dresses she needed. And there was a big pile of
money.

"That night the government cars drew up at the Minister's
house in time to take him to the train, and when he and his

family arrived they found a Mexican band at the station playing the national anthem. President Huerta was there to give
him all the éclat of a going away on a very important mission
for Mexico. As this Minister thought he was big enough to stand
in Huerta's shoes, Huerta determined the best place for him
was Paris.

"Another story Mr. Murray told was this: For a time Huerta
made love to the Catholic church and thought he had won their
favor, but later the influential leaders of the church came to
the conclusion that peace could not come in Mexico except by
the withdrawal of Huerta. And so they commissioned a Bishop
of an outlying State, who had been on friendly terms with
Huerta, to tell him that he ought to resign. This Bishop, who
was a very tactful man, made an appointment and went to
Huerta's house and they had an agreeable time talking about
all sorts of matters. Finally the Bishop came to the point; as
tactfully as he could and as courteously, he told Huerta that the
leaders of the church felt that he ought to serve Mexico by with-
drawing and letting someone else take his place.

" 'I think you are quite right,' said Huerta, 'and I intend to
resign.'

"Elated at the success of his mission, the Bishop talked a while
longer, and then, wishing to make a report to his associates, he
said: 'And, General Huerta, when will you resign?'

"The General replied: 'Whenever the people of Mexico, in the
way in which they can legally express themselves, demand my
resignation, and not until then. I have heard no such demand,
but I am ready to resign whenever they say so.'

"This troubled the Bishop very much, and after finding that
he could do nothing more with the General, he made ready for
his departure.

" 'Before leaving,' said General Huerta, 'seeing that I am a
good Catholic, although I do not live up to all the tenets of the
church, I wish you to give me your apostolic blessing.'

"The Bishop was in no mood to bless Huerta, but he felt he
could not refuse the office of the church, and so Huerta slumped
on his knees before the Bishop, and the Bishop in Latin (which
Huerta did not understand) gave the blessing that is always
given in the Catholic church to the incense. I do not recall
exactly the words, but they are something like this: 'Bless, Oh
Lord, we beseech Thee, that which is about to be burned.' "

CARRANZA—"THE FIRST CHIEF"

It was Wilson's pressure against government by assassination that gave powerful help to Carranza, Pancho Villa, and Emiliano Zapata, who had taken up arms against Huerta. This combination drove Huerta out of office, and he found refuge in the United States, where he died not long after.

I felt that I knew Carranza from talks with Lincoln Steffens, who spent much time in Mexico and was credited with having been a close adviser of Carranza, called "the first chief" before he became President. I had also talked about him with John Lind and with Charles A. Douglas and Luis Cabrera, Carranza's two attorneys in Washington who were trying to secure his recognition. Cabrera later became Attorney General of Mexico and was, while I was in Mexico, one of the leading lawyers of the republic. It was Cabrera who satisfied my curiosity as to how Carranza came to his death. I asked him directly about it, and at the time wrote home as follows:

" 'There was no chance for Carranza to win in his attempt to select as his successor Bonillas,' he said. 'Bonillas was a good man but made no popular appeal. Beside, Obregón had his heart set on being President and he had most of the Army with him. It was all-powerful. Carranza alone stood between Obregón and the presidency and therefore Carranza must be put out of the way.' Mr. Cabrera didn't say that Obregón gave orders for the killing of Carranza, but he said someone close to him did, and his clear intimation was that morally Obregón was the author. 'The man who was responsible for the killing was never punished,' he said. 'In fact, ever since, he has been receiving the salary of a retired General and living quietly,' added Mr. Cabrera significantly.

" 'How was Carranza killed?' I asked. He gave me a long account, the substance of which was that the Obregón forces were in pursuit of the Carranza forces. Obregón was at Tampico. His forces, under command of Colonel Cárdenas (now President) in a sector south of Tampico, were about seventy-five miles from Tlaxcalaltongo, where General Carranza was in camp. A detachment of Obregón's soldiers were near by, and Cabrera urged Carranza to move his forces, telling him his life was in danger. Heavy rains decided him not to leave that night. Carranza and his officials were sleeping in small cabins adjoining a ravine. About ten o'clock a man, claiming to have a message for Carranza, entered his cabin, remained long enough to see the location of the bed in which Carranza was sleeping. About one o'clock at night firing began in the camp. Two shots were fired through the thin wall of the Carranza cabin, striking him in the stomach and inflicting terrible pain. Two other shots were fired, entering the breast and heart of the General, from which he died. It was claimed that, seeing the first shots would prove fatal, General Carranza took his pistol at the head of his bed and killed himself. Cabrera puts no faith in that. He says that as soon as the news reached his cabin that Carranza was dead he slipped out the back door of the cabin in which he was sleeping and hid for ten hours in the underbrush in the adjoining barranca. That saved his life and he managed to get back safely to Mexico City. The members of Carranza's cabinet who accompanied the remains to Mexico City were arrested and put in jail as soon as they reached the city. Nobody was punished. In Army circles the Obregón partisans were not sorry, if indeed they were not glad.

" 'Was Carranza as pro-German during the World War as the world believed at the time?' I asked Mr. Cabrera. He said he was not pro-German or pro-Ally or pro-anything except pro-Mexican. He wished to keep Mexico out of any alignments with any of the warring countries. He added: 'It was the Zimmerman note that created the story that Carranza was pro-German. In fact, Carranza never had an intimation that such a note had been written until it was printed in all the papers. Carranza had too much sense to believe it possible under any circumstances for California and Texas to return to Mexico; it was a blunder of Zimmerman based on ignorance. He knew nothing of conditions in the New World as his absurd letter proved.' "

THE TOWERING OBREGÓN MEMORIAL

I knew less about General Álvaro Obregón, who succeeded to the presidency and secured United States recognition after long negotiations. But when I reached Mexico I found that he was remembered with affection by the Mexican people and loved by his soldiers and their wives. Every year I attended a stately service at the foot of the towering Obregón Memorial. His friends on such occasions denounced his assassins, who had killed him near that place.

Once in conversation with Ramón Beteta I asked his estimate of Obregón.

"As a young man I disliked him heartily," he said. "I had never seen him or known him. It was a sort of collective dislike. I was very close to Carranza and was with him at Tlaxcalaltongo, Puebla, when he was assassinated."

I asked, "Did you believe that Obregón had anything to do with the assassination?"

He answered by saying, "He profited by it, and at the time there were people who thought he might have had a hand in it. Shortly afterwards I went to Sonora, where I was born, and when I arrived Obregón invited me to live in his home and I was with him several months and I changed my mind entirely about him. He had the most agreeable manners and was one of the most popular Generals and Presidents Mexico has had." He added, "You may hate a man very much collectively, but when you know him, you may change your mind about him."

PORTES GIL'S "FIFTY YEARS OF MEXICAN POLITICS"

My cordial relations with Emilio Portes Gil began when he was in the Cárdenas cabinet as Minister of Foreign Affairs, and continued with growing friendship. He had become Provisional President in 1928 upon the assassination of Obregón in July of that year. He served as Governor of Tamaulipas and President of the National Revolutionary party, and in private life continued to be influential. He wrote an autobiography, *Fifty Years of Mexican Politics,* which gives interesting information of Mexican political history behind the scenes.

WHY PRESIDENT ORTIZ RUBIO RESIGNED

Pascual Ortiz Rubio was the only civilian to be elected President between the Revolution (1910) and 1946, and he did not last long. He lost the support of agrarians because he discontinued the distribution of lands in three States, and he lost the favor of Calles because he would not take orders. On the day of his inauguration Ortiz was the victim of an assault which left a scar on his face. He had the satisfaction of knowing that during his administration Mexico entered the League of Nations. We became friends as did our families. It was the general belief that, dissatisfied because

President Ortiz Rubio showed a measure of independence, General Calles, who had been designated by Congress "Maximum Chief of the Revolution," announced the President's resignation without consulting him and the President acquiesced.

I asked Ortiz Rubio why he resigned. He told me that a conspiracy was started against him in Congress because he opposed abuses and that when General Calles made no effort to stop the conspiracy, "I had the following dilemma—of dissolving Congress which could immediately dishonor me as happened to Presidents Comonfort and Victoriano Huerta; or of resigning my position, by which I could avoid that shame and shedding of blood and loss of reputation to my country. I decided to follow this second course, and presented my resignation on September 5, 1932."

FOUR RECENT PRESIDENTS

During my term of office, the three Presidents of Mexico, with all of whom I had pleasant official and personal relations, were Abelardo L. Rodríguez, Lázaro Cárdenas, and Manuel Ávila Camacho, each of whom completed his term and retired in accordance with the orderly processes of democracy. The constitutional process continued with the election in 1946 of Miguel Alemán to succeed Camacho, the second civilian to be elected to the presidency in almost a century. I had known him well when he was Governor of Vera Cruz and Minister of *Gobernación* in the cabinet of Camacho.

PLUTARCO CALLES, "THE SUPREME CHIEF"

My early association with General Plutarco Elías Calles, who was widely known as "The Iron Man," "Maker and Unmaker of Presidents," and officially designated "The Supreme Chief," convinced me that he had won place because of real ability and wide knowledge. But he fell from his high estate when, becoming rich, he lost faith in the people and opposed Cárdenas' labor and agrarian policies.

Shortly after I began acquainting myself in the State Department with the duties that would devolve upon me in Mexico I found that the career men who had been to Mexico believed former President Plutarco Calles was still the dominant man of Mexico. "He makes and unmakes Presidents and Congress does his bidding," they said. The same idea had been sold to President Roosevelt. History of the period seemed to justify that belief. It was borne out in Mexico in my first months.

"You must get in close touch with 'The Iron Man,' General Calles," was the advice of members of my staff when I reached Mexico. "Mr. Morrow got nowhere until he had won Calles."

"But," I said, "Calles was then President and, of course, directing public affairs. How would President Rodríguez feel if an 'ex' was treated as being the supreme power?"

The reply was, "Calles made Ortiz Rubio President and ousted him. He named Rodríguez who leans on him. There should be no hesitation on that score. The word of Calles is all-powerful."

GUARANTEE OF GOOD RELATIONS

I was naturally gratified when, on May 6, I received a letter from General Calles in which he said:

"I am filled with satisfaction that President Roosevelt, who has confronted the distressing situation with such vision and courage, should have appointed you as the Ambassador of the United States to my country, for your culture and humanitarianism are a guarantee of the good relations which should exist between the two peoples. It will give me a real pleasure to clasp your hand and to consider myself numbered among your friends."

CONGRATULATED BY CALLES

On August 9, on the invitation of General Calles, I went to his home in Cuernavaca. He had been appointed by President Rodríguez one of a committee of three to recommend the measures that should be paramounted at the approaching Pan American Conference. Of our conversation I sent a memorandum to Secretary Hull:

"I was delighted to find him so well informed and so enthusiastic about the possibilities of the Montevideo Conference. He thinks the economic questions should be kept to the fore, and some sort of a Pan American or credit system should evolve that would greatly increase the commerce between the countries and stabilize the currency. General Calles is, as you know, the 'big man' in Mexico. I spent nearly two hours with him. I have never come in contact with a Latin American who seemed to have such a clear mind, so well balanced, so frank, so courageous in expressing views, and evidently so sincere in his readiness to take risks to bring out policies for the common weal. Whatever is done in Mexico this year or next will not be contrary to what Calles wishes done. I find Dr. Puig is in complete accord."

I reported to President Roosevelt that General Calles had great faith in his policies and had said, "As a logical consequence of such policies there will be a better distribution of the public wealth which will prevent its monopolization by the few, but which will bring happiness to the great majority."

Above, Mrs. Daniels gives a luncheon in honor of Señora de Cárdenas, wife of the President of Mexico. *Left to right,* Mrs. Daniels, Señora de Cárdenas, and Señora de Hay, wife of the Minister of Foreign Relations. *Below,* Ambassador and Mrs. Daniels celebrate their golden wedding at the Embassy.

Above, Ambassador and Mrs. Daniels receive guests at the American Embassy. In the group are (*left*) Señor Ezequiel Padilla, Minister of Foreign Relations, and (*center*) Señor Jaime Torres Bodet, Mexican writer and diplomat. *Below,* on the steps of the Chancery, General Federico Montes, Chief of Police of Mexico City, pins badge on Ambassador Daniels, when making him Honorary Chief of Police of Mexico City, November 16, 1938.

VI

ABELARDO L. RODRÍGUEZ

GENERAL ABELARDO L. RODRÍGUEZ began his administration in 1932, after Ortiz Rubio resigned. General Rodríguez was a successful business man, had been a partner of Calles, and was rated a millionaire.

It was expected that Calles would be the power behind the throne and Rodríguez would do his bidding. In the first period of his administration they saw eye to eye, and when I reached Mexico, the opinion prevailed that Rodríguez took orders from Calles. By 1934 it became apparent that Rodríguez was, in fact as well as in name, President of Mexico. He encouraged capital but held the balance even. He restored dotation of land, which had been suspended, and caused 82,000 heads of families to receive land and loans to assist in its use. He gave impetus to public education and decreed that all education in secondary schools should be secular. In some cases he sent soldiers to protect teachers in the church-school controversy. He supported Narciso Bassols when his educational policies were denounced by the Archbishop of Mexico, who commanded all parents to refrain from sending their children to the public schools. When the fury was so great that Bassols was forced to resign, Rodríguez "kicked him upstairs" by making him Minister of *Gobernación*.

One of the most modern high-school buildings in Mexico City is named for Rodríguez. I visited it with the President. It is built on the site of an old Spanish prison, of which it was said, "Who enters here leaves hope behind." The contrast is great. Now it is the entrance to hope and opportunity.

In the months before his retirement in December, 1934, I was pleased to find in many things that President Rodríguez and I were simpático. The friendship forged in those months has continued and is cherished.

NEW DEAL AND SIX-YEAR PLAN

Public men often reveal their real selves and their policies in private conversation more than in public utterances. I found this was true of President Rodríguez on two occasions—first when he and Señora de Rodríguez invited my wife and me to visit the agricultural school in San Miguel Tenancingo and later when we visited them in their home in Cuernavaca. Of these visits and of the views of Rodríguez I wrote President Roosevelt (August 17, 1934):

"President Rodríguez is as familiar with all the plans and experiments of the New Deal as any American, probably more familiar than most of our countrymen, for he has been busy with problems that are not dissimilar. He is enthusiastic in his praise of your policy and believes it will help Mexico and all other countries, as well as the people of the United States. He compared the Mexican Six-Year program with the New Deal and said they had a common objective. In some things, as for example, giving land to men who work the haciendas, Mexico is looking to do more for the forgotten man than you have been able to do. For one thing, in putting people on the land the forgotten men here have been forgotten many more years than in our country and more must be done to somewhat make up for the neglect of the leaders for five hundred years. When, thanks to Andrew Johnson (by the way, a North Carolina President), the homestead law gave a chance for every American to get a farm, the land that the Indians in Mexico had held in common 'since the time whereof the memory of man runneth not to the contrary' was being taken from them and given to 'Los Científicos,' who ruled the country with rods of iron.

"This thought recalls the conversation that followed about the necessity of a governor, president, or other executive knowing at first hand how the people live, their conditions, and what is needed to give them a more abundant life. In that conversation Mrs. Rodríguez said that she had been intrigued by, and was always interested in, the story of the English King (or was he a Scotsman?) who dressed himself as a hunter and went into the cottages and lived among his people in order to know how to become a good ruler. The President said, after an inquiry by me, that his experience as a soldier in the Revolution had taught him the true situation of the people of his country, how little they had, and how they had been neglected. It is his vivid recollection of his comradeship in the Revolution that keeps him knowing how they need land, irrigation, tools for farming, schools, freedom, better wages, liberty—the things he says that the Six-Year Plan undertakes to bring in the reach of all, particularly those who have never had a chance. Some people say that this is a political pose on his part and on the part of his political associates, but if you had heard him you would have been convinced, no matter how far off is the goal, that he really wants a better day for the workers of his country. And if you could hear the criticism of the policies by power owners and the agents of rich concessionaries you would know it was no more a pose than your great power program.

"I was impressed with what he said about the Catholics in their dealings with these people. He spoke in severe criticism about the priests compelling the poor people, with hardly enough to feed their families, to give the first fruits of all they produced to make the church rich. My wife said, 'I know some people in America who do that—give a tenth of all they make to the Lord.' The President paused at that statement, but added, 'They do so voluntarily and out of their abundance. The priests took what was needed for a bare existence from the Indians who were forced to give.' It was this policy of the Catholic church and the fact that, having direction of schools, they kept the bulk of the people in ignorance, which makes him oppose what he regards as the dangerous policies of the Catholic church. One can in Mexico be a good Catholic in the spiritual life and rejoice in the better day the Revolution has brought to the mass of the long-neglected people. I like the word 'forgotten' better than 'neglected,' for in our country and in Mexico some bad things have been wrought, as the poet says, by 'want of thought rather than by want of feeling.' The people simply were forgotten by those who should have kept their needs and rights in remembrance."

GETTING RID OF SLUMS

The thing that made the worst impression upon a visitor entering Mexico City was the fact that so many people were housed in shacks, or, as we call similar places in the United States, slums. Rodríguez was anxious to do something about this. I wrote home (September 16, 1934) concerning an occasion in which modern new homes were opened to Mexican workers:

"After a long address by Aarón Sáenz, Governor of the Federal District, and music and the reciting of a poem by a lady with histrionic talent, the men were called to the rostrum and handed deeds to the homes built by the government. The government bought a large tract of land with a park in the center and built homes surrounding it. There is a large park and a school building near by. Each house has hot and cold water and modern conveniences. It costs 2,651.99 pesos. The government pays some part of the cost, about enough I suppose to care for the parks and plans, etc. The cost to each worker is 22 pesos a month until he pays 2,651 pesos. He then owns the house. The deed or legal conveyance includes an insurance policy so that if the worker dies before making all the payments, the insurance company pays the balance and the widow does not lose the home. On Saturday 108 houses were thus turned over. They are new, neat, and clean. This is the beginning of an attempt to wipe out unsanitary houses in which workers have lived from time immemorial—like the slums in our country which President Roosevelt is trying to wipe out by aiding in the building and repairing of houses. President Rodríguez told me that over 500 other houses would be completed shortly. Only workers can get these new houses. They are selected from many applicants on the basis of character and ability to keep up the payments. The turning over of the deeds was made a function. Many hundreds were present and as the name of each person who had agreed to purchase the house was called, he walked up and was given his deed. There were a few women purchasers. Some men wore overalls and some were dressed in their Sunday best. It was hailed as another step by the Government to aid the workers.

"When a reporter quoted me, after a visit to General Calles at Cuernavaca, as saying that 'General Calles is the strong man of Mexico,' President Rodríguez—not pleased—wrote me the following letter:

" 'Hermosillo, Sonora, November 5, 1934. My esteemed friend, Ambassador Daniels: I have read in *El Nacional* of the 3rd inst. the declarations which you made after your visit to General Calles, and I wish to express my appreciation of the statements made with reference to the economical status of Mexico and the prosperity which is now enjoyed, due solely to the revolutionary policies which have been definitely established and

to the institutional system which prevails in accord with our
principles and legal standards. Your admiration for General
Calles is held by all of us who fought during the Revolution
and we consider him the leader of the Party now in power and
as the one who orients the general policies of the Party. However, in an amicable way and guided by the friendly relations
which bind us, I wish to call your attention to the fact that the
manner in which the press has published your statements—
which I feel must not have been literally thus expressed and
doubtless inspired by very good intentions—may be hurtful to
the coming administration and to its constitutional self-respect,
since it may leave the impression on those who are not prepared to understand conditions or on foreign countries where
Mexico's present situation is unknown, that administrative matters are also in the hands of Calles, something which he has
never desired nor has it been true, because happily for him, for
the men of the revolution and for the country, we are now living under a well-organized political regime in which all democratic institutions function normally. As I have said above, I
wish to make this friendly explanation which will doubtless be
helpful in defining the real situation in our country, although
I presume that your declarations only expressed your personal
beliefs and were not given out officially by you as Ambassador
of the United States. Please accept, Mr. Daniels, my expressions
of high esteem and of personal friendship.

"A. L. Rodríguez.' "

"I made this answer:

" 'November 8, 1934. Dear Mr. President: Please accept my
thanks for your friendly letter written in Hermosillo, which
was handed to me by Dr. Puig, Minister of Foreign Relations.
I duly appreciate the spirit of your letter and your thoughts in
regard to a possible wrong interpretation of the statements attributed to me. I regret that the newspaper published a so-called
interview with me. I certainly did not make those statements
nor any others to the young reporter at Cuernavaca. As he spoke
in Spanish and I only speak English, I did not answer his questions, but Secretary Schott of the Embassy, who accompanied
me, answered his questions, as we were entering the hotel. Mr.
Schott informs me that the statement to which you refer was
not made. As a newspaperman myself, I have never wished to

correct a reporter publicly, knowing that as a rule when these young men make a mistake, they do not do it intentionally.— I congratulate you for the economic stability of Mexico under your administration, which has merited the recognition of bankers from other countries, as you may see from the enclosed article which appeared in the "New York World Telegram," and also of your own countrymen. I hope to have the pleasure of seeing you on your return to this city.—Thanking you for your expressions of personal friendship, reciprocated by me, I am yours with high esteem and best personal regards. Sincerely,
                                        " 'Josephus Daniels.' "

This incident was not publicized until the letters were printed in the life of Rodríguez, by Francisco Gaxiola.

A LUNCHEON THAT WAS CALLED OFF

In the spring of 1934 Mr. Ralph Morrison, of San Antonio, Texas, who knew Mexico through his near-by residence and through his investments in Mexican utilities and other enterprises, called at the Embassy. He had lately returned from London, where he had gone with Secretary Hull as a member of the Monetary Conference. He gave me some of the inside history of the conference and was critical of the assumption of Raymond Moley who, he said, acted as if he were the President's spokesman, whereas Secretary Hull was the accredited spokesman for his country. Mr. Morrison was an enthusiastic supporter of Roosevelt, and a close friend of Jim Farley, and had made a large contribution to the Democratic campaign. This made us simpático. "I know Mexico," he said "and will be glad to aid you in any way." He said he was an old friend of General Calles and advised me to do what Morrow did—cultivate close relations with Calles, who, he said, still was the supreme leader in Mexico.

A day or two later, having in the meantime gone to Cuernavaca to visit Calles, he called and said that, hearing I was shortly to go to Washington to a review of the fleet as a guest of President Roosevelt, Calles wished to give a luncheon for my wife, myself, and friends and send greetings to President Roosevelt. The guests were to be the members of the cabinet and their wives; the Dean of the Diplomatic Corps, who is the Ambassador from Argentina; and the Ambassador from Spain and the Minister from Great Britain;

Mr. Norweb (the new Counsellor) and his wife from the American Embassy; Mr. Ralph Morrison of Texas. I rather thought the idea of the luncheon originated with Mr. Morrison. However that may be, it was quite agreeable to me. Mr. Morrison suggested that it would strengthen ties and insure cordial relations if at the luncheon I could present a note of greeting to General Calles from President Roosevelt. I wrote the President and he sent the note. Upon my next call at the Foreign Office, Foreign Minister Puig informed me that General Calles had commissioned him to extend the invitations and make all the arrangements.

Later there came a near-explosion and the invitation was withdrawn; the luncheon was never held; I did not make the speech I had written; General Calles did not respond; and the letter of President Roosevelt was unread and was locked up in my confidential papers. There had been no publicity about the proposed luncheon and there was none when it was called off. It was long after, when Francisco Gaxiola wrote a book entitled *El Presidente Rodríguez,* that the story was given of "the lunch that wasn't."

The reason given to the few who had been invited was that General Calles had suddenly become ill and was going for rest and care to California. The Mexican papers carried this news item from Cuernavaca: "General Calles is ill. His temperature is 104. He is forbidden to make any engagements. He is still unable to see anyone." That was two days before the date set for the luncheon he was to give in my honor. Therefore the luncheon was postponed. It never came off.

The real reason was, as Foreign Minister Puig told me, that when President Rodríguez heard that Calles had invited me, and that President Roosevelt was to send Calles a letter of greeting, he said, "If any such luncheon is given I should give it and if a message is to come from the President of the United States it should come to the President of Mexico." Dr. Puig had supposed that because of the intimate relationship between the President and Calles, Rodríguez would welcome the plan. Puig had long been close to Calles, had been his campaign manager, and was said to follow where he led. It was supposed that he owed his place in the cabinet to Calles. The necessity of calling in the invitation to the luncheon greatly embarrassed Puig and he spoke frankly of his unenviable situation. I should—and would if I had been a professional diplomat—have understood that I ought not to have asked President Roosevelt to send the message except to the Mexican President. But protocol never meant much to me. Besides, knowing Puig's devotion to both Calles and Rodríguez it never occurred to me that there could be any objection by Rodríguez.

But recent statements to the effect that Calles, "the Iron Man, was really the captain of the ship" had got under the skin of Rodríguez, who was not taking orders. He sensed that if I accepted the invitation to this luncheon, to which Ambassadors and Ministers of other countries had been invited, and if I read a letter from President Roosevelt to General Calles, it would give color to the report that Calles was the shaper of Mexican policies. He asserted the dignity of his office and served notice to Puig and Calles that they could not "plough around him." There was no withdrawal of friendship with Puig and Calles. But they knew that the man in Chapultepec Castle was the President of Mexico. The incident caused no coolness or break in the cordial relations between the Mexican President and the American Ambassador.

SPEECH NOT MADE

I had written a brief speech which I was to have made at the luncheon. Here is the undelivered speech and here is the letter from President Roosevelt, which nobody ever saw and few knew had been written:

"I wish in this presence to express my own and my wife's appreciation to you, General Calles, for this gracious courtesy. The opportunity, upon the eve of a short vacation in the United States, to foregather with you and your friendly countrymen in this hospitable home at the conclusion of the first year of my service as Ambassador to Mexico, is cherished by both my wife and myself. Service here has made the last twelve months most agreeable. Welcomed upon arrival in a manner to warm the heart of the new Ambassador by President Rodríguez and Foreign Minister Puig and other high officials of Mexico; greeted shortly after arrival by you, General Calles, with whom I was privileged to exchange views touching the similarity of some of the provisions in the unfolding New Deal and the maturing Six-Year program, both of which look toward improvement and progress of the forgotten men on both sides of the Rio Bravo; and shown many kindnesses by official and unofficial Mexicans who have opened their hearts and their homes to my wife and myself—these experiences have made our stay here happy and pleasant.

"After spending a few weeks at home, conferring with the officials of my government upon policies which will more firmly knit together the peoples of these adjoining republics—now better neighbors than ever—and seeking to interpret to my country something of the forward-looking spirit which dominates the Mexico of today, we shall look forward upon our return to a fuller enjoyment of an association which has caused us to love Mexico and the Mexican people.

"Learning that today I would be an honored guest in your home, my long-time colleague and present chief, President Roosevelt, has asked me to convey to you his felicitations and present you with this letter which he sends with his esteem."

THE WHITE HOUSE
WASHINGTON

March 22, 1934

My dear General Calles:

I am requesting my old friend and colleague, Ambassador Josephus Daniels, upon the eve of his departure for a short stay in Washington, to convey to you my cordial greetings and felicitations upon the peace and growing prosperity of Mexico in these difficult days—a happy condition to which you have made large contribution.

It has gratified me during the year I have been in office to acquaint myself, through official sources and otherwise, with the progress your country has made and is making along the lines of social reform leading to social justice and the education and welfare of the Mexican people.

Hoping to have the pleasure of seeing you in Washington during my Administration, I am

Very sincerely yours,

FRANKLIN D. ROOSEVELT

His Excellency
GENERAL PLUTARCO ELÍAS CALLES
Mexico City, Mexico.

That luncheon which never came off was a significant event in Mexican history. More than any other event, I suspect it marked the beginning of true constitutional government, without any "Strong Man" standing in the scene behind the presidency.

VII

LÁZARO CÁRDENAS

I LITTLE THOUGHT when, as the newly arrived Ambassador from the United States, I called on Lázaro Cárdenas in April, 1933, at his office of Minister of War in the cabinet of President Rodríguez, that I was speaking to the man destined to inherit the mantle of Benito Juárez as the deliverer of Mexico from the rule of the privileged classes—a rule which had kept millions of Mexicans in the chains of poverty and ignorance for centuries. He was little more than a name to me, and my call was in line with other courtesy calls on all members of the cabinet. I did not even know his career—from jailor in a little Mexican town to General in the Revolution, Governor of his State, and President of the National Revolutionary party. He looked young for a cabinet officer—he was thirty-eight—but they pick them young in Mexico. He was a soldier without uniform, erect in bearing but looking more like a business executive than a man who had led battalions in battle. He received me with reserved courtesy. I expressed my thanks to him for sending a General and a carload of Mexican soldiers as escorts from the border to Mexico City. He said he had only carried out the order of the President, given in the desire to make certain I would know I had come to a country of friends.

Career officers told me at the Embassy that Cárdenas had been put in office by General Calles, who had picked presidents and cabinets for a decade. Later there was talk that Calles might make him the next President, but few that I talked with felt he was big enough for the job. They said he would have no chance unless Calles were assured he would carry out the Calles directions. Even then, however, I thought the strong jaw and twinkling eye indicated one who would be his own man in the National Palace if chosen by the people.

There were also premonitions of change from the Calles leadership. The dissatisfied murmured that Calles had gotten rich (and they intimated by ways that could not stand the light), and some said by gifts from the oil men who were allowed to violate Section 27 of the Constitution. There was suppressed gossip that his great hacienda near Mexico City had been the gift of Ambassador Morrow, who was said to have hypnotic influence over Calles. There was little public evidence of any of this critical gossip, however. Calles was master, or was supposed to be, when the historic Querétaro Convention met in December, 1933, and adopted the Six-Year Plan. It included promises to distribute land and water rights "until the needs of the rural population are satisfied."

Those who distrusted the old "Iron Man" believed that the convention had gone farther than Calles had desired when he publicly rang clear in favor of the Six-Year Plan. But many believed that he was sincere. Even so, others felt that the promises given to secure votes would not be carried out. They thought it was only a platform to cheer the underprivileged, promising land, education, labor rights—made to get in on but not to stand on.

But it was on that platform that Lázaro Cárdenas was nominated for President, though Calles had preferred the nomination of Pérez Treviño, a Conservative. Cárdenas was honest, the soldiers liked him, and he had a good record in the Revolution—a *sina qua non* for political preferment in Mexico. The Six-Year Plan was incarnated in Cárdenas, who was nominated by the convention that applauded it.

The campaign differed in only one particular from former ones. Without any break with Calles and with no opposition, by airplane and train and automobile Cárdenas visited every State and almost every neighborhood from the Rio Grande to the Suchiate. He had practically no opposition. He had the people, "Yes, the People," the Calles machine, and the Army. In the election (1934) he received 2,268,562 votes to a negligible number for the opposition. His party elected every member of the Chamber of Deputies and 49 out of 58 seats in the Senate.

During the campaign people had asked, "Why rush all over the country conferring with voters who have never before been solicited by a presidential candidate?" Cárdenas sensed that he would need the people when Calles and his following would try to submarine the Six-Year Plan. He looked to the future. Cárdenas sent word ahead, and the peasants were encouraged to tell him what they wanted. In every village, as the Indians gathered around him, sitting on the ground in their midst he would ask them, "What do you need in land, schools, seed, roads, health?" And the dispossessed were not slow to petition for their needs. Cárdenas had a record made of their requests with their names and villages, and after he was elected he was scrupulous to grant the requests whenever possible.

THE SIX-YEAR PLAN

The Six-Year Plan adopted by the National Revolutionary party for the presidential term 1934-1940 contained the following provisions (among others) with respect to a nationalistic economic policy:

> Mercantile and productive activities will be regulated by: preventing foreign companies from continuing to monopolize existing mineral deposits; facilitating the activities of Mexican miners; discouraging the exportation of mineral concentrates; establishing central mills and smelters, under State supervision; stimulating national enterprise in the petroleum industry; increasing the production of petroleum; changing the system of granting concessions, and refusing them when they oppose national interests; and preventing the exportation of products which are returned in a semi-manufactured state.

While politicians on the make felt that the platform was made "to get in on but not to stand on," Cárdenas thought it was a compact between the candidate and the people.

Many—most of the influential Mexicans in Mexico City and Americans in business and some in the Embassy—saw in Cárdenas only a serious and unimaginative man who, having long followed Calles, would be a rubber stamp in the Palace.

Was Cárdenas to forget the pledges in the Six-Year Plan? That was the interrogation point in the latter part of 1934 and 1935. Most people thought so who on November 30, 1934, heard the rather heavy inaugural address delivered without emphasis or suggestion that the old order was in for a drubbing and Calles was soon to be out of the picture, exiled from the country he had long ruled.

As I rode back from the inaugural ceremonies my mind was

President Cárdenas reviewing a military parade, September 16, 1938, stands on the balcony of the National Palace. President Cárdenas is on the right of the microphone. In the central group, *left to right,* are General Camacho, Dr. Ramos, of Cuba, President Cárdenas, Ambassador Daniels, Ramón Beteta (behind Ambassador Daniels' left shoulder), and Felix Ordaz, Spanish Ambassador.

Above, two former Presidents: *left,* Emilio Portes Gil, who was also Foreign Minister under Cárdenas; *right,* Pascual Ortiz Rubio, first civilian to be elected President (but soon resigned). *Lower left,* J. Ángel Ceniceros, Acting Minister of Foreign Relations and later Ambassador to Cuba. *Lower right,* Eduardo Suárez, Minister of *Hacienda,* and financial leader of the administrations of Cárdenas and Camacho.

in doubt, but I recalled the one flash in the address. It sounded to me like a note of consecration. He closed his otherwise unimpressive speech with the only dramatic effect in it, saying in tones that I thought had a note of defiance: "You have elected me to be your President. Your President I will be."

Was that notice to Calles that he had come to the end of his supreme power? I sensed it but found my associates saying; "They all talk like that but they all eat out of Calles' hand and take orders from the 'house of power' in Cuernavaca."

I wondered, but had a hunch that in the declaration, "Your President I will be," Mexico had found a militant successor to Juárez, Mexico's greatest President.

Cárdenas had formed what was called a "Calles Cabinet," including a not-very-able son of Calles. This indicated that Calles was still in the saddle. I made my usual calls on the new cabinet members, and I remember that I was to be severely denounced for making an official call on Garrido Canábal, the misfit Secretary of Agriculture. When I visited Tabasco while he was Governor of the State, he boasted of the schools he had established, of the improvements he had made in agriculture, and of the fact that no intoxicants were made or sold in his State. This pleased me. But I observed with a sinking of the heart that he had closed all churches and driven out the priests. When I called on him, as I called on all other members of the cabinet as a courtesy, he caused our pictures to be taken together. It was printed, and vicious critics said I was congratulating the enemy of religion.

As Cárdenas entered upon his term of office, I wondered, and I hoped, that the New Deal in Mexico, embodied in the Six-Year Plan, would run concurrently with Roosevelt's New Deal in the United States. I was to see that "Your President I will be" was notice to Calles that boss control had come to and end and that the Six-Year Plan was to bless the underprivileged of Mexico.

I did not have long to wait to see that a New Era had dawned in Mexico.

BREAK BETWEEN CÁRDENAS AND CALLES

In my nearly nine years in Mexico, where the unexpected happens and sensation follows sensation, the one that caused the most excitement among Mexicans was the sensational break in 1935 between Cárdenas and Calles and the subsequent expulsion of ex-President Plutarco Calles from the country by President Cárdenas.

Both these Generals had served in the Revolution, in the National Revolutionary party, and in government. The Cárdenas cabinet, when announced, included zealous friends of Calles. The break came when Calles saw that the new President was carrying out his pledge: "Your President I will be." Calles had so long "called the figures" in the Mexican political dance that he could not brook being relegated to the background. He had preferred Pérez Treviño to Cárdenas for the presidency but had yielded when the younger elements were determined to nominate Cárdenas. He had not liked the ultra-liberal Six-Year program but had acquiesced, thinking he could sidetrack it as he had done like pledges before.

In the first days of his administration Cárdenas seemed to be running true to the old form—looking to "The Iron Man" for guidance. His cabinet was of the old Calles group, and in his first public declaration for agrarianism, education, and a better life for the masses, he stated as his goal: "In short, there will be realized in its totality the doctrine for which General Calles has been fighting to make Mexico a strong and responsible country."

Did he think Calles was still fighting toward this goal? Or was he trying to keep his support by flattery? Or was it a warning to "The Iron Man" that the Six-Year Plan would be carried out *nolens volens?* Some said, "Calles is still in the saddle." Others said, "Cárdenas is laying down the law." But most people said that Cárdenas was a zealot for the Six-Year Plan and nothing could divert him from carrying it out. The last guess was the true one.

It was noticed that if there was to be a break, "The Iron Man" would have to dissolve the tie by repudiating his early record. And that is what occurred. It was not long before Calles made the issue. He warned Cárdenas he was going too far and too fast, sending him word through Senators to "slow down." He publicly condemned Cárdenas' attitude.

Becoming rich, Calles had built himself a glittering white palace in Cuernavaca, not far from the unpretentious old Mexican home of Morrow. Critics called the street where Calles and his associates lived in splendor, "Ali Baba Street" or the "Street of the Millionaire Socialist." From that base, which his many followers thought was an impregnable fort, Calles gave out statements of criticism of the policies Cárdenas was carrying out, emphasizing his dissent to the labor policy and the distribution of land to the peasants, declaring with a note of threat as to the Cárdenas program, "It will carry us to disaster."

One statement attributed to Calles, which stung and caused most resentment, in addition to his criticism of Cárdenas for devotion to the Six-Year Plan—a pledge both had made—was Calles' reference to the fate of President Ortiz Rubio, who had refused to be an executive puppet. The clear, hardly-veiled threat was that unless Cárdenas took orders from "The Iron Man" he would be deposed as had been Ortiz Rubio. Cárdenas made no reference to this threat of being ousted, but he summoned all his resources and employed them quietly and successfully to end the sway of Calles. Immediately after some members of his cabinet had paid a visit to Calles and some Senators were echoing the Calles charge that the Cárdenas program "will carry us to destruction," Cárdenas took a drastic step. When the members of his cabinet met, he requested—it meant an order—everyone to write out his resignation. That action spoke louder than any words the determination of the chief executive.

Those in the cabinet who were his supporters approved the drastic action. Cárdenas went further. He announced dismissal of General Medinaveytia as chief of the military zone of the Valley of Mexico and General Joaquín Amaro as Director of the National Military School, on charges of "seditious and rebellious" activities; thus he balked any possibility of a military coup. To all other officials, this was notice without words of the fate in store for all who wished to sabotage the Six-Year Plan, which Cárdenas held as sacred as the pious Israelites held the Ark of the Covenant. His calmness and decisive action and his resolve to put out of commission all except those loyal to the party program were proof both of his faith and of his courage. Public sentiment, vocal and organized, supported Cárdenas. The Federation of Labor passed a resolution demanding that Calles be turned over to a tribunal of workers for trial "for working against Mexican labor."

"I GO BUT I RETURN"

General Calles, meanwhile, had withdrawn from the troubled political scene by going to California for his health, saying, as he left Mexico, "I am departing, leaving all the responsibility for public affairs to those who have the responsibility in their hands." But it had a note of "I go but I return" in it. During his absence, his supporters busied themselves in trying to arouse public sentiment against Cárdenas. When Calles suddenly returned from Los Angeles, his followers welcomed him at the airport. It was the fulfillment of his farewell remark. All officials who welcomed him soon found themselves out of office. Calles was greatly improved in health. Upon his arrival he was quoted as saying:

"Because of the storm of insults and calumnies hurled against me and what is called the Calles regime, giving a wrong construction to facts and events, I have decided to break my silence, because should I not do so my attitude would be taken as cowardice and lack of dignity, which do not exist.

"During the four years I was President, I believed then and I continue to believe that I interpreted the opinion of the revolutionary group that carried me into power. I am further convinced that that group will accept with me all the responsibilities that may arise therefrom."

He declared it his intention to remain in Mexico despite the massing of 80,000 workers who paraded before the National Palace and demanded his expulsion. He described Cárdenas' address as "Communistic" and "filled with passion." He denied he was going to form a new party but said its formation could not be prevented. While the hostile demonstration went on, he played golf and then returned to his home as Mexico City was seething with excitement. It was heightened by the discovery of 10,000 cartridges, 57 rifles and submachine guns at the home of Luis Morones, the discredited Minister of Labor when Calles was President. Morones was put under arrest. He said the guns had been in storage since 1923 and added that "it is infantile to believe we are going to start a revolution with such old arms." He said, "In my opinion General Calles is in serious danger. We can expect anything." That was December 21, 1935.

EXPEDITED CALLES' LANDING

But it was April 10, 1936, before the worst that Morones expected occurred. Of the part that the Embassy played in promoting the entrance of Calles and his party into the safe refuge of the United States, I wrote home as follows:

"On Friday at about two o'clock A.M., Mr. Aguirre had Miguel wake me up and told me that Mr. Smithers, a close friend of Calles, had gone to see him to ask him to give me a message from Calles to the effect that he had been arrested and did not know what they intended doing with him, but in case of deportation wanted me to telegraph the State Department, so he would not have trouble with immigration officials when he reached the border. I accordingly sent a telegram at once to the State Department as requested. Shortly thereafter I talked to Mr. Smithers myself and he repeated what Mr. Aguirre had already told me. I advised Mr. Smithers that a telegram had been sent and he returned to Gen. Calles with that information. At 8:30 A.M. I was advised by Mr. Smithers that a plane containing Calles and three of his followers had left for Brownsville. That morning also Minister Hay called and said that Calles and his followers had been sent out by plane and should reach Brownsville around noon. He said he hoped the U. S. Government would permit them to enter the country as political refugees. I told him that I had communicated with the State Department by telegram and that I would communicate with them again telling them of his request. I then telephoned Washington and it was arranged for Calles and his party to land in Brownsville, and I understand they left there at once en route to California.

"The fact that President Cárdenas took steps last December to insure that no harm should come to General Calles when 80,000 men marched down the avenue under banners denouncing Calles and had later said the presence of Calles caused no alarm in Mexico—these things had caused general belief that nothing would be done about Calles along the old Mexican line of silencing opposition by deportation or otherwise. It, therefore, caused great surprise when General Calles was deported. The reason assigned was that he and his associates were guilty of acts which had caused disturbances and hostility to the economic policies for the welfare of the workers, culminating in dynamiting a train in the State of Vera Cruz and labor troubles organized by Luis Morones, one-time Minister of Labor when Calles was President. Nobody thinks Calles was counselling the dynamiting of the train but that his associates had lighted a fire which went further than they contemplated. Calles denies he was active in opposition to the Government and was in no way responsible for the troubles.

He sent word to Cárdenas: 'I am not responsible for the troubles. It is the unwise policies of Cárdenas that have caused the uprising in Mexico.' "

THE END OF "THE IRON MAN"

On the previous night around midnight, while General Calles was reading in bed at Santa Barbara, his hacienda, General Rafael Navarro, chief of military operations in the Valley of Mexico, accompanied by twenty soldiers and eight policemen, entered. Asked what brought them there at that time of night, the commanding general said, "You are to take a long airplane trip from Mexico City early in the morning."

Calles replied that he did not wish to fly, and General Navarro said, "You are an Army officer and so am I. When you were Commander-in-Chief I obeyed your orders. I obey my superiors. President Cárdenas has directed me to have you at the airport at six o'clock and see that you are on the plane that will take you to Brownsville. There are soldiers in your yard. Resistance is impossible."

Accepting the situation General Calles replied, "I am at your orders. I consider myself your prisoner. I have no forces at my disposal and I do not need them. You may take me in an airplane or before a firing squad. I do not consider myself responsible for the conditions through which Mexico is passing. The government is responsible."

So saying he turned over in bed and resumed his reading until the time fixed for his departure, when, under heavy military escort, accompanied by his family, he went in his car to the airport with a military guard. By direction I had caused to be sent them on their arrival at Brownsville, Texas (the four who had been sent out of Mexico), the necessary papers, and the American Consul met them. So they were safe from harm on United States territory. There they issued a public statement, signed by P. Elías Calles, Melchor Ortega, Luis N. Morones, and Luis León, in which they said:

"The desire of the government, whatever declaration it may make to the contrary, is to socialize the machinery of production, disregarding the private property rights that guarantee our institutions, and to establish a collective system in agriculture similar to the Russian system. We repudiate communism, as we consider it not adaptable to our country and because the Mexican people refuse to accept it."

While excitement was at feverish height as the news of the expulsion and the airplane flight became known, President Cárdenas issued a statement, which was, in part, as follows:

"When the situation reached such an extreme stage as to impede the march of our institutions and to frustrate the most noble end of the State in our social struggle, it appeared indispensable to the Federal Executive, in view of their criminal work, to abandon its attitude of watchful waiting and to adopt measures to prevent disturbance of a greater magnitude which, if not averted, would threaten to break down our collective organization and endanger the conquest we have achieved in exchange for so many sacrifices.

"I deferred intervention until it could be seen without equivocation that the authors of this agitation persisted in their nefarious task

"Therefore, I considered the circumstances demanded, as imperative for the public welfare, the immediate departure from national territory of General Plutarco Elías Calles, Luis Morones, Luis León and Melchor Ortega."

Arriving at Los Angeles, defiant in exile, Calles issued another statement, declaring: "The Government is attempting to set up a dictatorship on the Russian plan. And because I opposed it, I was exiled."

THE WOMEN TOOK A HAND

A short time after Calles had been exiled a group of two hundred peasant women, most of them barefooted and with children in their arms, seized Santa Barbara (the hacienda of Calles), but when officials were summoned they returned to their homes. It was predicted that the government would take over the property. Not so. Years later, with permission to return to Mexico on condition that he refrain from participation in politics, Calles returned, his property intact, and lived there quietly until his death.

WHAT IS A COMMUNIST?

In calling Cárdenas and his other opponents "Communists," the ex-Iron Man was following an American custom as well. I had observed at home that when a man, elected as a progressive, was headed to reaction, the only answer he made to those criticizing his going back on his professions, was to hurl the epithet, "Communist," in seeking to justify his falling from grace by such insult to his critics. And sometimes it worked!

As I read the "defi" of Calles, knowing there were not enough Communists to carry a single district, either in Mexico or in the United States (I never saw one in Mexico except Diego Rivera though there were others), I asked myself: "If there are Communists in Mexico and the United States, what kind of animal is he like? What is the definition of a New World 'Communist'?"

That question recalled the answer given by Lord Lochiel, of Scotland, a member of the Cameron clan, who won renown in World War I. Visiting his Cameron kin in North Carolina, he was relating an incident in Scotland, in which he made reference to "the Communists." I expressed surprise that there were such animals among the canny Scots. He said: "Only a few." To my inquiry: "What is a Communist?" Lord Lochiel essayed a definition, but before it was completed said: "No that will not do," and made several trials, but none suited him. At last he threw up his hands in despair at giving a definition and said: "O, a Communist is any damn fellow you don't like."

FASHIONABLE GAMBLING HOUSE CLOSED

Cárdenas' first act of a dynamic nature, which won my admiration, was his invoking of the law against gambling by shutting up the fashionable Foreign Club, where so many people had been fleeced that the business men, not all Cárdenas admirers, applauded.

That order created consternation in the ranks of the "high fliers," some of whom were politically prominent. It was said that certain men in high stations profited by the operation of the Foreign Club, which had been fitted up for receptions and parties of all kinds.

Cárdenas acted with his customary directness and swiftness and it was effective. One night the dice and cards and the gambling devices were going at full blast and elegant parties were being held as the unwary were being fleeced. The next night all was darkness. The lights were out, the garlands gone, and all had departed. The owners knew that appeals were useless for they realized that though Cárdenas was no Puritan, he had determined to end the fleecing of

people at the Foreign Club and nothing would move him. (Later
he did the same thing at Cuernavaca.) He knew the fondness of
many Mexican people for games of chance and he knew that the
high lights and glittering halls would cause many to lose their earn-
ings. He saved them, and business men applauded. If officials were
making profits, they dared not admit it. Mexico's Monte Carlo was
out.

CÁRDENAS SPEAKS AT OPENING OF CONGRESS

Of the opening of Congress, which was in session three hours as
compared with former sessions lasting five hours—I wrote to my
sons:

"Sunday was the great day when President Cárdenas delivered his message to the new Congress. All the Secretaries of the
Embassy and your mother went. For the first time in many
years the President rode down the streets in an open automobile
with no troops or secret service men in his car. This illustrates
his faith that he is in no danger. The exercises lasted from 10
A.M. until nearly 1 P.M. The President read his speech in a very
low tone, with no change in inflection and no emphasis. The
President of Congress followed in better voice. As the President
left the Chamber he saluted your mother and me. The members
of Congress are younger than with us—only five gray-headed
and eleven bald-headed men out of the 170. The President
stressed Socialistic Education, dotating land to the Indians and
the organization of the *campesinos* as a sort of reserve of the
army. The giving of land to them goes on and the President
declared it would continue until every *campesino* (tenant farmer
or worker on the farm) had been given land. We have protests
from some American owners that their property is being con-
fiscated."

CÁRDENAS STRONG FOR NEW DEAL

Of my last real talk with President Cárdenas before going to
Washington in the spring of 1935 I wrote home:

"On Friday I spent an hour with President Cárdenas, who
sent messages to President Roosevelt. He admires our President
very much and says he wishes he could give the New Deal of
America to Mexico. He dispelled any idea that he is sympathetic to communism. He is chiefly concerned to give education

to all the children and land to the landless. He is a sincere man devoted to improving the condition of the Indians. He is himself part Indian and has poise and speaks in a soft voice. He said when I returned from the United States he wished me to go with him on a visit to his home in Michoacán, 'the most beautiful part of Mexico.' He talked freely of the labor and religious troubles and believes both will be composed."

CÁRDENAS GIVES HIS VIEWS ON EDUCATION AND RELIGION

Ambassador Morrow thought he had settled the religious controversies in Mexico when the Pope agreed that the Archbishop should register with the government the priests who were to officiate, and bells were rung in celebration of the reopening of the churches in Mexico City, Puebla, Guadalajara, Monterrey, Cuernavaca, and other places. But the differences were deeper, and periodically there arose trouble because of excesses and wrongs on the part of some public officials, some perfervid priests and other Catholics, and certain politicians. Differences over church questions, the agrarian policy, and public education would not down. The best statement of the attitude of President Cárdenas was given to me in a heart-to-heart talk at his small home, "The Pines" (he declined to live in Chapultepec Castle), in October, 1936. Of that historic visit and conversation I made the following report addressed to the Secretary of State:

"I have the honor to report that on Wednesday afternoon, October 7, 1936, upon invitation, I called with Colonel Marshburn, our Military Attaché, to have tea with President Cárdenas at his private home 'Los Pinos.' On several occasions I had talked with the President about the agrarian and religious problems, particularly the latter. Recently I had represented to the Minister of Foreign Affairs the serious objections of my government to the dotation, without payment, of American-owned lands to *campesinos* of Mexico. President Cárdenas told me that General Hay had communicated my representations (see despatch No. 3939 of September 17, 1936) to him and he wished to talk with me about the matter and to assure me of his earnest desire, in so far as he could, to meet the wishes of my government as I had conveyed them to General Hay. At much length he discussed the agrarian situation in Mexico and his desire to meet the views of our government in every way that was within his power. He said that he was prepared to say that in the next budget he would make provisions for the payment for lands which had been in the possession of Americans and that he hoped to follow a plan that he believed would be 'acceptable to you and to the American owners.' He plans to include funds for such payment in his budget of January 1, 1937. He is now having a special study prepared to ascertain how large a sum may be set aside for such payments. He said more than once that he would put in the budget as large a sum as the condition of the Federal Treasury would make possible, and he repeated that he believed we would regard it as 'satisfactory.'

"President Cárdenas discoursed upon what he regarded as Mexico's three most important problems. In order he named them thus: 1. Educational; 2. Economic; 3. Religious. 'With due regard to our educational and economic needs.' he said, 'we will pay as much on the agrarian claims as we possibly can, and when payments are begun, they will be kept up.'

"I told the President that at this time the two situations which disturbed the perfectly friendly relations between the two countries were the division of American lands without compensation and the feeling in the United States that full religious liberty was denied in Mexico. The latter, as I had told the President on other occasions, lessened the prestige of Mexico in the nations of the world. He spoke at length, and evidently after much thought, about the religious situation. He was very earnest in repudiating the suggestion that Mexico was either communistic or atheistic. He said he believed religion was the foundation of morality, and that he had stood for no persecution.

" 'You have observed,' he said, 'that in every State as new Governors in sympathy with my administration have been elected, more and more churches have been opened and a policy of moderation is growing all the time.' He enumerated six or eight States in which churches had been reopened, among them Sinaloa, Chihuahua and Colima, adding that he was desirous that the more moderate policy should extend to all the States of the Republic.

" 'You must have observed,' added the President, 'a disposition on the part of the present administration to relax any stringent laws affecting religion, and that is the fixed policy of the government. We are neither pro- nor anti-clergy. While realizing fully the necessity for religion, and believing that morality and education are necessary corollaries thereto, we have always insisted that the clergy must confine its activities to its religious sphere and not attempt to use influence in the domain of politics or government. You should realize that there is a difference between the clergy and its actions in the United States and in Mexico. The Church here has often been politically-minded, and when it directed education comparatively few of the people were educated. Without universal education we recognize that progress and prosperity cannot reach the whole population. Therefore we are building schools and carrying the opportunity of education to all the children in every part of the republic. We recognize that a better future for Mexico depends upon general education.' He added that in other days many of the clergy had not been in sympathy with the movements for social improvement of the great masses of the people. Primarily, he said, he was interested in educating his people and that for many decades the leaders of the Catholic Church here had been in full control of the educational policy and that for that reason 85% of the people were illiterate, and that he was determined, above everything else, to see that the children enjoyed the advantages of education.

"Continuing, President Cárdenas said that several prelates of the Catholic Church had come from his family and that some of them were more interested in politics and control of government than in the social improvement of the people. 'It was because of this that we were not in agreement,' he added. He then stated that the Mexican clergy are sharply divided as to the course that should be pursued in Mexico, and 'it is because of this division among them that they have not been able to agree upon a successor to the late Archbishop Díaz.' . . .

"President Cárdenas then said there were good openings in Mexico for investors, manufacturers and business men from the United States. He enumerated cheaper raw material and a lower scale of wages than existed in the United States and expressed the hope that these advantages would incline my countrymen to larger investments in Mexico. This gave me the opportunity to tell him that the Embassy had received many inquiries concerning a Mexican Expropriation Act now pending in the Congress. I told him that because of its vagueness investors and business men and manufacturers feared it might give the right, and in some cases it might be exercised, to take private property from its owners. I told him that the publication of that proposed measure had caused much apprehension among Americans and other foreigners doing business here. I added that unless the measure was drawn with great clearness and gave assurance that private property would be protected, instead of the further investments he desired, there would be such fear as would decrease investments and manufacturing plants and purchase of property here.

"The President replied that he was glad of an opportunity to discuss with me the proposed act, the contents of which he said had not yet been made public. He assured me that before taking any property under the proposed measure he would guarantee that an arrangement would be reached which would be entirely satisfactory, both to the owner of the property and to me as representing my country. 'The law is being carefully studied,' he went on to say, 'both by a special committee of Congress and by very able men whom I have named. Nothing will be done until I have the result of these considered studies. The terms of the law, when and if enacted, will not apply to private industry.' He was emphatic in his statement that Mexico desires and needs United States capital to develop Mexican industries and assured me again that in every case of such *bona fide* investment in Mexico complete protection would be afforded the investors.

"The President talked so freely and at such length that he had not observed that the tea which had been brought was getting cold, and, with a laugh, his secretary asked, 'Do you like your tea hot or cold? If the former we will send for more tea.' I drank it tepid.

"As I was leaving, the President invited me at some future day to accompany him to the base of the volcanoes where a hotel for visitors and a road to Popocatepetl and Iztaccihuatl were in process of construction. He asked, 'Does the altitude affect you?' I replied that I had a good heart and never felt any perceptible difference between low and high altitudes. 'I have a good heart physically and spiritually too, I hope,' I added and we both smiled.

"In reporting the views of the President, summarized in a conversation of an hour and thirty-five minutes, I have sought from memory to give his words. I may not always have succeeded in getting his exact words, but at least they are as near as I can recall."

ROOSEVELT'S PRESENT TO CÁRDENAS

I found that in almost every New Deal and Pan American policy Cárdenas and Roosevelt saw eye to eye as this letter home (October 23, 1937) shows:

"On Friday, I had a long talk with President Cárdenas at the National Palace about several policies in which the State Department is interested. He is always cordial and agreeable. He knows his Mexico and has patience and courage—about the two best virtues any man can possess.

"I carried him one of the most beautifully bound and printed books I had ever seen, which President Roosevelt had asked me to deliver to him with his compliments. It contained, printed in elegant style, the speeches that President Roosevelt made on his South American trip. It was in both Spanish and English. President Cárdenas is in full agreement with President Roosevelt in the matter of the Nine-Power Treaty and the arbitration of the dispute between Nicaragua and Honduras. He told me he had directed the Mexican representative who is going to Brussels (Isidro Fabela Alfaro) to see the head of the American delegation at Brussels before the conference on the 30th."

CÁRDENAS JOINS ROOSEVELT TO PREVENT WAR

Toward the end of 1938 President Roosevelt, apprehending the danger that threatened the world, sought united action to prevent war. Of his attitude and Mexican coöperation I wrote (October, 1938):

"On Monday night, in response to a telegram from Washington enclosing a message from President Roosevelt to the leaders of Europe, urging that they continue their negotiations until a peaceful solution was reached, I went to see General Hay and told him that President Roosevelt would be glad if President Cárdenas would join him in a like message. General Hay said he would see the President and he knew he would be sympathetic. The next day Cárdenas did send the message; and afterwards Beteta called at the Embassy to bring me a special message from President Cárdenas to President Roosevelt, in which he suggested that all the Pan American countries should unite in an agreement that in case of war they would not sell any raw materials or munitions or anything else that could help the warring nations. He even said that although Mexico had an agreement to sell oil to Germany, it would forego the profits of such a transaction, if other nations would agree to keep aloof from the warring powers and prevent their getting anything which would enable them to carry on the war. I am afraid the United States would not agree to that. One of the things that make me hate to think of a war in Europe is the propaganda that would go on in the United States for us to get into it or help, in order to get high prices for our wheat, cotton, and munitions."

ROOSEVELT SENDS GREETINGS TO CÁRDENAS

In November, 1939, I wrote:

"Returning from Washington I went to the National Palace to see President Cárdenas and conveyed to him the greetings of President Roosevelt, who had asked me to say to General Cárdenas that he hoped during his term of office he and General Cárdenas could get together and exchange ideas and felicitations. Cárdenas was very much pleased and said he would be very glad to see President Roosevelt at any time and place as soon as the situation in the world permitted such a conference. He asked me how long I thought the war would last. I told him that when I was a young man I was frequently given to prophesying but that as most of my prophecies did not come true, I had decided to let Elijah do all the prophesying. He said that having had long experience I might be able to prophesy now better than when I was young but I told him I doubted it.

"We talked about many things of common interest to the United States and Mexico and I told him that President Roosevelt had been very much gratified at the coöperation of the Mexican delegation at the Panama Conference and that Mr. Welles had told me he and General Hay got along well together and saw eye to eye in every way in improving and increasing the good relations between Mexico and the United States and all Pan American countries. The President told me that he had been in communication with Ambassador Castillo Nájera, who had had a conference with Mr. Hurley and other oil people, and he expected that Mr. Richberg would be coming down to Mexico shortly and he hoped they would find a solution for the matter."

CÁRDENAS TELLS HOW THE WAR WAS INVOLVING MEXICO

As war clouds gathered, the need for the strengthening of the Good Neighbor ties of Pan American countries was seen to be imperative. I talked often of the importance of this hemispherical solidarity with the Foreign Office and with President Cárdenas. Of a visit to Cárdenas in the fall of 1939 I wrote:

"On Thursday by appointment, I called to see President Cárdenas and we discussed at length the war situation in Europe and the attitude to be assumed by the Pan American nations with reference to it. He said that he had early discussed with the Foreign Minister the importance of continental solidarity and would appoint representatives of his Government to be present at Panama to unite with the United States and other nations to that end. 'However much,' he said, 'Mexico might wish to be free from everything that occurs in the European war, it cannot be indifferent because it touches even the remotest part of the world.' As an illustration of this he spoke of the fact that Mexico had made a contract with Germany to furnish rails to complete the road being built in the south of Mexico, in the State of Campeche, which were to be paid for in oil. He said: 'Now we cannot get them and our work on that railroad awaits our ability to get them from some other country, though from Germany we could get them by barter. Not only the railroad construction must be halted but this means loss of employment, at least for the time being, for the men employed in the construction of the railroad.'

" 'This,' he said, 'is only one example of how the war affects people who have no connection with it and are remote from it.'

"In the course of the conversation I made the suggestion, and told him I knew that was the heart's desire of President Roosevelt, that all matters at issue between the United States and Mexico might be settled; that as long as they remained open they were more or less a running sore, and I hoped that without delay the two countries could agree on some method of adjusting these differences, some of them of long standing, and added that if we could not agree on some of these very difficult questions, a way should be found for arbitrating them so that they might not disturb the relations between the two countries. President Cárdenas said he was in hearty accord with this and would give it serious consideration and would wish to see me again."

CÁRDENAS APPROVES OF TOWNSENDS' WORK AMONG INDIANS

In accordance with a rule to call on President Cárdenas just before going to Washington, I followed that course in 1940 and wrote in my Diary (May 7) as follows:

"On Saturday by engagement I went to the Palace to see President Cárdenas. I always drop in to see him just before I go home on vacation and he always has a message for President Roosevelt. He was very agreeable and talked very freely about conditions. He expressed the hope and belief that some settlement of the oil controversy could be reached without arbitration and said that the agreement with the Sinclair ought to make possible agreement by the other companies and that Mexico would be very glad to discuss with them some similar arrangement.*

"I talked with him about the Indian Congress and the Indian Institute to be established here in which he is very much interested. Being partly Indian himself he naturally considers plans for their welfare almost more than any other person would. In the course of the conversation he said he was very much pleased with the work Dr. Townsend and his young people are doing in training the Indians who do not speak Spanish and had seen their good work in Chiapas. I told him that the day before one of the young men who has been teaching the Indians in Chiapas called to see my wife and gave her one of the hats worn by the Indians in that region, with a picture showing how they were worn. I said they were worn on the side of the head and tipped over one eye much as American and Mexican women wear their hats today and I told the President that apparently the present styles did not originate in Paris or London or New York, but came from the Indians of the State of Chiapas."

ROOSEVELT SENDS GREETINGS AND A MESSAGE TO CÁRDENAS

Upon my return to Mexico from my vacation in the United States I made my first call on President Cárdenas, of which I wrote (June 29, 1940):

* The story of the oil controversy is told in Chaps. XVIII-XXIV.

"Before leaving Washington President Roosevelt asked me upon my arrival to call on President Cárdenas and convey a message of courtesy and one of high regard and friendship. I therefore made an engagement to see the President at the National Palace on Friday and conveyed Mr. Roosevelt's message and then we talked about the greatly advertised threat of Nazi agents here and the importance of solidarity on the part of the twenty-one republics of this continent to prevent any penetration either by anything like the Fifth Column or by European countries wishing to get a foothold of land or economic power.

"The President said his government was vigilant to prevent any Nazi agents or Communists from doing any harm in this country and asked me to give him any information we might get indicating such subversive activities. I gave him one incident which indicated something was being done in the way of manufacturing grenades secretly and he asked me to keep in touch with him and give him any information we got, so that in addition to anything his people discovered he might have anything that comes to the attention of the Embassy. He was very much interested in the approaching Havana Conference and wished me to say to my Government that Mexico would coöperate fully in the policies and plans which might be adopted there for the protection of the Western Hemisphere."

CÁRDENAS REJOICED AT ROOSEVELT ELECTION

I was gratified to find most Mexicans joining in celebrating Roosevelt's reëlection, and wrote (November 12, 1940):

"On Wednesday morning I had a telephone message from General Hay saying that he wished to call at the Embassy at 10:30. He came, accompanied by Licenciado Leñero and General Lamont, President Cárdenas' private secretary and military aide respectively. General Hay said he had been commissioned by General Cárdenas to call and express his congratulations upon the reëlection of President Roosevelt and to ask me to inform Roosevelt of his gratification and that of the Mexican people that he was again to guide the ship of state for four years. He said he wished also to express his own felicitations and his deep admiration for President Roosevelt; so did the others who called with him. During his whole term I have talked often with President Cárdenas and found that he always had deep faith in President Roosevelt and his New Deal policy.

I think Cárdenas feels that he has carried out in Mexico some of the same ideas, particularly his devotion to helping the many men who have so long been forgotten. It was the similarity of goals that has made President Cárdenas feel so warmly toward our President."

PRE-WAR SOLIDARITY

During the difficult period after war began in Europe until his term of office expired President Cárdenas was vigilant to prevent Nazi propaganda, and in every helpful way coöperated with the United States in providing materials for strengthening Pan American military preparedness. His provision, followed and enlarged by President Camacho when war came, made the United States and Mexico not only Good Neighbors but allies in combating totalitarianism.

A MEXICAN CINCINNATUS

When his term expired President Cárdenas retired to his farm in his native state of Michoacán. When in 1941 a Mexican paper stated that he was trying to control politics, Cárdenas harked back to the medicine he had given Calles, who had tried to be the power behind the throne, and said cryptically, "We know the way to deal with men who attempt to meddle in politics after having been President."

He has since lived quietly on his farm; but he was like Cincinnatus of old, for when the Day of Infamy at Pearl Harbor stirred his patriotism, Cárdenas wired to President Camacho: "As a result of the painful event of the declaration of war between the United States and Japan, I am honored to place myself immediately at the disposition of your government." He was named "Minister of National Defense" and directed the land, air, and sea forces of Mexico during the whole of World War II. This justified my confidence in his devotion to democracy and his friendship for the United States, which had been impugned in the hectic controversies of 1938-1940. It made me feel that I had appraised his true place in history, when upon leaving Mexico in November, 1941, I wired Cárdenas a farewell message of affection. I said: "You have made your place in history alongside of Benito Juárez."

CÁRDENAS WOULD NOT ACCEPT GIFTS

Not long after the oil expropriation Ambassador Castillo Nájera was called to Mexico City by the President to confer on the oil impasse. I asked him to lunch. Nobody else was present except my wife. He told us many interesting stories about Cárdenas. The Ambassador was a surgeon in the Mexican Army during the revolution and was the doctor on the staff of Obregón, Calles, and other revolutionary leaders. He told us an incident which has probably been sticking in the craw of President Cárdenas all these years. He said that when Cárdenas was made military commander of the Tampico district years ago, shortly after he took command a representative of one of the oil companies called to see him and told him that his predecessors had always given protection to the oil companies, an assistance which they appreciated, and they had shown their appreciation by some gift, and added that they wished to welcome him as a new military commander, and make him a present; and they tendered him quite a large sum (I think he said 25,000 pesos).

Cárdenas answered that he had come there to fulfill his duty as an officer in the army and as such to afford protection to the whole district and all in it, natives and foreigners, but that he could not accept any gifts from anyone, but would be very glad always to have them call and would render any service that his country ought to render. He declined to accept the check. Castillo Nájera said that proved to Cárdenas what many people in Mexico believed, to wit: that in those days the oil companies dominated by offering graft to officials who were charged with public duties where oil wells were in operation.

VIII

CAMACHO AND THE ELECTION OF 1940

G ENERAL MANUEL ÁVILA CAMACHO was chosen President in the most heated contest of a decade (in 1940), which culminated in bloody encounters in the City of Mexico and some other parts of the country. He emerged victorious without rancor and without a stain. I was in Mexico only about a year of his term which embraced the period of World War II, but I kept up with the team work of Mexico and the United States in which both countries were ready to give the last ounce of devotion as partners in securing victory. They were difficult years for Mexico and called for a chief executive who was possessed of ability to unite all elements and solve the problems that came with war. President Camacho measured up to the requirements of those days that challenged sacrifice and demanded patriotism.

He had the calmness to resist pressure and to hold the scale even. The close relations established by his predecessors between the United States and Mexico were strengthened. Mexico was truly an arsenal of the raw materials of war which it possessed in abundance and which were freely placed at the service of the allies. The war won, President Camacho and Foreign Minister Padilla won world gratitude by leadership in coöperation for world peace, as Padilla's speech for unity had won him fame at the Rio de Janeiro Conference.

I remember the day of the election of Camacho as the most tense of all my time in Mexico. I stayed—as did all the Embassy staff—off the streets in pursuance of our policy to remain strictly aloof from the bitter politics of that campaign. However, we knew that it was not only a bitter fight between Camacho and Almazán, but also a crucial campaign. It was a campaign between those who wished to continue the Cárdenas policy and the promises of the Six-Year Plan and those who wanted to go back to the old pre-revolutionary order.

I knew both candidates and had had friendly relations with them.

Camacho was Minister of War in the Cárdenas administration. My first official dealing with him was when Mexico, becoming airminded, wished to buy planes in the United States and we were happy to aid in every way we could. I remember one day discussing the mechanization of armies with him, particularly the cavalry, to which Mexicans gave great emphasis. He said that as better roads were built in Mexico the number of the cavalry would be reduced, but that the Mexican soldier dearly loved his horse and the Army was paying much attention to the breeding and training of horses for cavalry service. A Mexican man would rather ride a horse than do anything else, the Minister said, so that even if cavalry were out of date it would be very hard to dispense with it.

I had first met Almazán as soldier, too, when I was a guest at his mountain home, Chapingua, overlooking the City of Monterrey, in 1934 and had social contacts with him at the home of his brother in Mexico. I had been greatly interested in the model military barracks under his command near Monterrey. Two things there intrigued me:

1. Provision was made for the wives and children of the soldiers to live within the enclosure in houses constructed by the soldiers. This gave a family life in a place of military training.

2. By their own labor the soldiers had built the quarters, had laid off the drill grounds, and had called for no appropriation or outside workmen.

Reviewing the troops there, I recalled a story I had heard accounting for the popularity of General Obregón during the Revolution. The Revolutionary Army had no Quartermasters Department, no supplies, and soldiers lived "on the country," their wives foraging for them and cooking their meals wherever they chanced to be. Obregón made it a rule to invite himself to take meals with the wives of the men and was so warm in his praise of their food, "the best ever," that he won all their hearts.

Almazán won some of the same sort of affection. He had all the dash of a soldier. Camacho, an able official, had skill and wisdom but no dramatic qualities. Camacho had been regular in every way, and in politics had always followed the lead of the National Revolutionary party. Almazán's political record was not so clear and was weakened in the campaign by charges that church leaders, oil men, and not a few Americans who were resentful over agrarian

Above, President Cárdenas, at a dinner which Ambassador Daniels gave in his honor. *Below,* Former President Cárdenas congratulates his successor, President Ávila Camacho, and hands him the traditional tri-color band which the President wears.

Above, the central figure on the balcony is President Ávila Camacho, to the right is Ambassador Daniels, and next to him is Miguel Alemán, Minister of *Gobernación,* who was elected President in 1946. *Below,* Ambassador Daniels congratulates Señora de Ávila Camacho on her husband's becoming President. At the far left is Ezequiel Padilla.

and oil seizures were putting up money for his campaign. It was never in the cards that Almazán could be elected. In the Madero days, Almazán for a time was with Madero but was never trusted by Carranza. He made the fatal blunder of pledging allegiance to Huerta and was promoted by Huerta to General of Divisions, the highest rank in the Mexican Army.

Almazán made no formal platform but promised stabilization, guarantees to capital, cancellation of socialistic education, no surrender to the oil companies; though as to the latter he was not clear as to what he would do.

In its issue of September 7, 1940, the Catholic magazine *America* carried an article by Bishop Kelly, eulogistic of Almazán, saying, among other things, that Almazán "desired to restore a healthy austerity to public service as Franco has done in Spain." As the Mexican government and most of the people were hostile to Franco, this comparison did not help Almazán. Bishop Kelly was not the only man who predicted that Almazán would do in Mexico what Franco had done in Spain. A Franco paper *A.B.C.,* in Madrid, printed a picture of Almazán with the caption, "The future President of Mexico is a Friend of the Caudillo," and declared, "Almazán will begin the reconstruction of Mexico on the same lines as General Franco did in restoring Spain."

There were people, including officials of the ousted oil companies, who had been waiting for "another election" as another chance to get what they wanted. Also some priests and laymen who longed for the old days when the Roman Catholic church had all power and great wealth wanted a change, and organized themselves along with the elements that hated the agrarian, education, and oil policies of Cárdenas. But the loudest cries for Almazán came from the elements which worked to destroy the growing influence of organized labor. To them were added the "outs," who wanted to get "in." And behind these influences was the secret aid of influential parties in the United States, which longed for the good old days when they could get rich from exploiting Mexican resources and pay substandard wages, and which felt that Mexico was drifting into Communism and was in danger of becoming a Bad Neighbor instead of a Good Neighbor.

The lines were early drawn for what was a campaign of marching and parades and clashes between opposing factions. Mexicans dearly love fiestas and parades, and the political campaign partook of both, plus great bitterness, which was not free from fighting and shooting. Almazán had determination behind his campaign. He had winning ways and was hailed in many parts of the country as the coming man.

The Old Guard of the Revolution, which embraced the forces that had ousted Huerta and had put Carranza, Obregón, Calles, and Cárdenas into office and had never met defeat, united in support of General Camacho, who had been a young officer in the Revolution and had served well as Secretary of War. He had no angles, spoke softly, preached no radicalism and was as far away from Communism as it was possible for a man to be. Moreover when the attempt was made to line up the Catholic vote solidly against him, it could not be done. He quietly said, "I am a believer," and his wife was known to be a devout Catholic. As the campaign grew fast and furious, I warned all members of the staff, and told those Americans who asked my advice to remain far removed from even talking about the campaign and the election. Most of their social associates were anti-labor and pro-Almazán. As the day of voting approached, the tension was so great that it could be felt in the air. The chief sporting events of Mexicans, elections and bull fights, are both held on Sunday. As the day of decision approached Almazán threatened that he would lead a revolt "if an attempt is made to thwart the will of the people." That aroused his supporters to fever heat. On election day the fear of wholesale bloodshed was general. Great crowds gathered at the polling places. People marched from church to the polls.

On Sunday, July 7, the day of election, our reports showed sharp fighting between the partisans of the candidates. Even in the Embassy we could hear loud explosions as of bombs. The streets outside resounded with the movements of cavalry and police. Writing home at that time (July 13), I said:

"This has been the most hectic week of my stay in Mexico and the most distressing also, and disappointing. I had hoped that the election would pass off without disturbance and the result would be accepted without resort to bullets, but the revolutionary spirit of Mexico which has flamed so fiercely in the past is not altogether gone and the two opposing forces, unwilling to get together to secure a fair election, chose to resort to methods that resulted in the killing of many people and the wounding of many more. Both sides claim that the majority of the people favored their candidate, and there is a rumor that when Congress convenes in September there will be an attempt to seat two sets of Congressmen, one favoring Ávila Camacho and one Almazán. Some people think it may result in serious conditions, but as Congress does not meet until September there is cooling time.

"Quite a number of journalists from the United States have been here during these election days and some of them have sent off very exciting and sensational reports. Things were bad enough without adding to them. Another type of American is the one who has been here for a short time and thinks he knows more about Mexico in three days than journalists and Americans who have been here for years, and some of them have been sending back very exciting reports."

The closing of the polls did not end the contention. Some weeks after the election (August 26, 1940) I wrote in my Diary:

"Ever since the election the city has been full of rumors about a possible uprising, revolution, etc. The Almazanistas have organized in a secret place their own Congress and electoral college and General Almazán has said, in a statement from Havana, that he would take office as President the first of December. Some of his supporters here expect him to arrive for the opening of Congress and claim that the Congress of his supporters is the legal Congress and their electoral college the legal electoral college and demand that he be given the certificate of election. If so, the supporters of Ávila Camacho, who are in charge of the Chamber of Deputies and seem to have the support of the Government, although President Cárdenas up to this time has made no statement, are expected to deny admission to the Almazanistas, and if the latter appear in force there are predictions of trouble. I have heard so many predictions of revolution since I came here seven years ago, none of which came off, that I am hoping that history will repeat itself and Mexico will be saved from a revolution and serious trouble."

Rumors and fears continued through the summer. On September 5th. I made a note in my Diary:

"All during the week there was a feeling of uneasiness caused by many rumors that there would be trouble on Sunday, September 1st. In anticipation that Almazán might try to carry out his statement that he would return and take possession of the Congress, the Government made unusual preparations and there were many soldiers and many *campesinos* from the country gathered ready to repel any attack made against Cárdenas and the new Congress. Either because the Almazán people had other plans or because they did not feel that September 1st was the best time to stage their attempt to take possession of the government, everything went off very quietly. In view of the fact that the Almazanistas held a Congress and secret session about which nothing was known on Sunday and an announcement to this effect had been made the previous week by supporters of Almazán, the newspaper reporters asked me which Congress I would attend—whether I would be present at the opening of the Congress in the Chamber of Deputies where President Cárdenas was to deliver his annual message. I told them that I had accepted the invitation to attend Congress as I had done every year since I had been here and that General Cárdenas had been elected six years ago and his term did not expire until December 1st of this year, and I would of course accept the invitation to hear him deliver his message to Congress. Practically all of the diplomats took the same position and were present. There were no untoward incidents and much enthusiasm for Cárdenas, who made known that he would accept the action of Congress in counting the votes for President—that is the Congress he was addressing, which was composed almost entirely of supporters of Ávila Camacho."

It was not easy for members of the Diplomatic Corps to stay in an ivory tower of diplomacy in those days. At about the time of the meeting of Congress I wrote as follows:

"Mr. Zawadsky, Minister of Colombia, called to see me and requested me, as Dean of the Corps, to call a meeting of the Corps so that all could come to an agreement with reference to granting asylum. A few nights before, about midnight, two Mexicans, ardent supporters of Almazán for President, had gone to the Colombian Legation and asked for asylum, alleging that their lives were in danger from the Government because they were supporters of the candidate not approved by the National Revolutionary party. The Minister said that under the

Havana Convention which had been ratified by his country he was compelled to take them in. I asked him if he knew their lives were in danger, and if any mob had tried to capture them. He did not know; he accepted their word of their peril. He wanted the heads of the missions to meet and adopt a uniform policy. I told him that if the meetings were held I could not take any part in it, because the Government of the United States had not ratified the agreement as to asylum, and that we granted asylum only when the person came pursued by a mob and it was necessary to open the doors to protect him from assault; but that under our practice, as soon as he was admitted, we would have to notify the authorities of the country, and turn him over to them. He was very insistent and at the Brazilian Embassy reception he and several others of the South American diplomats said they felt that whenever I was requested to call a meeting of the Corps I was compelled to do so. There were no precedents on file in the Embassy here; so I wired the situation to the State Department and asked them to let me know what the policy should be in these circumstances. Otherwise, I would not call a meeting of the Corps. The answer was one of approval of the course I had taken, but in substance advised me not to bring the matter to an issue if possible, and if it became insistent and the members of the Corps felt that I was not acting up to my duties as Dean, I might absent myself from the city for a few days. In the meantime, the Minister of Colombia told me that when he admitted these men to the Legation he wrote to the Foreign Office and they had not shown him the courtesy even of a reply, but had directed the Mexican Embassy in Colombia to bring the matter to the attention of the Colombian Foreign Office, informing that office that there was no danger to any Almazán supporter in Mexico and therefore no necessity of asylum. He resented the reporting of this matter to his government through the Mexican Minister. However, a little later the Foreign Office wrote him a letter. I told him this letter was coming to him, and he said that if the proper explanation were made he would not press the matter. I take it he was satisfied with the letter from the Foreign Office, for I heard no more about it. The incident might have grown to a troublesome issue."

Of course, the official announcement of Camacho's election did not satisfy the Almazán partisans—in Mexico or outside it. Bishop

Kelly claimed that 85 per cent of the five million voters had cast their ballot for Almazán and that he would set up his government "in some place secret from the raids of the Cárdenas police," and wrote: "Rival congresses can only make for violence. It is anticipated that in the above circumstances Almazán will return to his stronghold in Monterrey. Without foreign intervention on his behalf Cárdenas cannot maintain himself against Almazán. If the situation deteriorates to violence, Cárdenas cannot count on his Army."

THE ALMAZÁN JUNTA AT SAN ANTONIO

Some Almazanistas spoke openly of the revolution to put Almazán in the Palace, saying: "The people will know what to do. We do not have to urge them on; we have to hold them back until the proper time."

Undoubtedly, as long as he hoped at all, Almazán depended upon empty assurances given him by citizens of the United States who had helped to finance his campaign. His followers did have secret meetings, and it was reported that he would come to Mexico City with tens of thousands of supporters and take the oath of office as President on December 1st. Many people expected him to do so, but when the hour came it was evident that though Cárdenas had said nothing during the excitement he had made certain that the Almazanistas would not be able to carry out their threats.

I wrote in my Diary:

> "As I rode down the Paseo de la Reforma to witness the inauguration I observed great crowds of people, calm and resolute. There was not a cry among them for Almazán. The only possibility of the coming of General Almazán to the presidency would be through bloody revolution. General Camacho was the choice of the majority of the voters. He has the coöperation of the people and will coöperate with the United States. Mexicans want peace. They know from experience the destruction which attends revolution and they—or most of them—agree with the old Spanish proverb: 'Better a poor president than a good revolution.' "

TWINS IN RESISTANCE

Speaking in New York at the celebration of the enactment of the Bill of Rights, I was able to assure the people that the United States and Mexico had cemented the Good Neighbor relationship. I said:

"Coming home a short while ago from Mexico, before the Day of Infamy that precipitated war, President Camacho commissioned me to convey to President Roosevelt the assurance that his country would be found standing with our country for the liberties they both cherish. These executives see eye to eye. Since then, President Camacho has mobilized land and sea forces to protect the Pacific Coast from penetration or invasion under the command of another patriotic Mexican leader, his predecessor in the presidency, General Lázaro Cárdenas, a soldier and statesman of proven courage. Already Japanese ships have been seized, and Mexican and Americans on the West Coast are coöperating to meet any threat on the Pacific. Not only so, but four former Presidents of Mexico have volunteered for active service in the field. President Camacho has notified the German, Italian, and Japanese ministers that his country has broken relations with the axis nations, and the great majority of Mexicans are as opposed to totalitarian rule as the people of the United States. They will resist to the utmost the destruction of their liberties. As one long resident there, I have never doubted that the alien influences, once active, would be ousted and that Mexico and the United States, having honorably completed negotiations which settled most differences, would fight shoulder to shoulder.

"Let me here express my confidence in and admiration for President Camacho and his able Minister of Foreign Affairs, the Honorable Ezequiel Padilla, whose early perception of the gulf that separated democracy and autocracy and whose eloquent espousal of continental solidarity have won the admiration of all lovers of freedom. Ezequiel Padilla and Cordell Hull speak the same language of courageous patriotism. We are honored today by the presence of the ranking member of the Mexican cabinet, my good friend and the good friend of our country, the Honorable Miguel Alemán, Minister of *Gobernación*. He brings the assurance that these two republics are twins in resistance to the foes of democracy."

IX

ALEMÁN AND VERA CRUZ

OOKING back on my years as Ambassador to Mexico, I have a
feeling that Vera Cruz has a meaning of good luck for me.
Actually I think the Vera Cruz incident, which brought protests
against my appointment in the beginning, made it possible for me
to prove early that I was not quite so bad as I had been painted.
Also it was in Vera Cruz that I had an almost miraculous escape
from death. I think of Vera Cruz in remembrance as a place where
I found good luck and good friends.

On the insistence of career associates I had avoided any official
appearances in Vera Cruz. But passing through the city on a trip
to and from the United States, I learned that all the Catholic
churches were closed. I had seen more of Vera Cruz than many
Mexicans knew. One night before taking the steamer to the United
States I had quietly, unknown to anyone—and over the protest of
the consul—driven out to the monument to the cadets who died
when I sent the fleet there and placed a wreath upon it. I felt in
my heart that these young men had died bravely for their country,
which they believed was being invaded.

I had said nothing about such visits nor about the closed churches
which I had seen there, but one day in conversation with President
Cárdenas, I said, "General, the people of Mexico are the poorest
advertisers in the world."

"What do you mean?" he asked (not being a newspaper man,
though in his boyhood he worked in a newspaper office).

"A good advertiser puts his best goods in his show window and
boasts of them," I replied, "but you Mexicans display what does
you most harm."

Still he did not understand what I was driving at and asked to
what I referred. I told him that every visitor to Mexico from the
United States and Europe by water landed at Vera Cruz, and it
made a bad impression when they saw no church open for worship.
They returned home saying that Mexico kept all the churches

AL CAER LA TARDE DEL 1º DE DICIEMBRE DE 1936, CERCA DE JALAPA EDO. DE
VERA CRUZ, VIAJANDO SR. S.E. JOSEPHUS DANIELS EN UN TRANVIA, VENIA UN TREN
MUY GRANDE EN LA MISMA DIRECCION; Y POCO FALTO FALTO PARA SER ATRO-
PELLADO. TODOS LOS QUE VENIAN MIRANDO EL PELIGRO. SALIERON RAPIDA-
MENTE DEL TRANVIA, SOLO EL SR. DANIELS Y OTRO QUE ALLI SE HICIERON AMIGOS
QUEDARON DENTRO: NO PASO NINGUN SERIO ACCIDENTE POR LO QUE SE DEBE
EL MILAGRO A SAN CRISTOVAL. Y A EL SE DA GRACIAS.

Above, Miguel Alemán (*center*) at his inauguration as Governor of Vera Cruz.
Alemán stands between Ambassador Daniels (*right*) and Luis I. Rodríguez, personal
representative of the President of Mexico (*left*). *Below,* the retable painted by the
artist Pancho to commemorate Ambassador Daniels' narrow escape from death.
There is a translation on page 91.

Above, settling a Diplomatic Headache. A conference on the Claims question. *Left to right,* General Eduardo Hay, Mexican Minister of Foreign Relations, Ambassador Daniels, Lawrence Lawson, and Gustavo P. Serrano (Photo Acme). *Below,* General Hay handing Ambassador Daniels a check for the initial payment on American Agrarian Claims.

closed. I added, "Of course I know that is not true in most other parts of Mexico, but the visitor to Vera Cruz reports only what he sees in your chief seaport, and people abroad feel that your country countenances denial of religious worship."

He saw what I was driving at and told me I must have learned that under a former Governor there had been a serious conflict between the chief executive of the State and the Archbishop of Vera Cruz, and this conflict had produced the situation to which I referred.

"But," Cárdenas added, "a new Governor has been elected in the State of Vera Cruz and I think the old clashes will end and the situation will be changed for the better."

A few days later my secretary came in and said: "Judge Miguel Alemán, the newly elected Governor of Vera Cruz, has called and wishes to see you."

My acquaintance with him was slight. After some general conversation—few men in Mexico get to the main purpose of their visit quickly—Judge Alemán told me he had been elected Governor of the State of Vera Cruz and he had called to express the desire that I honor the occasion by my presence and make an address to his people on inauguration day. I was happy to accept, but when some career officers in the Embassy learned of the invitation and my acceptance they "went up in the air." They urged me not to run what was a serious risk by going to that State, where thousands would be gathered, and warned that some resentful Mexican, who had not forgotten that I sent the fleet to Vera Cruz, might seize upon the occasion to get revenge. I made light of their fears and went gladly to the capital city of the State. I was treated with every courtesy and kindness and was thanked for my Good Neighbor address. The day was beautiful. The Military Commander was General Jara afterwards Minister of Marine in the Cárdenas cabinet, a friend who years afterward visited me in my home in Raleigh.

I asked no questions, but I always had the hunch that it was at the suggestion of President Cárdenas that the newly elected Governor of Vera Cruz asked me to make an address at his inauguration. I was told it was without precedent that an Ambassador from a foreign country had been invited to speak at the inauguration of the Governor of any state in Mexico. The precedent having been broken, I was invited to have a part in the inauguration of other Governors.

Judge Alemán was chairman of the political campaign committee which secured the nomination and election of General Ávila Camacho as successor of General Cárdenas as President of the Republic. Alemán entered the cabinet of Camacho as Minister of *Gobernación,* the ranking post in the Mexican cabinet. Our relations were on the most-favored-nations clause of the Good Neighbor compact, and my wife and I had the privilege of breaking bread in their home and of welcoming them to the Embassy with frequent exchanges of views both official and personal.

LOOKING DEATH IN THE FACE

While on this visit to Jalapa, the capital of the State of Vera Cruz, I narrowly escaped death in the afternoon. With Governor Alemán and others I rode out through large coffee plantations to Coatepec to visit the plant of the power company.

While returning on a trolley car and coming down a steep descent of the road, on the same track a freight train appeared behind us. Its engineer lost control and the train was rushing down the incline and seemed about to demolish the trolley. I was talking with Mr. Jorge Pascal, son-in-law of General Calles, and had not noticed that the heavy train was coming down on us until I saw all the other occupants of the speeding trolley, with fright written on their faces, rush to the end of the car and jump to the ground. I turned to see the cause of the fright and stampede. When I saw the heavy train bearing down on us I felt sure that my time had come. Should I jump off into a steep gulch on the side of the track, or meet death by remaining in my seat? In a second I decided that not to jump meant death or injury and that the same fate would await me if I jumped. Every other person on the train jumped off except Mr. Pascal and myself; he remaining, as he said, to be with me to the end. Fortunately, Providence apparently had Mr. Pascal and me in His keeping. When the big engine was within a few feet of the rear end of our car, the engineer was able to stop it. I was within six feet of death. When I saw how near I had come to the end, I almost collapsed from the shock. I never expected to leave that car alive and I am sure I offered up silent prayers.

The Mexicans attribute such escape from death to St. Christopher.

When the news of deliverance reached the artist, Pancho, he painted a retable in colors and sent it to me with the message that I owed my life to St. Christopher. His retables are found in many churches, an especially beautiful one in the church of Vera Cruz. They are placed as testimonials of marvelous escape from accidents or cures from illness. Underneath the picture showing his conception of the near-tragedy (he erred in not putting the trolley and the train on the same track) he printed in Spanish:

"On the evening of December 1, 1936, near Jalapa, State of Vera Cruz, His Excellency Josephus Daniels was traveling in a street car; a very large train was traveling in the same direction; and he was almost run over. All of those on the street car, seeing the danger, rapidly left the car, only Mr. Daniels and one other who there had become friends stayed inside. There did not occur a serious accident. Therefore the miracle is due to San Cristóbal and to him thanks should be given."

It was framed in one of Spratling's famous tin frames from Taxco. I gave it a place of honor in the Embassy and it now hangs in my Mexican room in Raleigh under the oil portrait of Juárez and pictures of Rodríguez, Cárdenas, Camacho, Alemán and other Mexican leaders. I regard it as an emblem of my luck in Vera Cruz which began and steadily improved throughout my years in Mexico. (A photograph of the retable appears in this volume.)

More precious than any tangible mementos that I possess, however, is my memory of the generous spirit of some Mexicans who had the best reason to remember with bitterness the American landing at Vera Cruz. Not long before Governor Alemán asked me to come to Vera Cruz, I had been shown such generosity by a noble-hearted Mexican. I wrote in my Diary (January 10, 1935):

"Wednesday night we went to dinner with Mr. and Mrs. Martínez Zorrilla. Mr. Zorrilla and several brothers were educated at Cornell and were members of its winning athletic teams. When his sons were ready for college, he and his wife rented a house and lived at Ithaca, New York, until the sons graduated.

"During the evening the host took us to the Cornell room in which were athletic trophies members of the families had won at Cornell. In an adjacent room I noticed the portrait of a very handsome young man in naval uniform. I asked about him and then was deeply regretful that I had spoken. The young man was his brother who had been killed when the naval vessels and marines entered Vera Cruz, and had been posthumously cited for bravery. I started back as if I had been struck. But Mr. Martínez Zorrilla put his hand on my shoulder gently.

" 'It was the fortune of war,' he said. 'We cannot avert such tragedies. I do not blame you.'

"It showed a beautiful spirit. If any Mexican had cause for resentment to me and the Wilson administration, it is the Martínez Zorrilla family, but they understand and acted with generosity."

There was a sequel that warmed my heart. Some time after that night, Mr. Martínez Zorrilla called at the Embassy to invite us to the approaching marriage of his son and said they wished me to be a witness.

"But you do not wish the American Ambassador to be a witness?" my wife asked.

"No," replied Mr. Martínez Zorrilla. "We want our friend, Mr. Daniels."

Mexico is a land of friendships and true sentiment. They do not forget. After I retired as Ambassador, Mr. Alemán met me in New York and at the request of President Camacho presented me with a beautiful silk Mexican flag. It hangs now in my home in Raleigh.

"I am instructed by President Camacho," Mr. Alemán said, "to say that he sends you this flag with his esteem and asks you to promise you will never live a day without being under the folds of the Mexican flag."

In July, 1946, when Mr. Alemán was chosen President of Mexico, he sent me a message expressing hope that I would return to Mexico and be present at his inauguration. He assured me of even a greater welcome than when he gave me the freedom of his State when I was present at his inauguration as Governor of Vera Cruz.

X

THE SHRINE OF MADERO

I HAD been interested in the Madero movement in 1910, which unhorsed Díaz and sent him into exile in France, where he died. The murder of Madero by Huerta's men did not kill the spirit of Madero in the life of Mexico. His spirit still leads in the movement of Mexicans to liberty and opportunity. I therefore was glad when it was suggested by Robert Hammond Murray, veteran newspaper correspondent, that I do myself the honor of calling on Madero's widow at her home.

She was living quietly and gave a cordial welcome to my wife and myself, and won our admiration. She said I was the first American Ambassador she had met since the distressing scene in 1913 when she called at the Embassy to plead in vain with Ambassador Henry Lane Wilson to save her husband's life, as he could have done. He was impervious to her entreaties. She was evidently pleased that we had called to express our regard and admiration for her husband. We were accompanied by Señor Antonio G. Canalizo, whose wife is a sister of Madero. Writing home about the visit (May 14, 1933) I said:

"Mrs. Madero lives in one of the most beautiful places you ever saw. Like all Mexican homes of the old style, you never would judge the character of the house by the front. All the beauty in their homes and in their gardens is reserved for private inspection and enjoyment. If you did not know that Mrs. Madero lived there, you could not help but have an understanding from the minute you entered the house that it was a sort of shrine, with Madero as a saint. In the room into which we were first ushered there is a full-length portrait of Madero wearing the insignia of the office of the President. In the piazza overlooking the garden is a bronze bust of him, and all around the place the Madero spirit reigned, showing that the widow, while living herself in the present, is more than a woman— she is an institution, quietly keeping alive the spirit of her husband.

"She is a very pleasant and agreeable little woman with gray hair, and a very sweet smile, and she looked as if she had come out of a cameo. She served us with tea made from tea sent her by her brother, Mr. Romero, from Japan when he was Ambassador there fifteen years ago. He was present while we were in the home and is a very attractive man. He was not only Ambassador to Japan, but for a brief time was in Washington and in one or two European countries. He and she both speak English very well.

"I wish I was able to describe the garden to you. There are more flowers in that one garden blooming now than you would find in all Hayes Barton at this time of the year. There are shrubs and trees brought from all over the world, and crape myrtle, etc. etc. Your mother may write you about the flowers because she knows more about such things than I do.

"As we sat and sipped our tea, we were beguiled by the mocking birds in the garden. Two of the birds have been trained so they can render the Mexican national air, which they did while we were there, and perfectly. One or two others sing popular Mexican songs. It was most remarkable. They have not such raucous voices as the parrots, but gave the national air and other songs melodiously.

"There are two particular shrines in this house, one a real chapel, such as they formerly had in all Mexican homes of the wealthy classes. Over the altar was a picture of the Virgin of Guadalupe. I think Mrs. Madero hesitated a little about taking us into this chapel, but her sister-in-law, Mrs. Canalizo, suggested it and she seemed very pleased. Before we entered the chapel they excused themselves for a moment and when they came back they had something black to put over their heads— lace scarves probably. They stood before the altar a second and then Mrs. Madero pointed out the different things in the chapel. We were told that it was illegal to have religious chapels in the house unregistered. Mrs. Madero said with a smile, 'We bootleg religion.' From there we went into an adjoining room, where there is a picture of Madero and one of Pino Suárez, his Vice-President, and wreaths with ribbons 'To the Martyrs of the Revolution, Francisco I. Madero and Pino Suárez.'

"This is the most interesting afternoon we have spent, and in a historic setting that was most beautiful. Your mother quite fell in love with Mrs. Madero and I think it was reciprocated. You know how your mother walks into the hearts of people."

This visit, and all I learned in my stay in Mexico, confirmed my opinion that Henry Lane Wilson (a so-called American Ambassador but really the spokesman of big business) was in league with Huerta to prevent the success of Madero's administration, and was, in spirit, *particeps criminis* in the death of Madero. By taking the position that it was not his mission to interfere in Mexican internal problems, Wilson virtually gave Huerta the signal to do what he pleased. At the same time Wilson was keeping the wires hot to Washington urging the recognition of Huerta. In private Wilson was quoted as having said: "Madero belongs in an insane asylum and shooting would be too good for Suárez."

So it happened that while the Ambassador to Mexico was putting on a celebration for George Washington's birthday, Huerta was having Madero and Suárez assassinated, as they were being taken to the penitentiary (as it was given out) "for better safety," so that they could be killed "while attempting to escape."

I remembered the aftermath of that crime. Woodrow Wilson, indignant at the conduct of Henry Lane Wilson, recalled him and declined to recognize Huerta.

As I left the Madero house that day, I felt that Madero, the noble idealist who lighted the fires for a better Mexico, still lived. His slogan in his campaign, "Effective suffrage and no reëlection," is emblazoned on every official document in Mexico.

THE FIRST GESTURE

Mrs. Madero expressed to a mutual friend, with deep feeling, the kindly thought which prompted us to call upon her, especially as it was the only gesture ever made by any representative of the United States Government to indicate regret for what Henry Lane Wilson did, substantially in the name of our government, and certainly in his misuse of his official power and authority.

HOW MEXICO GOT THE BEST OF JAPAN

Through our association with Mrs. Madero—my wife and she became good friends—I came to know her brother, Señor Romero who related incidents of interest not in the books of those tragic days. Writing home (August, 1933) I gave this story by Señor Romero:

"President Carranza sent Romero as Minister to Japan, and his first duty was to obtain from Japan the money which it owed to Mexico.

"Huerta, it seemed, had made a contract with the Japanese that they should furnish munitions to the amount of 30,000,000 pesos at the time when he was struggling to maintain his government. He paid the first two installments and received a portion of the munitions, but not all that he had paid for. When the third installment came due, he defaulted, and Japan quit shipping, but it had made all the munitions, which were ready for shipment, awaiting payment. When this did not arrive, they filled their warehouses with Huerta's orders. Minister Romero, upon arriving in Japan, asked the Japanese government to reimburse Mexico for the sum they had received for which arms had not been furnished. In the meantime it seems that Russia was very desirous of securing the munitions, which had been ordered for Mexico. Huerta failing to pay the bill, Japan had sold all these arms to Russia at a very large profit; for example, a contract for a gun with Huerta was $20. for each one, and they sold the very same guns to Russia for $55. Mr. Romero demanded that this profit, or part of it, should go to Mexico, or the guns, for which Mexico had already paid, should be given to him so that he could send them to Mexico.

"I asked him how he ascertained that Russia had paid that price. He smiled and said, 'My early education in California stood me in good stead when I went to Japan. I had a Russian schoolmate at college [I think he said the University of California, but maybe it was Stanford, I have forgotten], and we studied together there for several years and became good friends. When I arrived in Japan I found that my Russian schoolmate was the man who had bought the guns for his government from Japan, and he told me what he had paid for them. I asked him if he would give me a statement to that effect. He did more than that; he gave me a photographic picture of the contract. Armed with that I was able to present the case, but it took five months to get action. Japan could not deny they had sold the guns ordered by Mexico for $55. each, when Mexico had paid for part of them at $20 each. So, after long deliberation, strengthened by this evidence given me by my old schoolmate, I got a certified check for $300,000, American money, on the Chase National Bank of New York, which I sent to Carranza. It came to him at a time when the treasury was empty and he lacked money to carry on the campaign. At that time, of course, the relations between the U.S. and Mexico were strained and the Japanese officials naturally supposed that I had feelings of enmity toward the U.S., and everywhere I went they would make some reference to the great Colossus of the North, which was trying to oppress Mexico, thinking it would be very pleasing to me. Of course I listened and said nothing, for there never was a time when I had any such feeling toward the U.S.'

"Mrs. Madero was much interested in the picture she had seen of your mother taken wearing the Tehuana costume, and asked her for one of the photographs, which your mother promised to send."

XI

FOREIGN MINISTERS

I N THE regular order, the chief access to the official life and the
spirit of the country to which an Ambassador is assigned is
through intercourse with the Foreign Minister. On him he makes
his first call. The Foreign Minister arranges for the presentation of
the new Ambassador's credentials and holds conferences with him
weekly and sometimes oftener. My association, more or less close,
with the American Secretaries of State Bayard and Gresham in the
Cleveland administration, and Bryan, Lansing, and Colby in the
Wilson administration had acquainted me with the processes of
diplomacy between a foreign Ambassador and the head of the Foreign Office of the country to which he is assigned.

Much of the success or failure of an Ambassador depends on his
relations with the Foreign Minister, who can be sympathetic and
advance the just representation he makes, or may bar the way to
achievement. I was fortunate in that, instead of assuming always to
have the last say, the four Mexican Foreign Ministers from 1933 to
1942—Dr. José Manuel Puig Casauranc, Emilio Portes Gil, Eduardo
Hay, and Ezequiel Padilla—were men of wide public experience
and understanding—simpático as well—who made access to the
President easy and in important matters arranged direct approach
to the Chief Executive. They sometimes suggested discussions among
the three which were helpful and fruitful. It enabled me upon my
yearly—or more frequent—conferences in Washington with President Roosevelt to convey the attitudes and views of the Mexican
Chief Executive; likewise, upon my return to Mexico, to acquaint
the Mexican President with the policies and aims of the President
of my country. Inasmuch as personal conferences between chief
executives are not feasible, this medium creates understanding.

MEXICAN AMBASSADORS TO WASHINGTON

As soon as my appointment was announced, the Honorable González Roa, Mexican Ambassador at Washington, one of Mexico's

ablest and most experienced statesmen, called to assure me of a welcome to his capital and to acquaint me with the matters pending between the two countries. We journeyed together to speak at the Pan American Society at New York, and later in Mexico City we pondered the everlasting question of Claims, which had troubled our predecessors for over a century. Later, when Dr. Francisco Castillo Nájera, a medical doctor and trained diplomat, succeeded to the ambassadorship in Washington, we established happy official relations which burgeoned into sincere friendship. Perhaps we were two of the happiest diplomats in the world in November, 1941, when the two countries reached agreements that settled the most vexing differences that had existed between the two countries. After I left Mexico, he became foreign minister under Camacho, one of the ablest and most versatile who ever held that portfolio.

A DOCTOR IS SECRETARY OF STATE

When I arrived in Mexico I fell into the hands of another official of the medical profession, the Secretary of Foreign Relations, Dr. José Manuel Puig Casauranc. In Mexico, much more than in the United States, doctors of medicine are found in public office. Puig, as a member of the House of Delegates, was imprisoned by Huerta who had usurped power. He was an able man in medicine, legislation, and diplomacy. He knew the United States well, having practiced medicine in Arizona and served as Mexican Ambassador in Washington.

When some objection was made to receiving me as Ambassador because of the Vera Cruz incident, few Mexicans knew anything about me or my political philosophy. One man—and one in the most important post—did, and he was Dr. Puig Casauranc. He told the President that my book, *The Life of Woodrow Wilson,* showed that I was a liberal who was in sympathy with the democratic aims of the Mexican Revolution and said that my book evidenced devotion to the long-forgotten rights of the under-privileged. He quoted my approval of Wilson's declaration that America would never annex a foot of territory by force and my opposition to those Americans who wished to impose their will on Mexico in the critical days of 1913-1921, and my belief that Mexicans had the right to govern themselves without pressure from any other Government.

Dr. Puig told me that before my arrival he had sent for the students, and talked to them concerning my appointment, and that, although at first they were bitterly resentful of my order at Vera Cruz, they had left agreeing to coöperate with the government and stating that they were in accord with its action. I was gratified when he said that Señor Gutiérroz Zamona, who is a descendant of the Governor of Vera Cruz at the time of the occupation in 1846-1847, and who was President of the National Confederation of Students, indicated his sympathy with the attitude of the government.

"THE AXIS OF WESTERN CIVILIZATION"

I found, in my early association with Foreign Minister Puig, that he not only knew my country and his own, but that our minds ran in the same direction in feeling that there was need of a spiritually humane doctrine created by and for all Pan American nations. Talking one day about the need for solidarity and neighborliness in the hemisphere, destined to grow in the days ahead, Dr. Puig gave me a toast he had made to America in 1931, when he was the Mexican Ambassador to the United States. It is worth preserving:

"America! Our America, without distinction of race or language, must become more and more united. Without boasting and without the slightest offence to Europe, it must be recognized that the axis of the western civilization is turning; that it has already turned from where it was only a quarter of a century ago. We believe that axis is now at the point of passing, from North to South, to the American Continent."

THE FUNERAL OF THE MONROE DOCTRINE

In spite of the historical fact that the Monroe Doctrine kept South American countries free and saved Mexico from the perpetuation of the Maximilian Empire, I was surprised to hear criticism of that sheet-anchor of Americanism in Mexico. It was voiced openly by Foreign Minister Puig at a banquet (January, 1934) in his honor when he returned from the Montevideo Conference. He said, "I have been to the funeral of the Monroe Doctrine." He also said, "With absence of any intervention now guaranteed, the best and most cordial relations will now exist between Pan American countries." He was warm in his praise of Secretary Hull.

Why did Mexicans criticize the Monroe Doctrine? At another time Dr. Puig answered that question: "The United States used the

Monroe Doctrine to prevent European nations from taking territory on the Western Hemisphere, but put no inhibition on its own annexation of Texas and California after the Mexican War and on the Big Stick policy, which was anathema south of the Rio Bravo."

SAID AMBASSADOR WAS IN GREAT DANGER

No more polite people live than courteous Mexicans. Here is an illustration, as I wrote home at the time:

"Dr. Puig, Minister of Foreign Affairs, is a doctor by profession and practiced medicine in Mexico and for a time in New Mexico. When he learned that my son, Dr. Worth Bagley Daniels, of Washington, D.C., was a guest at the Embassy, he invited him to accompany me on my next visit to the foreign office. We had an hour's talk about the Cuban situation and other matters and then Dr. Puig said to Worth: 'Your father is in great danger here, serious danger, of becoming in Mexico what Bismarck said was a dangerous position for any diplomat to hold.'

"He took down Colonel House's book 'Intimate Papers' in which Colonel House quoted Bismarck as saying that it was always a dangerous thing for any diplomat to be exceedingly popular in the country to which he was accredited. Of course this was a very pleasant way of trying to make Worth feel that his father was getting along well."

"STRANGE MEMORIAL OF A BELOVED BROTHER"

On the night of my birthday (May 18th), with a distinguished company your mother and I went to dinner at the home of Dr. Puig. Writing to my sons, I said:

"I can't describe how delightful the food was. Some of it was of a character we had never tasted before. The ice cream came on in the shape of a volcano with a fire burning on the top.

"After the dinner we all repaired to the library, or perhaps it would be better to call it a museum library, as it has so many things of interest in it. A beautiful, very large, center table of Italian marble with carved legs and adornment was the pride of Minister Puig. His son told me that Dr. Puig had been six years building the house and furnishing it, and it could well be believed, because he had gathered there many interesting objects of Mexican artists and others—the best to be found in the country.

"There is a head of an Indian woman carved out of a piece of wood which is very beautiful. On the floor in one end of the room is a figure of an Indian woman, with the color rather of the North American Indian. It is very unique and is made of wood. Dr. Puig told me who made it—some Mexican sculptor of real genius. There are many other things in the room, nearly all illustrative of Mexican art.

"But the *pièce de resistance* is a metal frieze, perhaps half a foot wide, which in a way is a story of Dr. Puig's life and incidents in his life. I did not take the time to examine it at all, but there were two parts about it which Dr. Puig's son explained to me. One was the picture of a man talking to two boys. 'It is the story of the wolf,' Dr. Puig's son said, 'My brother always thought the wolf would get away and would be harnessed to a wagon and take him in safety. I always thought the wolf would eat me up.' And there is the picture of the little boy in a wagon and the wolf pulling it; and there is another picture of the wolf standing over a boy, ready to devour him. 'My father,' said the son who was explaining the frieze to me, 'never intended to complete it during his lifetime, and left part of the panel vacant. But when his brother died (burned to death in an automobile accident) it was months before my father ever smiled. The blow was so severe that it affected him deeply. Afterwards he decided to finish this panel as a memoir to his brother. There is a picture of the whole funeral scene, with a laurel wreath, and a coffin being borne to the tomb, and other things making it truly a memorial.'

"Dr. Puig told me that he had been in the cabinet ten years and he had saved nothing. 'The house in which I live belongs to my wife. All the money I have in the world is less than $6,000. I have never cared for money and have served my country from other motives.' "

AMBASSADOR WILSON SAVED MEXICAN LIVES

After his retirement, Dr. Puig told us—at a quiet dinner at the Embassy—many unpublished stories about the Revolution. Of that conversation I wrote home (December 18, 1934):

"During the conversation we fell to talking about the revolution in Mexico. He said that Huerta had put all the members of Congress in the penitentiary. He was of the number. 'We execrated Henry Lane Wilson, who was regarded as responsible for the death of Madero, and who was Huerta's closest friend and confidant. One night about three o'clock I was ordered from my cell to go before the Judge. I did not know whether I was to be shot or what. I had been told in the prison that Henry Lane Wilson had upon his own motion asked Huerta not to shoot us. We had agreed that we wanted nothing from him for we regarded him as an enemy. I told the Judge that I wished no clemency based upon intercession by Henry Lane Wilson. He had sent for me only to get my declaration and not to shoot me.' Dr. Puig added that, even though the Mexicans despised Wilson, he rather thought it was Wilson's intercession with Huerta that saved their lives. Huerta saw that the killing of Madero had created resentment in the United States and that if he killed the congressmen it would intensify the bitterness against him."

DR. PUIG DIED OF A BROKEN HEART

In the middle of May my earliest friend in Mexican public life died. I wrote home (May 10, 1939):

"On Friday I went to the funeral of Dr. Puig Casauranc. You will recall that he was Minister for Foreign Affairs when I was appointed to this post. He was the soul of courtesy and consideration and a warm friendship sprang up between his wife and your mother. He had been suffering from heart trouble and had gone to Havana and died suddenly there. He was one of the most versatile and accomplished men in Mexico. He had served in Congress, as Ambassador, Minister of Education, and Minister of Foreign Affairs. He met the fate of many men who give their lives to politics and public service. He was manager of the campaign of General Calles for the presidency and wrote a life of Calles at that time. In recent years with Cárdenas as President, having been a strong Calles man he was rather out, and neither the Calles people nor the Cárdenas people claimed him. It seems that when Calles broke with Cárdenas, he made a statement that Cárdenas was carrying the country to ruin and Puig wrote a letter to Calles urging him that there be no break. This offended Calles and his friends, who said that Puig had been ungrateful for all that Calles had done for him, and as he had been a Calles man, the Cárdenas people did not want to put him in a position of much importance.

"At the funeral I was talking with a lady who knew him very well and she said, 'What he died of was not physical heart trouble. He died of a broken heart because he was devoted to public life and when the doors closed to him he was never happy again.' When he retired as Ambassador to the Argentine, he went to New York and took a course of several months and came back here to practice gynecology and I think the lady was right; he was never happy. I am distressed at his death."

EX-PRESIDENT IS MINISTER

When Cárdenas became President he named former President Portes Gil as Secretary of Foreign Relations and José Ángel Ceniceros, later Ambassador to Cuba, as Sub-Secretary. Portes Gil retired when the cabinet resigned in a body at the end of six months, and Ceniceros was Acting Secretary for five months. I had long known Portes Gil and found him and Ceniceros able and agreeable Ministers with whom I was pleased to deal. They were able lawyers, experienced officials, too. Portes Gil, former President of the Republic, had long been a leader. When he resigned, he became the head of the National Revolutionary party, a post of great importance in Mexico.

MEXICO'S TWO GREATEST MEN

At a dinner given at the Embassy in honor of Portes Gil, when he became Foreign Minister, I talked with Señora de Portes Gil (young and good looking), and about that conversation I wrote home:

"After the dinner (of course we had no wine, for we never do, and Portes Gil does not drink), the Minister from Peru, who is an ardent Catholic and a severe critic of the policy toward his church, and Portes Gil and I were talking. We were talking about great men. Portes Gil said Morelos was the greatest soldier Mexico had produced and Juárez the greatest civilian. This was in response to my question: 'What is your estimate of Benito Juárez?' After saying he was Mexico's greatest civilian leader, Portes Gil launched forth in a summary of his achievements. I saw my Peruvian friend, Ambassador Rafael Belaúnde, look uncomfortable as Portes Gil placed as highest among the deeds of Juárez his decree that made all church property the property of the government (the Church at one time owned over half of the property in Mexico) and curtailed the powers of the priests, some of whom had been active in politics and government.

"He proceeded to say that the full carrying out of the Juárez policy, thwarted during the reign of Díaz, was now being put into effect. He is an Indian, and didn't notice that my Peruvian friend was squirming, and he defended the policy as essential, to carry out 'the principles of the Revolution.' That is the set phrase for any policy the government adopts. Nobody who was not in sympathy with the Revolution (embracing the overthrow of Díaz and the subsequent fighting here) from Madero to Cárdenas, has any influence with the government. Recently several hundred officials, who were not regarded as real revolutionists, lost their positions. 'None genuine unless the name is blown in the bottle.' They go further, and if a man is believed to side with the Catholics in the matter of 'socialistic education,' he is *persona non grata*.

"After Portes Gil left, my Peruvian friend and I agreed that the policy of the government in denying full religious liberty was contrary to the spirit that ought to prevail everywhere. The Catholic hierarchy for 400 years allowed no Protestant preaching here. They opposed Juárez, stood by Díaz, and in the Revolution were with the old *'Científicos.'* This sticks in the craw of the revolutionary leaders, some of whom feel like punishing Catholics because so many of their leaders opposed the Revolution and still do not favor 'revolutionary principles,' though the rank and file of the people (Catholics, too) vote for 'the principles of the Revolution.' "

AN ENGINEER IS FOREIGN MINISTER

In December, 1935, General Eduardo Hay, an engineer by profession, became Secretary of Foreign Relations and served until December, 1940. He had held office under every President since Madero. Our acquaintance began when he was Revenue Commissioner, and our friendship ended only with his death. He served in the hectic days following oil expropriation. He was a forthright, downright, honest, and frank man. In war and peace he made full proffer of devotion to the revolutionary principles of his country. He bore on his person wounds received when as a youth he was a soldier in the Revolution. He showed me the official record reporting him dead on the field of battle. He was proud of his record. When I reached Mexico he was one of my first callers, and our friendship strengthened when he became Minister of Foreign Relations. He was full of reminiscences of the revolutionary days from Madero's time. Of some of them I wrote home (April, 1936):

"On Monday, April 6th, I went to the Escargot (The Snail) for a luncheon given by Mr. Hay, Minister of Foreign Affairs, in honor of Mr. Oscar W. Underwood, U.S. Commissioner of General Claims, Mr. Shand and Mr. Lay, his assistants, who have been here some days discussing the principles they can agree upon with reference to Uncle Sam's 1,000 claims and Mexico's 600. Officials of the Foreign Office and the Mexican Commissioner and his assistants were present. The luncheon was excellent. I drew Minister Hay out about his experiences in the Revolution. He was Chief of Staff of Madero, was close to Carranza and Obregón, friendly with Calles and Cárdenas. I told Underwood: 'You see in General Hay the original revolutionist, who has been in office under every administration since Díaz was driven out.' He told thrilling stories about Carranza and Villa, both of whom he knew well. I wish I had been forehanded enough to have a dictograph under the table so the stories might have been preserved. Underwood greatly enjoyed the recital of incidents, some of which were most remarkable. General Hay was not over-modest in relating his part. He thinks Villa was a genius of a truly Mexican type, fine officer for a small body of soldiers, but lacking tactical ability when his army became large. 'He had more men than Obregón at Celaya, he said, 'but did not know how to dispose them to win.'"

GIFT OF PROPHECY

Having been a soldier in the Mexican Revolution and a student of European problems and its wars, General Hay asked me one day soon after World War II began, "How long before the United States will be in the War?" He added, "You cannot keep out. As sure as fate the United States will be drawn in." I replied that I did not believe that my country would be drawn into the maelstrom

—that we had sworn after the Armistice "never again," and that I hoped the war would be confined to the European continent. My hatred of war in 1916-1917 had made me think my country could keep out of World War I, and I was the last member of Wilson's cabinet to give up the hope that we could honorably keep out. Again in 1938 the wish was father to the thought. But while I still hoped (up to Pearl Harbor) that Uncle Sam would not be drawn in, General Hay was telling me, on the day after the Germans reached Paris, that it was a world conflagration which would see every country in the conflict, even those in all Pan America directly or indirectly. I disagreed with his early prophecy:

> " 'I am a student of world affairs and of wars,' he said, 'and it is as certain as that tomorrow's sun will rise that the United States will be involved and that the Nazis cannot be defeated until the United States is a partner of the allied countries.' "

HEAD OF THE BRAIN TRUST

General Hay was fortunate in having as Sub-Secretary the ablest of all the younger officials in Mexico, Ramón Beteta Quintana, a congenital liberal, who was the most dynamic member of Cárdenas' Brain Trust. He was the soul of progress, of frankness, of the doctrines that were regarded by many as revolutionary. Seeing alike, as we did, the need in our world for change that would improve the lot of men too long forgotten, we became close friends.

My first real contacts with him were when he became Sub-Secretary of Foreign Relations. His good English and my poor Spanish made conversation easy, and we soon came to discuss other matters than those of diplomacy. He was a liberal who never compromised. He was broader than the popular slogan, "Mexico for the Mexicans," but he was a flaming apostle of the agrarian policy of "The land belongs to those who work it." He was a right arm to Cárdenas in the long and bitter controversy over oil and land expropriation. He made few public appearances, being more the pen of the revolutionary party than its voice, but when he spoke nobody doubted that he knew what he was talking about and that he could not be persuaded to "sell the truth to serve the hour." When the Conference of Consuls of the Republic of Mexico met at the Embassy, attended also by high ranking State Department officials from Washington, I invited Beteta to address the body. It was at a time when *The Lamp* (an oil paper) was blasting everything Mexican and fighting the Cárdenas administration, and when the United States Government was pressing for payment for lands of Americans dotated to the agrarians. Instead of the expected and usual courteous words of welcome, he plunged into the agrarian and oil questions with a vigorous defense of the wisdom of the Cárdenas acts.

When he had finished a militant defense of Mexico's agrarian, land, and educational policies, I observed that it was not pleasing to some of the Consuls who had come into the service in the era of Dollar Diplomacy.

"He should not have been invited if he was going to denounce the American attitude. He talks like a Communist," said a career man. My answer was, "It is best for all of us to know at first hand the policy of Mexicans about the matter at issue between the governments. I asked him to speak without limitation. I am glad he spoke his mind and his country's mind freely. I do not think any of us agree with all he said. I certainly do not, but I am like Voltaire, who, though not believing what a man said, would make any sacrifice to enable him to speak. I wished Beteta to 'take down his hair' and tell us what stand his government takes on controversial issues."

It was not the sweet diplomatic talk expected, like "hands across the Rio Grande," and the "Yes and No" talk too often heard when diplomats get together. Upon the inauguration of Camacho in 1940, Beteta became Sub-Secretary of *Hacienda,* and in 1944 he was Chairman of the Alemán Campaign Committee. In 1946 he became Minister of *Hacienda,* the same post as Secretary of the Treasury in the United States.

MOST ELOQUENT PAN AMERICAN

Upon the inauguration of President Camacho (December, 1940) the new Secretary of Foreign Relations was Ezequiel Padilla, truly called "the most eloquent orator in all Pan America." He had been educated at Columbia University, had served in the cabinet, in Congress, and as Minister to Rome. He was to be the spokesman of his country at the Pan American Conference in Rio, and was to voice the aspirations of all Pan America at San Francisco and at the Chapultepec Conference. It was a pleasure to be associated with him and his able Sub-Secretary Jaime Torres Bodet (who was later, as Minister of Education, greatly to reduce illiteracy in Mexico) in undergirding the Good Neighbor policy and laying the foundation for coöperation in the coming World War II, which we envisioned before the Day of Infamy at Pearl Harbor. Torres Bodet was advanced to Foreign Minister upon the inauguration of Miguel Alemán in December, 1946.

My relations with Ezequiel Padilla, which were to be close when he became Foreign Minister, had been on a friendly but not intimate basis. I had visited his home, where he and his wife were gracious hosts. It was graced with many works of art brought from his stay as Minister to Rome and with Mexican treasures. I found him one of the most brilliant of Mexicans. He had held high office under several Presidents. When he printed an interview with Calles at the time of the break between Calles and Cárdenas, he was criticized by the more ardent Cárdenas supporters; but he had received his first political recognition from Calles and was not a man to forget a friend. I had been pleased once or twice when I had heard him speak, but had never fallen under the spell of his eloquence until March 8, 1941, when I attended a session of the Mexican Senate at which he defended President Camacho's policy of unlimited coöperation with the United States at a critical period. I can still hear the cadence of his voice as he spoke to his fellow Mexicans:

> "It would be deceiving ourselves to deny that the United States is the only nation in this hemisphere with military power strong enough to meet the threat against American liberty. The destiny of America is to fight. Conscious of the cause which it embraces, the Mexican nation is determined to share that destiny. . . .
>
> "The symbol of our national life should not be that of Lot's wife who was turned into a pillar of salt for looking back on the flame of a dead city. Our symbol should be Pallas Athenas, the goddess of democracy, who faces the danger and from whose gleaming lance flies to the sky the banner of liberty. . . .
>
> "Can our Indian and Mestizo population dream of the contempt to which they would be subjected in a world governed by the Germans, who consider themselves masters of all races of the earth?"

Almost the same enthusiastic applause greeted that speech, which gratified me, as did the notable tribute given when he captured the great Pan American gathering at Rio de Janeiro in 1942, when he won the title of "The most eloquent of Americans." I sent his speech in the Senate to President Roosevelt, who was heartened by it. In the spirit of that address the relations were cordial and coöperative, and we became affectionate Good Neighbors as we planned the joint preparedness which was essential after Pearl Harbor.

THE BLOW THAT "ALMOST KILLED FATHER"

In the early part of 1941 a terrible earthquake almost destroyed Colima and adjacent country near the Pacific Ocean; 80 per cent of the houses were destroyed or injured. President Camacho and other officials flew to the scene, aid was sent, and the Spanish refugees sent $20,000 and others contributed to the relief. I telegraphed the State Department and suggested that our government help and I was sent $10,000 by the American Red Cross. The money was turned over to the Mexican Red Cross. In a few days I was informed that the American Foreign Affairs Committee of the House had unanimously approved an appropriation of $200,000. I hurried with pleasure to convey the news of that generous gift to the Minister of Foreign Relations. I was never more astounded than when Señor Padilla said that Mexico was grateful for the spirit behind the act, but as Mexicans had the matter well in hand it would reject the offer of the money if appropriated. I knew of the suffering, and the next day I called on President Camacho, who repeated what Señor Padilla had said—that Mexico alone could "care for the situation." Of that action I wrote (May 7, 1941):

"I believe this attitude was taken from a sense of false pride, and I talked to Mr. Quijano, President of the Mexican Red Cross, about the matter. He did not say so, and was very guarded in his words, but I think he agreed with me that later on there would be needs that had not been met and that the money could be used to re-house these people in comfortable homes and take care of them in the rainy season. That was my hunch. The next time I saw Mr. Padilla I said, 'This is the first time in my life I ever heard of anybody declining money. If the earthquake had taken place in North Carolina we would have employed experts to show that unless we received aid we would starve!' But he and the officials of his government were declining to take money which would have enabled them to re-build on a better scale. The next day the Sub-Secretary, Mr. Torres Bodet, sent for me and repeated what Mr. Padilla had said: that they would not accept it. I think he was afraid, after I saw Mr. Quijano, that I might take steps by which the money would be put down their throats despite their pride. I am quite sure that later on the people of that section, when they are living in the open and houses have not been built, will be quite critical of their government officials for declining an offer which would have put them in a good position."

Later a number of young Quakers from the United States went to Colima and helped the stricken peoples. Mr. Ray Newton, head of the Friends Service Committee, found there was need of his young men who rendered their service freely and without compensation. When I told Mr. Newton of the refusal to accept $200,000 from the United States he was as much astounded as I had been.

A ROYAL GIFT

In my home hangs a portrait made of me in 1941 by the Mexican artist, Armando Drechsler. It was a gift from Minister Padilla. As I was leaving the Foreign Office one day, Padilla said, "Come into my private office—there is something there I wish to show you." It was a portrait of the Minister.

"How do you like it?" he asked.

I thought it was a perfect likeness and a beautiful work of art and so told him.

"I want you to let the artist make a portrait of you," he said.

I replied, "There is one in the Navy Department at Washington paid for by Uncle Sam, and I am not rich enough to have this artist paint me."

"I wish to make it a present to you," Padilla said, "and the artist will be proud if you will give him a few sittings."

Not long after, in a rarely beautiful old Spanish frame, the portrait was praised by visitors to the Embassy. It was so good that at the request of President Camacho I asked President Roosevelt to sit for a painting when the artist came to Washington.

At a farewell dinner given by the Diplomatic Corps when I retired as Dean of the Corps and Ambassador to Mexico, Minister Padilla uttered expressions that warmed my heart.

Sometime after, coming to the United States, Señor Padilla paid me a visit in Raleigh, where with friends we welcomed him and he won the hearts of all who met him. He delivered an address at the University of North Carolina, where he made a hit.

"I am going," he told me, "to do something I have never tried to do—make an address to an English-speaking audience in English, and I am nervous about it."

He need not have been. His English was perfect and he held the audience. At its conclusion, at the hour for questions, he won applause by an apt reply. President Frank Graham, prefacing his question by saying the whole world had been entranced by the eloquent impromptu speech at the conference at Rio, asked: "How long does it take to prepare an impromptu address?"

Quick as a flash, Señor Padilla shot back, "Thirty years and fifteen minutes."

In the San Francisco and Chapultepec Conferences Señor Padilla more than sustained his reputation for eloquence and devotion to world peace.

Part Three

═══════════════════════════════

FIRST SETTLEMENT OF CLAIMS

XII

"JARNDYCE VS. JARNDYCE"

"Claims to the right of them,
Claims to the left of them
Volleyed and thundered at."

THIS paraphrase of "The Charge of the Light Brigade" was
ringing in my ears as I finished my days of novitiate as a diplomat preparatory to entering upon the duties of Ambassador to
Mexico. The amount of the claims against Mexico by people of the
United States—claims that had been tabulated, and the end was not
in sight—aggregated $499,708,539.27, and Mexico had filed claims
against the United States in the sum of $243,894,800.32. These had
been filed before the various commissions which had functioned for
a score or more years at a cost ranging around a quarter of a million
dollars a year, without being in sight of completion of the filing
and adjustment.

As I got deeper into the maze, there came a cable to the Department for me, through the Mexican Ambassador at Washington,
from the Mexican Foreign Minister, saying that upon my arrival
it was the great desire of the Mexican Government immediately
to initiate formal conversations on a settlement of the claims for a
lump sum. Dr. Puig stressed that the prompt solution was "necessary to eliminate constant tension which hindered the most perfect
coöperation between the two countries in economic and political
matters." The cable also wished the Ambassador to "initiate with
me the need of settlements of international waters."

Before getting that message, I had feared that the interminable
claims and counterclaims which overflowed the archives were such
that I had been catapulted into a Western Hemisphere *Jarndyce*
vs. *Jarndyce,* a case which had gotten musty in the British archives,
but was taken out now and then to confuse all new officials and
then was restored to the company of office rats. But Dr. Puig's message relieved my apprehensions as I took note of the tons of documents that would have almost made a bridge across the Rio Grande.

The multitude of claims of all sorts appalled me, but I was almost drowned when I tried to find a landing in the rushing floods of water disputes on the Colorado and Rio Grande. The Joint Commission on the Colorado, to which I was to devote many anxious nights and days, seemed to have reached an impasse. The American Commissions had recommended that no more water be allotted to Mexico, after the construction of Boulder Dam was completed, than it had been receiving before; while the Mexican Commission had demanded a much larger amount. Years before, when I was in Colorado, I had heard rumblings of trouble among the Western States as to their claims in the division of the waters of the Colorado within the borders of the United States. At that time, however, I little dreamed that I would one day be almost drowned in the roaring waters.

I soon learned that, to complicate the situation, the "waters" into which Foreign Minister Puig so calmly wished to plunge me were such that the situation was now reversed. In the case of the Rio Grande, the boot was on the other foot, inasmuch as Mexican tributaries furnished a larger portion of the waters of the Rio Grande available for irrigation and other purposes than the American tributaries, while American needs were far greater than those of Mexico. I soon saw that a principle applied on the Colorado River in our favor would inevitably be invoked by the Mexicans which would be unfavorable to Americans on the Rio Grande. In my inexperience it seemed easy to settle the whole matter by measuring the water and giving what each country needed.

But even more did I find myself disturbed when I tried to work out a "prompt solution" of the network of tangles which was called "The Chamizal Controversy." This controversy grew out of what was claimed to be "the abrupt and sudden change of the current" of the Rio Grande River between El Paso in Texas and Juárez in Mexico. Six hundred acres, by this convolution of the waters, was transferred to the American side of the river. The treaty of Hidalgo made the boundary line between the two countries "the middle of the river." The Rio Grande had been gradually changing its course. The owner claimed that the land belonged to him even if the current had transferred it to Texas. Mexico backed his claim. Uncle Sam held that only in case of sudden change of bed does the river cease to be the boundary and contended that in international law erosive alterations in the bed made no change in boundary lines, but nonerosive changes do. Uncle Sam claimed that land in United States territory was subject to Texas laws.

The situation was more difficult because Americans had built on the land in the city of El Paso. I was told by officers and lawyers in the Department that if the land was actually in the domain of the United States, no outsider could justly claim it, but they said the Mexicans insisted that title went with the land even if it had been carried by the currents out of the domain of Mexico. That was what Dr. Puig insisted I should take up, as soon as I arrived, for prompt settlement. To be sure, there had been commissions and hearings galore. In fact, by agreement of the two countries, the question had been submitted to arbitration, the head of the Arbitration Commission being a distinguished Canadian, M. La Fleur. To Uncle Sam's surprise the award was adverse to the United States. The Arbitration Commission dissolved, and the government of the United States refused to accept the award, saying it was both impossible of performance and utterly void in law. They also contended that by prescription the land belonged to the United States because of having been in its borders since 1848.

I asked my diplomatic mentor: "How could the United States decline to accept the award when it had consented to the arbitration and to the arbitrator?" His answer was not very convincing then or now. I was to find resentment at the refusal of the United States to abide by the finding of the arbitration, all during my many negotiations with Mexicans. Whenever I stressed that they were not living up to a certain agreement, they would invariably ask, "Did you not refuse to accept the arbitration on the Chamizal tract, after being a party to the selection of the Canadian as arbitrator?" And I had to confess that Uncle Sam was living in a glass house. That failure on our part embarrassed all negotiations looking to settlement of claims in Mexico. "If you would have equity, you must do equity."

Submerged in the mass, as I dug through documents, I nevertheless set out for Mexico in the confident belief that, by doing away with mañanas and costly commissions, these matters which had defied solution for scores of years could be "promptly" adjusted and that the payment of a lump sum, suggested by the Rodríguez government, was "just around the corner." It was good for me that I am an inveterate optimist. Otherwise, with the glimpse of this and the other lions in the path that awaited me, I might have thrown up the commission before entering upon the duties of the post.

I was not alone in the desire for early agreement, for when I conveyed the information that the Rodríguez government was keen for a lump-sum settlement, the American press hailed that method as ushering in a new day when all the vexatious questions which had grayed the hair of Ambassadors Sheffield, Morrow, and Clark would give no like trouble to the new Ambassador and the new administration. Presto change! A lump sum would act like rubbing Aladdin's lamp. Is it any wonder that, buoyed up by Foreign Minister Dr. Puig's confidence, I looked forward to an early lump-sum agreement which would be a "settlement" with a spirit of social and human justice and with truly fraternal spirit, and to the establishing of "permanent standards" between the two countries for a future friendship and coöperation? And so, in the earnest desire for "the best coöperation in the world," I asked Herschel Johnson, head of the Mexican division, to send this cable to Counsellor Lane in charge at the Mexican Embassy:

> "In order that it may be ready for his inspection immediately upon his arrival in Mexico City, Ambassador Daniels requests that you assemble all the available data concerning the terms on which claims between Mexico and other countries except the United States have been settled."

I thought this might be a formula that would aid in prompt settlement. Therefore upon my arrival I was in possession of the desired information, which showed that the Mexicans had paid on foreign revolutionary claims 7.92 per cent to Belgium; 7.57 per cent to Germany; 2.98 per cent to France; 2.74 per cent to Britain; 2.46 per cent to Spain, and 4.05 per cent to Italy. In other words, Mexico had paid ten million pesos in revolutionary claims aggregating 382 million pesos. I was not early disillusioned of my optimism, for shortly after my arrival I received an exhaustive communication (a little exhausting because of its length), in which Minister Puig set forth his government's position. I was gratified, and so wrote him, that he had quoted with approval extracts from my *Life of Wilson,* touching Wilson's attitude upon the fundamental rights of Mexico. During the bitter denunciation of Wilson's policy of "watchful waiting," Wilson had said of the Mexican situation: "I am more interested in the fortunes of oppressed Mexican men and pitiful women and children than in any property rights whatever." And he had declared he had "no sympathy with exploitation."

I wrote Dr. Puig that I was gratified that our minds were running in the same channel—and they were, as to a lump sum—but it took a dreary long time and much *mañana* before the size of the lump sum could be agreed upon by both countries. And in the years I sweat blood over the long-drawn-out negotiations, the unconscionable claims of some Americans and Mexicans. I was not long in learning that not a few claimants were like the North Carolina farmer, who, when the railroad killed a scrub cow, brought suit for the value of a cow that gave the finest milk and brought a thousand dollars on the market. The hoggishness of some claimants was beyond imagination. The smaller claimants deserved payment, but they were often overshadowed by those who, like the North Carolina farmer, wanted $1000 for a $10 cow.

In my first long discussion with the Foreign Minister, he instanced a claim growing out of the occupation at Vera Cruz. He said the State Department would not let him see the documents, claiming they were confidential. How they came into the possession of the Mexican government, he did not know. They had been introduced by the United States' agent before the Claims Commission. He said that "it was evidence that the agent of the United States was so intent on winning a small claim that he was willing to overlook the possibility of creating a serious situation for his government." Dr. Puig agreed to present Mexican figures for a lump-sum settlement by May 1. On April 22 Dr. Puig sent me a long letter covering twenty-seven pages reviewing the controversial matters and concluded by proposing again the formula of a "given lump sum." My Solomon Grundy expectation of ending the negotiations and reaching a settlement in the spring did not materialize. We all agreed "in principle" and wrote long notes, not the sort that Lansing wrote to prevent action by verbiage, but because the Mexicans wanted a sum much smaller than we could approve. And we talked and talked and used reams of paper, much of it reciting ancient history. I had the advice and counsel of Colonel A. Moreno, who had an encyclopedic mind, particularly as to the whole claims situation, from the time that Poinsett represented the United States in

Mexico in Jackson's administration. I never needed a fact or figure that Colonel Moreno did not have it at his tongue's end.

When *mañana* was about to get me down, Dr. González Roa, the very able Mexican Ambassador to the United States, who was his country's authority on claims, came to Mexico, and in person we talked over the desirability of an agreement on a lump-sum settlement exactly as we had done in Washington in March. After several suggestions, Dr. Roa proposed a settlement that would reach twenty-six million dollars based on the following percentages: General Claims, 8 per cent; Special Claims, 2.65 per cent; General and Special claims, 12.2 per cent. As European companies had settled on 2.65 per cent, Dr. Roa thought the United States should do likewise.

The black-letter lawyers in the State Department wrote as long and technical notes as the Mexican Foreign Minister, and both introduced elements that blocked the negotiations. Dr. Puig said the best thing to do was to "wait until Ambassador Daniels has an opportunity to discuss the matter with Secretary Hull," and was "confident that after such a conference a lump-sum settlement could be reached."

And so Christmas came with nothing achieved. I advised meeting the Mexicans more than half way as had the European governments. I pointed out that the two claims commissions that had been unable to effect a settlement had cost the United States Treasury nearly two million dollars, without either our country or the claimants getting anything, and I added that there was a deficit in the Mexican Treasury and if we could force a promise of a larger sum there was no prospect or possibility of payment. I added, "As long as these matters are not adjusted, they will constitute a running sore." But the legalists in the State Department, not in harmony with the Good Neighbor policy, preferred to get the promise of a pound of flesh nearest the heart.

Finally, on April 24, 1934, a convention was signed by Dr. Puig, for his government, and by me for the United States, to replace the Special Claims Commission that was created in 1923, and Mexico agreed to begin payments of $500,000 a year until $7,000,000 was paid. While the approval was pending in the Senate, I appeared before the Committee on Foreign Affairs, explained in detail the significance of the Convention, and answered interrogations of various members, and in response to a request by Chairman Key Pittman, wrote a letter on May 26, 1934, in which I pointed out that all the claims in debate originated between 1910 and 1920—the tragic years following the overthrow of the Díaz regime, when Mexico lacked stable government. The amount of settlement, 2.65 per cent, was the same accepted by the European governments and I stated that some of the American claims were of doubtful validity. I stated that by "accepting this settlement we would go a long way toward demonstrating our friendly and neighborly disposition and help materially to further a solution of other important questions." I have preserved the original of a letter signed by Luis Quintanilla enclosing a check for $522,240 in payment of the first annual installment. Mr. Quintanilla was a leader of the Brain Trust.

TIRED OF BEING A DEBT COLLECTOR

Many times I felt like saying what Consul Ben Cable said when I asked why he resigned from the diplomatic service. He replied, "I am tired of being a debt collector." When the oil, church, and claims questions were not being pressed, payment of the railroad debt was urged by the Bondholders' Committee, of which Thomas W. Lamont, of the Morgan firm, was chairman. It was a large sum (into the hundreds of millions of dollars) and had been standing for a long time. Many times I wished that Mr. Morrow, with Svengali power, had hypnotized Calles to settle other problems as he had done for the oil companies, if only for a time. In April, 1936, George Rublee, who had aided Morrow in the church and oil negotiations, accompanied by Mr. Laylin, representing the International Bankers' Committee, came to Mexico to renew the negotiations for a settlement. They intervened with Secretary of *Hacienda* Suárez and Montes de Oca and at one time were confident of making a settlement. When the proposal fell through, they wished the Embassy to take it up with the government. I wrote Washington that I had not taken the course suggested for the following reasons:

1. It took a full year to secure $500,000 a year on the Special Claims treaty and other payments would be falling due.
2. Our Government had sent Oscar Underwood, Jr., to Mexico in an effort to adjust and secure the payment of General Claims, and this was pending.

3. I was using all diligence to secure payment for lands taken from American citizens under the agrarian laws.

4. The Mexicans claim that the Bondholders' (Lamont) Committee is holding a large sum of money which belongs to Mexico which it has been demanding.

I strongly felt that the claim of the Bondholders' Committee should not take precedence over the other matters in process of adjustment, particularly since Mexico's fiscal situation would not permit it to meet all the claims. Moreover as 80 per cent of the bondholders lived in France, I had thought that the French Minister should take the laboring oar. (He was leaving the matter to the United States because Lamont, an American, headed the Bondholders' Committee.) Inasmuch as French citizens had loaned the money without any understanding that Uncle Sam would be the collector, I felt that the Embassy had as much as or more than it could accomplish to get the payments due my own countrymen first.

Mr. Rublee was earnest to serve his clients but not insistent; Mr. Laylin, who had prepared graphs and tables showing how Mexico could pay, acted as if collecting the debt of his clients was the chief and only duty of the Embassy.

WAS THE OFFICIAL CORRUPT?

In my early discussions when trying to adjust claims with Foreign Minister Puig, I had my first intimation from Mexican sources that the old Spanish custom of "rake-off" for officials was not entirely obsolete. Speaking confidentially, he said that while he was sweating blood to save $50,000 for his country in the settlement, there were officials who were set to get $11,000,000 for claims during the Revolution. He seemed greatly incensed at such action and indicated that he believed somebody had received two or three million dollars by mulcting the treasury. He added, "General Calles gave me his word that he knew nothing about the transaction." I did not feel at liberty to ask—since he had initiated the conversation—that he name the suspected official, and he did not volunteer the name. I wondered why he was exonerating General Calles, who had not been accused, except that he was supposed to be the power behind the throne. I am sure Dr. Puig suspected a certain official who was said to have gotten rich in office.

In the old days it was commonly believed that officials felt they were entitled to a "rake-off" and gossip persisted in Mexico that the old plan had not been entirely eliminated.

Gossip was the chief industry in Mexico City, as it is in Washington, and most of it was manufactured out of whole cloth, but General Cárdenas evidently thought that where there was so much smoke there was some fire, for after he was elected President, in his controversy with Calles he declared, "Any man who goes into public office poor and comes out rich advertises his venality."

A POINSETT RULE TO FOLLOW

I had so many requests by Americans to urge the payment of their claims or other requests of one kind or another that I found it necessary to look carefully into them to learn which were just and which were fantastic. There were many of both sorts. I had no stomach to fight for the payment of the claim of one American who filed a claim for $42,000,000 for the profits he expected to make on a patent, or of those who asked payment for a large part of Los Angeles, which they claimed to own.

I adopted the rule which Rippy says was followed by Poinsett, our most brilliant representative to the Mexican Republic—as thus stated by Rippy:

"He was vigorous in upholding the rights of American merchants, and in many cases his prompt action produced results. If, however, a claim was found to be fraudulent or unjust, he was quick to acknowledge the fact and apologize."

Many of the claims had sound basis. The Agrarian Commission, named in 1938 after Hull's strong note, agreed upon fair appraisals, Lawson for the United States and Serrano for Mexico. Their recommendations were included in the 1941 over-all agreement between the two countries.

LONG-DESIRED TREATIES RATIFIED

For a quarter of a century and more there were attempts to secure treaties that would be of mutual advantage to both the United States and Mexico, but most of them failed until the adoption of the Good Neighbor doctrine accelerated agreement. As the first fruit of that policy, in April, 1934, as already told, a treaty was signed between Mexico and the United States by which Mexico paid $500,000 a year in settlement of claims by citizens of the United States between 1910 and 1920. Though the percentage was small, it was higher than had ever been agreed upon before in the negotiations between Mexico and the United States or European countries.

Since then, twenty treaties, long desired, or agreements (in addition to the oil and other important settlements signed in Washington, November, 1941) were proclaimed between 1933 and 1941, including these:

On Statistics of Causes of Death

The Universal Postal Union

Adherence to the Anti-War Non-Aggression and Conciliation Treaty

Silver Agreement

Adherence to the International Institute of Agriculture

Treaty for Protection of Artistic and Scientific Institutions and Historic Monuments

Protocol of Inter-American Conciliation

A Convention on Extradition, signed at Montevideo

Convention on the Rights and Duties of States, which includes as Article 8: "No State has the right to intervene in the internal or external affairs of another."

Convention on the Regulation of Whaling

Convention on International Air Transportation

Convention of Nationality of Women

Membership in International Labor Organization

Convention and Protocol on Narcotic Drugs between Mexico and the United States

Protocol of General Claims, Mexico and the United States

Convention for the Protection of Migratory Birds and Game Mammals, Mexico and the United States

Convention between Mexico and the United States providing for the recovery and return of stolen property.

Treaty Between the United States and Mexico on Assistance to and Salvage of Vessels in Territorial Waters

Convention on the Rectification of the Rio Grande

A treaty providing for the termination of Article VIII of the Gadsden Treaty, by which the United States acquiesced in the request of Mexico that it relinquish such unexercised rights of of the United States as to construct a plank and railroad across the Isthmus of Tehuantepec

Part Four

EDUCATION AND RELIGION

XIII

LIGHT FOR DARKNESS

I N the matter of education the Cárdenas government planned on a large scale, larger than could be achieved in a six-year period. But it was probably on the theory that "not failure but low aim is crime."

In 1936 there were twenty-seven boarding schools for Indians. Seventy-five per cent of the rural schools established that year were in Indian districts. Three hundred and fifteen public libraries were established for workers. In that year there were 10,596 schools and 15,347 rural teachers, and the budget exceeded fifty million dollars.

In 1940 the Cárdenas administration spent 363 million pesos on public schools. In 1910, when the Revolution began, 70 per cent of the people of Mexico were illiterate. That is the worst indictment that could be made of those who had direction of the schools before the Revolution. By 1940, illiteracy was reduced to 45 per cent. The number of children in the public schools was 1,800,000.

Beginning under Madero, rural schools had been steadily increased in number. In 1933 Frank Tannenbaum, of Columbia University, who studied the schools by spending weeks in them, wrote of the movement: "It is the most modern, yet the most delicate and sensitive large-scale movement of cultural stimulus and social awakening that can be recorded in America and perhaps in the world."

On his return from Mexico in 1936 John Dewey declared: "There is no educational movement in the world which presents a more intimate spirit of union between the school and the activities of the community than the one found in the Mexican Rural Schools."

Coming from a State whose chief interest was centered in the education of the people, with emphasis on compulsory attendance in the public schools for all children (parents could send their children to private or church schools), I was interested in everything touching education in Mexico. I early came into close association with educational leaders, including the successive presidents of the

University of Mexico, visited the agricultural, normal, and public schools from Tabasco to Chihuahua, and rejoiced in the increasing opportunity to obtain education for the children in all parts of the republic. I learned by visits that in the hot countries some school work was carried on out of doors, with no houses. Some of the schools had farms or gardens attached, where the children grew vegetables, raised ducks and chickens, and prepared their own lunches. More than once I shared lunches with Indian boys and girls in their recess periods. Sometimes there were beehives, and the children ate the honey as well as the products of the farms and gardens and orchards. Children learned agriculture by growing crops. Some schools were the centres of the community life, with night schools for adults as well as regular schools for children. In some parts the children and parents together built the school-houses on plots of land given by some land-owners. Blackboards, benches, and desks were home-made at first. The schools were called *Casas del Pueblo,* and many were truly the houses of the people. Neighbors came together to exchange views, and women gathered for social plans of better living.

I found schools that were truly "socialistic" in the terms of the Constitution, making the school the Social Centre. In some I found conditions that I wished could be transferred to American rural communities, but more often I found lack of the best advantages. I was not long, however, in learning that, around that word "socialistic," battles were raging. Priests charged that under that word there were teachers who scoffed at religion. And there were some whose criticism of religion justified the charge, but I found that most teachers were concerned with teaching children the rudiments and trying to create better social conditions. Sometimes bloody war was waged where priests believed socialism was another term for atheism. More than once the President had to send troops to protect the teachers. But nearly everywhere I went I found faithful teachers giving the sort of instruction imparted in American public schools, plus practical courses on farm or garden.

The main opposition to the public schools was from religious leaders who believed education was a function of the church and that any education by the government would tend to create doubt or antagonism to the church. They stressed that "socialistic education" tended to Marxism and false doctrine. There were sticks of dynamite in that word "socialistic," which exploded to the injury of public education. Some teachers, incited by hostility of the priests, did deride the attitude of the church and construed "socialistic" in a way that led from the church. But they misinterpreted the word "socialistic" as much as did the priests who denounced it as synonymous with atheism. In spite of it all, the children attended the schools, illiteracy was decreased, and religious faith was not crucified. It cannot be done. Russia tried it in Trotsky's day, only to find that the religious instinct is immortal.

MEXICANS AND AMERICANS GO TO SCHOOL TOGETHER

At every commencement of the American School in Mexico City, Superintendent H. L. Cain asked me to deliver the address, and I was glad to come in touch with the hundreds of fine young people as they received their diplomas. This school was established by American residents in the city, mainly to educate their children in their mother tongue, but it was open to Mexican children, who were glad of the opportunity to master English along with their other studies. Children of Presidents Obregón and Calles had been students. All students were required to take Spanish, and it was a requirement that Mexican history and civics should be taught in the Spanish language. All graduates were proficient in both English and Spanish.

In my address (June, 1933) I departed from the usual honeyed advice to graduates, and was gratified on the day after to receive the following letter from the Minister of Foreign Relations:

Translation
"SECRETARY FOR FOREIGN AFFAIRS
  MEXICO
"Personal and Unofficial
                                                    "June 23, 1933.
"His Excellency
   Mr. Josephus Daniels,
   Ambassador of the United States,
   Mexico, D.F.
"My dear Ambassador Daniels:
   "I cannot refrain from writing you a few lines after reading the English text of your address last night at the American School, as published by *El Universal*.

"Your sincere and courageous statements relating to the 'captains of frenzied finance' and in general to the masters and captains of the old era are particularly valuable coming as they do from the lips of the representative of a country where until recently the teaching of blind worship of the Golden Calf was almost obligatory. Please believe that it gives me genuine pleasure to be able to confirm once more the opinion which from the example of your life and the text of your works I have always had of you. Please believe also that you have rendered a real service to the youth of the American School among whom I know are many Mexicans—who, to strengthen their essential optimism hear now from you that 'none of the masters of the old era can be factors in world restoration except those who have come by bitter experience to see their error and are ready to worship at the shrine of the only true God: Equality.'

"I also dared, as Ambassador in Washington, to speak to the youth of Marshall College at graduation exercises, presenting to them all the dangers and attractions of the different things which the captains of industry would present to them, in general, the methods of the old era, to enmesh them in their selfish and anti-social designs. And I cherish as one of the highest proofs of the understanding and the tolerance of the noble American nation that, even in those days when the 'new deal' had not yet been accepted and when even in my country there were timorous or ingenuous souls who thought that my address would be profoundly displeasing to the American Government and people, the Senate of the United States decided to publish my speech integrally in the Congressional Record.

"In Mexico, Mr. Ambassador, the words which you spoke can produce only applause, esteem and even gratitude, because they reveal faith in the new ways and stimulate beliefs which fortunately are already firm convictions among us.

"Please accept, my dear Mr. Ambassador, my most sincere felicitation and an expression of my personal gratitude because your words will serve to guide the youth who attend the American School and stimulate the social revolutionaries of Mexico.

"Very sincerely,
"PUIG"

VISIT TO CHAPINGO SCHOOL

As I had long been a trustee of the Agricultural College in North Carolina, I was glad to go with Agricultural Minister Francisco S.

Elías to visit the Chapingo School of Agriculture about twenty miles from Mexico City. I quote from my letter (1933) to my sons:

"Minister Elías pointed out how the Government was giving title to lands between Mexico City and Chapingo, in the hope that by cultivation, particularly by the planting of alfalfa and like crops, much of the dust which is at times (just before the rainy season) so unpleasant in the city could be prevented.

"The avenue of approach to the Agricultural College is bordered, I think for about a quarter of a mile, by fresno trees. They are somewhat like the ash trees we have—very tall and beautiful, and through them we could see a long way ahead.

"We spent a couple of hours there inspecting the barracks and going over the 480-acre farm and seeing the fine cattle. I have hardly ever seen finer bulls. They have a large herd of cows, which give enough milk for the students. I wish our children to know that we saw fifty chickens come out of the shells and a little lamb a few hours old.

"The college boys are doing the same things that college boys do at the State College in Raleigh, and if they had been speaking the English language, you could hardly have told any difference. They are all dressed in khaki and are there to learn how to be farmers, or rather how to teach others to be farmers.

"The plan is to send the best young bulls and cows to the other agricultural schools of the Republic, so as to improve the stock.

"The College is located on what was once the hacienda of former President González. He was President sometime in the early 80's, and must have been quite a sport. Certainly he had one of the most beautiful haciendas in all the world. One of our guides told us that instead of being called a hacienda, it ought to have been called a harem. There is preserved the car in which he rode on the railroads when he was President. In its day it must have been very fine, but it is now long out of date.

"Perhaps the most interesting place we saw on our visit was the chapel. On all these haciendas they had private chapels where the priests officiated. They had priests who lived right on the haciendas, and in the case of the very devout they had a priest living in the family. The chapel at Chapingo is now the chapel of the College. Public schools here have no religious services now; so the chapel at Chapingo if used at all is probably used only as a meeting hall. The chapel is famous for its murals by Diego Rivera. Dr. Puig told me that he thought Diego Rivera's paintings in this chapel were the best examples of his work to be found anywhere. He uses colors very broadly as you know, and in this chapel he seems to have carried out his motif better than anywhere else. Perhaps the most striking figure is a very large one at the end of the chapel, which you see upon entering, of a nude woman with beautiful hair. It is said to be a perfect likeness of his first wife. Rivera took liberties in this chapel as he seems to have done in New York, but here the people are so proud of his art that he was given free rein. There is no Rockefeller here to put the bit on him and tell him how far he can go."

SCHOOLS AT ORIZABA AND SANTA ROSA

I had heard about a school built by the operatives of a cotton mill at Santa Rosa and about the night school conducted by the labor organizations in Orizaba. My wife and I gladly accepted an invitation tendered by Editor Antonio P. Araujo to visit Orizaba (February, 1934). On the visit I wrote home:

"After the official reception, dinner, etc., we went to the plant of the Electric Power Company, owned by the Electric Bond and Share Company, the same concern that owns the Carolina Power and Light Company in Raleigh. We went down 1,000 feet on a very steep incline railroad, and when we arrived at the plant, which is in the center of one of the most beautiful valleys you ever saw, through which runs the Rio Blanco (White River), it seemed we were as near paradise as could be on this earth. The valley is several miles long, perfectly green, and the mountains tower thousands of feet above, also dressed in green. There is a beautiful guest house on top of one of the hills, and as you walked around you could gather grapefruit, oranges, gardenias, and all sorts of flowers and fruits, and hear birds singing. It was an ideal place.

"That night we went to the Centro Educativo Obrero, which was established by the labor people of Orizaba, and there we found 1,000 people at school—some of them grown men and women studying with their children, spelling out words. I was told that some of them, after working all day on a farm, walked three or four miles to the school, and father and son were learning together. These people were denied any chance of education until after the revolution and now they are eager to learn. You know how eager anybody must be to work all day and walk miles to school and then walk back home at night.

"There was a delightful entertainment program prepared for us by the pupils, with singing of Mexican airs and 'My Old Kentucky Home,' sung in honor of Southern visitors, rendered well by the class in English.

"The next morning I went out to Santa Rosa. I had heard something about it and found it was truly an object lesson which might be made the pattern for many labor communities in our country as well as in Mexico. In the last year of the Díaz regime the workers in the textile factory at Santa Rosa, who were working sixteen hours a day on very small pay and being herded in shacks, went on a strike for better conditions. Díaz sent a trainload of soldiers down, who fired into the strikers and killed eighty-nine. 'That was the beginning of the revolution in Mexico, certainly in the southern part,' said Mr. Araujo to me, as he pointed to a monument in the center of the town, which had been erected to the men who had lost their lives in an effort to receive decent pay and decent treatment. Now you find there that the owners of the mills (they are French people) have built stone houses for the operatives to live in and are charging very small rents. However, quite a number of the operatives have built their own houses, which are very simple but comfortable. The mayor and the aldermen and the school authorities (all labor people) met the car when I arrived at Santa Rosa and showed us through the school and the school grounds. The school building is quite a large one, built of stone, of two stories. It was built entirely by the contributions of the workers. They first bought a large lot of several acres, with plenty of room for a playground, and then constructed the building. They now contribute 1 per cent of their wages to carry on the school. After they had built the building and were carrying on the school, the State sent them teachers. The head of the school looked like a scholarly, intelligent, and enthusiastic leader. Of course these people are all Indians. They are now at work increasing the capacity of the school and it was interesting to see how much pride the laboring men who escorted us about took in the school and school grounds.

"After we had seen the school, they said: 'We want to show you our baseball diamond; it is the finest in Mexico.' It is a splendid park with elevated seats for spectators.

"Then they took me to the bank, which is run by the labor organization; and to the library which they conduct, with a thousand or so books; and then to the coöperative stores, where they sell everything at cost.

"Mr. Araujo contrasted the situation there with what it was in 1909. It is really a revelation and a revolution."

"SOCIALISTIC EDUCATION"

Of the demonstration for "Socialistic Education" staged in front of the National Palace in October, 1934, I wrote:

"Sunday dawned bright and clear. It was the day fixed for what had been advertised to be a monster parade to demonstrate that the mass of workers were in favor of the socialistic education embodied in the amendment to Article III of the constitution. There had been various demonstrations against it here and elsewhere in the country, culminating in strikes in a number of schools which had been closed. This parade was to be the answer. Yesterday the paper carried a notice that the Catholics would stage a procession the same morning to the Guadalupe Church. Here were the elements of a clash, at least for trouble, and it was freely predicted that trouble would follow. Instead, the demonstration was as quiet and peaceful as an Armistice Day parade. The police saw to it that there was no mass procession to the church. The worshippers were divided into small groups, each going to the church, but no large body going together. The people agreed, following, I am sure, the advice of Archbishop Díaz, who had written a letter to *El Nacional,* that he had advised only peaceful insistence on the rights of the church.

"The demonstration for socialistic education was reviewed by high officials of the government, and addresses were made by labor leaders. A member of the Embassy staff told me that a young lady teacher in the public schools, a devout Catholic, was in trouble as to what to do. She was afraid that if she did not march she would lose her position and she did not wish to fail in devotion to her church. A friend to whom she applied for advice said: 'Go on and take your place in the procession. You will not be less a Catholic by obeying orders of your Government.' She was in the parade.

"At its conclusion, President-elect Cárdenas made a brief address which was broadcasted in which he pledged himself and the country to enforce socialistic education. The main speeches were made by leaders of organized labor and country workers."

WHAT IS "SOCIALISTIC EDUCATION"?

You cannot understand the educational policies and the disputes over education in Mexico without having regard to the educational plank in the Six-Year Plan (if you can then). It is the chart of the officials elected by the party in power. It reads:

"Education imparted by the State shall be socialistic, and, in addition, shall exclude every religious doctrine, shall combat fanaticism and prejudice, and to this end the school will organize its teachings and activities so as to permit the creation in the young of a rational and exact conception of the universe and of social life."

Some of the public school opponents insisted that "socialistic" meant "communistic," which was stoutly denied. Some priests said that "shall exclude every religious doctrine" meant atheism. Almost every possible construction was made. Its ambiguity lent itself to such interpretations. Much depended on the teachers as in all schools. Church people insisted that "shall exclude every religious doctrine" was anti-Christian and charged, without proof, that this was the daily salutation existing in public schools:

"Good morning, teacher! There is no God!"

"Good morning, children! There never was a God!"

The Government said socialistic education was in keeping with the practice in public schools in the United States.

SQUABBLE OVER EDUCATION

The determination of the government for universal education in the public schools and the demand of Catholics to continue their church schools caused frequent clashes and much misrepresentation. On November 23, 1934, I wrote:

"You hear so much gossip here in the antagonism over socialistic education that you do not know what to believe. Last night at a dinner given by Dr. Madrazo, head of the Public Health Department, your mother asked him why the government did not correct the statements appearing in the American press, such as the statement that socialistic education sends young children to hospitals to witness the birth of a baby. He said that one false story followed so close on the heels of another that it was impossible to keep up with the yarns that were invented and circulated. 'Only to-day,' he said, 'a story was broadcast here and sent to the United States that girls in the public schools were stripped and made to dance before the boys as a lesson in sexual education.' He seemed to think it impossible for truth, even with seven-league boots, to be able to overtake such lies.

"On the other hand, you hear stories equally fantastic telling what priests are doing. And on both sides real evils exist. Colonel Marshburn, Military Attaché, who had been with the Mexican Army on manoeuvres lasting several days, tells me of a terrible incident in a small town. It seems that two teachers were sent to that town to take charge of the public school, and the church school was ordered closed. The priest brooded over it so much that after preaching a rambling sermon which the Colonel says showed he seemed to have lost his poise, the next night he went to the house of the two newly-arrived teachers, one a woman, and shot and killed them both. Marshburn thinks he was demented. Readers are inclined to accept such incidents as typical, just as the German atrocities were regarded in World War I. Of course they were and are exceptional. And such outbreaks are rare and are generally personal rather than inspired either by the Church or by the State."

"INDIANS CAN'T TAKE EDUCATION"

The difference between government leaders and Catholic leaders over education and the clashes between them caused a well-known writer to visit Mexico in the latter part of 1934. The government leaders declined to give him a statement, and he thought they were standing in their own light in not making their positions known. I wrote home (November, 1934) that he had told me he had dined with a wealthy Catholic lady who told him that she had advised all her friends not to send their children to the public schools. She promised that she would pay their fines and protect them, and said that she would open her home and large grounds to the children, provide a teacher, and thus outwit the government's determination to have exclusive control of primary education. She said she and other like-minded people would follow that plan. This course did not appeal strongly to the visiting writer. He told me of talking to others (Catholics and non-Catholics) who were hostile to the policy of the government. He said they told him that the Indians were incapable of taking an education and that the country was imperiled by the attempt to give them advantages they could not embrace. The same people, he said, were hostile to the government's agrarian policy and thought it would ruin the country. He inferred that they thought the country was made for the few thousand educated and well-to-do people, the only drawback to it being the thirteen million Indians, for whose weal the Revolution was fought, and for whose education and welfare the sincere leaders of the Revolutionary party were laboring.

PRIEST WORRIED

Almost every summer we were glad to welcome Monsignor James A. Magner, then a teacher in a Catholic school in Chicago and later called to a high position in the Catholic University in Washington City. We became real friends. At one of his first luncheons at the Embassy—almost before all were seated, and without being asked, he said grace. As grace was asked at every meal in the Embassy, my wife inquired, "Do you have to ask a blessing unrequested at many tables?"

He answered, "Unfortunately, I do these days."

Of his visit in 1936 I wrote home:

"On Tuesday I had a long talk with Father Magner, who took lunch with us. He had been to Mexico several times before, and this time has been spending several weeks here making a study of the church and school situation. He is very much disturbed, particularly about the socialistic education. His church people here have told him that the public schools compel the teachers to teach there is no God and the socialistic education is atheistic. For centuries the Catholic priests have controlled education in Mexico and they naturally feel they are greatly wronged when the Government forbids any church school and requires any private school which it licenses to teach socialistic education. Nobody has ever defined socialistic education and the principal of the American School here, which has increased its attendance, tells me that he is not called upon to teach anything along the line which Father Magner says they are compelling teachers to teach. As far as his school is concerned, Professor H. L. Cain said they engage Mexicans for part time to teach history and other branches and employ more Americans for full time than Mexicans. There has been no suggestion to him, he said, along the line of religious education. Even before the law was passed requiring socialistic education, the American School, like our public schools in America, did not teach religion but of course they are far from teaching irreligion. The Catholics believe that religion should be taught along with other studies and that failure to do so will bring up a generation that does not believe in God. Father Magner says there are teachers in the schools in Mexico who are teaching there is no God, even though the authorities deny this. Father Magner is a scholarly man and I enjoyed very much talking with him. He has been standing in his city and in his church for social reforms and is in entire sympathy with the goal of the social program of President Roosevelt."

THE UNIVERSITY OF MEXICO

The University of Mexico is the oldest institution of learning on the American continent, having been founded in 1553. Situated in the center of the city, and with meager support, it largely confines itself to the classics and to training for the learned professions. Many of the faculty practice their professions and teach only at stated periods. The government established technical and normal schools, feeling that the chief need was in that direction.

Returning from my North Carolina home, where as a trustee I had taken some part in uniting the State University and Colleges under one administration, I suggested to Manuel Gómez Morín, the scholarly new President of the University of Mexico, that his institution would fully meet the need of the new day by continuing the professional schools in the heart of the city, but building on the heights overlooking the city (owned by the government) a modern university, with textile, engineering, normal, and technical departments, with fields for athletics, all under one direction. I was enthusiastic about such a plan and made some drawings which I showed to the new President. I pointed out that by the plan suggested he could make the University of Mexico the head of a great public educational system of the republic. Nothing came of my suggestion either because money was lacking or because Mr. Morín believed in the old-time strictly classical university, and was not interested in the University of Mexico's becoming the head and light-fountain of a national public school system, reaching from top to bottom. Later a movement was inaugurated to build a great university center with plenty of land for buildings and athletic fields on a site overlooking the city in almost the same way I had outlined to President Gómez Morín.

PUBLIC HIGH SCHOOLS

I never lost an opportunity to show my interest in education, particularly in the public schools. I wrote (September, 1940) of a visit that showed the great progress made:

"On the Thursday preceding Independence Day all the Diplomatic Corps attended an outdoor celebration in which high school children and others went through gymnastics and other evolutions. I never saw anything more beautiful. I suppose there were five hundred, and at least half of them were young women in various picturesque costumes. I was seated next to Ramón Beteta, the Undersecretary for Foreign Affairs, and when I remarked upon how well the young women drilled and the beauty of their singing, etc., he said, 'When I was going to school in Mexico City (and he is in his early forties) there were only eight girls in the high schools of this city. Now there are twelve high schools for girls.' He said that illustrated the progress Mexico had made in public education in these years."

AMERICANS AT SUMMER SCHOOL

In addition to visiting most of the agricultural colleges in the republic of Mexico, every year I took part in the Summer School attended by teachers and students from all parts of the United States and Mexico. It grew to an enrollment of 1,000 students under the direction of Dr. Pablo Martínez del Río, distinguished graduate of Oxford. It brought to Mexico every summer a group of earnest American students, avid to learn Spanish and acquaint themselves with Mexican literature and history. Attendance opened a new world of knowledge to the visiting students and extended the study of the Spanish language. Two of the most stimulating teachers of Pan American history were Víctor Velásquez and Señora Amada Morán de Constantine. Every year the teachers and students—Americans and Mexicans—were invited to a tea at the Embassy.

ANTI-ALCOHOLIC CRUSADE

Recognizing the evil of intemperance, the government sponsored an anti-alcoholic campaign by organizing in one year 400,000 children in the public schools, who were taught the ill effects of drink. This crusade was directed by Luis G. Franco and backed by President Cárdenas and Dr. José Siurob, Minister of Public Health. There was a movement to quit the cultivation of the maguey plant, from which pulque is made, and to plant the land in food crops.

The Secretary of the Mexican Bible Society declared: "President Cárdenas has combated the vices of alcoholism and gambling," and rejoiced that by his acts "for the first time the Bible enters Mexico free of duty," and that "through President Cárdenas freedom of expression and worship are a reality in Mexico."

NEW WAY TO ABOLISH ILLITERACY

One of Camacho's first appointments was that of Jaime Torres Bodet as Sub-Secretary of State. He did not remain long in that post but long enough for me to assess, from official and personal contact, his fine qualities as he and Secretary Padilla made a strong team in the Foreign Office. He was soon promoted to be Minister of Education where, under the direction and support of President Camacho, he has carried out the most original plan to decrease illiteracy ever undertaken by any government. The Camacho administration has continued strengthening the public schools so as to reach all children, and this new policy has attacked the serious problem of teaching the many illiterate adults. These people have to work and manifestly can not go to school, though I saw a number going to night schools at Córdoba. Even so, the government did not have the money to establish as many additional schools as would be required.

The plan of adult education is to require every literate person to teach an illiterate person how to read and write, thus opening the door of education to thousands of Indians who had never had the opportunity of securing an education. A fine of fifty pesos was imposed upon every person disregarding the law that every educated Mexican must teach some untutored one to read and write. That would seem to be little enough return to give in return for enjoying knowledge. But some who regarded education as a decoration or a

Above, Ambassador Daniels delivering an address to the Faculty and students of the Summer School of the National University in Mexico City, July 1, 1940. Seated *left to right,* are Don Pablo Martínez del Río, Director of the Summer School, Don Roberto Medellin, President of the University, and Don Mario Cuevas, member of the University Council. *Below,* Ambassador Daniels discussing the agrarian problem of Mexico with Rexford Tugwell, Assistant Secretary of Agriculture, and Arthur Constantine, Correspondent of International News Service. *Below,* Arthur Constantine introducing Ambassador Daniels to a student at the University of Mexico, with whom they discuss the objections of some students to the appointment of Daniels.

Upper left, Amada Morán de Constantine, teacher of Spanish literature in the Summer School, and director of the Pan American Round Table of Mexico City in 1935. *Upper right,* Katharine Knox, of the Embassy Staff, carries Old Glory in the parade of flags of Pan American Nations, on the anniversary of the Mexican Revolution, November 19, 1939. *Below,* School children gather at the statue of George Washington, the only North American so honored in Mexico.

lever rather than as a trust, did not like it. Afar off I have been interested in its working and was glad to learn that 700,000 once-ignorant Mexicans are now literate, and the good work will be pursued until adult illiteracy has become a thing of the past for most Mexicans.

This method of ending illiteracy might well be adopted in other countries. Speaking recently of what is another step in social revolution, Minister Bodet said:

"The unity of a dignified and a prosperous country cannot be based on elements that have as their only links with mankind a brotherhood of anguish, misery, and suffering. This program is awakening within every man the constant promise of independence, honor, and happiness that we expect when we think of the future of Mexico. That has been and shall be the unifying purpose in this national campaign against illiteracy."

XIV

THE CHURCH AFTER THE REVOLUTION

THE people of Mexico are generally religious and predominantly Roman Catholic. Priests came with Cortés and brought Christianity to the people. For a long time there were no Protestant churches. Practically all education was in the hands of the priests. And there was opposition when a few Protestant churches were built. Many Catholics will tell you, "This is a Catholic country and our church inculcates Christianity. Why should there be other churches?" Protestants would reply, "The United States was started as a Protestant country, but soon welcomed all creeds. The same religious liberty should exist everywhere."

SIX STUMBLING BLOCKS

It did not take long to learn six things:

1. That the regulation of schools and religion is the problem of Mexicans and the Mexican Government alone, and an Ambassador has no right officially to seek to influence Mexican voters.

2. That the problem in its acute phases was laid on the American Ambassador's doorstep by Catholics and Protestants at home and by some in Mexico. He was urged to "use his good offices." Nobody directly asked intervention but "hoped the Ambassador could find a way to ameliorate the situation."

3. That some Catholics and Protestants would do anything for their religion except live it. They would fight for it, denounce men of other creeds, give their substance to it, observe its rules or rituals. But when it came to illustrating it by "doing unto others," some acted as if they only accepted the old saying: "Orthodoxy, my doxy; heterodoxy, your doxy." Even so, when their zeal made them bitter against others, most of them thought they were "doing the Lord's own work."

4. That some politicians would seize on an occasional bad utterance or action of a perfervid priest and attribute it as the fixed policy of the Catholic church; and some priests or prelates would

charge all officials with being animated by desire to destroy the Catholic church because of the irreligious policy of a few officials.

5. That nobody could write an account of the cross-currents of a question that created more heat than light, and that it was necessary to say as to every statement, "but on the other hand."

6. That there are many people in Mexico, as in all countries, who are not affiliated with churches.

It was often, as my experience proved, "You'll be damned if you do and you'll be damned if you don't." In my long years in Mexico I never injected into official dealings American requests for action as to church matters. But from the day I arrived until I laid down the office, I took every occasion to express my conviction that democracy, freedom of religion, and public education were a trinity that alone would bring light and leading to a free people. I had many heart-to-heart talks at his home with President Cárdenas about situations in Mexico not consonant with this trinity and expressed the hope that Mexico would be blessed by the right of all men to education and the exercise of their religion.

I was gratified that American visitors and Mexicans of all creeds met on common ground in the American Embassy and felt that their problems had sympathetic response. All knew of my own church affiliation as an old-fashioned Methodist, who tried to practice the religion that makes all Christians brothers. On my first Sunday I attended the Union Evangelical Church, composed of English speaking Protestants, and was a regular worshipper where the Reverend Charles R. McKean was minister. In many places in Mexico, I worshipped in Catholic churches and, upon certain occasions, in the Cathedral in Mexico City.

CATHOLIC AND METHODIST SAINTS

If I were to name two of the most saintly Christians, with love and charity for all, whom I have known in my long life, I would name my sainted Methodist mother and Catholic John Burke. The first shaped whatever of good intentions guided my life, and the last so well exhibited the virtues of devotion to his religion and his church that I turned to him for a right judgment in the religious differences in Mexico. He had been present at the conference at San Juan de Ulúa between Morrow and Calles, out of which came the agreement that the Archbishop could register the priests with the Mexican government and they could then officiate in their churches after a long lapse. Let me place on permanent record what I wrote to my sons when Father Burke "fell on sleep, and was not, for God took him." I wrote home (October, 1936) as follows:

"I was very much distressed this morning to read in the paper of the death of Father Burke. He knew more about the religious situation in Mexico than any other member of his church and had been commissioned by the Pope on more than one occasion to try to bring about an understanding, and had been instrumental some years ago, when there was an impasse between the Church and the State, and all churches in Mexico were closed, in securing the reopening of the churches and the return of priests, or at least as many priests as were permitted by the laws at that time. Every time I went to Washington I always went to see Father Burke and found him deeply interested and troubled about the situation in Mexico. He always talked about it with sweet reasonableness and confidence that the day would come when conditions would be improved. He looked more like a saint than any man I have ever known. It was only a few days ago that he was made a Monsignor and I wrote him a letter of congratulation. I sent the following telegram today to Mr. Montavon, who is the counsel of the Catholic Welfare organization, which was under the direction of Father Burke.

"Mr. William F. Montavon,
  National Catholic Welfare Conference,
  1312 Massachusetts Ave., N.W.,
  Washington, D.C.

México, October 31, 1936.
"I will thank you to convey my deepest sympathy to those who, like myself, loved and honored Father Burke. Our friendship, begun in the World War days, was very dear to me. I found him wise in counsel and noble in spirit and holy in life. I rarely visited Washington without spending an hour with him. Each visit was a benediction. His face reflected the beauty of the religion of the Christ who was his exemplar. He was wise beyond human wisdom. I regret that distance prevents my being present at the funeral service."

WHEN THE CATHOLIC CHURCH WAS RICH

When Juárez seized all church property and gave the title to the government, his supporters said that the Roman Catholic church in fee simple and in mortgages owned over half of the property in Mexico. I was asked many times if that was true. There was no answer that was not questioned. In his book, *The Ejido, Mexico's Way Out,* Eyler N. Simpson gave this estimate:

"The Church's sources of revenue were numerous and diverse. In addition to the customary sums received from tithes, gifts and bequests of money and property; parochial fees for marriages, funerals, baptism, confession, and for masses . . . ; special collections to honor some patron saint; alms gathered by the monasteries; dowries given to convents of nuns, and so forth, the Church derived additional funds in other . . . ways. The personal services and labor of the Indians were used without limit; large sums were gained from legal practice by members of the clergy . . . ; the clergy . . . engaged in commerce of all sorts. . . . In 1796, the income of the clergy in the capital city alone was $1,060,995. This income, capitalized at five per cent, would give a property valuation of $21,219,893. . . . One writer estimates the income of the clergy in 1800 at $13,000,000, which . . . would give $260,000,000 as the valuation of productive property."

DIFFERENCES BETWEEN CHURCH AND STATE

When I reached Mexico I shortly found that correct knowledge of the religious situation was difficult because the laws were such that there existed differences in each of the twenty-eight States. In Mexico City, for example, only twenty-five priests could legally officiate. However, I attended several services in the Cathedral, where more than fifty priests were celebrating. In a few states no priests officiated, and in others very few. In most places churches were open, but the big State of Vera Cruz still had all the churches closed when I reached Mexico in 1933.

During my term of office I was gratified to see churches opened in Vera Cruz and other States and an amelioration of much of the bitter feeling that had existed. Most of the trouble in the succeeding years grew out of the opposition of some Catholics to what was called "socialistic education," and the determination of some priests to control education. That was the chief difference that stood in the way of the settlement of the acute differences between the government and the Catholic Church. As told in the preceding chapter, President Cárdenas felt that the education in the public schools was the only certain way to end illiteracy. Catholic priests resisted that position. That was the main clash. Of course, the old hostility to the law enacted in the Juárez regime "that all churches, and property belonging to the churches, were *ipso facto* the property of the State," irked both Catholics and Protestants. As to the actual practice, though in law all religious property belonged to the State, the Catholics and Protestants had direction of the services in most states, and were generally free from any government suggestion or action.

THE EXTREME CHURCH VIEW

Undoubtedly in Mexico, as in other countries, there have been religious leaders who upheld aristocratic rule, and some high church officials have given expression to a lack of concern for the social betterment of the poor, in marked contrast to Pope Leo's humane social encyclical. The declaration that Mexican revolutionary leaders quote most often as justification for denying the old-time power to the church is contained in this pastoral by Archbishop Orozco y Jiménez of Guadalajara:

"As all authority is derived from God, the Christian workman should sanctify and make sublime his obedience by serving God in the person of his bosses. In this way obedience is neither humiliating nor difficult. We do not serve the man; we serve God; and he who serves God will not remain unrewarded. . . ."

"Poor, love your humble state and your work; turn your gaze towards Heaven; there is the true wealth. Only one thing I ask; of the rich, love; of the poor, resignation."

THE RELIGIOUS LAWS

The laws relating to priests and other ministers and to church property, which were protested by the Pope in the days of Juárez, and later by religious leaders in the days of Calles, as well as in recent years, may be thus characterized:

1. The law that vested titles of all church property in the government was part of the so-called *reforma* movement in Mexico,

which culminated in the constitution of 1857, and all who officiated were required to register with the government.

2. The law requiring registration of priests and other ministers was enacted under Calles. It stated the number of priests who could officiate in the republic; or at least gave the government the power to determine that number.

3. The law does not discriminate as to the various religions. That is, it gives power to the Executive concerning all priests, regardless of the religion to which they belong.

ARCHBISHOP DÍAZ WANTED MORE PRIESTS

The first religious leader with whom I had contact was Archbishop Díaz. He looked the leader and gentleman he was. The Archbishop was a full-blooded Indian from the state of Jalisco— short and thick-set, with a strikingly intelligent face. Accompanied by Colonel A. Moreno, a member of the Embassy staff, a broad-gauged Catholic, we talked interestingly over a cup of tea, about conditions in Mexico. He spoke to me with frankness and criticized the attitude of his country in limiting the power of the church and in socializing education. He pointed out that the number of people going to the Catholic church was so great that the few priests were unable to fulfill their holy function. But he never asked me to intercede. He said he only wanted me to know that the church had a side and one that should be considered. He had been quoted as saying—but not to me—"They accuse me of stirring up the people against the government. They say that if I should ever appeal to the multitudes to rise up they would overthrow the government." But he was too wise to wish that belief put to the test and did not wish revolution. Mr. Arthur Constantine, Dean of American correspondents, once speaking of the Archbishop, related this incident:

"He was one of the rarest examples of church prelates in the Catholic world. He was a Jesuit. It is forbidden in the Order of Jesuits for one of their number to accept offices of the Church. Once, in a dispatch to the *New York World,* I referred to him as a Jesuit. Many Catholics among the readers of the *World* sent me a telegram scolding me. I took the telegram to the then Bishop Díaz and showed it to him. He dictated a reply to the *World.* He said he had been designated a Bishop by the Pope himself—that the Pope's authority, of course, took precedence over the rules of the Jesuit order."

Archbishop Díaz was at one time the victim of an act by a super-zealous, subordinate public official that caused great indignation. The law in Mexico forbade a priest or minister to officiate outside his diocese. Called to minister in another State, the Archbishop responded to the call. He was taken by agents behind the Lomas de Chapultepec and kept there over six hours. He told friends that he expected to be assassinated. Upon his release he was almost in a state of collapse. When the higher-ups in government heard of the indignity to which he had been submitted, he was released. But he did not forget it, and he regarded it as an inexcusable wrong. On my next visit to the Foreign Office I ventured, wholly unofficially, to express my feeling of the bad effects such an act was having in my country as well as in Mexico. I found that the Minister entertained the same feeling and was relieved that the Archbishop had been released.

MY ONE RELIGIOUS INTERVENTION

Of course an Ambassador has no right or permission to tell Mexicans how they should conduct their domestic affairs; and, while I always unofficially expressed my belief in the religious and educational policy prevailing in the United States, I refrained from any attempt to tell Mexicans what policy that country should pursue.

Only once did I risk overstepping the mark set for diplomats in respect to a church service, and that was on the occasion of the death of Archbishop Díaz in the summer of 1937.

When the Archbishop died, I called at his residence—we were near neighbors—to offer my sympathy to his household. To reach his home I had to pass through a street crowded with weeping women, who bemoaned the passing of the Archbishop. The next day I received a call from the Archbishop's Secretary, Señor Alberto Carreño. He was a gifted writer and devoted to the Archbishop and to his church. He made a request of me of such a nature that my heart could not permit me not to accede to it. There was a law in Mexico that no priest or preacher could appear in the street in the robes of office and there could be no religious funeral processions on the streets. Therefore the body of the Archbishop could not be taken from the residence to the Cathedral, attended by priests and church officials. The Archbishop's secretary told me that he and other church officials felt that the rule ought to be waived with respect to the Archbishop, but that the government officials had declined the request. In his extremity he said he felt he could appeal to me to use my good offices to ask the government to permit the Archbishop to be taken by his priests and officers and other Catholic friends to the Cathedral for the funeral services. He sensed that this appeal would be sympathetically received and he was right. I told him I would do anything in my power to see that the permission was granted.

I called upon the Dean of the Diplomatic Corps, a Catholic, who felt as I did. "Leave it to me," he said. "I will obtain the permission."

I heard nothing further and some time later learned that his request had been rejected. About night the Archbishop's Secretary called at the Embassy and told me of the impasse. I resolved, even if I broke all diplomatic rules, to make an appeal to President Cárdenas not to permit an inhibition that would be condemned all over the world where it would be known. I called that night at the home of General Hay, the Foreign Minister, to acquaint him with my feeling that I must make the appeal to the President of the Republic. When I arrived at his home, I found that he was entertaining a large dinner party—that the company had just gone in to dinner—and the man at the door told me he could not disturb the Minister. I therefore penned a note telling General Hay that I must see him immediately for a few minutes on a matter of importance. He left his guests, escorted me to his study, and asked what was so immediate and important. I explained the refusal of the cabinet officer and told him I felt so deeply about the matter that I was going to register an appeal to President Cárdenas, but would not do so without first communicating my purpose to the head of the Foreign Office, who was the medium of approach by foreign diplomats.

"You seem excited and I never saw you so wrought up," he said, and then asked, "Are you a Catholic? What makes you so interested in the Archbishop?"

"No, I am not a member of the Catholic church," I said, "but I hope I am a Christian and have fellowship with Christians of all faiths."

I proceeded to tell him that a refusal to grant the request would outrage the sensibility of people everywhere and cause criticism of the government. After I had stressed to him what brought me there, I said, "I wish with your knowledge now to make the appeal to President Cárdenas."

"But you cannot see the President tonight. He is not in the City."

"I know," I replied, "that he is at Cuernavaca, but I am going there at once to lay the matter before him." Seeing my deep interest and persistence, he said, "Leave it to me. I will communicate with you shortly." Not long afterwards he telephoned me that the request had been, or would be, granted. There was marked respect by all on the avenue, thronged with people, as the funeral cortège moved from the residence to the Cathedral. The night before, I had been called to Washington, but the Embassy was represented by the Counsellor and Secretaries.

When I next saw General Hay and he again expressed surprise at the great length to which I was ready to go in the matter, I told him that I was ready to go to any length to secure the humane action toward a great Catholic leader, even if it should result in overstepping diplomatic rules and regulations. I added I knew that General Hay's heart and that of President Cárdenas would respond to my own if I presented the request as a humane act, and one that if refused would bring down criticism on their country which they and all of us would sincerely regret. It warmed my heart to receive the expressions of approbation from the friends of the Archbishop.

TREATMENT OF CATHOLICS REPREHENSIBLE

One of my later Catholic callers was Father Parsons, who had written "An Open Letter to Ambassador Daniels." He related his views on the treatment of Catholics in Mexico, which he pictured as reprehensible. He asked nothing specific to be done officially but expressed the hope that unofficially I would be able to be helpful.

METHODIST CHURCH IN OLD CONVENT

As there were no English-speaking Methodist churches in Mexico City, we attended a Union church composed of most English-speaking Protestants. Of my first attendance at the service of a Methodist church attended by Mexicans I wrote home:

"Sunday night, in response to an invitation from Bishop Pascoe, who is Bishop of the Methodist Church in Mexico, your mother and I attended a service at the Methodist Church (Iglesia Metodista Mexicana) on Gante Street. It was the closing service of a convention called the 'Nacional Evangélica,' composed mainly of teachers of the various schools in Mexico which had been established by American religious or educational societies. This church was once a part of a large convent. About 200 delegates attended the convention. Twenty States were represented. The services were all in Spanish, and of course we could not understand very much of what was said, but we could enjoy the music. The tunes were those we were accustomed to, and if we could not get the words, we could get the spirit.

"The sermon was preached by Dr. Vicente Mendoza. He has been preaching for over thirty years and at the end of the service we met him and other leaders of the movement, introduced by Bishop Pascoe. Dr. Mendoza said, 'I love this boy,' putting his hand on Bishop Pascoe's shoulder. 'When I was a young man I was a student in the University. I did not believe in any religion. I was very near to being an atheist. This boy's father, a Methodist preacher who had come to Mexico from England, brought me into the light and the knowledge of Christ and it changed all my life.'

"After he left, Bishop Pascoe said to me, 'This is a very remarkable man. He has been preaching over thirty years, part of the time in Los Angeles. He told you that he was converted under my father's preaching. I will add something to that. When he professed conversion and joined the Methodist Church here, his father disowned him and he took his mother's name.'

"The church was crowded and it was very interesting to see how devout most of the Indians were. The choir rendered the 'Hallelujah' chorus with spirit and beauty. After the service we took the Bishop and his wife and children home."

WANTED TO PAY FOR CHURCH PROPERTY

Although no church organization under the old Juárez law—and the later constitutional provision—could own any property used for religious purposes, the Methodist representative in Mexico was persistent in his insistence that I bring pressure to bear upon the government to pay for the school-houses built by the church. It seems that the Methodists had conducted a normal school and had trained preachers and also teachers, mostly Mexicans but some Americans, who had taught in the Mexican schools and had done good work. I asked my Methodist brother, "What are the Mexicans doing with the school buildings they have taken over?" He said they were training Mexicans to teach in Mexican schools. He added that under the laws of Mexico none but Mexican citizens, or those trained in schools licensed by the government, were permitted to teach in Mexican schools. This practically put these American-owned normal schools, built by Protestant churches, out of business, since their graduates were forbidden to teach.

I answered the Methodist preacher by asking, "Instead of asking money for the buildings, why don't you give them freely and gladly, since your service is no longer desired and the Mexicans feel they can train all the teachers their schools need? Why not say, 'We came here when you lacked school facilities for your people and were glad to train teachers for your schools. If you no longer need these schools, we are ready to retire and give you the property.'" I told him that if we pressed for payment, the Mexicans would say, "All the Yankees want is money," and hearts will be closed to the gospel message.

He acted as if he thought I was very generous in giving away other people's possessions. He said it was indefensible that Mexicans could take church school property without paying for it. I told him that demanding money would block the usefulness of property taken over. I told him he knew that under the laws of Mexico no church could own property.

CLAIMED NO CHURCH CONNECTION

Bishop Pascoe, with whom I had served as a delegate in the Methodist General Conference, and others gave me the Protestant position. Writing home of my talk with Bishop Pascoe, I said:

"'Our chief trouble here,' Bishop Pascoe said, 'is as to the schools.' The Minister of Education, Mr. Narciso Bassols, comes, according to Bishop Pascoe, from a very strong Catholic family, and the Bishop thinks he extends no favors or consideration to Protestant churches and schools. The school question is very much on the Bishop's mind, and he said that he was having an appointment with President Rodríguez to bring the matter to his attention. I told him that I thought that was a very wise course to pursue. I was very glad he did not ask me to take the matter up.

"A few weeks ago Miss Laura Temple, who has long been the head of a Methodist Church school here (the Sara L. Keen) called to see me. She stated that her school had been closed in accordance with the law that no school shall be permitted which is run by a religious organization. She was objecting to the school's being closed, claiming that it is run by the Women's Missionary Society and has no church connections, and asked me to arrange an interview for her with the Minister of Education. I did so.

"Miss Temple's school was formerly a church institution, I believe, though I am not sure, but at any rate it has been supported for some time by the Women's Missionary Society, and she claims that her school should be allowed to run, as it is within the law. She says she has even cut out saying grace at meals or having any Bible reading.

"However, as I told her, when she came to see me, I thought she was trying to draw a very narrow twilight zone line between support by the Church and support by the Missionary Society. I said that my mother was a very active member of the Missionary Society all her life and took great interest in the missionary movements and in raising money for the Society, but I doubted very much if she would have been willing to do this unless she thought these schools in Mexico, China, and elsewhere, were teaching religion. In fact, I thought she would have considered them a little heathenish if they forbade the reading of the Bible to the children in the schools. The Missionary Society in our part of the country was supported by the Church and, while the women's money was kept separate, they made reports to the Conferences. I can hardly see, therefore, how Miss Temple can support her position that her school has no connection with any religious organization."

WOULD PRACTICE NO EVASIONS

The church and school question bobbed up almost as often as claims. On March 27 I wrote home:

"On Sunday night Miss Sallie Lou McKinnon, head of the Methodist Missionary Society, and Miss Ingram, a Methodist teacher from Saltillo, were at the Embassy. Miss McKinnon is a daughter of my old friend Sandy McKinnon, of Robeson

County, N.C. Your mother had known her at Junaluska. She is a fine woman, wholesome and sensible. She had come down to attend a Methodist meeting and confer about the situation with reference to schools. No church schools are allowed here, and Miss McKinnon said, 'We will not practice any evasions.'

"Some churches have been advised to transfer the church property to individuals and say it is not church property and that the institutions are not religious institutions. This is called 'bootlegging teaching or preaching or mass.' Miss McKinnon wisely sees that any such evasion does not square with Christian principles and would hurt the church. Unfortunately some other church people do not see this. She wishes the church to serve here in ways that are needed and not otherwise. Miss Ingram, of Saltillo, who was with Miss McKinnon, has been a teacher in a Normal School in Saltillo a long time. Both are now convinced that as the government is providing Normal Schools, and gives teaching certificates to their graduates, there is no longer any need for church schools to attempt to carry on that character of work. The social work and hospital work are welcomed and needed. These two sensible ladies are working in the right direction."

EXPULSION OF THE BISHOP OF CHIAPAS

On one of his frequent visits to Mexico I expressed to Ambassador Castillo Nájera my concern over the expulsion of the Bishop of Chiapas. I wrote of this:

"Mr. Carreño was long Secretary of the late Archbishop Díaz and an active leader of the Catholic church. He was much troubled because the Bishop of Chiapas had been expelled from that State. For several years no churches had been open in that State, but a few weeks ago it was printed that churches had been opened and that the Bishop had returned. Mr. Carreño said the Bishop thought he had the right to return. He is now in hiding in Mexico City. In view of the absence of any such persecution in recent months, and President Cárdenas' statement that he had inaugurated a policy of moderation, this arrest and expulsion of the Bishop is disturbing.

"The Ambassador was troubled when I told him about the expulsion of the Bishop of Chiapas. He said: 'I do not believe President Cárdenas knew of this. He promised me to pursue a course of moderation. I am to see him at Cuernavaca tomorrow and will talk to him about how this injures the standing of Mexico.' "

COULDN'T PREACH IN CHURCH HE BUILT

The church question, next to oil and claims, was, like the poor, always with us at the Embassy, even if we could not affect Mexican laws. On one phase of it, I wrote (July, 1934):

> "Among the guests at dinner was Bishop Creighton. He was Episcopal Bishop here for five years but had to leave when the government demanded native-born ecclesiastics.
> " 'I came into the country,' he said, 'with an agreement not to officiate in any church, and it is hard not to do so when many of my old parishoners are so kind to me.' He mentioned a church he had built. 'I will not even go there, for the people would not understand why I did not preach to them and administer the communion.' "

CATHOLIC BISHOPS DENOUNCE PUBLIC SCHOOLS

The church-school situation flared up again in January, 1935, as I wrote:

> "The morning I reached Austin, returning from a trip to Washington, the paper carried under big headlines the substance of the Pastoral letter of the Catholic Bishops of Mexico, directing Catholics not to send their children to government-supported schools and declaring that to do so constituted 'a mortal sin.' Burleson showed it to me and felt that it portended trouble in Mexico. 'It is a Church declaration against the Government,' he said, 'and may cause great trouble and may involve you.' He is as good a friend as he is a good hater. 'I have influence in Washington,' he said, 'and I will go to Washington any moment you wish me to do so.'
> "Here in Mexico, the letter seems to have created little impression. The government took no steps to prevent its being read in the churches and has since wholly ignored it. There are schools in Catholic homes conducted against the law, but so far the government has taken no action about them. The truth is that the people as a whole—the workers—are seeking to secure better wages and better living conditions. Their wives go to church and most of them support the government even though remaining Catholics. Present comforts have more weight with

many than a declaration that sending their children to the government schools constitutes 'a mortal sin.' "

DID NOT THINK ANY CHURCHES OPEN

I was constantly to learn of propaganda in America that no Catholic could worship in Mexico. Writing home (January 9, 1935) of a visit by Thomas Hickey, of San Francisco, I related:

"Mr. Hickey is a Catholic and expressed surprise that the Cathedral and other Catholic churches were open. 'I thought they were all closed,' he said. 'That is the opinion in the United States.' We both regretted the propaganda and the closing of churches in a few States in this country. None have been closed and no priests denied the right to hold service in the Federal District. The Federal government has no power in the States, and several of them have passed stringent laws, one, for example, denying the right of any priest to officiate unless he is a married man. The hostility to the clergy and capitalists (they are usually coupled together by revolutionary speakers) is very great among a certain element of the governmental leaders. And it is said that at Catholic churches Sunday morning a paper was read from the Archbishop of Mexico (he lives in San Antonio) threatening the excommunication to all parents who permitted their children to attend the public schools. As no other schools are lawful, except private schools which teach 'socialistic education,' you see the impasse."

CHURCH AND STATE DIFFERENCE

Before I became Ambassador I was told that Mr. Andrés Osuna was the ablest and most influential Protestant leader in Mexico. Of his visit and views I wrote in September, 1935:

"I had a call on Friday from Mr. Hauser (who represents the American Methodists in Mexico) and Mr. Osuna, a Mexican Methodist, who has been the representative of all the Protestant churches in this country. I had received letters from the Missionary Boards of both the Northern and Southern Methodists asking my advice about what to do about their schools in this country.

"Mr. Osuna says the law is plain—all property purchased by churches or mission boards is national property. Representing the churches, he has asked President Cárdenas to pay for the

Upper left, Monsignor Pascual Díaz Boreto, former Archbishop of Mexico. *Upper center,* The Reverend James A. Magner, author of *Men of Mexico. Upper right,* the Reverend John J. Burke, C. S. P., S. T. D., General Secretary National Catholic Welfare Conference. *Below,* Ambassador Daniels, with his Excellency, Luis María Martínez, Archbishop of Mexico, and the Honorable Michael Doyle, American member of the World Court. Taken at the Embassy, June 7, 1939.

Above, the heart of Mexico City from Montezuma to Alemán. On the left is the Cathedral of Mexico, and on the right the National Palace. *Below,* Hospital de Jesús, the oldest hospital in the Western Hemisphere.

church property. In the Rodríguez days, the government promised to pay the Presbyterians for their school property taken over in Mexico City, but up to this hour nothing has been paid. As the law makes no provision for payment, I doubt if the government has any funds from which to make the payment promised by a former president or cabinet officer. Mr. Osuna thinks Cárdenas would like to aid the Protestant schools, as he says Obregón and Calles did, because in none of their schools was there opposition to the government.

"He then told me an interesting story. At one time, he said, during the Obregón and Calles regimes, there was a fear on the part of these two leaders that the United States would either withhold recognition or withdraw it. 'I was requested,' he said, 'by General Calles to go to the United States and acquaint the Protestant churches with the true aims of the government, so they would not join with the Catholics who were fighting the government.'

"Both Obregón and Calles told him they opposed the Catholics because they organized to drive the Revolutionary party from power—they had no opposition to Protestants because they refrained from political action. 'I went to New York,' said Mr. Osuna, 'and talked with the leaders of the Protestant churches and told them they had nothing to fear in Mexico—in fact their schools and churches were doing a work that was needed—and if they kept within the law, they need have no fear. I spoke in over 150 places and the preachers repeated my assurances in thousands of churches. This work I did prevented any fight on the government in Mexico by the Protestant churches in the United States, and was appreciated by Obregón and Calles.

"Mr. Osuna showed me a memorandum he had given President Cárdenas requesting that the school buildings taken over be paid for by the government. 'There is no need to ask him to permit the schools to be continued,' he said, 'for the law is all-embracing. But I think he would like to find a way to pay for those which have no religious instruction now and have obeyed the law.'

"I told Mr. Hauser and Mr. Osuna that, in my opinion, if all the school buildings established by religious organizations were by law government property, the best thing the church boards in the United States could do would be to say to the Mexican authorities: 'We came here to help educate young Mexicans when there were not enough schools. We were welcomed and came to do good. Now that you say the government is in a position to take over all education, we present you with our school property and hope it may assist in the education of all the children in Mexico.' I think both agreed, but Mr. Hauser did not think the Boards in the United States would be willing. They have asked my advice and that is the unofficial advice I will give them."

Later in urging the same policy on Bishop Ivan Lee Holt of Texas, who was in charge of all Methodist churches in Mexico, I said that the mistake of Mexico for five hundred years had been that the schools had been controlled by the Catholic church, and that, whenever education was controlled by any church, only a very small proportion of the people received any instruction, as was evidenced by the fact that at the end of the Díaz regime 86 per cent of the people of Mexico were illiterate; and that the only hope of Mexico, as of every other democratic country, was public schools for everybody with universal education required. Already, I told him, by reason of the public schools in Mexico, illiteracy has been greatly reduced, and if the government could continue the building of public schools and get better teachers, the day would come when Mexico would have an educated constituency. This is essential for real democracy. You cannot have a good democracy with an illiterate constituency.

TWO BY TWO LIKE EARLY CHRISTIANS

In some instances my advice that Methodists retire from the educational field and devote themselves to evangelization among the Indians was taken. Not long after giving this advice, I wrote (December 10, 1938):

"Dr. Meadows, head of the Baptist Hospital at Puebla, tells me that his church is working along evangelistic lines by sending out men two by two, much as in the old days in Europe, and that they are having good success. These two men live with the people, show interest in their affairs and help them. Usually one of them knows something about medicine and wins the confidence of the people in that way and preaching the gospel. I think that as the schools of the Protestant churches reach so few people, if they are to make headway in Mexico it must be in evangelization by travelling through the country and living with the people. Conducting schools is very costly, particularly when the Mexican government feels that it should control public education."

RELIGION AND WOMAN SUFFRAGE

As sidelights on religion, education, and woman suffrage, as viewed by old-time Mexicans, I wrote home as follows (September 21, 1935):

"On Tuesday night we went to supper with Víctor Velásquez and wife. He is a brilliant lawyer, a devoted Catholic, and has been in fear that the government might deport him because of alleged utterances he made at the University Summer School. He denies, and has affidavits supporting his denial, that he made the critical statements attributed to him. He has represented the Catholics in their contests with the government. He told me an incident showing his belief in God's direction of the affairs of men. During a sharp controversy in Vera Cruz, the Bishop asked him to represent the church in pending litigation. He told the Bishop that it would injure him and his professional success to do so, but said: 'If you say it is my Christian duty, I will do as you say.' The Bishop told him to let him seek the direction of God in prayer, and after doing so said he would advise Velásquez of his duty. 'It is your Christian duty,' he told Velásquez, 'and God will care for you.' On the day he was to go to Vera Cruz to represent the church, Víctor said a company called at his office and gave him a $7,500-retainer to represent them. 'So you see the Bishop was right,' he said.

"Telling of his experience in the Vera Cruz controversy, he said that a bullet fired in the church barely missed him and the Bishop, showing the protection of the God they were serving. He showed me a fine portrait of 'The Holy Father' which he values highly. He is a delightful and agreeable man, and his wife is lovely and charming. They are of the old order, important in the Díaz days, and strong Catholics, whose devotion to their religion excites admiration. One of the guests at the dinner was a beautiful and intellectual lady of the old Spanish order who told your mother she was an advocate of suffrage for women in Mexico. Your mother told her that I was the original and militant advocate of woman suffrage in our family. She added, 'In the United States, votes for women has not changed things much, for women usually vote with their husbands and fathers.'

" 'Why are you so ardently in favor of woman suffrage?' I asked the Señora.

" 'Look at what woman suffrage has done in Spain—the women overturned the government and restored the rights of the Catholic Church.' She then launched upon a severe denunciation of the Mexican educational and religious policies which showed that she believed the present order would be overturned if women had the ballot. 'I know you don't agree with me,' she said. I told her that I strongly believed in full religious liberty and in universal education. She and most of those who prospered under the Díaz policies live in the hope that in essence they will one day be restored."

MORE CHURCHES OPEN

In keeping with my promise to write often, on April 7, 1936, I wrote President Roosevelt:

"On Palm Sunday thirty-nine Catholic churches were open in Mexico City, which is fifteen more than have been open at any time since I came to Mexico, and the crowds who thronged the churches carrying palms were the largest the oldest inhabitants said they had seen.

"On my trip to Southeastern Mexico I found churches open at places where they had been closed. This shows that the Cárdenas policy is being carried out. Of course there are counter currents. Fuel was added to the flames of those who are opposed to the church by the killing of a certain number of non church goers in Jalisco this week. They were said to have been led by a priest."

BISHOP OF VERA CRUZ IN HIDING IN MEXICO CITY

It became known that the American Ambassador would welcome any and all, and I had visitors of all kinds. Of a rather interesting visitor I wrote home (August 8, 1936):

"On Monday of this week I had a call from Father O'Brien, who is a member of the faculty of the University of Illinois and who has been here some time particularly studying the religious situation. He is a high-class man and I have enjoyed association with him. He said to me some days before he called Monday that he found that some of the Catholics here, in view of an address I made once praising universal education, had an idea that I had endorsed socialistic education, and that he wanted some of the most prominent ones to meet me so that they would understand my true position. He brought with him the Bishop of Vera Cruz. The State of Vera Cruz is in the control of men who have long had a conflict with the Catholic church and there is no Catholic church open in the city of Vera Cruz, and a short time ago there were none open in other parts of the State. If there are any open at all it is only very few, and the Catholics there, who are very numerous, have been active trying to get the President and the State Government to change the course and permit freedom of religion in that State.

"The Bishop of Vera Cruz does not live in his diocese and has been in Mexico City for some time. I have heard that at first he was in hiding here. Last summer Mr. Brown, who was one of a committee of three that came here to investigate the religious situation, told me that he had visited the Bishop of Vera Cruz in his humble home here, where he was living almost in squalor, and that as he talked with him he felt that he had gone back to the days of the catacombs when men who worshipped Christ had to hide. He thought very highly of the Bishop of Vera Cruz.

"The Bishop talked freely to me about conditions in Vera Cruz. He said that the present Governor of the State was an excellent man and if left to himself he would be more liberal; that the situation in Vera Cruz was that when the Catholics applied to the State Government for permission to open churches they were told that it was a matter to be taken up with the President in Mexico City, and when they would take it up in Mexico, they would be told that the Constitution gave exclusive right to each State to regulate the number of churches and priests or preachers, and so between the two, each one throwing the responsibility on the other, they had been unable to secure the right to worship. The Bishop seemed to have no bitterness, but to be feeling that there was no immediate hope for better things. However, I think he still carries on and I have no doubt that some of his priests are holding services in Vera Cruz, in other words doing what they call 'bootlegging' in religion. That is to say, that priests are holding services in private homes. Under the former Governor they were arrested frequently for this 'bootlegging,' but I believe under this Governor (Alemán) no active effort is made to do what President Cárdenas would call 'persecution.'

"President Cárdenas has stopped the arresting of priests but of course he says he must carry out the law, and the law leaves it entirely to the State governments to say how many churches and priests there shall be. In Chiapas and a number of other States where the laws are against the Church, of late churches are open and priests are officiating without authority and without interference by the State governments. In other States like Querétaro, where there have been no churches open, the laws have been changed and churches are open in the capital and other towns."

AN IRISH CATHOLIC OF THE REAL OLD STOCK

As further instances of religious and educational "bootlegging," one fine Protestant lady told me her school was not supported by the Methodist Missionary Society organized by the church. And some Catholic women—maybe nuns—conducted schools that under strict construction of the law would have been catalogued as church schools. Of one of the latter (by her invitation I attended its commencement exercises one year) and its head I wrote home (October 10, 1936):

"I had an interesting call on Thursday from Miss Mary E. Stapleton. She is the director of the Helena Herlihy Hall school. During the summer Father O'Brien was down here from the University of Illinois and brought Miss Stapleton in to see me. She is a fine type of vigorous, upstanding Irish woman. The school has been conducted by Catholics for a long time. The school goes on as usual and I suppose under restrictions. Everybody refers to it as a Catholic school, although the law does not permit church schools. She told me she was very much more interested in training the character of the children and for right life than in teaching them arithmetic, history, etc. She brought with her two ladies, one a teacher in the school and the other the mother of the teacher who was visiting her from Cleveland, Ohio. What they wanted was to cast their absentee vote for President and have it certified, as the law requires, by an official authorized to administer the oath. I arranged for Steve Aguirre to take them over to the Consulate. Of course I did not ask them how they were going to vote, though I wanted to. It would never do for an Ambassador to be a politician; so I had to exercise great control not to talk politics to them. When they returned, Mr. Aguirre told me that all the formalities had been complied with and they had both voted for Roosevelt. Of course I could congratulate them then and found they were both pretty staunch Democrats. Miss Stapleton invited me to visit her school some time and I shall try to do so. She says she has 700 or 800 students."

STAIN UPON CÁRDENAS ADMINISTRATION

Great indignation prevailed early in 1937 when the news came of a terrible situation in Orizaba in the State of Vera Cruz. I wrote home about it (February 13, 1937):

"Wednesday I had a call from Mr. Barragán of Vera Cruz. He was the gentleman who accompanied Aguirre and myself when we went to Jalapa, to attend the inauguration of the new Governor of the State. He told me about a terrible affair in Orizaba. It seems a priest was officiating without authority of law, and had a large company of worshippers present while he was celebrating mass. The police entered the place and when there was a commotion began to fire, and killed one young woman and wounded others. It was a horrible affair and has created quite a revulsion of feeling in Mexico City. The President says it is a stain upon his administration, and that he will remove it; he sent half a dozen men down to investigate. The Governor himself went to Orizaba to look into the matter. The people were so outraged that all the churches which had been closed were forcibly opened and they entered the churches. The police had been arrested and put into jail. The situation is very grave."

NEW ARCHBISHOP CONSECRATED

The middle of April (1937) the new Archbishop was consecrated and of the services I wrote home:

"At 9:30 I went with Mr. Boal and Mr. and Mrs. Bursley (they are all Catholics) to the Cathedral to the consecration of the new Archbishop, former Bishop of Michoacán (home of President Cárdenas). Archbishop Martínez is highly esteemed and it is hoped there will be improved conditions in religious affairs. A few minutes after the Archbishop began his sermon, a section of the floor near the altar fell in and dropped a distance of twelve feet into the basement carrying a number of people, a dozen of whom were painfully hurt. It caused much commotion for a time but Red Cross nurses took away the injured. No one in the part of the Cathedral where I was sitting knew what was the trouble. The services were continued when quiet was restored, and the Archbishop preached his sermon as if nothing had happened.

"Upon leaving I said to the Catholic secretaries: 'After this morning nobody can doubt that I am in good standing (and of long standing) in the Catholic church.'"

CHURCHES OPEN IN EVERY STATE BUT ONE

In August, 1938, replying to a letter from Laurence Duggan, Chief of the American Republics Division in the State Department, I told of trying to assist Jews who feared deportation, and thus discussed the religious situation:

"I told President Cárdenas that Mexico was hurting itself most because there remained churches closed in a number of States. It has been a great satisfaction to me that after these talks, which were, of course, informal and unofficial, the churches are now open in every state in Mexico except Tabasco.

"In fact, so great has been the change that in the State of Chiapas, where they have a fool law that no priest could officiate unless he is married, churches are open and priests who obey the rule of their church that they remain celibate are functioning."

This letter was written to answer a letter from George S. Sullivan charging that I had interested myself against a government move to expel Jews but had refused to concern myself "with the violation of fundamental rights of Catholics in Mexico."

A VISIT TO BISHOP MARTÍNEZ

During all my stay in Mexico I made it a rule to talk to influential leaders and learn how they felt about conditions in Mexico so that I could carry this information to the President and others interested. I always called on the Catholic leaders in Washington who kept in touch with Mexican affairs and conveyed the views of church leaders as they related to the present status. On May 21 (1937) I wrote:

"On Monday afternoon I called to see Archbishop Martínez. ... He is an Indian from Michoacán, the same state as

President Cárdenas. I understand that at one time they attended the same school. I found him very agreeable and it seems that his selection was the best that could have been made. Like President Cárdenas, he leans to moderation and says that conditions with reference to the church here have improved and he hopes that every State will permit the opening of the churches so that people may worship."

THE PONTIFICAL MASS BY MANY PRIESTS

By invitation I attended some special religious service every year at the Cathedral in Mexico. I wrote (March 20, 1939):

"Last Tuesday I went to the Pontifical Mass for the coronation of Pope Pius XII. A committee of laymen of the Cathedral had called previously and extended a special invitation and I understand a like invitation was extended to all the diplomatic missions. The mass was set for ten o'clock and with American devotion to punctuality we arrived at that hour, but the Archbishop seems to regulate his schedule by the old time and we were there an hour before he and the priests entered. There were many priests and many young Mexicans who were evidently training for the priesthood and their attendants. Only one other Ambassador beside myself was present and very few members of the Diplomatic Corps. Six from our Embassy were present. We did not leave the Cathedral until one o'clock. It was pretty cold in this vast place and it was pleasant to get out in the sun. The Archbishop spoke at length on the virtues of the former Pope and of the new Pope. I told some of the secretaries who are Catholics that it took a heretic like myself to get them to go to church."

METHODIST CARRIES CANDLE IN CATHOLIC CATHEDRAL

Of the last special service I attended at the Cathedral, I wrote (April 17, 1941):

"I had a special invitation from the Archbishop of Mexico to attend the Easter services at the Cathedral. Usually most of the Diplomatic Corps is invited and I have been in the habit of going. I was told that the services would begin at nine o'clock and arrived a few minutes later to find that it would begin at ten. I did not get home until nearly one. At the end of the long mass, preceded by the Archbishop and about seventy-five priests and diplomats, I went with the Minister of Venezuela in the procession through the Cathedral, carrying a candle. Imagine me in the procession with all these priests in their rich gold-trimmed vestments and all the distinguished people who attended the Cathedral celebration. When I arrived at home, after I had been rising up and sitting down for three hours, we had company for luncheon, and thus ended a hectic week."

ATTENDED MASS FOR PADEREWSKI

Before the United States entered World War I, and during the war, I had frequent calls from Paderewski, the great Polish pianist, who was burning with zeal to see Poland made a free and independent state. It was also Wilson's and my heart's desire at Paris—and Wilson brought it about. This common tie was strengthened when I entertained Paderewski in my North Carolina home, and I was glad in Mexico to do honor to his memory, as I wrote home (July 21, 1941):

"On Friday I went to the Church of Our Lady of Lourdes to attend a mass for Paderewski. Nearly all the members of the Diplomatic Corps were present and many others. It was a very impressive service. The Minister of Poland stood just before the altar during the whole service like a statue, not even batting an eye. There were two solos, one by a man and one by a lady, both with very fine voices."

Y. M. C. A. AND Y. W. C. A.

There is hardly any part of the world where the youth are not reached by the Young Men's Christian Association. The leader of that and other religious movements, Dr. John R. Mott, was for many years as much at home in China or Africa as in the United States. Soon after I reached Mexico I visited the Y. M. C. A. and took part in its good work. I found that the Y. M. C. A. in Mexico, long guided by Secretary Taylor, was one of the most vital religious agencies, blessing many in the youth movement. My wife was glad to have a part in the work of the Y. W. C. A., having been a worker in the national organization in the United States, wearing the Y. W. C. A. uniform in her travels to camps and training bases in World War I. The Y. W. C. A. in Mexico City was organized in 1923. The trustees include British and American women residing in Mexico. The board has always been principally

Mexican. It has done a notably good work, educationally, culturally, and morally among the women of Mexico.

The new building was formally dedicated on July 7, 1933, my wife having a part in the ceremonies. I was present. It was made possible largely by the bequest of $100,000 by Miss Olivie Eggleston Phelps Stokes, a resident of Pasadena, California and Washington, D. C. It was the gift that enabled Mexico City to have the first Y. W. C. A. building of its own without a debt in Latin America. In her lifetime Miss Phelps Stokes had each year paid the salary of the secretary.

Among the founding members was Mrs. Fred Adams, an English woman long resident in Mexico, and her husband was a trustee. They created a trust fund of some $380,000, which will come to the Association upon the death of those relatives who receive the interest on the fund during their lifetime.

In the early part of January, 1940, we were glad to welcome to the Embassy Dr. Mott, a brother Methodist, who came to Mexico to a religious gathering that lasted for several days. He gave inspiration to all workers in the Y. M. C. A. and Y. W. C. A. and stimulated evangelical zeal by his addresses in the Gante Methodist Church. I recalled that in the Wilson administration, Dr. Mott had felt impelled to decline President Wilson's tender of the office of Minister to China because he had consecrated his life to religious work at home and abroad. His visit to Mexico was a benediction and my wife and I enjoyed his presence in the Embassy. Of this visit and its sidelights, I wrote (January 16, 1940):

> "On Friday we were very glad to welcome Dr. John R. Mott. I have known him for fifty years and have been in touch with him every now and then. He is the world's greatest globe-girdler; he has been to Asia a dozen times, to Africa almost as many, and to Europe more often than that, and knows the universe about as well as most of us know our own town or State."

"THE LORD WILL PROVIDE"—THE TOWNSEND LINGUISTIC GROUP

An acquaintance began in November, 1933, which ripened into deepening interest when Mr. Cameron Townsend and an associate called to present me with a Bible he had translated into the previously unwritten language of a tribe of Indians in Guatemala. He had taught them to read it. The Townsends—his wife and my wife became good friends—were a new type of selfless missionary. They and a group of a score of young people would go into a remote section where seldom a Catholic priest, or Protestant preacher, had penetrated, live with the Indians, eat and sleep as they did, and with the aid of some young Indians translate a portion of the Bible into their hitherto unwritten language and urge the Indians to accept Christianity. I asked them what organization furnished the money. They said, "We do not trouble about money. The Lord will provide. Our business is the translation of the New Testament. When it is learned what we are doing, the money comes." I wrote Mr. Townsend, "I have not seen such faith—no not in Mexico."

My wife took great interest in the work of the Townsend group and always invited them to tea at the Embassy when they were in Mexico City. Once we spent the day at their cottage in a small village remote from Mexico City.

PRESIDENT CÁRDENAS GAVE APPROVAL AND AID

Of the character and details of the work of the Townsend group, also known as Linguistics, I learned much from a conversation with a young member of the group, and I wrote the following letter home (September 26, 1936):

"The most interesting conversation I have had this week was with Mr. Eugene A. Nida, a young man who majored in languages at the University of California and who, with eight other young men from the United States under the direction of Mr. Townsend, are here to work with that department of Education which is establishing schools in the remote Indian villages where the Indians still speak their tribal languages and have never learned Spanish. President Cárdenas is showing great interest in these long-neglected Indians who cannot read or write any language and, through Mr. Townsend, is opening schools for such instruction in various parts of the Republic.

"Mr. Nida told me that he would leave for Chiapas in a few days and would go with a Mexican who spoke Spanish to a town in that State to begin his work. He said there were 7,000 people in that community, of whom only 100 spoke Spanish, the balance speaking the same tongue that was spoken when Cortés arrived, and the people have made a little progress. He said the President was anxious that they should be taught to

THE CHURCH AFTER THE REVOLUTION

read and write in their own tongue but that teachers should also introduce the cultivation of new foods so as to give what we call in America a 'balanced' ration.

"The Indian raises nothing but corn and beans and this is not considered wholesome. Mr. Nida told me that he was taking down with him various seeds and that his main business would be to teach agriculture. I asked him how he would do this and he said in conjunction with the schools that would be established. He would work with the teachers. He does not know the Indian language where he is to teach and the Mexican who is to go with him does not know it, but he thinks that having mastered four or five languages at the University of California it will be comparatively easy for him to master it. In fact he had already been studying it some, and illustrated the difference between the Spanish and the Indian tongue.

"This is a most interesting experiment and it is strange that it has not been attempted long before this. When you consider that out of 16,000,000 people in Mexico 14,000,000 are either Indian or *mestizo* and something like 2,000,000 still speak the old Indian tongue and live in the old Indian way, it is evident that the future of Mexico is dependent upon the improvement of the Indian, both those who have learned Spanish and those who still live in the same style as 500 years ago.

"I was interested to know whether Mr. Nida was in any sense a missionary. I asked if the Townsend group represented any church or missionary work. He said, 'You know Mexicans in their public schools do not have any religion taught and I am not here for that purpose, though of course the spirit of religion is always present.' I asked him what church he belonged to and he said he belonged to the 'Church of the Open Door' in Los Angeles. I had never heard of this church and asked him something about it. 'Well,' he said, 'I guess it is about like the Presbyterian church. Most of the people I know who belong to it are Presbyterians.'

"While we were talking, Counsellor Boal, who is a Catholic, asked him whether there were any priests in this country where he is going. He thought not. He said that in the adjoining region there were some priests, and that while most of them that served the Indians would go there only occasionally to celebrate mass and therefore made very little impression on them, there were some other priests who had been very helpful and were consecrated to their work."

PRACTICAL RELIGION ADVANCED BY THE LINGUISTIC GROUP

Little was known of the Linguistics in Mexico City. On October 2 and 7, 1940, I wrote home:

"On Tuesday, September 24, your mother invited the Townsend group and others for tea. Mr. Townsend is head of the Summer Institute of Linguistics in Arkansas, which trains young people for missionary work. After they have this training they come down to Mexico and go in couples into sections of the country where the Indians speak the same languages as they did five hundred years ago and have very few modern methods of living. . . .

"At the tea we were very much interested in the talk made by Dr. Elena Trejo, an Indian woman from Guatemala who has studied medicine in the United States and has been licensed to practice. Mrs. Townsend told your mother that seventeen years ago she and her husband were working in a remote Indian section of Guatemala translating the Bible into the Indian tongue, when a young Indian girl without any education, who had never seen shoes (Elena Trejo), came into the school. She was very bright and quick, learned English readily, and afterwards took a course at the Presbyterian Missionary School in Guatemala. She had a fine mind and decided that she would study medicine and go back to her people in Guatemala. She earned her way through high school and college in California by working as a nursemaid and otherwise, and later by lecturing, got her degree and then went to Puerto Rico for her internship and was offered a good position by the U. S. Government in one of the hospitals there, but her heart was set on going back to her own people, who still worship the moon and the sun. She wants to carry to them the light of learning and the light of Christian religion.

"Dr. Trejo's talk was most illuminating and interesting and heartening. It showed the possibilities, when an Indian, who had never been out of her little village, became an educated woman and a very useful member of society. She is one of the smallest women I have ever seen, with the brightest eyes and pleasantest expression. She said she had a dream when she first entered the school in Guatemala of becoming a doctor and that that dream was realized, and now she has a dream—she doesn't know where the money will come from or how—of getting a small hospital in the village from which she came and furnishing medical treatment to her Indian relatives and friends and carrying the Gospel to them.

"The Townsend group is trying to help President Cárdenas bring a better way of living to the Indians, who have shown capacity to learn and who, when educated, make good mechanics, engineers, doctors, lawyers, legislators, and presidents."

THE PROTESTANT CHURCHES

The Protestant movement in Mexico began in 1857. In 1859 some Catholic priests formed a group called "Constitutional Fathers" because of their sympathy with the new liberal Constitution. In 1861 a layman, Ramón Lozano, separated himself from the Catholic church, and a priest, Aguilar Bermúdez in Mexico City and Dr. Julio Prevost held meetings in Zacatecas, and celebrated holy communion in their homes and offices. The first organized Protestant church in Mexico was established by the Baptists in Monterrey in 1864. Other churches followed. Dr. Butler, a Methodist, quoted President Benito Juárez (he was of full Indian blood) as saying: "The future happiness and prosperity of my nation depends on the development of Protestantism. I could wish that Protestantism would become Mexican by conquering the Indians; they need a religion which will compel them to read and not spend their savings on candles for the saints."

The coming of Protestants into a country that had been converted to Christianity by Catholic priests was resented by some priests and others. Protestant preachers declared that they and their congregations "suffered social ostracism" and other persecution. The number of Protestants is small and statistics are not available. In 1930 the total membership, divided among twelve denominations, was said to be 130,322, distributed as follows: 22 per cent Methodists; 19 per cent Presbyterian; 13 per cent Baptist; 8 per cent Adventists; with a smaller percentage of other denominations. In 1941 it was said that the total membership was 300,000.

THE SALVATION ARMY ENTERS MEXICO

I had long known of the good work of the Salvation Army and regretted that when William Booth wished to minister to those who were "down but never out," the Methodist leaders in Eng-

land lacked the vision to go along with his plans. This caused him
to leave the church and establish the Salvation Army. Though
active nearly all over the world, the Salvation Army did not come
to Mexico until January, 1939. Of that coming I wrote (January
28, 1939):

"One of the interesting developments here is the establishment of the Salvation Army as an institution in Mexico. I had
a call from Ensign Fange of the Salvation Army this week,
accompanied by the Reverend Mr. McKean. They were getting
up their budget for this year and wished a contribution. I was
glad to subscribe. They showed me a picture of the Salvation
Army building here which was erected, they told me, by the
gift of one man. Ensign Fange says that what has surprised
him was that members of the Salvation Army were permitted
to wear uniforms on the street. You know in Mexico no priest
or preacher or nun can wear any clerical garb on the street. He
accounted for the fact that the Salvation Army people were
allowed to do it because they sought no memberships in any
church nor to proselyte, their only object being to bring physical
and spiritual aid to those who are down and out."

I rejoiced in the work of the Salvation Army and wrote again
(October 7, 1940):

"I had a call on Tuesday from Mr. Hauser and Señor Guzmán of the Salvation Army. About two years ago the Salvation
Army came to Mexico and began work, after the visit by one of
the Captains who had formerly been on duty in Raleigh. They
showed me pictures of their buildings and gave me a statement
of the excellent work the Salvation Army is doing among the
down and out. They reach hundreds of people and have dormi-
tories for people who haven't anywhere to sleep. I am not certain if this is not the best way for the Christian religion to be
propagated by Protestants in Mexico and other like countries
where the average man has been so long neglected. In the early
days of the Protestant missions here, they always established a
church and tried to carry the gospel to the people, but I think
they are going to carry it better by Salvation Army workers
than through the old organized church ways. In other words,
instead of people going to church, Christian missionaries come
to the people in their homes and show them that their mission
is to the poor who have been so long neglected, often by both

Catholic and Protestant churches. For that reason I was glad to see the Salvation Army people come in and it is very gratifying to find that they have done a great work and that it is increasing. So far as the Government authorities are concerned, they seem to have welcomed this character of Christian work. The Salvation Army does what no other organization undertakes."

CATHOLICS COULD NOT BUILD THEOLOGICAL SCHOOL

The Mexican law that did not permit Protestants, or Catholics, to build and conduct theological seminaries to train young preachers and priests was, I always thought, a policy that ought to be ended. Of it and a visit of Catholic leaders I wrote (July 22, 1939):

"A few days ago I received information from Washington that Monsignor Ready and several Catholic Bishops were coming to Mexico City this week to hold a conference with Archbishop Martínez about a theological school for young Mexicans who wish to become priests which has been established in New Mexico. Of course, under the laws of Mexico there can be no religious schools in Mexico, and in view of this fact, for quite a number of Mexicans who wish to be priests, a school has been built just across the border. When I knew it was going to be built I suggested to General Hay that it would seem to me to be much better if Mexico would grant the right to build it in Sonora or Chihuahua or one of the other States near the border in Mexico; that the money would be invested in Mexico and in the support of the institutions; and that it would be a good gesture. But he said that it was positively against the law and he hoped they would not ask for it. They did not, and of course they built the school in the United States. Tonight I am going to dinner at the University Club as the guest of Archbishop Martínez. There will be two bishops from the United States and Monsignor Ready. The Monsignor is a very fine man. I have seen him often in Washington. He succeeded Father Burke in the Catholic Welfare organization and is a forward-looking man—much more so than most priests and preachers as to economic and public-welfare conditions.

"While these bishops and Monsignor Ready have come down here in the interest of the theological school, the Mexicans, who still believe the Catholic church would like to get into politics here, do not feel that this is the real reason, but that they are conferring with Catholics here who would like to see a change in the government. As far as I know that is only a suspicion; I have seen no evidence that they are doing anything except purely church work. However, in the next campaign for President, which is going to be pretty exciting, the government officials believe that they will have to meet the opposition of an element in the Catholic church which wishes to get into politics.

"I am told that there is a distinct division between Catholic laymen here and priests, the more conservative of them saying that inasmuch as active persecution has ceased and priests are officiating and everybody who wants to go to church can do so, the turn is toward larger liberty and ultimate independence and freedom of church from either participation in the government or restraint by the government. The other and more militant Catholics wish to take sides and support a candidate for President who, if he is elected, will promise to restore conditions as to the church as they existed in the Díaz days. It is said that this element wishes the church to get behind the candidacy of Almazán. So far this is all gossip, but where there is so much smoke there is generally a little fire."

CATHOLIC DIGNITARIES DINE AT EMBASSY

I valued the friendship of Archbishop Martínez highly and always before going to Washington conferred with him so as to let his coreligionists know the situation as to church matters in Mexico. More than once he was a guest at the Embassy. Of a dinner for visiting dignitaries of the Catholic church, I wrote (August 2, 1939):

"On Monday night we gave a dinner at the Embassy for the Bishops and other dignitaries of the Catholic church who were in Mexico City. Prior to that I communicated with Archbishop Martínez and asked him to give me a list of the visitors and any others connected with the church that he thought it would be well to invite. We had a fine dinner and those present were as follows:

Leopoldo Ruiz y Flores, Archbishop of Morelia
Miguel Darío Miranda, Bishop of Tulancingo
Guillermo Tritschler, Bishop of San Luis Potosí
John Mark Gannon, Bishop of Erie
James A. Griffin, Bishop of Springfield (Ill.)
Monsignor Micahel
Father Dugan

Sr. Ingeniero Jorge Núñez, Protocol Commissioner
Sr. Roberto Bürckle
Sr. Juan Lainé

"Archbishop Martínez was unable to attend because of ill health. After the Mexicans had left, the American Bishops and priests and I had a long talk about the religious situation in Mexico. They asked me many questions, and I tried to give them the picture of the changes that had taken place and the attitude toward the church and the improved situation. I told them that whereas five years ago the situation was so tense that in six or seven States of Mexico the churches were not open for worshiping, now they were open in every State, even in Tabasco, where conditions had been so bad, and that while no laws had been changed, any person in Mexico who wanted to worship was free to do so and there was no active persecution anywhere. I also said the trend was for even greater freedom without any change in the laws. However I told them what I think is perfectly true, that if it should chance that in the coming presidential election the church should enter the campaign supporting any particular candidate, it would be the worst thing that could happen for the Catholic church. I told them there were two elements among the Catholics here—one purely spiritual which wanted nothing but freedom of religion, and another which wanted to control elections, do away with public schools, and restore the old close connection between church and state. If Catholics as religionists went into politics it would react against a growing liberty and freedom of worship which is so essential to religion.

"I ventured to tell them that the attempt by a few Catholics in Mexico to induce American Catholics to give support and help to any candidates in Mexico would check the growing improved situation. I said: 'We Americans cannot take any part in Mexican politics; if we should, it would invite here what happened in the United States when Grover Cleveland gave the British Minister his walking papers because he assumed to say what America should think or do.'"

WORST CHURCH SITUATION IN MEXICO

Writing home, I quoted the pastors of the churches here as being discouraged because—where English is spoken—only a handful of Englishmen and Americans go to Church. I said:

"Not long ago a visitor talked about the church situation in Mexico and asked me what was the worst phase of it. 'So far as we Americans are concerned, the worst thing about the religious situation in Mexico is that very few of the members of the American and British colonies go to church,' was my reply. 'We talk about how we prize religious freedom and the right to worship, but when many of our people come to Mexico they set a bad example in church-going.'

"I quoted to a Catholic friend who said, 'Do not confine that statement to Protestants. There are many Catholics who never go to church except to the required confessional once a year.'

"Later, when I was repeating these statements to my friend Rabbi Stephen S. Wise, he looked sad saying, 'I regret that this lack of devotion to religion exists in many Jewish families.'"

XV

AFTER THE CALM, THE STORM

Y first year had been smooth sailing, and when I went to Washington in the spring of 1934 I was able to report that the long controversy over Special Claims (dating from the ancient days), which had cost hundreds of thousands of dollars in commissions and other ways, had been settled and Mexico had made a down payment of half a million dollars; progress had been made in other negotiations; and there was not a cloud on the diplomatic horizon as far as Mexico and the United States were concerned.

It is always the unexpected that happens. It is equally true that a blow comes from a source least expected and against which no foresight could prevail. One day, not very long after I had gotten back to Mexico, I picked up my paper to read that two members of Congress had introduced resolutions that the American Ambassador should be recalled because, allegedly, he had approved an attack upon Catholics in Mexico. About the same time the papers reported that Martin H. Carmody, head of the Knights of Columbus, had upon the same charge called on President Roosevelt to order my recall.

I was not long left in ignorance of what had prompted the resolution in Congress and the action of the head of the Knights of Columbus. These gentlemen had been informed that on a certain day in 1934 General Plutarco Calles, former President, had made an address denouncing the Catholic church, and that a few days thereafter, speaking to a group of American scholars and students attending the Seminar in Mexico City, I had quoted and approved his speech. Of course no man who knew me and my record believed the false report. But those legislators and Knights and some prelates who seemed to want my head on a charger, or without one, could have ascertained that in a long life I had enjoyed the confidence of all Catholics who knew me and had enjoyed friendships which would have been withheld if I had been capable of the narrowness attributed to me.

I asked myself: "Is it possible I am the man being held up as a bigoted critic and enemy of a great church?" I recalled that it had so chanced that in my official life my closest advisers belonged to that church, and also in private life some of my dearest friends were of that faith. In the Cleveland period, when I was Chief Clerk of the Interior Department, my chief assistant and close friend was William H. DeLacy, a devout Catholic, who became later a Judge in the District of Columbia. When I was called upon as Secretary of the Navy in the Wilson administration to name a Chief of Operations, the highest rank and most important directive post in the American Navy, I chose Captain William S. Benson to be my closest Naval adviser and administrator and later recommended him as Naval adviser to the Peace Conference in Paris, where he was Wilson's strong right Naval arm. I did not select Benson because he was a Catholic, though I knew his church relations, but because, after considering all the high ranking officers of the Navy, I deemed him the best fitted. I even gave the place to a Captain when consideration of rank would have called for an Admiral. I was gratified years afterward to accompany that leader of the Knights of Columbus to Baltimore when the Order of St. Gregory the Great, Military Division First Order, from Pope Benedict was bestowed upon Admiral Benson by one of my dearest friends, Cardinal Gibbons, in the Baltimore Cathedral. It is the highest order conferred upon laymen and was in recognition of Benson's integrity and virtue as a Catholic gentleman and officer. Admiral Benson was a prominent Knight of Columbus, was devoted to his church, and incarnated the best virtues of the Christian religion.

At the moment the demand for my recall was being made, the Counsellor of the Embassy, Pierre Boal, and my personal secretary, Stephen Aguirre, were members of the Catholic church. None of these associates owed the official relationship to church affiliations. It just chanced that I was blessed with their appointment. They were as dear to me as if they had belonged to my own church. And as I thought on some of the bitter attacks, I also recalled that my first act as Ambassador had been to overrule the action of an American Consul who had declined to issue passports to Mexican young women who wished to go to Catholic institutions in the United States for training. They received the passports.

I also asked myself, if I had been the man depicted, would Archbishop Díaz have been my guest at the Embassy and talked with me freely? However, as the storm raged, I declined to make such references or to make any public statement in response to the charges except through official channels. I never doubted that, when all the facts were known, those who were most violent would be convinced they had acted upon false reports. My chief regret was lest some politicians might seek to arouse church opposition to Roosevelt in the next presidential election.

REACTION TO CAMPAIGN FOR RECALL

How did I react toward this tirade of denunciation from some Catholic papers, Catholic priests, and bishops, bitter attacks in the press, and resolutions in Congress demanding my removal from office? I knew that these attacks were based on the belief that Mexican officials were bent on destroying religion; and that the priests, believing it was a war like that between the Moors and the Christians, had rallied to the defense of their faith. The priests had accepted the incidents in Bishop Kelly's *Blood-Stained Altars* as representing the fixed attitude of Obregón, Calles, and other revolutionary leaders. They regarded the closing of all the churches in Tabasco by Garrido Canábal and the closed churches in Vera Cruz as the policy of the new order in Mexico. They did not know that many churches were open, that the wives of some politicians who were fighting the churches' attitude toward government and education, were going to mass regularly, and many of them were going to confessional every day. They did not know that, while some politicians were against religion, nearly all were animated chiefly by a desire for complete separation of Church and State and the end of church control of education. An influential political leader said:

> "For hundreds of years the Catholic church (there are few Protestant churches) had virtually directed the government of Mexico, sometimes clerics also being Viceroys, and, in spite of the constitution, had regained control in the last years of Díaz, with the result that there were magnificent silver and gold-ornamented costly churches (over 300 in Cholulu, a small place) while the great body of the impoverished people lived in unsanitary shacks and had no health protection for their families and few schools for their children. There are faithful and consecrated priests who labor for the souls of the people, but they

have no power to give liberty, education, opportunity, and health to the people. It is the domination of government by the church we are fighting."

However overdrawn that indictment was, and unjust in some parts of Mexico, the people followed the National Revolutionary party in order to get schools, land, and better living conditions. The spectacle was seen in Mexico of hundreds of thousands of Indians and mestizos going to mass in the morning and then going direct to the polls and voting for candidates for office who were denounced as enemies of the church. That sounded like a paradox. It was not so regarded. If these uneducated Indians had been vocal they would have explained: "We are Christians who wish freedom to worship without church restraint upon our voting to get our share of the good things of life."

But Americans, hearing only the propaganda that Cárdenas was trying to destroy religion when he wanted only to separate Church and State, were aroused to hot indignation and took it out on me because I was a 1934 disciple of Jefferson. I kept cool under the attacks, strengthened by the reflection that because Jefferson had separated Church and State in Virginia he was heralded as an infidel by the Puritans of New England. What had aroused Jefferson's antagonism to the union of Church and State in Protestant Virginia in colonial times? It was the fact that the established church haled Baptist and Quaker preachers into court and had them sent to jail for, as Patrick Henry said, "the crime of preaching the gospel." And I had not forgotten that the Puritan church in New England banished Roger Williams because he would not conform. Having carried Christianity into Mexico, some Catholic priests and prelates and laymen felt that the church was entitled to be the exclusive fountain of Christianity in that country, as in colonial days the Puritans in New England, and the Episcopalians in Virginia would recognize no nonconformists. And I, in all things, was a congenital nonconformist.

I was not surprised that priests and others in Mexico, and co-religionists in the United States, believing that hostility to religion was general in Mexico, should feel a sense of duty to stop persecution. When I saw thousands of Catholics in Mexico going freely to worship in their churches, I regretted chiefly that it was not universal and that full religious liberty did not exist in Tabasco and other States and in every country under the sun.

I had seen zealous preachers in my own day in my own church in my own State seek church control of schools. I had witnessed an eloquent Bishop of my church (the Methodist) go into the pulpit and denounce Thomas Jefferson as an atheist and an enemy of religion because Jefferson had built a state university and separated education from church control. And the Bishop thought verily he was doing the Lord's work, and he was a zealous Christian. And so I reflected that Catholic priests who were inflaming the people against Mexico were likewise honest. But I knew that just as Methodists in North Carolina refused to follow their zealous Bishop, and just as Massachusetts had repented of banishing Roger Williams, and Virginia Episcopalians were ashamed of jailing Baptists for preaching the gospel, the day would come when Mexico would guarantee freedom of religion and provide a system of public education for all the people.

No, I did not seek officially to tell Mexicans what to do, because that would have been in conflict with the Montevideo declaration, to which the United States was a party. But I did not hesitate, whenever opportunity permitted, to present to President Cárdenas, Archbishop Díaz, Bishop Pascoe, to all and sundry Catholics and Protestants my conviction and to urge the fullest freedom.

ATTACK BASED ON MISINFORMATION

I little thought on July 27, 1934, when I made an address at the Seminar, a yearly gathering of teachers and others from the United States headed by Hubert Herring, that my advocacy of public education would bring down on my head the wrath of leaders of the Knights of Columbus and some Catholic bishops in the United States. A day or two before, I had read a brief extract from an address by General Calles. I quoted and commented favorably on these words by Calles: "We must enter in and take possession of the mind of childhood, the mind of youth"—a statement that to my American mind was simply equivalent to advocating universal public education. However, later in that address, which was not printed in full in the paper from which I quoted, General Calles had made some criticism of the Catholic priests. I was charged, without justification, with having approved "the attack on the church."

I began my address at the Seminar by saying that, as I was driving on a street in Mexico, my attention was arrested by a building on which was the sign "Horace Mann School." I said it was significant that in Mexico, which was devoting one fifth of its revenue to public schools, a school was given the name of America's most famous apostle of public education and added:

"Experience through many centuries has taught mankind that no other agency than Government has brought the advantages of education to all the children of any country. Civic and religious organizations have promoted education of some of the people and have preserved records and advanced love of learning. But nowhere at any time has universal education carried its blessings alike to the children of the poor and the rich, unless public schools, supported by taxation, were opened freely to all the children of the country. Indeed, these blessings have come in largest measure only where compulsory taxation of all the people for public education was accompanied by compulsory attendance by all the children. That is the educational goal of all countries where government is based on the consent of the governed."

From these sound declarations, part of my lifelong creed, I never departed in the least. It was in this connection—a speech which had long been my chief theme in the United States—that I said that General Calles in a brief sentence had employed what Jefferson had envisioned a century ago. It was some time after, when my perfectly unassailable presentation of the truest Americanism was twisted into an attack on the Catholic church, that the head of the Knights of Columbus demanded of President Roosevelt that I be recalled as Ambassador for having approved attacks on that church.

WHAT CALLES SAID

I never saw any other part of the speech by Calles, except the extract I quoted in my address to American scholars, until it was printed in the Baltimore *Catholic Review* under a seven-line streamer (October 17, 1934):

PRESIDENT ROOSEVELT WE CALL YOUR ATTENTION
Josephus Daniels Come to Judgment

As it appeared in that paper Calles had said in his address:

"We must enter into consciences and take possession of them: the conscience of the children and the conscience of the youth; for the youth and the child must belong to the Revolution.

"It is absolutely necessary to drag the enemy out of his trench. The Conservatives are the enemy; and their trench is education, their trench is the school. It would be a grave and cowardly dereliction of duty not to snatch our youth from the claws of the clericals, from the claws of the conservatives; and unfortunately the schools in many States and in the Capital are directed by the clerical and reactionary elements.

"We cannot leave the future of the country, the future of the revolution in enemy hands. With all their trickery the clericals cry: 'The child belongs to the home; the youth belongs to the family.' Egoistic doctrine! Child and Youth belong to the Community, to the collective body; and it is the revolution's inescapable duty to attack this section, and dispossess them of consciences, to uproot all prejudices (i.e., religious beliefs) and to form the new national soul.

"For this end I urge and exhort all the governments of the republic, all the authorities of the republic, all the revolutionary elements of the republic, that we give definitive battle, on whatsoever plane and to whatsoever limit, in order that the consciences of the youth shall belong to the Revolution."

LEARNED OF THE AGITATION

The first I knew of the uproar in the United States was when Acting Secretary William Phillips informed me of it and asked what I had said. I quoted my remark and added that I had not known of any other statement in the Calles address except the brief one I had quoted with approval. That explanation by a State Department head did not satisfy Mr. Carmody and some others. An agitation against me was whipped up into a campaign for my removal.

On February 9, 1934, Representative Connery introduced a resolution demanding my recall. He called the attention of the House to "a public report of an address by Josephus Daniels," in which the Ambassador was said to have described the philosophy of former President Plutarco Elías Calles as typical of that of Jefferson. Mr. Connery said:

> "The American people have a right to know fully what the Ambassador to Mexico means when he compares the educational policies of Calles with the policies of Thomas Jefferson. Does the American Ambassador favor communism in Mexico?
>
> "I believe that the Honorable Josephus Daniels and other representatives of the American Government in Mexico, who, for some unknown reason are coöperating with the tyrants of Mexico to enslave the Mexican people, should be summoned back to the United States and be forced to tell the truth of the rotten conditions which exist in the country at this time."

Representative Hamilton Fish, Jr., declared (November 30) that he would demand the recall of Josephus Daniels from Mexico when Congress convened in January. Fish criticized the administration's non-intervention policy in Mexico. He declared that he would demand a vote on a resolution, defeated in committee eight months ago, calling upon the president "to use his good offices to bring about religious liberty and freedom of worship in Mexico." Mr. Fish referred to Mr. Daniels as "that eminent and deserving Democratic Ambassador who has too long misrepresented American policies and tradition in Mexico City."

Representative Higgins followed and some Republicans demanded action.

UNJUST AND UNWARRANTED

When Representative Higgins demanded my removal, denouncing my call on Secretary of Agriculture Garrido Canábal, a Red Shirt and an anti-church leader, President Roosevelt wrote him that he was acting "upon a distortion of the facts," and added:

> "Shortly after the inauguration of the present administration in Mexico, Ambassador Daniels paid courtesy calls on all of the members of the new Cabinet among them the Secretary of Agriculture. These visits were fully reported by Ambassador Daniels in his despatches to the Department of State, and I can assure you that to interpret his actions otherwise than as the performance of a courteous formality is as unjust as it is unwarranted by the facts."

A little later Representative Fenerty, of Pennsylvania, attacked me alleging I had failed to protest against religious persecution in Mexico and called for my removal. He said in the House:

"It is difficult to see how we could be worse represented in any land by such a man as this, one who is either too ignorant to know his responsibilities, or too much interested in the political descendants of the Mexican bandits in whose behalf he sent our fleet to Vera Cruz in 1914, to care what happens to the oppressed Mexican people.

"Our erratic Ambassador blandly says: 'They (Mexican officials) deny there has been any religious persecution.' As a sample of Ambassadorial stupidity, Mr. Speaker, there is a choice morsel for you.

"Actually, this list of official outrages upon Mexico's persecuted people shows thousands upon thousands of crimes, from murder to mere overnight kidnappings, have been committed by the government officials in the name of communism and atheism in Mexico. Our Ambassador somehow never hears of them.

"Mexico is dedicated to a system of socialistic education that instills hatred of Americans into the minds of the young, that boasts that God is excluded from Mexico, that brings the most perverse forms of degenerate immorality into the class rooms, and compels the children to greet their teachers with the morning salutation: 'Good day, teacher; there is no God.'

"Daniels has turned press agent for Mexican Communists."

STORM GREW

In spite of my disclaimer, the storm grew. Some Catholic newspapers attacked me for allegedly favoring anti-church activities. Catholic students in New York University loudly asked for my recall, and the New York Assembly unanimously adopted a resolution memorializing President Roosevelt to protest to Mexico "against alleged persecution of Catholics in that country." Monsignor H. L. Lang scored me as an enemy of the church, and Archbishop Hayes called on priests to preach on "Church Persecution in Mexico," and offer prayer "to put an end to the cruel, tyrannical and even diabolical persecution of our church in Mexico." On the day they were to hold these meetings, some irresponsible fanatic threw a bomb into the Embassy grounds in Mexico City. This caused the Mexican

Government to put police dressed like peons in the near-by streets to protect the Embassy.

WHAT CARMODY CHARGED

Mr. Carmody, in his letter to President Roosevelt, asked that the government "exercise its good offices in behalf of persecuted Catholics in Mexico." The letter declared that the Mexican government "directs aggressively a continuous propaganda throughout the United States to promote its Soviet philosophy of government," and charged that the Mexican government was openly hostile to "our form of government, our free institutions, and our principles of civil and religious liberty."

Criticizing the State Department for remaining "silent and inactive," in the face of protests from various individuals and organizations, Mr. Carmody said that several Mexican States had forced Catholic churches to close altogether, that "their priests have been murdered, imprisoned, or banished," and that "atheism and red communism" are taught in the schools. "Because of these persecutions, thousands of refugees are being forced across the Mexican border into our country and forced to seek the charity of the United States."

CONGRESS FOLLOWS HULL

To my great surprise, Senator Borah introduced a resolution to investigate the religious situation in Mexico, saying that it was "fit and proper to protest the anti-religious campaign and practice of the present rulers of Mexico," adding that the Senate "views with the gravest concern ruthless persecution of helpless men and women who have become the innocent victims of anti-religious persecution." He called on the Mexican Government to cease denying "fundamental rights," and authorized a sub-committee to conduct hearings.

Secretary Hull, in a letter to Chairman Pittman, strongly opposed the passage of the resolution, but neither Hull nor Pittman would make the letter public. It was understood that Hull reiterated his view that the United States should not interfere in the affairs of another country.

The Executive Committee of the Federal Council of Churches of Christ in America adopted (March, 1935) a resolution opposing

Borah's resolution for an investigation of the religious situation in Mexico. The Committee's resolution was as follows:

"In the absence of sufficient authentic and unbiased information, we do not undertake at this time to pass judgment on various aspects of the controversy between the Mexican government and the church. On two points, however, our convictions are clear:

"1. We take a vigorous stand in support of religious liberty in all groups both in Mexico and in every part of the world.

"2. We record our strong opposition to the resolution introduced into the United States Senate calling for an inquiry into the religious controversy in Mexico. We would regard such action by our government an unwarranted interference in the internal affairs of another nation."

Congress took no action on the Borah resolution.

NOTHING IN SPEECH TO SUPPORT CHARGE

While what I had said to the members of the Seminar was being venomously discussed, the Honorable Ernest Gruening, who was present and heard the address and knew Mexico well, wrote me:

"I note with surprise that you had been made the target of a barrage—evidently carefully timed—because of your alleged support of attack on the Catholic church. I was even more surprised when I realized from reading the newspaper account that the basis of these charges was contained in words of greeting addressed to the Seminar last July. I had the good fortune and the pleasure to be present on the occasion and I would be most happy to testify that nothing seemed more remote from the purport and obvious purpose of that address than the intent with which you are charged."

SENATOR CHAVEZ DEFENDS

While the resolutions were pending in Congress, Senator Chavez, of New Mexico, who knew Mexico better than any other legislator, replied to Representative Kennedy's attack. Kennedy had offered a resolution which would require Secretary Hull to answer a series of questions. It was tabled by the House. Senator Chavez said: "I feel confident that an account of Mr. Daniels' work in Mexico and his dignified and humane efforts in protecting American interests should satisfy any fair-minded body of inquirers."

UNDER WRONG IMPRESSION

Not only did members of the Knights of Columbus demand intervention as to religious practices in Mexico, but a friend of mine in New York wrote to me that in the fall of 1935 the Secretary of that organization demanded that the embargo on arms be lifted so that Mexican Catholics could arm themselves. In the previous summer, when I was at home, a Catholic Bishop had said to me, "It is a shame that the American government puts an embargo on arms so that no effective resistance can be made by the Catholics of Mexico." I told the prelate he was laboring under a wrong impression. He thought the Wilson and Coolidge embargoes, limited as to time, were still in force, and I added, "The only deterrent against Mexicans' getting arms from the United States is the vigilance of the Mexican government against the importation of arms, but that in spite of the efforts of the government some arms had been smuggled in."

MUNDELEIN'S REBUKE

While some priests and prelates and members of the Knights of Columbus were demanding intervention, Cardinal Mundelein, of Chicago, stated emphatically: "No individual Catholic, Bishop, or priest, nor organization of laymen or Catholic newspaper has the right to speak for 20,000,000 Catholics in this country in matters of politics; only the Bishops of the country together, in conference or in council, and they have not done so, and so we do not wish our words to be interpreted in that sense."

Cardinal Mundelein was understood, according to a statement in the New York Times, to have had three purposes in speaking out so earnestly: to rebuke the political priests of his faith, notably Father Coughlin; to rebuke laymen, such as officials of the Knights of Columbus, who had criticized the President for policies—toward Mexico, for example—on which the policy of the church could be stated by its hierarchy alone; and to endorse his conception of the President's effort to spread the blessings of American prosperity.

President Roosevelt had planned to come to Mexico and had received a pressing invitation from the President, but on February

1, 1935, I wrote him that, in view of the attitude of some American Catholics, I would suggest that he delay his visit, saying: "If you were to come now, religious feeling might be aroused to the highest pitch. Some prelates and others would insist that you take up the religious and other matters about which there is a controversy. If any official is to receive criticism let it fall on me." And I added:

"The difficulty here is that the leaders of the National Revolutionary party, which in effect is the Federal Administration, charge that the clergy are actively in politics, directly or indirectly, and are trying to overturn the Government. They point to the 'Cristero' rebellion in 1926, which they say was engineered by the Catholic church, and to the murder of President Obregón, which they charge was inspired by church leaders. Their attitude is in substance that, 'Unless we teach the children the principles of the Revolution, the clergy will teach them to believe in the old order of Church control of education and government, and the reforms of the Revolution will be overthrown.'

"On the other hand, the church's attitude may be compressed thus: 'The government is seeking to enforce atheistic education which denies the existence of God and it is communistic in its aims. It is persecuting the Church and we must not submit.'

"Apparently the best members of both factions are sincere, the one thinking the Revolutionary government would be overthrown by the church, and the other thinking the government would uproot religion. This makes an impasse. Neither side is open to reason. Last year, in a talk with General Calles, I pointed out to him that unless religious freedom was guaranteed, and the fact made known, Mexico would lose the prestige it had gained in the world. He insisted that the policy of the government was not opposed to religious freedom, and that if the government must change its laws and its policies to obtain the approval of other countries, it would have to stand the danger of such loss."

ROOSEVELT'S HISTORIC ANSWER

Replying to Mr. Carmody's letter, President Roosevelt set forth with clearness in an unanswerable way the policy of our government. It was exactly in accord with my course from the day I reached Mexico and I wired him, "Bravo!"

His letter is the chart for America for all time in dealing with other nations. It is as follows (November, 1935):

The White House
Washington

My dear Mr. Carmody:

I have received your letter of October 25.

Without commenting upon the language of your communication under acknowledgment and without reference to the accuracy of the statements or conclusions which you advance, I shall inform you once more of the attitude of this administration in the matter of the policy pursued by the government of Mexico toward religious activities in that republic.

The right of the United States citizens resident or travelling in foreign countries to worship freely, to conduct services within their houses, or within appropriate buildings maintained for that purpose, is desired by this government. There has not been brought to this government during the past year a single complaint by any United States citizen that such opportunities in Mexico have been refused him.

In respect to the rights enjoyed by Mexican citizens living in Mexico, it has been the policy of this administration to refrain from intervening in such direct concerns of the Mexican government. That policy of non-intervention I shall continue to pursue.

While this government does not assume to undertake any accurate determination of what the facts in such domestic concerns of other governments may be, this policy of non-intervention, however, can in no sense be construed as indifference on our part. I repeat what I stated publicly in San Diego, California, on October 2, last:

"Our national determination to keep free of foreign wars and foreign entanglements cannot prevent us from feeling deep concern when ideals and principles that we have cherished are challenged. In the United States we regard it as axiomatic that every person shall enjoy the free exercise of his religion according to the dictates of his conscience. Our flag for a century and a half has been the symbol of the principles of liberty of conscience, of religious freedom and equality before the law; and these concepts are deeply ingrained in our national character.

"It is true that other nations may, as they do, enforce contrary rules of conscience and conduct. It is true that policies that may be pursued under flags other than our own are beyond our jurisdiction. Yet in our inner individual lives we can never be indifferent and we assert for ourselves complete freedom for ourselves, complete freedom to embrace, to profess, and to observe the principles for which our flag has so long been the lofty symbol. As it was so well said by James Madison, 'We hold it for a fundamental and inalienable truth that religion and the manner of discharging it can be directed only by reason and conviction, not by force or violence.' "

This statement I now reiterate to you.

Inasmuch as you have referred in your letter under acknowledgment to the policy pursued in such matters as this by previous administrations and have meant specifically the administration of President Theodore Roosevelt, it may not be inappropriate to call to your attention the statement of the former President Theodore Roosevelt contained in his annual message to congress, December 6, 1904.

"... Ordinarily it is very much wiser and more useful for us to concern ourselves with striving for our own moral and material betterment here at home than to concern ourselves with trying to better the condition of things in other nations. We have plenty of sins of our own to war against, and under ordinary circumstances we can do more for the general uplifting of humanity by striving with heart and soul to put a stop to civic corruption, to brutal lawlessness, and violent race prejudice here at home than by passing resolutions about wrongdoing elsewhere."

You and I abhor equally, I trust, religious intolerance, whether at home or abroad. For my own part, however, I decline to permit this government to undertake a policy of interference in the domestic concerns of foreign governments and thereby jeopardize the maintainence of peaceful conditions.

Sincerely yours,

FRANKLIN D. ROOSEVELT.

The letter of President Roosevelt satisfied most of those who had been protesting. Mr. Carmody denied that he or those associated with him would bring the question into the presidential campaign. Now and then there was a revival of the criticism, but it was confined to a few.

COMMITTEE OF THREE CREEDS INVESTIGATE

The reports that reached the United States of serious outbreaks because of the church controversy resulted in the creation of a "Committee on Religious Rights," an unofficial organization of Catholics, Protestants, and Jews to investigate. This committee of three came to Mexico in June, 1935, to study the religious problem. It was composed of Dr. William Franklin Sands, of the Foreign Service School of Georgetown University (a Catholic), Dr. Philip Marshall Brown, a member of the Faculty of Princeton University (a Protestant), and Carl Sherman, Attorney General of New York when Al Smith was Governor (a Jew). Mr. Sands was First Secretary of the Embassy in Mexico in 1908 and was familiar with the Mexico of that period. This committee talked to officials, priests, and citizens of standing. As they were leaving Mexico, I did not ask what their report would be. During their stay I gave them such information as they requested. Writing to President Roosevelt (August 3, 1935) I said:

"The report of the Committee of Religious Rights is not ready, but Mr. Sands, the Catholic member, in a letter to Colonel Callahan, stated: 'What I want you to know is: That Government officials assured me that Daniels has never let up for a minute stressing the importance of a solution to this religious problem. . . . President Cárdenas told Daniels that he could not change the law but there would be no religious persecution.'

"Yesterday Mr. Edward Reed, Chief of the Mexican Division of the State Department, sent a confidential copy of the rough draft of Mr. Sands' report. Accompanying the draft Mr. Reed sent a confidential memorandum in which he says:

"'Concerning Mr. Daniels, Mr. Sands expressed the opinion that our Ambassador has been most unjustly maligned. Mexican Foreign Officials told him that Mr. Daniels had gone far beyond what might reasonably have been expected of him in trying to bring about an adjustment of the religious controversy. Mr. Sands was sure that these statements were correct and he wished to do something about the matter in justice to Mr. Daniels. Mr. Daniels, however, had insisted that he keep silent on the subject of his activities unless authorized by the Secretary of State to make a statement in regard to them. Incidentally, Mr. Sands indicated that he was familiar with the purport of Ambassador Daniels' recent conversation on religious matters with President Cárdenas.'

"I do not know what will be the final report of this committee, but I surmise it will stress the deplorable situation in Tabasco, Vera Cruz, and other States where there has been bitter conflict between Catholics and Revolutionary leaders. In

Upper left, Miss Sallie McKinnon, called the Methodist woman Bishop. She wanted no money. *Upper right,* the Reverend and Mrs. Charles R. McKean, at entrance to the Union Evangelical Church. *Below,* Ambassador and Mrs. Daniels entertain at the Embassy one of the Townsend groups, described on pages 167-71.

General Board of Religious Education of the Methodist Church of Mexico. *Front row, left to right,* Dr. Juan N. Pascoe, Professor Baez Camargo, Mrs. J. P. Hauser, Dr. Wade C. Barclay, and Professor Juan Díaz Galindo.

the meantime I thought you would like to read the impression of the Catholic member of the committee."

SWEEPING CONCLUSION NOT JUSTIFIED

Later when the Committee reported that they were confirmed in their opinion that the government desires "not merely the suppression of alleged abuses in any church but the extirpation of all religion in the country," I wrote to President Roosevelt (December 18, 1935):

"I do not think that sweeping conclusion is justified by the situation here, though the action of a number of States in closing all churches is as indefensible as it is indicative of the continued fight upon the Roman Catholic Church by some of the revolutionists. Since that time churches have been opened in Querétaro and services have been renewed in other States. The fight is not against religion as such; it is more a hang-over of the fight between the revolutionists and Catholic priests which blazed out in the revolution of 1910 and afterwards. Mr. Sands was here in August, 1929, and upon his return to the United States wrote a long letter to Colonel Patrick H. Callahan giving his impressions. In the course of the letter Mr. Sands says: 'Archbishop Diaz was asked if it is true that "the Church" in Mexico is in politics.' He answered: 'In politics? I am in politics up to my neck and intend to stay there! How do you suppose we are to get anti-religious laws repealed except by politics?'

"Catholic church leaders today deny they are in politics, and, even when admitting that this is true, the government officials say that they are ready to return to their old activities if they were not restrained by the government's measures."

CHURCH NEGLECTED OPPORTUNITY

When the storm had subsided I had a call from a distinguished jurist (a staunch Catholic) from the United States who had quietly spent a month in Mexico in a survey of the religious situation. He said: "I was requested by leaders in my church to make an independent survey of the religious situation in Mexico. The saddest thing about my observations here is that my church has failed to make the best of its great opportunities to educate and improve the conditions under which so many Mexicans are forced to live."

MOST SERIOUS RELIGIOUS SITUATION

While the Knights of Columbus and others were demanding that the United States government assume the right and power to compel Mexico to change its laws, a prominent member of the American Colony brought a visitor from New York to call on me. The visitor asked: "What is the most serious aspect of the religious situation in Mexico?"

Instead of trying to lead him through the maze of the heated controversies I replied, with an implied criticism of his host and others like him who played golf on Sunday and did not go to church, "The one which troubles me most as an American is that many members of the American Colony do not go to any Church."

As these gentlemen were leaving I was moved to say: "In view of what I have said and the bitterness engendered by religious differences I am tempted to believe that the sage was right who said: 'Most men will do any and everything for their religion, even fight for it; there is no sacrifice they will not make for it. There is only one thing they will not do for their religion—they will not live it.' This applies to many Catholics, Jews and Protestants—more's the pity!"

AN AMBASSADOR'S SUCCESSFUL ERROR

After President Roosevelt's sound declaration and the denunciation of the agitators, the *Baltimore Sun* reviewed the incident, closing as follows:

"An errant Tarheel dropped into the office the other day for the purpose of claiming credit. 'You people are singularly blind to the extraordinary qualities of that ornament of the Old North State, Ambassador Josephus Daniels,' he declared, reproaching *The Evening Sun* and Marylanders generally. Unappeased by assurances that all Tarheels are considered extraordinary in this vicinity, he elaborated his argument:

" 'That treaty settling the land payment problem he negotiated last week is pretty nearly a miracle of diplomacy. Why, has it occurred to you that he has persuaded the Mexicans into doing of their own free will what the Nazis have compelled the German Jews to do, that is, pay for the damage their oppressors have inflicted upon them?

" 'The Mexican contention from the start has been that we

stole every foot of that land and that our title-deeds never were worth the paper they are written on. All the same, Josephus has got their names on the dotted line and they are going to cough up.

" 'How did he get away with it? Obviously, he has contrived somehow to get to the point where the Mexicans will take his word for anything, and I believe he did it through what everybody denounced as a terrible diplomatic blunder.

" 'You remember the time he made his public school speech, which the Catholics thought was intended to be an attack on their church and so sent petition after petition to the President demanding his recall?

" 'Of course, everybody in North Carolina knew Jo Daniels never meant to attack anyone. We all knew that speech by heart. He had been making it every time a schoolhouse cornerstone was laid in North Carolina for forty years. So when they asked him to lay a cornerstone in Mexico City, he simply got out the old speech, dusted it off a bit, struck out the words Perquimans county and substituted Mexico City and fired her off in fine style.

" 'There was a passage in it where he said that North Carolina's real wealth is not her money or her land but her children, that her first responsibility is to these, her wards, and so forth. Well, nobody ever thought anything about it at home, nor did he think anything about it when he substituted Mexico for North Carolina. But the church that claims Mexican children as her wards, thought he did it purposely, and there was a fine uproar.

" 'Now, Josephus is a pious man, and looks it. He doesn't drink, he doesn't smoke, he doesn't swear and he attends church regularly. I believe half the Mexicans, especially the anticlericals, suspected him of being a papal delegate in disguise— until the row broke. After that, though, there was no doubt that wherever he came from, it was not from the Vatican. Perhaps the anti-clericals began to suspect that he was one of them in disguise.

" 'At any rate, he has been solid with the ruling outfit down there ever since the uproar. I tell you right now, a man who can make capital of his own mistakes like that is unusual, even for a North Carolinian, and I want you to give him credit.'

"So here it is."

Part Five

THE SIX-YEAR PLAN

XVI

"THE LAND BELONGS TO THOSE WHO WORK IT"

THE Revolution in Mexico was accompanied by the slogans "Land and Liberty" and "Effective Suffrage—No Reëlection," and "The Land Belongs to Those Who Work It With Their Hands." The country had been cursed by officials who kept themselves in power without popular election, and Madero's demand was for full suffrage and an end to long terms in office. Up to this day no official in Mexico can be reëlected. But the shibboleth that rallied the people was the promise of land to those who tilled it. Up to 1910 the land was owned in large estates by a few *hacendados,* and the workers had no chance to become landholders. The men who led the Revolution said that those who owned the land had obtained it by favor. Sometimes their acquisition of it was as indefensible as when the Spanish took it by force and compelled the Indians to work for them under conditions akin to slavery.

WORKERS GREW POORER AND POORER

In his informing book *The Ejido, Mexico's Way Out,* Eyler N. Simpson, who spent several years in Mexico, tells how the masses grew poorer and poorer. He says that in 1908 the minimum daily wage was 23.5 centavos. While wages remained the same for nearly a century, corn rose in price approximately 179 per cent, rice 75 per cent, flour 711 per cent, wheat 465 per cent. The workers on the farms did not even receive in money the starvation wages. Every hacienda (plantation) had a "pay roll" store and big profits were made. The result is thus stated:

> "By the first decade of the 20th century Mexico had become a country of peonage and poverty. 'The poor peon never holds in his hands a piece of silver money. The son receives at an early age the chains which bound his father and passes them along in turn to his sons. The monthly salary of the workers is converted into a series of marks in a book which the poor peon cannot understand, nor tries to understand.' . . . The re-

sult was one of the most luxuriant harvests of the weeds of special privilege the world has ever seen."

It was said that when in 1910 Madero started the Revolution (always spell it with a capital R) one per cent of the people owned 90 per cent of the arable land of Mexico, and over 95 per cent of the heads of families were landless. One family held 988,400 acres and the thousands who tilled it were later even deprived of their *ejidos,* or common lands. In the state of Morelos eighteen families held practically all the cultivated soil. The law was cruel to the poor. No Indian in debt could leave the farm, and if he died in debt his son must work until the debt was paid.

With the victory of the National Revolutionary party the promise was the dotation of land to "those who worked it." Obregón began distribution, but the fulfillment of that promise was slow until President Cárdenas was elected, though all Revolutionary leaders had pledged in the Six-Year Plan to give land to the workers. Calles began to keep the pledge but later said it was not feasible. Portes Gil distributed 1,000,000 hectares; Ortiz Rubio, 1,702,796; Abelardo Rodríguez, 876,133. Up to the time of Cárdenas, 8,158,929 hectares to 671,400 persons had been distributed since the Revolution. During his term Cárdenas gave 1,020,495 persons 18,352,275 hectares.

As the chief executives, acting under the pledge of the Revolution, dotated land to those who worked it, they never said the words "give the land." They said, "return the land," and declared that restitution of the land was being made to those from whose ancestors it had been snatched.

There was bitterness on the part of the *hacendados* at the distribution of lands they had long held. From the day I arrived I presented claims for lands taken from American citizens. The Embassy heard all Americans who were dispossessed of their lands, and naturally they felt a sense of the wrong done them, and I shared their feeling. A few—a very few—acted as did one American, about whom I wrote:

"I had a call today from the head of a big company holding thousands of acres of land, who has been in Mexico a long time. He told me that the government, in carrying out their agrarian policy, had not taken much land from his company, which

"THE LAND IS NOW YOURS." General Gildardo Magaña, Governor of Michoacán (*standing*) reads the announcement which delivers the properties to the peons. *Extreme left,* Julian Rodríguez Adame, head of the National Bank of Ejidal Credit; Cárdenas with hands crossed; *right* from Cárdenas, General Francisco Mugica, Minister of Communications and Public Works; *next right,* Antonio Villalopos, Chief of the Labor Department.

Above, Vicente Lombardo Toledano (*left*) president of the Confederation of Mexican Labor, and Alejandro Carrillo (*right*) secretary of the Confederation. Toledano is Dean, and Carrillo Secretary of the Workers University. *Below,* the inauguration of the Workers University, session of 1944.

owns I don't know how many thousand acres, much of it very good timber land. 'My plan,' he said, 'is to recall that I am in Mexico and that if I want to get along, I have to make friends with these people and not antagonize them. For example, they wanted to take some of our land and divide it up under the agrarian law. Instead of making a fuss about it, as some people do, I conferred with them about it and we gave up some land without any trouble. But of course,' he added with a smile, 'we kept the cream.'"

THE LAGUNA AGRARIAN DEVELOPMENT

The Laguna development about Torreón was one of the largest properties divided. I visited it before it was taken for division among the Indians who had worked as peons on it. Naturally, coming from a cotton-raising section, I was interested in that part of Mexico where cotton was the main crop. I had heard much about the lands around Torreón and in March, 1934, wrote home:

"We turned our faces toward the great irrigation projects and big cotton haciendas, as the guests of Messrs. Plácido, Juan, José, and Jesús Vargas. One of these gentlemen (Plácido) is the head of the Road Commission, and he, with his brothers, has a big hacienda. He told me that they had 9,000 acres. 'How much of it is cultivated?' I asked. 'All of it,' he said. 'This was a desert country (most of it still is) until the irrigation works were started some years ago. Now there is a section, perhaps 100 miles square, where big crops of wheat and cotton are grown. The yield is one bale to the acre. We use no fertilizer. Our river is to our country what the Nile is to Egypt. The silt that comes down with the water enriches the soil.'

"We drove for miles along the river. In some parts there was not a drop of water—most of it dry sand. Occasionally in the deepest places there was a little water, but very little—not enough to do any good. I was told that not a drop of rain had fallen there since last September. And how dusty it was! Sometimes during the rainy season this dry river bottom overflows with an abundance of water, and the irrigation ditches are full to overflowing. Sometimes there are three feet of water over the land. This seeps in and helps in the long dry season. But the river does not furnish sufficient water for the increased acreage and in recent years 500 wells have been dug, and it is this water that gives a steady flow of abundance of water. As far as the eye can reach it is a flat surface, well watered, and we could see the wheat waving and the young green cotton pushing its way up in the long—very long—rows. Cotton blooms in May and matures in July and August. One half of the crop of the irrigated land is in cotton and the other half in wheat. If one crop fails the planters have something to fall back on.

"If there are any small farmers, I did not happen to see them in a twenty-five-mile drive. The Vargas brothers have 9,000 acres. A few haciendas contain 25,000 acres. The workers live in a village near the house of the hacienda owner, and go out from the central place to till the land, reap the wheat, and pick the cotton on their hacienda. They have the most modern machinery for threshing, etc., of wheat. This hacienda is a farm, machine shop, store, in fact a town with all town facilities. There is electric power all over the farm. The plant is owned by the Electric Bond & Share. All the pumping (and there is a great deal) is done by electric power. Farmers are complaining that the rates are too high. Torreón and the irrigation district consume more power than the entire city of Monterrey, an industrial center.

"A delicious lunch in a house with the windows opening on the patio where flowers were in bloom and where beautifully plumaged birds sang throughout the lunch. You see that far from any city we had music with our meal! Quite a company, and good food. Then a visit to the large gardens—a vineyard of many acres, but now showing just a little green.

"'You should have come a month later to enjoy the grapes and to see how green and beautiful is a vineyard,' said my luncheon host, proud of his fertile hacienda. By hedging, etc., he said he realized 11 cents for his crop last year. He thinks it will bring 15 cents this year. What did I think? I told him the Henry Grady story that 'Cotton is a fool.' They are almost as wholly centered on cotton as is the Delta country or as were Edgecombe and Wilson and Halifax counties, in North Carolina before they began to grow tobacco. However, they are too wise to depend on one crop—they go half and half on wheat and cotton."

TORREÓN LANDS GIVEN TO INDIANS

That was in 1934. In 1936 President Cárdenas expropriated thousands of acres, gave it to the peons, and provided loans and machinery so that they could work it to advantage. That dotation was widely criticized and defended. The government said the large owners had gotten it by favor for a song and that it should revert to the State. The owners of the big estates declared they had obtained it under Mexican laws, invested large sums to make it productive, and cried out loudly against "the confiscation." As a sample of the vigorous protests I wrote in my weekly letter home (November 24, 1936):

"I had a visitor last week, Colonel John Tabor of Great Britain, who is a Vice President or some other officer of the English company which owns thousands of acres of cotton-growing land in the Laguna District near Torreón, which has been dotated by the government to the agrarians. Of course he and the other owners of land in that section are very much perturbed about this and he had come from England to see if it could be prevented.

"He had not been talking very long until he made the request that I take the matter up with the Mexican government and try to change their policy of dotating this land to the agrarians. He said that Americans owned some of the bonds of the corporation. I did not much like the idea of his coming to me when he is a Britisher, and I told him that I had talked with the British Minister, Mr. Murray, about the matter and that the Minister was doing everything that could be done and I advised him to talk it over with his own Minister.

"In this connection President Cárdenas is determined that every person living on this land (they are all Indians and have been working it for years) should own a part of it, leaving to the original owners something like 150 hectares. The President has been in that section for two weeks, not only looking into the division of the land but also considering loans for the Indians so that they can own mules, and the purchase of cotton gins, etc., etc. They found here that the policy of giving land to the Indians when they had no money or implements was not working well. Most of the objection to the agrarian system by Mexicans was that many Indians who received the land did not work it. President Cárdenas is undertaking to see that as they get land they also have the necessary implements and enough money to live on until they make a crop. Nearly all the land in the Laguna District belongs to the English company, or to Mexicans. Not many Americans owned land there and the Americans have made an agreement with the authorities by which they retain their 150 hectares (about 370 acres) and have been allowed to select the part of the land they wished to keep for themselves. They knew they could not keep all the land and so they made a virtue of necessity and reached an agreement."

SUCCESS CLAIMED; DENIED

I never had the opportunity to visit the Torreón lands after they were taken from the large companies and the Indians started to farm on their own. Conflicting reports came about the operations. "It is a great success and demonstrates the wisdom of dividing the big estates," said those who believed in the policy. "It is destined to fail because the men to whom it is given lack the ability to make the experiment a success," said others.

It evidently appealed to some Americans, as is seen from this extract from a letter I wrote home (April, 1941):

"Last year I wrote you about Mr. Ray Newton, of the Society of Friends, of Philadelphia, who had sent a large number of young men and women to Torreón, where the government had divided the big estates. President Cárdenas was trying to help these *campesinos* in building simple homes and schools. These young Quakers took off their shirts and went to work to build schools and houses, and some of them became teachers and in many ways were very helpful. I talked with Mr. Newton when he came down, and while everybody else was decrying the experiment at Torreón and saying it was a failure, he thought it was going to be a success, and though the first year they had a very difficult time because of the drought, this year. Mr. Clarence Senior, representing the same Friends Society, came down and called to see me and said there were 100 young college students who would leave college in June who would like to come to Mexico, and offered their services to work in the rehabilitation or reconstruction of the town of Colima and the surrounding towns which had been damaged by the earthquake. He said it would cost the Mexican government not a penny; that they would pay their way from the United States to Colima and pay their living expenses. The only thing the

Mexican government would have to pay would be the materials used in the construction. The Minister of Foreign Relations accepted the offer of these Quakers and Mr. Senior is to make arrangements with him today as to when they shall go and what they shall do."

XVII

LABOR GETS ITS MAGNA CARTA

Having been vouched for by William Green as a friend and co-worker of organized labor when I went to Mexico, after the news had reached Washington that some labor men protested my appointment, I had an open sesame to the labor leaders on the the affairs of the republic.

Under the leadership of Vicente Lombardo Toledano and Alejandro Carrillo, the Workers University of Mexico was organized with Toledano, a scholar of note, as Dean, and Carrillo, editor and member of Congress, as Secretary. The Confederation of Mexican Workers under their inspiration became powerful, having over a million members. There were State Federations of Labor in every State in the republic. Agricultural as well as industrial workers were organized. The greatest success was in the organization of the workers in the petroleum industry. Their demand for better pay, resisted by employers, won the approval of the Labor Board and was upheld by the Supreme Court.

It was claimed by labor that no man had been elected President in Mexico in a decade who did not receive labor's support. They rallied to the advocacy of the election of Calles, Cárdenas, Camacho, and Alemán.

Continuing a friendship born in Mexico, I had the pleasure of welcoming Toledano and Carrillo as guests in my home in Raleigh when they were in the United States conferring with labor leaders.

LABOR LEADER WINS HEARERS

The most talked-of meeting in Mexico in the early fall of 1938 was the session of the International Industrial Relations Conference. Of it I wrote (September 7, 1938):

"That afternoon I went to the Palace of Fine Arts to attend a session of the International Industrial Relations Conference. This conference is headed by Miss Mary van Kleeck, of the Russell Sage Foundation, who is strongly in favor of liberal labor legislation and is seeking all over the world to secure better conditions for labor. I asked Miss van Kleeck what she thought would be Russell Sage's reaction if he saw that his money was being used in a direction which most big employers think is going to ruin industry. This proves that the dead hand cannot control. Russell Sage never had an impulse to help labor— quite the contrary—and yet his money is enabling Miss van Kleeck and other forward-looking advocates of better conditions of labor to advance the interests of the very people that he never thought of; but it is the best use of his money that has ever been made. In view of the fact that this organization is called ultra-socialist and radical, some of my friends at the Embassy thought I ought not to attend, as it might look as if I approved some of the more radical views that would be advanced. However, as you know, I have been a militant progressive all my life and have not hesitated to throw my lot with men and women who are trying to improve conditions of the average man, and if that called for criticism I have never sought to evade it.

"I heard two of the best addresses I have heard at a public assembly since I have been here. One was by Mr. Nathaniel Weyl, of New York, on 'International Trade.' He understands the difference in conditions between our country and Latin America better than anyone who has spoken on that subject, and I could wish that his views might be widely disseminated in our country. They were backed up by facts and figures. The crowning address of the day and one of the most eloquent and interesting I have heard from mortal tongue was that of Miss van Kleeck. She summed up the work and aspirations of the conference and gave a résumé of the progress in rural electrification and the benefits that will come from it. She is a master of good English and has a sweet womanliness, along with vigor, that charmed all who heard her. One of the officers who went with me and who felt we ought not to go, after he heard her was quite enthusiastic. I told him I thought she vamped him."

GUESTS AT THE EMBASSY

When I attended the session of the Labor Conference, at which John L. Lewis and Miss van Kleeck were present, some correspondents berated me for going because, they said, it encouraged communistic policies. My reply was that I went in response to an invitation from the Mexican Foreign Office. I added: "I also invited Mr. and Mrs. Lewis and Miss van Kleeck to dine at the Embassy and invited some Mexican labor leaders, who were not any more communistic than the correspondents were Fascists."

After all, the Embassy belongs to the American people and was open to all Americans—labor leaders, capitalists, officials and other visitors. My wife, whose judgment was singularly discerning and correct, found Mrs. Lewis and Miss van Kleeck ladies whom she was glad to welcome to the American Embassy.

WHAT BROUGHT LEWIS TO MEXICO

After John L. Lewis returned to the United States, ubiquitous William R. Davis told a member of the Embassy staff that Lewis had really come to Mexico to confer about organizing a new Confederation of Labor that would displace Toledano's organization. "Lewis will furnish the advice and I will furnish the money," said Davis. It sounded fantastic at the time, but later, when I learned that Davis was contributing money in a presidential campaign in the United States and Lewis was bitterly attacking President Roosevelt, I decided that there may have been basis for what I at first regarded as gossip.

Long denied decent wages or good living conditions, Mexican labor won power and influence, first under Calles, when bad leadership lost its place, only to regain it and strengthen it under Cárdenas, when it won its Magna Carta. Like some labor leaders in the United States, there were those who forgot the maxim, "It is excellent to have the strength of a giant, but it is tyrannous to use it as a giant."

Labor was a strong influence to advance the liberalism which ousted the old order. It helped give Mexico a place among the nations which were discarding caste and opening doors of opportunity to those looking longingly and almost hopelessly out of darkened windows.

Part Six

LIQUID GOLD

XVIII

"CHAPOPOTE" TO PETROLEUM

S oon after I arrived in Mexico, I visited, upon the invitation of oil operators the fields in the Tampico area and saw the magnitude of the oil industry in the republic. In World War I, I knew of the dependence of the allies upon the Tampico field and had provided for the protection, by American Naval ships, of tankers to the North Sea. I recalled that in those days Woodrow Wilson rebuked American oil men who tried to induce him to dictate by force Mexico's policies. B. M. Baruch, head of the War Industries Board, told me at the time that when some oil men tried to induce our government to "take over that part of Mexico in which the great oil wells were located," Wilson asked: "You mean to say that unless we move into Mexico and take by force the oil properties located in her territory, we will not be able to conduct war?"

Someone answered, "Yes."

The President then said, "Well, you will have to adjust yourselves to a war with what oil reserves you have or whatever you can buy in the markets. Germany raised the same point when she invaded Belgian territory. We cannot do the same thing."

THE INDIANS CALLED PETROLEUM "CHAPOPOTE"

Oil in Mexico was discovered by accident something over seventy years ago. It has brought wealth (mostly to British and American companies), and employment to many; it has threatened a rupture of good relations with Britain and the United States.

The name of the Boston captain who made the discovery is unknown. While his ship was anchored at the mouth of Tuxpan River, the Captain asked the Indians for something to use for calking the water butts. The natives furnished a resinous tarry substance called "chapopote." As it was being used, it caught fire. Oil, called "rock-oil," had recently been discovered in Pennsylvania and the captain opined this stuff was oil. He took a small quantity to Boston, a company was formed, and soon two wells, "Chapopote Nuñez" and "Cerro Viejo" were opened. The quantity offered was small, and the Bostonians, not seeing into the future, refused to furnish more capital. There is a tradition that the sea captain had such faith in the oil wells that when his America declined sufficient money for exploitation and development, he was so troubled that he killed himself. The superstitious believe his spirit returns to the scene of his frustrated dream.

The Indians used chapopote as incense medium, and in place of candles for light. During the Spanish rule the famous oil field, "Potrero del Llano," which was to produce more than a hundred million barrels, was discovered, but the Spanish knew nothing of its value.

ALL OIL BELONGS TO THE PEOPLE

Since 1783 in all Spanish dominions all mines and subsoil wealth had been the property of the crown. It was explicitly stated that the State owns the "bitumens and juices of the earth." Even in Maximilian's day, the principle of national ownership of subsoil rights prevailed. Díaz violated the century-old rule and surrendered the right to subsoil properties. That gave many millions of dollars to foreign oil exploiters. Until the British and Americans had avid eyes on Mexican oil, there had been no thought of abandoning the principle derived from Spain that all subsoil rights belonged to the government. In Britain and in the United States the possessors of land owned down to the bowels of the earth and up to the sky. Not so in Spain or Mexico or other countries with Spanish laws. When the British and American oil promoters saw the riches in the subsoil of Mexico, they induced President Díaz to change the laws and transfer the subsoil rights to the possessor of the land.

Encouraged by this change in the law, W. D. Pearson, of England, afterwards Lord Cowdray, E. L. Doheny, of the United States, afterwards figuring in the Teapot Dome scandal, and others began around 1901 to buy up or lease oil lands for a song from Mexican farmers who did not know they possessed liquid gold in the subsoil. These oil men had a sixth sense in discovering oil and had a like scent for getting concessions. By 1910 production had reached 193,397,500 barrels.

REFINED OIL EXPANSION

The riches of oil in Mexico were not fully realized until E. L. Doheny obtained 283,000 acres in the Tampico area, on which the first well gushed in 1904. The oil literally spurted out of the ground, and oil promoters from Britain and America rushed to Mexico to obtain the liquid gold. By 1924 the American stock in oil companies in Mexico had reached 448,157,836 pesos; the British, 204,408,322; Dutch capital, 88,639,949; and Mexican capital, 23,519,964. By 1938, when expropriated, the British companies claimed their properties in oil exceeded 500 million dollars, and the United States companies estimated their holdings as around 400 million dollars.

COUNTRY'S PATRIMONY TO FOREIGNERS

Díaz turned over the patrimony of his country to foreigners. He exempted from taxation the machinery imported by them, and capital invested in oil was exempt from taxation, as was the manufacture of by-products. For eleven years the foreign oil companies were not required to pay one cent of taxes on their property, except as agricultural lands, notwithstanding their fabulous profits. When in 1912 President Madero imposed a small tax and Carranza a "production tax" and later an "exportation tax," the total taxes imposed by Mexico were one fourth the tax imposed in the United States. In 1934 the wages paid American oil workers in the United States were more than four times greater than wages paid for similar work by oil companies in Mexico, and the workers had to live in squalid huts.

WHAT MEXICANS GOT

There are many stories of how much, or rather how little, the Mexicans who parted with their land received. They did not know its value. The Pearsons and Dohenys drove the best bargains they could with owners ignorant that beneath the topsoil they had great wealth. Here are some of the ways old-time concessionaires are said to have acquired and exploited the oil lands, as told by a high Mexican authority:

1. The owner of a lot in Chinampa, Vera Cruz, got only 150 pesos a year and the lessee produced 75,000,000 barrels;

2. The Huasteca Petroleum Company, owner of the famous Cerro Azul property, was paid 200,000 pesos. It produced 181,870,538 barrels of oil;

3. Four properties in Tuxpan produced 50,757,677 barrels of crude oil, and the owners got a small royalty after long litigation;

4. The owners of Amatlán, which produced 7,000,000 barrels, obtained the property for a rent of 3,000 pesos per hectare, or 112.50 pesos per year. The company admitted that it obtained seven million barrels on this lot, for which it actually paid only ten pesos.

5. The Juan Casiano property was leased from a native Indian woman for 1,000 pesos a year. The Huasteca Company obtained 100,000,000 barrels of crude oil. When the owner threatened litigation, Doheny paid her $40,000.

These are a few of such early leases by foreign prospectors that helped to arouse the indignation of the people to the Díaz regime. Many more cases of getting the cream of oil properties for next to nothing from Mexicans ignorant of their true value—some accounts true and some fantastic—when they became known, created a wide-spread sentiment of resentment against permitting Mexico's most precious wealth to be gobbled up for next to no adequate compensation by foreigners. On their part, the oil pioneers said they bought or leased on a gamble and spent much money on leases from which they got no returns. The defenders of Díaz said he knew little more about the potential value than the exploited peons—that he was activated by the motive of inducing foreign capital to develop Mexico's resources, and in order to induce them to do so it was necessary to annul the century-old Spanish law retaining the subsoil to the nation. As a further inducement he assigned a government geologist to report on the possibilities, and later the Doheny interests secured his service, and he became known as "the Mexican father of oil production." However, the bald fact stood out that foreign oil men had come into the possession of Mexico's greatest wealth without paying anything like its value, that they had been given largesses in the shape of tax concessions and other favors, that the wages paid to workers in the oil field were scandalously low although in keeping with the Mexican standard, and that the laborers in the oil section lived under wretched conditions as to housing and health protection. The resentment toward seeing foreigners and a few Mexicans getting the cream and the Mexicans hardly getting the skimmed milk rose to a crescendo in the days when the famous Cerro Azul property produced 181,870,538 barrels, for which the original owner received only 200,000 pesos. That mounting indignation helped to create the Revolution led by Madero in 1910 and was in a large part responsible for the return to the old subsoil law.

REASSERTED SUBSOIL RIGHTS

In 1917, after Huerta, who was supported by the oil men, was ousted, Mexico reasserted its ownership of the subsoil and incorporated it in the new Constitution at paragraph 4, article 27, quoted in part:

> "In the nation is vested direct ownership of all minerals or substances which in veins, masses, or beds constitute deposits whose nature is different from the components of the land, such as . . . solid mineral fuels, petroleum and all hydrocarbons, solid, liquid or gaseous."

Mexicans held that this provision did not destroy a right, but, on the contrary, sought to reëstablish it. Mexicans contended that foreign owners had only concessions that permitted them to develop Mexican mineral deposits. They contended that the government at any time had a right to revoke Mexican concessions. They contended that "Mexico did not expropriate the petroleum. She could not expropriate that of which she is the owner."

In addition to Article 27, Carranza issued decrees, requiring lessees or purchasers to show clear title. The oil companies resented this, and later secured annulment by Calles, only to lose out in the Cárdenas administration. Article 27 also provided that only Mexican citizens and corporations could obtain concessions of mines, and could concede that right to foreigners only if such foreigners would not invoke the protection of their own government and would respect and obey Mexican laws and the decrees of Mexican courts.

Mexicans believed that many troubles suffered by Mexico were caused by a struggle for petroleum concessions. They declared that during the Harding Administration the motto of Washington was "The Standard Oil Company Above All."

I asked Thomas Lockett, the Commercial Attaché, to obtain information bearing on oil, particularly as it related to operation of

Americans. He reported that Mexico was rich beyond almost any other country in oil. In 1933 there was produced 22,824,523 barrels of light crude oil. From 1901, the time when oil production actually began on a large scale, until 1933, the total production was 1,698,-861,178 barrels of crude oil. Nearly half of the total production in 1933 was by the British Companies. As the government of Mexico was obtaining considerable revenue from oil, the oil question did not become acute until the big strike in the oil fields in 1937-1938.

Frank L. Kluckhohm, correspondent of the *New York Times,* stated the history of the acquisition of oil lands in Mexico when he wrote in his book *The Mexican Challenge:*

"Through bribery and corruption, and by obtaining occasional diplomatic aid from their governments, the large oil companies exerted pressure upon the Mexican government. Despite frantic protests to the contrary today, there is every reason to credit the assertions of Mexican regimes that foreign companies sought to dominate them in order to maintain the position of absolute individualists and to be permitted to run their own affairs in their accustomed highhanded manner. The arrogance of the large oil operators during the Díaz period carried over into the epoch of the Revolution."

XIX

PRELUDE TO EXPROPRIATION

WHEN I came to Mexico I knew that the Morrow-Calles arrangement as to foreign oil companies had been hailed as a great triumph for Ambassador Morrow, as it indubitably was, for in it Mexico virtually made void the famous Calvo Clause * as it related to oil and in effect relinquished the government's subsoil rights in oil. It was a far-reaching victory as to the main contention of British and American oil companies, but it left uncertain some things desired by the oil companies. As soon, however, as the more zealous Mexican revolutionaries understood how their Constitution had been set at naught—and they hardly realized it for some years —there was much under-cover resentment at the "taking over" of Calles by Ambassador Morrow and an endless current of determination to regain all that was possible for the Mexicans. It was not until the spring of 1934 that oil men told me that the oil question had not been "permanently settled," as many Americans believed.

Mr. Jack Armstrong, Secretary of the Association of Producers of Petroleum in Mexico, called in March, 1934, to tell me about a semi-official organization which had been formed to develop the petroleum lands in Mexico. He said that the government had turned over to this newly organized company all the oil lands belonging to the government (which included all the subsoil rights of lands adjacent to rivers and oceans) and all the government's oil equipment in its plants in the Tampico district, and that it was proposed to put the government in the business of drilling for oil, refining, and selling it. He said that the government officials were saying that though Mexico furnished the raw product, foreign companies got all the profits and had all the trade in Mexico growing out of petroleum.

Mr. Armstrong talked of the old theory, which the oil men have opposed ever since the adoption of the Constitution, a theory which

---

* This clause required the full submission by foreigners to the laws of Mexico without recourse to their own governments.

held that subsoil rights belong to the government of Mexico. The oil companies, he said, were troubled because, if the government carried out this plan, it would have a great purchaser for its oil in the government-owned railroads (or rather government-managed railroads) and all the government agencies which were then supplied by the oil companies. Mr. Armstrong left me a long memorandum giving the position of the oil companies. He said that in Tampico a judge had held titles illegal which had long been respected. He believed that attacking titles was one method the government was employing to oust foreign oil companies. I asked him if the companies had valid titles. He said:

"They are as good as anybody else has. Most titles here could not stand the severe scrutiny which owners or lessees in the United States could invite. Inasmuch as the titles have been recognized for years, the present attack is only a method by which it is hoped to give Mexico the control of oil fields possessed by Americans and Englishmen."

WANTED EMBASSY TO KNOW

Mr. Armstrong said the Mexican government had failed or refused to confirm title to 1,500,000 hectares of pre-constitutionally acquired leases and freeholds, and the oil men wished me to intercede to secure the government's fulfillment of the "oral agreement" which they said confirmed their claims. He also showed me a map which he said indicated another government method of taking oil that would injure the foreign oil operators in Mexico. Under the Constitution of Mexico all streams and a certain portion of adjacent lands and waters belong to the government.

"Many of the streams," he said, "are dry except in the rainy season. Foreign oil companies have operated where there are no real rivers. If the government enforces its claims to all streams and adjacent lands, the foreign companies will lose 40 per cent of the good oil fields."

He wanted me, without mentioning any particular case, to intercede with the government to check the action of the courts in this attitude toward oil lands adjacent to streams. I told him that our government could not complain of decisions by the legal processes of the courts and that his only remedy would be appeal to the Mexican Supreme Court. He said that he only wished me to know his fears, which he said were not groundless, so that I might be able to check the dangers in ways that would be proper and effective.

STANDARD AFRAID OF DOHENY TITLES

In April (1934) Mr. Anderson, of Standard Oil, discussed the worry of his company. I wrote:

"I had a long talk with Mr. Anderson, of the Standard Oil Company, about the troubles the oil men say they are having. I talked also with two representatives of the company who have come here from New York. The government has discontinued granting concessions until they make a full study of titles. The cases are in court and these gentlemen have evidently come down to make a big fight to hold property on which they have *prima facie* titles only and to prevent the government's taking over all oil under river beds and the beds of streams. The Standard bought out Doheny's holdings when he got in trouble. The government claims Doheny did not have valid title on much of the land of which he had possession."

WISH REDUCED TARIFF RATES

In the summer of 1934 I was made more and more aware of the fears and desires of the American oil companies. In July, Judge McMahon and Harold Walker, representatives of the Standard Oil Company, told me that their company was nervous because the government had taken over large oil fields operated by an English Company, on the ground that the titles under which they claimed ownership were defective. They were also suing for the oil already extracted. They said if the government was doing that to English companies, they feared American companies might be declared to be in like situation. Judge McMahon told me of a decision of the Supreme Court, which he called an "outrageous judgment by which all oil companies must pay $250,000.00 of back taxes."

They made no requests. What they chiefly talked about was the hope that, under tariff reciprocity, oils could go freer from Mexico to the United States. Prior to the passage of higher tariff rates, much oil from the Tampico and Vera Cruz districts went to the United States. At that time most of it went to Europe and South America. "Our government urged Americans to invest in Latin American companies," said Judge McMahon. "They did so and now they are unable to realize on their investments because of the prohibitive tariff." Mr. Walker called attention to the fact that Secretary Hull, then a member of Congress, opposed the higher rates. I told them that when in Washington I learned it was proposed to take up reciprocity with Mexico in the late fall.

OIL TITLE DECLARED DEFECTIVE

In August Stanley B. Rice, of Tampico, told me that his company had taken out 7,000,000 barrels of oil, but had been notified by the government that it had no legal title and the Minister of National Economy had taken it over. I asked about his title. He said he operated under leases given many years ago. The owner was dead—had many children, legitimate and illegitimate. Originally a small amount was paid in royalties, but since the costly litigation no royalties had been paid. "We are out unless we can get help, for the courts have ruled against us," he gloomily said.

THE BRITISH FEARED THE WORST

In November, 1934, Mr. J. A. Assheton, President and General Manager of El Águila Oil Company, who said he was going to England for two months, wished me to know that recently the courts had given judgment against his company for a large sum on the allegation that they had been extracting oil from properties to which they had no valid titles though they had been in possession of the land for fifty years. He said all oil companies were fearful they would have to pay millions of dollars for oil they had extracted from lands on which they did not hold valid titles. The British Company had appealed to a higher court, but Mr. Assheton feared the worst. All the oil companies were making common cause, he said, and hoped to at least win as to back payments, even if they lost lands upon which they had not been drilling.

WASHINGTON NONCOMMITTAL

On December 11 (1934) Edward L. Reed, Chief of the Mexican Division of the State Department, sent me a memorandum which contained the following:

"Harold P. Walker, Vice President of the Huasteca Oil Company, thought the matter of confirmatory concessions, covering properties to which the titles held by the companies have been

found to contain technical defects, could be greatly facilitated
if the question be discussed privately between Mr. Reuben Clark
and General Calles. It was his idea that Mr. Clark should be invited by Ambassador Daniels to visit him in Mexico, and while
there Mr. Clark should go to see General Calles, accompanied
by Mr. Smithers, whom Mr. Morrow and Mr. Clark had used
as an interpreter in their previous discussions with General
Calles on the subject.

"Mr. Walker was confident that Mr. Clark would have no
difficulty in convincing General Calles that the latter's agreement with Mr. Morrow was being disregarded by the Mexican
officials, and he was equally sure that a word from General
Calles in the proper quarters would immediately straighten matters out.

"Mr. Walker said he apprehended little difficulty in persuading Ambassador Daniels to adopt this 'extraordinary' course, because the Ambassador was not a man to let personal pride stand
in the way of an understanding on an international sore spot."

Mr. Reed added that he had said he "did not believe Ambassador
Daniels would acquiesce in this plan without the Department's consent," and that he "felt certain that the Department would not
commit itself in the matter."

APPEAL ONLY TO COURT

Upon receipt of that letter, I wrote the State Department:

"The only recourse open to the oil companies is by appeal to
the Mexican courts. We have no more right to demand any
specific decrees by the courts for our nationals than Mexicans
in the United States would be justified in asking the State Department to request the Supreme Court to render a certain
decision."

Later, Mr. Armstrong, speaking for all the companies, formally
made the request that former Ambassador Clark be invited by me
to come to Mexico. He said the companies would pay all Mr. Clark's
expenses and fees but he would be working "under the Embassy."
He repeated the contention that the Mexican Government had "disregarded" the agreement which President Calles and Ambassador
Morrow had "reached in 1927." He said Mr. Clark was present when

this oral agreement was made and he would confirm it. A memorandum was furnished me by the oil men as follows:

"We are advised that Mr. Clark is unwilling to capitalize his knowledge or influence as former Ambassador to Mexico, but we believe, if asked by you to do so, he will seek an interview with General Calles and will endeavor to secure confirmation of the verbal agreement expressed above. To do this successfully, it is respectfully suggested that you might invite him to Mexico to discuss the antecedents of this matter; for him to take this opportunity to present his respects to General Calles and to use that opportunity to tell General Calles of the doubts and fears that exist and to ask him frankly what he may tell you as regards the understanding referred to."

My response was that I could not comply with the request—that if Mr. Clark came down as their attorney to press their claim, he must do so as any other attorney without Embassy sponsorship. I added that if Mr. Clark came, I, of course, would show him every courtesy, as I held him in high esteem, but could not as an official request him to come. Of course I had no knowledge of any "oral agreement." But an examination of the records showed that in March, 1928, Secretary of State Kellogg said that the Department "felt as Ambassador Morrow did" that "such questions as were raised should be settled through due operations of the Mexican administrative departments and the Mexican courts."

Mr. Clark came and represented his clients. I did not present him and he did not report to me the result of his negotiations. He was highly esteemed by Mexicans and American residents in Mexico and deservedly respected by Mexican officials. He and Mrs. Clark were entertained at the Embassy, and a formal dinner was given them by old friends in the American colony, which my wife and I attended. Some high Mexican officials also attended. Clark's mission, however, did not bring to an end the differences about oil.

Before I was asked to join in inviting Mr. Clark to come to Mexico, I wrote the State Department:

"A wise man once said, 'All oil stinks.' He must have been referring to the devious ways, violating laws as well as morals, by which big companies have obtained a near monopoly of the oil."

When asked about Clark's coming to secure confirmatory concessions, I said I would regard retaining an ex-Ambassador for such purpose as scandalous and I did not believe Mr. Clark would lend himself to it. If he should come, unless otherwise advised by the Department, I would advise him to go home and not stand on the order of his going.

I cannot forget that when Woodrow Wilson was trying to drive out Huerta, British and American oil companies were partisans of Huerta, agitating for intervention and backing Albert Fall. I agree with Sumner Welles' statement that "American capital invested abroad should be subordinate to the authority of the country where it is located."

OIL STRIKE REACHES IMPASSE

Upon my return to Mexico (September, 1937), I found that a strike in the oil fields had reached an acute stage. The oil operators told President Cárdenas they could not pay the increased wages demanded. The operators had served notice on the government, rather indirectly via New York, that if the government stood by the demands of the workers they (the operators) could not continue the operation of their oil fields. The government was dependent largely upon the income from the taxes on oil. This made somewhat of a crisis. The President had appointed a committee of experts, all Mexicans, to examine the books of the oil companies to ascertain whether their income was large enough to justify the additional wages demanded by the workers. When I discussed the situation with Foreign Minister Hay he expressed the opinion that the oil companies were quite able to pay the increased wages and thought everything would work out well.

SAID GOVERNMENT COULD NOT OPERATE

By November the situation was worse. I had a long talk with Mr. Anderson, of the Huasteca Petroleum Company. He said that all of the oil companies were united in saying that if the Government held with the labor unions and compelled the operators to increase wages 26,000,000 pesos a year, it would cause them to lose money. They thought that the financial situation of the government was such that it could not afford to be stiff, because if the oil companies shut down, the government would lose large revenues and also would invite the very strong protests of the American and British governments. Under the laws of Mexico, if a mine or oil field is not operated, the government can take it over, and I asked Mr. Anderson if he did not fear that. He seemed to think that if the government did take it over they could not operate it, or if they could operate it they would have no sale for their oil because they could not obtain tankers or tank cars.

"NOBODY DOES THAT"

The oil people were nervous as 1937 ended. Mr. Walter Scheuden, of the Sinclair Oil Company, called at the American Embassy in December. I asked him why oil companies and other companies here always waited to grant increased wages until there had been a strike and why they did not anticipate by paying as high wages as they could afford. He frankly said, "Nobody does that, and if we pay as high wages as other people pay that is all that can be expected of us."

WHAT BOTH SIDES SAID ABOUT OIL

As the New Year opened, the contention over the demand of the workers in the oil fields for more pay and many changes grew more serious. The government experts declared that the oil companies could and must pay additional wages amounting to about 26 million pesos annually. The oil companies expressed a willingness to pay 13 million pesos annually additional. The government officials said they had evidence that the oil companies in Mexico practiced various devices to conceal their profits. For example, they alleged that some of the companies sold their product to a subsidiary corporation, which they owned, for 85 centavos a barrel when the market was 1.25 and that this denied to local corporations the profits which they actually made.

SUPREME COURT UPHOLDS OIL WORKERS

The oil controversy reached a head in March, and I wrote to my sons (March 5, 1938) as follows:

"This has been a very strenuous week. The Supreme Court has upheld in every particular the contention of the oil workers and has directed the oil companies to pay the increased wages amounting to 26,000,000 pesos a year. The oil companies say that this is more than they earn and that they cannot and will not pay it. It looks like a complete impasse. Unless a compromise can be found before next week the natural course of events will be that the Government will appoint a receiver for the properties of the oil companies and continue to operate the plants and pay the increased wages and if any money is left over the companies will get it.

"The situation is acute and it looks like an irresistible force against an immovable object. The oil men believe that the government is backing the labor people in making excessive demands in order to confiscate the property and turn it over to the government."

THE OIL IMPASSE

As the year 1938 moved on, the impasse between the foreign oil owners and the workers got worse. As I wrote home (March 12, 1938):

"The contending parties are about a million dollars apart in the wage schedules for the future and it seems a shame that there should be an impasse and a break when they have bridged most of the chasms and neither party is willing to go far enough to secure a compromise agreement. Of course all I could do was to talk to the various parties and try to help bring them together so they could talk over the situation in the hope that they might agree."

The conferences continued between Cárdenas and the oil executives, who definitely stated that they would not and could not abide by the decree, alleging that because of the vagueness of the language the increase would be more than the 26 million pesos. It was stated in the press that Cárdenas offered to guarantee that the increase would not exceed 26 million pesos.

There was much talk and gossip about what was done or said in the conferences. Some oil men said that at the last minute they had agreed to pay the 26 million pesos increase in wages, provided certain objectionable provisions were omitted. "But we were told too late," said one oil man. At the same time Finance Minister Suárez, in detailing the last-minute negotiations between Cárdenas and himself on one side and the oil companies on the other, said that the companies flatly refused to pay the increase as directed by the Supreme Court, though they suggested an increase up to 22 million pesos but conditioned it upon other unacceptable conditions; and that only after such refusal did Cárdenas issue the decree. I had hoped against hope that an agreement would be reached. To one oil man who called on me, I said, 'I give no advice, but if I were the oil companies, I would pay the increased wages." He said it was impossible and the companies would never pay the wages the Board had approved.

In the early spring it was obvious that something was about to happen in the oil controversy. But most observers expected that at the worst the oil properties would be operated by receivers to carry out the wage decree.

XX

BOLT FROM THE BLUE

I was sitting in my study in the Embassy on the evening of March 18, 1938 when representatives of the American and Mexican press came to the Embassy and asked to see me. They were excited and surprised, and I was surprised also when they told me that earlier in the evening President Cárdenas had announced on the radio that he issued a decree expropriating the properties of American and British oil companies in the republic, accusing them of "a conspiracy" against Mexico.

The President said he was acting under Article 27 of the Constitution of Mexico. The conspiracy, he alleged, grew out of their organized refusal to abide by the laws of Mexico as construed by Supreme Court decisions upholding the Labor Board's findings of an increase in the wages of oil workers. The climax came after months of wrangling between the oil companies and the workers and ineffective negotiations between the government officials and the officers of the oil companies. The announcement astounded listeners in Mexico and those who received the news beyond its border. It startled men in the chancelleries on both sides of the Atlantic. There followed a bitter conflict that lasted until November 21, 1941, when settlement was finally reached between the United States and Mexico. The expropriation decree rattled the windows of the British Parliament, where government was in partnership with the oil interests affected. There were reverberations in the editorial rooms of some newspapers, whose columns, under scare headlines, blistered the Mexicans as "thieves and bandits." In the oil world there was unrestrained wrath as executives of the oil industry in the United States demanded that Uncle Sam "do something" to compel restoration of the property to the owners at once or else—meaning that force should be employed and war with Mexico, if necessary, to "teach the Greasers 'Thou Shalt Not Steal.' "

Actually—little as we might like it—President Cárdenas was acting under clear and well-understood Mexican law. The Constitution of Mexico, for many years prior to the expropriation, had required as a condition precedent to business activity by foreigners in Mexico, that they accept the "Calvo Clause," which, as already stated, required the full submission by foreigners to the laws of Mexico without recourse to their own governments.

The announcement of the expropriation gave the jitters to most diplomats in Washington and elsewhere. They had imbibed the doctrine enunciated by Theodore Roosevelt. The Rough Rider President ran rough shod over Colombia, calling the people "jack rabbits" and the people of Bogotá "contemptible little creatures," and had sent soldiers south of the Rio Grande without saying "by your leave." Even in the twenties, Calvin Coolidge had asserted, "The person and property of a citizen are part of the general domain of the nation even when abroad." The policy of the State Department had generally been the Big Stick and Dollar Diplomacy until Franklin Roosevelt repudiated such imperial and military practices and replaced them with the Good Neighbor doctrine.

However, though the official legalists muttered and urged the Big Stick, the White House and the Secretary of State were not stampeded. It shocked Cordell Hull, who deserved the title of "The Just." The air was thick with rumors that because I had not told Washington the expropriation would take place or had not used the Big Stick, I was to be recalled and a tough man sent to head the mission who would "tell the Mexicans where to get off." One wag said, "Ambassador Daniels is the boy who stood on the burning deck whence all but him had fled," and "the deck is burning from expropriated oil."

TWO OFFICERS KEPT THEIR HEADS

In this war of nerves and jitters, fed with gasoline from the headquarters of the oil companies in London and New York, two American public officials—there were others in and out of office—kept their heads while all about them were losing theirs. They were Franklin Roosevelt in the White House, who had proclaimed the Good Neighbor doctrine, and Josephus Daniels, the walking delegate of that doctrine, in the Republic of Mexico. The success of that policy was their supreme heart's desire, a consummation held more precious than all the dollars in the New World or all the diplomatic precedents of history. These two men in responsible positions knew that the Mexican officials were not all thieves nor the oil officials all saints.

When President Cárdenas, without notice that reached the Embassy, went on the radio and announced the expropriation of the oil properties, I said truly, that it was "a bolt from the blue." I regretted the action. I had kept the State Department fully informed, but neither the Embassy officials nor the officers of the oil companies had been given a hint that expropriation would follow the failure of the companies to accept the Supreme Court's decision. On the contrary, oil companies expected, and had so expressed themselves to me, that a receivership would follow. I had also been told by the Secretary of Foreign Relations that if the companies did not accept the court decree he expected a receivership would follow.

The President of the United States and the Ambassador to Mexico had heard the thunderclaps from oil before. For seven years, while heads of the American Navy, they had been compelled to wage a constant war to keep oil magnates from obtaining the power to drain the Naval oil reserves in California and Wyoming. They succeeded, only to see, early in the Harding administration, the Teapot Dome scandal break when that precious reserve was sold by a crooked official to grasping oil operators.

In the present emergency, when denunciations were hurled, and predictions of war with Mexico were headlined, President Roosevelt at Warm Springs calmed the tumult by refusing to be stampeded into seizing the Big Stick and brandishing it. Instead, two weeks after the expropriation act of President Cárdenas, the Associated Press carried this story:

"WARM SPRINGS, GA., April 1.—(AP)—President Roosevelt reported today negotiations with Mexico over the seizure of American oil properties were proceeding satisfactorily.

"At the same time, administration sources said the United States would show no sympathy to rich individual Americans who obtained large land holdings in Mexico for virtually nothing through bribery and claimed damages for seized property far in excess of what it cost.

"The President talked to reporters while sitting in his automobile under a portico of Georgia Hall, administrative building of the Warm Springs infantile paralysis foundation.

"Asked about the Mexican situation, Mr. Roosevelt said President Cárdenas of Mexico had just sent a note to the American State Department and the situation on the whole was developing in a satisfactory manner.

"Sources close to him re-defined American policy with respect to land and other property seizures by Mexico over a period of years.

"These authorities sharply differentiated in acquiring title to thousands of acres, and those Americans who had invested meager savings in small ranches and farms below the southern border and, like the wealthier classes, lost their properties under the Mexican land distribution system.

"While no sympathy would be shown the rich individuals who obtained their lands illegally, the United States had insisted and would continue to insist on full and fair indemnification of the small ranch owners.

"Mexico, it was added, had assured this country the latter group would be taken care of.

"As for the American oil companies, whose properties were taken over when they failed to abide by a Mexican court decree ordering wage increases, the administration sources reiterated that they were entitled to damages equivalent only to actual investment, less depreciation.

"Indemnification in their case, it was said, should not include prospective profits or, in other words, what the properties might be worth five years from now. This attitude was described as based on the same principle the Roosevelt administration has been following with respect to holding companies."

OIL MEN ASKED TO NEGOTIATE

In Mexico, after sending the information to the State Department, without waiting for instructions I called on President Cárdenas and discussed the acute situation which the expropriation had brought about, expressing surprise and regret at the action, and stressing that my government would insist upon payment by Mexico for the properties expropriated. It was then, before I could go further, that President Cárdenas gave me his assurance that his government would take the necessary steps to make payment to the companies and requested me to ask them to confer with him to negotiate as to the valuation and the terms of payment.

OIL MEN WANTED INTERVENTION

A few days after the oil expropriation I flew up to Washington to convey the feeling in Mexico and get the reaction by personal talks with the President and Secretary Hull. A fellow passenger in the plane was an official of the Standard Oil Company, and this conversation took place between us.

"What is going to happen about the oil property expropriated?" he asked me.

"You have been in Mexico longer than I; what do you think?" I replied.

"It is up to the State Department to find means for the restoration of the property to its owners," he answered.

"By what course—sending Marines or other intervention?" I asked, having heard suggestions that the big oil companies wished use of force if necessary.

"It is up to Washington to find the way. We are leaving the plan to the State Department," was his reply.

I found when I reached Washington that some of the oil officials had already started to build propaganda fires under the government to compel a return of the properties. They praised Secretary Hull's strong declarations and opined that when Mexico could not be warned by tufts of grass that Hull would soon be throwing stones. But, though Hull was irritated by the expropriation and the manner of it and wrote condemnatory notes to Mexico and never receded from his thesis that "universally recognized rules of law and equity" required "prompt and adequate payment," he never could be moved from his position that Mexico had the right—though he did not approve its exercise—to expropriate with "prompt and adequate payment." This caused the oil companies to say, "The Government let us down."

SECRETARY HULL'S NOTE

In the early days of the expropriation I felt that my dear friend, Cordell Hull, on one occasion let his Tennessee temper lead him into undue sharpness in a message to the Mexicans. I was a little surprised, not at his position, but at the tone in which it was stated, when I received instructions from him to present the following message to the Foreign Minister:

TELEGRAM SENT

March 26, 1938.

2 p.m.

"AMEMBASSY,

"MEXICO CITY, (MEXICO).

"Please deliver not later than Monday, noon, to the Minister for Foreign Affairs a note reading textually as follows:

"In his First Inaugural Message in 1933 President Roosevelt announced that QUOTE in the field of world policy I would dedicate this Nation to the Policy of the good neighbor—the neighbor who resolutely respects himself and, because he does so, respects the rights of others—the neighbor who respects his obligations and respects the sanctity of his agreements in and with a world of neighbors. UNQUOTE.

"During the last five years, I feel sure Your Excellency will agree, my Government has repeatedly evidenced its fulfillment of that pledge, both in general and in specific cases. Moreover, because of the universal applicability of the basic principles upon which this policy is premised, they have had the support of other governments of this hemisphere. These principles include a real friendship between nations, complete confidence of the respective governments and peoples in each other, the adjustment of difficulties by processes of negotiation and agreement, fair play and fair dealing, and the wholehearted disposition to co-operate each with the other for the promotion of their mutual interests and mutual welfare. My Government has repeatedly expressed to the Government of Mexico its conviction that, as has been generally recognized by other governments, this policy of equity and of reasonable and just treatment cannot of its nature be a one-sided policy. As shown in its application by the American Republics generally, this policy must of its very essence have a reciprocal character if the peoples of the New World are to progress steadily toward a higher level of international relationships.

"It will be agreed, I think, that my Government has been mindful of the high social objectives of your Government. Both of our Governments have endeavored to better the conditions of living of their respective citizens. My Government is confident that the American people, who have been giving frequent indications of their friendship for and good-will toward Mexico and the Mexican people, fully sympathize with these objectives.

"It is apparent from the statements which His Excellency the President of the United Mexican States has repeatedly made that he believes that in order to improve the standard of living of the Mexican people as a whole, a development of national resources is essential. For such development, capital has been required. Very substantial amounts of American capital have in the past been made available to the Mexican people, resulting in the development of natural resources and the establishment of industries not previously existing which have provided an increasing scale of wages for the Mexican people and increased revenue for the Mexican Government.

"His Excellency the President of Mexico has frequently stated, even during the present year, that the Mexican Government welcomed the investment of this capital, to which it would give all guarantees under Mexican law.

"My Government recognizes the obligation of all American interests in Mexico to play their reasonable and relative part in promoting the policy of the Mexican Government and the welfare of the Mexican people, but despite the consistent endeavors of the Government of the United States to cooperate in every mutually desirable and profitable way with the Government of Mexico, my Government has noticed with anxiety the increasing number of instances of disregard of legitimate and uncontroverted private property interests of its nationals. This has been particularly true with respect to the carrying out of the agrarian policy of the Mexican Government, pursuant to which land holdings, both large and small, owned by American citizens, in many instances, have been taken and turned over to Mexican nationals without the payment of compensation to the American owners of such lands. My Government has made repeated representations to the Mexican Government regarding this situation and has pointed out in all such representations that, while it has not been disposed to question the right of the Mexican Government to take over and distribute large holdings of real property, such action should not amount—as it has in effect—to the confiscation of such property, but that under every rule of generally recognized law as well as equity the rightful owners are entitled to the payment of just compensation, having a present effective value to the owners from whom the properties are taken.

"In addition to these difficulties pertaining to the agrarian policy, a large group of American claims against Mexico, some of which date back over a long period of years, remain unadjudicated despite efforts of this Government to reach some satisfactory adjustment of them.

"Finally, we have the occurrence of recent date of the taking over by the Mexican Government of large investments of American nationals in the oil industry of Mexico, amounting to many millions of dollars. The position which my Government has so frequently presented to the Mexican Government regarding the payment of just compensation for land taken pursuant to the agrarian policy applies with equal force with respect to the oil properties that have just been expropriated. This does not mean that the Government may later pay as and when it may suit its convenience. Having in mind the treatment that has been accorded the American owners of land, my Government must of necessity view with concern and apprehension the most recent act of the Mexican Government.

"My Government reserves for itself and for its nationals all rights affected by the proceedings under which the oil companies have recently been faced with an award of the Labor Board, sustained by the Supreme Court of Mexico. Furthermore, my Government reserves for itself and its nationals all rights affected by the decree of expropriation.

"My Government has taken attentive note of the statement that President Cardenas is quoted as having made on March 23 that QUOTE We are not going to refuse to pay for what is expropriated. We are acting on a high legal and moral plane in order to make our country great and respected. UNQUOTE.

"In view of that statement by the Chief Executive of Mexico, my Government directs me to inquire, in the event that the Mexican Government persists in this expropriation, without my Government undertaking to speak for the American interests involved, but solely for its preliminary information, what specific action with respect to payment for the properties in question is contemplated by the Mexican Government, what assurances will be given that payment will be made, and when such payment may be expected. In as much as the American citizens involved have already been deprived of their properties, and in view of the rule of law stated, my Government considers itself entitled to ask for a prompt reply to this inquiry.

"My Government also considers that the time has arrived for

a similar understanding regarding the payment of American nationals whose lands have been, and are being, taken pursuant to the agrarian policy of the Mexican Government."

HULL

NO RESORT TO NOTE-WRITING

I was not only directed by Secretary Hull to deliver this note to the Minister of Foreign Relations but specifically given the deadline for the time of delivery. As a good messenger I obeyed orders, though I had received the assurance immediately after the expropriation from President Cárdenas that Mexico would do exactly what Hull's note demanded, and I had so informed the State Department.

When Foreign Minister Eduardo Hay finished reading the note, he expressed surprise that Secretary Hull had felt called upon to give Mexico so long a message of arraignment of his country and indictment of its policy. He was particularly disturbed by the use of the word "confiscation." He said: "This note seems to have been written without the knowledge of the oral assurance made to you by President Cárdenas." He informed me that, after conferring with the President, he would feel compelled in answering the note to give an elaborate history of the relations with the United States and defend the course his country had pursued. He said he would have to go into particulars of how the oil companies, paying substandard wages, had violated their pledge to observe the Mexican laws, and refused to obey the decree of the Supreme Court, and had defied the action of the chief executive of Mexico and had "conspired" against the Mexican Government.

While I was in full accord with Secretary Hull's insistence upon payment for properties expropriated, I could not feel that a resort to note-writing would achieve the results sought, particularly since both the Foreign Minister and President Cárdenas had plighted their word orally to do what Hull asked in his note.

Seeing that we might be in for long and inconclusive note writing, I said to the Foreign Minister: "Since the President has promised payment for property expropriated, it may be as well to consider the note as 'not received' and I will convey again to my government the promise to pay."

CÁRDENAS MAKES OFFICIAL PLEDGE

Secretary Hay later handed me this statement, which he said President Cárdenas had directed him to give me:

"That the Mexican Government is fully able to pay the affected petroleum companies the indemnities which may be due hem for the irrevocable expropriation of their properties.

"That the Ministry of Finance will receive and give consideration to the representatives of the companies as soon as they present themselves to that Department for the purpose of entering into discussions in the premises.

"And the Mexican Government, in order to effect these payments, will not await the final appraisal of the amount of indemnity legally due the companies."

LETTER BY PRESIDENT CÁRDENAS

On March 31 President Cárdenas wrote me the following letter:

"My government considers that the attitude adopted by the Government of the United States of North America in the matter of the expropriation of the petroleum companies reaffirms once more the sovereignty of the peoples of this continent, which the statesman of the powerful country of America, His Excellency President Roosevelt, has so enthusiastically maintained.

"By this attitude, Mr. Ambassador, your President and your people have won the esteem of the people of Mexico.

"The Mexican nation has lived in these last few days through moments of trial in which it did not know whether it would have to give rein to its patriotic feelings or to applaud an act of justice of the neighboring country represented by Your Excellency.

"Today my country is happy to celebrate, without reservations, the proof of friendship which it has received from yours and which will be carried in the heart of its people.

"Mexico has always wished to maintain its prestige, carrying out its obligations, but elements which did not understand Mexico placed obstacles in the way of this high and noble purpose. Today a new dawn breaks on its future with the opening to it of the doors of opportunity. You may be sure, Mr. Ambassador, that Mexico will know how to honor its obligations of today and its obligations of yesterday.

"Mr. Ambassador, it is a satisfaction for the Mexicans to have the friendship of a people which, through its President, continues to support the policy of friendship and respect of each nation, a policy which is winning for your country the affection of many peoples of the world.

"President of the Republic,

LÁZARO CÁRDENAS.

"Mexico, D.F., March 31, 1938."

HULL'S MEMORANDUM

When I made report of my conversation with the Foreign Minister to Hull, he said his note would, therefore, not be given to the press, agreeing not to make public the note at that time and not at all if satisfactory arrangements were made. However, when later (July) the newspapers made a great to-do about my having "suppressed" Hull's note, he told me he had not understood that it was to be regarded "as not received." He made this statement of his understanding:

"It was the understanding the Department of State that publication of this note would be withheld for a few days to accommodate the desires of the Mexican Government, which desired of its own initiative to submit a note on the oil expropriation matter without making reference to the note from the United States Government. It was the intention of the Department of State definitely to withhold publication of the note in the event a satisfactory solution of the problem were found.

"It was not contemplated that the note would be suspended or withdrawn, inasmuch as it was delivered and received in the regular procedure in such matters. The Department of State has instructed that the Foreign Office be informed that it desires to remove whatever ambiguity may have existed in the minds of the Mexican Government and that the Minister for Foreign Affairs be informed that the Government of the United States has always considered, and will continue to consider the note as regularly delivered and valid in every respect.

"The Department further instructs that General Hay be informed that, in view of a misunderstanding that has arisen, an endeavor will be made, in responding to press inquiry, not to mention that particular communication."

I gave my views fully to Secretary Hull in many telegrams and letters of which the following is one:

Mexico, April 2, 1938

"My dear Mr. Secretary:

"In my telegram of this morning (No. 99, 9 A.M.) I said that I would send you by air mail some views about the oil settlement for your consideration.

"If the oil companies will proceed to negotiate with the government and find a solution for the matters at issue, they will be not only serving their own interests and the interests of their stockholders, in this present grave situation, but they will be helping to preserve peaceful conditions and economic stability in this country and promoting the friendship between Mexico and other countries.

"There are distinctly two elements here connected with the oil companies and other big foreign interests. The first accepts the doctrine which you laid down in your statement at the press conference the middle of the week: to wit—that as a sovereign country no nation had a right to object to the policies of the Mexican government even to the point of expropriation, provided compensation was made for the property expropriated. As you know, practially all the oil companies here, certainly all the big ones, are Mexican corporations. The responsible men in the management of these corporations recognize that they are doing business under the Calvo Clause and that when they call upon their governments for diplomatic assistance in protest against Mexican laws, they are not only violating their own pledge not to do so, but they are demanding to do business in Mexico in violation of the constitution of Mexico. These men, or at least some of them, while regretting that Cárdenas made what I regard as a great mistake for his own country as well as for others concerned, feel that the expropriation of the oil properties is something that has been accomplished and is irrevocable. Having made the expropriation and having been guaranteed in ways that were unprecedented in Mexico the support of his countrymen, I do not believe there is any power under the sun that could make Cárdenas recede from his decree. I know that some of his best advisers thought he was making a mistake and regretted it, but these men are as ardent in support now, since the question in Mexico has come to be regarded as a question of preservation of national sovereignty, as are those who urged him to take the position which brought about the seriousness which has given us all great trouble in the last few days. This element of oil people and other foreign investors, as well as Mexicans who have large properties, see the dangers inherent in conflict, not only to their pocket-books but to the peace of the country, and they are willing to make some sacrifices before they would do anything that might cause an uprising here, which they know full well would make impossible the collection of compensation of any kind for their property.

"There is another element which busies itself in spreading propaganda all over the country that if the oil companies and other foreign investors will stand firm and buck the government a revolution will follow, Cárdenas will be displaced and a new man, a strong man of conservative tendencies who will take orders from the oil companies like Díaz and Huerta, will take his place, and under such rule their properties would be restored and labor demands would be crushed and we could return to the halcyon days, as they call them, of Díaz. Of course you and I know that in the halcyon days of Díaz he gave away, or parted with for money or favor, the rich natural resources of his country to his favorites, many of them foreigners, so that when the revolution drove Díaz out practically all the oil, all the silver, all the gold, all the hardwoods and other basic national resources belonged chiefly to foreigners and to the favorites of the Díaz régime. Not only so, but though Díaz had induced foreign capital to build railroads and other things that were of value to the country, at the close of his twenty-five year rule the great body of the people were hungrier and more naked than they were when he began. Land was held in large bodies, one family alone owning eight million hectares. The body of the people were landless, ignorant and hopeless. That was what the halcyon days did for the mass of the people in Mexico, and at the same time the *Científicos,* both native and foreign, lived in splendor and luxury, many of them spending much of their time in Paris and Madrid when they were not in Mexico City. This condition of affairs, as you know, and the iron hand upon any liberty of speech or liberty of conscience, finally caused such a mild-mannered *hacendado* as Madero, such a don as Carranza, and the uneducated men like Villa and Zapata, who were cruel in the highest degree, to rise up and demand the driving out of Díaz and of Huerta under the slogan of 'Land and Liberty.'

"I urge you as strongly as I can that every proper influence should be brought to bear upon the American oil interests to sit down with Mexican authorities and try to reach an equitable and just arrangement by which Mexico can pay for the oil properties in the only coin they have—oil. President Cárdenas tells me, as I have written you, that if they are agreeable to this he will not take advantage of the expropriation law which gives ten years to pay for the property, but in a way that would guarantee the oil companies their share of the oil, the oil would be divided as it is taken from the ground, part to the Mexican Government and part to the oil operators, and that without waiting for a final appraisement of the value of the property. Whatever was realized from the oil that would go to the oil companies would be received by them as payment in part for the property expropriated.

"I have not felt at liberty to proffer advice to the oil representatives. In the first place, they have not asked it, but they have kept us posted as to what they were doing until lately, when it is now understood that the policy of the American companies will be determined in New York and of the British companies in England.

"Pardon me for this long letter, but I am so confident that the wise course is for the oil companies to seek a possible solution rather than fight, that I thought I ought to give you the benefit of my observations based on my experience here.

"Always with my warm regards,
"Sincerely yours,
"JOSEPHUS DANIELS."
"The Honorable
Cordell Hull,
Department of State,
Washington, D.C."

SECRETARY HULL'S STATEMENT

In response to inquiries at his press conference following the expropriation, Secretary of State Hull made a statement early in April saying that while the American government did not undertake to question the right of the government of Mexico in the exercise of its sovereign power to expropriate properties within its jurisdiction, the American government would insist upon fair compensation of the "assured and effective value" to the American nationals from whom this property was taken.

From that sound position the American government could not be budged, though for three years officials of the State Department had conferences with the heads of the oil companies and with representatives of the Mexican government hoping they could agree upon a prompt and just settlement and payment for the properties expropriated.

I was so insistent upon early negotiations that when the officials of the Standard Oil Company dallied and would not even discuss values, I proposed to Acting Secretary Sumner Welles that I go to see John D. Rockefeller and put the matters that were disturbing friendly relations squarely up to him and ask that he end the *mañana* policy. But the State Department hoped that course would not be necessary and did not approve my suggestion.

CONFIDENCE IN SOLUTION

In a note to the State Department President Cárdenas had said: "Mexico will know how to honor its obligations of today and its obligations of yesterday." Hull matched that with a statement voicing confidence that, in view of the attitude expressed, "a rapid, satisfactory and equitable solution of the pending problem between the two countries can be found." On April 2 a State Department note requested to "be advised directly of the Government's plan for payment." When the Finance Minister, Suárez, said that Cárdenas was ready to "set aside a certain per cent of the proceeds from the sale of oil to be placed in a fund for payment when the value was agreed upon," the State Department replied that the assurances were not adequately responsive and did not cover the method of payment of such compensation.

WOULD ACCEPT OFFICES OF THE UNITED STATES

On April 19 Sub-Secretary Beteta told me President Cárdenas had instructed him to give me this statement:

"The Government of Mexico will treat regarding the amount and form of payment due the petroleum companies with their representatives in Mexico; but will accept the unofficial and friendly offices of the Government of the United States in case the latter offers them for the two-fold purpose of making manifest the good will of Mexico and of avoiding as far as possible the campaign which might be conducted against it abroad."

ONLY CASH OR PROPERTY RETURNED

The attitude of the oil men was thus stated by Mr. Anderson, of the Huasteca Oil Company: "The reaffirmed position of the oil companies is that Mexico must pay the full indemnification in cash or return the properties. No time payments will be considered."

I advised oil men to negotiate. One oil executive scorned the invitation, saying: "They would make an offer so low it would be insulting. And even if they agreed to pay a fair price, the government hasn't enough money. It would be a waste of time."

My reply was, "Suppose you are right. If so, that is an additional reason why you should accept the invitation to negotiate. If a ridiculously low price is tendered or if it is demonstrated that Mexico could not pay, your position would be improved. If you refuse even to discuss the matter, you put yourself in an indefensible position." But none of the oil men would accept the invitation of Cárdenas to confer as to payment.

One reason given by the oil companies at first as to why they could not accept the offer to negotiate with the President was that they wished to test their rights in the courts. Three or more actions were instituted, but the Supreme Court, having upheld the finding of the Labor Board, gave adverse decision in the litigation.

ROOSEVELT PLEDGED FRIENDLY COÖPERATION

On April 24 in a message to Deputy León García, the majority leader of the Mexican Chamber of Deputies, President Roosevelt expressed "our common determination to solve our problems in a spirit of friendly coöperation." On July 22, 1938, Secretary Hull wrote a note proposing arbitration. While dealing specifically with the agrarian question, the note asking arbitration, by implication, extended also to the oil disputes. He said the proceedings would be under the provisions of the Inter-American Treaty of Arbitration of 1929. The arbitration would determine "whether there has been compliance by the Government of Mexico with the rule of compensation as prescribed by international law in the case of the American citizens whose farm and agrarian properties in Mexico have been expropriated by the Mexican Government since August 30, 1927, and, if not, the amount of and terms under which compensation should be made by the Government of Mexico." There followed much correspondence—the State Department insisting upon "prompt, fair, and adequate payment," and Mexico promising to make such payment if and when the oil companies would consent to an agreement as to valuation. The State Department thought the Mexicans were adopting a *mañana* course and the Mexicans, while gratified at Hull's announcement of the principles involved, felt he was tough with them. He combined firmness with patience. As nearly always happens, the note-writing got nowhere. Finally it was agreed by all parties that Donald Richberg, the attorney of the oil companies, and President Cárdenas would meet man to man, discuss the whole problem, and seek to reach a satisfactory agreement.

THE ISSUES AFTER EXPROPRIATION

Actually there were three differing points of view with regard to all the questions raised by expropriation:

1. The oil companies held that the property belonged to them in fee simple and that Cárdenas had been guilty of confiscation of their property and should be compelled to return it. The British government demanded restitution and declined to consider payment. The American companies insisted their government should exert whatever pressure necessary to compel Cárdenas to retract his decree and let them operate the property.

2. The Mexican government contended that all subsurface mineral or oil belonged to the government and that no laws in conflict with Article 27 of the Constitution were legal. They contended they were upholding the Constitution and laws which the oil companies had flouted. Here is Article 27:

"The ownership of lands and waters included within the limits of the national territory is vested originally in the nation, which has had and has the right to convey title thereof to private persons, thereby constituting private property.

"The nation shall have at all times the right to impose on private property such qualifications as the public interest may demand, as well as the right to regulate the development of natural resources, which are susceptible of expropriation, in order to preserve them and equitably to distribute public wealth.

"In the nation is vested direct ownership of all minerals or substances which in veins, masses or beds constitute deposits whose nature is different from the components of the land, such as minerals from which metals and metalloids used for industrial purposes are extracted, beds of precious stones, rock salt and salt lakes formed directly by marine waters, products derived from the decomposition of rocks, when their exploitation requires underground workings, phosphates which may be used for fertilizers; solid mineral fuels, petroleum and all hydrocarbons, solid, liquid or gaseous.

"Only Mexicans by birth or naturalization and Mexican companies shall have the right to acquire ownership of lands, waters and their appurtenances or to obtain concessions to develop mines, water or mineral fuels in the Republic of Mexico. The nation may grant the same right to aliens, provided that they agree before the Department of Foreign Relations to be considered Mexicans in respect to such property, and accordingly not to invoke the protection of their governments in respect to the same, under penalty, in case of breach of this agreement, of forfeiture to the nation of property so acquired."

The Mexicans, resting upon the Constitution, said the real issues were whether the oil companies could defy Mexican laws, treat with contempt the judgments of Mexican courts, pay such taxes as they saw fit and reject labor awards by invoking the pressure or intervention of their governments.

3. The United States government disapproved the expropriation but accepted the right of Mexico as a sovereign country to expropriate under its own laws property for public use, provided it made prompt and adequate compensation.

BRITISH STIFFNESS KICKED BACK

While the American government was telling Mexico it would not object to its carrying out its laws authorizing expropriation if prompt and assured compensation was made, the British took the course of being tough. Their Minister in a long note (April 8) told the Mexican government its action was "tantamount to confiscation carried out under a veil of legality," and declared that "the only remedy for the expropriation is the return of the expropriated property to the companies." This followed a news cable from London: "Great Britain is acting with ferocious zeal. She has lined up with the oil companies instead of with the United States."

Shortly after the expropriation, Owen St. Clair O'Malley, the British Minister, came to see me, seeking to secure joint action in demanding restoration of the oil properties. I pointed out that we had asked for just and prompt compensation, whereas his government had demanded a return of the property itself, eliminating the question of compensation. Therefore we could make no joint representation.

A little while later the Minister presented a note to the Mexican government demanding immediate payment of $361,737 which the note said was a debt owed by Mexico four months overdue. He added that non-payment indicated that Mexico could not indemnify the British for the expropriation of the oil properties. It was astounding that with a claim for four or five hundred million dollars pending, Britain should write a letter demanding a comparatively small sum. Mexicans regarded it as an affront.

I had not heard of this *faux pas* until in May, when upon calling at the Foreign Office, General Hay showed it to me and also gave me a copy of his reply. His reply was New York exchange for the $361,737 demanded and a letter in which the British Minister was spanked by what General Hay thought was masterly strategy. Showing resentment of O'Malley's suggestion that Mexico's action was reprehensible, General Hay in his note reminded the Britisher that there were countries richer than Mexico which owed large debts on which they had defaulted—a plain reference to Britain's disregard of its obligation for war loans due the United States.

Hay read me that paragraph and he looked "as pleased as Punch" at his "getting the best" of the Minister—as pleased as if he had swallowed a canary.

The British Minister got his $361,737 and not a cent for his claim of five hundred million dollars for the oil of British companies. He also got something that created a ten-day sensation: the Mexican Government broke off diplomatic relations with Great Britain and O'Malley left for home.

XXI

MEXICAN REACTION

W ITH the expropriation of foreign oil properties, a wave of delirious enthusiasm swept over Mexico, heightened by bitter denunciations from other countries, as the people felt that a day of deliverance had come. On March 22, upon the call of the Confederation of Mexican workers, some two hundred thousand people passed in compact files before the National Palace acclaiming President Cárdenas and carrying banners such as: "They shall not scoff at Mexican laws." Old inhabitants said there had never been such manifestations of the unity of the Mexican people in the history of Mexico as followed the appeals to the people to uphold the Constitution and the sovereignty of Mexico. It was shared by people who lost sight of oil in their belief that Mexicans must present a united and solid front.

Closing his address to the multitude, Cárdenas told labor men they deserved the support of their government, and counselled them to discipline their ranks, increase production, and avoid insolent attacks—"to prove there is a real, individual liberty justly demanded by the Mexican people."

Many thousands of students in the Mexican University organized an enthusiastic parade. Its Rector, speaking to President Cárdenas, said: "The University offers you its solid support in this moment when the fatherland requires the unity of its sons. It comes to offer the youth of Mexico to be with you as you are with the honor of Mexico."

CATHOLICS RAISE FUNDS

Noticeable was the enthusiasm of Catholics, many of whom had been critical of the Cárdenas government, in raising funds to support his expropriation move. On Sunday, April 30, the Archbishop of Guadalajara advised from the pulpit that it was a "patriotic duty to contribute to this national fund." It was announced (April 3) that Archbishop Martínez had promised a "letter on the oil controversy during Holy Week." On May 3, a circular, approved by archbishops and bishops, was published, exhorting Catholics to send contributions. All over the country in churches collections were taken to help pay for the seized oil properties.

WOMEN MAKE EXPROPRIATION A "NATIONAL RELIGION"

Women in Mexico have generally followed an old slogan: "The place of woman is in the home." That was the attitude of women in the early part of April, 1938. Then, as by a miracle, suddenly they became vocal in their patriotism. Cárdenas had made approval of the expropriation of oil a sort of national religion. The people believed—and had grounds for their opinion—that their patrimony had been given for a song to foreigners who refused to pay living wages to the men who worked in the oil fields. When the men gathered by the hundred thousands to show allegiance to Cárdenas after the oil expropriation, the women poured out of their homes by the thousands to voice their ardent support of the leaders who had somehow made the people feel that the oil exploiters were the enemies of their country. What could they do? President Cárdenas had given his word to me on the day after the expropriation that payment would be made. The people were zealous to see that his pledge was kept. What could the women do? Pitifully little toward the millions needed, but all Mexico in a day was full of the spirit of the widow who gave her mite and was commended, having given her all as giving "more than all the rest."

Something the like of which has rarely been seen in any country occurred on the twelfth day of April. By the thousands, women crowded the Zócalo and other parks and in companies marched to the Palace of Fine Arts to give of their all to the call of their country's honor. It was a scene never to be forgotten. Led by Señora Amalia Solórzano de Cárdenas, the President's young and handsome wife, old and young, well-to-do and poor—mainly the latter— as at a religious festival gathered to make, what was to many, an unheard-of sacrifice. They took off wedding rings, bracelets, earrings, and put them, as it seemed to them, on a national altar. All day long, until the receptacles were full and running over, these Mexican women gave and gave. When night came crowds still waited to deposit their offerings, which comprised everything from gold and silver to animals and corn.

What was the value in money of the outpouring of possessions to meet the goal of millions of pesos? Pitiably small—not more than 100,000 pesos—little to pay millions—but the outpouring of the women, stripping themselves of what was dear to them, was the result of a great fervor of patriotism the like of which I had never seen or dreamed. It was of little value for the goal. It was inestimable in cementing the spirit of Mexico, where there was a feeling that the Cárdenas move was the symbol of national unity.

AMERICAN CONCERNS BOYCOTT MEXICAN OIL-PRODUCING ORGANIZATIONS

Two American acts after expropriation especially offended Mexicans. In this situation in which all indignation was not on either side of the border, these acts seemed items of tough economic pressure from north of the Rio Grande.

Not long after the Mexican government expropriated the oil properties, the government needed to buy pumps and parts for machines made in the United States to operate effectively. Their order was refused. I was told of the boycott, as I wrote home (October 29, 1938):

"Thursday, when I was at the Foreign Office, Mr. Beteta, the Undersecretary, told me that he was very much concerned. The night before he had attended a meeting with reference to the petroleum situation, and the head of the government organization said he had sent orders to a number of manufacturers in the United States who had been furnishing pumps and all sorts of machines and parts to the Standard Oil and other companies which had been operating in the Federal Petroleum District; but that the American companies sent the money back and would not fill the orders. They regard this as a boycott by American manufacturers in retaliation for the government's expropriation of the oil fields. Beteta said that the government had expropriated the oil fields for good and sufficient reasons and intended to pay for them; but they would not be returned. He said: 'I am chiefly concerned because if United States manufacturers and dealers refuse to sell us the essentials for carrying on the oil work, they throw us into the arms of Germany, where we can swap oil for this machinery, etc., that we need.'

"He felt very strongly about it, and said he would send me a list of the orders which had been rejected. 'If we were asking any favors,' he said, 'as to credits, etc., we would not feel bad about it—but when we offer the cash and then the manufacturers who have the material for sale reject the orders, it looks as if the oil companies are dominating to such an extent that the manufacturers will sell to everybody in the world except Mexico.' He added: 'It seems that your country objects to our selling oil to Germany, Italy, and Japan; but the Standard Oil is selling all the time to these countries without any protest and with the consent of the government. We wish very much we could sell our oil to democratic countries; we have no sympathy with the totalitarian policies of Italy and Germany; but if the United States and England boycott us we shall have no alternative but to trade where we can.' "

MEXICANS INCENSED AT BLOW TO SILVER

The sudden discontinuance of buying Mexican silver by the United States a few days after the oil expropriation was received by Mexicans as a punishment for the expropriation and as a plain threat: "Return the oil properties or take the consequences."

It was a severe blow to the Mexican treasury, for the silver export tax was sorely needed, and at the time I wrote Washington that the question of purchasing silver should be considered on its own merits and should certainly not be made to seem a device for punishment.

In 1933 Mexico was receiving 26 cents per ounce for its silver and in 1933-1934 exported 95 million ounces in various forms for which it received 24 million dollars. Later (in 1938) the prevailing price reached 70 cents, which for the full production of the mines would have brought the mine owners 66 million dollars, with increased taxes to the treasury.

The effect of the stoppage was serious because 100,000 heads of families were employed in silver mines; the government received 10 per cent of its revenue from it; the National Railways received 17 per cent of its income from that source; and silver provided the major source of foreign exchange. As against silver mining giving employment to 100,000 heads of families, the oil industry employed only 16,000.

Not only were officials of the Mexican government indignant at the body blow, but the silver mine owners, mostly Americans, who felt they were being made to suffer for the deeds of the oil companies, were also infuriated. They owned 80 per cent of the Mexican mining industry which spent millions in the United States for mining equipment.

I talked to some silver mine owners who felt that they were being made the goat. They said it would deny many workers employment and would distress all the mining districts. The protests of the American mine owners were carried to Washington and the discontinuance of the purchase of Mexican silver was of short duration. The effect of the stoppage increased the determination of Mexicans not to be influenced by any outside pressure. However, one silver mine operator had a different opinion, about which I wrote home (November 19, 1938):

"This is a queer world. Mr. and Mrs. Lockett were in Pachuca last week and were entertained at luncheon by Mr. Kuryla, of the Real del Monte mine. When he returned Mr. Lockett told me that he had never in his life heard people so violent in their denunciation of President Roosevelt. Mr. Lockett told Mr. Kuryla that if anybody in the world ought to be grateful to President Roosevelt it was the silver mine owners. Lockett told him: 'Before Roosevelt began to buy silver you were getting 32 cents. Now you are getting 42 cents and at one time you were getting over 50 cents. You are enjoying the best subsidy of any people in the world and yet you are more against his policy than anybody else. Why is it?' Of course there was no answer. When people are very partisan in their politics they are not very reasonable, as we have found out at home as well as in other countries.

"The last time I saw Mr. Kuryla he asked me what I thought was going to be the future policy about silver in the United States. I told him I thought the government would continue to buy silver, but that whether they would continue to buy except from mines in the United States I did not know; that there was a strong sentiment against buying it from Mexico, Canada and other countries. I told him I did not know whether that would materialize but that he knew as well as I did that Americans (in fact 90 per cent of the mines in Mexico are owned by Americans) get the cream of the money paid from the United States Treasury for silver, though of course Mexico was benefited because the mines gave employment to thousands of workmen and brought taxes into the treasury.

"Mr. Kuryla said to me: 'Though I am a silver miner, I am troubled about silver in the future, because all of this silver is being put into the ground in the United States and not used. My experience in life and my reading show that when there is no use for any product it loses its value and as years go by and the millions of pounds of silver are dumped in the ground and locked up and soldiers are engaged to protect it, it loses its value. Is that to be the future of silver?' "

MAN OF MYSTERY

In every drama there must be a heavy villain, just as they say that in all successful business enterprises there must be a wicked partner and in politics a crooked politician. Before the oil expropriation, the Mexicans named the foreign oil magnates as the heavy villains, while the oil men gave that place in the cast to Cárdenas and Toledano, and staged William Rhodes Davis as accessory after the fact. Davis appeared on the scene not long after the expropriation. Little was known of him except that he had roamed the world on what he thought would be a sea of oil. He loomed upon the center of the stage, taking two parts: to the big oil companies, after expropriation, he was the heaviest of heavy villains; to the Cárdenas administration, the deliverer in the time of need. Out of resentment for the expropriation and the hope that Mexican operations would fail, markets for Mexican oil in the United States and in Britain suddenly dried up. Without markets the Mexicans would be drowned in their own oil, and the expropriation would fail. Some people regarded Davis as a Mulberry Sellers; others, as a rich oil promoter who would furnish needed markets for Mexican oil; and others as a glad-hand Nazi agent or as a crook. He was a composite.

The Mexican government had no market for its flowing oil except for domestic consumption and the dribbles they could sell in such Pan American countries as were not under obligation to buy from the old oil companies. In that critical situation Davis dropped down as if from the skies, as the Mexican oil administration saw it. But, to the old oil companies, he came as a devil from other regions. He had been an oil operator in England until, having clashed with the big oil companies, he lost out. Then he went to Germany. The First National Bank of Boston backed Davis to use blocked markets, which the bank had in a German account to help build a refinery. Germany was in desperate need of oil, and so was Italy. The Mexican government oil concerns were in sore need of a purchaser for their surplus of oil. In that situation Davis arrived in Mexico and quickly made arrangements to buy Mexican oil for Germany. At once the oil interests of Britain and the United States said that Davis was a Nazi agent and that if Mexico had dealings with him it would demonstrate that it was a Nazi sympathizer and against the countries which were at war with the Nazis and the Fascists. As giving proof of this charge, Jean Schacht, son of Hitler's former head of the Reichsbank, Hjalmar Schacht, appeared in Mexico. He was seen much with Davis, though he asserted he came to Mexico on a pleasure trip.

The Mexicans welcomed any purchaser of their oil. They were ruined without an outlet for the supply. Davis made a contract to supply the Nazis with Mexican oil. Associated with Davis was Joachim Hertslet, who worked in engineering deals that made it possible for the Nazis to get oil out of Mexico. Long after, Marquis Childs wrote of seeing Davis in Mexico City at that time:

> "When I saw Davis in the blue-and-gold presidential suite of the Hotel Reforma in Mexico City in 1938, he still talked of the far-reaching international trade he was directing. While he talked, telephone calls came from London, Hamburg and Washington.
> "In reality he was a ruined man, intriguing with the evil force of nazism out of the bitterness of his resentment and frustration. And always he and his associates talked of how much more oil the Germans had got, in the years of preparation for conquest, from the big British and American combines than they got from Davis."

Was Davis a Nazi agent? He was shadowed by the British secret service in Bermuda and Portugal on his way to Berlin in 1939. Whether the British were trying to prevent Davis from buying oil from Mexico or suspected him to be in league with the Nazis is not known. It may have been both, but it has been stated that Davis arranged for the payment of a $5,000-radio-hook-up in 1940 when John L. Lewis delivered his bitter attack on Roosevelt and tried to get Labor to oppose Roosevelt's reëlection that year. Davis did not use his own money, if at that time he had money to spare. And it is not known that Lewis was informed that friends of Davis paid the bill, though Drew Pearson has said that John L.

Lewis complained to Assistant Secretary of State Berle because F.B.I. men covered Davis's apartment in the Mayflower Hotel.

Many years afterward it was revealed in investigation by the United States Department of Justice that Davis was used by Foreign Minister Joachim von Ribbentrop in the Nazi organized effort to defeat President Roosevelt for reëlection in 1940. The German Foreign Minister explained that it was "essential to defeat Roosevelt because he, more than any other American, was capable of making sweeping political decisions" that would not be pleasing to the Nazis. To this was added testimony that in 1939-1940 the chief objective of the Nazis was to defeat President Roosevelt in 1940. In 1936 when Davis was trying to organize a big oil company, he was quoted as claiming to have "made available" $291,286 to an amount to elect Roosevelt and certain senators. If so, it was without the knowledge of the White House and if and when he sought White House favor, Davis got no recognition. Davis was also said to be trying to put on a three-cornered deal between Mexico, Germany, and the United States involving surplus cotton. No "pent-up Utica" contracted his soaring adventures.

CELEBRATION OF ANNIVERSARY OF EXPROPRIATION

On the anniversary of the expropriation (March 18, 1939) two thousand people attended a banquet in the bull ring in celebration, and on Sunday seventy-five thousand people gathered in the Zócalo with banners, and heard speeches by President Cárdenas, syndicate workers, and others to celebrate "the historic decree." The ringing of the Hidalgo bell was said to be the signal for throwing off the foreign yoke. The syndicate workers and Señor Rodríguez, President of the Mexican Revolutionary party, created great enthusiasm by their attacks on imperialistic policies. President Cárdenas' speech was mild in comparison, but he upheld the course he had pursued, said that no backward step would be made, and indicated that the negotiations going on between him and Mr. Donald Richberg, attorney for the oil companies, would be successful, leaving operation in the hands of the government.

His speech was enthusiastically received, particularly when he denounced the oil companies for launching a fiery campaign through the foreign press in an endeavor "to crack the domestic economy." He defended "the reincorporation of the oil subsoil rights to the hands of the nation." He declared that the oil companies had "made it a practise to obstruct the enforcement of the most fundamental laws by way of diplomatic coercion or mercenary revolt." He declared, "The potential wealth of Mexico, purely hard Indian labor, exemption from taxes, economic privileges and tolerances on the part of government constitute the essential figures of the great prosperity of the petroleum industry in Mexico."

At the same time flags were flown on the towers of the Cathedral which faces one side of the Zócalo. On one of the towers was a large Mexican flag with the eagle and snake. On the other tower was a great flag of the Mexican Revolutionary party, and high above all was a banner reading: "The PRM extends greetings to President Lázaro Cárdenas, Redeemer of Economic Independence." I do not recall ever before seeing a political banner on the Cathedral.

XXII

AMERICAN PROPAGANDA

As an organ of propaganda against Mexico, to build up hatred of that country to a point which they thought would cause Uncle Sam to send in Marines to force a return of the expropriated petroleum, the Standard Oil Company of New Jersey began the publication and free distribution of a paper called *The Lamp*. It did not confine itself to oil discussion but sought to inflame sentiment in the United States against Mexico by parading every crime or incident that would injure the standing of Mexico in the United States and to broadcast every item to injure the Cárdenas government clipped from subsidized and other papers in Mexico and the United States. Also it sought by scare heads to frighten possible investors in Mexico. It demanded a discontinuance of silver purchases in the hope of bankrupting the Mexican treasury. As an example, it printed again and again from American papers articles beginning with such paragraphs as, "There is Mexico stealing everything it can lay its hands on." One headline over the silver purchase was headed, "Sop for the Brigands." Most of the clippings were credited to papers little known.

The cartoons were, if possible, more insulting. They represented Mexicans as of a lesser breed, whose chief business was brigandage and lawlessness and theft. No reader of *The Lamp* could have any conception of Mexico other than as a country occupied by uncivilized and degraded people who were happy only when robbing American investors. One characteristic cartoon—not the worst—represented the Mexican as a chicken thief, oil company property being the rooster he was carrying on his back. The thief was represented as saying: "Honest, Sam. I will pay you back some day." I would not degrade this volume by reproducing any of these repulsive cartoons. Started for the purpose of creating sentiment to compel Uncle Sam to take out his Big Stick, *The Lamp* degenerated to intemperate abuse of all things Mexican, which probably so disgusted fair-minded people as to "kick back and knock its owner over." Certain it is that *The Lamp* did not, as its promoters hoped, stampede Uncle Sam to repudiate the Good Neighbor doctrine and his Montevideo pledge.

The Lamp inveighed against lending money to Mexicans. It claimed that the oil properties of America and Mexico were worth $2,000,000,000 whereas a joint commission years afterward agreed that they were worth only forty million dollars and both countries approved the appraisal. This sheet sought to scare Mexico by printing under big headlines that because of the expropriation the tourists were avoiding Mexico.

It printed stories with fake or manufactured date lines; for instance, a disputed figure (credited to the Richmond, Texas, *Courier*) stated that the number of tourists in the year after oil expropriation fell from around 100,000 annually to 24,997. It estimated that the tourists spent an average of $19,000,000 in the year before expropriation and dropped to less than one half of that amount because of the action of Cárdenas. The article, as did many of them, contained this plain false statement: "The blunt refusal of the Mexican government to make any settlement with the owners..." though they knew, the day after expropriation, through me, that President Cárdenas promised to pay and requested the representatives of the oil companies to discuss the amount to be paid. As evidence of the viciousness of the articles, they suggested "that American tourists might wonder whether their private personal property, such as baggage or motor cars, might not be jeopardized if taken into Mexico."

In view of such slanders, repeated in issue after issue and meant to injure Mexico, the wonder is that the tourists trade did not completely dry up. Many of the articles charged Mexico with "stealing" and "pillaging," and paramounted every crime committed in any part of Mexico.

GOVERNMENT AGENT DUPED

Not only did *The Lamp* and the papers it quoted from misrepresent Mexico, but some American government officials lent a willing ear to false gossip. In June, 1940, President Roosevelt, saying that he had no evidence of its value, wrote me that "one of the government information services" sent in this report:

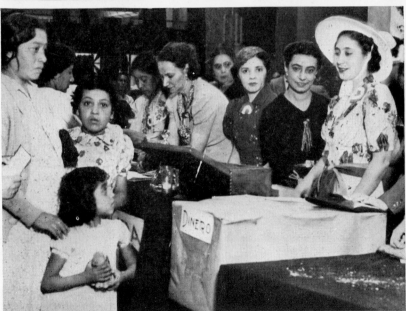

Above, General Hay, Foreign Minister, (*left*) and Vicente Cortez Herrera, Director of Petroleum (*center*) meeting to discuss problems following expropriation. *Below,* Señora de Cárdenas (*extreme right*) leads the women's movement to contribute their jewels to support the expropriation of oil.

Above, an oil well near Tampico. *Below*, one of the oil fields in Mexico's "Golden Lane."

"President Cárdenas, despite public utterances, is very close to the Nazi Government and the Communists who are operating in Mexico. Cárdenas, according to the informant, has seen to it that the Police Department in Mexico City is infiltrated with Communists and pro-Nazis. Cárdenas, it is indicated, has stated that he is purposely misinforming Ambassador Daniels as to his feelings with reference to Nazi and Communist efforts in Mexico."

I answered that the President might be sure that "we keep our eyes open," and informed him that every statement by the government agent was false; that Cárdenas was "vigilant to ferret out any attempts at subversive influence"; that "the German big shot, Dietrich, was leaving the country," and that the suggestion that Cárdenas was "purposely misinforming Ambassador Daniels" was a repetition of oil reactionary gossip; that "I was in touch and there was no foundation for the reflection upon the Police Department." I added that "the report showed the government agent had been taken in by those trying to sabotage the Good Neighbor Policy."

"SILLY LIES" DENOUNCED

While *The Lamp's* oil was broadcasting anti-Good-Neighbor articles, much of it false and defamatory, William Edward Zuch wrote a denial of some of the sensational stories to the *Christian Century* in these words:

"Let me state categorically that no oil has been poured on the Gulf and burned, no ports have been leased to the Japanese for naval bases, no fascist air fields have been built in Yucatan or Campeche, no pipe line has been constructed across the Isthmus of Tehuantepec to supply Japanese warships with oil, no rebel armies exist in the mountains, bandits do not infest the main highways, no ... but why go on denying all these silly lies that a gullible American public seems to relish?"

MAGAZINE SHAMELESSLY LOST ITS VIRTUE

The lowest depths to which propaganda against the country's policy and against the government's officials ever reached, was that of the old *Atlantic Monthly*, which had been a favorite of mine all my life, when it was degraded into lending itself to the oil interests by a special edition in July, 1938. While President Roosevelt,

Secretary Hull, and the American Ambassador were seeking to secure the just compensation for the oil, promised at the time of the expropriation, we were bombarded by the wide circulation of a special issue of *The Atlantic Monthly* devoted to misrepresentation and slander and hate by a magazine which had, in its long history been the favorite medium for carrying the writings of the best authors. It fell from the heights to the deepest abyss and won the contempt of all who felt that a journal which people had long trusted had lost its virtue, as it had, in upholding the campaign of the oil companies which wished the United States to go to war with Mexico.

That July issue contained sixty-four pages under big headlines, "THE ATLANTIC PRESENTS TROUBLE BELOW THE BORDER." Every page smelled of oil. In vain did any reader look for one page, or one poem, or one article of the old *Atlantic* flavor. Bad as the contents were, the most flagrant offense was that the magazine did not state what its true purpose was—to serve the oil companies wishing to force Uncle Sam to pay the oil men four hundred million dollars for properties worth only fifty millions. It declared its purpose to "promote a better understanding among readers below and above the border," whereas nine tenths of the articles were attempts to create hate between Mexico and the United States. In all the sixty-four pages there was not even an intimation that the trouble was precipitated by absurdly low wages and the refusal of the oil companies to obey the decree of the Supreme Court. That issue of *The Atlantic* was full of insulting cartoons representing Mexico as a nation of brigands, communists, and thieves, who set out to destroy the Good Neighbor Policy. Not a Mexican was shown who did not look like a thug or a thief. It declared that Mexico showed "racial degeneration." From any and every source it scraped up and printed a raft of stories showing how Mexico was retrograding—had retrograded—and the reader, if he believed half that was printed, saw Mexico as a debased country. One offensive cartoon pictured Mexico as doing what Hitler had done in Austria, Japan in China, and Mussolini in Spain. It paraded letters signed by some of the eighteen thousand workers who wished to go back to the old wages and conditions but was careful not to say that, out of the eighteen thousand, only seven took that position. The first two pages, which are reproduced elsewhere in this book, indicate the attempt to hold Mexico up as a nation of contemptible people.

TURNS STATE'S EVIDENCE

In February, 1941, I wrote in my Diary: "Sedgwick, editor of *The Atlantic Monthly,* thinks serious situation exists in journalism. *Chicago Tribune* thinks of nothing except money."

THE CEDILLO REBELLION

While this propaganda was at its height, there broke out what the American papers called "revolution" but which Mexican officials called "a rebellion" in San Luis Potosí as General Saturnino Cedillo, resigned from the cabinet, declared opposition to the Cárdenas government, and took the field against it. Did the oil men promote it? The government officials headed by Cárdenas said so. There were reports that the Nazis were behind it, and color was given to the charge by reason of the fact that for years an officer named Van Mecker, said to be in touch with Hitler, was the director of Cedillo's private army, and it was reported that the rebels had German and Italian planes.

I was in Washington when Cedillo started the uprising. A member of the Embassy staff wrote me that he had "every confidence that President Cárdenas will bring it to a successful conclusion." He added:

> "Since President Cárdenas went to San Luis Potosí to beard the lion in his den, it seems that almost everyone here has been determined that there shall be a revolution in Mexico as a result of the Cedillo situation. The petroleum companies as well as other vested interests have promoted every conceivable type of rumour and reports in the effort to intensify the situation. In fact, there is no doubt in my mind but that recent broadcasts from San Antonio on the subject of Mexico and Cedillo have been instigated by the petroleum interests. The same thing applies to broadcasts which have been originating in the United States."

While this revolution was heralded as the beginning of the often predicted downfall of the Cárdenas regime, the Chief Executive quietly entered the city of San Luis Potosí, walked up the streets unarmed, and called on the people to disown the rebels. Strange to say, many heard and complied, and the revolution that was to turn him upside down "died a-bornin' " Cedillo had taken to his heels. But while the excitement lasted, it looked like a real rebellion.

A PREDICTION FULFILLED

Shortly before the Cedillo abortive uprising in San Luis Potosí, writing to Secretary Hull I said (September 6, 1937): "Secretary Hay, referring to Cedillo's leaving the cabinet and the danger he might be used by disaffected elements to start a rebellion, said, 'It would be crushed. You know the difference between a rebellion and a revolution. A rebellion under Cedillo would not go far because it would reach only the soldiers he controlled in San Luis Potosí. A revolution can come only when the people are ready to unite to overthrow the government. That condition does not exist.' "

WAITING FOR TWO ELECTIONS

During the long months when the oil companies were filling the papers with propaganda against all things Mexican, their representatives in Mexico sought out correspondents, who came for stories, and gave them their side of the case but not generally for direct quotation. Here is an example of what correspondents heard. H. R. Knickerbocker, a well-known correspondent, wrote a series of articles for the Hearst papers. I talked with him and wrote the Secretary of State:

"You may be interested in these sidelights on Mr. Knickerbocker's visit. (1) He told me that representatives of the oil companies said that if necessary to compel Mexico to pay for the oil properties expropriated, the way should be opened at the border for arms to be brought in by the oil companies or any other parties.

"(2) He said he had been told by oil men here that one reason the oil companies had not pressed for settlement earlier was that they were waiting for two elections.

"I asked him, 'What elections?'

"He replied: 'One in the United States and one in Mexico.' He said oil men here believed there would be a political reversal in the next election in the United States and the new President would throw the Good Neighbor policy overboard. 'The oil men here,' he added, 'are quite confident of that.' "

The two elections in 1940 brought disappointments to these prophets, for both the United States and Mexico registered a determination to hold fast to the Good Neighbor doctrine as practiced since March, 1933, and to carry out the Six-Year Plan.

REASONS FOR GOOD RELATIONS

While paid propagandists (some went to Mexico to write what their employers paid them to write) inculcated hate of Mexico in the United States, the best correspondents, who came to Mexico to report the truth, served their country well. One of the ablest columnists America has known, Raymond Clapper, whose death occurred while he was on duty in the Far East during World War II, in his letter (April 21, 1940) wrote:

"The reason relations with Mexico are so good is that the present Mexican Government is smart enough to see that good relations are to its interest.

"I should add a second important reason. It is Uncle Joe Daniels, the American Ambassador. By all of the rules he should be the most unpopular ambassador we have ever had. For as Secretary of Navy under Wilson, he sent the fleet to Vera Cruz. He doesn't speak a word of Spanish—says he is too old to learn.

"Yet no ambassador has been more loved by the Mexican people. The reason is that they are convinced he is sympathetic and that he is not trying to gouge them. We have had ambassadors who have conceived it their duty to concentrate on nagging the Mexican Government, serving as a kind of police court lawyer for the oil companies. The oil companies don't like Daniels. They resent his not acting like the British did. The British became very snooty over the oil expropriations and as a result were requested to go home—where they still are. They have to do their propaganda work here now through an unofficial agent. He is smart and has plenty of spending money, so he gets along.

"Ambassador Daniels could have been tough with the Mexican Government, but it wouldn't have got the oil properties back. Nothing is going to get the oil properties back. Expropriation Day is the big national holiday here now. But the Mexicans do not take it out on the American Government and for a good deal of that we can thank Uncle Joe Daniels.

"He is an old-fashioned country editor, a William Jennings

Bryan Democrat, and happens to be just the kind of a person who inspires confidence among the Mexicans who are going through their Bryan period. This friendly feeling had made it possible for the Government of President Ávila Camacho to start playing ball with the United States.

"The whole story of that can't be written yet. The recent agreement permitting American Army planes to fly over Mexico and to use Mexican landing fields is only the beginning. There is much more going on, looking toward defense of the Northern Hemisphere.

"It may be a little hard on the oil companies but they have made a good thing out of Mexico for a long time and now there are bigger issues at stake, as anyone can see who will think for a moment of the place Mexico must occupy in our defense.

"We are getting what we need here through the co-operation of the Mexican Government. That is better than having to fight a war against a pro-Nazi Mexican Government to get it."

XXIII

RICHBERG LOSES; HURLEY WINS

IT was just one year after the oil expropriation that the oil companies retained Donald Richberg to open negotiations with the Mexican government looking to a settlement. His coming was approved by the Mexican government, and the United States thought it a favorable indication that an agreement would be reached. The discussions started auspiciously. President Roosevelt asked me to convey a message to President Cárdenas of his sincere hope that a just agreement could be reached. When I conveyed the message, Cárdenas sent his thanks and said he shared the same hope as Roosevelt. He added that he believed details could be worked out "after the question of value is determined and accepted." I wrote Roosevelt that this question of value was the lion in the path. But Richberg came heralded with hope. He and his wife were introduced to Mexicans in a dinner at the Embassy. Then President Cárdenas himself gave a formal dinner in Richberg's honor at Chapultepec Castle, attended by the chiefs of the government. No private foreign mission ever began so auspiciously.

After Richberg's first talk with President Cárdenas, which I reported fully to Washington, Richberg told me that he had "veered away" from all talk of values and ultimatums and made his suggestions "as sweet as possible." He told me that his clients had given him "no leeway even to discuss the valuation of the properties." The goal for which the oil companies were insistent was a long-term contract (fifty years suggested) of operation by the oil companies with some undetermined division of profits. Their bait held out to Cárdenas was that when the suggested fifty-year contract had expired, the properties would all belong to the Mexican government. Richberg elaborated on "this generous provision." Commenting on it, Secretary of *Hacienda* Suárez said, "With control of operation by the oil companies, the only thing left at the termination of the contract would be a hole in the ground. They would have drained the oil to the last drop." Secretary Suárez said the proposal reminded him of the story of the condemned man who told the king that if he would spare his life he would teach the king's donkey, which accompanied him everywhere, how to talk in ten years. The king spared his life and he agreed to return on the morrow and begin to teach the donkey to talk. "You know you cannot teach the donkey how to talk," said a friend who accompanied him. "Why do you promise to do that?" The man replied, "In ten years, one of three things will happen: (1) The king will be dead; (2) The donkey will be dead; or (3) I will be dead."

My own unexpressed opinion was that it would be like the boy eating an apple, who, when asked by his little brother for the core, said, "There ain't goin' to be no core."

Richberg's orders were that for the duration of the contract, the amount of taxes and wages could not be changed, and if wages were increased, such increase should be paid out of the government's percentage of the profits of the company to be organized. In the early discussions, Cárdenas understood that the value of the oil properties would be agreed upon first and the Mexicans would have the chief direction of the operation and insisted on that, while the oil companies understood that they were to have control.

Cárdenas insisted that, in any plan, American and British companies should be consolidated, so that Mexico would deal with only one company instead of sixteen. After talking with Richberg, I advised Washington that "an agreement can only be reached by mutual concessions." I regarded it as impossible that any government could fix the scale of wages or the rate of taxation for half a century.

WHY NEGOTIATIONS FAILED

The pleasant negotiations in Mexico City did not result in agreement, and Richberg flew to New York to consult his clients amid an aura of optimism. Later the conference was carried on for days at Saltillo, and the papers announced a settlement which caused much rejoicing. But it turned out not to be true, and there was some acrimonious discussion as to which side was to blame for the failure. The negotiations were doomed to fail, because the oil companies refused to discuss valuation. Oil men demanded operation and a guarantee of no increase in wages or taxes for the life of the contract. Cárdenas was equally firm in demanding the fixing of value first of all, and would not agree to insure that the taxes and wages

Cover page of *The Atlantic Monthly*, favoring the oil propagandists for being
tough with Mexico.

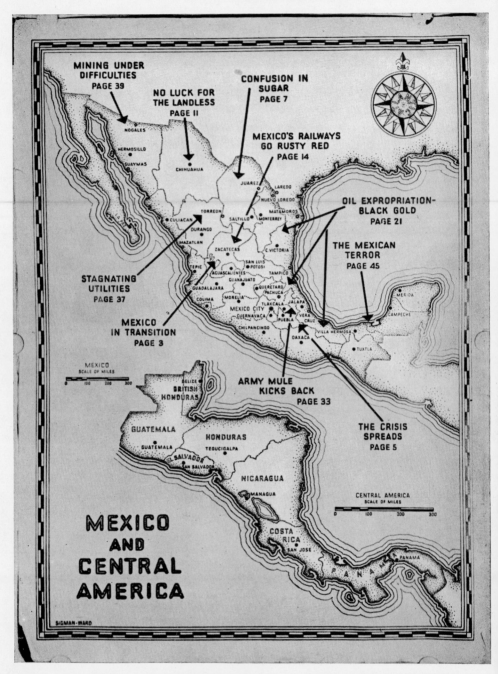

Titles of articles in *The Atlantic Monthly*'s issue of propaganda against Mexico.

would be static. Each hoped the other would recede and, until the last, both hoped this would occur.

The impasse continued until November, 1941, when, at the insistence of President Roosevelt and President Camacho, both governments finally acted without the coöperation of the oil companies. They agreed upon a valuation and Mexico began payment. It could have been adjusted as well in the year 1938 on the basis finally agreed upon, if the oil companies had accepted Cárdenas' invitation conveyed through me to the oil companies to negotiate with Mexican officials on the valuation, with a promise by Mexico of payment.

PAT HURLEY CAME, SAW, CONQUERED

While Richberg and representatives of other oil companies were failing to talk with Cárdenas, another kind of negotiator arrived in the person of General Pat Hurley, representing the Sinclair Oil Company. He had married the beautiful daughter of my old shipmate, Admiral Henry B. Wilson, and we were glad to welcome the Hurleys to the Embassy. I found he had not come bristling with demands or in the hope that the Marines would be sent down to compel the return of the properties. He was a realist and knew that the interest of his company depended upon the policy of give and take. President Cárdenas and his cabinet members liked him and his desire to reach an understanding. Cárdenas, who is an Indian, was pleased to learn that Hurley likewise had Indian blood. Hurley also played up the fact that he, like Cárdenas, was a soldier. They both talked directly, brusquely, shouted at each other, disagreed, agreed, exchanged an *abrazo,* and parted as fast friends. The result was that Hurley received a fair price for the Sinclair Company and did not join in the campaign of vilification of all things Mexican. His willingness to confer and accept payment was not relished by the big oil companies that had not learned that the days of the Big Stick were over.

XXIV

DAY OF DELIVERANCE

NOVEMBER 19, 1941, might go down in the annals of Mexico and the United States as the Day of Deliverance. On that date final agreement was reached, just before I retired from office. It was agreed that experts should be appointed by the two countries to "determine the just compensation to be paid to the nationals of the United States of America whose property rights, or interests, in the petroleum industry were affected to their detriment by acts of the Government of Mexico subsequent to March 17, 1938." It was stated that the oil companies "would retain full liberty of action."

On November 19, not only was there agreement on the plans which resulted in the satisfactory settlement for the oil property, but there was the consummation of fair agreements upon the long-standing agrarian and most other claims by each of the neighbor countries. Both countries reached an understanding also as to the perplexing silver purchases, agreed in principle on a reciprocal trade agreement, the stabilization of the Mexican peso, and the expediting of the engineering construction, as a link from the Gulf to Panama, which would constitute an important part in the Inter-American Highway, well advanced in Mexico and in other American Republics. The Mexican government made a cash deposit of $9,000,000 "on account of compensation to be paid to the affected companies and interest," and arrangements were made with the Treasury Department and the Export Import Bank to aid in financing the arrangements and the payment of substantial sums on the adjusted claims.

Upon the signing of these agreements—by Cordell Hull for the United States and Castillo Nájera for Mexico—a statement was made by Secretary Hull that dissipated the clouds that had long hung over the complete friendship of both countries. He said: "They [the agreements] mark a new milestone of great importance in the cause of solidarity between the two countries of the New World." He declared also that they constituted a "concrete proof that problems existing between nations are capable of mutually satisfactory settlement when approached in a reciprocal spirit of good will, tolerance, and a desire to understand each other's points of view."

It was stipulated in the agreement that "both governments agree to consider unappealable the joint report resulting from the agreement of the experts, and, in consequence, as definite the compensation and interest fixed in the report."

It was fortunate for all concerned that the United States was represented by Morris Llewellyn Cooke, an able, distinguished, and just economist and expert, known as Uncle Sam's Number One Trouble Shooter. The Mexican expert, Manuel J. Zevada, was a man of equal ability and standing. They were chosen to act "according to equity and justice" and to reach a conclusion for "a fair assured effective value."

Within five months (April 17, 1942) by diligence and justice the two representatives agreed that the amount Mexico should pay to oil companies was $23,995,991. In the early days after the expropriation, spokesmen of some of the companies had put a valuation of from three to four hundred million dollars on the properties expropriated.

MAÑANA POLICY ENDED

While I was anxious because of my wife's health to resign my post I was intent upon an early settlement of the oil question. I talked to Roosevelt about it. "The Good Neighbor Policy is at stake," I told him. "If the oil matter drags on, Mexicans will think that pressure is being put on them that is akin to intervention. Unless the oil matter is settled now (and if we wait for the oil companies to agree to confer, it will hang on indefinitely) Mexico and all Pan America will lose faith in the Good Neighbor Policy. We have already lost much by the delays. We should act now." And I added: "My term ends in a few weeks, and I wish to see this matter settled before I leave office. I feel that I have fought for a settlement too long to feel that I can retire comfortably leaving this matter hanging."

Roosevelt replied, "You are right. See Hull. I am sure he feels as deeply as we do that the time has come for action."

I put up the same argument to Hull that I had to the President. He had long hoped—and so had Roosevelt and I—that voluntarily the oil companies would agree to accept an appraisal by experts, and we had patiently urged such action. But they had talked and talked and pursued the policy of *mañana*.

A short while before November 19, Hull said he was happy to inform me that a solution to the long-vexing question was being shaped by the two governments. I could then retire with a feeling, "Let Thy servant depart in peace," satisfied that a just settlement had been agreed upon.

BON FIRES SHOULD BE LIGHTED

The day after the settlement had been signed by Secretary Cordell Hull for the United States and Ambassador Castillo Nájera for Mexico, Lombardo Toledano, labor leader of Mexico, said: "Bon fires should be lighted throughout Latin America because for the first time a small country (Mexico) and a big country (U. S. A.) have sat down at the Council Table and ironed things out without the use of force."

Part Seven

THE BANKER AND THE COWBOY

XXV

A BANKER DIPLOMAT

T HE situation in Mexico is difficult and grave," said President Coolidge in 1927, when he appointed his old classmate at Amherst, Dwight Whitney Morrow, to become Ambassador to Mexico. He knew from as far back as their college experience that Morrow had tact and charm. He recognized that the reason for Morrow's success as a member of the Morgan firm was that, added to ability and large knowledge, he had a genius for bringing people together, and getting what he wanted. It was said of him, "Morrow cannot see two men in dispute without letting his mind experiment on ways and means of bringing them together."

A friend stated that his method was "to strip away nonessentials and twist the gimlet of his inquiry toward just principles." It was said of him that "he liked people, not only in the objective, but in the personal sense. He liked individuals." And also, "He was the gayest, wittiest and most entertaining of companions; even his periods of abstraction, when he perpetrated absent marvels, were endearing."

PROBLEMS THAT CONFRONTED MORROW

The four problems Morrow had to deal with when he reached Mexico (October, 1927) were the same that confronted all his predecessors and successors—collection of claims against Mexico by the United States and its citizens; the delicate church question pressed by Catholics in America; agrarian policies; and the oil question, which was perennial. His predecessors had failed. They had found an irresistible force opposed to an immovable object—a situation that had long baffled President Wilson, who had drawn a graphic picture of American profiteers standing in the way of agreements and understanding:

"There are those who wish to possess Mexico, who wish to use her, who regard her people with condescension and a touch of contempt, who believe they are fit only to serve and not fit for liberty of any sort. Such men cannot and will not determine the policy of the United States."

But they had horned in particularly from the first gush of liquid gold, when British and Americans got the richest oil lands.

Could Morrow, by sympathetic interest and the courting of Calles, accomplish by charm what Sheffield and others had failed to do by forthright argument, with the Big Stick in the offing?

HAM-AND-EGGS DIPLOMACY

Ambassador Morrow went to Mexico heralded as "a Wall Street banker and debt collector." One paper said, "After Morrow come the Marines." He did not fail to see that he must disprove such statements, which, if they correctly diagnosed his position, would block his mission before it had begun. He sought "to love the country into accord," and set about making friends with President Calles, saying to his comprehending wife, "I must get the President behind me at each end." He knew Coolidge would give him a free hand, having given him only one instruction: "Keep us out of war with Mexico!" With the backing of the Presidents of both countries, he felt he could not only prevent war but build up concord and friendship—and he did both for the time being.

Fortunately for Morrow, President Calles had aroused opposition from "land owners and liberals," and he was as anxious to get Morrow "behind him" as Morrow was to win the coöperation of Calles. That mutual desire was advanced by what came to be known as "Ham-and-Eggs diplomacy" at breakfasts in the American Embassy. Calles also invited Morrow to breakfast at his ranch, Santa Barbara. Calles asked him to come alone, and Morrow tactfully consented that Jim Smithers, a partner of Calles, should be the interpreter, as Calles did not speak English and Morrow did not speak Spanish. Morrow talked of irrigation and went with Calles on a trip to the Calles Dam at Aguascalientes and to the Don Martín dams, with genial Will Rogers as the life of the party.

FRIENDSHIP NOT FRUMMERY

When Lord Reading became Viceroy of India, he is reported to have said that there were three ways to rule India—one was by force, one was by deception, and the third was by "frummery." The first

Above, the "Man of Mystery," W. R. Davis (*right*) conferring with Mexican government representatives Prieto Souza (*left*), and Fritz Flanby on expropriation of oil lands. *Below,* Donald Richberg, representing expropriated oil companies, being questioned by Mexico City newspaper men after his conference with President Cárdenas. *Inset,* Patrick Hurley, who as representative of the Sinclair Oil Company, reached an understanding with the Mexican government.

Secretary of State Cordell Hull and Mexican Ambassador Castillo Nájera signing the agreement settling oil, agrarian, and other claims, November 9, 1941. In the background, *left to right,* Eduardo Suárez, Mexican Minister of Finance; Antonio Espinoza de las Monteras; Roberto Cordova; General Christobal Gruzman-Cárdenas; Salvador Duhart.

left blood in its train; the second succeeded only until the people caught on to the deceit; the third appealed to the love of glamour and parade.

Morrow did not win by "frummery" in Mexico, but he was mightily helped by the glamour and humor of Will Rogers, who accompanied Calles and Morrow in an inspection of irrigation and agricultural projects and used his lariat to win applause for himself and admiration for the Ambassador who was his host. Will Rogers meant more in Morrow's winning Mexican regard than has been appraised. To that showmanship was added the acceptance of the Ambassador's invitation to Lindbergh to fly to Mexico, where he was the toast of the country. The Embassy became a sort of lover's bower—and "all the world loves a lover"—when Lindbergh wooed and won Anne Morrow, the gifted daughter of the Embassy. Mrs. Morrow was truly a Co-Ambassador, whose tact, wisdom, and friendliness won all hearts, and it pleased the people of Mexico that her daughter became a teacher in a public school in Mexico City.

ROMANCE AT THE EMBASSY

The people did not see that Morrow had planned the coming of Rogers and Lindbergh in an appeal to the Mexicans' love of the fiesta spirit and to ingratiate himself with the leaders and the people. It did more than all the formal notes and protocol ever conceived by the old school of diplomacy. And when romance was added to adventure, Morrow shone in reflected glory as well as in astute diplomacy. While basking in the spectacular, showing his true interest in Mexicans, which was genuine and sincere (the people sense whether friendship is affected or comes from the heart), Mr. Morrow kept always in view the goal of his inflexible purpose. It was to try to collect claims (he did not succeed any better than his predecessors) and to secure and undergird the claim of American oil companies to the ownership of much of Mexico's petroleum wealth.

To obtain that goal he knew he must create an atmosphere of friendship. Most of all he had his heart set upon winning the confidence and coöperation of President Calles, who was regarded then, as a French ruler regarded himself when he said, "I am the State." Morrow won Calles, not alone by "Ham-and-Eggs" breakfasts and the like, but also by genuine interest in the policies Calles favored. Some said he hypnotized the Mexican President. Confidence and a desire to please "the great and good friend" of the Embassy was at its height, and Calles broached his desire to secure an adjustment of the oil controversy. Morrow was ready with the plan that Calles followed, which nullified the Mexican Constitution and virtually made the Mexican oil laws into a copy of those which prevailed in the United States. And in so doing Mr. Morrow felt he had preserved valuable property to his countrymen and brought Mexico and the United States to a common basis in the regulation of oil. To be sure, some of the oil men bemoaned that they had not gotten all they were entitled to, but they understood that what Morrow had induced Calles to do was virtually to annul that provision of the Constitution which gave all subsoil rights to the State.

A CHURCH MODUS VIVENDI

Morrow reached Mexico at a time when no priests were functioning in the churches. When the government had decreed that all priests must register before officiating in the churches, the Pope, as their spiritual leader, ordered them not to submit to the authority of the State. As they would not register, the Catholic churches, while open, had no spiritual shepherds. In a country where most people were Catholics, that created a situation which had reverberations in Rome and in the United States. Mr. Morrow was confronted with the need for a *modus vivendi*. Shortly after he arrived, he found a diplomatic coadjutor in Father John J. Burke, who spoke for the Catholic hierarchy. He wanted the churches opened. Calles would not agree unless the priests would obey the laws and register with the State. Morrow wished some settlement to end the impasse —and so, on a ship in Vera Cruz Harbor, Ambassador Morrow, President Calles, and Father Burke, each having the gift of diplomacy, mulled over the situation. They met in good feeling.

In that conference on the ship, Father Burke said to Calles: "I wish to remind you that the Catholics were among the earliest patriots in Mexico and, in fact, led for independence. It was a priest, Hidalgo, who first rang the bell for independence."

"Yes," commented Calles, "I know he was a priest, but the authorities of your church excommunicated him because he wished for independence, and they were responsible for his death, for he was shot in sight of the church which had decreed his excommunication."

"But," answered Father Burke, "he was excommunicated from the church, not for his participation in the Hidalgo revolution, but because he was the father of children, and no priest could lawfully have a family."

Retorting, General Calles said: "If at that period the church had turned out every priest because he was the father of children, there would not have been many priests left to officiate in the churches."

When asked, "Why does the government keep the churches closed?" Calles replied, "The Mexican government has never forbidden priests to officiate or closed any church. They can be opened tomorrow if priests obey the Mexican law requiring members of all professions, including the clergy, to register. The trouble is that your highest authority, the Pope, has forbidden the priests to obey the laws of Mexico. Therefore, it is the church which is responsible for the lack of religious ceremonies in Mexico—not the government."

This preliminary talk did not look as if agreement was near, but the truth was that Calles was looking for a way out without surrender, and so were the leaders of the Catholic church. And Mr. Morrow, with consummate diplomacy, suggested an arrangement that, for the time being, caused the resumption of services by the priests in Mexico City and some other parts of the republic.

According to statements, carrying out this arrangement, made by Archbishop Ruiz (June 22, 1929), "as a consequence of a statement made by the President, Portes Gil, the Mexican clergy will resume religious services pursuant to the laws in force." The agreement was that the Bishops could register the priests with the government, but only those named by the church authorities could officiate.

MORROW AND THE LAND QUESTION

Ambassador Morrow looked with no favor upon the Mexican doctrine of the Revolution that the land belonged to him who worked it. He wrote to the State Department:

"The whole agrarian question seems so complex that I had hoped I might be able to persuade President Calles that Mexico has already taken more land than was needed for peons available to go upon it, and that the Mexican government without definitely changing the policy could now stop taking new lands and devote the energy to improving the land already taken and to other reforms."

MORROW'S GROWING REPUTATION

After winning the victory and securing the oil for the oil companies and the return of priests to churches, Morrow sailed for London as a delegate to the Disarmament Conference. That added to his growing reputation and influence. Upon his return from Europe he showed, as a college man, interest in the University of Mexico. He asked to be permitted to make a donation; I think it was $50,000 but it may have been more. This added to the Ambassador's popularity.

CLOUD OVER LAST DAYS

Upon sailing for Europe Morrow had directed Captain Lewis B. McBryde, Naval Attaché and able economist, to make a study of Mexico's financial structure and draft a plan by which the Mexican government could carry on its fiscal affairs with special reference to securing enough revenue to meet its socialistic need and pay its foreign debt and other claims. The report was elaborate, a complete set-up for Mexican taxation and fiscal operations.

Morrow then wrote the President of Mexico and the Minister of Foreign Relations (and it was strange that he should do so after his successful diplomacy, but a Morgan partner could not resist the temptation to direct financial policies), suggesting that Mexico adopt the plan evolved by Captain McBryde, who, though he had studied the Mexican financial structure, or lack of structure, was not regarded in Mexico as entitled to direct its Minister of *Hacienda* and Congress. The McBryde plan would revolutionize the Mexican system, but Morrow urged it and wrote, "I feel that the policy of dealing with the debt as a whole is the only one that conserves the interest of Mexico itself and the interest of all its creditors."

The letter offended the astute financier, Señor Montes de Oca, Minister of *Hacienda,* and Ortiz Rubio declared it "improper" (*inconveniente*). Realizing that he had trespassed upon a sacred preserve of Mexican finances, Morrow withdrew the letter at once, but it had made a breach which was not healed. "The unhappy incident," says Morrow's biographer, Harold Nicolson, "threw a cloud over his last days in the country which he had loved so deeply, and for which he had done so much. It did not, however, detract from the value of his achievement or leave behind any personal rancor."

DID NOT LIKE MORROW'S SUGGESTION

As I was leaving the Government Public Health Building one day (it is one of the best of public buildings), where as American Ambassador I had gone to speak when a plaque in honor of John D. Rockefeller had been unveiled in appreciation of his gifts to public health in Mexico, an American who had lived long in Mexico said, "It was Mr. Morrow's opposition to the construction of this building that lost him favor in official and medical circles in Mexico."

I asked, "Why?"

He replied, "I have never heard it verified or disputed that when the Mexican Government was planning to spend a large sum on the Health Center and Building, Mr. Morrow protested that until they had paid their debt to America they ought not to invest in so costly a public building."

Their answer was to enlarge their plans to show that no outside influence could cause them to alter the policy of the government.

A MORROW BRONZE PLAQUE

A peculiar honor was given to Ambassador Morrow not long after his death. At the request of Mexican friends, as a token of affection, presented by Javier Sánchez Mejorada, President of the National Railways, a bronze plaque was placed on the Embassy. It bears the likeness of Mr. Morrow with this inscription:

DWIGHT WHITNEY MORROW

"Ambassador of the United States of America in Mexico from October 1927 to September 1929.

"He nobly fulfilled his mission, loved and understood Mexico and won the affection of the Mexicans.

"Homage from his friends in Mexico 1932.

XXVI

TWENTIETH-CENTURY UNCLE SAM

I KNEW before I went to Mexico of the warm place my old friend, Guillermo Rogers, had in the hearts of Mexicans. His Indian blood made him at home in an Indian country. He had welcomed Lindbergh to Mexico when the aviator received the greatest demonstration ever. Some credited him with making the match between Lindbergh and Anne Morrow. The Mexicans are a romantic people and love fiestas and heroes. They named a school after Lindbergh; they toasted the bride-to-be and felt they had a hand in the lovemaking.

But the Grand Diplomat of love and aviation was Guillermo Rogers, who roped himself into an abiding place in Mexican hearts, as he had in his own America, by his wit and wise-cracks and philosophy. Dwight Morrow, Will Rogers, and Charles Lindbergh made a trinity that Calles and most Mexicans could not resist.

Will had visited in our home in Raleigh and often expressed his admiration for my wife, telling us that in her spirit and humour and poise she reminded him of his sister. This story illustrates the inimitable Will Rogers:

After dinner in our Raleigh home my wife excused herself for not going to hear him at the auditorium because her son had just returned from the hospital and she did not feel that she could leave him. But later, learning of his mother's purpose, Josephus telephoned for a taxi and hurried her to the auditorium. She arrived late and, as she was going down the aisle to her seat, Will espied her. He stopped in the middle of his act, dislodged his chewing gum, and called out to her: "Come in, Mrs. Daniels, Come in. We have a seat for you near the front." As, quite embarrassed, she walked to her seat escorted by the usher, Will, turning to the audience, said, "Folks, I'll tell you why Mrs. Daniels is late. I took supper with her and she had to stay home to wash the dishes."

Will had intended to come to visit us at the Embassy, even if he couldn't bring another Lindbergh. Unable to come, he wrote the following characteristic letter (June 27, 1933):

"Dear "Uncle Joe" Ambassador, and Ambassadoress

"Well of course you wouldent be hearing from me if I dident want something. But I have been pretty good and havent bothered you for quite a while. But I did something which I never did, or dont do, at all and that was to give a letter of introduction, and I want to beat it there with this apology. One of our studio officials, a very good friend of mine for many years, his daughter I think is going there for a short course at your University, and her mother is with her, so I promised him I would give them a letter to some one down there. Well I used to have a lot of friends down there, but when I went back after the last revolution I had picked the wrong side, and I dident know a soul. So I had to make good with em, so I am giving them one to you. Hope it wont be too much bother. She is a very nice person.

"I been wanting to get down there myself and see you all. In fact I may blow in any time. I love it down there, and I bet you folks do. You seem to be doing a fine job. You have not only kept them from jumping on us, but you have kept them from jumping on themselves. Do you stay in the city all time, or do you go down to "Corn-e-vaca". (spelled wrong but sounds right).

"Your old friends the Democrats are about to make name for themselves up here. They have surprised even themselves. They dident know they was that good. If they would just keep out of conferences they may last, but it takes a strong administration to live through a conference. If I was President I wouldent even confer with my tailor.

"Well I sho wish you good luck, and hope you like it there. Ask Mrs. Daniels how she remembers all those diplomatic Bohunks names when she gives a dinner. I would hang tags on some of those Chinese, Nicaraguans, San Salvadorians, and Apaches.

"Well one thing you cant get any notes from home, Moley has gone, and poor Cordell (I am afraid he has been gone since March 4th).

"Yours.

"WILL ROGERS."

I wrote him, inviting him to come down, and added the following:

"I had by grapevine telegraph a story from Washington which is one of the best I have heard of late. I cannot use it, for you know an Ambassador cannot think or say anything without submitting his thought or words to the State Department for approval. But here is the story, which you can use or throw in the waste basket:

"A little while ago when George Creel was in Washington Huey Long was introduced to him, and, with the Louisianan's usual desire to be different from anybody else, he said: 'Oh, Mr. Creel. Yes. I am very glad to see you, I have read some of your writings and I will say to you that they are rotten. Doesn't it surprise you for me to say that?'

"Creel turned to Long and said: 'No, that does not surprise me. I did not suppose you could read.'"

I had another like letter from Will Rogers who said:

"I want you and my main friend down your way (Mrs. Daniels) to say hello to Mrs. Ned Wortzel and her daughter, to say hello to them, take the flag and bail 'em out of any devilment they get into. This lady's husband is the one I work for at this moving picture business. It's them that's kept me from going to Raleigh, North Carolina, every year and shaking down your townsfolk. So you or some of your gang see that they don't get in the bull ring while the bull is still there.

"Yours with best wishes which you don't seem to need."

Later when Charlie Curtis, as told in another chapter, came down representing a shady client—a medical quack who had a radio unlicensed, I wrote Will:

"It is reported that your Indian cousin, Charles Curtis, is coming down here as a representative of Dr. Brinkley. I do not know how true it is, but if he should come, you might be here to pair with him, you represent the people and Charlie his Kansas constituent. Of course this is confidential, or *entre nous,* or just between friends."

Above, Ambassador and Mrs. Dwight Morrow, with Charles Lindbergh and their daughter Anne. *Below,* Plutarco Elías Calles, when President of Mexico, and Ambassador Morrow at a fiesta.

Above, Pueblo Indian delegates attending the Inter-American Conference on Indian life, are entertained at the Embassy. *Below*, Ambassador and Mrs. Daniels attend an Indian Congress.

Will telegraphed:

"Tell Curtis howdy. Don't let them vote static out of radio. That's the best thing in it. If your Conference is not better than London, kindly push all delegates in bull ring next Sunday.

"(Signed)—Guillermo Rodríguez
alias
"Will Rogers"

Will knew how the Mexicans liked him and he reciprocated the feeling and had it in his mind to come to see "my best friend down there"—my wife—and make the Embassy and all Mexico happy. Not long before he went on his fatal flight to Alaska, he sent me word that if I'd give him a rain check on the invitation he'd come down soon.

Soon after, he died. When I visited his wife in California, she told me that she had a strange feeling about the trip on which he was killed: "It was the only time in my life I wished Will not to go on a flight. Will sensed my fear, and said, 'Wiley and I will be as safe in the plane and in Alaska as if I were at home.' But I could not dispel the premonition and recalled it when the sad news came."

Knowing of our friendship with her husband, Mrs. Rogers sent us a photograph of Will. It has a place of honor on our mantel, and is the most perfect likeness I have seen of any man. It appears in this volume.

In the years that have passed, I have felt, as have millions of his countrymen, a sense of personal and public loss. We have had nobody to take his place who could shoot folly as it flies, show up stuffed shirts, and hit the nail on the head with such precision, and thus help to guide the thinking of his countrymen. He won the thanks of his generation. I always think of him as a model Uncle Sam, a wise and "homey" philosopher.

XXVII

ARE DIPLOMATS "SACRED" PERSONS?

As soon as I was appointed I set about trying to learn something about the history of diplomacy, the status of a diplomat, and what was expected of an Ambassador. And so I consulted my friend, David C. Mearnes, director of the Reference Department of the Library of Congress, who furnished me heavy tomes by erudite writers, from which I learned that it was an old calling, a little lower than the angels. In a test case in South America it was held that "a diplomat is a sacred person." Cicero said: "The inviolability of an Ambassador is protected both by divine and human laws; they are sacred." Dr. James Brown Scott, President of the Institute of International Law, said: "Machiavelli had the view that morality had nothing to do with the affairs of nations, and that nations were to be governed by their own interests."

Brunnus held that Ambassadors could claim the right of inviolability "only so long as they behaved themselves." "Diplomats may trace their ancestry to divine lineage, the angels or messengers of God," says Graham H. Stuart.

"SENT ABROAD TO LIE FOR HIS COUNTRY"

There are many other definitions by writers and statesmen. One, which was used in the era when a diplomat was supposed not to be truthful and straightforward, was: "He is an official sent abroad to lie for his country." That definition was in the back of the mind of Bismarck who, when instructing a class of young diplomats about to be sent to foreign countries, is said to have given them the following as his last admonition: "Lastly, gentlemen, I must admonish you never, no matter what may be the temptation, to depart from the truth. Always and everywhere you must stick to the truth." But before dismissing them, the old German autocrat added, "And then nobody will believe you."

MR. DOOLEY'S DEFINITION

I then turned to one of my chief mentors, Mr. Dooley (Finley Peter Dunne). When George Harvey, famed for wearing knee-breeches and for telling the British that the United States "entered the war to save its skin," was serving in London, Hennessey asked Mr. Dooley, "What is an Ambassador?" To which Mr. Dooley replied, "An Ambassadure, Hinnesey, is a man that's no more use abroad than he would be at home."

A BRITISH DEFINITION

A Britisher at the head of a mining company in Mexico in 1913, when there was discussion about Wilson's refusal to recognize Huerta, said that Wilson should follow the accepted rule of diplomacy. Asked what it was the Britisher said: "Diplomacy is the financial promoter and guard of financial interests of the country and the citizens of the country for which the diplomat is acting—it is to utilize the mistakes or weakness of the country to which they are accredited as opportunities for acquiring advantages for investments of their own government or its nationals. This has always been the national British concept and method for its diplomats and consular officials."

In his *Requirements for Success in Diplomacy* Howard Nicholson, a British diplomat, among other things enumerated these: "Concentrate less upon comparative ethics and more upon the problem of human behavior at periods when humanity is strained.... Should possess foresight, obduracy, a faculty for insisting upon the most inconvenient processions, charm, immense curiosity, courtesy, truthfulness, sobriety on all fitting occasions, capacity for enduring long dinner parties, a complete sterilization of all human vanity."

As I read the long catalogue, I recalled that the Indiana poet had defined the requirements of an editor in this question: "Can he be all and do all with cheerfulness, courage, and vim?" I had succeeded fairly well as a country editor without meeting those prescribed tests, and I thought I'd chance an assignment as a "Shirt-Sleeve Ambassador" without measuring up to the standards prescribed.

AMBASSADOR MORROW'S JOKE

Mr. Morrow was, in the old term used by career men, a "Shirt-Sleeve Diplomat," in that he went to his post from his law office and banking house without training and service up the grades. He would have retorted in kind as he did by calling career men "cookie pushers with the milk of Groton still on their lips." He invented this witty catechism for his family:

> "Question: 'Do you know what an Embassy is?'
> "Answer: 'The home of the dodo.'
> "Question: 'And who is a dodo?'
> "Answer: 'The dodo is somebody who is dead but doesn't know it.'"

RIGHTS AND PRIVILEGES

Having exhausted these authorities to assure myself of what was expected of a Shirt-Sleeve Ambassador newly appointed, I later discovered that Dr. Harlow S. Person, author of *Mexican Oil,* notes that there has been a change from "the classic days when diplomacy —more or less secret—was largely confined to the exchange of views between monarchs usually represented by their heads of foreign relations departments," to "the beginning of a diplomacy based on enlightened global national interest" with "the introduction of the skill of experts in matters involving controversy."

PROFESSIONAL AND SHIRT-SLEEVE DIPLOMATS

Beyond all these views and definitions, however, in the bright lexicon of career officers in the Foreign Service there are only two kinds of Ambassadors: (1) Those who come from the ranks, having made a profession of diplomacy; (2) Those chosen outside the ranks, such as politicians, statesmen, industrialists, college men, and high-brows without previous experience among the cloistered professionals. Most career men believe all ministers and ambassadors should go up by successive stages, just as Navy officers go from midshipmen to the rank of admiral. They think the appointments should be made exclusively from the professionals.

Undoubtedly long training helps in the meticulous and technical duties of the office, but it does not give broad experience in public affairs. Also it tends to make one a creature of tradition and protocol. However, I have known some professionals who added the qualities of broad statesmanship and richly deserved promotion to preside over Embassies. It would be a crime not to advance such

To Ambassador & Mrs Daniels
With sincere good wishes
Betty Rogers

Will Rogers, Twentieth-Century Uncle Sam

Ambassador Daniels, in a skit presented at the Embassy, advises diplomats to discard spats, etc., and to dress and act more like Uncle Sam. Secretary Robert McGregor is Uncle Sam and Secretary Stephen Aguirre is the old-time diplomat.

men, say, as Herschel Johnson, to mention a North Carolinian whom I had an opportunity to evaluate.

In the popular mind there are two types of Ambassadors: (1) Stuffed-Shirt and Spats Diplomats; (2) Shirt-Sleeve Diplomats.

The first go up often by seniority, and the second by political appointment. By that definition Benjamin Franklin, Thomas Jefferson, the trio of the Adams family, and other great men would be Shirt-Sleeve Diplomats because they did not go through the professional machine—and so would James Bryce, the ablest of British Ambassadors in Washington in my day—as well as other great and near-great heads of missions.

Franklin Roosevelt became President and Cordell Hull became Secretary of State, "chosen to direct the foreign policy," without diplomatic experience. But Hull's legislative experience and Roosevelt's legislative and executive experience gave them an insight into world affairs incomparably greater than that obtained by any career diplomat. The nearest to a career diplomat we have had as Secretary of State was Robert Lansing, whose vision was narrowed by adherence to precedent. Like Roosevelt and Hull, I had not been through the protocol course—experience in politics and as Secretary of the Navy was compensation for lack of technical training. But that did not take me out of the classification of a Shirt-Sleeve Diplomat. My observation and experience in Wilson's day and in the Roosevelt administration convinced me that there is need in the Foreign Service for more men with wide experience in public office who by association know the spirit and tempo of the American people—a knowledge which is lacking in many professionals.

LONG-WINDED DIPLOMATIC NOTES

I was early introduced to that bane of diplomacy—long, elaborate, didactic notes in which some diplomats take delight and which are more "for the record" and display of knowledge of precedents and international law than for clarification and prompt action. On April 29, 1933, soon after I got to Mexico, I wrote in my Diary:

"Foreign Minister Puig came to the Embassy to see me. We had a long talk on cigarettes, education, and the Economic Conference. He then gave me in Spanish a twenty-five-page note saying: 'I dictated it all myself and bring it to you as one writer to another.' It dealt with Claims. His chief concern is to secure an *en bloc* settlement in lieu of the Jarndyce-vs.-Jarn-dyce method employed for years. I promised after having it translated and digested to have a talk with him about his suggestions."

I was appalled at its length and wished it were diplomatic to blue-pencil most of it after the practice of editors. But such a suggestion from an amateur would have violated the most sacred tenets of protocol. After wading through the interminable document, with citations and history, I found that it summed up to a desire for an *en bloc* settlement which was in accord with my views. But it took reams of paper and long notes and a whole year to reach a settlement. Puig was not the only one, at that—our State Department was sometimes as verbose.

DIGS UP MORE SNAKES THAN IT KILLS

Most diplomatic note-writing digs up more snakes than it kills. It originated in an era when there was no telegraph, no cable, no wireless, and no way of quick connection between the Foreign Offices and the diplomatic representative abroad. It continues with verbosity when, if an Ambassador is worthy of trust, the matter could be discussed between him and the Foreign Minister after a telephone conversation with the home secretary. If an Ambassador is fit to be appointed as the President's spokesman in a foreign country, he ought to be entrusted with the negotiations face to face, after being made acquainted with the policy of his government. Instead, the legalistic bureaucratic officials in the Foreign Office at home often regard the Ambassador or Minister as a well-paid messenger boy and at times wish to instruct him, without consultation, to deliver a peremptory note to the Foreign Minister. When he complies, all the satisfaction he gets is that the Foreign Minister says, "Next week I will furnish you a note giving my Government's reply." And sometimes this exchange goes on interminably, without result. This is true even when not done, *à la* Lansing, "with deliberate purpose." This practice is to relegate an Ambassador to the rank of a messenger unless he is on such good terms with the Foreign Minister that he can reach an understanding before the long-winded note is read. In nine times out of ten, diplomatic notes should be relegated to a garret for outgrown garments.

NOT A MESSENGER BOY

It always irritated me to get a note saying: "You are hereby instructed to deliver the enclosed note to the Mexican Government."
I felt like replying: "A ten-cent messenger boy could do this job
as well and the Government could save $17,500 a year by engaging
his services instead of having an Ambassador on duty here." But
I was obedient to orders and, except on one or two occasions, made
delivery, though I felt sure the order did not come from the President or originate with the Secretary of State. Fortunately only a
few such orders "to deliver this note" were sent, and the Secretary
of State trusted me, believing I had enough sense to represent the
Government's policies and to speak in the President's name without
specific directions. There are times certainly when the written note
should be employed and records should be preserved, but long and
verbose note-writing has caused more wars than it has prevented.
There has often been more rattling of swords in the Foreign Offices
than in War and Navy Departments. That was seen in the year
1916 and the early part of 1917, when the State Department of the
United States was carrying us into war by note-writing, while the
Secretary of War and the Secretary of the Navy were declining to
go along with the State Department, both desiring to prevent war
as long as it could honorably be avoided.

DOES AMBASSADOR OUTRANK PRESIDENT?

In the nearly nine years I held the post of Ambassador in Mexico,
I often wished—but dared not say so—that I had been a diplomat
in the good old days when it took months for instructions to come
from the State Department—though only twice was I troubled
with instructions which I decided to forget. A good "forgettery"
should be added to the requirements of a diplomat. The only one
I completely ignored came at the time when President Quezon, of
the Philippines, was coming to Mexico as the guest of that republic. I had known him in Washington when we were comrades
in the fight for early Philippine independence. We were both Wil-
sonians. Shortly before his arrival I received the following order
from the State Department:

"In connection with President Quezon's visit, the Department
desires to invite your attention to certain facts and rulings which

have been brought to the attention of other diplomatic officers in those countries in which President Quezon has traveled since his inauguration on November 15, 1935, as President of the Philippine Commonwealth. Although under the Independence Act of March 24, 1934, a large degree of self-government has been accorded the Philippine people, the Philippine Commonwealth created under the terms of the Act *is not an independent state* and the United States still exercises sovereignty over the Philippine Islands. The President of the Commonwealth is not, therefore, entitled to honors usually accorded to a chief of state. The only official of the United States entitled to such honors is the President of the United States.

"Whenever honors are rendered to any official of the Philippine Commonwealth and the flag of the Philippines is displayed, the flag of the United States should also be displayed, in a position to the right or higher than the Philippine flag.

"Also, as a representative in Mexico of the President of the United States, you take precedence over the President of the Philippine Commonwealth."

I put that direction in my pocket and paid no attention to it, not even acknowledging its receipt. Quezon, who was regarded as the President of a Spanish-speaking republic, was the honored guest of a Spanish-speaking republic. It would have been the height of presumption for me to tell the Mexican Government that they must give me a seat higher than that of their distinguished guests. Protocol can be ridiculous. When it is, diplomats should have the sense to put courtesy above protocol. That ought to be listed among the qualifications of an Ambassador. If not, he ought to use his common sense and remember that he was a gentleman before he became a diplomat.

NO CENSORED SPEECHES

Upon the occasion of making an address shortly after my arrival in Mexico, a Secretary of the Embassy told me that it was a regulation of the State Department that a copy of every speech made must be sent to the State Department for approval before delivery. I replied that inasmuch as I never finished a speech until a few hours before delivery it would be impracticable to send it to Washington unless it was sent by wire; adding, "None of my speeches are valuable enough to pay the telegraph toll." So I never sent one in advance but always in the pouch following delivery.

Moreover I said to myself that I saw no good reason to rely upon a clerk of the State Department, unfamiliar with the situation in Mexico, to emasculate what I felt an Ambassador should say. Besides, I was commissioned as the personal representative of the President and Secretary of State, neither of whom would have either the time or inclination to read the many addresses I was called on to make. I might have escaped some criticism by sending for revision but I would have been saying nothing worth saying after the bureaucratic elimination.

Only once did I send a speech before delivery and that was when Ambassador Castillo Nájera and I were to speak on the Good Neighbor policy in the United States. I said, with some changes in phraseology and additional historical allusions, what I had said many times before. Washington approved with a few verbal changes—a waste of time!

Between April and Christmas in 1933, I made fourteen formal addresses, in addition to the one at the presentation of my credentials, to many organizations and on patriotic occasions. These were in addition to talks to clubs and brief words of welcome to scores of visitors and Mexicans who were received at the Embassy.

DIPLOMACY À LA MULE

I never thought that the Embassy would be troubled about mules. I had grown up in a cotton country where mules were essential. I saw none in Mexico until I went to the cotton-growing section of Torreón. Later, when those lands were dotated to the men who worked the land, the mule question confronted me. The former owners of the land, mostly British, wishing to save something, sold their mules to Americans, who started to take them to Texas. Then the trouble began. The Indians who had been given the land said they could not raise cotton without mules, and a heavy export tax on mules was levied by the Government—almost prohibitory. The purchasers protested that the export tax on mules made it impossible to take them into Texas. By direction of the State Department the Embassy embarked on mule diplomacy to try to get the tax removed. No success. The *Hacienda* Minister said that compensation for the mules would be made—but never said when. Cárdenas wanted the tax to be prohibitive so that the mules could be used to cultivate the land in Mexico he had dotated to the Indians.

In all matters relating to mule diplomacy I remembered the old Southern injunction: "If you go to the funeral of a mule always stand at the head."

Writing Assistant Secretary Moore, I said:

"I am ready to carry out any instructions of the Department except to approach the mule from the rear and among the staff there are no muleteers. Can the department furnish experts in mule diplomacy? If so, they should be given the old time Southern admonition:

"'You should reason with a mule;
You should never beat him
That would only heat him
You should reason with a mule.'"

Mr. Moore replied:

"It appears that according to the Mexicans the mule is all right when he stays in Mexico but becomes all wrong when he starts toward the Rio Grande. When Texas Congressmen call I will tell them that the Mexican Government is as stubborn as the mule."

CASTE AND SNOBBERY

There is need for an end of such diplomats as Emerson described as having "an aristocratic bias which usually puts him in sympathy with the continental courts." The United States has been misrepresented by diplomats who had similar tendencies to speak for the privileged and wealthy classes. In America the diplomatic caste system grew up patterned on English imperialistic caste, contrary to all the boasts of British and American democracy. Some diplomats, instead of representing the aspirations of their country, have misrepresented them, and a few have been affected by a sort of class or money snobbery which has prevented the promotion of the good relations for which they were commissioned.

Referring to certain diplomats in past eras, an old-time journalist in Mexico said:

"Some come here and act as if they represented nobody in the United States except the oil, mining, steel and like monopolistic parts of the United States. Not only so, but in their social life they seem not to know they are sent to interpret their country to Mexicans and promote understanding, but to associate almost exclusively with a class that lacks touch with the Mexicans."

JOINED TO THEIR IDOLS

It would require an atomic bomb to change any old official practice. As a rule career men are "joined to their idols." Once I urged that the Embassy be enlarged and made the clearing house for all Mexican information, and made such recommendation to Washington. Instead, every consul in Mexico sends his dispatches direct to Washington and the Embassy learned about the reports afterwards. I found that the Military Attaché felt that because of instructions from the War Department he must send political and other reports having no reference to military affairs direct to Washington. This was true, to a less degree, of the Commercial Attaché. I was up against an archaic stone wall of tradition, which prevented a central clearing house in Mexico. Later the Commercial Attachés' offices were transferred from Commerce to the State Department. Unity, economy, and promptness would be advanced by making the Embassy the only governmental agency reporting to the Departments at Washington.

LAUGHING STOCK OF THE WORLD

In an address on "Diplomacy As A Career," Hugh Robert Wilson, Ambassador to Germany, said in an address at Milton Academy in 1941:

"There were notable figures in early American diplomacy, figures of which the American people are justly proud, but the great majority of our representatives abroad were men who brought little credit to the American Government and people. ... Generally speaking, they were the laughing stock of the world. The cases are rare when it is better to have an outsider."

The only "outsider" he specifically approved was Benjamin Franklin. He did not disapprove by name of such distinguished "outsiders" as John Adams, Thomas Jefferson, John Quincy Adams, James Russell Lowell, Charles Frances Adams, John Hay, Thomas F. Bayard, Whitelaw Reid, Thomas Nelson Page, John W. Foster, Walter Hines Page, Robert Worth Bingham, Robert Underwood Johnson, William E. Dodd—to mention only a few of the long list of eminent "outsiders," omitting those able ones now living.

It is a list longer than that of those able "insiders" who served with distinction. A comparison of the Shirt-Sleeve Diplomats, with the career men would utterly confute that unjustifiable statement that "generally speaking, they were the laughing stock of the world."

TOOK CROWBAR TO BREAK INTO THE DIPLOMATIC CORPS

It was not in my province but when capable young men in North Carolina wrote, thinking I could aid them to secure positions in the diplomatic service, I protested to Washington that only 19 per cent of the diplomatic staff from all the states were given to Southerners, though the law looked to division in proportion to population. New York had one hundred and eight and North Carolina only eight.

It was once said that it almost took a crowbar to force an entrance into the diplomatic ranks unless an applicant had the Groton or Harvard background or their equivalent. The result gave the North Atlantic states a monopoly in the diplomatic field, but often their representatives did not know America whole.

DRESS AND ACT LIKE UNCLE SAM

I found, indeed, some secretaries and career diplomats who, while not oiled and steeled, were more the representatives of steel and oil monopolies than they were of the American people. There is need for a change. Men should be appointed who have demonstrated ability, rather than only those who, trained in a school of diplomacy, know little of the affairs and needs of their country.

I gave expression to this in an address (September, 1940) at the Consular Conference in Mexico, attended by all the consuls in the Republic of Mexico and their wives. I urged the consuls and secretaries to eschew spats, mufflers, canes, silk hats, and formalism, and seek to act and look like Uncle Sam. In my talk I said that, as they formerly dressed and talked, they were as like the diplomatic personnel from European countries as two peas. And I added that a few were noted for being more English than their confreres representing John Bull, and more French than those of La Belle France. I added that I had heard some wanted diplomatic gold braid uniforms, which Uncle Sam would not recognize.

In order to impress this truth at a dinner to consuls, foreign service officials, and the Embassy staff and their wives, a skit was put on in the Embassy, which enforced my point. I induced Secretary Steve Aguirre to wear the old-time protocol dress—topcoat, silk hat, spats, white vest, and narrow shoes—and walk and talk like a stuffed-shirt diplomat; and, as a counterpart, I got Secretary Robert McGregor to wear the traditional Uncle Sam dress. To the amusement of the party, each played the typical part, which stressed the superiority of the American to the European dress and attitude. Among the amused spectators were two ranking officers direct from the State Department—A. M. Warren and Herbert Bursley and their wives. They said the stunts pulled off were as good as a circus.

ROOT'S MISTLETOE SUGGESTION

After the show—that word describes the acting of Aguirre, McGregor, and me—an old-time officer asked me, "Did you ever hear what Secretary Root did to the suggestion of a uniform for career men?" I had not. He said that some career officers in Washington presented a pattern of a proposed uniform for members of the Diplomatic Corps, one of them wearing it to show how it would become the officers. After looking it over, Mr. Root said, "There is one thing lacking." Asked what it was he answered, "A mistletoe should be pinned on the coat-tail." That ended the diplomatic uniform.

"I feel undressed going to a grand function dressed as a head waiter when all other diplomatic officers are distinguished by their red, purple and gold braid," said a young officer. I referred him to my speech, "Look and Act Like Uncle Sam," and to Mr. Root's suggestion. I heard no more of it.

STOPPED A CONSPIRACY

There never were more friendly and jolly comrades than the men and women who represented their countries in Mexico. They were not so serious that they did not take time out for social pleasures. There was a sort of camaraderie that made for happiness. As accredited representatives to a foreign country, they had common aims and made a delightful society of their own, mingling with each other and often with Mexican officials. As an example of the spirit of good feeling and fun that made life in another country agreeable, I quote what I wrote in my Diary (September 5, 1939):

"On Wednesday night the members of the Diplomatic Corps gave a farewell dinner to the Dean of the Corps, Ambassador Roças and Señora de Roças at Paolo's. Some seventy were present including the wives. As I succeed Señor Roças as Dean, I was asked to preside and make the address, to which Señor Roças replied. It was a very interesting party and at the conclusion I thought I would have a little fun; so I put on my badge of honorary Chief of Police of Mexico City and informed the party that news had come to me from sources I dared not ignore, that at least seven members of the Corps had entered a conspiracy to kidnap Señora de Roças before the time of her departure from Mexico, and that like information had come to me that part of the Corps were planning to kidnap Madame Goiran, wife of the French Minister. Both these ladies are beautiful and I put my hand on the head of each one of them and said: 'As the honorary Chief of Police of Mexico I will not permit the members of the Corps to conspire against these ladies; if there is any kidnapping to be done I will do it myself.' "

Part Eight

INDIANS AS GOOD NEIGHBORS

XXVIII

OLDEST AMERICANS

Every visitor to Mexico (where nearly all the people are either full-blooded Indians or are part Indian and part Spanish), seeing that Indians of some tribes have the color and eyes of the Chinese, asks the question, "Where did they originate?" I asked that question. The answer given by most educated Mexicans is that years ago they came across from Asia, which was connected by land with Alaska, and drifted down the Pacific Coast until they reached the promised land of Mexico. But there are other speculations. That and the burial place of Cuauhtemoc, last of the Aztec emperors, have long been matters of speculation. I asked questions when I reached Mexico, and in a letter home wrote of differences of opinion:

"Count Byron Kuhn de Prorok (I am informed he was plain Mr. Byron Kuhn until he bought the title of Count de Prorok), who is heralded in the papers as a professional excavator of buried cities, reports that he is returning from the States of Chiapas and Tabasco bringing six cases of fossils, which he excavated in the buried cities of those States. He says these cases will be studied by paleontologists and he states that they will prove that American races are indigenous and did not immigrate from Asia, Africa, or Europe to Mexico. He thinks that the cave man roamed the jungles of Mexico one hundred thousand years B.C. He believes at last the tomb of Cuauhtemoc, the last ruler of the Aztecs, has been located in the jungles. He says he came upon the stratified remains of the primitive man. He says that Cuauhtemoc, the last of the Aztec Emperors, was captured by the Spaniards and tortured to make him divulge the location of his great treasures. All of which is very important, as Horace Greeley used to say, if true.

"On the same day that this Count tells us that the cave man lived here one hundred thousand years B.C., Dr. Daniel Rubin de Borbolla, a Mexican anthropologist, upholds the theory that the Indians in this country migrated from Asia. He says his theory is based on the human remains in the famous Monte Alban tomb.

"In connection with Cuauhtemoc's tomb, the late Mrs. Zelia Nuttall, a well known archaeologist here, advanced the theory that the Monte Alban tomb containing all the jewels was the tomb of Cuauhtemoc, who was known to have been captured by the Spaniards south of Mexico City while he was on his way probably to Guatemala. She held this theory because so many of the jewels found represented an eagle falling, and Cuauhtemoc means falling eagle. Mr. Caso, the discoverer of the jewels, does not agree with this theory. In the days of the Aztecs there existed two orders of warriors, the 'Eagles' and the 'Tigers,' and Mr. Caso thinks the jewels of Monte Alban probably belonged to some high official of the 'Eagle' order, who had been buried in the Monte Alban tomb. Mr. Caso (who is one of the foremost archaeologists of Mexico and is now Director of the Museum here) also believes, with Mr. Borbolla, that the races on this continent originated in Asia. He believes, however, that when they reached this continent, by the way of Alaska when there was a land connection there with what is now Asia, they were in a very primitive state, so that they have been on this continent for a very long time; that at the time they came here they had hardly reached the stage of fishers and hunters, and were far from the agricultural civilization."

PROGRESS OF THE MOST BACKWARD INDIANS

The most interesting and informing day my wife and I spent outside of Mexico City in 1933 was when we saw the results of a revolution in the condition and education of Indians in the near-by State of Hidalgo. I learned so much that increased my knowledge of what education could do for the most primitive Indians that I wrote about it to President Roosevelt, knowing that he and Eleanor would share my own and my wife's enthusiasm. Here is the letter which tells a story that should live:

"December 2, 1933

"Dear Franklin:

"Knowing your deep interest in public education and your large contribution to improvement in New York State while you were Governor and Mrs. Roosevelt's active efforts in the same direction, I know you will both be inclined to envy the very interesting trip my wife and I made on Saturday.

"Thursday when Frank Tannenbaum was at the Embassy for Thanksgiving dinner, he told us a story about the progress of a group of Otomí Indians in the State of Hidalgo, which interested us.

"The Otomí Indians, very numerous, have lived in less than a hundred miles of Mexico City since Aztec days. It distresses you even now to see the shacks (one room) in which most of them still live. Formerly many of them lived under cactus plants and most primitive thatched little houses. They eked out a miserable existence, some of them finding employment at the haciendas at starvation wages and the others getting scant subsistence out of a soil which, without water, is barren. Madero came into Mexico City, accompanied by a real earthquake, as well as a political one, and the ignorant and aloof Otomí Indians never heard of what was going on, so I was told. If they heard of Huerta's murder of Madero, of the American occupation of Vera Cruz, or of the other revolutions, it meant nothing to them, and they carried on in their simple homes as usual.

"When peace came, the leader of the Otomí Indians heard that the Government at Mexico City was giving lands to the Indians. So he and a company of Otomí Indians journeyed to Mexico City, went to the head of the Agrarian Commission and said they had come to get land which they had heard was being given to the Indians.

"'Land is only set aside for Indians who have a community; you live widely apart and have no community and, therefore, under the law you can get no land,' was the answer to the application.

"The reply was, 'What can we do to become a community?'

"The sympathetic Secretary of Agriculture said, 'Build you a schoolhouse.' So they went back and built a stone schoolhouse, and then came back and were given land remote from the public roads.

"Not long afterward the child of this resourceful Indian leader became ill. He took the child to a hospital in the nearest big place, where an operation was performed (I think it was appendicitis), and the operation was successful. Returning home, the chief called the Indians of his neighborhood together and said, 'We must have a hospital here where our sick can be treated.' How? There was only one way. They must build it themselves. They set to work and, each man giving one day in the week, they completed the small stone hospital which we visited on Saturday. As you may suppose, it was simple in construction, but made of stone it is durable and clean and neat.

"The trouble in that rough section—in fact in most of Mexico —is the lack of water. They could not raise crops without water. The only water in that neighborhood was controlled by the owner of the old hacienda and it was not a large supply. 'We must have water,' said the Indian leader. How did they get it? They made pipes enough to reach the mountains and laid them so that water was brought from a long distance. This made it possible to increase their crops, and water was supplied to the hospital and the school, and will afford a supply for the homes of the one hundred and forty families served by the school at La Estancia. They have a swimming pool at the school and a beautiful lake near by.

"Then, under the inspiration of this leader, they built a road twelve miles long to connect their lands with the highway. It is a good road, too, as I can testify. They are now building stone and cement homes for the community of one hundred and forty families.

"Mr. Tannenbaum, who spent some time among the Indians when he was in Mexico before, invited us to go with him Saturday to visit this Indian school near Actópan. We left about 10 o'clock and were met at Actópan by the head of the rural schools for the Republic, and the director of the rural schools in the State of Hidalgo, and also the director of schools in the district of the school which we were to visit. This latter gentleman is director of fifty-four schools in the State of Hidalgo in this district of Actópan. The director had notified the teacher and his wife that we were coming, and also the chief Indians of the community. After we had made an inspection of the hospital, of the school, and of one of the houses which had been recently built, we were invited to dinner. The dinner had been prepared by the Indians in their homes and brought to the schoolhouse. There was a barbecued lamb as the *pièce de resistance,* and every kind of Indian food eaten by the Indians of that section. They brought it in pottery jars of Indian workmanship, and it was better prepared than any Indian food I had seen or eaten. We ate very heartily and I think too much for digestion, barely tasting the pulque. At the other end of the room the Indians who had brought all the food were served at another table. It was interesting to see how they enjoyed the food. My wife sent her greetings and thanks to their wives.

IN MEMORIAM

Bronson H. Rumsey   Daniel S. Roosevelt

Above, between Ambassador Daniels and Secretary Aguirre stands Manvilio Islas, the Indian who carried Miss Constantine on his back down the mountain when the plane crashed. *Below,* the framed picture of the two aviators killed in the crash, Bronson H. Rumsey and Daniel S. Roosevelt, which hangs in the Fraternidad School in Canonitas built in their memory. (Story on page 315.)

Above, flier Francisco Sarabia, just before taking off on his non-stop flight from Vera Cruz to the New York Exposition in June, 1939. On his way home, he was killed. (Story on page 318.) *Below,* floral wreath from the American Embassy sent to the Sarabia funeral.

There was only one other woman present, a teacher in the school.

"The schoolroom had impressionistic paintings after Diego Rivera—a long way after—giving a history of the community. First: a picture of the Indians, ragged and uncombed, without any land, working for the Spanish proprietor of the hacienda, who has his lash to make them work; then step by step the progress was depicted, as to how they got land, how they built a hospital, how they built a road, and then ended with the educational system. The painter may not have been very good, but the picture was certainly expressive of the revolution that had taken place in that community. On one side of the schoolroom were pictures, evidently made by the Indian teacher, showing the effects of alcohol on the human system. The first picture was an Indian drinking; then two Indians, after drinking too much, fighting and the policeman putting one of them in jail; and then the children, ragged because their father spent the money for pulque. I could not imagine a more impressive lesson on the evil effects of drinking than was presented in the pictures in this schoolroom.

"Later in the day we drove many miles over roads (some of which were not good) to the location of the Agricultural College of the State of Hidalgo. I was told that when Calles became President his purpose was to establish such a college in every State. Eight of them were established and this is one of them. There were over two hundred pupils. They pay nothing for education or room or board. The plan is that from the fifty-four rural schools in that part of the State the teachers select a given number of the brightest and smartest pupils from among the boys and girls who would be graduating, and they would be sent to the Agricultural College for instruction. There is a large farm connected with the college, belonging to it. The students work on this farm. There is a dairy and all sorts of agriculture indigenous to that State. They make enough on the farms to pay for half the cost of their support and education; the balance is paid by the State.

"The head of the college had spent two years in Boston and spoke English fairly well. At a signal, a bell rang and all the students, and about a hundred rural schoolteachers gathered in the chapel and the principal of the college made an address. He said: 'I will speak in Spanish because I can express myself better,' and his speech was translated. It was a very excellent speech, such as you might expect from any head of an agricultural college in our own country, telling the story of what had been done and what they hoped to do. Then I was called upon for a speech, and I told them I would follow the example of my friend, the head of the school, and speak in English because I could think better in English than in Spanish, and my speech was translated. After these exercises and after going through the school and the dairy, etc., they took us to what they call a model house. It is the type of house which the best Indians are building all through that country. It was new and white and clean. As beautiful a girl as I ever saw was our escort through the house. Her eyes shone with pride as she pointed out the *brasero* and all the fittings and equipment of the house. In the rear there was a garden with nothing in it except what is indigenous to that section, with borders of organ cactus, etc. It was a revelation and showed what education and training can do with a race of people who have been kept in more or less slavery for a hundred years and not given a 'look in.'

"The three men who were with us, the Inspector, and the leaders of education, were as nice looking men as you would find anywhere in the United States, intelligent and smart, and well dressed. They are doing here on a smaller scale exactly what McIver, Alderman, and Joyner and others did in North Carolina forty or fifty years ago in the beginning of our educational renaissance. Nobody could see what had happened here without being certain that if the revolution had done nothing else, this justified it."

MALINCHE, A MEXICAN JOAN OF ARC

As a boy I had been fascinated by Prescott's story of the Indian— the Malinche or Mariana maiden—who was the *alter ego* of Cortés. As interpreter and deserted lover of the Spanish conqueror, she made possible his conquest, but her contribution to the success of Cortés has never been fully realized in Mexico, in Spain, or elsewhere. Writing home (January 15, 1935) I said:

"We had a quiet week, with your mother and me delving into folklore and histories of Malinche. You know she was the Indian woman who was interpreter, guide, philosopher and friend to Cortés and the mother of his son. Your mother has reached the conclusion that she was a sort of Joan of Arc, and that without her aid Cortés might have failed in his conquest of Mexico.

Near here is an hacienda where Malinche lived after she was cast off by Cortés, his Spanish wife having arrived. You have rarely seen your mother so interested in anything and she wants me to help her 'do' a book or magazine article on this remarkable Indian woman who she thinks has been neglected—or misrepresented—to the glory of the male Cortés. It is an intriguing piece of Mexican history, with its romantic background.

"On Saturday she went out to Santa Monica, the hacienda given to Malinche by Cortés, and Miss Niles, who went with her, took some pictures. Malinche's bath is in a good state of preservation, as are portions of the house and the chapel and the beautiful garden. It was a royal present and gives evidence of Cortés' gratitude to Malinche. I think he probably told her, 'I would marry you, but my wife will not let me.' "

THE EARLY MEXICAN IDEA OF THE CREATION

In February, 1937, we went to the Round Table to hear Señor Manuel Cruz of the Foreign Office speak on folklore. He was reared in Chihuahua in an atmosphere of tradition and folklore. His wife was born in Greensboro, North Carolina. Señor Cruz gave the Indian idea of the creation of man as follows:

"In the beginning the Creator became lonesome and decided to create man for fellowship. He fashioned him out of clay in his own image and then put him in the oven to harden. There was too much fire in the oven, and the clay figure came out a black man. This did not suit the Creator, so he made another image and again put it in the oven to bake; but this time there was not enough fire and the figure came out very white. This did not please the Creator; so he made another clay figure and put it in the oven, and the heat was just right and this time the man came out red, an Indian. And the Creator was very happy that he had made a companion who would give him fellowship."

AMERICAN INDIANS VISIT MEXICAN INDIANS

Though only the Rio Grande separates the Indians in the United States from those in Mexico, there has been little intercourse. They spring from the same ancestors but do not speak the same language. Of the most interesting visit of Indians from New Mexico to Old Mexico I wrote home (June 9, 1941):

"On Wednesday night we had one of the most interesting and I guess one of the most unique affairs at the Embassy. There are about seventy-five American Indian students from a school in Albuquerque, N. M., here on a ten-day visit. For a year they have been saving their money to make this trip and were able to do so on their own account. Dr. Sofia Eberle, who is the Superintendent of the Indian Schools of that State, and a number of their teachers are here with them. We invited them to come to the Embassy Monday night for a buffet supper. Dr. Eberle said they had never been in such a large house and that that of itself would make it a very interesting evening for them. I think your mother enjoyed it almost more than any other party she has been to in a long time and she had everything in fine shape. You know she takes more interest in entertaining people who are not generally entertained and who are ambitious to make a way for themselves than in the ordinary social affairs. We were very much interested in these young Indians, and most of them seem to be quite intelligent. On Saturday night we went to the Palace of Fine Arts, at the request of the Department of Indian Affairs here and Dr. Eberle, to attend a performance in which these Indians gave many of their dances. It seems that there was some mix-up, for we were invited for 9:30, but a Chinese magician—I call him a sleight-of-hand man —had engaged the theatre and his performance did not end until 11 o'clock; so we did not get away from the dances until nearly one o'clock in the morning. They put on a pretty good performance, but it did not pay us for staying up so late at night. The Indian Department here gave them many entertainments and tried to show them everything, and gave them places to live in the military barracks, etc."

"CIVILIZATION IS A FAILURE"

Is civilization a failure as the road to happiness? In answer to that question I wrote (May, 1941):

"I had a very interesting call on Wednesday from three professors of the University of Michigan: Drs. Hartweg, Broadkirk, and Cantrell. Some time ago we obtained permission for them to visit the State of Chiapas and collect specimens of birds and animals for laboratory work. They have been in Chiapas for some weeks and were on their way back home. They were telling me some of their experiences.

"One day they saw a native man coming in, carrying on his back a load of salt sustained by a tump-line across the forehead. He looked different, and they talked with him. He said he had gotten the salt at some point very far away and had toted it on his back all the way to the market place. Further inquiry led them to find the following set of facts: This Indian was an orphan and had a wonderfully bright mind. Some people in Chiapas who came in touch with him felt he was too smart a boy not to be given a chance of education; so they sent him to school and afterwards he was enabled to go through the University of Mexico and graduate. While he studied he made such an impression upon a French professor that when the school was over this professor took the boy with him to Paris, thinking it would enlarge his horizon, and complete his education. After some months spent in Paris, where he graduated at the Sorbonne, this young Chiapas Indian departed for his native State, and since then has lived exactly as he did before he went to school. He gets enough salt to take to town now and then, to pay for all he needs. When someone asked him why he had returned to Chiapas, he said that he had tested civilization and found it so much a failure—that he had seen that the people of Mexico City and Paris had not been improved by education and progress, but on the contrary, were greedy and did not illustrate the virtues he had supposed they would have as educated people —that he returned to Chiapas. In view of the fact that all the educated and so-called civilized people in Europe are now employed in using all they have learned and achieved in killing each other, I am asking myself the question: Is not the Chiapas Indian right? At least, they say, he is happy and contented, and wishes nothing that belongs to anybody else. If Thomas Jefferson was right in saying that the great end of life is the pursuit of happiness, should we not all—sans education and sans so-called civilization—return to the primitive life? I submit it to your consideration. For myself, with all its evils, I believe I prefer electric light and a hot bath, and above all things the safety razor, the greatest invention for the happiness of man in the history of the world."

STORIES ABOUT PANCHO VILLA

From the first I was interested in Pancho Villa; in fact had been when I was Secretary of the Navy. One night in Washington we were at a dinner during the hard "Watchful Waiting" days, and my wife was the dinner partner of General Hugh Scott. A past master in Indian affairs, he had been sent by Wilson to make a survey of the conditions in Northern Mexico. He had spent some time with Villa and had a good opinion of his fighting ability. That was before the murder of the American engineers shocked us. General Scott had told my wife many incidents about Pancho Villa which intrigued her, and she repeated them to me later. This interested her in Villa, and when she learned his favorite song was "Adelita" (she thought it Mexican for Adelaide, which was her name, and loved it best of Mexican songs), she would call for it and say banteringly, "Villa and I have something in common, seeing that I am something of a Revolutionist."

I made it a point in Mexico to draw out Mexicans who had known him, and heard many hair-raising stories about him, some of which were doubtless true.

One Sunday in September General Juan Cabral, a Sub-Secretary in the cabinet, and other friends dined at the Embassy. General Cabral told several stories of Villa. I found them interesting and wrote home:

"Villa was one of the strangest men you ever knew. He could enthuse his followers and make them do anything. He was a good fighter. Toward children he had the tenderest heart, and yet he could kill people without the least qualm. For example, one day, he was going to a certain place with his troops and he gave orders that there should be no noise and nobody should fire a gun. Contrary to this order, one of his soldiers on top of a car fired a gun, whereupon Villa pulled out his weapon and shot the man dead. 'There was a story,' said General Cabral, 'which I cannot vouch for, but which I think is true, that on one occasion Villa said to one of his followers: "I want you to leave at once and go to a certain place." The man said: "But, General, I cannot go." "Why not?" asked Villa. "I cannot leave my wife and child." "Is that all that will keep you?" said Villa, and got into his car and rode over to the man's house and killed his wife and child and then said: "You have no excuse now, so go on." One day Villa is said to have held up a rich person and to have taken thousands of pesos from him. Once he took a payroll of a mining company (2,000 pesos) in silver dollars and gave the money to a party of children he met on the road, going to a picnic. He had no desire for money except to carry on his military operations, and he would be generous one day and shoot people to whom he was generous the next.'

"I was sorry I did not have a dictaphone so that I could have had a record of all the hair-raising stories told."

TENDER HEART AND BLOODY HAND

One of the most interesting men in Mexico was Jim Smithers, and I had many talks with him. He had been a partner of General Calles and their relations were intimate. He often was the spokesman when Calles was "The Iron Man" and after he had lost his power.

Once when he was at lunch with an American editor who desired to meet "The Colonel House of General Calles," Jim told a story which I wrote in my Diary:

"At at certain place where Villa was in command, one day when he was having a council with his staff, a weeping woman, who was almost hysterical, managed to break into the room where the conference was being held. Villa was evidently displeased that she had been allowed to enter, but as she was there he listened to her. She told him her husband was in jail and had been sentenced to be shot that day, and she had come to plead for his life. She was weeping and in great distress and Villa heard her and then said: 'Madam, give yourself no concern, I give you my word of honor as a soldier and a gentleman, the life of your husband shall be saved,' and she went out. She had not gone twenty paces from the room when Villa turned to one of his orderlies or soldiers and said: 'Rush over to the jail and have that blankety-blank-blank man shot at once. I am so tender-hearted I could not resist the appeal of his wife. The best thing to do is to shoot him quickly.' "

PRIZED PORTRAIT OF JUÁREZ

A place of honor was given in the Embassy to a portrait of Benito Juárez, often and truly called by Mexicans "the George Washington and Abraham Lincoln of Mexico." Certainly no man has lived in Mexico whose memory is so cherished by the great body of the people. In addition to other services that endeared him to the rank and file of Mexicans, his saving Mexico from becoming an Empire subservient to France when Maximilian was set up as

Emperor of Mexico, had made him beloved by all. Both my wife and I were more intrigued by that patriotic Indian after visiting Oaxaca, his birthplace. It was also the birthplace of Díaz, who ruled more than a quarter of a century. But while Oaxaca honors Juárez in his native State, the visitor would not know Díaz was born there unless someone told him. There is no memorial of the long-time ruler who started out as a patriot and ended in exile because he permitted the patrimony of his country to be possessed by foreigners. For a long time my wife sought to obtain a portrait of Juárez to hang with those of Wilson and Roosevelt in the Embassy, but without success. One day early in 1920 a gentleman called at the Embassy carrying a large package and asked to see my wife. He carried an oil portrait of Juárez, which hangs in an honored place in Wakestone, our home in Raleigh. The gift of that portrait is regarded as a priceless possession; eminent artists have pronounced it a fine work of art. Writing about it (February, 1940) I said:

> "We received a present last week from Señor Jorge Enríquez —an oil portrait of Benito Juárez, very fine and of unusual interest because it is one of the very few that were painted of him while he was President of Mexico and for which he consented to sit in person. Señor Enríquez is a close friend of President Cárdenas. He had heard some time ago that your mother was trying to get a good picture of Juárez, and he was good enough to present it to us."

INDIAN BLOOD RULES MEXICO

I knew that originally the only inhabitants of Mexico were Indians and had read their history. With the coming of Cortés and with his conquest, there was no such emigration of the Indians to the far west as in the United States. They were not nomadic and most of them were rooted to the soil. As the years passed, the blood of Spaniards and Indians mingled so that today nearly all the population is pure Indian or Mestizo. All speak Spanish except these tribal Indians in remote sections who have no written language. The Indians predominate in Mexico. A whole book could be written of my association with them, their simple virtues, their patient endurance under the Spaniards who used them to work their haciendas, and their progress in the arts and in education.

"GREATEST PROTAGONIST OF THE INDIAN"

At the first Pan American Congress held in Mexico in the Spring of 1940, John Collier, U. S. Commissioner of Indian Affairs, authority on the Indians, declared:

"No individual, public or private, in these current years, has more massively or more significantly served the Indian—and therefore—more has served all the nations of the West, and therefore more has served human justice and the spirit of mankind, than President Cárdenas has done in the six years behind. Among living men he is the greatest protagonist of the Indian."

INDIANS ARE SIMPÁTICO

My earliest understanding of the goodness of Indians, often far from the surface, came through my wife's love of Indian sarapes, Indian pottery, Indian art, which came to her from her woman's love of shopping and bargaining. She loved to go to the market, to the towns where Indians gathered with their wares. And some began to come to the Embassy, where real friendships were formed over giving and taking orders for the rare things unknown Indian artists created. Out of these contacts she learned much Indian lore, and the relations were simpático. "If you would understand the Indian," she would say, "you need only to show pleasure in what they fashion and make. They feel your friendliness and there is no chasm that is not bridged."

She loved to tell a story by Edward Verdier. She said that in essence she could duplicate it in her dealings with the Indians. Here is the story:

"For years Joe González, a short, thickset Mexican with a golden smile, mowed my lawn and kept the garden a thing of beauty. Then he was lured away by a job paying almost twice as much; my pleas and letters, even my offers to meet his new wages, had no effect.

"In my free time, I worked desperately trying to keep the weeds down and the hedges trimmed. Finally, a neighbor, Pan American consul in California, noticed my losing battle and offered to write a letter in Spanish for me to Joe González —a letter that would persuade him to come back.

"I was highly skeptical, but the day after I mailed the letter, Joe was again working in the garden. 'I glad be back,' he said, bobbing his head happily. 'I not know you write Spanish. Very nice.'

"I could hardly wait to ask my friend what magic words he had used. 'It was very simple,' he said with a shrug. 'I just wrote that the trees were bowed with grief, their leaves were falling like tears. The roses were turning their faces away from the sun and losing their sweet perfume. The birds were sad and did not sing their lovely songs, for Joe was no longer here to make the garden so beautiful.' The consul smiled. 'I felt sure he would be simpático.' "

A MEXICAN LEGEND

I had never heard of a Golden Mexican Legend which made Mexicans put the true value on a Good Neighbor, until I went to Mexico. The tradition antedated Roosevelt's proclamation of the Good Neighbor doctrine. When I ran across it, I told Mexican friends—and often repeated it in public addresses—that San Isidro must have had experiences with bad neighbors. The legend runs as follows:

"San Isidro was plowing his garden one spring day. He looked up and saw an angel, who said to him: 'The Lord wants to see you, Isidro. Come with me.' He answered that he was busy. 'I can't go now. You tell the Lord that I am late in getting my corn planted and that I'll see him when I have finished.'

"The angel retired but soon another heavenly messenger appeared in the field and said: 'The Lord wishes to see you immediately, Isidro, and directs me to say that if you do not come at once, He will send hot winds and drought that will wither your corn.'

"Isidro, dripping with perspiration in the hot sun, continued plowing, pausing to send back the message: 'I've seen hot winds and droughts many a time before. They don't bother me. I can bring water from the river. Tell the Lord I can't come now, but I will see Him when I have finished planting my corn.'

"Not long afterwards another heavenly courier with stern mien tapped Isidro on the shoulder and said: 'I am commissioned to tell you that the Lord does not like your attitude, and sends word to you that unless you come with me right now, He will send a plague of locusts to devour your corn from the top and a plague of cutworns to eat its roots.'

"Isidro did not stop plowing; but sent back the answer: 'That does not frighten me. I've had plagues before, but by use of fire and hoeing and hard work, I've harvested my crop all right. You tell the Lord I'll finish my plowing tomorrow and will see Him when my work is completed.'

"The messenger from the skies disappeared, and before the fourth messenger descended he had finished several furrows. This last angel had the appearance and bearing of authority. As he flapped his wings and walked along the furrows to keep step with the stubborn plowman, the angel spoke sternly: 'The Lord isn't going to argue with you any more, Ysidro. He commands me to tell you that if you do not come with me without a moment's delay, He will send you a bad neighbor.'

"That threat terrified San Isidro. He called, 'Whoa!' to his burro, who stopped short, and he wrapped the reins around the plow handle. The look in his eye showed that fear had taken possession of him.

" 'The Lord says unless I come He will send me a bad neighbor, does He? I cannot stand that infliction. Life isn't worth trying to live, with a bad neighbor. You tell the Lord I can stand hot winds and droughts, locusts, cut-worms, and all kinds of plagues. I can endure anything but a bad neighbor. I'll go with you right now,' and he stopped short in the middle of the row, not even waiting to unhitch the burro from the plow."

THE VIRGIN OF GUADALUPE

On every anniversary the appearance of the Virgin of Guadalupe's visit to Juan Diego (December 12) my wife and I joined the throngs that filled the "Shrine of our Lady of Guadalupe" in Mexico City. Thousands of Indians in groups walked many miles to engage in this religious festival and made obeisance to the Virgin, crawling on their knees to the altar of the beautiful church.

THE BEAUTIFUL STORY

On the morning of December 9, 1531, an Indian called Juan Diego, crossing the barren slope of Mount Tepeyac (at that time called Tepeyacac) in Mexico, heard strains of lovely music and beheld a vision of wondrous beauty. In radiant colors, and dazzling light, stood a beautiful lady. She spoke gently to him and bade him approach. When the Indian overcame his fright, the lady told him she was the Virgin Mary and asked him to tell the Bishop she wished a church built upon the spot where she stood.

Juan Diego hurried to Bishop Fray Juan de Zumarraga, who was incredulous and asked for a proof. On December 12 Juan Diego returned to the barren mount. The Virgin reappeared and sent him back to the Bishop with his *tilma,* or cloak, filled with roses which she had miraculously caused to bloom on the rocky hill. Unseen by anyone, he carried the roses to the Bishop and upon opening his *tilma* to deliver them, the image of the Virgin was found miraculously depicted upon his cloak. The sign convinced all of the sacred nature of the apparition. Great multitudes came to venerate the holy picture. The Shrine was erected and December 12 set apart as a day of religious festival in honor of Our Lady of Guadalupe. Over the main altar of the church hangs, framed, the original likeness of the Virgin.

Part Nine

TRAGEDY AND BROTHERHOOD

XXIX

KINDNESS IN TRAGEDY AT CANONITAS

In April, 1939, two young students from the United States, Bronson H. Rumsey and Daniel S. Roosevelt (a nephew of Mrs. Franklin Roosevelt), flew down to Mexico in Mr. Rumsey's plane on a pleasure trip. They made a number of flights about the city, and on April 18, with Miss Tito Constantine as a guest, flew toward the Orizaba high mountain. A fog enveloped their plane in the heights near Canonitas in the State of Puebla; there was a deadly crash as it struck the mountain. The plane crashed and both the men were killed, their bodies being badly mangled. Miraculously, Miss Constantine escaped death, though she was painfully injured. An Indian, Manvilio Islas, a farm worker plowing in a field near by, hurried to the scene. He lifted the body of Miss Constantine on his back and carried her five miles over a rocky and rough trail to a home where she received every tender care until she could be removed to a hospital.

Robert McGregor, of the Embassy staff, directed to proceed to the scene of the accident, made arrangements for the transfer of the bodies to Mexico City. In his report he tells the story of how tenderly the Indians carried the body of Miss Constantine to the home where she was taken: "The Indians unfolded the tragic tale, telling how the injured girl was found in a ravine and borne by a peasant to a spot of safety and there rested against a tree; how the bodies of the two men were borne upon improvised litters and carried to a native shelter in the vicinity of the crash; how later Miss Constantine was taken on the back of the peasant, Manvilio Islas, to Canonitas and from there further in an improvised litter to another village to a hospital."

Arriving before dawn, Mr. McGregor and Consul John W. Wilson found the village Chief, Manuel Díaz, and one hundred others of the village assembled at the scene of the tragedy. The trail was rock-strewn, tortuous, and steep. Without command and in silence the bodies of the young men were covered by the Indians when they reached the scene of the tragedy. On the shoulders of Indians, taking turns, they were taken to the village church in Canonitas in the early morning, where people silently watched until the bodies could be taken for burial in their far-away homes. As the bearers of the mangled bodies entered the church, solemn bells tolled and the chief said, with tears in his eyes, "It is the tolling of sadness." An altar was constructed, decorated with garlands of vines, while at the head of each litter were lovely wild flowers. Before the little cross were wild flowers, and candles were lighted. All of this was done by the Indians. Tragedy had come to Canonitas. Honor and gratitude for their tender ministration was shown the people of Canonitas. That story which touched hearts was told in McGregor's report, which was literature.

HOW INDIANS INCARNATED THE GOOD NEIGHBOR DOCTRINE

As soon as the bodies of Rumsey and Roosevelt were sent to the United States for burial, accompanied by Secretary Stephen Aguirre, I went to Canonitas to express appreciation to the kind people for the goodness and aid at the time of the tragedy. I had previously invited Señor Islas to the Embassy and assured him of the appreciation of the families of those in the crashed plane, and told him they would not forget to show their gratitude.

Upon our arrival the bells on an eminence in the centre of the village were rung, and the people poured out of their little adobe houses (there were also many visitors) and crowded in front of the church where the bodies of the two aviators had been tenderly placed when they were brought down from the mountain after the plane had crashed. I told the assembled Indians of the gratitude of all America and thanked them for giving the most practical evidence of a good neighbor that had been seen, uniting the two countries in bonds of friendship. I repeated an Indian legend which showed that they early understood and practiced what later the leaders of the two countries had adopted.

After the ceremony I took Islas aside, told him the Rumsey family wished to show appreciation and asked him what he would like best. He first said that as he was a very poor man he would like to have a piece of land and a mule. He paused, and lifting his four-and-a-half-year-old child in his arms, said, "But most of all I would like to make certain that my son shall receive a good education." He got both.

THE RUMSEY-ROOSEVELT SCHOOL

The families of the young men wished to make some permanent token of gratitude to the kind people of Canonitas. Mrs. Franklin D. Roosevelt sent a gift and the Rumsey family consulted me as to the kind of large gift that would be most helpful and appreciated by the people of the community. I advised the building of a public school as a memorial to take the place of the small and inadequate one there. The families were glad to contribute the funds. When the modern school house was completed, I went with General Maximino Ávila Camacho, Governor of Puebla, and other influential political leaders; General Eduardo Hay, bringing a message from President Cárdenas; and others to present formally, in the name of the donors, "the House of the People," as public schools in Mexico are called. Governor Camacho accepted the building, expressing gratitude to the donors and promising that the school would be cared for as a tie between the two countries, as well as a center of public education. A very large crowd attended the dedicatory services. At the end of the assembly hall hangs a frame containing a picture of Rumsey and Roosevelt. A tablet is embedded in the wall over the main entrance inscribed to their memory. The building has four ample, light and airy class rooms, equipped with modern desks, and an assembly hall. The school was named "Fraternidad" in token of that spirit of brotherhood to which the fathers of the children of Canonitas bore ample and simple testimony.

XXX

A MEXICAN EAGLE FALLS

Mexicans were thrilled—and so were Americans—in June, 1939, when Señor Francisco Sarabia made the most spectacular non-stop flight from Vera Cruz to the New York Exposition. It was regarded in that day as second only to Lindbergh's famous flight across the Atlantic. As he was seeking to get his plane to rise in the airfield at Washington on his return, something inexplicable happened and he was killed.

A short time before leaving on that trip, he called at the American Embassy. He had a winning way. I was attracted to him and wished him a happy voyage and a safe return. I sensed he didn't know what anxiety or fear was, and after he had said "good-bye," I called him back and laying my hand on his shoulder said, "Twenty-five years ago I took my first flight and rejoice in the progress you aviators have made. But may I say this word to you?" Being answered in the affirmative, I said, "Be careful," and repeated it three times. He smilingly said he would remember that good advice.

When the news reached Mexico, the country was "like Niobe, all tears." I wrote of the feeling of Mexicans that followed his tragic death (June 12, 1939):

> "The death of Sarabia, the aviator, who had made such a fine flight from Mexico to New York, has cast a gloom over the whole country. People here were so proud that a Mexican had made a flight against such odds, and they highly appreciated the honors given him in the United States. They were looking forward to giving him a grand welcome upon his return as a hero, and when the news came that his plane had plunged into the Potomac, people were distressed and some of them beside themselves. The afternoon paper *Ultimas Noticias* printed that several members of the Mexican Chamber of Commerce had declared that Sarabia's death was due to sabotage and they were bitter in assailing Americans. This paper carried a very sensational story and it inflamed some people.

"The next morning a crowd gathered in the Zócalo, and intemperate speakers made such demonstrations against Americans that the Chief of Police sent quite a number of policemen around to the Embassy and also some motorcycle police, to guard the Embassy, thinking something might happen. About that time the news came that some of the crowd had gone out to the American School and thrown rocks through the windows of a classroom, hitting one Mexican boy but not doing much damage. The children of Sarabia attended that school. The Chief of Police sent police to the school and soon the crowd dispersed.

"He was very vigilant to protect any American places, and ever since, in front of the Chancery, there have been police, and one night some of them remained all night. General Montes was very much outraged at those who had thrown stones at the American School and held the meeting at the Zócalo. He was determined to take every precaution.

"When I called on General Hay at the Foreign Office that day he was irritated at those acts and said that his country was very grateful to President Roosevelt and all American officials for their very great kindness toward Sarabia, and he wished me to convey the thanks of his Government. He spoke in very severe terms of what he called the 'damned fools' who had created the disturbances here."

When this furore was at its height, Señora de Sarabia, awaiting the arrival of the body of her husband, which was brought with every honor in an American Army airplane, escorted by Major Caleb Haynes, son of my old friend of Surry County, North Carolina, manifested a spirit that quelled the manifestations occasioned by incorrect reports. She was received at the Embassy by my wife, whose experience in the death of her Naval brother, prepared her to extend sympathy and consolation to the widow. Señora de Sarabia wished me to convey thanks to President Roosevelt, the officials in Washington, and all Americans for the honor shown her husband in America, and for the distinguished escort that brought his body to lie in the soil of his beloved Mexico. The poise, wisdom, good sense, and gratitude of the widow of the Mexican eagle dissipated the hectic and foolish resentment of an ill-informed, excited group. This is a case where one sensible woman, rising above her grief, saved a dangerous situation.

Part Ten

HAVEN OF THE EXILED

XXXI

MEXICAN SYMPATHY WITH LIBERALS EVERYWHERE

I NDIAN to the core in blood and tradition and Spanish in culture
and nomenclature, the Mexicans held true to both. It was mainly
Indians and Mestizos, with a few Spanish liberals, that backed
Hidalgo when he rang the bell, the "*Grito*," which sounded the
death knell of what the Spanish called New Spain, out of which
developed the Mexican Republic.

I found that the revolutionary party leaders were in sympathy
with every liberal movement and showed particular interest in
Spanish-speaking liberals. I observed this first in the contest between
Fulgencio Batista and Ramón Grau San Martín in Cuba when,
having ousted the old order, Batista kept himself in power by force.

I was to learn of the Cuban situation (1933) from a fellow journalist, then Ambassador to Mexico. Ambassador Massip told me that
during the Machado regime, he regularly contributed to a leading
newspaper, and of the restraint upon writers he said:

> "I was permitted to write about anything I wished—Russia,
> Germany, science, art, or literature—provided I did not write
> about the thing I was most interested in, which, of course, was
> securing a good government in Cuba, which would bear in
> mind the interests of the plain people as well as those who own
> most of the sugar plantations and public utility companies.
> Along such lines as vitally touched Cuba's welfare, I could not
> write a word."

Of that conversation I wrote home (October 1933):

> "Mr. Massip was a strong friend of Grau San Martín and
> believed that the new government in Cuba will attract to it other
> elements and will succeed. If Ambassador Massip was in the
> United States he would belong to our 'brain trust' and would
> be a stout champion of Roosevelt, whom he admires very much.
> He spoke about the disclosures in the Senate investigation of
> how certain American bankers had enriched themselves at the
> expense of Cuba by the sale of bonds to their customers, always

protecting themselves. He thinks that there is much rottenness in the bond deals between the Cuban Government and American bankers, and hopes that all will come out well."

Mexican leaders were as heartened, when Roosevelt cut the ties that denied Cuba full independence by annulling the Platt Amendment, as were the Cubans. They were depressed when Batista ousted Grau San Martín. I shared the view of the Mexican officials. To show how they feared intervention in any Pan American country and how deeply they felt, I quote from my Diary (1933):

"Wednesday night, just as I was sitting down to supper, I received a call from the Department of Foreign Relations asking me to come down at once. I did so and found Dr. Puig very much disturbed by some telegrams he had received from the Mexican Embassy in Washington, which seemed to indicate that President Roosevelt was to intervene in Cuba under the Platt Amendment. Dr. Puig had sent a very strong telegram to Mr. Hull, saying that he hoped there would be no intervention and particularly telling him that he (Dr. Puig) knew about the five men that composed the new Cuban government, and he thought they would be able to preserve order. Any suggestion of sending Marines into Latin American countries stirs the people of Mexico as nothing else could do. There is a feeling that the 'Colossus of the North,' as they call the United States, is so powerful that it could dominate if it chose to do so, and there is always a fear that if they send Marines into one country, it may spread, and Latin American independence and territorial rights may be placed in jeopardy.

"Later at the Brazilian Embassy I found out that all the Latin American diplomats were deeply interested in the Cuban situation, and without exception they feared and were much opposed to intervention in Cuba.

"Most of them told me that intervention by the United States in Cuba would strain, if not break, the friendly relations between the United States and Latin America. One or two actually thought that if it was necessary to intervene, the Montevideo Conference, which now promises to be so fruitful, would fail. One or two of them, indeed, thought it ought to be called off if intervention occurred. They are acting together with Dr. Puig in the hope that they can help the authorities in Cuba to restore order so that there will be no necessity for invoking the Platt Amendment.

"I assured the troubled Pan Americans that Roosevelt was only concerned to aid in a difficult situation in Cuba, and that they need not fear intervention in that or any other country as long as Roosevelt was in the White House."

OLD ROYALISTS DISSENTED

Before Franco came to power, Spain was represented in Mexico by a distinguished journalist and diplomat, Álvarez del Vayo. We became great friends. But while the Mexican Government was in sympathy with him and with the republican government in Spain, the small group of Spaniards in Mexico who clung to the old order were bitter against the expulsion of the King. This was impressed on me at a dinner party during the Radio Conference. My partner was a charming lady, whose mother had been a lady-in-waiting to the Queen of Spain. When I said I regretted the report that the Ambassador might not return to Mexico, she said with icy coldness, "I do not know the Ambassador from Spain to Mexico."

Later I learned that her father was exiled with the King and lived in a chateau in France. She told me that she had five children and taught them all herself, which was hard work. I wanted to ask her why she didn't send them to the public schools but sensed that a public school was anathema to all Spaniards who had been near the throne.

She showed no enthusiasm until I told her that my friend, Claude Bowers, American Ambassador to Spain, had written me of the magnificent palace in which he lived in Madrid—saying that the nobleman who owned it was glad to rent it to him at a reasonable sum because, being used as the American Embassy, it was assured protection. She brightened up then and said the widow of the nobleman lived in Mexico. Her description of the special room containing works of the old masters and of the gardens was given with an enthusiasm that for the moment made her feel she again dwelt in marble halls. She asked me pointedly if it wasn't "better to have a King who had a sense of responsibility than the new irresponsible rulers without background."

TWO CUBAN PRESIDENTS VISIT MEXICO

I was glad to have a talk (in March, 1934) with Grau San Martín, who, after he had been defeated for President of Cuba by the Batista forces, visited Mexico. I found him a scholarly man, measuring up to the standards I had felt he incarnated when I had hoped he would win in Cuba. Upon arrival he had severely criticized the United States, alleging it was dominated by international bankers and saying that most of the land belonged to American sugar corporations. The Foreign Office deplored his use of Mexico as a place to criticize the United States. He also said that "Cuba must follow Mexico and see that the people have land."

Later, when Reyes Spíndola, the Chargé d'Affaires in Cuba, returned to Mexico (March, 1934) I asked him about the situation. He said, "If Grau San Martín were to land in Havana now, 50,000 people would welcome him to power. He will be elected President after the turmoil is over. Grau San Martín is of the same type as Madero—an honest, sincere idealist—but lacks experience in dealing with men."

In one respect Spíndola was a prophet for "after the turmoil was over" Grau San Martín became President of Cuba.

When the Cuban President Batista came to Mexico with all honors, I recalled that the Mexican officials had been sympathetic (and so had I) with Grau San Martín, though Batista was well received by Mexican officials and a formal dinner was given him at the American Embassy.

The visits of President-elect Alfonso López, of Colombia, and President Quezon, of the Philippines, were both occasions of manifestations of Latin American solidarity as well as of brotherly welcome. I had met President López, a very able man with a vision, in Washington and had invited him to dine at the Embassy when he reached Mexico.

I had known President Quezon when he was a delegate in Congress from the Philippines, and was glad to renew an association in which we had been yoke fellows for Philippine independence in the Wilson administration. At a dinner given in his honor at the Embassy, he recalled those days, spoke of his lasting regret at the failure of what he called the "Wilson League," of his approval of the New Deal policies in the United States and the Six-Year Plan in Mexico, and said his country could profit by these experiences.

He was accompanied by his wife and daughter and General Douglas MacArthur. As we had known General MacArthur when he was Chief of Staff under Secretary of War Baker, we were glad to welcome him.

"It is a pleasure to greet you, General," my wife said as we met him.

With a smile he said, "Cut out that General business and call me 'Doug' as you did in Washington days."

But she insisted on giving him his high rank.

QUEZON'S TRIBUTE TO CÁRDENAS

In his visit to Mexico in 1937 President Quezon gave this appraisal of President Cárdenas:

"General Cárdenas, in my opinion, is one of the greatest Presidents that Mexico has had. Under his efficient and honest administration, his wise and strong direction, and thanks to his great heart of human kindness, opportunities are being given to the Mexican people such as they have never had before to better their economic, cultural, and political condition ... President Cárdenas is today the strongest man in Mexico, but his power does not rest in any fear which he inspires in the Mexican people, nor does it depend upon the bayonets which he has at his command. He rose to power without shedding a single drop of blood, and no blood has been shed during his regime from political motives. His power rests solely upon the support and confidence of his people. . . . During my short stay in Mexico I also noticed the great change which has taken place in the attitude of the Mexican people toward the United States. The distrust and aversion which Mexicans formerly felt toward North Americans has disappeared, and a feeling of trust and friendship has taken its place."

But the high-water mark of Spanish-Mexican solidarity came when Franco, the stooge of Hitler and Mussolini, was placed in power. Not a great while before, Franco's brother had been a guest at the Embassy and told me he was a liberal. I guess he had a difficult time when his reactionary brother came into power, but I heard he hoped that out of it all his brother would bring good to Spain.

When the officials of the Republican government in Spain, which had driven out the King, were expelled by Franco's army, Mexico became a friendly refuge to the fleeing Spaniards. Twenty thousand found welcome in the land where the Spanish language was spoken, the people sympathizing over their cruel expulsion by those who wished to make Spain the training ground for the war Hitler was planning.

Nothing interested me more or roused my indignation so much as the driving out of the Republican government. It was a reflection upon diplomacy that every diplomat accredited to Spain, except Claude Bowers and one other, favored recognizing Franco and had no sympathy with democracy.

From the first, and throughout the Spanish war, Mexico, under the leadership of Cárdenas, adopted an attitude of unswerving support for the Spanish people in their fight for democracy and against the fascist usurpers. It supplied some ammunition and light arms to affirm its belief that the Spanish Republic, the legitimate government, had the right to buy arms anywhere in the world and to protest against the policy of non-intervention. I rejoiced that Mexico refused to recognize Franco and regretted that my country had not taken the same course.

Diplomatically Mexico always stood, in the League of Nations, as a firm supporter of the Republican cause. In both the League Council and the Assembly it voted for aid to the Spanish people, victims of fascist aggression.

After the Spanish War ended, Cárdenas opened all doors of Mexico to the Spanish Republican exiles whose situation had become critical at the outbreak of World War II. Between fifteen and twenty thousand Republicans came to Mexico, either directly from France or from other Latin American countries where they had taken refuge. Cárdenas declared on several occasions that if means of transportation had been available, he would gladly have welcomed all the Republicans living in France, not only because they were outstanding fighters for democracy, but because they would have contributed to the cultural and economic life of his country. General Ávila Camacho, who succeeded Cárdenas as President of Mexico, continued the policy of his predecessor toward the Spanish Republicans.

In a letter of June 12, 1939, I wrote:

"Thursday I had a call from Sir Richard Rees, of England. He tells me that he has been working with Cárdenas and others trying to find homes for the Spaniards who cannot return to their country. A ship bringing eighteen hundred is expected at

Vera Cruz early in the week. Negrin, head of the Loyalist Spanish Government, and Álvarez del Vayo, former Secretary of State, have been here several days talking with the President and the Minister of *Gobernación,* and Sir Richard Rees understands that they have made arrangements to receive these people and scatter them in different parts of the Republic. He says they have the money to take care of themselves and that money is being raised in England and he supposes also they will raise some in the United States.

"I asked Sir Richard if they were taking any of these people in Canada or in the British colonies. He did not know, but thought Canada would not be a very suitable place. This is a case where everybody wants to help people who are persecuted, but they want to send them to some other country. Of course, they speak Spanish and naturally most of them would prefer to be in Spanish-American countries, and if they had money and would go into agriculture, it would be a good thing for the thinly populated countries, as well as for these Spanish refugees. The trouble is that most of them who have arrived so far have been so-called intellectuals and it is not believed that they have any idea of tilling the soil."

Of one distressing incident that came to my attention, I wrote (March 18, 1940):

"On Saturday I had a call from Julio Álvarez del Vayo, who was given a passport to go to the United States. He applied for it some three weeks ago but was given the third degree at the Consulate as to whether he was a communist, and about the time the matter was under consideration at the Consulate, there came a telegram saying that he and his wife had been sentenced to imprisonment in Belgium for violating the regulations. He explained the matter to me, showing that the French authorities gave him permission to enter France, but afterwards, for some reason he did not understand, the government officials held that he had gone into France from Belgium without legal authority. My guess is that, seeing that there is a conflict between the Prieto and Negrin factions belonging to the old Spanish Republic, the enemies of Álvarez del Vayo may have been responsible for this order of imprisonment for himself and his wife. He was very much disturbed about it, particularly on account of his wife.

"Secretary Hull telegraphed that Álvarez del Vayo was not

a communist but quite the contrary, and finally he was given a passport in transit. He expects to go from New York to Chile within sixty days. He was the Spanish Ambassador here when I came to Mexico, a lifelong journalist and a very accomplished man, and we became very good friends. I do not know anybody for whom I have greater sympathy. He is a real liberal democrat and put his life in jeopardy to try to give self-government to Spain. Of course Mussolini and Hitler, by throwing their forces on the side of the reactionaries in Spain, defeated the republican government, and they had to leave Spain. There are 80,000 such refugees in France; Álvarez del Vayo and others are trying to secure homes for them in Pan American countries. Seven thousand have come here and others are expected. Discussing his own situation and that of his expatriate countrymen at a time when he had been under a gruelling upon the charge that he was a communist, he said to me, with tears in his eyes, 'I hope you will never know what it is to be a refugee.' These Spaniards who sought to have a free government in Spain remind me of Edward Everett Hale's story, 'The Man Without a Country,' although they are without a country through no fault of their own; only because they bravely and courageously sought to lift Spain out of the monarchy which had brought it down from one of the great countries of the world to one of the weakest.

"My indignation at the totalitarian countries in Europe which have destroyed the national life of the smaller countries blazes higher against the destruction of Spain than of any of the other small countries, if I can make that distinction between them. My reason is that Spain could have been saved if France and England had acted promptly, and if Spain had been saved the other small countries might not have had to fall as victims of imperialistic powers."

DISTINGUISHED SPANISH REFUGEES ASK HELP

I saw much of the officials of the Republican government of Spain who found refuge in Mexico. As throwing light upon the situation in Spain and their hopes, I wrote (November 4, 1940):

"On Tuesday I had a call from a committee representing the Spanish refugees, headed by Diego Martínez Bárrios. All of the members of this committee, who are now refugees in Mexico, were either members of the Azaña cabinet in Spain or held other high official posts in the Spanish Government until Franco's victory compelled them either to go before a firing squad or to leave the country. These gentlemen managed to get away by plane. I asked General Miaja, who was in charge of the defense of Madrid for several months, how he got out and he said by the skin of his teeth, in a plane.

"I have never been in contact with a committee of gentlemen who impressed me more favorably than this committee of Spanish officials of the Republican government of Spain, perhaps because of my deep sympathy with the Republicans and my indignation that the so-called democratic governments sat quietly by and permitted Spain to be captured by Hitler and Mussolini. They called as a committee because the news had come to them from Spain that five or six of their colleagues in the cabinet and in the government had been convicted and sentenced to death by Franco's government. They were in deep distress about it and said there were no charges against any of them except that they had supported the republican form of government and said there was no hope of saving their lives unless the governments in Pan America would unite and try to bring pressure to bear to get Franco to set aside the death sentence. They had been to see the Ambassadors and Ministers of all the Pan American countries and said they were well received and believed that they were willing to coöperate.

"What they wanted was for the United States government to make an appeal to Spain to spare the lives of these men. Whether the government at Washington would feel that it was justified in asking Spain to do something for Spaniards I do not know. Sometimes governments do request clemency, but it is generally for their own nationals. However, I feel so deeply that every effort ought to be made for these men who were to be executed for no crime except favoring the kind of government they thought was best for their country that I forwarded their petition to the State Department expressing the hope that an effectual door might be opened which would save the lives of these members of the Republican goverment."

SPANISH REFUGEES FEAR FOR ASSOCIATES

The Spanish Refugees in Mexico never lost sight of two things: (1) fear that their comrades in France would be liquidated; and (2) the expectation of returning to Spain and restoring the

Republican government which had been overthrown by Hitler and Mussolini.

I was always glad to see them. Of one visit I wrote (June, 1941):

"There are seven or eight thousand Spanish refugees in Mexico most of whom had to get out of Spain when Franco destroyed the Republican government, and I have been quite interested in them though I have not seen much of them. On Friday I had a call from Señor Serrano Pareja and a group of these refugee intellectuals—men who had held high office and professors of universities, scientists, etc. They are very much disturbed because they say many of their colleagues and others were driven out of Spain and are now in France, and they understand that Franco is to order them back to Spain and they say that means that many of them will be 'purged,' or, as the Germans say, 'liquidated,' which are words now employed to mean put out of the way. I read them a letter which I had received from Mr. Hull, to whom I had presented this matter some time ago, and gave the substance of it to them in writing, showing why we could not compel the protection of these people, but that our government would do anything it could to aid these unfortunate people. I have the deepest interest in them because at the time of the revolution in Spain I was in close touch with Claude Bowers, our Ambassador to Spain, who kept me informed about the situation, and who felt that the policy of France and England particularly, and our country to some extent, was a mistake. Every official in Europe of a democratic or near-democratic country who in these days did not use every ounce of power possible to uphold the Republican government of Spain under Azaña is now reaping the terrible harvest which he might have prevented. Spain was the training-ground for the Hitlers and Mussolinis, and until recently there have been leaders in Britain who thought they could buy Franco, forgetting that he was already owned soul and body by the totalitarian countries, and it came out last week that England had lent him 12,000,000 pounds, believing that they could thereby prevent his giving permission to the Nazis to go through Spain in their desire to take Gibraltar."

If there was a stupid diplomacy, it was in the attitude of democratic countries during the revolution in Spain.

Mexican support for the Spanish Republic took a new turn in

August, 1945, when Dr. Juan Negrin and Señor Julio Álvarez del Vayo went to Mexico City to negotiate an accord with other Republican leaders to reëstablish the Spanish Republican institutions in exile. After conferences with President Camacho and General Cárdenas, Dr. Negrin and Señor Álvarez del Vayo received assurances that the Mexican government was ready to give moral and political support to this endeavor. It extended the right of extraterritoriality to the Spanish Cortes and made the Council Room of the City Hall available to the parliamentarians for their first meeting. In an impressive gesture of amity, Mexican troops paraded in the capital to honor Señor Martínez Bárrios, who was elected provisional president of the Republic by the Spanish deputies.

A few days later the Mexican government accorded full diplomatic recognition to the new Spanish Republican government headed by Dr. José Giral and turned over to him a fund of several million pesos which it had been holding in custody.

At the meetings of the United Nations Security Council, the representatives of Mexico have been consistent and outstanding fighters against the present fascist regime in Spain and for the Spanish Republic.

XXXII

THE SCATTERED NATION

THE NUMBER of Jews in Mexico is not large, but as everywhere I found they furnished a few men eminent in the professions and successful in other callings. I heard of no anti-Semitism in Mexico, but every now and then I had letters from my friend, Rabbi Stephen Wise, reporting that Jews in Mexico were not treated as they should be, and received calls from Dr. Ulfelder, an able Jewish doctor in Mexico City, concerning the same subject. This feeling and fear increased as the power of Nazi anti-Semitism spread in the world.

When I was Secretary of the Navy the Jews felt I was the best means of approach in Wilson's cabinet—perhaps because my given name, Josephus, is Hebrew. They had the same feeling in Mexico. Writing home about the situation (January, 1938) I said:

"Quite a number of people from Southern Europe, many of whom are Jews, came into this country many years ago when Mexico was desirous of obtaining agriculturalists who would improve the farming situation. They are now threatened with expulsion. They came in as agriculturalists but most of them are said never to have seen a hoe or a farm. They have gone into business and some of the small merchants and manufacturers say that they are underselling them and ousting them. They are demanding of the Government that the Jews be expelled because they are here under false passports. I have taken this matter up with the authorities several times and find the higher officials are not in sympathy with any wholesale policy of deportation, but people who are in competition with these Jewish merchants are demanding that they be deported.

"Under the former Minister of *Gobernación* there was a secret service force that went to see all of the Jews and Syrians and demanded that they show their passports. The Jews say that some of these men were more desirous of securing blackmail than of enforcing the law.

"On Monday I called to see Minister García Téllez, and told

him that if all the people of Southern Europe, particularly the Jews, who came in as agriculturalists upon the invitation of the country, were expelled, it would be like putting a man in a canoe in the ocean without chart or compass. He said: 'Yes, it would be like sending them to sea in a ship with leaden sails.' He has stopped all of the active work of the secret service men and is making a study of the situation."

JEWS FEARED DEPORTATION

The fear among the Jewish group that they might be expelled from Mexico was constantly recurring. Writing (October 22, 1938) I said:

"I had a talk Wednesday with Mr. Wolf, a prominent Jewish merchant of Pittsburgh, who has been here for some time and is much concerned about the report that Jews are to be expelled from Mexico. I talked again to the Minister for Foreign Relations about it, and he said there was no crusade here against the Jews and would not be; but that immigrants who had come in illegally—that is, had come in on the understanding that they would be farmers and did not farm—would have to be deported under the law, whether they were Jews, Catholics, or Protestants, or what-not. The trouble about it is that if they should be deported, there is nowhere they could go. The countries from which they have come will not receive them, and if they were put on a ship at Vera Cruz to go back they would not be received on the other side. I hope the Mexicans will not apply their laws so as to work hardship and injustice on people who, once admitted, have nowhere else to go."

JEWS FOUND MEXICO IS FOR MEXICANS

Writing once more (November 9, 1938) I gave a sidelight as to the attitude of Mexicans toward the Jews in these statements:

"The Jewish situation here has been the one uppermost and most distressing of late. I had a call yesterday from Mr. Nathaniel Weyl, who had been to Michoacán and thought he could arrange for Jewish societies in the United States to put quite a number of Jews from Germany on land where they would raise fine cattle and have good dairy farms, which would not compete much with the Mexican farmers. About the time they were making this arrangement, an immigration order came out from *Gobernación* defining the number of immigrants who can come into Mexico from the various countries. Its provisions state that the aim of Mexico is to welcome only immigrants who come here to become full citizens and identify themselves completely with Mexico and its future.

"Of course, insisting that they should become Mexicans in every particular and have Mexican families was interpreted by the Jews as shutting the door to them, because as a rule Jews don't marry outside their race and faith. The goal of Mexico is 'Mexico for the Mexicans,' and foreigners who stay here a long time are expected to make themselves amenable to Mexican laws and customs and not call upon the government of their country for assistance. They hold that this puts them in a superior position to Mexicans."

CRY ON STREETS "DOWN WITH THE JEWS"

Early in 1939 several Jews from New York came to Mexico with a plan to find a place of refuge for Jews driven out of Germany. I told them they should get the approval of the Commission, headed by Myron C. Taylor, in service in London. Writing home (February 6, 1939) I said:

"Last week, after a brush between a Jew and a Mexican, a thousand people gathered on the streets and shouts of 'Down with the Jews' were heard and some windows were broken. The government people say that this and other demonstrations against permitting soldiers who have fought in the Spanish war coming to Mexico were really organized by opponents of the Cárdenas administration and was political rather than anti-Jew. However, there is undoubtedly a strong feeling here against permitting Jews who engage in trade to come into Mexico, chiefly among the small merchants who say that the Jews have come into Mexico as agriculturalists without intent to farm, and that they are taking trade from Mexicans because they undersell them."

JEWS REFUSED ADMITTANCE INTO MEXICO

When the Jews were suffering the most cruel persecution from the Nazis in 1940, those who could get transportation sought refuge in Mexico. I wrote in my Diary (September 21, 1940):

"Early in the month I had a call from Mr. William Mayer, who is president of the Jewish organization of this city. He came in connection with a telegram I had received from Rabbi Stephen Wise about some 80 Jewish refugees who had arrived by ship at Vera Cruz from Portugal, and were not permitted to land. They all had visas given them by the Mexican Consul at Lisbon, with the understanding that they were to be received. I spoke to the Minister for Foreign Relations of the unfortunate situation of these men without a country. He said nothing could be done about it; that *Gobernación* had ruled they could not be admitted, and the President had approved the view, and the Minister of that Department was adamant in his decision. He did not say that the Mexican Consul at Lisbon was corrupt, but said he had no authority to issue these visas, and he added in strict confidence that the man was no longer an official of the government. It was reported that he had received one hundred dollars apiece for each of these visas. It was a cruel thing to do. These poor people had come over believing they could land, and had to be turned away."

NAZI AGITATORS AGAINST JEWS

Diego Rivera, the celebrated artist, came, in his customary vigorous style, to the defense of the Jews and urged President Cárdenas to grant them protection and asylum. He said he was proud of his Jewish blood and attributed the opposition to Jewish immigration to "the Nazi penetration." He charged that the German residents in Mexico were forced to pay 5 to 25 per cent of their profit to the Nazis. He proved his faith by opening his house to Leon Trotsky, the most famous Russian Jew. One day he said: "It is a pity Cortés brought so few Jews to Mexico. They have won high place. The majority of the well-to-do families in Monterrey are of Jewish origin, although all have been converted to Catholicism."

Dr. Wise asked me about the Jewish population. I did not know but quoted the United Press as saying: "there are about 100,000 spread over the Republic of Mexico with three synagogues."

XXXIII

CONFEDERATES IN MEXICO

As a son of the South, with a hazy knowledge of the attempt of Commodore Matthew Fontaine Maury (the first scientist in the American Navy and inventor of the deadly electric torpedo while with the Confederate Navy), General Kirby Smith, and other Confederate leaders, to find a new homeland in Mexico, I was early interested in that adventure. From school days when my favorite study was *Maury's Physical Geography,* the life story of that Naval officer intrigued me.

As I went about Mexican States, every now and then I was invited into a home whose owner would say, "My grandfather was a Confederate soldier who after Appomattox sought to start life over again and emigrated to Mexico along with Commodore Maury and other Confederates, who thought they would have no chance to rebuild their fortunes in the South." Not a few elected to stay permanently. Some had married Mexican wives and reared their families and were happy in their new home. They remained—but most of them trekked back when Maury, following Lee's example, became Professor of Physics at the Virginia Military Institute in Lee's Lexington, Virginia, and General Kirby Smith returned to become President of Sewanee College in Tennessee.

Not long after I was at home in the Embassy, I received a call from the son of General Kirby Smith, who had married in Mexico, and had friendly relations with him and his daughter, Mrs. Edgar Skidmore. His grandson was a midshipman in the Naval Academy at Annapolis. Later I visited the Smiths at Oaxaca, and we became good friends. He talked very interestingly of the movement of which his father was a leader.

CONFEDERATE PAPERS IN MEXICO

One of my interests in Mexico was collecting the history of this romantic but futile Southern movement. I discovered that there had been a Confederate newspaper in Mexico City. Concurrently with Emperor Maximilian's appointment of Commodore Maury as Imperial Commissioner for Colonization, a Confederate weekly in English, *The Mexican Times,* was established in Mexico City. It announced that it would "advocate immigration and all constructive measures for the development of Mexico."

The editor was Henry W. Allen, a wounded Brigadier General of the Confederate Army and former Governor of Louisiana. He employed two Confederate printers. Expecting punishment by Federal authorities, he went to Mexico in 1865 with $500 borrowed money, saying, "Banishment is desirable because a banished man has the choice of places in which to dwell." When he was presented to Carlota, she said, "The poor Confederates have my heartfelt sympathy." Maximilian gave the editor a subsidy of ten thousand pesos "to popularize immigration" to what Allen called "the garden spot of the continent."

Among the advertisements was one of "The Confederate Hotel, largest two-story house in Córdoba." The chief editorial was a boost of Mexico as "an ideal home for emigrants from the United States and Europe ... who wish rich production and cheap lands." The reader was made to feel that Mexico was almost a Paradise, with "climate of eternal spring.'" There was a special appeal to those "in the United States whose fortunes have been swept away by the terrible tempest that has so long raged in that afflicted land, to those who have drunk the cup of bitterness to the very dregs." The Confederates were assured that "the fortunes which you have lost can be regained here." Stress was laid on freedom of religious worship. It closed with: "The destiny of Maximilian is fixed. The Empire is an accomplished fact." The invitation to immigrants read: "One can go to church in the morning, to a bull fight in the afternoon, and to hear an opera at night." The appeal closed with: "This is the finest country on the face of God's earth." Papers in the United States were said to "teem with accounts of people coming to the country of Mexico."

The arrival of Confederate immigrants was featured in *The Mexican Times.* It was said they were coming in such numbers that "there will be no longer any use for French soldiers to help Maximilian maintain law and order." The paper's sanctum was the headquarters for old Confederates, a sort of club where they exchanged experiences about Dixie. The paper praised monarchies, and the

Monroe Doctrine was called "a gas bag that would be punctured." It declared, "North American insolence and aggression may become insufferable," and Yankees were roasted in every issue. When subsidy from the Government was withdrawn and the Confederate paper folded up, there were only thirty-eight paid subscribers.

A new editor, at first free, and then a supporter of Maximilian, secured a number of subscribers, but when the Emperor fell and Confederate immigration was discouraged, the editor said, "Incomprehensible, unfathomable, intangible, and unnatural Mexico! Neither can foreigners, nor can yourselves understand the people that populate your land."

Alfred Mordecai, engineer of the Mexico railroad in 1866, writing to relatives in Raleigh, North Carolina, made frequent references to Maury and other Confederates in charge of Maximilian's immigration department. He wrote:

> "I showed Maury the newspaper script you sent me about Maximilian and he says it is true what is said about schools, etc. I have no doubt that he is doing all that can be done by means of decree, etc., but I have great doubt about his measures' being carried out by his Ministers, and Maury is more hopeful about immigration, especially from the United States, in consequence of the condition of things in the South, present and prospective. He reported to Bishop Hawks, of North Carolina, that a missionary bishop, or Episcopal minister would be well received.
>
> "There are Confederates here very anxious to do something, but it is difficult without capital. Many of them are on the railroad either as engineers or conductors."

THE MAURY MISSION TO MEXICO FAILED

Maury was in the Virgin Islands when he heard of the total collapse of the Confederacy, having reached there from Europe where he had been in a semi-diplomatic character. He hurried at once to Cuba, directing a letter "At Sea, May 25, 1865," to the U. S. Officer of the Gulf Squadron. He said he would consider himself "a prisoner of war, bound by the terms and conditions which have been, or may be, granted to General Lee and his officers." He was strongly advised not to return to the United States. His brother-in-law, Dr. Herndon, wrote him, "The eminent part taken by you in the cause would make you a decided object of that 'vengeance against leaders' so plainly proclaimed and so plainly visible."

The United States Minister to England, mindful of the mission of Maury abroad for the Confederacy, said to a friend, "All Maury's friends should advise him against going back to the United States yet. The feeling there is very bitter against him, and I believe the consequences of a step of that kind on his part at this time would be very unfortunate for him."

These friends doubtless knew that it was Maury's torpedoes against the Federal Fleet that "paralyzed and rendered that formidable fleet impotent during the whole time that Richmond was beleaguered by Grant with his armies and the whole Federal host on land."

As further evidence of the effectiveness of Maury's plan for harbor defenses of Southern ports, Gideon Welles, Secretary of the Navy, in his report (December 4, 1865), said that "the Navy lost more vessels by torpedoes than from all other causes whatever." Of the value of his electric torpedoes Maury wrote, "I mined the James River with them; they destroyed every Federal vessel that attempted to pass them, and kept the powerful fleet at bay during the siege of Richmond by General Grant."

Maury was as well known in Europe as in his own country and was no stranger by reputation to Maximilian when he conceived the idea after Appomattox to build what he thought would be "a new Virginia in the tropical land of Montezuma." He took this course because, as he wrote to a friend from Mexico City (August 8, 1865), he believed the victors would practice "*Vae Victis!*" and said, "The time has come and the doom is now resting upon the fair city [Richmond] and is spreading over a goodly land." He gave as his reason for going to Mexico:

"In contemplating this shipwreck of country, kinsmen, and friends, I recognized among the debris of the wreck the very materials that are required to build, upon good and solid foundations, the Mexican Empire. Never, since the Revocation of the Edict of Nantes, has such a class of people been found willing to expatriate themselves. From such a wreck Mexico may gather and transfer to her own borders the very intelligence, skill, and labour which made the South what she was in her palmy days—except her bondage.

"Though many of the negroes have been set free, and, owing to the abrupt manner of doing it, have run riot, and are afflicted with both pestilence and famine, there are many of them still true to their masters. Let us encourage the owners of these to emancipate also, and then say to the former: 'Now bargain with such as are willing to accompany you to Mexico as apprentices, bound to serve as agricultural and other laborers, until they can learn the language of the country, and make themselves acquainted with its customs and its laws, while they are being instructed in the cultivation of the staples that are new to them, and then emigrate with them to these fertile lands.' At the expiration of this term of service—say seven years —the apprentice will have earned a home as one of the rewards of his labours, and will be able to take care of himself.

"For this, I am now charged by certain of the vindictive prints of the North with 'plotting' to reopen the detestable African slave trade. The negro was set free in Mexico more than a generation ago. The Emperor, the laws, and the people are all opposed to slavery; and anyone who could be so wicked as to desire to reopen the African slave trade, might as well attempt to 'plot' with the British Government, as with this, for that purpose. Nothing seems too absurd for the sensational press of New York.

"Mexico is a country of perpetual harvests. On the way from Vera Cruz to the capital, I saw corn in all its states, from the time of its scattering by the hand of the sower, till it was gathered in the arms of the reaper. But agriculture is in a rude state. I saw them plowing with a stick, and sawing with an axe, hoeing their corn with a shovel, and grinding it with a pebble. A few of our clever farmers, bringing with them their agricultural apprentices, would give new life and energy to the country. By sprinkling the Empire with settlers of this sort, they and their improved implements of husbandry and methods of culture would serve as so many new centers of agricultural life, energy, and improvement.... You may well imagine the effect, therefore, upon the prosperity of this country, and the stability of the Empire, which would follow the introduction of a few thousands of these very laborers, guided, as they should be, by the skill and experience of their former masters...."

The scheme of a large emigration of Confederates to Mexico which was hailed with approval and support by Maximilian failed for two reasons. The first and chief reason was that it was not approved by General Lee, whose word was law with most of those who had followed the fortunes of the Confederacy. He wrote Maury (September 8, 1865):

"I look forward to better days, and trust that time and experience—the great teachers of men under the guidance of our ever-merciful God—may save us from destruction, and restore to us the bright hopes and prospects of the past. The thought of abandoning the country, and all that must be left in it, is abhorrent to my feelings, and I prefer to struggle for its restoration, and share its fate, rather than to give up all as lost. I have a great admiration for Mexico: the salubrity of its climate, the fertility of its soil, and the magnificence of its scenery, possess for me great charms; but I still look with delight upon the mountains of my native State. To remove our people to a portion of Mexico which would be favourable to them would be a work of much difficulty. Did they possess the means, and could the system of apprenticeship you suggest be established, the United States Government would, I think, certainly interfere; and, under the circumstances, there would be difficulty in persuading the free men to emigrate. Those citizens who can leave the country, and others who may be compelled to do so, will reap the fruits of your considerate labours, but I shall be very sorry if your presence will be lost to Virginia. She has now sore need of all her sons, and can ill afford to lose you."

The second reason was the failure of the Maximilian Empire in Mexico, which should have been foreseen. Long before he was executed (June 16, 1867), in July, 1866, Maximilian wrote Maury, then in London, that "it was found necessary to abandon the cherished policy of colonization of Confederates in Mexico" and in August wrote Maury congratulating him on the laying of the trans-Atlantic cable, for which "a debt of gratitude is owed to your genius." The Emperor closed his affectionate letter with: "I am pleased at announcing to you that I have appointed you Grand Cross of the Order of Guadalupe."

Maury wrote the Emperor of "the deep concern I feel for your success in one of the noblest undertakings that ever animated the human breast."

I find it difficult to understand Maury's admiration for the inept Maximilian and can account for it only by the fact that, when feeling that *"Vae Victis"* would be his portion if he returned to his Southern home, he found hospitality and honor and friendship with the Emperor and Carlota.

THE AMERICAN CEMETERY

A few of the men who followed Commodore Maury and General Kirby Smith in the track of Confederates to Mexico in the late sixties are buried in the American Cemetery. On every Memorial Day (May 30), at the request of relatives, my wife placed flowers on the grave of one who went from North Carolina.

This beautiful and well-kept cemetery, in the very heart of Mexico City, was long ago set aside by the United States War Department as the last resting place of men of the American Army who died in service or in residence in Mexico. A few other Americans are buried in this God's Acre. It is well cared for by an officer of the U. S. Army.

On every National Memorial Day, the ladies of the American Colony members of the Alan Seeger Post of the American Legion cover the graves with a wealth of flowers, and the American Ambassador, in a memorial address, pays tribute to the Americanism of the men buried there.

Part Eleven

VISITORS TO MEXICO

XXXIV

THE GOOD NEIGHBOR IN PERSON

M EXICO CITY had become in 1940, like most other great cities of the world, a scene of struggle between the forces of fascist reaction and those of democratic resistance. There never was, I think, the slightest question about the democratic loyalties of the mass of Mexicans and their government. They had given welcome to the exiled Spanish Republican government. The chief Mexican officials had been among the builders of American solidarity. The whole program of the Revolution was antagonistic to any Fascist ideas. Mexico had had all the dictators it ever wanted to see. But in 1940, nevertheless, there were those in the lunatic fringe of reaction who sought to serve Hitler in arousing antagonisms against the United States. Their efforts came to a climax, I think, with the visit of Henry Wallace; and the triumphant visit of Wallace marked with great clarity the futility of all their efforts. No man could have served so well as Wallace as a symbol of democracy to Mexicans, whose whole revolutionary program centered around the efforts of Mexico to help the common man.

But Wallace's visit was an exciting time, nevertheless. He had a cordial welcome from the time he crossed the Rio Grande until he reached Mexico City. He was accompanied from Washington by the Mexican Ambassador to the United States. Everywhere Mexicans—especially the *campesinos*—greeted him with spontaneous and ceremonial affection. I had sent representatives from the Embassy to accompany him and waited to welcome him at the Embassy. It was at the moment of his arrival there that the Fifth Column struck. It was a complete surprise but one which did no damage to Wallace or democracy.

Long before he arrived, the crowd gathered to welcome him. There was no sign that there was anything but friendliness in its mood. Fortunately, considering the secret animosity hidden in the crowd, it gathered before the Chancery, supposing he would enter the offices there. Instead, the Wallace procession came the other way and at a smart pace turned into the residence gate. Wallace was already inside before some of those in the crowds substituted stones for confetti. Neither Wallace nor I saw the sudden tumult outside the walls. Indeed, no real damage was done though Colonel Gordon H. McCoy, the military attaché, was struck with a blackjack on the shoulder. (Incidentally, he knocked his assailant down with one blow of his fist.) Outside, however, it was a brief but noisy time. Inside, I remember that the Embassy looked more like a county fair than a diplomatic establishment because many Indian farmers had brought their corn to show it to Wallace, not as visiting Vice-President, but as a world-recognized authority on the breeding of corn. During his whole visit he held a sort of corn clinic for all comers.

My good friend, Betty Kirk, able young newspaper woman, who was in the riotous crowd, told about it later. She said:

"Men and women were shouting 'Down with the *gringos* who meddle in our affairs!' A Mexican woman, with hate-filled eyes, plucked my sleeve and said eagerly, 'Are you German?' Before I could answer, she shook her fist at the Embassy and yelled: 'Death to the *gringos!*' This was the tip-off, and while the other correspondents were inside the Embassy, scrambling to get to phones, I stayed outside and watched Hitler at work in Mexico.

"Another Mexican shoved into my hands a printed sheet screaming 'People, Awake, Do Not Sleep!' and declaring that General Almazán was being held prisoner after being forced to make the declarations in which he renounced his claims to the presidency. This and other handbills which I gathered that night incited Mexicans to 'riots and more riots until we win or die.' I recognized them instantly as being the handiwork of the same agents that had kept up an anti-Jewish, anti-United States propaganda throughout the desperate summer months. Then, as I stood on that corner watching the mob being dispersed by motorcycle police armed with tear-gas guns, I saw Kurt Kaiser, the Nazi dictator of the German School, prowling among the mob. The next morning I learned that also present at the Wallace riot were Baron Karl Friedrich von Schleebrugge and George Nicolaus, alias Campicini, Hitler's top hatchet men in Mexico City."

Above, President Camacho (*left*), and Julio Álvarez del Vayo, former Spanish Ambassador to Mexico, a liberal who in Mexico headed the Spanish Republic in Exile. *Lower left,* Ramón Beteta, Under Secretary of Foreign Relations under Cárdenas; Under Secretary of *Hacienda* under Camacho; and Secretary of *Hacienda* under Alemán. (Apex Photo.) *Lower right,* Miguel Alemán, Governor of the State of Vera Cruz, 1936; Minister of *Gobernación* under Camacho; *El Presidente,* inaugurated December 1, 1946.

Upper left, Señor Abelardo Roças, Brazilian Ambassador, outgoing Dean of the Diplomatic Corps, with Ambassador Daniels who succeeded him. *Upper right,* Ambassador Daniels and Señora de Roças. *Lower left,* the Ambassador welcomes Mrs. Wallace to Mexico with an *abrazo.* Miguel Alemán is behind Mr. Daniels. *Lower right,* Ambassador Daniels, on his last day in Mexico, says good-bye to Señora de Ávila Camacho, wife of the President of Mexico.

I knew the mob was not representative of Mexico. The Mexican attitude was clearly seen in the great manifestations of popular affection for Wallace, as when, at the inauguration of Camacho, at which he represented Roosevelt, the Mexican Congress rose in a spontaneous ovation as Wallace entered the hall. Knowing how unusual such an ovation was, I was deeply pleased, as were other members of the American delegation to the Camacho inauguration, including Representative Sol Bloom, Chairman of the Foreign Relations Committee, and Representative Maury Maverick of Texas. Later both Bloom and Maverick were invited to speak at a special session of the Congress.

Throughout this visit, Wallace and his delightful wife seemed to me more threatened by the fatigue of overwhelming welcome than anything else. For Wallace the time was an almost uninterrupted succession of receptions, speeches, dinners, and other occasions. I stood the pace, but I must admit I was glad that I felt no official or hospitable duty, after such racing days, to get up when, after going to bed at midnight, he got up at seven o'clock in the morning to begin the day with several sets of tennis with his Mexican and American aides. Wallace seemed never to tire.

"There cannot be too many meetings of men of good will," he said.

And I think I never heard the Good Neighbor doctrine, to which I devoted my mission, better stated than when he addressed the Mexican Congress. "The most practical ideal for the people of this hemisphere," he said in Spanish, "is Pan-Americanism. Without hemispheric solidarity we can have no assurance of peace. Without peace, we cannot build in orderly fashion for that prosperity of agriculture, labor, and business which we so keenly desire."

His speaking in Spanish pleased his Mexican hearers and added to the enthusiasm of the applause which followed his speech. His visit was a great occasion for Mexico. It added substantially to the popularity of the United States. I rejoiced in both. But there was personal satisfaction for me—and my wife also—in the Wallace visit. Soon after Roosevelt came to the White House, I had met Henry Wallace at luncheon beside Roosevelt's desk. I made an entry in my diary at the time—"an able man." But on that visit of his to Mexico, I had a chance to feel as an individual what the Mexicans sensed as a nation—his honesty, his enthusiasm, his knowledge, his good will, and his driving power for better things for people every-where.

In so crowded a visit, there would seem to have been little time for easy friendliness and talk within the Embassy. Yet I remember the Wallace visit as one in which we did have such times. We told Henry and Iola good-bye with affection and also, when as an old Liberal I saw Henry Wallace go away with the cheers around him, with admiration for his effectiveness and meaning in the liberal politics and policies of our times.

XXXV

THE AMERICAN EMBASSY A MECCA

I N THE nearly nine years we were in Mexico City, many distinguished guests honored us by breaking bread at the Embassy. There were a score of governors, including our own Governor J. Melvin Broughton and his wife and his predecessor as North Carolina's chief executive, the Honorable O. Max Gardner and his wife. There were distinguished friends from the States who made regular visits to Mexico. We welcomed politicians and artists, business men and editors, statesmen and vacationists. We had every sort and kind, from Mrs. Woodrow Wilson to William Randolph Hearst, from Connie Mack to William Allen White, Zimbalist to Senator Robert R. ("Our Bob") Reynolds.

Indeed, far from home the Embassy in Mexico was in many ways a sort of listening post about things at home. People came from all parts of the United States—indeed, the world—to tell us stories about both home and Mexico. Sometimes the table at the Embassy seemed utterly American or almost completely Mexican. And at other times it was surrounded by a great variety of people.

One Thanksgiving Day, I remember, we extended the celebration of the American festival to guests from China, Russia, Mexico, and other countries. Of the dinner I wrote home:

"We tried to keep Thanksgiving Day as we do at home, and your mother had two pumpkins on the table and corn and wheat and oats galore. Part of these decorations had been given us at the Pan American luncheon the day before, but the pumpkins she had bought. We had as our guests people who represented almost all parts of the world: Mr. Zimbalist, the violinist, who has been here for some days on a second tour and who is very popular; he was born in Russia and became a citizen of the U. S. and married Alma Gluck the singer; Mr. Samuel Sung Young, the Minister from China; he was born in San Francisco of Chinese parents and is a very folksy and friendly man; Mr. and Mrs. Lowry of Washington, D. C.; Mr.

Lowry is here getting data to write the 'Life' of Mr. Morrow; Mr. Frank Tannenbaum, who has made a particular study of the agrarian problem in Mexico, and who brought me a copy of his new book on the *Revolution in Mexico,* which he had autographed."

MRS. WOODROW WILSON

When in Washington my wife had invited Mrs. Woodrow Wilson to make us a visit. Early in 1937 I had a telegram from Mrs. E. T. Meredith, wife of Wilson's Secretary of Agriculture, saying she and Mrs. Wilson were en route. I wired them they must be guests of the Embassy, but received no answer. Before daylight I went to the station to meet them, but they had left the train before I arrived. I visited several hotels and was about to advertise:

LOST, STRAYED OR STOLEN—WIDOWS OF PRESIDENT AND CABINET OFFICER

when I looked into the Hotel de Genève and saw these two homeless widows in a strange land sans a room or baggage. Mrs. Meredith had wired for rooms, but there was not a vacant one in the hotel. I took them to the Embassy and told them it was the only place for them in Mexico. Of their visit I wrote home (February 20, 1937):

"You know in how much esteem your mother and I have always held Mrs. Wilson, and I admire her more as I find out how whole-hearted she is. We have had opportunity to talk over many things of the old days in Washington. She knows pretty much everything that happened and has strong opinions. She has given me the inside of some matters on which I only had partial information. She is not only well-informed, but she is just in her judgments and when she thinks anyone who owed loyalty to her husband had been disloyal, she feels very deeply and expresses herself very strongly but only to her intimate friends.

"I went with Mrs. Wilson and Mrs. Meredith to Puebla. It seems to me it was the most beautiful day I have ever seen, neither warm nor cold and so clear that we could see the mountains better than I have ever seen them since I have been in Mexico. As soon as we arrived at Puebla the Governor, knowing that we were coming, had motorcycle guides to meet us, and we were entertained at lunch at the Colonial Hotel, visited the Palafox Library, the museum, the Cathedral and other points, winding up at the Santa Monica Convent. This convent was not known of until about three years ago, being hidden in the middle of a city square. It is one of the most interesting places I have ever seen.

"Some of the nuns lived there fifty or more years, never putting foot out of the convent grounds. They were buried there, and in a box they had some fifty skulls that had been found there. It is now a sort of religious museum. I suppose they have five hundred paintings—all of the Popes and Bishops and other dignitaries of the Catholic Church, and some scenes, mostly religious. There are vestments of all kinds, for the celebrating of all the sacraments, made of the most beautiful materials and the finest needlework.

"We took Mrs. Wilson and Mrs. Meredith to Xochimilco. The day was perfect. They were entranced as they felt they had gone back to the days of Montezuma. Mrs. Wilson said it was worth the long trip to see this Aztec Venice, as she noticed that the Indian boatman had artistically woven her name, "Edith," in flowers, as the name of his boat.

"In the afternoon, by special arrangement, we visited the Palace of Fine Arts to see the Tiffany curtain and painting, etc. After we had seen the curtain and the paintings in the salon on the second story, the guide started to take us to the top story to see the duplicate of Diego Rivera's paintings—the ones that were painted for the Rockefeller Center in New York. Most visitors here go to see them. To do so they have to climb very steep steps. Mrs. Wilson balked at the climb, and said, 'I'll wait to see them the next time I come to Mexico.' "

WILLIAM RANDOLPH HEARST

Of a distinguished journalist visitor I wrote home (March, 1941):

"On Monday of last week I had a call from Mr. William R. Hearst, who with two of his sons and their wives and Marian Davies and others are spending several weeks in Mexico. During the call we naturally talked about the situation in Europe and about Hitler, whom Hearst had seen, and I said I would not imagine he would be interesting. Hearst said, 'I think Hitler has some humor. I recall when I was visiting him (this was before the war) and spoke about his political party which had come into ascendancy, he said to me "You contributed to making my party strong." Astonished, I asked him what on earth I had to do with the party. He said: "Some years ago you paid me for contributing some articles to your newspapers in America and I used the check you sent to finance the party, so you are somewhat responsible for it." '

"Also in the course of the conversation Hearst referred with a smile, perhaps cynical, to his land holdings in Mexico and said, 'I suppose we will lose them. They have taken some of the land already and I suppose they will take it all, piece by piece.' However, he has been very fortunate in not having his big estate divided. He has always retained on his staff here not only American lawyers, but Mexican lawyers with a pull, and very little of his land has been expropriated in comparison with that of other Americans. To be sure, his properties in the northern part of Mexico are more suitable for grazing than for agriculture and his properties in Campeche are chicle forests and not very well suited to agriculture. However, he seemed to shrug his shoulders and to accept what was coming without a grimace."

Not long before that, one of Mr. Hearst's agents had been to see me, and I wrote in my Diary about his visit:

"On Thursday I had a call from Mr. Frank Lathrop, of San Francisco. He and his wife, who is a charming lady and good-looking, were in Carmen last spring when we were marooned there for some days, and so we saw a good deal of them. Mr. Lathrop is the representative of Mr. Hearst for all of his properties in Mexico and they are very great. He is said to own a million acres of land, one of the best gold mines in the country, and a very large acreage in hardwoods in Tehuantepec and Campeche, together with many thousand acres of chicle forests. Mr. Lathrop had come down because of some regulations of the Forestry Department of the government looking toward conservation. The owners of the chicle forests are very much perturbed about these regulations, which permit them to take out only 25 per cent of the amount they have heretofore been sending to the United States. Mr. Lathrop said that he thought he had things arranged for the balance of this year but as to what would happen next year he did not know.

" 'Do you know where all the social reforms in the United States had their birth?' he asked me. I was not able, off-hand, to trace the genesis of all social reform; so I had to answer in the negative.

" 'They were born in the brain of Mrs. Phoebe Hearst and carried on by William Randolph Hearst,' he said.

"That rather floored me. I think a person who is employed by a man like Hearst must, of course, carry on what his employer wishes him to do in order to keep his job, but I have never thought he should genuflect to the extent of endowing a person like William Randolph Hearst with all the nobler attributes. For ten minutes he undertook to prove his statement by such adulation of Hearst as you never heard. He said that Mr. Hearst had never sought to exploit any of his properties in Mexico; that his chief and whole desire was the welfare of the people whom he employed and so forth and so forth and so forth.

"About the only great things he has ever done for Mexico have been when his father persuaded the Díaz government to give him all this property or sell it to him for a song, and to print forged documents some years ago which put the President of the Republic in a very bad light and which later he was compelled to admit were forgeries."

THE KANSAS PHILOSOPHER

There were some visitors who came back to Mexico almost every year and to whose coming my wife and I always looked forward with delight. One of the chief of these was my old, dear friend William Allen White, the noted editor of the *Emporia Gazette*. As two country editors and as long-time observers of politics, he from the Republican and I from the Democratic side, we always had many stories to swap and much to talk about. We were equally devoted to Mrs. White. We somehow felt more at home when they were in Mexico. Of one conversation I wrote home:

A WIDOW'S SINGULAR DEVOTION

"We have greatly enjoyed talking with Mr. and Mrs. White, who returned to Kansas yesterday. He says that he finds that twice a year he must go away for a month's complete rest, and if he does so, he can work the other ten months as well as ever. He told me something of his history. His father was an Ohio Democrat, and during the War he sided with Vallandigham and others who opposed coercing the South and were persecuted and called 'Copperheads.' He was named for William Allen, late Democratic Governor, who was kin to Judges Oliver and Will Allen of North Carolina, a grand old Democrat. 'My mother,' said White, 'was Irish and an intense abolitionist, who was called a "black Republican" from New England. She sent herself through college and went to Kansas to teach school. My father, a doctor, moved to Kansas. She was thirty-nine years old and my father was older when they were married. I was the only living child.' Mr. White related this incident after saying that his father and mother never dared talk politics—too partisan to trust themselves; 'and when the subject was broached, I have seen my father rise from the table and walk out on the porch to keep from a discussion in which he feared he might say something he might regret,' Mr. White added."

Here is the incident, quite remarkable, which he told me:

"In 1884 when Cleveland was elected, the first Democrat since 1856 (omitting the election of Tilden)—the few Democrats in our town decided to hold a celebration and a torch-light parade. My father had died the year before. My mother reflected upon the happiness such result would have given her dead husband, went down the street, and bought dozens of big candles and illuminated every window in our house, one of the largest in the place. And then, stout Republican that she was, when the Democrats marched and shouted, my mother went into the darkened kitchen, not looking out, and cried all during the evening.

"Mr. White spoke of this as showing how love for the departed husband prompted her to do honor to his political convictions after he was dead. 'If he had been living,' he added, 'she would never have shown that consideration for his views.'"

GENERAL WANTED WINE SERVED

It was my good luck to succeed Mr. Reuben Clark as Ambassador. For one thing he is an Elder in the Mormon Church and his religion does not permit him to use or serve intoxicants. Mr. Morrow had no such scruples as some Mexicans who enjoyed his hospitality told me. I found the Embassy dry and kept it so, a principle I had followed in Washington when Secretary of the Navy. I never heard it criticized except by an American Army officer. Of his criticism and the aftermath I wrote home (July 23, 1934):

"An incident of the dinner we gave to Dr. López, the new President-elect of Colombia, who was here last week, has just been told me by Mr. Newbegin. General Johnson Hagood, the second high ranking officer of the American Army, with headquarters at San Antonio, was here on leave, and we invited him and his wife to the dinner. I had met him when I was in San Antonio, July 1st. He is a native of South Carolina. After the dinner, speaking to Major Marshburn, our Military Attaché here, and others of our staff, he vigorously declared that it was a lack of proper consideration to South America for the Ambassador to invite them to a formal dinner and not serve wine or champagne. Major Marshburn said that he could not agree, seeing that upon principle I had never served anything intoxicating when I was Secretary of the Navy at Washington and had put the order into effect whereby no wine could be served on any naval vessel.

"During the same evening Ambassador Belaúnde from Peru —a stickler for form—said to one of our Secretaries, pointing at General Hagood: 'Who is that guy over there who has the bad taste to come to the Ambassador's formal dinner to the President-elect of Colombia wearing street clothes? Doesn't he know enough of the proprieties to dress in the customary way for such an occasion?'

"A Secretary answered that General Hagood was the second highest ranking officer in the American Army, and being here on a visit had not brought any evening clothes.

"'It makes no difference,' said the irate Peruvian diplomat. 'Unless he could dress properly, he ought not to have accepted the invitation.'"

BERTITA HARDING TOOK US BACK TO DÍAZ

The best story of Maximilian and Carlota in Mexico, by one whose parents were close to the wearer of the crown of Emperor, was written by Bertita Harding. Of Mrs. Harding I wrote:

"On Wednesday night I went to the American School auditorium to hear Mrs. Bertita Harding, author of *The Phantom Crown.* It is one of the most interesting books of the Maximilian period. Mrs. Harding detailed the story of how she came to write the book. One of her parents was Hungarian and the other was German and her mother was commissioned by Franz Joseph to come to Mexico and try to secure the jewels and other things which Carlota had when she was living in Mexico as Empress. Of course that was after Carlota had gone back. Mrs. Harding said that with the assistance of the Mexican government her mother obtained many of these jewels from various sources and also a number of valuables which had been given Carlota by Napoleon and by people of Mexico. Mrs. Harding's mother carried them all to Franz Joseph, who would receive none of them except those which Carlota had before she came to Mexico, even declining to receive any of those given her by Napoleon III. Franz Joseph gave all of these other valuables to Mrs. Harding's mother and Mrs. Harding has them now and in her lectures in the United States she exhibits them."

RUSSIA NOT ALL BLACK OR WHITE

It was interesting to hear Julian Bryan, a writer and lecturer, talk about Russia. When I was in Paris the year before, Ambassador Bullitt had depicted Russia to me as so bad that it had no redeeming trait. Mr. Bryan painted a different picture, as I wrote home (August, 1938):

"Perhaps the most interesting man I have met in a long time is Mr. Julian Bryan. He is a writer and lecturer, formerly a journalist. He has been in Russia a long time and seems to know more about the Russians and to give them a more just appraisement than anybody I have seen. Most people who go through Russia think it is all white or all black. One man will tell you it is a Utopia and another man will tell you it is a Hell. Last summer when I was in Paris I was astounded at the bitterness of Ambassador Bullitt, who had recently been Ambassador to Russia. When the Roosevelt administration came in, Bullitt, who was a personal friend of Roosevelt and who had been in Europe right after World War I, and was very conversant with the situation in Europe, urged Roosevelt to recognize Russia and was very enthusiastic about the future of that country. He went to Russia where he was the only Ambassador, according to Mr. Bryan, who was received by Stalin and was regarded by the other Ambassadors as the petted child of the Russian government.

"I gathered from Mr. Bryan and from what Mr. Bullitt said, that the latter expected Russia to pay the money that had been loaned to the Kerensky government. It was not done, and

Bullitt became convinced that Russia was headed for the worst sort of communism and was hostile to the democratic governments. At any rate, after his enthusiastic advocacy of recognizing Russia, he showed the bitterest disapproval when he talked to me about it in Paris. According to him there is nothing good in Russia. According to Mr. Bryan there is much good in Russia. Its treatment of children, its schools, and many other things show Russian progress. At the same time he pointed out that in many things it was backward and there were many black things about it. He illustrated this by a number of incidents; and because he didn't think everything had to be all black or all white and seemed to know what he was talking about, I sensed that his appraisement was better and fairer than that of any other visitor to Russia."

EX-AMBASSADOR FLETCHER'S STORIES

In January, 1939, Henry P. Fletcher, who had been Ambassador to Mexico in the Wilson Administration, paid a visit to Mexico and was cordially received. We had been friends for years and we were glad to welcome him. Of his visit I wrote home:

"During the dinner he told me two very interesting stories. One was how, when he was in office either as Ambassador here or as Undersecretary, he had secured, as Mrs. Doheny's gift, the donation of the land on which the Chancery was built. He said Doheny could do nothing much with the property and it was a very good thing for the American government.

"The best incident Mr. Fletcher told was about how Pierpont Morgan gave his home in London to the American government for an Embassy. He said that the elder Morgan had made an offer but the State Department had not acted on it, and one day the younger Morgan called him up when he was Undersecretary of State and said: 'The tender of the residence in London to the government to be used as an Embassy by my father is withdrawn.' Fletcher said that the State Department was very anxious to have the building as an Embassy, and he added, 'There is a letter in the mail, signed by President Harding, accepting the tender and your withdrawal comes too late.' 'I had White House stationery at my elbow,' said Mr. Fletcher, 'so I wrote a letter to Mr. Morgan expressing great appreciation of his generous offer to give his residence to the government for an Embassy and accepted it.' I immediately took the letter over to the White House and got President Harding to sign it and rushed it off to New York. It was by this narrow margin that we saved the property for the government.' "

At the dinner given for Mr. Fletcher, among other guests were Mr. and Mrs. Knickerbocker. Mr. Knickerbocker was a Hearst correspondent who had been highly commended by Assistant Secretary of State Messersmith. I wrote of him:

"He does not have any confidence in the Good Neighbor policy and thinks the United States ought to be very rough and use the Big Stick on Mexico. Indeed, he went so far as to say that they ought to allow the oil companies and others to bring arms into Mexico to compel the government here to protect American interests. I took it from our conversation that he expects to write a series of articles and that he came here with fixed opinions, as do most correspondents, and was looking for data to justify the things he heard before he left the United States."

JAMES R. GARFIELD ASKS WHY WILSON RECOGNIZED CARRANZA

There were not many visitors to Mexico so delightful and interesting as James R. Garfield, son of the President. My wife and I were happy to invite him to the Embassy on his frequent visits. Of our conversation about the days of Carranza and Wilson's recognition I wrote rather a full story home (February 7, 1934):

"Mr. Garfield, who had interests in Mexico and still has business and clients here, told me that in the critical days here he and others sought to aid in bringing an end to the Revolution. 'We saw that Villa was impossible and it was the same with Carranza. Therefore I conferred with Secretaries Garrison and Lansing, who approved a plan to ask a score or more men in Mexico to take charge and agree upon the best man for President, who, recognized by the United States, would be able to set up a stable government. This was done, and I so reported to Lansing and Garrison. They were enthusiastic in approval, and I asked them to present it to the President and secure his approval.'

" 'You must present it to the President,' they both said. This astonished me, for I thought, of course, that Wilson would listen to members of his Cabinet rather than to a Republican outsider.

"Mr. Garfield paused in his recital and turned to me and

asked, 'Why do you suppose Wilson's two members of the Cabinet hesitated to urge the solution they approved to settle the Mexican trouble?'

"I told him that my opinion was that neither Lansing nor Garrison was in agreement with Wilson's zeal to help out the 85 per cent of Mexicans who had never had a look-in as to the government of their country; that I believed at heart they would have welcomed intervention. Conscious that Wilson did not think they were in sympathy with his ideals and policies, they did not believe Wilson would look favorably on any plan they presented. That seemed to surprise Mr. Garfield.

" 'What happened then to your plan?' I asked.

"He said, 'Lansing and Garrison said they would arrange for me to have a conference with Colonel House, who had the President's ear and confidence. It was arranged, and I went up to Wood's Hole and presented the plan with as much clearness and earnestness as I could, telling House that Carranza and Villa must be eliminated, and a group of the best Mexicans allowed to pick out the man to lead Mexico into peace and stability. Colonel House had talked to Wilson, and I gathered that Wilson would be favorable to the plan presented. I felt sure the trouble in Mexico would soon be ended by the approval of the plan. I waited but had no answer. A little later I went to New Mexico to appear in court and was almost stunned one morning when I picked up the paper and read that Wilson had recognized Carranza. Why on earth did he do it?' he asked as he paused.

"I replied that the chief reason was that the A B C representatives, whose good offices Wilson was glad to accept, came to the conclusion that Carranza had won out in his fight and was so entrenched that he could more certainly set up a stable government than anybody in sight.

"I never asked Mr. Garfield who the score or more men were who had been selected to pick out a President for Mexico, dependent upon Wilson's approval. They were doubtless men of influence who wanted peace, but I am inclined to think they would have selected a man who was more acceptable to the *Científicos* and near *Científicos* and foreign concessionaires than to the 85 per cent who had been exploited since the days of Cortés. Mr. Garfield represents big interests, having many claims against Mexico, and is hostile to the operation of the agrarian laws. I asked him if he did not think Mexico was

right in taking portions of big haciendas, and dotating them
to the men who till the soil, by paying the assessed value of
the land for taxation.

" 'That sounds all right,' he said, 'but in some States the
amount of taxes assessed by the tax assessors or tax collectors
had little relation to the real value of the property.' He therefore
did not think this assessed value was fair, even if the bonds
to be given for the land were valuable. He thinks that if an
American obtained land here, under the laws in force when
he obtained it, no matter what the cost, he should not be deprived of it except at such price as he was willing to take.

" 'What about the 100,000- to 1,000,000-acre tracts which came
through favoritism or bribery or the like?' I asked.

" 'I advised the leaders of the revolution,' he said, 'to tax oil,
land, and mines, and shut the door to future obtaining of natural
resources by favor, but told them they should not try to undo
the past; that I had advised that course in the United States
when I was Secretary of the Interior.'

"Mr. Garfield is a charming man and honest, with some
T. R. progressiveness, but he would not make a way for the
peons to get land. And that is the basis of a future stable and
prosperous Mexico."

SENATOR BOB REYNOLDS IN A CHARRO SUIT

A few men in the United States Congress took time off, as they
said, to get the truth about Mexico at first hand. Some were serious,
like Senator Chavez, of New Mexico, who was a frequent welcome
visitor. He spoke the language, and got the facts.

But there were a few like Senator Bob Reynolds, of North Carolina, a fellow Tar Heel, who spent his time in Mexico divided
between being a play-boy, having hundreds of his pictures taken in
rented caballero suits, making a speech to the Senate, in which he
was so fulsome in praise of all things Mexican that his memorandum
was used in tourist publications. I knew his measure. Nobody could
help liking friendly "Our Bob," who had gotten into the Senate
from North Carolina on a fluke and gotten himself reëlected by
voting regularly for the New Deal, though, when safely reëlected,
he became an Anti-New Dealer. He became obsessed with the
thought that he must save America from contact with other nations,
and organized a party that was a joke; it was a jumble of anti-

foreignism, Townsendism, Father Coughlin, mixed in now and then with some real Americanism, but the latter was submerged.

Senator Reynolds wired in from Vera Cruz that he was enroute to Mexico City and asked me to hold his mail. Of course we invited him and his daughter to be guests at the Embassy. (She learned more about Mexico than the Senator.) One day he did not go out of his room. I asked him what was keeping him in confinement. He said, "Come and see."

And there, lying about on the chairs and bed, were scores of postal cards containing a picture of Bob dressed in a *charro* suit. The cards were addressed to constituents in North Carolina living in a remote mountain cave, or a Buck's Swamp, or Hanging Dog, or a like address. On each card was a message of regard signed, "Our Bob."

I asked him, "What's the idea?"

He replied, "The voters back home to whom I am sending these cards never had a card or letter from a foreign country. When they get this picture with me in characteristic Mexican ornamented costume, they will prize it and say that 'though away in a foreign land, old Bob is thinking of his friends back home.' And every one of them will spread themselves to get votes for Our Bob at the next election."

One day the Senator and his daughter set off for Acapulco, a seaside resort on the Pacific. The next thing I heard was a sensational story in the paper that he and his daughter had been held up by bandits in a part of the road that was infested with robbers, and Bob had been robbed of $500 and his daughter of jewelry. Returning to the Embassy, Bob related his experience as if it had been a picnic, and in a bantering way my wife said, "Bob, there is a good advertisement for you, but nobody in North Carolina will believe you had $500."

He assented, for he loved publicity so much that he would have paid $500, if he had had it, to get the front page play-up in all the papers, even if the story troubled Mexicans, whom he had, while in their country, adulated to the skies. Upon his return to the United States, Senator Reynolds parroted the charge that Mexico "sells the petroleum that is the property of business men of the United States." He changed his tune of praise in the Mexican Senate and was critical of the policies of Mexico. He had never read Article 27 of the Mexican Constitution, which vested all subsoil property in the government. He knew nothing of the background and the exploitation of the people by the early oil prospectors, or the fact that the oil men had forfeited their pledge to abide by the Mexican laws.

When my Mexican friends, who knew I had engineered his request to address the Senate, expressed surprise that he seemed, on arrival in the United States, to convey an unfair impression of their country, I had to tell them that neither in North Carolina, nor elsewhere, did anybody, not even Bob himself for long, take Bob seriously. He beamed love of Mexico while in their country, and, on his return to the United States, oil men filled him with tales of "confiscation," and he repeated them. But the Mexicans said: "The world does not know that his mind is chameleon, and after the honor we gave him it is mortifying to have him turn on us."

I told them that in another month, with a better story, Bob might be expected to repeat his speech in Mexico that pleased the Senate. I shared, however, my Mexican friends' chagrin.

CONNIE MACK'S BASEBALL OUTFIT

By 1937 Mexico City had become baseball-conscious and I wrote home (March 6):

"We have had some very distinguished visitors, the most distinguished being Connie Mack, Manager of the Athletics. He is here with thirty or forty young men who are being trained, and they are having several games with the Mexicans. Among the boys he has here are six or eight from North Carolina and we invited them to tea yesterday at the Embassy. They were nice chaps and did credit to the State. One of them was introduced as Mr. Yount. 'Where are you from, Mr. Yount?' someone asked him, and I said, 'Mr. Yount is from Catawba County, North Carolina.' 'How did you know?' asked Mr. Yount. 'I know all the Catawba County names and know most of them are Dutch, and I expect I knew your grandfather who was State Senator from that county many years ago and was a good friend of mine,' I replied."

While I was the baseball fan in the family, a genuine friendship sprang up between the genial Connie and my wife. He dropped in often at the Embassy, and his stories about the great American

THE GOOD NEIGHBOR IN PERSON

Above, Vice-President Wallace congratulates President Ávila Camacho on December 2, 1940. Señora de Ávila Camacho is on the left. *Below,* toasting President Ávila Camacho's health. *Left to right,* Cuban Ambassador Carbonell, Ambassador Daniels, President Ávila Camacho, Vice-President Wallace, almost concealed behind Mexican Ambassador Castillo Nájera. The glasses contain champagne.

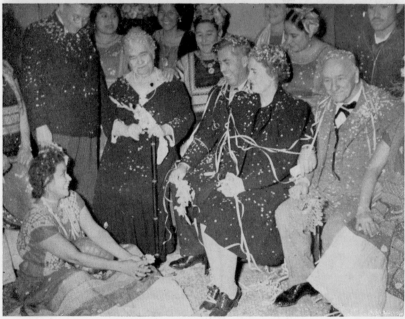

Above, Vice-President and Mrs. Wallace with Ambassador and Mrs. Daniels at the American Embassy. *Below,* a party at the Embassy, with young ladies dressed in Michoacán costumes.

game and how he came to give his life to it were interesting. He was "All American."

ARTISTS LOOK BENEATH THE SURFACE

Among the many kinds of people from every part of the world who come to Mexico—artists to catch the gorgeous colors of an ever changing sky and flowers and fauna and picturesque Indians—and scholars—and scientists—and businessmen, I met while I was in Mexico more people from distant places than in the same time in Washington City. And some exploring visitors knew more about the hinterland than residents of Mexico City, few of whom have gone beyond the plateau.

I was intrigued by the experiences of a gifted artist, Dana Lamb, and his wife, June Cleveland, with whom we became very good friends. They knew more about the Yaqui Indians in Tiburan, along the Cuatzocoales River, in Chiapas and Tehuantapec and other places hard to reach, than any Mexican except some scientists, engineers, and General Cárdenas, who, in an uncontested campaign, visited every State and learned what the people needed and wanted so that he could act with firsthand knowledge. In Mexico and the United States too many high officials think they know what to do without going out among the people.

Mr. Lamb knew all the customs and ancient practices among the tribes, some of which had no written language. For example, he found caste more fixed than in European military camps. He told how, at Miramar Beach, the dancing in the pavilion was in strictly class lines. The classes never mix, for if a man belongs to the first class and associates with the second class socially, he automatically becomes *déclassé* with his own group. Americans on first coming into the country are assumed to belong to the first class, but they, too, are subject to the rules. If they are seen to associate with what are regarded as lower classes, they immediately become social "untouchables" in the eyes of the ruling caste.

The Lambs were Enchanted Vagabonds, who in a small boat went in and out of streams and rivers, fished and talked with the people, took pictures innumerable and called their nomadic jaunts a "Great Adventure." They were the first people I knew in Mexico who had penetrated into the inner thought of the Yaqui Indians who are the most warlike of all the tribes. Even today they remain aloof. Why? Mr. Lamb told me:

"The old chief launched into the story of the Yaquis. 'They were a strong proud race,' he said, 'but the Spaniards, when they came into the country, instead of recognizing their pride and trying to understand them, did nothing but mistreat them and steal their lands. So the Yaquis struck back' His hatred of the white oppressor and the governments who had tried to crush the Yaquis was mirrored in his face as he talked. They permit no racial intermixture by marriage outside the tribe; and practise a religion that is best described as a thin veneer of Catholicism over their ancient pagan worship."

In our home in Raleigh hangs a beautiful colored drawing of the Chancery, executed by Mr. Lamb, who presented it to my wife.

XXXVI

THE CHANCERY A CLEARING HOUSE

T HE Chancery was regarded by many as the clearing house for more things than any diplomat thought could cross its threshold. Its business was to interpret America to Mexico, to give aid whenever possible to American citizens, and to illustrate good neighborliness. But many people regarded it as a carry-all, and I closed my ears to no request, keeping the door open and putting its services at the call of all who felt they stood in need of its good offices. And letters galore came not only from Mexico but from the United States.

BRIBE-GIVER AS BAD AS BRIBE-TAKER

Americans had heard so much of "greasing the palm" of officials that some thought the old methods of paying for service could be revived. One morning an American business man, representing an important company back home, called at the Embassy to get help. He said he had been trying for weeks to get a contract signed with the Mexican Government—that it was a perfectly good arrangement for both sides—but he could not get action. He said, "Last night a Mexican of prominence told me that the responsible official was waiting to be paid a sum for his private pocket, and if I would give him $5,000 in cash the contract, worth many times that amount to my company, would be promptly signed. I'd be glad to pay it and end this Mexican business and go home."

He then asked me the point-blank question: "Would you advise me to pay it?" I replied by asking him if his automobile was at the Embassy door. He said it was. I then inquired: "Have you that much money with you?" He said he had. Then I said: "Lose no time; get in your automobile and drive as quickly as you can, contact the official and bribe him."

I paused and my visitor arose as if to take this advice. After what I tried to make an impressive pause, I resumed: "Go at once and pay the amount of the bribe *provided*—provided—you are as damned a rascal as you are advised the Mexican official is. A bribe-giver is as bad as the man who takes the bribe."

My visitor, face flushed, drew back and I continued:

"It may be that the official would accept the bribe and you would get the contract, but you would be guilty of inducing him to violate his oath and barter his country's honor for money. But the chances are that the official is honest, and you would have no defense when haled into court on the charge of trying to bribe an officer.

"Our duty in Mexico—as Americans who claim to do business on the plane of honesty—is to respect the laws of Mexico and not put temptation in the way of officials. I hear some Americans speak slightingly of Mexicans and say some officials have become rich by selling what belongs to their country to foreigners. Sometimes that has occurred, but if we buy what belongs to Mexicans by bribing a dishonest official, how can we look Mexicans in the face after such criticism?"

Later word came to me that this business man on his return to New York related the conversation to his associates and said: "I thank God we have an Ambassador in Mexico who talks and acts that way."

AN AMERICAN GO-BETWEEN DISCHARGED

One day, early in my service, Mr. Thomas Lockett, Commercial Attaché, informed me of the righteous wrath of a Mexican official because he had been informed that an official or an employe of the American Consulate had told an American contractor he could expedite his business with a Mexican department of government by making a gift of a certain sum of money to a Mexican official. When this was traced down to a clerk, he was promptly dismissed, and apologies were made to the Mexican official. There had been no delay, although the money racket was that of an employe of the American Consulate.

"It's an old Spanish custom which was imported to Mexico, this rake-off for officials, and you cannot eradicate it," said an American old-timer.

"At least we can stamp out corruption in our Consulate and cooperate with honest Mexican officials who are trying to eradicate the evil and succeeding in the main," was the answer. He was incredulous.

SPANISH AND AMERICAN SWINDLERS

I had some experiences which convinced me that Barnum was right when he said a sucker was born every minute. Not a few Americans who bit at the seductive offers to get rich quick put their troubles on the door of the Embassy. My surprise was that men who had held high position in the religious and educational field could be taken in by the oldest crooked game familiarly known as "The Spanish Swindle." I will cite the two instances that gave me the most trouble:

The first dupe was a Methodist minister in California. He had come to Mexico and got in trouble by responding to this characteristic letter that was sent out to many Americans supposed to be gullible enough to think they could get something for nothing. Here is the letter that brought that preacher to Mexico to cry out his stupid cupidity, begging that no publicity be given because "it would ruin me back home":

"Dear Sir:
"A person who knows you and who has highly spoken about you has made me trust you a very delicate matter on which depends the entire future of my dear daughter as well as mine.

"I am in prison sentenced for bankruptcy and I wish to know if you are willing to help me save a sum of $285,000.00 which I have in bank bills inside of a secret place in a trunk that is deposited in a custom house in North America.

"As soon as I send you some undeniable evidence it is necessary for you to come here and pay the expenses incurred in connection with my process in order to lift the embargo on my baggage and thus recover a suit case which contains the necessary documents (a baggage check) that we need to take out the trunk that contains the cash and which is deposited in a customs house in the United States.

"To compensate you for all your troubles I will give you the *Third Part Of Said Sum.*

"Fearing that this letter may not come to your hands I will not sign my own name till I hear from you and then I will entrust you with all my secret.

"For serious reasons that you will know later please reply via air mail. I beg you to treat this matter with the most absolute reserve and discretion. Due to the fact that I am in charge of the prison's school I can write you freely and in this way.

"For the time being I am only signing 'L.'

"I cannot receive your reply directly to the prison so in case you accept the proposition please airmail your letter to a person of my entire trust who will deliver it to me safely and rapidly. This is his name and address. . . ."

Instead of gathering any part of the fabled $285,000, he found himself arrested and charged with fraudulent complicity. He appealed to the Embassy to extricate him from a position that showed he was a silly sucker. And he was not the only one. It became necessary to ask the press in the United States to expose "The Spanish Swindle" operations and to warn suckers.

The second, and the one hardest to understand, was the case in which I was called upon to secure the release of a retired American college president from charges of trying to swindle a New York slicker plying his trade. He was the ideal caricature of a professor who lives in a world of books and learns nothing practical from them. This teacher had won the regard of students and parents. Just before his retirement, the rich mother of one of his students, in gratitude, gave him a large sum of money. I am not sure whether it was $50,000 or $100,000. The sudden wealth went to his head. A New York sharker, making money by fraudulent representation, told the professor that there was a bonanza in buying hardwoods in Southern Mexico—that he could buy a tract of such land for $50,000, out of which half a million dollars could be cleared. The Professor bit—gave the slicker a large part of the money for the down payment—with the understanding that the professor would later go down, inspect the land and trees, and close the deal. On his way to see his bonanza he learned from a fellow traveller that he had been sold a gold-brick and that he had been the victim of what was worse than a Spanish swindle—a Yankee robbery. Indignant, he returned to face his deceiver, who had the professor arrested on the charge of violating his contract by refusing to pay the balance of the agreed price. It seems the professor had signed a promissory note. He was like a babe in the woods, or rather a sucker in jail—the victim, charged with being the culprit. It was all that James R. Garfield, Ohio lawyer on a business trip to Mexico, a friend of the professor, and the Embassy could do to get him out of the clutches of the crook and the law. In the meantime the professor's wife and daughter, humiliated and distressed, were in Mexico City. I never felt such pity for suffering victims of folly.

When the swindler learned that I was "on to his crookedness," he called at the Embassy and, with affected indignation, swaggeringly demanded that I protect him as an American citizen instead of taking sides with the duped professor. He said that as American Ambassador I had no right to take sides between two American citizens. When I told him the Embassy stood only to protect American citizens from their stupidity, such as the professor had shown, and from fraudulent representations, he strode out threatening to report me to Washington as refusing protection of an American citizen trying to collect an honest debt. I never heard of him again. When the Mexican authorities sought him he had vanished. Garfield saved part of the money for the professor, who, a sadder and wiser man, with his sick-at-heart wife and daughter, returned to the United States.

I never heard from the New York crook, or his Mexican partners in the hardwood swindle until sometime later he went to the home town of the duped college professor and "tried to raise trouble." When he was invited by the attorney of the professor to go into court, "where the whole affair would be aired but not to your advantage," he disappeared.

EXPECTANT MOTHER OF TWINS UNBEKNOWN TO HER

In January (1934), I wrote to my sons this example of the strangest of requests:

"Many curious letters come to the Embassy. A ten-page letter came in today from a lady in San Francisco, written in a good hand. In the course of the rambling letter, showing a mind without a rudder, she says: 'Thought transference is being used to rot us mentally and to make us ill and kill us as well. The four fundamental churches are supposed to agree that I am an expectant mother of twins, *unbeknown* to myself. Thought transference is being used to make the babies stillborn.'

"She wanted the President to order troops to give protection and tell her when and where to move in order to get rid of this

troublesome thought transference. It is beyond me to understand how she could be an 'expectant mother of twins unbe-
knownst' to her, and I have no power to give her protection.
I suppose the only thing to do is to put it up to the President.
People seem to think he can know the unknowable and un-
screw the inscrutable."

NOT AN AUTHORITY ON COCKTAILS

Of a strange request (and me a Prohibitionist) I wrote home
(February 8, 1938):

"A little while ago I had a letter from a man in Milwaukee
asking me to give him the ingredients of several cocktails which
he said were used in Mexico, and to advise him as to the relative
merits of Mexican cocktails and whether the ingredients could
be obtained in Milwaukee. I have had many requests of various
kinds since I have been in Mexico, but this one stumped me. I
had no wish to be quoted in Milwaukee as a man who was
advising as to cocktails. So, thinking that the authorities in
Washington were engrossed with serious matters and something
in a light vein might interest Franklin Roosevelt and Cordell
Hull, I sent a copy of the letter to Cordell Hull and one to the
President. Here is a copy of my letter to the President and his
reply.

"Personal.

"Mexico, January 25, 1938.

"Dear Franklin:

"I am enclosing you a copy of a letter I am writing Cordell
Hull today, making inquiry as to the duty of a diplomat in
regard to a new service requested of an Ambassador. As you are
not as staunch a prohibitionist (if propinquity makes the difference) as Cordell or myself, he may be asking your advice
before making an official ruling. Should Milwaukee citizens
continue to drink the stuff that made Milwaukee famous, or
should I encourage the use of ardent spirits by importing the
recipe for a Mexican beverage.

"If neither you nor Cordell feel capable of an answer, please
ring for Solomon. I await instructions.

"Respectfully,
(Signed) "Josephus Daniels."

"The White House,
Washington.
February 1, 1938.

"Dear Chief:

"You have raised a nice question for the career men in the State Department to answer. How could you expect mere politicians like Cordell and myself to prepare a reply?

"However, if I were in your place I would tell your Milwaukee friend, first, that if Milwaukee is to maintain its national reputation, it should stick to beer and not go in for hard liquor. Secondly, that you would get him the information about those Mexican drinks if you could but that not claiming to be an expert on cocktails you might send him the wrong directions and that this would be a disgrace you do not want to subject the Embassy to. A third undiplomatic reply might work equally well: 'Come to Mexico and try the dirty stuff yourself.'

"As ever yours,
(Signed) "F.D.R."

QUACKS AND STATIC

Mexico City was the almost constant scene of every variety of conference, official and otherwise, between Mexicans and Americans. But the first I saw was one between radio experts of both countries. Most such conferences were attended, not only by officials but by attorneys and others watching out, not for international agreements, but the interests of individual clients.

One day in 1933 former Vice-President Charles Curtis, of Kansas, called on me and commended highly Dr. Brinkley, the radio advertiser of a goat-gland operation, who had been forced to leave the United States and was operating a station just across the Mexican border.

"You know," Curtis said, "my friend and client, Dr. Brinkley, has a claim on you. He was born in North Carolina."

Patriotic North Carolinian that I am, I was not able to respond very heartily to the news that Brinkley was from my own State. Like other states, North Carolina had its share of charlatans, and its citizens were content to lose such to other States—including Bleeding Kansas.

Brinkley, however, proved to be not only a quack but a troublesome fellow in the way of any satisfactory accord at that time between the United States and Mexico on the division of radio wave-length.

Curtis' visit approximately coincided with the meeting in Mexico of the Pan American Radio Conference. It was attended by the best technicians and ablest men in communications from the whole hemisphere. Naturally, as former Secretary of the Navy, I had early been deeply interested in wireless communications, and during World War I, when its operation was a government function under the Navy, many of the important developments had been made by experts under my direction in researches financed by the government. I had felt that radio should remain a government function, and the part played by Brinkley at that time did not change my mind. His goat-gland programs, which were supplemented, in blasts across the border, by claims for a cancer cure, seemed to prove more important at that conference than the views of the radio experts.

The American delegation, headed by Octavius Sykes (a graduate of the Naval Academy in the class with my wife's brother, Worth Bagley), came to Mexico anxious to stop Brinkley from broadcasting from Mexico after he had been driven from the air in the United States. I detailed Harry Norweb, Counsellor of the Embassy, who had represented the United States at other international radio conferences, to attend the session as the representative of the Embassy.

At the conference the Mexicans insisted upon having twelve exclusive channels, including five on the border. The Americans felt that the Mexicans should have a smaller number of clear channels, with none on the border which would permit such broadcasting to the United States as Brinkley was doing. That time, Brinkley won temporarily, and the conference failed.

Among the Americans who came to see me (not including Charlie Curtis) there was a suspicion that Brinkley had paid well for his Mexican concession. Some Mexicans in high places loudly condemned the Brinkley concession and suggested that some sub-officials may have had their palms greased. Undoubtedly it was a case where a disreputable individual was successful for a time in thwarting the aims of the more enlightened men in both countries. That is an aspect of international relations—in more fields than radio—which the best diplomats sometimes encounter.

The chief purpose of the radio conference failed. But no one would have thought so when delegates were making congratulatory speeches and signing a document which had scarcely anything in it except some minor agreements in technical matters.

Why did it fail? I remember that Jim Smithers, the American partner of General Calles who had a finger—or thought he did—in every Mexican pie, gave an explanation at the time. He did not mention the possibility of graft. But he diagnosed the situation with some shrewdness.

"The Americans," he said, "came down with an impossible ultimatum which the Mexicans understood as an attempt to dictate what they should do with stations in their country. The Americans virtually demanded that Dr. Brinkley be put off the air and insisted that Mexico should have no broadcasting stations on the border that could carry messages into the United States. This demand made failure certain from the beginning."

He smiled as if he possessed all inner knowledge about Mexican affairs. "A weak or small nation is always sensitive," he said.

Part Twelve

FRIENDS IN MEXICO

XXXVII

THE AMERICAN COLONY

I WAS given two diametrically opposite pieces of advice in Washington, as I was leaving for Mexico, by officials and others who had spent some time in Mexico:

1. "Do not cultivate the American colony. Its influential leaders are representatives of big corporations who will have no sympathy with Roosevelt's New Deal, Good Neighbor policy. Their support would do you more harm than good as Ambassador Sheffield found out. He was liked by the American colony and got nowhere in negotiations with the Mexican Government."

2. "The friendship of the American colony will be an asset to your happiness and success. To be sure, some of the richest will wish you to get favors for their companies, but you will not need to follow such counsel. Most of the members are good Americans and will give you cordial hospitality and friendship if you show yourself friendly. Morrow made the mistake of ignoring the American colony too much, as Sheffield erred in thinking like those who wished to direct Mexican policies."

Shortly after our arrival, a committee of the American colony called to extend welcome from "fellow Americans" and tender a dinner, which was held at the Country Club, made festive for the occasion with more flowers than my wife and I had ever seen. The Mexican music, new to us, delighted my wife. The spoken welcome at the dinner at the Country Club was given by H. A. Basham, a leading lawyer, who presided. He said he and others had taken up their abode "in this land of opportunity and marvelous beauty, finding the Mexican people to be most hospitable and kind." He spoke in high terms of my predecessors, Morrow and Clark, and their ability to understand the viewpoint and requirements of the American government and its people, and said, "We know it to be your highest and sincerest purpose to bind still closer the friendly relations between the two countries," and in "this noble undertaking permit me to pledge to you on behalf of the American colony our most hearty coöperation and support." He quoted with cordial approval the address by President Roosevelt at the Pan American Union, and won my heart by his tribute to my wife, using prophecy when he said, "In this land of most hospitable, kind-hearted people, of perennial sunshine and beautiful flowers, we anticipate your new friends will become old friends and your love for Mexico will be second only to that of your own country."

This was the auspicious beginning of delightful association. Our mutual love of the land of our birth was stronger, I found, than our differing attitudes toward social and political questions. And nearly nine years of friendly association proved I correctly judged them.

Such a group, however, was composed of all kinds of Americans. There were simple, hard-working people among them. The colony was recurrently—if temporarily—freshened by newcomers from the North, many of them very liberal in their attitude toward Mexico and Mexicans. By and large, however, the permanent colony, as it could be seen in the American Club and other such gathering places, were just about the same sort of well-to-do people who wish to maintain the *status quo* as one would meet in a similar club in the United States. In general they were conservative—sometimes reactionary, but I always found them, as individuals if not as political and economic philosophers, men and women given to friendliness, hospitality, and kindness. As a group, as they have shown by building and maintaining the American Hospital and School and other benevolences, they are a generous and charitable people. I recorded my conversations with some of them in letters to my sons at home.

One American manufacturer surprised me by his support of the New Deal, not only in American politics but in his own plant in Mexico City. He told me with satisfaction about the situation in his factory, which later, on an inspection trip, was also reported to me by the head of the labor unions there. There were some good and interesting rules; for example, if a worker's suggestion saved money for the company, he received a share of the saving. There were other such rules. They worked well, my American friend said, and he approved the laws requiring factories to provide hospitalization and training opportunities for their employees.

This American, I regret to say, could not be regarded as typical. Of another equally prominent American in Mexico, I made a note in my Diary:

"He has not a very high opinion of any Presidents since Díaz, but said that, of them all, Obregón was the least bad. He believes that the destiny of Mexico is for our government to annex it. He thinks the writing of notes asking for payment, even the withdrawal of recognition, would be only half-way measures attended with ills and evils and that the only solution that is possible for permanency and the protection of American property here is that we should suddenly and at a number of points at the same time, take charge of Mexico. He thinks if it were done with great efficiency and suddenness there would be no effective resistance. Anything short of that, he said, would be followed by bloodshed and would be ineffective. I am quite sure that in this very frank and confidential statement to me, he voiced the feelings of many of the big American investors here. The expropriations of property have increased this feeling, although probably it was more intense in Huerta's time when Doheny and Cowdray backed Huerta. Some other Americans who are very much afraid they will lose their investments feel that if the United States would be firm and threaten to withdraw recognition that would be sufficient, but many wish for the strong hand."

AMERICAN CIENTÍFICOS AND DÍAZ

Two of the richest Americans in Mexico were George W. Cook and Harry Wright, with whom I had cordial relations. As a picture of these Americans and of a home that was quite like a museum, I wrote to my sons:

"Last night your mother and I were invited to dine with Mr. and Mrs. Harry Wright. They belong in spirit to what was called in the Díaz days the *Científicos,* who thought that a few people were born booted and spurred to ride on the backs of others. All the people present were what we would call "big business" in the United States.

"The conversation at the table largely ran upon the Morgan investigation and the action of Congress in making all debts payable in legal tender money and not in gold of a certain weight and standard of fineness. Mr. George W. Cook, who was a close friend of Díaz, and who is said to go to bed every night hoping to wake up the next morning and find Díaz back in the castle, could not find words strong enough to denounce the action of Congress about the gold payments. As to the Morgan

investigation, he considered it an outrage to smear an American
company which had done more for the world in this century
than any other one concern. Mr. Wright said the investigation
of Morgan would do more harm to the United States than anything that had happened to it.

"Of course I listened for a while, but I could not be silent
when they were making Bolshevists and almost anarchists out
of the present Congress, particularly since I was in perfect harmony with what Roosevelt and Congress has been doing. Two
of the guests were Englishmen. They did not say much, but
they seemed to chime in with what Mr. Cook and Mr. Wright
thought. Whereupon, hoping to get some division in the Anglo-
Saxon alliance in Mexico, I quoted the decision rendered by the
highest court in Great Britain, which affirmed the action in that
country of making debts payable in the legal tender money of
the country, and not in gold as heretofore. Your Englishman
is a great believer in the laws of his own country and its courts,
and very justly so, because I expect the courts there as a whole
render justice more evenly than anywhere else in the world,
and I noticed these two Englishmen sat up and listened very
attentively when I quoted the recent decision in the English
Courts, fortified by several Judges, including the Chief Justice.

"Mr. Wright has a most remarkable house. The dinner was
served on the gold plate that belonged to Díaz. There are over
two hundred pieces in the set, with a centerpiece that I suppose
is gold plated (I do not think it can be solid gold). On the
plates from which we ate is Díaz' monogram. I asked Mr.
Wright how he obtained this set, in the back of my head
wondering if some of his friends looted Díaz' home when
Díaz went away. He said that, contrary to the popular opinion,
when Díaz left Mexico he was a poor man; that all the talk
about his sending millions to Paris was propaganda by his
enemies; and that Mrs. Díaz really had to sell their plate and
other things to obtain money to live on. She did not want to sell
it herself, and would not let it be known that it was being sold,
but gave it to a friend of hers who was a prominent jeweler
in Mexico City, so that it could be sold quietly and without
anybody's knowing it for a time. This jeweler was a friend of
Mr. Wright's and asked him to come and look at the plate. He
did so, and the next day he asked Mr. Cook if he had seen it.
Mr. Cook had not seen it; so he went with Mr. Wright. After
looking at it and ascertaining the price, Mr. Cook said: 'It has

been offered to you, Mr. Wright, but if you do not buy it, I will.' Whereupon Mr. Wright bought it. He is very proud of being its owner and very proud also of having been a friend of Díaz. He told me that when Díaz left Mexico City, he went out in his, Mr. Wright's, automobile.

"On leaving, Mr. Cook said to me, 'After you have been here a few months, you will have a different opinion of some of the characters in Mexico than you probably entertained when you came.' Mr. Cook probably referred to the fact that, like Mr. Wilson, I had an admiration for Madero and the leaders of the revolutionary forces who ousted Díaz and Huerta. He thinks Díaz was one of the greatest men the world has produced and said he was the only man who could give Mexico peace for thirty years."

Of another conversation with Mr. Cook I wrote in my Diary:

"Mr. Cook is an outspoken anti-New Dealer. He said that the only hope for foreigners in business here is for the Mexicans to feel that Uncle Sam will protect his nationals here. 'Mr. Roosevelt's declaration withdraws that protection,' he said. 'Who knows whether the other Pan American countries will coöperate in case orderly government falls down?' Mr. Cook, a very agreeable gentleman, got rich here in the Díaz days, and was called 'the merchant prince of Mexico.' He greatly admires the Díaz regime; believes in a country with distinct classes; and admires no government that Mexico has had since the days of Díaz.

"In the course of his conversation, Mr. Cook said that when President Wilson sent the Naval ships to Vera Cruz, looting began in Mexico City, and in his store, and he concluded it was time for him to get rid of his business. So he sold out. Inasmuch as I was Secretary of the Navy and ordered the ships to Vera Cruz, Mr. Cook, inadvertently and wholly unconsciously, was telling me that my order was responsible for driving him out of business. As a matter of fact it was the Huerta attempt to restore class (*Científico*) rule as in the Díaz days that brought about the trouble. But everyone must find a goat, who is responsible, and all select one they do not approve."

WHAT IS A GRINGO?

"Why do they call us Americans who come here 'Gringos'?" was a question tourists would often ask, hearing boys looking at them and saying, "Gringos." I told them it was no worse an epithet than some Americans used when they called Mexicans "Greasers," and that neither word was used by thoughtful men. I told them that originally "Gringo" was a word applied to the English who did not speak Spanish naturally. The meaning degenerated into one who talked unintelligently, or spoke gibberish, and then it descended further into a contemptuous epithet. However, the ignorant who use it usually mean only a foreigner who speaks English. No intelligent American calls Mexicans "Greasers."

THE 1936 ELECTION

There was gloom in the American Club in Mexico as a result of the 1936 election, though there was rejoicing in the cheerful American Embassy, where friends gathered to hear the news and rejoice. A few days later I wrote home:

"On election night the American Club here kept open house and on election day opened a ballot box in which all the members of the Club were invited to cast their ballot. The result was 117 for Landon to 11 for Roosevelt. I was told that in 1916, when Wilson ran the second time, the sentiment of the American Club here was about 99 for Hughes and 1 for Wilson. Two days after the election I went to the Club to a luncheon given by the directors of the Chamber of Commerce to an official of the Chamber of Commerce of Fort Worth. There is a very interesting Negro, Joe Joyner, who is the factotum at the American Club. He won the regard of Americans here during the Revolution because, as porter on the pullman from Mexico City to the border, he is said to have prevented the attempt to rob Americans on the pullman. He is one of the very few Negroes in Mexico City and is the best type of the kind of Negro we find in our clubs and hotels in the United States. After the luncheon at the Club, he said to me that he was very glad to see Mr. Roosevelt had been elected. He said, 'I told these gentlemen here at the Club when they were voting for Mr. Landon that the American Club would be the only place he would carry in the whole world.' He seemed very proud that he had made that prediction.

"On the night of the election as soon as it became clear that the President had been reëlected, I had a telephone message from President Cárdenas sending congratulations, and the next day I had a call from General Hay, Minister of Foreign Relations, and messages from most of the members of the cabinet and many others. Here in Mexico everybody seemed to be in favor of Roosevelt except a majority of the American Club and the *Científicos*.

"Your mother served a very nice supper and we got the returns promptly over the radio and the A.P. and U.P. were good enough to send us their bulletins. The Postmaster General of Mexico furnished us the bulletins, which were received over the wires, so that we had all the information, and almost as promptly as you had it in Raleigh. It sounds like a miracle, doesn't it?

"Since the election I have had calls and messages from many people here, expressing congratulations upon the result of the election, because of course they all knew of my deep interest in it and of the gratification the sweeping victory gave."

NOT UNITED POLITICALLY

It was interesting to compare the feeling about the election in the American Club with that in the Mexican Foreign Office. A few days before the election I wrote in my Diary:

"When I called at the Foreign Office on Thursday, General Hay asked me about the presidential election in the United States. I told him that I had no doubt that Roosevelt would be reëlected. 'As a Mexican official I can express no choice over candidates in any country,' he said, 'but as Eduardo Hay, speaking to Josephus Daniels, friend to friend, I will say that if I had ten million votes they would all be cast for Roosevelt.' He was expressing the views and hopes of most Mexicans who belong to the government and the National Revolutionary Party. They think the New Deal parallels their Six-Year Program. It does, in the spirit of giving a better chance to the forgotten man, though its policies are different. On the other hand, Big Business here, whether Mexican or American, is hostile to Roosevelt. Most Americans here who are prosperous either own or direct business for American owners—oil, mines, hardwoods, utility companies, etc. They share the views of their employers in the United States. They hate Cárdenas and they hate Roosevelt."

Though many of the members of the American Chamber of Commerce in Mexico were not pro-Roosevelt, shortly after the election I received the following letter from its President:

"The Board of Directors of the American Chamber of Commerce of Mexico, at the first meeting held since the presidential elections in the United States, passed a resolution instructing me to tender to you the congratulations of the Chamber because the outcome of the elections undoubtedly assures your remaining in your present post, and to thank you for your hearty coöperation with and interest in the American Chamber's affairs since you have been in Mexico."

CHAMBER OF COMMERCE A CLEARING HOUSE

The American Chamber of Commerce of Mexico City, of which I was Honorary President, and whose meetings I regularly attended, I found to be a clearing house, promoter of good will between the two countries, a Good Neighbor in advancing the exchange of commodities, and an integral part of international coöperation.

SCOTCH FOR THE AMBASSADOR

At the yearly banquets of the American Chamber of Commerce there was always a stunt that caused laughter. As prizes in the lottery were being handed out to holders of tickets I always drew a bottle of Scotch or other alcoholic drink, the gift of a dealer I had never patronized. Some of the Embassy staff envied what they called my good luck.

THE AMERICAN AND BRITISH HOSPITALS

Interested deeply, my wife often visited the hospitals, particularly the American Hospital, built by generous Americans. We were interested in the plan, under the leadership of Bolling Wright, of uniting the American and British hospitals.

MEXICANS MARRYING AMERICANS

Among our earliest and best friends in Mexico was Señor José Romero, who was the nephew of a former Mexican Ambassador to the United States. I had known him, when, as young men, we were both in Washington in the Cleveland administration, and we were glad to renew the association. His wife, the mother of eleven children, did not look twenty-five. When the daughter was to marry an American, I was asked to be a witness. Of the marriage I wrote home:

"In Mexico you are not legally married except by a civil marriage. Catholics, however (and most of the people here are Catholics), do not consider themselves married unless they have a church service. Therefore it is necessary to have two weddings. We were invited to the civil wedding and also to the church wedding, which took place the next day, but we went only to the civil wedding, where I was a witness. I draw the line at attending two marriages of the same people; I think one is enough.

"At the civil marriage only the bride and groom and their families and a few friends attend. At this one there were perhaps twenty-five or thirty people. The Judge or Justice of the Peace (I do not know which) came in very gravely, with his secretary carrying two large leather-bound books. He asked the bride and groom questions in Spanish, and they answered evidently satisfactorily. I do not know enough Spanish to know whether she said she would obey or not. I do not know whether that is required in the service here. Then when they answered satisfactorily to very long questions, the friends of the groom and friends of the bride signed the register as witnesses. I think it is as witnesses, but it may be that the friends of the groom have to sign his bond for him and the friends of the bride do likewise. Then everybody shakes hands, and the women all kiss each other, and some of the male relatives do likewise, and they go into the dining room, where they have champagne and refreshments and they cut a big wedding cake.

"I told the groom that as I had signed his bond I was telling the bride that if he did not take good care of her in the United States we would have him shot at sunrise.

"The sister of the bride, who told me that she was engaged to marry an American also, said that American men make better husbands than Mexicans, and she proceeded to say that as a rule Mexican husbands did not give their wives much privilege, and they expect matrimony to be what it was one hundred years ago before women were enfranchised. These daughters of the Romero family evidently have a notion that if they marry Americans they will wear the breeches as some American women do. However, I told her that there were American husbands and American husbands, and that if she thought all American husbands were ideal and model, she ought to read the proceedings of divorce cases and see how many of them were very unworthy and unfit, and then if she looked around her she would see that there are Mexican husbands who are just as good as Americans, for example, her father."

CRITIC BECAME PHYSICIAN

Critics upon acquaintanceship often became good friends. When I was appointed, this telegram was sent to President Roosevelt:

"Mexico City, March 13, 1933

"The President
"Washington, D. C.
"Why open old sores in Mexico's side appointing Josephus Daniels Ambassador to Mexico?

"DR. M. J. FERGUSON"

There was a sequel to this. In Mexico my wife and Mrs. Ferguson, both lovers of flowers, became good friends in the Garden Club, and the friendship extended to their husbands. I never intimated that President Roosevelt had sent me the above telegram. Once when I was taken painfully ill in the middle of the night with something that resembled ptomaine poisoning, Dr. Ferguson was summoned. He used the stringent remedies needed and remained until the cause had been removed. My wife, most anxious and distressed, had wanted, before calling Dr. Ferguson, to telephone her doctor son in Washington, Dr. Worth Bagley Daniels, but realized that long-distance treatment was not the urgent need. However, after Dr. Ferguson had "brought me through" by what I called drastic methods, she said, "And now I am going to call Worth by long distance." It was for her own satisfaction after the tension. Dr. Ferguson said, "Mrs. Daniels, your son probably has a hard day ahead of him. Why disturb his rest in the middle of the night and unfit him for his duties tomorrow?" But she felt it would calm and assure her if she could hear his voice. When she persisted Dr. Ferguson said,"I pray you, Mrs. Daniels, don't be a damn fool." That unexpected prescription both stunned and stopped her, and a hearty laugh removed the strain. The doctor's apologies were accepted. Ever after in the family and in the Embassy, if it was thought anyone was about to do something wholly unnecessary, the advice was, "Follow Dr. Ferguson's prescription." That, and "Don't violate Rule No. 6—don't take yourself so damn seriously," were the only standing orders in the Chancery and in the Embassy.

LEARNING ABOUT NORTH CAROLINA IN MEXICO

The old saying, "Go from home to learn the news about home," was verified one night in July, 1933, when we were dining with Mr. and Mrs. L. H. Parry. He showed me maps made by the English Government during the Revolutionary War, saying, "I think they will interest you." They did, more than he imagined.

In one map of North Carolina, was shown the section west of Orange County. My wife was quick to say, "There is the New Garden Quaker Meeting House where my great-great-grandparents lived when they first came to North Carolina."

He got out another map of Eastern North Carolina. What caught my eye was a bay adjoining Roanoke Island called "Daniels Bay." My Daniels kin landed on Roanoke Island when they came to the New World, and scores of them still live near the body of water called "Daniels" on that original map but now given another name.

My wife and I were surprised and gladdened to see maps locating the places where our forebears settled before the Revolutionary War. Mr. Parry was good enough to have several copies of the maps made, which I sent to the University of North Carolina and other educational institutions, and one to Cousin Melvin Daniels, who lives on Roanoke Island. I requested him to restore the name "Daniels" to the Bay.

There was a symbolism about those maps in the American colony in Mexico. They showed me more clearly than I had known before facts about the topography of old North Carolina. At the same time, the longer I stayed in Mexico and the better I knew the American colony there, the clearer it was that the colony, with its faults and virtues, is only a reproduction of like groups to be found in clubs and business and social circles in the United States.

XXXVIII

THE BRITISH COLONY

A COMMON tradition and a common language insure close relations between Americans and British people in whatever
part of the world they chance to be. This is true, no matter how
widely they differ, even though differences are deep-seated. Most
Americans in Mexico, as elsewhere, in close association with their
British cousins, held with Whittier:

> "O Englishmen!—in hope and creed,
>   In blood and tongue our brothers!
> We too are heirs of Runnymede;
> And Shakespeare's fame and Cromwell's deed
>   Are not alone our mother's.

> " 'Thicker than water,' in one rill
>   Through centuries of story
> Our Saxon blood has flowed, and still
> We share with you its good and ill,
>   The shadow and the glory."

Britishers carry "There's bound to be an England"—meaning the
ingrained British habits and principles and bathtubs and afternoon
teas, as well as adventures for oil and other natural resources.

In whatever part of the world they find themselves—and they go
everywhere—the Americans and British live up to their common
traditions, laws, and language. I found welcome and made cherished friendships in the British colony in Mexico.

For a hundred years "The British Society of Mexico" has embraced many from that kingdom who early invested in developing
Mexican resources. The largest number came with the discovery
and operation of the oil fields. In keeping with British tradition,
they brought with them old English customs—the early establishment of a church which grew into Christ's Church, first called the
Anglo-Saxon Church, which was dedicated in 1898 "in memory of
our most gracious Sovereign Lady, Queen Victoria." Benevolent

and other societies on the English pattern were organized, and hospitalization at Cowdray Hospital made it truly an institution of blessing, not only to members of the English colony but to all others. Of the 2,085 cases treated in one year, 1,306 were Mexicans. It was named for Viscountess Cowdray, whose husband, an early developer of oil, gave a million pesos for its construction.

The British Club is a center of social life for the British colony, and I often tasted its hospitality, being invited to the annual St. George and St. Andrew dinners as guest and often as speaker. In addressing the St. Andrew Society, I paid tribute to the thrift and devotion of the Scots, to their religion, to their leadership in education, to their large contribution in my State of North Carolina, including an appraisement of the people I always called "The God Blessed Macs":

> "If you could take the wings of the morning and fly to the uttermost part of the earth, it is certain you would find a Scotch pedagogue teaching the youths or a skilled Scotch mechanic applying machinery to industry, or a capable Scotch business man finding new markets, or a Scotch dominie in a kirk preaching Calvinism to dwellers in India's coral strand. And this Scotsman would be pursuing his vocation in his new environment as if he had never looked upon the lochs of the land of his birth, but if three Scotsmen were present they would have organized a St. Andrew Society. He would be following his calling without boasting or ballyhoo or self-advertisement. Modesty is a Scotch trait that is in the blood."

I also told this story, related to me by L. H. Parry, who had a pat story for every occasion:

> "An American, visiting in Edinburgh, became ill. His physician ordered him to a hospital. A blood transfusion was prescribed. A Scotsman agreed to furnish the blood. It was beneficial. The American improved and wrote the Scotsman a letter of thanks, enclosing a check for £50. Later the physician prescribed a second transfusion. The same man responded. More improvement. The American sent another letter of thanks and enclosed a check for £10. A third transfusion was ordered and the same Scotsman again gave his blood. The American, fully restored, wrote a letter of gratitude to his benefactor, but sent no money.

" 'I cannot understand your American patient,' said the Scotsman to the physician. 'When it was easy to give my blood, he sent me £50; when it was more difficult, he sent me £10; and the third time when it was even more difficult I received only a note of thanks,—no money. Can you explain it?'

"The physician, a Scotsman himself, replied: 'The explanation is easy. You see, Sandy, blood will tell.'

"It is eternally true that blood will tell."

A lover of books, a collector of old manuscripts, and, before coming to America, an associate in London of Ramsay MacDonald and Sidney Webb, George Conway had a library which I found absorbing. Among other items of his large collections was the original of a document signed by Cortés and the Conquistadors and material on Malinche. The latter interested my wife, who was writing a book on Malinche. When I tried in vain to buy a book written by our Minister, Joel R. Poinsett, it was Mr. Conway who secured it for me in London.

George Conway was head of the company controlling the public utilities of Mexico City, and I wondered if as an older man he had practiced the early liberal creeds of Ramsay MacDonald and Sidney Webb. I rather think his company would not have wished him to put them into effect in Mexico. Perhaps he left them in London. Regardless of his views, he was a delightful gentleman and was blessed with a fine wife.

COULDN'T HELP BRITISH MINISTER

Mexico City is a mile and a half nearer heaven—presuming that heaven is higher than Popocatepetl—above the sea level. It is the altitude which gives it the climate that attracts tourists from warmer countries in the summer and from the frozen north in winter. The elevation is responsible for the thin oxygen—and not a few rich residents give that as their reason for a separate establishment at Cuernavaca, or some place at a lower elevation.

Without design on my part, the Mexican tourists and immigration agents came to use me as "Exhibit A" in picturing Mexico City as the ideal winter and summer climate. It came about in this way. In the British Foreign Office it has long been a rule to permit the diplomats to retire on a pension some years earlier if they serve in a climate supposed not to contribute to normal health; as in the

Far East or the tropics. One day in the late thirties the British
Minister, supposing incorrectly that the United States pensioned its
diplomats and retired them earlier by reason of services in certain
climates, asked me to write a letter, or join him in a letter, saying
that the Mexican climate was such that one year's service for a pension status ought to be regarded as two years.

I told him that I would love to grant the request, but my experience as a resident of eight years would not justify such a letter
—that if I wrote at all, I would be forced to say that the climate
of Mexico City was as near perfect as could be, and I preferred it
to any I had known, except, of course, my home city in North
Carolina, and it was even better in the summer. Of course, I never
mentioned the reason why I could not join my colleague in the
letter he desired, but it leaked from the British Embassy, and some
weeks later General Hay complimented me as "the most popular of
all Ambassadors." Surprised, I asked why. He then told me that my
reply to the British Minister had become known and was Mexico
City's best boost for securing tourists. I had no such thought when,
regretfully, I could not join my English-speaking colleague in obtaining a climatic reason for early retirement. But I do not think
I could have changed my declination, even if my country had
pensioned its Ambassadors.

ENGLISHMAN SAID MEXICANS HATED AMERICANS

It would be unfair to suppose that an opinion of one Englishman
was representative of the estimate entertained of Mexican people
by Britons. There were strong ties between many Britishers and
Mexicans and some intermarriages, as was true of Americans. Therefore I was rather shocked, at a dinner where Arthur Stockdale, an
English mining engineer, and I were guests (July, 1933), to hear
him say:

"I was born in Mexico. I know all about Mexicans and Mexico. Every Mexican that breathes hates Americans—don't forget
that! You cannot trust a Mexican. These Mexicans will only
show you the beautiful side of the shield. They will never let
you see the other side which is worm-eaten.

"Mexican lawyers are the smartest in the world; they can
make black look white. They can fool anybody. The only
honest man in public life in Mexico in my lifetime was Díaz.

When he went to France Díaz left 50,000,000 pesos in the Treasury. It is propaganda that he took large sums to France. After Madero had been in office a little while it was all shoveled out."

He made a gesture of a man taking a shovel and pitching money as you would throw coal into a furnace, and continued,

"His family and people around him robbed the Treasury and he had not the strength to govern. It is better to have a competent man in public office with guts and brains than it is to have a good man who lacks these qualities."

HIS ESTIMATE OF MADERO AND MORROW

This Englishman, who put Díaz on a pinnacle, had a low opinion of Madero and did not think much of Morrow. He said, "Mr. Morrow allied himself with the worst type of Mexicans and did nothing for his countrymen—nothing!—nothing!—nothing! He was a little man, a stuffed shirt. He was a very delightful man, very charming, but he let the Mexicans have their way and it was a way that was injurious to his country."

I remarked that Mr. Morrow must have done some good things for his country to win the commendation given him. He replied, "Propaganda, every bit of it, well worked up. On account of it I cancelled my subscription to the *New York Times*. Morrow did save something for a few of the big oil men, but all other Americans were scalped."

BRITISH APPRECIATION OF LEND-LEASE

The British Woman's Charities Committee were most active and generous in every way to aid their country from the time war was declared. Of a remarkable sense of appreciation for the aid of the United States, I wrote home (May 19, 1941):

"I had a call from Mr. T. Ifor Rees, the British Consul General, who told me that the ladies of the British War Charities organization wished to have an appointment to come to the Embassy some night soon and present a silver token of the high appreciation of the British colony for the United States' passing the Lend-Lease Bill. It seemed to me, in view of the great efforts being made to get money together for British Relief in Mexico City and elsewhere, to present a silver token to the United States for an act which our Government took in the belief that it was important for the British and Americans to stand together against German aggression was not very timely —but the old saying is you must not look a gift-horse in the mouth. I hesitated to say all this to Mr. Rees."

Later I learned that he held the same view, but had not felt he could decline to convey the request of these good ladies. The presentation of the token was made without any formality or publicity.

BRITISH SENSE OF HUMOR

There is an ingrained belief that the British lack a sense of humor. Below are two stories that belie that impression. The first was told me by Mrs. George Conway, wife of the head of the foreign-owned power and light company, who spoke her mind freely.

"It is a shame," she said to me one day, "for foreigners to own all the best things in Mexico—the silver mines and oil properties." But she did not include public utilities of which her husband was the chief official.

Here was her story as I wrote it to my sons at home:

"Some years ago, the daughter of an employee of the Light & Power Company was in the Cowdray Hospital here very ill, and the surgeons said it was necessary for a transfusion of blood and they said that the blood of Mrs. Conway corresponded. She very generously, because she has a fine, generous, warm heart, offered to go to the hospital and give her blood. When the father of the girl heard of this, he, being a man who believed that any woman who drank a cocktail or played cards for money was a very devil of a creature, refused to permit her to give the transfusion of blood and said, 'I will never permit my daughter to be contaminated by having in her veins the blood of that cocktail-drinking, card-playing wicked woman.' Then, with a twinkle of the eye which is indescribable, Mrs. Conway said, 'And so I did not give my blood, and now his daughter, while she got well, has never been right in her mind. It may have served him right, but I am sorry for the girl.'"

"GOD DAMN JOSEPHUS"

Of the second story showing British humor, I wrote home (March 18, 1935):

"On March 9, Admiral Best, of the British Navy, who is in charge of the British ships on this side of the ocean, came from Vera Cruz, where his ship was anchored. He and his officers and crew were here for nearly a week. Your mother and I were invited to dine with the Admiral and his officers at the British Legation. I had met him when in Rosyth in 1919. He is a very agreeable gentleman, and told this story which I think you will enjoy:

"When the Prince of Wales was making the trip around the world, he was cruising on the ship of which Admiral Best was the Captain. When anchored in a harbor at a South American port, the Prince left the ship to take dinner ashore. In his absence the Captain of the ship invited a number of American officers who were in that port, to dine with him. He served every kind of wine and liquor and the Americans drank copiously. One of them drank to excess and stayed after the other officers left. As he was leaving, rather wobbly from too much drink, on being helped over the side of the ship, he pointed to a barrel-like affair standing near the gang-way. In the thick tones of a man in his cups, he pointed to it and inquired, 'What ish that?' He was told that it was a rum-head in which rum and water are kept ready for the sailors of the British Navy, who were given their daily tot; and after an especially arduous task, or in especially bad weather, a double tot. That seemed incredible to the American officer who belonged to a service where neither sailor nor officer could bring intoxicants aboard.

" 'What are these letters on the outside?' the intoxicated American Captain asked.

" 'They are "God Save the King",' he was told.

" 'What ish that for?' he asked.

"The Captain of the ship replied that it was to let the sailors keep in mind the fealty they owed to His Majesty.

" 'Itsh a dern good idea,' he said. 'A damn good idea. Do you know what I am going to do when I return to my ship?'

"The Captain answered in the negative. 'I am going to get a barrel, fill it full of lime juice. On the outside of the barrel I will have printed in very large letters, "God Damn Josephus," ' he explained.

"We all greatly enjoyed the story, and it has gotten wide circulation."

Above, Ambassador and Mrs. Daniels with Tyrone Power on the steps of the American Embassy. *Below*, Grace Moore, who was received at the Embassy by Ambassador and Mrs. Daniels.

Above, when stars fell on the American Embassy. In the group with Mrs. Daniels are Ann Sheridan, Norma Shearer, Kay Francis, Wallace Beery, Joe E. Brown, Johnny Weismuller, and Mickey Rooney. *Below,* the Ambassador makes his first contact with Mexican youth when members of the University of Mexico football team visit the Embassy.

The British Captain did not volunteer this story. In fact, after he related it to my wife, who insisted on his repeating it to all at the table, the Admiral said, "I don't think your husband would relish it." She replied, "You don't know him. He likes jokes on himself."

Afterwards, whenever I addressed old shipmates and told that yarn, I was sure to get laughter and applause. They remembered the famous—not so regarded by all—General Order No. 99 that I issued forbidding the introduction of intoxicants on any ship or Naval base.

XXXIX

THE FOURTH ESTATE

EVEN BEFORE I presented my credentials to President Rodríguez, I had been received as one of them by the resident members of the press and the American correspondents who "covered the Embassy." In a country where executives did not hold press conferences, newspaper men had to dig for news. Whenever I could help them I forgot I was in the diplomatic service and reverted to being a reporter. In fact I was never anything else.

All the great news agencies had correspondents—John P. McKnight, with a Cuban background; Clark Lee, who later won fame as a war correspondent in the South Pacific; and able Ben Myers, who at different times headed the Associated Press. William P. Lander, who spoke Spanish like a native, understood Mexico and could interpret her international relations, and was an authority on Latin American affairs, headed the United Press after the departure of popular Jack D'Armond. Arthur Constantine, dean of the corps, who had left his Massachusetts home as a young journalist and was correspondent in the Huerta days at Vera Cruz, married in Mexico and remained as head of the International News Service.

In addition to these representatives of the big three, the great journals of the world maintained permanent or temporary correspondents, among them such distinguished and outstanding writers as Frank Kluckhohn, Raymond Daniell, and Arnoldo Cortesi of the *New York Times,* Betty Kirk, of London and American papers, and Curtis Vinson, of the *Dallas News.* And every time any big news would break, flocks of special writers would fly down to give their angle to what was going on "down Mexico way."

To the Embassy press conferences came friendly and talented representatives of the Mexican press, Spanish-American reporters, and also Nazi writers, who not only sent the news, but when war clouds hovered became diligent Nazi propagandists.

While relations between Reporter Josephus Daniels, temporarily on duty as Ambassador, and correspondents and writers were always cordial, the press representatives were not free from reporting what they saw, and sometimes their reports were the opposite of the Embassy policy. But that made no difference, for all recognized that the first duty of a newspaper man was to tell the story straight, as he saw it. Reporters, friendly or critical—sometimes super-critical —never needed to make an appointment. The official reporters and the unofficial ones were simpático.

FIRST PRESS INTERVIEW

In my first interview with the press, I outlined the course I pursued through the years in these words:

> "The principles of parity of sovereignties and of mutual re-spect between the two governments in their dealings with each other are so fundamental with the peoples of the United States and Mexico that every right-minded man makes them his own. The two countries have common destinies. They should respect each other's territorial rights and seek to secure not only better understanding, but the closest association."

Reporting the interview, Arthur Constantine made this comment in his papers about my declaration:

> "This was in refreshing contrast with the slobbery and con-descension so characteristic of the school of good-willers and so offensive to intelligent Mexicans and Americans. It went to the point. It satisfied the Mexican conception of just and correct relations. It eliminated any fear that Ambassador Daniels had come to Mexico to swing the Big Stick."

WELCOME, MR. DANIELS

Mexican cartoonists joined the press and the people in a welcome to Mexico after I had presented my credentials and had made my address outlining the Good Neighbor doctrine. Mexicans said that this doctrine was in the spirit of their policies, which had grown out of the Revolution. One of the best of the cartoons was by Manuel Aguiles Caderes. It represented a Mexican holding his sombrero and, with a beaming face, saying, "Well-Come, Mr. Daniels." The artist gave me the painting from which the cartoon was made and it hangs in my study in Raleigh as the companion of one by Arias Bernal that appeared in *Hoy* entitled "Good-bye,

Boy," when after my resignation I was leaving Mexico City. Both are reproduced in this book.

COMRADES OF THE FOURTH ESTATE

After calling on the high officials of all departments of government, national and district, and being received with Mexican courtesy (none more courteous in the world) I felt that I could not be happy in the new surroundings without association with the Fourth Estate—men of my own profession. I decided to go to visit the editors of Mexico City.

The papers had announced that I would visit them at a certain hour and the streets around were crowded; the Associated Press and other newspaper men said, "When you have called officially and have been met by public officers, that is one thing; they are officially courteous. But this is a popular reception of citizens, who wish to show you welcome in Mexico."

The *Excelsior,* speaking of my visit, said, "For the first time in Mexico a high foreign representative democratically conveys his greetings and presents his respects to public officials without any formality," and added, "as Dr. Puig recently said, 'the new Ambassador of the United States has complied with rule six.'"

As my three sons were conducting our paper in North Carolina, I knew they would be interested in the Mexico City papers. I wrote them about my visit at the time:

"I have spent part of yesterday and today in the newspaper offices in this city. You know I am never quite at home unless I can hear the click of the typesetting machine and the whir of the press and the music of the typewriters preparing copy for the next day's paper.

"The papers in Mexico have been so generous in their treatment of me and their discussion of the matters that I have touched upon, that I wished to come in personal touch with them as fellow journalists.

"So an appointment was made and yesterday afternoon I went to pay a visit to Mr. Luis León, who directs *El Nacional.* That paper would be called in the United States the organ of the government. Here it is called 'the organ of the National Revolutionary Party,' which some people say is the government. All the officials belong to that party and General Calles is, as you know, the recognized leader of the party.

"*El Nacional* is in Mexico what the *Times* used to be in England. You can read it and know what the government is thinking about doing. And you can read it also and know what is in the minds of the leaders of the dominant party.

"When we went into the office of Mr. León, he was sitting at his desk with eight or ten gentlemen surrounding him, and I could see they were discussing something pretty important. They all arose and left at once. As they were doing so, I said to Mr. León, 'I suppose you are having a meeting of the staff of the paper.'

"He smiled and said, 'No, these are Deputies.' They were evidently discussing politics and plans for the forthcoming meeting of the leaders of the Revolutionary party, which is to be held shortly. Mr. León said, 'A paper of our character, which supports the Revolutionary party, is having more trouble just now than at any other time. We do not take sides in the nomination of candidates for the presidency, but all candidates who would like to be nominated for president, and their friends, wish us to aid their candidacy, and if we do not do so, they are apt to think we are against them. We are, therefore, having a very difficult time.'

"Mr. León asked me if I had seen the new Mergenthaler machine. It is a new invention. He has the first one that has been set up in any printing establishment in any country. The new machine makes type as big as the heading of a paper on the first page of any paper in the United States. With very great éclat and pride, he said, 'I would like to take you down and show you the working of that machine.' I was of course glad to go and found that a man from the Mergenthaler Company from Brooklyn was there. who had installed it. Mr. León went himself to the machine, pressed the lever, and the other parts of the machinery necessary, and in a second brought out a great line of type as big as the heading of *The News and Observer:* JOSEPH DANIELS. He left out the 'us.' That is a new name down here, as it is a jawbreaker anywhere.

"My next visit was to *El Universal*. By mistake we went in the back door. The building goes through from one street to the other, and, therefore, we saw the presses and the typesetting machine before we got to the offices. They are rebuilding their plant, and we had to go up stairways in the process of erection to get to the main office. When we arrived there, we found Mr. Lanz Duret and Mr. Eduardo Elizondo. Mr. Lanz

Duret is the president and managing director. The other gentleman, who is the editor, spoke English perfectly. We discussed all phases of journalism—editorial policies, advertising, circulation, radio, etc.

"I next went into the office of *La Prensa (The Press)* at 7:00 in the early evening. *La Prensa* is an independent tabloid. I was received by Señor Julio Zetina, the president and managing editor, who introduced me to his editorial staff. We went all over the plant and talked shop—the place the newspaper occupies in the making of public opinion.

"Leaving the office of *La Prensa,* on the same night I went to the office of *Excelsior*. This paper has the largest building of all the daily papers in Mexico City. I was received by Señor Rodrigo de Llano, director, and Santiago André Laguna, a reporter. I was introduced to Gonzalo Herrerías, managing editor; Carlos Díaz Dufoo, editorial writer, and all members of the staff. We all got in a bunch, as football players do, and talked about various matters. They all seemed to look up to Carlos Díaz Dufoo. He is the Dean of the Mexico City journalists. He looks like a judge, and I turned to him and said, 'All we young journalists come to you as to Gamaliel and sit at your feet.' That created quite a laugh and made us all friendly.

"After visiting various parts of the plant, particularly stopping to see the rotogravure press printing the Sunday's section which had a picture of the banquet given to my wife and myself at the Mexico City Country Club by the American Colony, they took us to the printing office, where they have a battery of linotypes. I was requested to see how many ems I could turn out on the linotype, and while I was sitting there I had my picture taken (of which I sent you a copy), which appeared in the *Excelsior*.

"The next day I completed my official visits to the daily newspapers by calling at the office of *La Palabra (The Word)*. This paper until recently had been a weekly and was devoted to the propagation of the Catholic position in the Republic. The Editor told me that he had been put in jail at one time for insisting upon his rights to say what he believed, and that the paper was now an independent paper. 'You see we have a very modest plant,' he said, 'and of course do not make money, but we are trying to make a paper that is truly expressive of the convictions of a large number of people in our country.'

"I was received by Señor Edmundo del Monte, managing

editor, and Señor Carlos Domínguez, a reporter. I had met Mr. Domínguez on the first day of my arrival and had given him an interview which he handled admirably, and I thanked him for it.

"There was some question at the Embassy as to whether I ought to call at the office of *La Palabra,* which had been generally against the present (Mexican) government. This paper holding such position, it was questionable whether the Ambassador of the United States should call upon a paper not in harmony with the government to which he was accredited. But, after talking it over, it was decided that I was visiting all the papers not as Ambassador but as a fellow journalist, and that to visit all the others and not visit *La Palabra* would be marked, and so I paid a visit there and was very cordially received. I was introduced not only to all the editorial staff, but also to the business staff, and they took a picture of me with some of the young ladies in the business office."

FIRST PRINTING PRESS IN THE NEW WORLD

My next visit was to Howard S. Phillips, editor of the oldest publication in Mexico, the monthly illustrated *Mexican Life,* who showed me the building, still standing, in which was installed the first printing press in the New World. It was brought to Mexico in the 1530's by Viceroy Antonio de Mendoza. About the visit to the site of this old press I wrote to my sons:

"On Friday afternoon I went to see Señor Guillermo Echaniz, at his place at Donceles 12 to see the first printing press operated in the New Hemisphere. He also had many interesting things connected with printing which he had collected, most of them very old. This printing press, which was put up in 1536, was used first to print religious publications. It had been preserved in some way and Señor Echaniz, who has a penchant for printing material, had found the parts of it and put it together. It is a very primitive press, on much the same pattern as the old Washington hand press which I used when I first began as a boy editor to print the *Wilson Advance.* As I looked at the old press, my mind went back to the days in Wilson, N. C., when the Negro, Stepney Buck, manipulated my press, and sometimes when I couldn't get anybody else to do it I manipulated the roller and I was as black at the end of the day as Stepney Buck, who was as black as the ace of spades. The building in which this press is kept is a very old one and I felt that it ought to be in a fireproof building and be taken care of and I wondered why the government did not consider it as a national monument and take it over."

Few journalists have been called to high station in Mexico. The two greatest officials—Juárez and Cárdenas—however, had early training in newspaper offices in their youth—Juárez as a bookbinder and Cárdenas as a printer.

HOW MUCH CENSORSHIP IN MEXICO?

I asked Howard S. Phillips, of *Mexican Life,* if the press in Mexico was free and he answered, "There was no official form of censorship during the administrations of Abelardo Rodríguez and Lázaro Cárdenas. On the contrary these governments tacitly encouraged an opposition press. This has not always been the case in the provinces, where local political 'strong men' have at times resorted to strong-arm methods in suppressing press opposition."

However, there were correspondents who thought otherwise and felt that the Mexican Department of Press and Publicity made regulations at times which were not consonant with a truly free press. There was resentment when visiting correspondents printed stories officials deemed unfair or slanderous.

STONEWALL JACKSON AND THE SEÑORITA

Being interested, I dug up the fact that the first English-language newspaper to be published on Mexican soil was the *American Star,* launched at Vera Cruz in 1847, under the aegis of General Winfield Scott's forces. The editors were George Peoples and Frank Barnard, both Texans. The *Star,* following the invasion army, was subsequently printed at Jalapa and Puebla, and continued publication in Mexico City during the year, more or less, of the occupation. Printed weekly, its columns were filled mostly by "hot shots," incidents and anecdotes *re* the officers and enlisted men of the expedition—it was no respector of rank.

One of these I read (but it was not authenticated), told about an experience of a Second Lieutenant Jackson, commonly known around the barracks as "Parson Jackson" because he was notoriously given to reading and quoting the Bible. Tradition has it that the

Lieutenant became quite infatuated with a Mexican Señorita and on nights off devoted himself assiduously to "playing the bear"— courting the young lady through the iron bars of her window. His attentions, while apparently welcomed by the young lady, were strenuously objected to by her family, in particular by some grown-up brothers. One night, date not recorded, the brothers *en masse* assaulted the young officer, which caused his ardor to cool. His attention thereafter seems to have been devoted more to his military duties and his Bible. In later years this subaltern climbed high and as General Stonewall Jackson won an immortal place in history. The *American Star* was printed in a large room of a building I visited, which still stands on the Zócalo facing the National Palace. When peace was signed and the American Army marched out for Vera Cruz, the *Star* also disbanded.

"TIME" EXCLUDED FROM THE MAILS

Twice censorship was applied that touched two important American journals—*Time* and the *New York Times*. I was able to secure a reversal of the order excluding *Time* from the mails, but the refusal of permission of the Mexico City correspondent of the *New York Times* to continue his assignment in Mexico came while I was in the United States. It was not reversed as to that correspondent, but when another correspondent of the *Times* was assigned to Mexico, the censorship was ended.

The article in *Time* (April 3, 1933) which aroused the animosity of Mexicans was as follows:

"Few of Mexico's leaders are white men. Calles is the illegitimate son of an unknown and a peasant woman; Ortiz Rubio is reputedly three-quarter Spanish, one-quarter descendant of Michoacán kings. President Rodríguez is a halfbreed, speaks Yaqui fluently. Both Cárdenas and Amaro are pure Indian. Observers have long noted the virility of the Mexican Indian blood, the emergence of an Indian dynasty in Mexican politics."

In my letter to my sons (May 25) I wrote:

"When I called at the Foreign Office some time ago, Dr. Puig said laughing: 'I wish to be indiscreet and speak to you about a matter unofficially.' So today I said to him: 'I wish to follow your example and to speak to you unofficially and to be indiscreet, if what I am saying is indiscreet.'

"I then spoke to him about a letter I had received from Mr. Luce, editor of *Time* in New York, referring to the fact that *Time* had been barred from the mails in Mexico, and expressing the hope that something could be done by which the order could be revoked, so that subscribers to *Time* could get it in Mexico as elsewhere. I showed Dr. Puig a copy of the letter.

"I had had an unofficial letter from Herschel Johnson, Chief of the Mexican Division at Washington, hoping that something could be done unofficially about the matter.

"The reason that *Time* was excluded from the mails in Mexico was because some weeks ago, it printed an article about the parentage of General Calles to the effect that he was born out of wedlock; the Postmaster General, who is a half-brother of General Calles, excluded *Time* from the mails. It was an article that ought not to have been printed and reflected upon General Calles' antecedents in a way that naturally offended all Mexicans. It turned out, in my conversation with Dr. Puig, that the order issued by the Postmaster General was on his own initiative.

"I made no official request of Dr. Puig about the paper, but he agreed to take it up and look into it. Unless *Time* is willing to make a correction, it is hard to see how the Postmaster General can be induced to change his order.

"I have always felt, even in the Wilson Administration when Postmaster General Burleson denied the mails to a newspaper without a hearing, that it was a dangerous exercise of one-man power. I think censorship is always dangerous, and that Jefferson was eternally right when he said that where the press was free, we would have free government, and if the press was censored and made subservient, all would perish."

I sent this message to Mr. Luce: "Be good and do not again reflect upon the parentage of any leader in Mexico. In fact omit such reflection upon any man anywhere. If false, it is inexcusable. If true, the man is not to blame who arrives in spite of the handicap."

Dr. Puig told me he had taken the matter up with President Rodríguez and, while they felt that there was justification for condemnation of the article, strictly as a courtesy to me as a journalist interested in the freedom of the press, the President had decided to withdraw the order banning *Time* from the mails. I told Dr. Puig that I thought this was a very generous and fine action on the part of the President and the Mexican government. My plea for the freedom of the press bore fruit—at least for a time.

KLUCKHOHN PERSONA NON GRATA

The act that created the greatest sensation in press and other circles was the expulsion in 1939 of Frank L. Kluckhohn, a correspondent of the *New York Times*. The genesis of the affair was the refusal to send, and censorship of, the Kluckhohn dispatches, by the Mexican Department of Press and Publicity, headed by Licenciado A. Arroyo Ch. and the Post Office Department.

Instead of press conferences, as in Washington where correspondents have access to the President and members of the cabinet, Mexico set up a Bureau of Press and Publicity through which all official news was released how and when they chose to do so. It was a practical censorship which irritated the correspondents and worked badly. It culminated while I was on leave in Washington, when the officials became indignant at some of Kluckhohn's dispatches, which they said were false and defamatory of Mexican policies. They were either censored or not permitted to go out. A. Arroyo Ch. justified the act by specifying one message which he said was sent after Kluckhohn had been informed it was false, and unjust to Mexico. Kluckhohn (June 16, 1938) wrote A. Arroyo Ch. that he was violating the international radio code and that henceforth all dispatches in the *Times* would be marked "censored." After writing that letter, Kluckhohn came to see Counsellor Pierre Boal, Chargé d'Affaires in my absence, and said he thought the only way to stop that arbitrary action was to make a definite issue of it. He expected it would result in his expulsion from Mexico under Article 33.

Counsellor Boal talked with Colonel Alfonso Gómez Morentin, Mexican Postmaster General, named the act of censorship and suppression, and told him such action would injure his country. Colonel Morentin said Kluckhohn's messages were false and defamatory but he would try to adjust the situation. He said he would recommend to A. Arroyo Ch. that they resume the sending of Mr. Kluckhohn's messages, and that in the future, if they had any doubts as to the accuracy or propriety of these messages that, instead of holding them up, they would simply issue a statement correcting the facts, and asking Mr. Kluckhohn and other correspondents to transmit such rectification to their newspapers.

NEW YORK TIMES CORRESPONDENT EXPELLED

I wrote home from Mexico (January 21, 1939):

"The first thing I learned upon leaving the train was that, the day before, Frank Kluckhohn had been sent out of Mexico by airplane by the government on the ground that he was *persona non grata*. He has been here quite some time as correspondent of the New York *Times* and a very bright young man, but the government officials for a long time have said that he made use of every item of news to injure the Mexican Government in the eyes of the American people. Last fall Undersecretary Beteta told me that Kluckhohn had gone to see him and spent an hour telling him how he (Kluckhohn) was in perfect sympathy with the progressive policies of Mexico; that he was a liberal and had been driven out of Spain because of his liberalism and that he was in hearty sympathy with the Mexican policy of helping the under-privileged. At that time Beteta told me that he thought that Kluckhohn was the worst enemy Mexico had and added: 'Kluckhohn's ambition is to be a martyr and to compel the Mexican Government to send him out of the country because of his articles.'

"I said to Beteta, 'I hope the Mexican Government is too wise to do anything of that character. It is impossible to censor the press. If you should send Kluckhohn out because you don't like what he writes you would find that the whole United States would condemn the action because our people believe that democracies must expect criticism and sometimes unjust criticism and that nothing is worse than censorship or shutting the mouths of the people who criticize.' He agreed with me.

"Therefore when I learned that Kluckhohn had been sent out I went at once to see Mr. Beteta and voiced my astonishment and indignation at such action. He said that he remembered what he had said to me before, but that the government had changed its mind after Kluckhohn had sent out an article which Beteta said Kluckhohn knew was false, saying that the government had taken over lands belonging to Italians in Michoacán and had paid 3,000,000 pesos for them, whereas they were taking American land without making payment. Beteta said that Mr. Lockett had investigated the matter and informed

Kluckhohn that there was no truth in the statement and still Kluckhohn had sent it out. Evidently there has been strong feeling about Kluckhohn's articles and this was the culminating act which caused the Government to be guilty of the worst thing it could have done for itself in expelling the writer. Undoubtedly Kluckhohn did give the Mexican government the worst interpretation of some of its acts. Even so, Mexico hurts itself by expelling a correspondent. Its remedy was to secure a rectification of any misinformation.

"The trouble here is that the Department of Press and Publicity gives out no news except that which is propaganda for the government, and naturally newspaper men resent the attempt to make them propagandists and this resentment tends to make them more critical than they would be if they could get the news as it is. In my conversation with Beteta I detailed the method employed in the United States, where the President receives the press once a week and Cabinet officers see them every day and respond to questions about public matters, reserving the right to say to correspondents when they ask questions about matters that the government feels should not be discussed in public at that time, not to answer the questions. I told him they would have a much better press if Mexico would adopt that policy."

In talking with Counsellor Boal about the feeling of Mexican officials toward Kluckhohn, Ambassador Castillo Nájera told him that he thought it was better to minimize the importance of Kluckhohn's note than to create an incident. The Ambassador was of the opinion that Kluckhohn wanted to be sent out of the country and that under no circumstances should the Mexican government take such action.

In one of his letters (December, 1938), presenting both sides of the situation in Mexico, Kluckhohn had said that "Washington having gone far toward sacrificing American investments, trade, and prestige in keeping peace with Mexico becomes aware of a Fascist danger in Latin America and wants to buy the support of these nations through a peace program, expending money to accomplish what an insistence of reciprocation and legitimate protection of American interests would have made unnecessary."

It was in my absence, after Kluckhohn had sent a dispatch which the Foreign Office said was without foundation, that I read in the press that Kluckhohn was "expelled," or "33rd-degreed out" as the paper carried it.

Article 33 of the Constitution, which had formerly been invoked, was not employed by Cárdenas. That strange article contained this provision:

> "The President of the Republic has the exclusive power to expel from the country, immediately and without trial, any alien whose presence he deems pernicious to the country. Aliens are not permitted to take part in internal political questions."

Earlier a newspaper correspondent who was leaving Mexico told me that Kluckhohn had stated to him that he had three purposes in view in coming to Mexico. One was to drive the Cárdenas government from power and one was to have himself expelled from Mexico—the correspondent said he had forgotten the third. I always felt that, if Kluckhohn had said that, he said it when he was "talking" and that this was not his real purpose or that of the *Times*. By talking I mean it was said in the sense that the word was employed by a man in "The Harricane" section of Wake County, North Carolina. As a witness in court he was asked if the statement he was making was not different from the one he had made the day after the crime was committed. He answered, "Yes, but I was talkin' then; I am a-swearin' now."

Like some politicians, there are newspaper men who over-speak themselves in private talk without expecting to be taken literally.

KLUCKHOHN'S OWN STATEMENT

Some months ago I asked Mr. Kluckhohn to write me his version of the incident that aroused resentment among journalists and believers in freedom of the press. He responded and gave me his version as follows:

> "You ask about my being expelled from Mexico. The facts were these:
> "Just before leaving for the United States on a brief vacation in 1938—and in fact on the day the Lima Pan-American Conference opened, I had published on the front page of the *New York Times* a news report that expropriated Mexican oil was to be sold to Germany through an entrepreneur of U. S. nationality. This story was correct.

"I had driven to the States in my car and had left it there, returning to Mexico by train in early January. On the morning of my arrival back in Mexico City, a brother correspondent told me he understood there had been an order at the border to prevent my reentering Mexico but the fact that I had, by chance, entered by train instead of automobile had prevented its execution.

"In the afternoon, I went to the Government Office of Press and Publicity, in company with William Lander, the United Press correspondent. Lander was asked by a sub-official to confer with the chief of the office—as it turned out a means of getting him out of the way. I left at this point and, as I stepped out the street door, about five men, who turned out to be policemen, grabbed me. I pushed the first to touch me away and struggled against the rest until they showed their badges.

"They put me in a car and took me to the Ministry of Interior. There I was held incommunicado for about two and a half hours, although I was otherwise politely treated. I asked permission to telephone the American Consul General and this was refused.

"Then I was taken before the Sub-Treasury of Interior who read a long document asserting, among other charges that I was 'in the pay of the capitalist classes' and was officially informed I would have to be out of Mexico in twenty-four hours or be arrested. I left the next morning for Brownsville, Texas, by plane. Mr. Stewart, then the Consul General, came to my house, conferred with Ramón Beteta, then Sub-Secretary of Foreign Relations, by telephone and helped me with arrangements.

"I am certain that had you been in Mexico at the time—and not away on a visit to the States, that I would not have been expelled. It was my impression, although I am not certain about it, that President Cárdenas himself was not fully informed about the matter or that matters were misrepresented to him. I felt a small Government clique, including one official who was quite close to the German Embassy at the time, were responsible.

"You yourself always took any criticism good-naturedly and my personal relations with Cárdenas, whom in many respects I greatly admired and with whom, on occasion, I had lunched alone, were always good. I know that you not only preached, but practised, freedom of the press. I felt that Cárdenas, more

than some of his minor officials, appreciated impartial reporting. I am sure that, with the universal respect held for you in
Government circles, you could have halted this summary action
without difficulty.

"In retrospect, I feel that you did a magnificent job under
trying conditions in Mexico and that the good feeling for the
States which you induced, during the long period you were Ambassador to Mexico, played a large part in cementing the ties
which led our two countries eventually to active participation
in the war together."

Years afterward Kluckhohn conversationally said to me: "At the
time I did not think your policy was wise, but in the light of later
events I wish to tell you that I believe you pursued the right
course."

"THE MEXICAN CHALLENGE"

In 1939 Mr. Kluckhohn published a book, *The Mexican Challenge,* in which he enlarged upon his telegrams to the *Times* and
closed his on-the-scene observation with this line: "For Mexico's
future is as uncertain today as it was the day that the Revolution
began." He detailed some of the acts of certain Mexican officials
in calling newspaper men on the carpet, and directing them to
"slant" the news. Kluckhohn said some of his messages were halted
by the government, climaxing his expulsion from the country. He
says it was "under a subterfuge." Criticising the Press Department,
Mr. Kluckhohn says: "President Cárdenas, on the other hand, has
always been glad to receive correspondents, give them views frankly,
and tell them that the thing he had to say was 'off the record.' His
statements have always been run, without comment, in newspapers
abroad. Once again his ideal attitude has been sabotaged by his
own order."

A BRILLIANT CORRESPONDENT

Kluckhohn was one of the most industrious and brilliant of
American correspondents. I held him in high regard and we talked
freely. On one or two occasions I ventured to advise him, when
I felt he was going too strong, and warned him to be sure of his
facts. I told him that some Mexican officials felt that he made use
of every incident to injure Mexico in the eyes of the American

Above, Ralph McGill, Editor of the *Atlanta Constitution* visiting at the Embassy.
Below, William Allen White, Dean of American journalists, discussing censorship
in Mexico and the United States with his fellow journalist, Ambassador Daniels.

Left to right, President Cárdenas, Betty Kirk (Mrs. Francis Boyer), newspaper correspondent, and A. Arroya, Ch., of the Committee on Public Information.

people. He was ambitious to score scoops and may have erred by accepting stories that were not authentic. It was not easy to get the truth about controversial matters in the hectic days after expropriation.

The talent shown by Kluckhohn, first in Spain and then in Mexico, flowered in his illuminating correspondence during World War II from the South Pacific and afterwards from Europe and South America.

THE LAST EXPULSION

I am moved to go into this matter at such length both because I wish to do justice to all parties and because nothing excites my indignation so much as for a government to censor the news and resort to archaic practices to punish a representative of a free press. I thought then that, as Mexicans believed the *Times* was opposing their policies as to oil, the expulsion of its correspondent might be aimed at that paper.

Though other correspondents visited Mexico and were far more critical than Kluckhohn, there was no further attempt at censorship. Upon the first opportunity I expressed strongly to President Cárdenas the same views I had urged upon Beteta. I asked no response but felt certain that no officials again would do in Mexico what some countries did in Europe before and after World War II when enlightened journalists were earnestly seeking full freedom of the press all over the world. And it was the last expulsion from Mexico!

XL

TIME OUT FOR STORIES

T HERE were serious days in my stay in Mexico, but the strain was often relieved by incidents and stories in official and social life. Some of them concerned visitors and some showed Mexican as well as American humor. The story that had the largest currency was called the "Don't-Drink-the-Altitude Story."

The Mexicans themselves—or some of them—were responsible for the altitude complex that affected many tourists. Whereas in the United States the query to a visitor is, "How are you?" some Mexicans ask visitors to the city, "How does the altitude affect you?"

That question suggests that altitude has its dangers, and some people think they must do something to ward off what the altitude may do to them. It is an alibi and is often invoked.

Perhaps the following incident that came to be quoted often illustrates what altitude is supposed to do to some visitors. In the second year of my stay, one morning my secretary came in laughing heartily—but let Robert Newbegin tell what happened the night before:

"I was at the Ritz last night with friends. It was a patriotic day and the dining room was full of gay groups, every table taken, and Mexican music regaled the diners. I noticed an American guest, rather unsteady on his legs, who had a night-club complex. He not only was drinking pretty freely with those at my table, but was going from table to table calling on everybody to drink with him and making merry in the fashion of an amiable and generous drinker at a night club. Presently he came to our table and said, 'Are you the secretary to the American Ambassador?' When he learned that I was, he asked me to tell the Ambassador that he had letters from several of his best friends in New York and would call the next day at the Embassy to present them.

"Look out for him, but I suspect he will sober up before presenting his letters of introduction. But he had a glorious time last night and it cost him a pretty penny."

A week passed by, and I had almost ceased expecting the New Yorker, when one morning, looking just as if he were fresh out of a Turkish bath, the gentleman presented letters from John W. Davis, Gordon Battle, and Henry Morgenthau, of New York, all speaking in the highest terms of the business man of the metropolis and requesting the extension of courtesies to their friend.

"I am glad to see you," I said in welcoming him to the Embassy. "I have been expecting you to call every day for a week. I hope you have found Mexico pleasant."

He answered, "Yes, I came a little over a week ago, expecting to present these letters at once, but I had hardly reached the city before the Altitude struck me, made my head swim, caused me sleepless nights, and made me wobbly and uncertain in my movements." And he proceeded to enumerate all the things Altitude had done to him that caused him to delay the call until he got acclimated. After finishing his catalogue he asked, "When you first came to Mexico, didn't the Altitude knock you out?"

"No," was my reply.

"You never felt it in any way?"

"No," I answered.

Thereupon he said he thought it very strange it had not affected me at all when it had floored him. "How do you account for it?" he asked.

I took a good look to satisfy me that he was the sort of man who could laugh at himself—the best test of a real fellow. Deciding he could take it, I replied, "I never drink it."

For a minute he looked blank and then burst out in laughter and cried out, "You are on to me!"

And we became good friends—minus Altitude. The story got wide circulation. Afterward when a visitor expressed fear that the Altitude might affect him, he was told that Ambassador Daniels had found a way to prevent Altitude's affecting any one. And the story was widely told to the music of much laughter.

When I found it had gotten wide circulation, I confided, jocularly to a friend, that there was more behind that Altitude story than appeared on the surface. As a congenital dry and an enemy of

John Barleycorn I was using it to discourage the drinking of intoxicants. The story was popular but was not used in the attractive advertisements of liquor that filled pages in papers and magazines.

LIQUOR IN COFFEE CUP

There were stories galore aimed at my being a teetotaler. At every banquet where prizes were given, I always drew a bottle of rum. It never failed to create a laugh, and people wondered what I did with the liquor. I never told them.

When Admiral Williams and a number of Naval officers were at a luncheon given by Mr. and Mrs. W. B. Richardson, one Naval officer—so Bill told me afterwards—said: "In view of the General Order by Mr. Daniels prohibiting drinking on board ship, I do not like to drink before him. Can't you put the alcoholic refreshment you are serving in a cup so that the Ambassador will think I am drinking coffee?" He got the beverage.

DRINKING TOO MUCH

Earthquakes in Mexico rarely do any damage to Mexico City because of the porous soil on which the city is built. One day as I was walking across the Embassy garden with Secretary Aguirre, the ground began to shake. I put my foot out and used my walking cane to brace myself when Aguirre said, "Mr. Ambassador, this is an earthquake." I replied: "Did you think I had been drinking too much?"

CALLED IT SPARKLING GIN

Harry Norweb, Counsellor in Mexico from November, 1933, to May, 1936, recalls the following incident about a visit of Alfonso López, President-elect of Colombia:

"Here is *one* incident that has always remained fresh in my memory. Señor López, in his tour through the Sister Republics and during his stay in Mexico, had of course been fêted as becomes a prospective head of State—and by the time he came to dinner at the Embassy (I think, just before his departure), he had been wined and dined to the limit of human endurance. At your board, however, he gained some respite in the matter of liquor—being presented only with plain water and a wine-glass of mineral water. (By the way, sir—at this distance of time and space, may I tell you that the glass of mineral water which you served at dinners was referred to by your irreverent but devoted staff as 'sparkling gin'?) Well, after the dinner for López, as we were chatting over coffee, he heaved a sigh of heartfelt relief and said to me: 'You know, at the end of a jaunt like mine, it's been a pleasure to spend one evening on the *alkaline* side.' I have always remembered this as an indication of how public men are martyred by public festivities, and also of how a foreigner can sometimes master the current idioms or slogans of our language."

"CREMA DE XTABENTUN"

There was no end to the fun over my dryness, though I found that President Cárdenas and other Mexican leaders "looked not upon the wine when it was red."

At an official luncheon at Mérida (a beautiful old city) there was served a deadly drink. It is called *Crema de Xtabentun*, a liquor produced by the fermentation of the white honey which the bee extracts from a small fragrant, bell-shaped flower called *Xtabentun*. It looked like pure water and a few drinks would knock a man out. A young man thought it would be fun to see me "full." A large glass was placed at my plate. My wife caught on to the trick, took the toastmaster into her confidence, and set a large glass of water to replace the liquor. I drank copiously. Those who had planned the stunt became afraid I would be drunk and continued to get word to me to drink sparingly. There was consternation when I drank enough to floor a hard drinker.

"Tell the Ambassador the danger he is in and to quit drinking so much," said one of the young men to my wife.

She replied, "He is all right. He can stand it."

They were surprised when I was cold sober after the potations.

THE ALPHABETICAL AGE

Some American visitors who lunched at the Embassy could not forget their political bias. In the days when the Roosevelt New Deal alphabetical agencies and policies were anathema to the economic royalists, we had as guests two very rich Americans. Though knowing the relations between Roosevelt and myself, one of the guests inquired: "What do you think of Roosevelt's alphabetical new fad which is ruining the country?" Overlooking his *faux pas,*

I replied, "You see I have been away from home so long that I cannot keep up with all that is going on. When I left Washington in March, 1933, the only alphabet that I heard anything about was the I. O. U. which had brought the country to the brink of bankruptcy."

His companion laughingly said, "The Ambassador has got the best of you." And politics was adjourned at that luncheon.

"MR. COOK MINUS HIS PANTS"

Boys will be boys even when they are grown tall and have gotten rich in Mexico, as the following from my letter home shows:

"On Friday I attended a luncheon at the University Club which was out of the ordinary. A few days before, Mr. Harry Wright called and said that one of the old-timer friends here, was leaving shortly for a trip around the world and he wanted to have a quiet little dinner for a dozen of his close friends and asked me to be present. He said they wanted to pull off a stunt for some fun at the expense of Mr. George W. Cook, President of the University Club. Mr. Wright said, 'You know Mr. Cook is a very reserved and dignified and cultured gentleman and the old-timers have had a picture made of him carrying out a story we invented about him years ago when he was younger. The story was that he appeared at the Club without any pants. We wish you to present the portrait to Mr. Cook.' I accepted the invitation, knowing, of course, before I went, that I would be the only person there who was not a 'Científico' or a sympathizer with the old 'Científicos.' "

NOT A DAY OVER A HUNDRED AND FIFTY-EIGHT

Closing a letter home about the celebration of the Fourth of July (1935) I added:

"I must tell you about the blow that almost killed father at the diplomatic breakfast on the Fourth, being the 159th anniversary of the Declaration of Independence. As the wife of the Belgian Minister was presented, I said, seeking to be agreeable and facetious: 'I am celebrating my 159th anniversary today. I do not think I look it. Do you?'

"She paused, giving me a critical examination before answering. After a long inspection she said, 'No, I don't think you look that old,' and then with a glance that showed she thought she was scoring she said, 'I am sure you do not look a day over 158.' She made a hit, a palpable hit."

THE END OF STAG BREAKFASTS

On patriotic occasions—for example on every Fourth of July—the Embassy entertained at breakfast the Mexican Cabinet and all members of the diplomatic corps. One day, in our first days in Mexico, I said to Madame Stadler, wife of the Belgian minister, "I do not like the idea of having these stag breakfasts and another year we are going to change the custom and invite the wives of members of the corps."

She replied, "That is a good idea. But why wait until next year?"

My wife agreed, so that later Fourth of July breakfasts had the added charm of the wives of the diplomats and the Mexican officials.

FOURTH OF JULY AT THE EMBASSY

On every Fourth of July, even when it rained, we gave a blanket invitation to all the members of the American Colony and American visitors to the city to come to the Embassy to an afternoon tea and help celebrate the natal day. There was always a large gathering. One year more than thirty-five hundred callers passed through the gate. The Declaration of Independence was always read by the President of the American Chamber of Commerce or the Commander of the American Legion. The only penalty on callers was to hear me deliver a brief Fourth of July address. But there was compensation, for every year patriotic ardor was stirred when Mrs. Walter Christié sang the "Star-Spangled Banner."

The highlight of pleasure at these celebrations for American visitors was the music by the Mexican *Típica* Band, led by Lerdo y Texada, the men and women were dressed in festive Mexican costumes and sang their patriotic and tender love airs with a spirit and understanding that were contagious. All visitors were entranced by the music of these gifted artists.

COULD MUSSOLINI REPEAL THE LAWS OF BIOLOGY?

Almost every night in the summer of 1937 we attended some dinner or had a dinner at the Embassy. Of one I wrote home:

"On Monday night we went to dinner at the Italian Legation. The Minister, Count Marchetti, is a bachelor and quite an agreeable man, with some humor and some sarcasm. At this dinner I sat next to Mrs. Hay, wife of the Foreign Minister, who was at the right of the Italian Minister. Our host was in a good humor and we spent the time in exchanging stories. One thing he said rather shocked the ladies. He asked Mrs. Hay if she knew that Mussolini had issued, or was intending to issue, a decree that every woman in Italy should have a baby every six months. You ought to have seen her face when she heard this. Mentally she was counting up the nine-month period and wondering how even Mussolini could reduce it. After the Italian Minister gave his attention to the lady on his other side, I said to Mrs. Hay that, inasmuch as Mussolini had repealed all laws relating to parliamentary government, and had abolished the League of Nations so far as Italy was concerned, and had become an autocrat in every way, perhaps he thought he might repeal the laws of biology."

INTERNAL INTERNATIONAL COMPLICATIONS

I wrote home (November 16, 1934):

" 'It is merely another case of the result of international complications' I told Dr. Puig this morning at the Foreign Office, when he asked if I had recovered from my slight indisposition which prevented my meeting him at the dinner last night given by the German Ambassador.

" 'How is that?' he inquired.

" 'I ate luncheon on Sunday at the French Club in an Armistice Day celebration: I lunched on Monday at the Italian Legation; and on Tuesday I dined with Californians. The result was that the international mixture gave me internal complications.' "

HOW DÍAZ GOT UNANIMITY

If you listen, you hear all sorts of strange stories and some of the strangest are true. One—probably legendary—told by the Revolutionaries who opposed Díaz, is that going into a town to quell a revolt, Díaz assembled all the men in the public square and made an address to them explaining his policy. At the close he asked if all agreed with him. All except two men gave the sign of approval. Whereupon Díaz shot the two discontented peons and remarked: "Now we are all of one mind."

LAUGHING BEHIND THE HAND

Mexican officials had an indirect way of showing their displeasure if foreigners were insistent upon telling them how to manage their affairs. Once a newspaper correspondent, invited to go on a special train with the President to a remote section of the republic, insisted on giving unasked advice. Growing tired of the suggestions, aides of the President told the correspondent that someone wanted to see him at the next station. It was in the center of a wide desert. When the train stopped, the correspondent was assisted to the ground. The train moved off leaving him standing there. When he finally got back to Mexico City he protested strongly to the President, who professed to be indignant that he should have been subjected to such treatment and promised investigation and punishment of the wicked perpetrators. And then he laughed behind his hand!

RULE NUMBER SIX VIOLATED

Early in May I had a call from a rich American who had made a fortune in Mexico. He told me that my success depended upon getting in close touch with President Rodríguez and he was the man who could secure such association. I wrote my sons that I felt he had violated Rule Number Six and added, "I guess you know what that Rule is. In case you do not, I am sending a little history of it written by Counsellor Arthur Bliss Lane:

"As I recall it, Mr. Morrow's account of the origin of Rule Six, as he personally told me on several occasions, was as follows:

"During the War, when Mr. Morrow was serving as adviser to the Allied Maritime Transport Council—which was composed of a British General, a French Admiral, and, I believe, Japanese and Italian representatives—some technical point arose one day regarding tonnage. The British General, who was chairman of the Commission, sent for a subordinate officer who was handling this technical question in person.

"In reply to the General's request as to what the facts were on this given question, the young officer did not confine himself to a specific answer, but elaborated on what his ideas were as to how the war must be won. He went on to say that unless his proposals for the winning of the war were adopted, the Allies would certainly lose.

"After listening to this uninvited discourse for some minutes, the General brought the young officer to order with the sharp command: 'Captain, you will please bear in mind Rule Six of this Council.'

"The young officer, somewhat taken aback at his superior officer's sternness, inquired, 'I beg your pardon, sir, but what is Rule Six?'

"The General's terse reply was, 'Don't take yourself too damned seriously.'

"When the meeting broke up, Mr. Morrow found himself walking out of the council room side by side with the General. He remarked to the General that the rule he had cited to the young captain was one of the most excellent rules he had ever heard. Mr. Morrow observed that if Rule Six were so good, he should be glad to know what the rules from one to five were. The General replied:

" 'There are no other rules.' "

MEXICANS GOT THE BEST OF THE OIL MEN

There were plenty of stories of how the Mexicans, supposed by some Americans not to be as shrewd as people north of the Rio Grande, often got the better of American traders. Here is an illustrative story told by General Manuel Peláez to Arthur Young, who told me the General chuckled as he pointed out that the oil men don't always get the best of Mexicans:

"Being hard pressed for money, General Peláez asked the oil producers in the Panuco section to give him a loan of a very large sum (I have forgotten how much but it went into the thousands of pesos). The oil men feared that if they granted that request, it would be the beginning of more requests, and that they would have to support the army. They did not wish to make a precedent of it and did not want to give up the money. On the other hand, inasmuch as the General was in control of that district and since their pipe lines and properties might need his protection, they were in a dilemma. They had a conference in New York to know what to do. And then a representative of all of them went to see the General on a certain day with a large sum of bills of the amount he had requested. But all that money had been issued by another regime and had been repudiated by Carranza. They thought the General did not know this, and the oil men said, 'General, we have decided to make the loan as requested, and here is the money,' and handed him the money. 'But,' said the General, 'that money was repudiated yesterday. It is of no value, and I cannot use it.' 'Oh yes, you can,' said the oil men, 'you are in control down here and you can compel the people to take it.' A new light shone in the General's face and he accepted the money. He used it to pay off his soldiers and instructed them to spend it all in buying goods from the Huasteca Oil Company's store, thus converting bad money into good money and compelling the oil people to furnish goods in the full amount of the loan he had requested."

A ROLAND FOR AN OLIVER

Anyone who thinks it easy to get the better of a Mexican will have a rude awakening, as this characteristic incident shows:

"The representative in Mexico of a U. S. industrial concern was complaining to a labor department official that his employees, although under contract, were now demanding things not covered in the contract. The American presented his case eloquently, emphasizing that in the U. S. people had a deep respect for contracts, and for the law. 'It would be extremely difficult,' he said, 'to explain to our Board of Directors, who are representatives of our citizenry, which has a profound respect for contracts, and for the law, the circumstances under which workers could demand things not contemplated in a written agreement, made under the laws of Mexico. I cannot overemphasize that in the U. S. we are a law-abiding people.'

"A twinkle came into the eyes of the labor official, and he said: 'Yes, I have been in your great country, and I think I understand fully what you mean. But tell me, señor, I am confused about one thing. You see, I was in your magnificent nation during the prohibition law, and I am confused about the reaction of the people there to this law, in view of the general respect and the abiding faith of the people of the United States in their laws.' "

INSISTED ON PAYING DOUBLE

"No, I will not pay anything but a peso—nothing else," emphatically declared a Rotarian to a taxi driver who had asked him half that sum. Not understanding Spanish, he made the surprised taxi driver take twice the regular fare. The price automatically went up to a peso for all Rotarians.

RESENTED ROOSEVELT'S CONGRATULATIONS

Many good stories were told by guests at the Embassy from the United States. Here is a good one I related in a letter to my sons and sent a copy to President Roosevelt:

"Mr. Dresser, Head of General Motors here, was talking to your mother about age and how wonderful it was some people lived to the century mark and the length of life was extending all the time, and said that his grandmother had passed 102 years. He said that when she celebrated her 102nd birthday President Roosevelt sent her a telegram of congratulation and good wishes. As she is an old-time and very ardent Republican, she greatly resented the intrusion upon her birthday celebration by a Democratic President and was very indignant and asked why he should seek to have part in an occasion where only her friends were welcome. When I see Franklin I shall tell him about the reception of his telegram of congratulation. I take it, of course, that some friend in the community wrote to the President or to his secretary and suggested that it would be a very nice thing to do, seeing this lady had gone two years over the century mark, to have a word from the President, but it didn't work. She wished no Democratic felicitations. Politics is deep-seated, and anybody who talks about adjourning it will have the same experience President Wilson had when he said, 'Politics is adjourned.' It may have been adjourned in that room, but it took up business the next day in a larger hall."

SENT ON TO ROOSEVELT

In the days of bitter controversy about the New Deal legislation at Washington—and I kept up with it all—Roosevelt was being pelted with verbal stones, and while he sometimes replied in kind, I wrote him:

"If at any time you desire to use some cuss words that are not hackneyed, I will give you some that came to the Embassy recently. A letter came from a party who had desired us to take some action which it did not seem we had authority to take. When we asked this party to submit proof before we could pass upon the matter, the answer came that what we asked for would require the party to submit to:

> " 'an illegal, unconstitutional, tyrannical,
> destructive, bad, confiscatory, and usurping
> act.'

"If you want to say anything rough about anybody, you can quote that as a Mexican way of giving strong expression without using any real cuss words."

EQUAL TO THE OCCASION

There was frequent badinage between me and Beteta. One day I had a letter from the Foreign Office addressed to the Embassy in which Santa Barbara, California, was referred to as in Mexico. I solemnly took the letter to Beteta and asked, "Since when did Mexico annex a part of California? This expropriation business is going too far." Beteta was equal to the occasion and replied, "The error of the stenographer is understandable since California was a part of Mexico before your government expropriation."

MEXICAN SENSE OF HUMOR

Here are two stories by Katherine Knox, of the Embassy Staff, showing that Mexicans have a sense of humor and know how to get even with their critics:

"During the time and talk of racial discrimination along the Texas border, one Mexican, who had stood about all he could take after seeing restaurants on the Texas side with such insulting signs as 'No Mexicans allowed here,' etc., decided to erect one in competition just across the border. The sign he posted read: 'Anyone can eat here, even Texans.' "

"The second anecdote shows up a typical tourist who went to Mexico and employed a native guide to take him around. While going through the markets, the American picked up a small orange and asked what it was. When the Mexican guide told him it was a Mexican orange, he, in a very deprecatory tone responded, 'Oh, but you should see the lovely, big juicy oranges we grow in the State of California.' The Mexican very politely answered nothing until asked a little bit later what was the name of another specific fruit. 'That,' he responded, 'is a Mexican peach.' 'Oh, my poor fellow,' responded the tourist, 'You should see the magnificent peaches that made the State of

Georgia famous.' The guide still answered nothing though his pride was beginning to mount. Further on, when asked the name of still another fruit, to which he responded that it was a Mexican apple, he could hardly contain himself when the tourist quipped, 'But, my dear friend, you should see the delicious apples produced in the State of Oregon. Why we even call them the Delicious Apple!' Finally they took a car and drove out into the country where they passed field after field of maguey (cactus) plants. It is taller than a man. When the American asked the name of that plant, the Mexican could hardly wait to answer with a beam, 'Why, that, Sir, is what we call a Mexican artichoke!' "

SHE DIDN'T OWN A BURRO

According to Hopkinson Smith, folklore and good stories cross all borders. Mijares Palencia, Governor of Puebla, told me the story of the man who didn't get the horse because he gave away the fact that his wife was head of the family. He thought it was peculiar to Mexico. Ned Woodul told me this story:

"A kind-hearted but inquisitive old lady travelling in Mexico met a couple city-bound. The husband was perched with comparative comfort on the rear end of a burro—the wife with a baby strapped on the front and a heavy load on her back, followed afoot.

" 'Why doesn't the wife ride?' the old lady inquired of the husband.

"He replied, 'She doesn't own a burro.' "

In another form this story was current in the United States:

"A German officer complained of American pullmans when he engaged a section.

" 'What is the trouble with them,' he was asked.

" 'My wife is very heavy,' he said, 'and it is difficult for her to climb into the upper berth.' "

A BOSTONIAN'S SPANISH

Ned Woodul also told me this story:

"A young lady had just returned to her home in Boston after a three months' course in Spanish at the Summer School in Mexico. Her friends were anxious to know how much Spanish she had learned. She replied that, true to Bostonian tradition and culture, she had confined herself to the business of study and that what she had learned was grammatically and otherwise correct and proper.

" 'But how much Spanish do you really know?' they insisted.

" 'Well,' she finally replied, 'I learned that *mañana* means tomorrow and *pajama* means tonight.' "

BOSTONIAN SECRETARY SPOKE BROKEN ENGLISH

My career secretary (and a good one), Robert Newbegin, rather prided himself, as all Bostonians are supposed to do, on his correct pronunciation of English. On one occasion this man from the Hub (spelled with a capital "H" in Boston) was taking a group of Texans through the Embassy. One asked, "Are you an American?" Newbegin replied that he certainly was "one of the real old stock," or words to that effect, and added that all secretaries in the Embassy were required to be American citizens.

Thereupon another Texan in the party remarked that he certainly did not speak English like an American. Newbegin proudly said, "I came from Boston and I might use a Boston accent."

The Texan then said, "Now I understand why you speak broken English."

WHERE TAXPAYER'S MONEY GOES

Secretary Newbegin furnished me this story:

"On one occasion, I took a group of tourists over to the Embassy residence to show them 'their home,' as the Ambassador always happily put it. After showing them the living room and large central hall, we entered the dining room where there were two large cupboards where the silver was on display including as it did, a number of beautiful trays and trophies which had been presented on various occasions for a variety of reasons including services to the Democratic party. One member of the group, after scrutinizing that magnificent display from a distance, gasped, 'Now you know where the taxpayer's money goes to—it is to supply Ambassadors with all this unnecessary silver.' I pointed out to him as tactfully as I could that he was in error and that that silver belonged to the Ambassador personally. Corrected, but by no means subdued, he said, 'Huh, got money of his own, ain't he?' "

"EVERYBODY LOVES YOU EXCEPT MY WIFE"

In Mexico the members of the diplomatic corps and their families live in an atmosphere somewhat resembling a colony, and there exists a spirit of comaraderie. They were often at each other's houses, and rarely a week went by when there was not association in their own homes or at dinner or banquets or fiestas. As illustrative of how sympathetic they were I wrote home (February 18, 1934):

"After the dinner at the Embassy to diplomats and Mexican officials when we were standing in the drawing room in a little group, including the Ambassador from Brazil and his wife and others, the Ambassador came to me and put his arm on my shoulder and said, 'I want to tell you that everywhere I go in Mexico I find that everybody likes you—the public officials, the private citizens, and the men and women. They like you very much.'

"And then, with a smile, he said, 'Everybody in Mexico likes you except my wife.'

"She is a beautiful Chilean and is quite popular with the men and fascinates many of them. When he said 'everybody likes you but my wife,' I said, 'That is what she tells *you*, but that is not what she tells *me*.' And of course we had a good laugh."

DID THEY GO FOR A WALK?

Bill Richardson tells this yarn:

"I remember very well one incident when the Garden Club of America came to Mexico. It was my pleasure to give the ladies a luncheon at the Casa Alvarado in Coyoacan, and you and I were the only members of the opposite sex. Some of the ladies were wives of very prominent men in the United States and one of them had sipped cocktails in such a way that she felt most happy, and, all smiles, she addressed you and said, 'Mr. Daniels, isn't this wonderful? There are only two men present for us hundred women. Couldn't you and I go out for a walk?' I don't quite remember your answer!"

SAVED SIX HUNDRED LIVES

The best story teller in the Diplomatic Corps (some of them were risqué) was Fin Lund, minister from Denmark. I frequently reminded him that "there is something rotten in Denmark." This is one of his prize stories:

"A Danish lady, taking an ocean voyage, made these entries in her diary:

"*First day out:* It is glorious and wonderful, the sea and the refreshing air.

"*Second day out:* I am thrilled. The Captain asked me to sit at his table.

"*Third day out:* Went on deck with the Captain at night. Under the stars, he made an improper proposal to me which outraged me and I clearly let him understand my sense of insult.

"*Fourth day out:* The Captain told me that unless I acceded to his proposal that had insulted me, he would sink the ship and all on board would be drowned.

"*Fifth day out:* I saved six hundred lives!"

NO MAN CAN ESCAPE A WOMAN'S HUNTING NOOSE

Of a rare luncheon on August 17 (1935) I wrote home:

"Your mother had a tea Monday and I had liberty. On Tuesday we went to the Pan American Round Table luncheon to hear Mr. Lucas de Palacio, Manager of the Ritz Hotel, speak on old inns in Mexico. He was formerly in the diplomatic service. His address was quite interesting and informing. There are many stories connected with the old inns. The Chairman of the Committee, Mrs. Lesher, told frankly, with flashes of humor, that as a young woman she went on a steamer down the Pacific Coast to Chiapas to marry Mr. Lesher, to whom she was engaged. When I was introduced, I suggested that all other wives tell their story, as they would show that though a man may take wings and fly to an inaccessible coffee plantation, the woman who has made up her mind to marry him will pursue him and find him and marry him. Returning home that afternoon, I read a story that recalled my remarks at the Round Table and wrote this letter to the President of the club, Mrs. Arthur Constantine:

" 'Referring to the suggestion that the members of your Round Table should successively, one at each meeting, follow the example of Mrs. L. at the meeting on Monday, and tell the story of how she captured and married her husband and kept him in captivity, I came across a statement by a German Baron in a story in *Collier's,* which I was reading last night, which you may wish to pass on to the married members of the Round Table to be considered in preparation of their confessionals. The remark attributed to Baron von Genther by Quentin Reynolds, the author, is as follows: "Well, I know of no case either in our time or in antiquity where a beautiful woman who wanted a man did not eventually succeed in getting him. Cleopatra set the precedent, I suppose. I tell you, no mere man is proof against the determined resolve of a woman. What were those lines of Browning's from *A Light Woman?*—'When she crossed his path with her hunting noose, and over him drew her net.' " ' "

A FARRAGUT STORY

In the War Between the States, Southern men like Maury and Farragut divided in their allegiance. I never heard until I was in Matamoros that Farragut's standing by the Union—"Damn the torpedoes, Full speed ahead"—cost him the love of his sisters devoted to the Confederacy. Vice Consul Krausse at Matamoros, whose maternal great-grandmother was an aunt of Farragut, related an incident I had not hitherto known. He said that "the Farragut family did not speak highly of the Admiral because he espoused the cause of the Union during the Civil War." His two sisters, then living in New Orleans, are said never to have spoken to the Admiral after the war. He came to New Orleans once after the close of the war to visit his sisters. Upon learning of his approaching visit, the sisters instructed their maid to tell him that they had no brother."

RODE IN A REPUBLICAN CAR

Some of the Embassy staff, when I was getting ready to go home to a Democratic Convention, asked if I let it be known that I made all my trips in Mexico in a Republican automobile. I had told them this story:

"Shortly after my appointment the agent of Mrs. Morrow advised me that the automobile used by my predecessor belonged to her, and asked if I would like to buy it. I was told that I could get it for $400 or $300.

"I said, 'There is my check for $300.' And the deal was closed. It proved I was a good Yankee Trader. I told Mrs. Morrow, on one of her periodical visits to Mexico: 'I have been riding in your

Republican car. It didn't do well until I had baptized it in the Democratic Stream, and I found the innards had to be repaired, or renewed pretty often.'"

I told her I thought this was due to its Republican origin, but she opined the Democratic chauffeur might be at fault.

In those days of economy (contrasted with the present extravagance, it sounds niggardly) the government did not furnish the Ambassador with an automobile or gasoline. Both had to come out of his salary, as did the bulk of the costly entertaining for the first years.

NO DEMOCRAT CAN ENTER HEAVEN

Mexicans and Americans living in Mexico love fiestas, and no critical period drives out their love of social pleasures and fun. Here is an illustration, in a way, that was original, as I wrote (June 12, 1939):

"After dinner we went into Mr. Wright's movie theatre, where he showed quite a number of excellent pictures. The chief one was one that Mr. Wright himself had designed and had gotten people to assist him, which he called 'The Great Reformation.' The motif of it was that your mother and I, riding donkeys, went up to the gates of Heaven, and Saint Peter, or the Angel Gabriel, I don't remember which, declined to admit us, saying no Democrats were allowed to come into Heaven, and that, plodding our way down from the gates of Heaven, we met Mr. Wright. He told us that nobody could go to Heaven riding a donkey, but that if we would go on elephants St. Peter would be glad to welcome us, whereupon we mounted elephants and were received.

"Mr. Wright had much fun working on this picture. Before your mother left, he borrowed from her one of my hats. It was very well done. He had Heaven peopled by Lincoln and Harding and Coolidge and Hoover, and the only Democrat in Heaven was Al Smith. Then he had a boat rocking and about to sink, in which he had Roosevelt and Woodrow Wilson and other Democrats in a very bad situation and in danger of drowning. Mr. Wright was in the picture as 'A Very Meek Man.' I said, 'I understand that perfectly; you have been reading the Bible and you saw that "the meek inherit the earth," and as you want the earth you are willing to be meek for the time-being.'"

THE RABBIT FOOT WORKED UNTIL . . .

It began the first year I was in Mexico. I hit upon an original and daring plan which I used until I left Mexico. It was a rabbit's foot for luck and brought me many cherished gifts. It began this way: In the early part of 1933, upon returning from the Agricultural College at Chapingo, I invited Secretary of Agriculture Francisco S. Elías and Mr. Hubbard to lunch at the Embassy. At the luncheon, when the waiter passed some oranges, Señor Elías asked, "Where did these oranges come from?"

I told him I did not know, but "somewhere in Mexico."

He replied, "You know, of course, that the best oranges in the world grow in Sonora." He was a native of Sonora and close kin to General Calles.

I answered, "You say the best oranges in the world come from Sonora, but without being discourteous to a guest I must say I do not believe a word of it."

When he recovered, Señor Elías said, "You don't believe it? Then I will send you a box to prove it." And he did, and I wrote him that there were none more succulent.

That incident gave me an open-sesame to getting other gifts than oranges. Some time later when I was in Uruapán at a luncheon given to the members of the Diplomatic Corps, the mayor asked me, "How do you like this coffee?" as I was taking a second cup. I replied that it was very good.

"Very good!" he said, as if I had not praised it enough. "Señor, this is the best coffee in the world. It is so good that in Paris they use it to add to poor coffee to make it palatable." And he proceeded to discourse on the coffee of Uruapán as superior to any that ever delighted the human palate.

Recalling my success in getting a box of oranges from Señor Elías, I said, "I heard what you said but I do not believe a word of it," and before he could be offended I related the incident wherein the Minister sent me a box of oranges to make good his boast. The Mayor listened but did not indicate that he took the hint. I went to the train feeling that I had not put it across with the Uruapán Mayor. However, I was wrong. When we entered our room in the train, my wife, a great lover of good coffee, cried out happily, "Look here, the mayor has sent us four bags of Uruapán coffee!" And it

Upper left, Miguel Lerdo y Texada, director of the famous *Típica* Orchestra, which has given many concerts at the Embassy. *Upper right,* a charming young lady who danced at the Embassy. *Lower left,* Cantinflas, Mexican comedian. *Lower right,* Roberto Soto, comedian of the Mexican Theatre, in the role of a *pachuco.*

Nacimiento (Nativity) arrangement and figures (*left*) carried at the head of the procession of the *Posada* given at the American Embassy on December 23, 1937.

delighted us for many weeks. My plan worked so well in other places that I thought about having it patented.

It had not lost its charm, but conditions made it unworkable at the steel town of Monterrey. After telling my story of getting gifts from other people by professing incredulity of their boasting about their favorite product, I said, "I understand you make the finest steel rails in the world." Applause. "But I don't believe it"—and before I could go further the president of the steel company arose and said, "Come over to the steel plant and you can have all you want—provided you will take them as they come, red-hot from the furnace." He got the best of me.

When I tried the trick at Tampico, it fell down completely. The Diplomatic Corps had made a tour of the oil fields of the Tampico district and were being entertained at a banquet and ball at the country club. Called on to speak, I told my stock story, which had paid large dividends, and closed by saying, "I am told that the oil wells in Tampico are the best in the world." And then I used the old gag of "I don't believe a word of it." I waited for someone to rise and say, "You don't believe a word of it? We will give you an oil field to prove we have the best." I am waiting still. The trick that got me the oranges and coffee never got me an oil well. The joke had lost its fetching force.

Long after, when Cárdenas had expropriated the oil fields, a friend from Tampico came to see me at the Embassy. During the conversation he asked if I recalled my Tampico speech in which I virtually asked to be given oil wells and drew a dry hole. I told him I did. He replied, "Since Cárdenas has expropriated all the oil fields, I wish to God we had given you some wells to prove our boasting." My rabbit's foot had ceased to work!

XLI

THE PLAY'S THE THING

I WAS introduced to Mexican love of the dramatic art on the night of September 29, 1934, when in a blaze of glory the Palace of Fine Arts was formally opened. President and Mrs. Rodríguez, the chivalry and beauty were there, and so were the People.

On the night that *La Verdad Sospechosa* by Juan Ruiz de Alarcón was rendered, every one of the thirty-five hundred seats was occupied, and the ecstatic joy of the people knew no bounds. The foundation had been laid in 1905, covering five acres of ground, and thirty years later we witnessed its opening. It had cost eighteen million pesos, and was the product of noted artists and architects of seven countries. The pure white marble was brought from Carrara, Italy, and native marble came from Mexican States. The most characteristic of the wealth of decorations and statues was called an architectural poem depicting the National Emblem—the great Mexican eagle perched upon a cactus with a snake in its mouth, a legend of the wandering Aztecs.

I was introduced to this perfection of art and architecture by Federico E. Mariscal, who was entrusted with the completion and installation of the interior of splendor.

The completed structure gave Mexico the most beautiful opera house in the world. Marble and gold shone resplendent. What was most impressive was the stage curtain, fifty-two feet in height, composed of millions of opalescent crystal mosaics. It was made at the Tiffany studios, reached Mexico about the time of the Revolution, and was kept in a safe place during those troublous days. The crystal curtain represents a wide window through which you seem to be looking out upon the luminous valley of Mexico. Lake Texcoco and the snow-capped peaks of Iztaccihuatl and Popocatepetl gleam in the sunlight.

As we gathered after the opening performance, Mexican friends told us that the neglected people had resented the Díaz expenditure of so much money in a marble palace, when there were no schools for the Indians and people lived in shacks.

After the Revolution, the leaders said: "Let the incompleted palace stand as a reminder of a reign that regarded only the Four Hundred *Científicos.*" I was told that, as designed, there were only four hundred elegant cushioned seats, "because there were only a few hundred whose education could permit them to appreciate the operas to be presented." But when the new government decided to finish the building, instead of four hundred velvet seats provision was made for thirty-five hundred available seats on the theory that music and art were for all the people. And the people thronged to hear classic as well as native music.

"I could but think, as the first performance in the marble theatre went on," said an old-time Mexican, "that there was being recreated the play rendered by the Indians upon the arrival of Mendoza, the first Viceroy from Spain, in 1535. That dramatic performance took place in the open-air theatre in the Zócalo. Many thousands of Indians were present, including the regally garbed Aztec nobles. In its way the splendor was as notable as tonight when we saw the brilliantly illuminated and glittering palace opened for the first time. Mendoza and the Spaniards with him gazed upon the pomp and ceremony with surprise and awe. This September night in 1934 did not out-do in brilliance the performance by the Indians in 1535."

We were to go often to the palace of enchantment, high-lighted when Grace Moore came to Mexico and won the hearts of all the people with her voice. The *Excelsior,* under the headline, "A Golden Voice Wins Mexico," said: "Take an orchid, take a band, take the applause of an enthusiastic Mexican and multiply it by a thousand and you have Grace Moore's trip to Mexico." Armillita, said to be the world's greatest bullfighter, killed a bull in her honor, a ceremony usually reserved for royalty or high government officials.

MUSIC, PICTURE STARS, AND GRACE MOORE

The Embassy grounds and the adjacent streets were thronged on Fourth of July celebrations and at the coming of distinguished visitors, such as Vice-President Henry Wallace, Presidents of Republics, and daring aviators. But none of them attracted so many people as did Ann Sheridan, Kay Francis, Hedy Lamarr, Paulette Goddard, Dorothy Lamour with Tyrone Power, Bob Hope, Wallace

Beery, and other stars who were received at the Embassy. They were almost smothered by the admiring crowds that wished a sight of their favorites. Equally did Mexican lovers of music give their hearts to Grace Moore and other American artists.

It was after these stars had conquered Mexico that Foreign Minister Padilla complained to my wife and other friends: "The Ambassador does not treat me right. When aged, high-brow ladies come here to gather material for stories on Mexico he sends them to me. But when Grace Moore and the glamorous movie stars and actresses arrive, he monopolizes them himself."

POSADA CELEBRATED AT THE EMBASSY

My wife was greatly intrigued by the *Posada,* a peculiarly Mexican Christmas celebration. The motif is: A number of people accompany Joseph and the mother of Jesus "great with child," seeking a place where the Christ Child can be born. Mary rides on a burro led by Joseph. The company stops, sings Christmas carols in front of houses, and asks admittance. They are rebuffed from house to house until finally they find entrance, as at the stable where the Saviour was born. It is an old custom, carried out in the old days with deep religious sentiment. Unfortunately, some moderns have introduced levity (I attended one where a Mexican taking the part of Joseph acted like a clown and got roars of laughter). But it still exists in its old beautiful spirit with those who look on Christmas as a holy festival. The word *Posada* means "Inn."

One Christmas, having become a lover of things Mexican, my wife decided to have a *Posada* (Christmas Fiesta) in the Embassy in the old Mexican manner. By the goodness of two beloved Mexican friends, Amada Morán de Constantine, who was a director of the Pan American Round Table, and Señora Luisa Iturbide de Rincón Gallardo, a large company of diplomats and others were delighted with the *Posada* given by these three—Luisa, Amada, and Addie Worth. The gifted Mexican ladies led in the arrangement and with the aid of experts their deft fingers built a replica of a stable and set it up in the Embassy. With beauty and dignity and sacredness and reverence the first *Posada* in the American Embassy ushered in Christmas.

The *Posada* was in the blood of those members of Mexican families. Señora de Constantine was a granddaughter of Don Ignacio

Mariscal, for thirty-five years Foreign Minister, and the daughter of Federal Senator Don Tomás Morán, and the wife of Arthur Constantine, Dean of American Correspondents. She spoke equally well in Spanish and English and was a lecturer in the University of Mexico. Señora de Rincón Gallardo was a member of the distinguished Iturbide family.

Mrs. Constantine speaking of the happy introduction of a Mexican custom into the American Embassy, said, "Mrs. Daniels had studied the Mexican Christmas tradition carefully, and the Embassy was the scene of the most beautiful and authentic fiesta of the Christmas season. The hospitality of the American Embassy at all times was something to be remembered. Mrs. Daniels opened her heart and home in the most charming manner."

A FLOWER HIS MONUMENT

A lover of flowers, my wife found happiness in the abundance of orchids and calla lilies, plentiful and cheap, and took pride in the fact that it was a Carolinian, a predecessor as head of the Mexican mission, who rescued from obscurity the Mexican Christmas flower, called the Poinsettia in honor of Minister Joel Roberts Poinsett. He took cuttings of it to his South Carolina home and lavished care upon them so that they have carried Christmas cheer all over the world.

Poinsett was the most versatile, dynamic, and able of all American diplomats to Mexico, but he is remembered mainly because Jackson had to withdraw him for having taken an active and influential part in the domestic politics of Mexico. In fact, he was credited with organizing a political party of York Rite Masons, which elected a President of Mexico. But it created a storm, for Mexicans are jealous of any outside influence in their domestic affairs.

LEGEND OF THE POINSETTIA

Making the Poinsettia the chief Christmas decoration my wife preserved this piece of lore by Violet M. Roberts:

"It was during Poinsett's sojourn in Mexico that he discovered a simple but beautiful little green weed which had as its flower a bunch of yellow pods that formed the center of a scarlet whorl. It was eight years later, in 1836, that the unknown weed was recognized by the country's leading botanists as a flower and given the name poinsettia.

"A charming legend explains the origin both of its beautiful color and of its use as a Christmas flower. It is said that in Cuernavaca, Mexico, it was the custom for every church and chapel to have a manger in which lay an image of the Infant Savior. On Christmas Eve the village folk flocked into these places to decorate in His honor with flowers.

"On one Christmas Eve, in the outer district of Cuernavaca, a small dark-eyed child grieved and mourned because she had no flower to take to the manger of the Christ. But as she cried a beautiful angel appeared before her and said, 'Lovely child, weep no more. Go pluck a weed from the roadside, bring it to the altar, and wait.' The little girl arose and did as the angel had told her, and when she had placed her weed on the altar it immediately became a vivid scarlet whorl.

"And, according to the Mexicans, that is why the poinsettia is today the most prized of all Mexican flowers for the beloved Christmas tide."

THE PICTURESQUE CHARROS

When the Spaniards arrived in Mexico they found that the Indians had the spirit of play and games of their own. But there were no horse races, which Mexicans later came to love so much, because a horse had never been seen in Mexico until Cortés rode one into the ranks of the Aztecs. Having never seen a horse, they thought the man and the beast were one, and fled before the strange animal.

One reason that the cavalry is so popular in Mexico is that the Mexicans dearly love a horse, and their chief sport has been in the saddle, dressed in picturesque *charro* suits. The Marqués of Guadalupe (a title given when Maximilian was handing out titles as in Austria) and other *charros* did me the honor of electing me as a member of the *charro* select organization of horsemen. But they didn't give me a horse. However, I wore the costume on stated occasions and enjoyed the association.

MEXICAN LOVE OF SPORTS

I early found friends among the University students, particularly those interested in athletics, some of whom had earlier joined in protest against my appointment. As a boy I had played baseball and as Secretary of the Navy I had been an enthusiastic backer of the Annapolis football teams. Knowing this, Arthur Constantine made an engagement for me to meet the University teams who called at the Embassy soon after I arrived. We formed relations that made them among my best friends. I coöperated with the Noriega brothers, pioneers in football, and others in obtaining coaches from Yale and other American institutions and in getting teams to come to Mexico. I recall that in a game between the University of Louisiana and the University of Mexico in 1933, I went on the field before the kickoff, and said to the squads: "Your game constitutes an important and significant contribution to international relations. Over and above your competition should be your collaboration to make this event a success. You, players of Louisiana College, represent the youth of the United States. You, players of the University of Mexico, represent the youth of Mexico. By your conduct the youth of two countries will be judged. Play hard, but play clean. The rules will be strictly enforced. A smashing tackle carries deep understanding."

The game of football did not come to Mexico until late, and it was not until the thirties that it gained as strong a hold in the cities and colleges as in the United States. The same is true of baseball. By 1940 it was so universal that I often stopped at open fields to see boys playing and rarely missed an intercollegiate game. One of the most distinguished and popular visitors to Mexico, always welcomed at the Embassy, was Connie Mack, who brought his teams down for a winter of practice.

I was happy in 1946 to learn that Jorge Pasquel, who had faced death with me in the State of Vera Cruz, with others had made baseball as popular in Mexico City as in the United States, securing some of the best players from across the border.

COULD NOT ESCAPE BULLFIGHTS

Why do Mexicans go to bullfights? To me it seemed strange and brutish that every Sunday afternoon they gathered by the thousands to see the toreador and the bull contend for the mastery. In the nearly nine years I was in Mexico I did not go to one, though once without knowing where I was going I found myself in a great stadium crowded with officials and others who had come, as I had, to witness the inauguration of a new Governor.

At one other time I thought that I could not get out of witnessing what I had determined never to see. All diplomatic representatives were requested to join President Cárdenas at a bullfight to raise money for some most worthy and patriotic cause. The plan was for the President, with the Mexican flag, to be in the center, and all Ambassadors and Ministers near, with the flags of their countries, so as to give it the glory of an international setting. Of course, I paid the price and could not properly absent myself without a lack of courtesy to the President. I had heard that President Cárdenas had no liking for bullfights, and it was not certain that he would lend his presence. On the morning of the event, I ascertained that the President was out of the city and would not be present. That made it proper for me to follow my desire not to go, and the United States was represented by secretaries, some of whom rarely missed a bullfight. I wrote home in 1933 how I narrowly escaped having a bullfight in my honor:

"Referring to Worth's experience at the bullfight [he became faint] I do not think I ever told you of how my diplomacy was put to the test with regard to a bullfight. Not long after I arrived here, a delegation representing the Brotherhood of Locomotive Engineers and other workers called to see me and said they wished to give me the distinction of having a bullfight in my honor. They said they knew of my close association with the railroad workers in the United States and wished to show their appreciation of my position. They were not then prepared to name the day, but said they would write me. In the meantime, after they left, I had a conference with some members of the Embassy staff as to how I could get out of it without offense. I said that I followed a Mark Twain rule: 'in case of doubt, tell the truth,' and, therefore, I thought the best thing to do would be to tell them that I appreciated very much their kindly feeling, but that I did not believe in bullfights and could not attend. The members of the staff thought this would be unwise, and I saw that it would be equivalent to telling them that I was rebuking their attendance at bullfights and calling it wrong. We learned later that they had also called on the Spanish Ambassador and wished him to be a co-honoree, so to speak, of the bullfight. Of course those who were to be honored were to pay a goodly number of pesos, so that a fund could be raised for the unemployed workers. Fortunately for me, it turned out that there was some disagreement as to this particular bullfight—as

Ambassador Daniels in *charro* costume and Mrs. Daniels dressed as a *China Poblana*.

The *Jarabe,* the folk-dance of the State of Jalisco. The young lady is dressed as a *China Poblana.* The gentleman, Don Carlos Rincón Gallardo, Marqués de Guada-lupe, is dressed as a *charro.* Ambassador Daniels essayed to dance the *Jarabe* but he was not as adept as the Marqués.

to the date or something of the sort—and it was called off without my having absolutely to decline.

"I made up my mind if ever I went to a bullfight somebody would carry me, and after Worth's experience I am all the more strong in this position. He said it would not have been so bad if it had not been for the disembowling of the horses. Somebody told me that the horses that are used for the bullfights are generally pretty poor specimens and could not live long anyhow. I understand that at the beginning the bullfighters come into the ring on beautiful horses and ride around in a grand parade. These horses are then left outside and the poor old animals are ridden in which are used during the actual fight, a number of them being killed in every fight."

ARTISTS PORTRAY HISTORY

Mexican revolutionary history stares you in the face at every turn, thanks to impressionistic artists who have portrayed it indelibly and colorfully on the walls of the National Palace and nearly all other public buildings.

Artists, judging by these murals, constitute the best propagandists of the Revolution. They painted for the masses. Their pictures aroused hostility to the Cortés conquest and enslavement of the Indians. They depict the later exploitation of the workers, and their murals likewise flay the *hacendados* and *Científicos* of a later period. The theme does not change—always it arouses resentment against oppression of workers and against all exploitation.

You cannot look upon the realistic pictures without a feeling that artists, better than orators or actors, have sensed why the people rose up under Hidalgo, Juárez, and other leaders of the revolutionary period. If there were no historians to recite the story of the cruelties of other days, no orators to inflame the passions, the speaking murals would literally shout of bondage and uprisings from Hidalgo's bell, the *Grito,* to the yearly ringing of the liberty bell in the National Palace.

While the technique today is modern, artists made pictures from earliest times. Corwyn, an authority on Aztec history, poetry, and art, from whose association I learned much, said, "Mexican artists thousands of years ago were at work doing what the Greek and Roman artists did several hundred years later."

My first acquaintance with Diego Rivera was at the time when we spoke at a celebration at Spratling's place in Taxco, where silver was fashioned into designs that pleased tourists. But my chief recollection is that neither Diego nor I scored that night—the palm went to an Indian apprentice, whose speech was so eloquent that I found oratory was not a lost art in Mexico.

THE DIEGO RIVERA SCHOOL OF ART

Everybody who came to Mexico wished to see the frescoes of Diego Rivera and to find out what Mexicans think of their famous artist, about whom so much has been said and written. Mexicans are proud of the distinction he has won, even those who are in utter disagreement with his political or economic views. Rivera's frescoes are seen in large relief, massive in historical pictures, in the National Palace, in the Department of Education, in the Public Health Building, in the Agricultural College at Chapingo, and in the Cortés Palace and the Morrow House at Cuernavaca and elsewhere. He is prolific, and his murals are vivid, mainly historical, depicting Mexican scenes from Montezuma to Expropriation. They paramount revolutionary events and leaders. They have a quality which can be described only as being of the Diego Rivera technique. In other words, visitors to Mexico say that he has created a Rivera school of its own.

The first of Rivera's murals that I saw were those that covered three sides of the Cortés Palace at Cuernavaca. They attract visitors and stand out in bold relief as if they protruded from the walls. Writing home about the paintings, I said:

"When Mr. Morrow was Ambassador, he commissioned Diego Rivera to paint a mural on the partially enclosed porch on the second floor at the back of the Palace, overlooking the valley and the mountains. This is a large porch running the entire length of the building and the painting covers the three sides and the ceiling. In an impressionistic way it tells the story of the conquest of Mexico by the Spaniards, with particular reference to the conquest of Cuernavaca. It shows the cruelty of the Spaniards, who are represented as driving the poor people to work like slaves, while they recline in hammocks. The guide told us the following story: He said that after Rivera had finished most of the paintings (for which Mr. Morrow is said to have paid $20,000) Mr. Morrow was examining them one day and he said to Rivera, 'You have made every priest look like a villain or a brigand. There were good Spanish priests in Mexico in the old days. I think you ought to include in the painting one of the benign priests who gave their lives trying to help the poor people, and not let people think they were all thugs and rascals.' Rivera is said to have shrugged his shoulders and said, 'Well, if you wish it, I will do so.' When Mr. Morrow came to examine the finished murals, he turned to the painter and said, 'I do not see any priest with a good face. I see you did not keep your promise and give the picture one priest who did not have a cruel face.' 'Oh, yes,' said Rivera, 'I have painted one good priest. Come, let me show you.' And he pointed out (and the guides point it out to you) the picture of the priest. You see nothing but his back. He wears a robe with the cowl over his head. Except for his priestly robe there is nothing to indicate that he is a priest."

AMERICA'S BIG THREE

American visitors are always taken to the Rivera paintings in the Education Department, which represent Rockefeller, Morgan, and Ford, the big three whom Rivera would call "capitalistic feudalists." He pictures the Indians, their muscles taut from strain and overwork, creating wealth, which is transferred to the coffers of these Americans, whom he depicts as getting the lion's share. In view of that painting, Mexicans here were surprised that Rivera was engaged to do murals in the Rockefeller Center. Some of them predicted what later occurred.

ROCKEFELLER REMOVED RIVERA'S PAINTING

In 1933 the papers had much about the murals Nelson Rockefeller had engaged Rivera to paint for Rockefeller Center. The public was startled when young Rockefeller ordered the destruction of the Rivera paintings because they contained a figure of Lenin among the great of the earth. Though I had nothing in common with Communists, I felt a sense of indignation when the papers carried the story that young Rockefeller had ordered the destruction of a work of art. Some papers said the young man expected the painter to make John D. Rockefeller, Sr., the central figure and was incensed that Lenin had the high place.

Not long after the destruction of the Rivera murals, Nelson Rockefeller and his wife came to Mexico. At a dinner at the Embassy I found he was, like his father, whom I had visited in New York and had worked with in the Y.M.C.A., an agreeable gentleman, whose sincere devotion to the spirit of the Good Neighbor doctrine endeared him to the Mexicans. I told him I liked the murals Ambassador Morrow had engaged Rivera to paint on the walls of the Palace of Cortés at Cuernavaca. Mr. Rockefeller, evidently feeling that he was on the defensive about the destruction in Rockefeller Center, said: "But in that case those who employed Mr. Rivera knew what he was going to paint." In his case his father paid Rivera a large sum to paint murals for Radio City, but did not know what the artist was going to paint.

Though young Rockefeller was not asked the reason for the destruction, or questions about the contract, I did have a talk, at a dinner at the home of Señora Iturbide de Limantour (a sister of Eduardo Iturbide and widow of Díaz' Minister of *Hacienda*), with Mrs. Francis Flynn Paine, who was in Mexico as a representative of the Rockefeller Foundation. She told me she secured for Rivera the opportunity to paint the murals in the San Francisco Stock Exchange, and induced both Mr. Ford and Mr. Rockefeller to give Rivera a commission. She felt that Rivera had violated her confidence because she had felt assured that his murals would be in line with American history and progress as accelerated by the discovery and large use of petroleum. She felt that when he accepted the Rockefeller money, it was a violation of the proprieties to give a leading place to Lenin, who represented views diametrically opposed to the American views which Mr. Rockefeller incarnated. She was indignant at what Rivera had done, and her resentment was increased because she had gotten him the commission and in a sense had vouched for his doing nothing that could offend his patron. Rockefeller said little, but Mrs. Paine was voluble in her criticism of Rivera.

Some new light on the murals that Rockefeller had engaged Rivera to paint was provided at a dinner given (September 12, 1933), by British and American friends to Counsellor and Mrs. Lane as they were leaving for Nicaragua, where Mr. Lane was to assume the post of United States Minister. I wrote home as follows:

"I took in to dinner the wife of a prominent American who had business connections in Mexico. I was very much interested to hear her tell about the misunderstanding between the Rockefellers and Diego Rivera. She had recently been to New York and had talked with Mrs. Rockefeller. It seems that Mrs. Rockefeller is greatly interested in modern art and it was she and not Mr. Rockefeller who was responsible for engaging Rivera to make the mural painting at the Radio Center in New York. When the painting was completed, this lady told Mrs. Rockefeller that the Mexican people did not think she (Mrs. Rockefeller) had any fighting spirit, and urged her to take the course she did of covering up the painting, because Rivera had used it to give glory to Lenin and the communists.

"When Mrs. Rockefeller was told that the Mexicans thought she had no spirit and was permitting Rivera to put something over on her, she and Nelson gave the order to cover up the painting. My dinner companion said she had a copy of the original drawing that Rivera made, which was presented to Mrs. Rockefeller before she made the contract with him, and the painting is not at all in keeping with this drawing, showing that he had gotten his money by false pretenses; that is, he made Mrs. Rockefeller think she was to get one kind of picture when she actually got another. She offered to show me this drawing sometime if I wanted to see it. I shall do so, for this is one controversy that will not down.

"At this point an American business man, who had lived long in Mexico, broke in and said it served Mrs. Rockefeller right; it served Mr. Ford right; it served all those Americans right in San Francisco, New York, and Detroit who had anything to do with Rivera, because he is a common, sorry man and his one purpose is to try to elevate communism. 'He is of the dirt, and I am glad they got stung by him,' he said. 'It ought to teach them a lesson to have nothing to do with him.' Neither the business man nor the lady thought that Rivera's art compensated for his communism.

"I had very little to say about it, because I saw that all the company at my table were on the Rockefeller side of the argument and there was no need to have a controversy with people who think that anybody who is not of the established order is more or less socialistic or communistic. It might have put me down in Rivera's class if I had told them what I thought about it.

"I judged from what this lady said, and I have heard from others, that John D., Jr., had nothing to do with making the contract; that he let his wife and Nelson run the whole business.

"I asked why they covered the painting up instead of destroying it, since it was so objectionable. 'You know,' she said, 'the public have short memories. It would have raised too much controversy to have destroyed it, and artists, who were not practical, would have sided with Rivera. By covering it for a time, until after the public has forgotten it, it can be destroyed and nothing will be said about it.' In this I think she is very much mistaken."

RIVERA—A CREATOR OF UGLINESS

Diego Rivera did not escape harsh criticism at home. His admirers said he painted life as it was. His critics said he selected the ugliest and neglected the beautiful and gloried in the nude, painting his own wife naked. *Excelsior* (May, 1933) said: "Diego's ugly things appear sublime to a few dozen crazy people. He is a promoter of ugly things and is a Communist. He paints ugly things because, being ugly himself, he thinks the world should be populated by homely types. His plan would produce a world of poor fools and ugly people."

NORTH AMERICANS PORTRAYED MEXICAN LIFE

It was not only native Mexicans whose murals and paintings told the story, for the eye of Mexico, from pre-Cortés days; some North Americans delighted us by their perfect delineation in water color, oil, and films. Ralph D. Gray won the Amateur Cinema League Camera-men honor with his film, *Fiesta Mexicana*.

An exhibition before a group of people, including Minister Padilla, which my wife and I enjoyed, was Gray's showing of the life of the native fisher folk of the Patzcuaro region, the blessing of the animals, the passion plays at Lent, the battles between the Christians and the Moors, and a score of others portraying Mexican life, old and new, in its perfection. Gray caught the color.

A CITY OF MONUMENTS

The capital of Mexico is a city of monuments from the heroic bronze equestrian statue of Charles IV of Spain, which stands in the center of the Avenue Reforma, to those of patriots who drove out the Spaniards.

There are two that appeal strongly to American visitors. The first is the massive statue of George Washington. In the passion of resentment that flared high against the United States in 1914, George was roughly handled but later was restored to his pedestal. On every February 22, members of the American colony and visitors join with the Embassy staff in putting a wreath at the base of the monument. It is the only statue of an American that I saw in Mexico.

The second was erected in 1925, many years after he lived, to Father Bartolomé. It bears this inscription: *"Stranger, if thou art a lover of virtue pause and worship, for this is Friar Bartolomé de Las Casas, Father of the Indians."* That Catholic friar is chiefly remembered because he is the author of the saying: "Unless the natives are given their land they cannot be saved." This is the genesis of the slogan of the Revolution: "The land belongs to those who work it with their hands."

The statues and monuments most revered by Mexicans are those of Father Hidalgo, the priest who rang the bell (called the *Grito*), which began the fight that secured independence from Spain; and of Juárez, the Oaxaca Indian, who put an end to Maximilian's Phantom Crown and restored self-government to the Mexican people. Though Hidalgo and Juárez are not knighted or canonized, their deeds and their spirit to incite liberty in Mexico are revered as are those of Bolívar in South America and Washington above the Rio Grande.

THE WILL ROGERS OF MEXICO

Roberto Soto was the first of the comedians to hold up public officials to devastating ridicule. Calles once served notice that no busybody official should molest Soto. I loved to see him and hear his hits. He literally exuded wit! I was quoted as saying, "Soto is Mexico's Will Rogers," and Will Rogers said of him, "He is an actor's actor." He was inimitable. Soto could be serious and devastating. I recall particularly the skit that had no little to do with driving a member of the cabinet out of office, and I remember that his skit on Garrido Canábal raised a storm that gave an impetus to Canábal's leaving Mexico. As Governor of Tabasco, Canábal had closed all the churches in the State and had driven the priests and nuns into hiding, and then had sought to atone by making it impossible for any intoxicants to be bought or sold in the State.

Soto in closing his skit showed Garrido Canábal with a long whip, swaggering before a cowering group of Tabasquens. He denounced them for their religion and inveighed against the clericals with vicious scorn. After a time an old crone tottered into the Plaza. Garrido stopped his shouting and ran toward her, crying, "Nana! Nana!" (Nurse). He took her tenderly by the arm, murmured endearments and helped her to a chair. She began to scold him. He tried to appease her. As she became more and more angry with him, he implored her to forgive him. "Tomasito, why haven't you been to Communion?" she demanded. He became abject. "Go to Church at once, Tomasito!" she ordered. He slunk off. Soto did Garrido's obedience to his old Nana with irresistible humility. The audience howled with understanding.

A MEXICAN COMEDIAN

Almost every Sunday, crowds of politicians and others went to hear Cantinflas skits. His very appearance excited laughter. He wore baggy trousers and a shirt too short, and the audience momentarily expected to see his pants drop off, but they never did.

The people laughed and applauded when he got off gags about public men. The report was current that when Charlie Chaplin was introduced to Cantinflas, he said, "I am proud to meet the greatest comedian of them all." Most Mexicans gave him that place. If a man said to you, "You are Cantinflas," it meant that you were making a great speech and saying nothing. The word ought to be adopted in the United States. It fits some public men.

Under the old order, based on old Spanish customs, a cat might look at a king, but no comedian could make sport of a high public official. Spanish officials, however, are not the only ones who resent having comedians make them the butt of ridicule. It was whispered and generally believed that President Harding withdrew a White House invitation to Will Rogers because the lariat-throwing comedian and philosopher made some act of Harding's look ridiculous to a laughing audience. Stuffed-shirt public men could not tolerate Will Rogers or Cantinflas. Big men took their jokes in their stride. Genuflection toward men in public office did not end entirely when the revolutionary leaders took over. Some of the new order did not relish being made sport of to the amusement of the populace. When I went to Mexico, there were stories of how Roberto Soto had kidded Calles' Labor Minister, Luis Morones, out of office, and I heard him make side-splitting digs at others.

In his role of bedraggled, lonesome bum, Cantinflas (christened Mario Moreno) gave the impression of having drifted in off the street, though he had graduated in law at the National University of Mexico. He had the distinction of having his name used as a verb. "To cantinflas" meant to tell much and say little and indulge in wild *non sequiturs*.

I recall that when Spanish War Minister Prieto visited Mexico, after witnessing Cantinflas he seriously advised President Cárdenas to forbid his joking, saying, "You ought to stop this. It was by permitting such ridicule of the Spanish Republican Government that we lost public confidence, and this resulted in our downfall."

Though Cárdenas was too wise to act on that advice, some less sensible officials did at one time order the closing of the theatre where Cantinflas performed, after hearing an acrid skit on Mexican election scandals. Backed by the people, Cantinflas declared the ban a violation of his civil liberties and it was soon lifted; his satire was so popular that the official had no support. Undoubtedly the constant rebuffs Cantinflas gave the German propagandists strengthened the Mexican sentiment against the Nazis. He was featured in the full-length moving picture *Neither Blood nor Sand*.

CREED PRESERVED IN POETRY

From earliest times poetry has been the favorite expression of the Mexicans. Songs and dances, accompanied by fife and drum, were the chief features of all Aztec religions, court, and other ceremonials. The Azetcs had put in verse their religious beliefs and had committed it to memory. Only in that way was it preserved when the newly arrived Spanish priests set the example of burning books. The creed of the Aztecs was engraven on their minds, and from many it has never been eradicated.

The Mexicans believe the tone of a bell becomes mellow with centuries of ringing. "They preach a sermon of beauty in their quiet way, an Angelus in the midst of our occupations," said a patriotic Mexican on the night of the *Grito* as we stood in the National Palace, awaiting the hour when the President, in the presence of a hundred thousand celebrants, would ring the very bell which was rung by the patriot-priest, Hidalgo, in the little town of Dolores Hidalgo on the night of September 15, 1810, when he called the people to assert Mexican independence.

FROM AZTECS TO CHÁVEZ

Music is in the blood of Mexicans. No event, whether religious, social, or political, is without music. It is of all kinds, from the tempo of Aztec days to the latest symphony conducted by Carlos Chávez, who was called to the United States as leader in the largest opera houses.

No reception or celebration at the Embassy was held without the presence of the *Típica* band under the leadership of Miguel Lerdo y Texada, whose friendship I esteemed and whose death I deplored. He was a real maestro. The members of the band felt at home at the Embassy, where they were welcome guests.

I recall how they laughed and applauded on our wedding anniversary when dressed in brilliant costume, I essayed with a señorita member of the band, the *Jarabe* in my *charro* suit.

STANDARDIZATION NOT LIKED

Mexico is a country of artists and craftsmen. They create for "the joy of the work" each one "in his separate sphere." If you order a dozen of anything—pictures of men or burros, silver articles with Mexican design, picturesque sombreros or *charro* suits—designers and workmen often suggest that it would be better not to have them all alike, but to permit the creator to vary the design. They do not like monotony or standardization. But of course, they are ready to follow the desire of the customer if he insists upon having all his plates or pictures of the same pattern. American desire for standardization threatens individual pattern and varied creations. An American long living in Mexico says, "American tourists, insisting upon standardization, threaten Mexican artistry in creation."

Part Thirteen

TRAVELS

XLII

KEEPING IN TOUCH

I N 1946 the American Congress enacted legislation looking to remedying the failure to keep in touch with home by members of the Diplomatic Corps whose duties called them abroad. It provided for stated periods of return to the United States. I put that principle into practice. Almost every year I spent my leave, not only at home as vacation but in getting in touch with the people, gauging public sentiment and having part in politics and other matters interesting my country. My first year in Mexico was happy and fruitful without a cloud as big as a man's hand.

A BUSY MONTH AT HOME

After the signing in the Foreign Office, with Minister Puig, of the settlement of the Special Claims and the setting up of a tribunal to handle General Claims (just one year after I began negotiations), my wife and I set out for home (April, 1934). We went to be present at the review of the American Fleet upon the invitation of President Roosevelt, and in Washington where, as chairman of the William Jennings Bryan Memorial Committee, I was to make the presentation of his statue and President Roosevelt was to accept it as it was unveiled, not far from the Lincoln Memorial and the Arlington Memorial Bridge.

THE PRESIDENT'S INVITATION

We had been looking forward to that home-coming since the day in February when I had received this letter from President Roosevelt:

> "THE WHITE HOUSE
> WASHINGTON

> "February 5, 1934.
> "Dear Chief:
> "It has been fairly definitely established that the fleet review will take place off Sandy Hook on Thursday, May thirty-first.

As you know this will mark the return of the fleet to the Atlantic Coast after an absence of over three years.

"In case there is any possibility of your being home at that time, it would be grand if you and Mrs. Daniels could join me at the review. Somehow I can think of nothing more wonderful than to have you standing beside me when the fleet goes by.

"All goes well here and I have distinct hopes that the Congress will adjourn by the early part of May. If everything else is quiet, I hope that I can leave on a cruiser towards the end of June and go via Puerto Rico, Virgin Islands, and the Canal to Hawaii and the West Coast. In the old days you stole a march on me for I never got as far as the Hawaiian Islands!

"Many thanks for that delightful birthday telegram.

                              "Affectionately yours,
                                   "FRANKLIN D. ROOSEVELT."

"HONORABLE JOSEPHUS DANIELS,
    American Ambassador,
    Mexico City, Mexico."

From my Diary I quote of our visit to the White House and our stay in Washington:

"When we reached Washington we drove to Worth's home to greet the family. We found that Mrs. Roosevelt had invited Worth and Josie to take lunch with us at the White House. Our rooms were in the corner overlooking the Treasury. We had been greeted by the officials and attendants at the White House, most of them having been there in the Wilson days when we were frequently there.

"Mrs. Roosevelt told us she had invited all our family in Washington to lunch with us—Worth and Josie, Addie's sisters Belle and Ethel, her brother Henry and David and David's wife to make a family party on our wedding anniversary. No courtesy could have been more appreciated. This was partly true because forty-six years ago that morning we had been married and two days afterwards had been received at the White House by Mrs. Grover Cleveland, and had been at the White House in Wilson's day at another of our wedding anniversaries.

"Upon our arrival at the White House an old-timer showed us to our rooms and said Mrs. Roosevelt would call later. Pretty soon she came in, without waiting to take off her hat. 'I did not know what hour you would arrive and I went out driving to be sure that Louis Howe would get some sun and air in the middle of the day.' She told us (knowing our interest, for Howe had been private secretary to Roosevelt when he was Assistant Secretary of the Navy and we occupied adjoining offices) that Howe had been sick for three months and that she and the President had been and were anxious about him. He had suffered a long attack of influenza. She had at one time feared it was a slight stroke. 'He has not eaten a meal with us for weeks and he lacks the will or something to get back to his old self.' She said it was necessary to insist upon his getting out; that the day before he would stay out only ten minutes but that she had managed to keep him out a whole hour and it had done him good. 'Nobody else can move him to go out and I was glad I could keep him in the air so long today.' She said, 'It is good to see you both again, to see you looking so well and Franklin and I are happy to have you with us.'

"In the afternoon Mr. and Mrs. Manton Wyvell (who had charge of matters about the Bryan statue unveiling and who was Chief Clerk of the State Department under Bryan) gave a reception to us at their house. Hundreds were present, including most of the Cabinet, diplomats, Congressmen and the Bryan family, who had come to the unveiling.

"At night we went to a dinner at the Mayflower given by our old friends, Secretary and Mrs. Daniel Roper, who had invited fifty or sixty of our old friends to meet us. We had wired Mrs. Roosevelt from Raleigh of this invitation, and Mrs. Roper had written to her about it; so it was all right to accept an invitation out to dinner on the first night of our stay at the White House. There we learned that an Ambassador on leave has no rank in his own country. Though we were the guests in whose honor the dinner was given, we were not in earshot of our hosts, the place of honor going to the French Ambassador and then to the Cabinet and on down as provided by the protocol.

"It made no difference to us and I was glad to talk to my dinner partner, the wife of the representative from Hawaii, whom I had met when we visited Honolulu.

"Shortly after our arrival, Addie gave Mrs. Roosevelt the lacquer tray she had brought for her from Mexico. She said she was going to take it to Hyde Park to use as a tea table and was glad to get so beautiful a present from Mexico.

"The next morning Mrs. Roosevelt came into our rooms. She said I would go with Franklin and Addie would ride with her to the unveiling of the Bryan statue. She had two ladies to luncheon in addition to the wife of Senator Sheppard. I took lunch with the President at his desk in his office. Light lunch—stuffed eggs. Wallace was also at the luncheon, and farm legislation and problems were discussed among other things. I was glad to be let in on some of the plans and discussion of great values. Smart man, Wallace.

"After lunch the President said, 'You must excuse me so that I can finish the speech I am to make this afternoon.'

"We left the White House at 3:50 for the unveiling, from under the South Portico. The President came out in his little chair, propelled by his assistant. He fixed his braces and got into the car. We talked of Bryan and how he had lived before his day. Reaching the stand, the President went in on the arm of his aide and I followed."

UNVEILING THE BRYAN STATUE

There was interest in Mexico when it was known in May, 1934, that I was going to Washington to deliver the address at the unveiling of the statue of William Jennings Bryan. As the foremost advocate of silver as primary money, Bryan was given a warm welcome when he visited Mexico, which is the greatest producer of silver in the world.

Bryan's old friends were there (though not many who had helped to nominate him in 1896 were alive) and members of his family. Among those present were the officers of the Association: the President, Josephus Daniels; the Vice-Presidents, William H. Thompson, Manton M. Wyvell and Patrick H. Callahan; and the members of the Executive Committee, Charles A. Douglas, Chairman, Thomas S. Allen, Daniel Bryde, Blair Lee, and Clifford Berryman. It gladdened me that my old shipmate, President Roosevelt, was to make the speech of acceptance for the government.

There were addresses by Harold L. Ickes, Chairman; the Honorable Blair Lee, an old companion in political battles; Gutzon Borglum, the sculptor; my presentation address. The speeches were climaxed by the acceptance speech of President Roosevelt, after Bryan's grandson, David Hargrove, had unveiled the statue. It was fitting that the prayer was offered by the Reverend Joseph R. Sizoo, who told me he was largely influenced to enter the ministry by an inspirational speech at his college by Bryan; and the benediction by Bryan's old friend, Bishop John W. Hamilton. In my address I reviewed at length the career of the Commoner, a near and dear friend. President Roosevelt's tribute was a classic. He said, in part: "No selfish motive touched his public life; he held office only as a sacred trust of honor from his country, and when he sought a mandate from his fellow citizens the soul of his inspiration was the furtherance of their interests, not his own, not a group, but all."

REVIEWING THE FLEET

Later in the month we journeyed to New York to review the fleet of the American Navy returning to the East Coast after a long stay in the Pacific. Of that event, which drew many thousands to New York Harbor, I wrote in my Diary (May 31):

"Up betimes, with breakfast in our rooms, and to the *Indianapolis* by 7:30 to the Naval Review, the first big review of the fleet on the Atlantic since shortly after the World War. I reviewed it then (President Wilson being in Europe) with Assistant Secretary Franklin D. Roosevelt with me.

"My wife was surprised that I was given a salute of nineteen guns as I went aboard, and Ruth, to whom it was an honor she had not seen before, said she and Frank were thrilled.

" 'I did not know you gave this salute to an ex-Secretary of the Navy,' my wife said to a Naval officer friend.

" 'This is not a salute to an ex,' he said, 'but to the Ambassador of Mexico.' They took a picture showing me receiving the salute and Addie standing by."

"It was a saluting day, with nineteen guns for the nine members of the Cabinet as they came aboard and twenty-one for the President as he was received with all the honors of music and guns, made and provided for the Commander-in-Chief when he came aboard. It was all familiar and dear to him, for he is a Navy man to the core. Mrs. Roosevelt and the President's mother, wives of Cabinet officers, and invited guests were on the *Indianapolis* (a 10,000-ton modern cruiser which was the reviewing ship), Frank and Ruth had been invited by Assistant Secretary Henry Roosevelt to go out with them on another ship.

"A rather heavy fog delayed the coming of the ships, but

the wind sprang up and the sun came out (Roosevelt luck) and the day became clear and beautiful. At nine A.M., when the fog was thickest, I told Attorney General Cummings that some Naval officers feared the fog would not lift in time for a clear review. With a merry twinkle in his eye, Cummings said: 'I will issue an order to the lawless fog to disappear by eleven o'clock.' I told him that if he could arrest and imprison a fog, which interfered with the President's program, I would believe he could get Dillinger and the other criminals who had long eluded capture.

"At eleven o'clock, the fog having lifted, I informed the Attorney General that I would no longer doubt his authority and capacity to govern on land or sea. The photographers snapped us at that moment when we were smiling over the incident. It was a fine sight to see the great ships swing into line, to see the upstanding sailors man the rails, hear each ship's band render the 'Star Spangled Banner,' and hear the twenty-one-gun salute to the President as they passed to receive the return salute by the beloved Commander-in-Chief. At the request of the President, I stood on his left and Secretary of the Navy Swanson stood on his right. It recalled to us the interesting days which knitted us together, days of getting ready for and aiding in the conduct of World War I. Then I was Secretary; Roosevelt, Assistant Secretary; and Swanson was Chairman of the Naval Affairs Committee in the Senate. We worked together in that crisis, and it made us all happy to be together again. As we stood there for hours (Swanson, not well, would sit down in the intervals, the President always saying: 'Claude, sit down a few minutes.') The President stood all the time. He was as fresh at the conclusion as if he had never had any infantile paralysis which even now prevents his walking or standing without braces. He was in a gay mood, and we all told stories, mostly connected with incidents during the days of the Wilson administration.

"While the President and Claude and I were laughing at a story, a photographer took a snap shot which preserved our faces in laughing merriment. When the pictures appeared later, a friend asked, 'I'd like to know what caused you and the President and the Secretary of the Navy so much hilarity during the review."

"I told him I guessed the photographer caught us just after the following occurred:

"I turned to the President, as the salute from the *New Mexico* died away and we were waiting for the next salute, and said, 'Franklin, do you remember the most difficult task committed to us during the years we were running the Navy?'

" 'Certainly,' replied the President. 'It was getting two million soldiers over to France without the loss of a single man en route to the battlefield, in spite of the menace of U-boats.'

" 'You are wrong,' I replied. 'That was easy compared to another job.'

" 'Then if I am wrong,' he said, 'tell us what was the most difficult task.'

"Swanson sat quietly listening as if wondering what the difficult task was.

" 'It was,' I said, winking at the President, 'trying to induce Claude Swanson to let us, over his opposition, spend Navy money at the Norfolk Navy Yard, at Hampton Roads or Quantico, or some other place in Virginia.'

"We all three laughed, because we recollected that hardly was the ink dry on any Naval appropriation bill before Swanson would call at the Navy Department and undertake to show that it was essential that most of the improvements contemplated should be carried out in Virginia. It may be that the photographer caught us at that moment. There is no telling, for the President told numerous stories, and so did Swanson, and we all were as happy and free from care as three boys out of school.

"The review over, we went below and had tea and real food. I was distressed to see that Swanson could not walk without aid, showing that the report of a slight stroke in one leg was true. In fact, though the President had been unable for years to walk without help, he could go up and down the gangway, holding on to the side-rails, better than Swanson. Addie had greatly enjoyed the day with Mrs. Roosevelt, wives of Cabinet officers, and others. It was nearly night when we reached the Plaza, and we suddenly found we were pretty tired. A hasty dinner and we were off to see *As Thousands Cheer*. It had been a long time since we had seen an American play. Frank and Ruth had seen it before but were glad to go again. I never saw a better take-off than the one when Hoover and his wife were leaving the White House; the scene between the Prince of Wales and his mother; and the one when John D. Rockefeller,

Jr., and wife were trying to get John D. to accept Radio City as a birthday present."

THE PARADE OF SAILORS

The next day (June 1) I rose early to accept the invitation of Mayor La Guardia to review the parade of the sailors up Fifth Avenue and to be present at the city's welcome to the officers of the fleet at the City Hall. Afterwards I spoke at a luncheon given the officers of the fleet by the Advertising Club. Of that day I wrote in my Diary:

"Mayor La Guardia introduced me as the man who was once 'the boss' of President Roosevelt. 'As much his boss,' I said, 'as any man ever was of a Roosevelt.' I then told them that a friend had asked me about the status of a diplomat. I replied that I had heard it said: 'There would be no need of an Army or a Navy if it were not for the mistakes of diplomats' and I observed that within two months after my appointment to the diplomatic corps, a large increase had been made in the Navy, with an increase also of the Army strength. Was it a coincidence? Or was it cause and effect?

"During our stay in New York I was a guest of honor at the annual dinner of the Survivors of the *President Lincoln*. That ship, commanded by Captain P. W. Foote, who was afterwards my Naval Aide, was torpedoed on the way home from France. They have a dinner every year and one of the crew came all the way from San Antonio to be present. It was like an alumni reunion of a college, with much jollity."

POLITICS NOT ADJOURNED

On that visit at the White House more was talked about than the Naval Review and the unveiling of the statue of Bryan. I quote from my Diary:

"Franklin and I talked politics, particularly who ought to be Chairman of the National Committee, seeing that Jim Farley would retire and devote his time to his duty as Postmaster General. His idea was to draft some man, not necessarily one who would conduct the 1936 campaign, to fill in. That didn't seem to be wise and I told him I doubted if any but a big man should be chosen. He mentioned several. I suggested that Jim Farley resign as Postmaster General and retain the chairman-

Above, banquet of the Presidential Electors in Washington, June, 1941. *Left to right,* Homer Cummings, Attorney General and former Democratic National Chairman; Mrs. Franklin D. Roosevelt, Ambassador Daniels, Vice-President Wallace, and Michael Francis Doyle, Chairman of the banquet. *Below,* reviewing Fleet from a battleship in New York Harbor in May, 1934. *Left to right,* Claude Swanson, Secretary of the Navy under Roosevelt; President Roosevelt, former Assistant Secretary of the Navy; and Josephus Daniels, Secretary of the Navy under Wilson.

Above, monument to William Jennings Bryan, unveiled in Washington, May 13, 1934. *Below,* President Roosevelt, as he accepts the statue of Bryan. Ambassador Daniels made the presentation speech. (Associated Press photos.)

ship. He did not think Jim would like to leave the Cabinet. He said: 'Think it over and see me again.' I asked him if we could not elect a Democrat to the Senate in Maine and said if President Sells, of Bowdoin College, would run he could win. He asked me to see him again about this probability as he had talked about Sells; that he would be a model candidate if he could be induced to run. 'He can be induced,' I said. 'See what you can do and let me know,' he said.

"I had a long talk with Postmaster General Farley on politics, in the course of which I asked him the question: 'If you could hold only one position, that of Postmaster General or Chairman of the Democratic National Committee, which would you prefer?' I told him that, in view of the President's attitude as to expecting all Federal officials to resign from the National Committee, I did not think it was fair for him to hold both places. He agreed. But before answering my question,, he went to the door and locked it so that we would not be disturbed, and then opened his heart to me. He said that naturally he appreciated the honor and the opportunity of serving in the Cabinet, that he had done well, enumerating some reforms which will make the Department self-sustaining for the first time in years, and that, inasmuch as he had come in for criticism as to the air-mail contracts, he would not like to resign before the good results of his administration were recognized by the country. He went on to say: 'In answer to your question, I would much prefer to be Chairman than Postmaster General. My wife is not enamoured of Washington life and prefers our old home life, and I am interested more in our party's victories in the future than in holding any job.' He then asked me: 'When do you think I ought to resign?'

"I told him it should be not later than the last of September, so that he could give all his time to organizing for the election in November without the Republican and independent press continually criticizing him for using public position to carry on political activities."

ATTENDED WHITE HOUSE PRESS CONFERENCE

It was on this trip to Washington, I joined fellow journalists as they went into the White House to the President's press conference. A reporter printed what took place as follows: The President, who once served under Daniels as Assistant Secretary of the Navy, saw him in the group and called out, laughing:

"What are you doing here, Mr. Ambassador? We don't allow diplomats at these press conferences."

Daniels drew himself up with pretended pride. "I am not here as a diplomat," he said, "but as editor of *The Raleigh News and Observer*."

"That won't do either," retorted the President. "We don't allow editors; only reporters."

Daniels would not be downed. "Very well then, I am here as a reporter for *The News and Observer*."

The President gave up. "All right, boss," he said, "take a seat."

BIRTHDAY DINNER AT RALEIGH

Between discussing Mexican affairs at the State Department with Cordell Hull and Sumner Welles, who were happy that the first settlement of claims in half a century had been reached, and talking about legislation with members of Congress, I took time to go home to attend and speak at the Commencement of the University of North Carolina, and to attend a birthday dinner given by the Raleigh Chamber of Commerce. I wrote in my Diary (May 18, 1936):

"At that dinner Howard Branch, Secretary of the Chamber, presented a gold-lettered, black leather volume containing letters of appreciation from prominent men who had been invited to the dinner in my honor. He read the one from President Roosevelt, who referred to his opportunity of measuring his chief when he was a subordinate. There were letters of cordial birthday greetings from the Vice-President, Speaker of the House, Cabinet officers, and ex-Cabinet officers, of cordial greetings, and generous compliments. Neither my wife nor I had heard of the book and the presentation was a pleasant surprise. Among the messages was one in Spanish sent by Dr. Puig, Minister of Foreign Relations. Toastmaster Marsh said that as Governor Ehringhaus was an adept in the Spanish language, he would read it. Amid much laughter the Governor tried to translate it.

"At every plate there was a picture of me on cloth woven on the Jacquard looms of the Textile School at the College by Ben R. Harris.

"There were songs: 'America,' of course, and others; and then a big cake, the gift of B. Streb, baker, was brought in by a lovely girl. It contained forty-six candles, one for each year of our married life. 'Blow them out and see how many grandchildren you are going to have,' cried the Toastmaster. (All of our sons and their wives were seated at a table near us.) Twenty-one candles glowed after my first trial at blowing. Two survived my second puff. Governor Ehringhaus interpreted that as twins, at which there was much laughter.

"Addresses of welcome were made by Governor Ehringhaus and by W. H. Weatherspoon, Vice-President of the Chamber. He gave a review of my life, and said some nice things, but he got the glad hand when he paid tribute to my wife, showing that I am an 'also ran' in comparison to her in popularity in Raleigh. 'She has blessed Raleigh,' he said, 'with a ministry peculiarly her own. She has sought to do good among her people and not in a manner to provoke public acclaim. By precept and by example, she has sustained in this community the best tradition of womanhood, of beautiful motherhood. With such a companion as this I wonder how any man could be other than great. I ascribe to her credit for what he has done.'

"My speech was one of affection and gratitude, and I said that Raleigh never looked so beautiful. I then touched upon the success of Roosevelt's New Deal and how it had dispelled the gloom and given the sunshine of increasing prosperity."

POLITICIAN AS WELL AS DIPLOMAT

I never lost interest in politics. No protocol or diplomacy could drive out of my life true political activity when I was in the United States. I kept up in the papers and, through correspondence, with the political tides and came home at each National Democratic Convention. I never took any stock in the notion that a man in office should lose interest in the politics or government of his country —a doctrine that has made many office holders slackers as citizens.

ATTENDING DEMOCRATIC NATIONAL CONVENTIONS

Not having missed a National Democratic Convention since 1896, immediately after the hot presidential election in Mexico, bloodstained in Mexico City, I went home for the 1940 convention, serving on the platform committee. I had gone to the convention in Philadelphia in 1936. All had been easy sailing then. At that convention Senator "Cotton Ed" Smith walked out because he "didn't want to hear a Negro preacher pray in a Democratic Convention." Reporters asked my reaction. I told them that I was like the man in the old spiritual, "Standing in the need of prayer, O! Lord! Standing in the need of prayer."

THE THIRD-TERM ISSUE

The 1940 Convention was very exciting. No President had been elected for a third term, and, though the delegates by an overwhelming majority favored Roosevelt's nomination, there was opposition led by Jim Farley and Carter Glass—the latter placing Farley in nomination chiefly as a protest to a third term. He got few votes. Having supported Roosevelt in 1932 and successfully conducted two national campaigns, Farley felt that Roosevelt ought to hand him the nomination. But few agreed, and Roosevelt was renominated with Wallace for Vice-President. There was quite a fight in the North Carolina delegation. I favored Wallace, but the majority of the delegation voted for Bankhead.

NOT TO GO TO WAR UNLESS ATTACKED

But the big fight was behind the scenes in the platform committee. Germany had started World War II. Some wanted the United States to go in, while others were vehemently against taking any step that might carry us into the war. The draft declaration was changed several times. I was strongly against war but did not wish to tie our hands by a declaration, advocated by some, against war under any circumstances. Finally, after much discussion, some of it heated, and telephone talks with the White House, the platform committee wrote this plank, which the convention adopted: "We will not participate in foreign wars and we will not send our Armies, Naval or Air Forces to fight in foreign lands outside the United States except in case of attack."

True to the platform, Roosevelt declared (October 23, 1940) in a campaign speech: "Throughout these years my every act and every thought has been directed to the end of preserving the peace of the world, and more particularly, the peace of the United States."

SECRETARY OF PEACE

I got away from the long sessions of the platform committee long enough to attend the Bryan Breakfast, a quadrennial honor to the

Commoner. Bryan in Wilson's cabinet was truly "Secretary of Peace." Writing of that breakfast in *Labor,* its correspondent said in part:

" 'Never in history has a sincere man spoken bravely in behalf of the oppressed without inciting the hate and opprobrium of those enjoying unearned possessions. The greater his sincerity, the more their vindictiveness.

" 'Jefferson was a Jacobin; Jackson was a demagog. It is the price a great soul must pay to ring true against caste, privilege and exploitation.'

"Thus spoke Josephus Daniels of North Carolina, ambassador to Mexico and famous as Secretary of the Navy for eight years during the Wilson administration and the World War.

"The stars of this unusual affair—which, by the way, produced more inspiring oratory than any gathering outside the convention itself—were Josephus Daniels and William Allen White—one a Democrat and the other a Republican.

" 'I never voted for Bryan,' said White. 'I do not make that statement as a boast, but rather in the spirit of the publican who entered the temple and prayed from afar off, "God have mercy on me, a sinner." ' "

WALLACE WON OVER OPPOSITION

Of a canvas of the delegates from North Carolina, I wrote:

"Sunday afternoon I attended a meeting of the North Carolina delegation. They elected me a member of the platform committee and then took up the question of who the delegation should support for Vice-President. All had been instructed for Roosevelt and the vice-presidency was the only thing up for decision. Governor Ehringhaus and Governor Morrison said the delegation ought not to act; that they ought to find out who President Roosevelt wanted and vote his choice. Two days later we had another caucus of the North Carolina delegation, and then it turned out that the delegation had learned that Mr. Roosevelt favored Wallace and most of them were up in arms against the Wallace nomination. Ehringhaus was strong for McNutt, Doughton and Barden were strong for Speaker Bankhead, and some of the others were for Wallace. One of the delegates came in and said he had just heard that eleven western States had held a meeting and declared against Wallace, whereupon

Miss Beatrice Cobb, National Committeewoman from North Carolina, made a motion that I call up Mr. Roosevelt and ask him to withdraw his recommendation of Wallace. I sidestepped any such duty. Governor Hoey said: 'They may nominate Wallace but they will never do it by my vote. I will vote for no Republican.' Morrison was almost as emphatic, saying that all this talk about Wallace helping the farmers was believed by nobody in North Carolina except Clarence Poe, and that whatever had been done for the farmers had been done by Roosevelt, and Wallace had nothing to do with it.

"Other delegates said they wouldn't vote for Wallace because he was a Republican; they would not vote for a man who was not a lifelong Democrat. I answered that Wallace had been born in a Republican home and that his father was a Republican Secretary of Agriculture, but that when Coolidge vetoed the agricultural bill which Wallace felt was the salvation of the impoverished farmers, he quit the Republican party and supported Al Smith for President after Smith had outlined a farm policy which was in direct contrast to that favored by Coolidge, and that he had supported Roosevelt in 1932, never thinking, when he supported Smith and Roosevelt that he might be called into the Cabinet. I added: 'If we had not received into the Democratic party thousands and hundreds of thousands of Republicans, the Democrats would have been in a helpless and continued minority, and I think we ought to rejoice that a man of Wallace's ability should have had the courage and independence to leave his party when he became convinced that it was refusing to recognize the terrible situation of agriculturists and did nothing to better it.' However, the delegation voted mostly for Bankhead, with a few votes for McNutt, and a half dozen others voted for Wallace.

"Roosevelt made a speech by radio to the Convention, but before he did so, Mrs. Roosevelt flew to Chicago and it was good to see her and talk to her as we sat on the platform together before she was presented. She made the best speech of the Convention—short and in excellent taste—and opened the way for the radio speech of the President, which was heard by every person in the great hall as plainly as if he had been in the room.

"The only real contests in the Convention were for the Vice-President. The galleries were clearly for McNutt—perhaps overwhelmingly—and many were also for Bankhead. They didn't warm up to Wallace at all; on the contrary his name was booed by hundreds of people in the gallery when it was presented and if the galleries could have controlled the nomination McNutt would have been the nominee. However, McNutt was a good soldier and when he saw that the Administration at Washington, of which he forms part, wished Wallace, he withdrew his name, or rather he undertook to, but the galleries, sensing that he was going to withdraw his name, prevented him from doing so. Finally he was permitted to have his way and withdrew his name from consideration. Most of the Southern delegates voted for Bankhead who, I think, was very much disappointed that he was not nominated. However, all the big States like New York, Illinois, Pennsylvania plugged their vote for Wallace and so did most of the Western States and before the first roll could be ended Wallace had a majority and then others withdrew so the nomination was made by acclamation.

"On the day of the nomination of Wallace I took lunch with him and we talked about everything except his candidacy. He is a very modest sort of man and I do not think would have pressed himself at all. He told me he thought it was the proper thing for the Southern delegates to support Bankhead. I sat with Mrs. Wallace on the platform while the voting was going on and it was interesting to watch her face. She was rather tense but did not act as if the result concerned her as much as it did."

WHEN ROOSEVELT TRIED TO GET INTO WORLD WAR I

Upon the third inauguration of President Roosevelt (1941) the members of the Electoral College held a meeting in Washington—an innovation conceived by Michael Francis Doyle, of Philadelphia, who presided at the banquet. Many electors were there, all the cabinet, and distinguished guests. I was asked to deliver an address and made a heartfelt tribute to President Roosevelt, my old Navy shipmate. A few days afterward I received this letter from President Roosevelt:

THE WHITE HOUSE
Washington
February 14, 1941

Dear Chief: —
I did read your perfectly grand speech at the Electoral College Banquet, and I am particularly glad that you brought out

that old effort of mine to get into the war—when I was only thirty-five years old.

Do you remember the other and final chapter? When I had nearly finished the inspection work on the other side in September, 1918, I think I wrote you or cabled that after I had come home and reported to you, I wanted to go back to Europe with an assignment, in uniform, to the Naval Railway Battery. Good old Admiral Plunkett had talked with me about it at St. Nazaire in France where the guns were being assembled and were nearly ready. He asked me if I could swear well enough in French to swear a French train on to a siding and let his big guns through. Thereupon, with certain inventive genius, I handed him a line of French swear words, real and imaginary, which impressed him greatly and he said that he would take me on, if I came back, in his outfit with the rank of Lieutenant Commander.

A little later, as you remember, I came back on the Leviathan with "flu" and a touch of pneumonia and was laid up in New York and Hyde Park for about three weeks. I got back to the Department, as I remember it, about the twentieth of October, told you of my desire, and you said that you could not conscientiously ask me to stay in Washington any longer. Then I went to see the President and the President told me that in his judgment I was too late—that he had received the first suggestions of an armistice from Prince Max of Baden, and that he hoped the war would be over very soon.

That ended the effort on my part because within a few days it was clear that some form of armistice would be worked out.

Love to you both,

Affectionately,

FRANKLIN D. ROOSEVELT

Honorable Josephus Daniels,
American Embassy,
Mexico, D.F.
jd:kct

XLIII

BATTLE MONUMENTS

I FELT honored to be named on the American Battle Monuments Commission to dedicate chapels and other war memorials and cemeteries near the fields where Americans fell fighting in France and other countries in Europe in World War I. The dedication was fixed for the summer of 1937 on the twentieth anniversary of the entrance of the United States into that war.

The Commission was headed by General John J. Pershing, who commanded the American forces in World War I. I found he was as beloved in France as in his own country. The untimely death of Secretary of War Newton D. Baker, was regretted afresh as we trekked over grounds which he had trod during the war. Brigadier General Benedict Crowell, Assistant Secretary of War, represented the War Department, Congress had named as members of the Commission Senators F. Ryan Duffy, Richard B. Russell, Ernest W. Gibson, Representatives Finis J. Garrett, Lister Hill, Walter Lambeth, and Charles A. Eaton. The other members were the Honorable David Reed, Brigadier General Clayton Hill, Colonel John D. Markey, Lieutenant Colonel K. H. Price, Mrs. Cora W. Baker, Mrs. Howard Boone, Brigadier General Kearney, Harry W. Colmery, and C. A. Ragon, with three chaplains, the Reverend Perry Smith, Father William P. O'Connor, and Rabbi Michael Aaronsohn—all chosen because of their war service. At all the ceremonies there were present representatives of the American Legion, who were the guests of the French Government.

Fourteen monuments were unveiled at sites glorified by American sacrifice, two memorial tablets were placed, and eight cemeteries consecrated. The ceremonies began with the unveiling of the Meuse-Argonne Monument at Montfaucon, commemorating the most important engagement of the American Expeditionary Force. It was attended by the President of France and a great company of French people, many of whom had fought in that greatest of battles.

Magnificent Memorials had been erected at the following places:

Monuments: Montfaucon, Montsec, Chateau-Thierry, Brest, Tours (where there was a memorial fountain) Bellicourt, Cantigny, Audenarde, Kemmel, and Gibraltar.

Memorial tablets: Chaumont and Souilly.

Cemeteries: Meuse-Argonne, Oise-Aisne, St. Mihiel, Aisne-Marne, Somme, Suresnes, Flanders Field, Brookwood.

As the largest number of American Legionnaires were present at the dedication of the memorial at Chateau-Thierry, where the Marines won everlasting glory, I think the Army generals who made up the program preferred that I should not speak there or at Belleau Wood for fear I would claim that the Marines won the war and prove it. As a matter of fact, the Marines suffered the largest casualties in the war at Belleau Wood. The beautiful memorial building at Chateau-Thierry is a notable tribute to the men of the Army and the Marines who died in the fighting that saved Paris. For this reason I think the Army generals thought I might start singing this addition to the Hymn of the Marines:

> "As we raised our flag at Tripoli
> And again in Mexico
> So we took Chateau-Thierry and
> The forest of Belleau."

At Cantigny, where I spoke, I found a marble marker erected to Lieutenant Robert B. Anderson, son of an old friend in my boyhood home in Wilson, North Carolina, and paused to lay a wreath on his grave and breathe a prayer. I closed my Cantigny address thus:

"In our grateful remembrance as we have stood beside the graves of thirty thousand of our countrymen whose bodies are buried in France, as we stood reverently in every cemetery, we have recalled the scene in Maeterlinck's 'Blue Bird' in which the grandmother in the Land of Memory tells her grandchildren that it has been months and months since she saw them, not since Hallowe'en, when the church bells were ringing. The children ask how could they see her when she was dead. The answer was, 'We are not dead until we are forgotten.' By that test, seeing in what loving remembrance the men buried here are held, we can truly say they are not dead because they are not forgotten."

At every place where memorials were dedicated in France, Frenchmen who had taken a distinguished part in the war delivered addresses. What delighted me most was that the patriotic French people, in and out of uniform, attended all the dedications and showed, twenty years afterward, that the friendships formed in the heat of war were enduring. The same thing was true in Belgium, where Ambassador Gibson and Prime Minister Paul Van Zeeland spoke, recalling the immortal poem, "In Flanders Fields" by Lieutenant Colonel John McRae:

> "In Flanders fields the poppies blow
> Between the crosses, row on row,
>   That mark our place; and in the sky
>   The larks, still bravely singing, fly
> Scarce heard amid the guns below.
>
> "We are the Dead, Short days ago
> We lived, felt dawn, saw sunset glow,
>   Loved and were loved, and now we lie
>   In Flanders fields.
>
> "Take up our quarrel with the foe;
> To you from failing hands we throw
>   The torch; be yours to hold it high.
>   If ye break faith with us who die
> We shall not sleep, though poppies grow
>   In Flanders fields."

I had always been exhilarated by the noble French *Marseillaise,* but I had not conceived of its power to lift men out of themselves until scores of times I heard, on consecrated French soil, the French national air played and sung by patriotic Frenchmen. There is a lift and a challenge in it that stirs the blood.

In the dedication at Surrey, England, there were addresses by Ambassador Robert Worth Bingham and the Honorable Alfred Duff Cooper, First Lord of the Admiralty, the Honorable Lister Hill, and military leaders. In all of these dedications, men who had served in the armies renewed their unity and bivouacked as in the high days of war.

The dedication of the Brest Naval Memorial was given a distinct Naval character by the presence of United States and French warships in the harbor and a large attendance of United States and French officers and men in uniform. That beautiful memorial stands high commanding the harbor of Brest, through which millions of American soldiers passed enroute to the front. I was particularly interested in that dedication, at which three French military leaders, Senator Richard Russell, and I were to be the speakers, because it was Navy day and because for the last year of the war it was at ancient Pontanezen barracks where many of the armed forces of our country were received and from which they embarked for home. That important post was commanded by General Smedley Butler, of the United States Marine Corps, under whom my oldest son, Captain Josephus Daniels, Jr., served. I had visited it early in 1919, when going to and returning from the Paris Peace Conference.

Most of the memorials dedicated were on ground made holy by the deeds of the two million men of the American Army, whose courage, added to that of the European allies, met and routed the hitherto undefeated Germans. This was fitting, for it was their unbeatable fighting which was decisive. The Navy made a great contribution, but the war was won on the Western Front.

At each celebration addresses were made by members of the Commission and other distinguished Americans and allied leaders and participants in the battles, beginning with the historic address by General Pershing at the dedication of the magnificent marble memorial at Montfaucon, where allied forces won immortality. President Lebrun of France, Marshal Pétain, Ambassador Bullitt and American Legion Commander Colmery highlighted the speaking, which culminated in a stirring message by radio from President Roosevelt. Fortunately all of these addresses have been preserved and constitute an invaluable part of the history of World War I.

The other navy memorial was dedicated at Gibraltar, where Rear Admiral Fairfield told the story of how, in an important period of the war, American submarines escorted 25 per cent of all convoys bound for French Ports and 70 per cent of all convoys bound for ports in the British Empire.

My mind had been in debate at the close of World War I as to whether the bodies of Americans killed in battle should repose in France, "sleeping where they fell," or should be brought back home to be interred in their native soil. However, after having seen the beautiful cemeteries in France, where many were buried, with the long lines of crosses "row on row," and where their graves are guarded and tended with loving care, I came to the conclusion that Theodore Roosevelt was right when he wished his son Quentin, who died in battle, to be buried where he made the supreme sacrifice. Nowhere in the world are there such suitable cities of the dead.

EQUESTRIAN STATUE OF PERSHING

This patriotic vacation was enhanced by the opportunity to come in contact with the people of other parts of France as well as those of Paris and to enjoy association with American members on the Commission, members of the American Colony, and hospitable Frenchmen.

I soon found that the two military men with whom I was associated who were held in highest esteem in France were Pershing and Pétain. They seemed as close as David and Jonathan. Together they graced the occasion when we placed a wreath on the grave of the unknown soldier and paid tribute to others at the Arch of Triumph. They pointed out to us the newly-constructed Maginot line, which was believed to be invincible, as we made our way through its underground tunnels and recesses.

The French wished to perpetuate in a lasting way the glory of Pershing and Pétain by equestrian statues standing at the entrance to Versailles. At a luncheon given to Pershing there was shown the model of the Pershing equestrian statue. The artist was present. It was a good likeness of Pershing but—let General Pershing tell how he felt: "This honor touches me beyond expression," he said, "and I am grateful to France and thankful to the artist. However, I must violate an American rule which says, 'You should not look a gift horse in the mouth' and say that I do not think I sat in the saddle as stiffly as the artist has placed me."

POLITICS AND DEBT TO AMERICA

In one province of France I found a deputy whose campaigning might be copied by candidates who are called upon to meet difficult questions. After the Armistice, when France had pledged to repay the money it had borrowed from the United States, there grew up a strong opposition in France to taxing the French people to pay the debt. Of this feeling a candidate was asked, "If you are elected what attitude will you take toward paying the war debt to the United States?" The candidate shot back, "We do not owe them anything," and made this ingenious reply:

> "The United States insured every soldier's life for $10,000 and for every one killed that money had to be paid his family. By exposing themselves in battle and getting killed, the French lost more lives than the Americans, and every time a Frenchman was killed America saved $10,000. So you see, as so many French saved the lives of American soldiers, we owe the United States nothing. In fact it owes France."

I do not know what influence that reasoning had, but France did not pay the debt.

NO BIBLE, NO JEFFERSON

Visiting the American Embassy library to consult the Bible and Jefferson's works in preparation for an address I was to make, I was pleased to find that the librarian was born in my county in North Carolina and was the daughter of a Baptist missionary. She was mortified when she had to tell me that there was no Bible or Jefferson in the library. Talking later to Ambassador Bullitt I told him that as Jefferson had been his predecessor in diplomacy in France he ought to see that Jefferson's works were available. He touched a button and directed the purchase of Jefferson's works for the Embassy Library. "But as to the Bible," he said, "the lady was wrong." To prove his statement he opened the drawer of his desk and took out two Bibles, one printed in English and one in French. He said he kept both handy. I do not know how it came up but I told him I was orthodox in believing everything in the Bible except one.

"What is that?" he asked, after saying he believed it all.

I replied by quoting the words, "The meek shall inherit the earth." I told him that my observation was that the meek, not only do not inherit the earth, but were pushed aside by the go-getting people and got little, while others grabbed the earth, some putting up barbed wire fences around it to keep others out.

"Have you read that text in the French Bible?" he asked. I had not. He then opened his French Bible and said that sentence read, "The debonair shall inherit the earth." He said that was the correct translation. He quoted the definition of a debonair person as "one of good disposition, gracious, kindly," and said, "They are the people to whom the Bible promises the earth." However, I recalled that if Spenser was right, there was no wide difference between being meek and debonair, for Spenser had written "Was never prince so meeke and debonaire."

BULLITT'S ATTITUDE TOWARD RUSSIA

I was surprised, when dining with Bullitt in his magnificent chateau near Paris, at the bitterness of his denunciation of Russia and all things Russian. I recalled that during the Paris Conference he had gone to Russia and later had expressed faith in the Soviet Union. When Roosevelt was elected Bullitt had favored its recognition. Because of his faith that we could and should get along with Russia, he was made Ambassador to that country. He had not only been disillusioned, but he spoke about Russia and Russians with a hostility that astounded me. Therefore, in 1946, when he became a violent opponent of any association or agreement with Russia, I was not surprised. What caused the change? Some said he went to Russia hailed as a friend and that he expected Russians to eat out of his hand, but that when they did not accept and follow his advice, he turned on that country and its people and became their most violent enemy.

TAR HEEL IN EMBASSY

Far away from my North Carolina home, incidents such as these pleased me. On the morning after my arrival as I reached the American Embassy, a familiar voice said, "Howdy do, Mr. Daniels. When did you leave North Carolina?" It came from a Negro doorkeeper, who formerly lived in Rockingham County. He spoke my language. He had gone to France in World War I, had remained, and was the American Embassy's door-keeper in Paris.

As I approached the desk of the receptionist in the Embassy a familiar voice said, "We have been expecting you, Mr. Daniels. When did you come?" It was Mrs. Elizabeth Deegan, of Asheville, North Carolina, a daughter of my old friend Senator Jeter C. Pritchard. Tar Heels stick together at home or abroad. This is the Mrs. Deegan who was arrested in the early days of German occupation in Paris (World War II) for giving protection to British officers. But she was too many for the Nazis and soon got back home and has remained in our diplomatic service. The third person I saw was the librarian from Wake Forest College, North Carolina.

GUIDE TO HISTORIC CHARTRES

The itinerary of the Commission did not take us to some interesting places outside Paris which I wanted to see. Again it was a North Carolinian who opened visions of the historic places—Robert Lee Humber, of Greenville, North Carolina. He had been a Rhodes Scholar at Oxford, and after completing the course and a year of travel, had gone into business in Paris and had married a French girl. He was my guide in an enchanting trip to historic Chartres.

VISIT TO LEAGUE OF NATIONS HOME AT GENEVA

The most interesting side trip on that visit to Europe was the one when—no speaking for three days—Walter Lambeth, a North Carolina friend and member of the Battlefield Commission, and I made a side trip to Geneva. I had been in Paris when it was decided that the League of Nations location should be on the lands overlooking Lake Geneva, and I had faith that in the atmosphere of free Switzerland the vision of a world organized for peace would bless mankind. We met the officials; we visited the magnificent buildings; and we sorrowed that the vision splendid had not been realized. But we hoped it would one day be the birthplace of the long-desired universal peace.

And in 1945, when the forty nations called by Roosevelt at San Francisco to plan for a world peace convention met, I felt that the place should be Geneva and the empty building should resound to "Peace on Earth, Good Will among Men."

DIPLOMACY AND POLITICS IN LONDON

It was a delight in London to be welcomed as if at home by Ambassador Robert Worth Bingham at the American Embassy with all courtesies and Tar Heel hospitality. Late into the night he and I reviewed the post-war period and rejoiced in the accomplishments of the Roosevelt administration.

It was at London that the news reached us that President Roosevelt had appointed Senator Hugo Black as Associate Justice of the Supreme Court. It delighted Lister Hill and myself because we greatly admired Black.

Upper left, Naval memorial in Brest, dedicated August 12, 1937. *Upper right,* Representatives Lister Hill, and J. Walter Lambeth, and Ambassador Daniels in Flanders Field Cemetery. *Lower left,* war memorial at Thiaucourt, Ambassador Daniels is at the left. *Lower right,* General Pershing and Ambassador Daniels at dedication of the American monument at Bellicourt.

Above, marker erected by the American Chamber of Commerce of Mexico City on the Laredo-Mexico City Highway at the highest point on the route. *Below,* at the celebration marking the opening of the highway. *Left to right,* Congressmen Thomasson and Burnham, Senator McAdoo, Ambassador Daniels, Congressman Cartwright, and Senator Dennis Chavez. Senator Tom Connally is second from the right and next to him is W. B. Richardson.

"I think," said Hill to me as soon as the news came, "that I will be a candidate for the vacancy."

"If so," I replied, "telegraph at once your intention and take the first fast steamer for the United States so as not to let other aspirants capture the field while you are abroad."

He needed no urging, and soon he and his charming wife, who had won the hearts of all members of the Battlefield Commission, were enroute for home, preceding the rest of us, in pursuit of the toga. It awaited him, and he has adorned it for years.

Bingham had won high regard in England and gave me the inside story of the monetary conference that failed. He was critical of Moley and warm in praise of Hull. Bingham's health had militated against his activity but not against his distinguished service, which was cut short by his early death.

In pursuance of an arrangement made in Paris, when I left London I joined Mr. and Mrs. Roy O'Connor, friends from Mexico, for a visit to the Emerald Isle. It was in fulfillment of a dream my wife and I had long cherished. An attack of arthritis forbade her taking the trip, but she charged me to look up her Irish kin. She was part Irish, which accounted for her humor and sprightliness, and she never let St. Patrick's Day pass without "the wearing of the green" and pinning the shamrock on every member of the family.

We arrived in Dublin the middle of August, when Ireland was a sheen of emerald bedecked with lovely flowers. Escorted by an Irish O'Connor—a passport to the race—I was intrigued by the beauty of the island and found myself agreeing with the Irish Governor of Hawaii. Asked (in 1919) his favorite color, the Governor said "Any color so it is green." We saw everything from Dublin to Cork, regretting that time did not admit of a trip to the Presbyterian part of the country in the North.

We "did" the ancient and interesting places in Dublin and all the castles and famous places as we motored to take my ship at Cork. I still call it Cork, though it has a new name, and I couldn't make my tongue say Eire, when I had always thought of the Emerald Isle as Ireland.

I had met Eamon De Valera when he was in the United States and had attended a banquet in his honor at San Francisco, though a friend told me a member of the cabinet should not give him such recognition. I had a long talk with President De Valera, and his charming and well-informed woman secretary. Among the things he told me was that the heart's desire of nearly all Irish was the uniting of the northern portion, still a British possession, so that all the country should be together under one government.

"How about Belfast and the section in the North?" I asked.

His answer was if there was a plebiscite a majority of the people outside of Belfast would vote for unity. I hope it will come.

I found our minister, Mr. Cudahay, living in a magnificent palace and enjoyed meeting him and his guests at a luncheon. Irish in lineage, he enjoyed being back in the old country and talked interestingly. The house in which he lived was later the home of the President.

My wife had charged me to look up her Clary kin, and I found some of them in Dublin and two other places. On the morning after our arrival, as we left an old church, where Mrs. O'Connor and I had gone to see some mummies, I ran right into the shop of "Patrick Clary and Sons, Liquors and Wines." Entering I asked to see Mr. Patrick Clary.

"I am his son, Sir," said a nice looking young man. After a chat about the Clarys, he said he had no doubt that his family and my wife's were related. I wondered if she would be proud of a relative engaged in "liquor and wines," seeing that we were prohibitionists. After leaving the place, I reflected that when I told her that her Irish Clary kin were liquor dealers, she might think I was putting one over on her. I returned and bought a pint bottle with the autograph of Patrick Clary on the label. It was the first money I had ever spent for liquor, but I found on my return to Mexico that it was well spent, for without that "Exhibit A," my wife would have doubted what I told her of her Irish kin.

Travelling south after leaving Dublin, we visited a beautiful old castle and garden near Birr in the county of Offaly. I asked a man on the street if any people by the name of Clary lived there.

"Certainly," he said. "There is the home of Timothy Clary, who was this week appointed by President De Valera as Revenue Commissioner of Ireland." He volunteered to take me to the house where two maiden sisters greeted me. I called them "Cousin." The brother was not at home and I sent him a message of congratulation. The next day, wondering if it would give him a laugh, I wrote him a note:

"Dear Cousin Timothy:
  (Cousin by marriage)
"A few days ago while in Dublin I called on President De Valera. He was very courteous. I asked him as a great favor to the Clarys in the United States to appoint you as Commissioner of Revenue for Ireland. He promised me he would do so. He is a man of his word and I congratulate you upon receiving the appointment.

"Faithfully
"JOSEPHUS DANIELS
"(Who married into the
Clary family)"

I had hardly got to Mexico City when I received a letter from Cousin Timothy Clary, expressing his deep gratitude that I had travelled to Ireland and had secured for him the position he desired. That's Irish for you!

On this visit I learned that Birr (or Rosse) Castle was the stronghold of the O'Clearys. The first Earl of Rosse was a nephew of Michael O'Cleary, one of the "Four Masters," who was a famous historian in the sixteenth century. His nephew was made Earl of Rosse and given a big tract of land in the center of Ireland, where in 1620 he built a castle, which we visited. When, upon my return, I described the castle and showed the pictures of it taken by Mr. O'Connor, my wife said, "I am sorry that when some of the family reached America they changed O'Cleary to Clary. That omission of the 'O' and the 'e' will deny me access to the castle."

Waiting for the steamer, I visited every point of interest in Cork, going over every part of the harbor where the American destroyers were welcomed early in World War I and Captain Taussig had said, "We are Ready Now," and proved it in the days ahead. I found that the American sailors had left behind them admiration for themselves in those critical days when the British and American Navies sailed as one fleet.

XLIV

THE LAREDO ROAD OPENING

I n July, 1936, the completion of the long-desired highway to the Mexican capital was completed, and in celebration there was a fiesta in every town and village from Laredo to Mexico City. While in Washington I had conferred with President Roosevelt and State Department officials about the United States participation. As President Roosevelt could not leave Washington, Vice-President Garner headed the celebrating delegation, with Senators W. G. McAdoo, Tom Connally, Representatives Johnson, Burnham, Cartwright, and Thomasson, distinguished representatives from the American Chamber of Commerce and many other organizations, including my old Raleigh friend, Charles M. Upham, head of the Road Builders Association. He built the first modern roads in North Carolina and was Consulting Engineer in Mexico when it started hard-surface road construction.

The completion of this highway (regarded as the first link on a highway from the United States to Panama) had long been looked forward to as an important link between Mexico and the United States. The construction of its seven hundred and seventy miles had been difficult in the mountain sections and very costly, and had taken toll of not a few lives. The historic official opening was staged in a manner in keeping with the importance of the construction of the unit from Laredo to Mexico City.

Of the continuous celebration—banquets, speeches, and fiestas—consuming several days, I wrote home (July 11, 1936):

"We were due to attend a banquet at Laredo at 9 P.M. but we did not get there until 5 A.M. the next morning. After breakfast we proceeded to the bridge over the Rio Grande, which is the dividing line between the two countries. Foreign Minister Hay spoke for Mexico and Vice-President Garner for the United States, and several others (I among them) made brief Good Neighbor talks. There were bands from the American military post and from Mexico, and many soldiers. The town was decorated with intertwined American and Mexican flags.

"Immediately after the ceremonies we entered automobiles and rode over the highway to Monterrey. There were fifty-six cars in the cavalcade that carried the party all the way to Mexico City. At Monterrey, General Almazán, Commander of the Mexican Post, welcomed us, gave the Vice-President a salute of twenty-one guns, and invited us all to lunch. That is a fine military post, all the construction work having been done by the soldiers. In Mexico that is the rule. After lunch General Almazán showed the party over the post and gave a review. After the review your humble servant and the Vice-President slipped away and got an hour's sleep. It was a life-saver, for Monterrey is about as hot as Laredo.

"Later in the afternoon we were taken up to Chipinque, the mountain home of General Almazán. It is about 6,000 feet above the city and is reached by a winding road. Arrived at the top of the mountain, a banquet was served, speeches were made, and there were Mexican music and dancing, after which Garner and I slept that night on the top of the mountain. It was delightfully cool in General Almazán's mountain home.

"Thursday morning the cavalcade started towards Mexico City. At every town and village, some of them very primitive, the people gathered in numbers with music and flowers. At Ciudad Victoria lunch was served in a park and the usual speeches of hands-across-the-river made. At night we stayed at Villa Juárez, where there was a good new hotel. As I was preparing to change my shirt before dinner I found that my bag was missing. It turned out that it had been put in the car of the Vice-President and had gone with him to Laredo. I borrowed a night-shirt and a Gillette and a shirt for the next day. Fortunately, the next morning my bag arrived, so that I didn't have to go the balance of the journey without fresh clothes. I threatened to have the Vice-President arrested and sent him word that the story of his visit to Mexico could be condensed in this sentence: 'Vice-President Garner came to Mexico and stole all hearts, and not content with that stole the clothes of the American Ambassador.' But when the bag arrived I was happy and decided not to have the Vice-President arrested. But he had a close call!

"When the people of Tamazunghale (pronounced as if it were spelled Thomas and Charlie) gave cordial greeting, I told

Senator Thomas Connally and Charles Upham it was in honor of the fact that they had derived their given names from this old town. They liked it so well they were reluctant to leave the only town that bore their names.

"We spent Friday night at Zimapán. Most of the delegates were housed in quarters of the Highway Commission. Mr. Boal and I were entertained in the house of Mr. Martínez, the tax collector for that District, and had a comfortable night.

"The next day was the Glorious Fourth. A delegation of American citizens residing in Mexico came out to take part in dedicating a memorial they had erected in appreciation of the hospitality they had received from the Mexicans in their stay in Mexico. This memorial is on the highest point of the road, about 8,000 feet high. There was music. At the request of the American citizens I presented the memorial and it was accepted by Mr. Hidalgo.

"Soon we were in Pachuca, the center of silver mines that have been operated since the days of Cortés. An elegant banquet was given and I made the principal address for the Americans and General Hay for the Mexicans after a most eloquent Mexican had delivered an address of welcome.

"Promptly on time, 5 P.M., July 4, we arrived at Guadalupe, where there were city dignitaries, a cavalcade of *charros* on fine horses, and women dressed in beautiful native dresses and mounted on horses. A chorus of several scores of young women sang hymns of welcome, and beautiful maidens in *China Poblana* dresses showered all the party with flowers. Thousands had gathered on the hills and the welcome was beyond description.

"Wonderful to say, the trip was made on time. We were scheduled to arrive at 5 P.M. and arrived two minutes before five. It was good to get home. Mrs. Garner and her granddaughter and the young Mrs. McAdoo with your mother had preceded us to the city, going on the train.

"Sunday afternoon we went to a pageant and dancing etc. at Chapultepec Castle, followed by a supper and then by fireworks on the lake. Monday was crowded with events and Tuesday Congress has a special session in honor of our Senators and Representatives and later a fine lunch at the Palace of Fine Arts.

"Mrs. Garner left Monday night, showered with presents and flowers. At the train was Mrs. Cárdenas (wife of the President) who had called the previous day, and many others, with a band. Your mother took Mrs. Garner to call upon Mrs. Cárdenas.

"The road is so splendidly engineered that before we knew it, with our engine actually enjoying a corkscrew climb, we had gone from 300 to 3,000 feet above sea level and were looking out toward the East, at what we then thought was a magnificent panorama. It was beautiful. At some places the road goes up to over 8,000 feet and at some points there is a sheer drop of 2,000 feet. The scenery is beyond description; it has been said by some globe trotters to be the most sublime in the world. Mr. Taft once said: 'Never say that any scenery is the most beautiful in the world. If you do, some day you will see something more beautiful.' Certainly a view of the dazzling heights just above sheer depths where nature has given its extreme expression makes the trip more than worth making.

"The company gone and the lights out and the parades over, we are living very quietly."

UNITED STATES PARTICIPANTS ATTACKED

Not even the notable events of the formal dedication of the highway from the United States border to Mexico City (July, 1936) caused a cessation of the attacks by a partisan paper on Americans participating. A correspondent of the *Brooklyn Tablet* roasted Vice-President Garner, and Senators McAdoo and Connally, who took part in the celebration, which partook of the nature of a patriotic fiesta on the new road, long desired, by the people of both countries. The writer said we were "selling out the heritage of American liberty, traditional Americanism and common humanitarianism." The paper made these quotations with the comment that we were betraying America:

"Said Garner: 'Mexico has made invaluable contributions to the progress of civilization.'

"Said Daniels: 'Mexico has accomplished great things. This highway is a symptom of the spirit of progress which inspires both the government and the people of this republic today.

" 'From this the highest point of the road, we may look north to the United States and south to Mexico. In the form of an open book this monument is placed to remind passing travelers that the history of progress is the history of transportation and communication, and on its pages will be inscribed a record of the present friendship, of the future deeper and broader mutual understanding between Mexicans and Americans.'

"Said Connally: 'Mexico has a great and heroic past and I congratulate you on the evidence of stability, order and peace within the republic.'

"Said McAdoo: 'A nation can be judged by the profound sense of stability and spirit of its people, the vision of its statesmen, and the genius and skill of its people. The great Republic of Mexico possesses three elements in high degree.'

"President Cárdenas in reply carried the burlesque to its logical conclusion. He said he had freed the people—on the same day ten slaves were murdered seeking liberty—and silenced the contingent of unfair protestants in the United States who 'misrepresented' Mexico. Ambassador Daniels he extolled for his 'austere, citizen-like virtue in expressing within the borders of his fatherland, and in opposition to adverse opinions from strong social groups, the truth about Mexico, many times the subject of calumny by baneful interests.' In other words, Mr. Daniels was seemingly applauded for being a tool of the anti-Christian, anti-American campaign in this country."

XLV

DIPLOMATS TOUR MEXICO

W E NEVER missed the *Grito* at the Palace, which was celebrated every September 16 in commemoration of Hidalgo's ringing the bell that began the war for independence. A hundred thousand people thronged the Zócalo, which was brilliantly illuminated, and officials and diplomats were entertained by the President in the Palace. It was at the 1935 *Grito* that President Cárdenas unfolded to me his plan to put the presidential train at the disposal of the heads of foreign missions so that they could visit all parts of the country and know its terrain and its problems. First he said, and with native pride, that he wished my wife and me to be his guests in his home State of Michoacán, which, he said, had the most beautiful lakes and the most beautiful scenery in the republic. Everyone thinks his own State surpasses all others.

Before President Cárdenas put the "Olive Train" at the disposal of the Diplomatic Corps, my wife and I had visited parts of Mexico as guests of Governors or friends, and had gone to most places in Northern and Eastern Mexico. I knew every State east and north of Guadalajara almost as well as I did the Northwestern part of the United States. These visits were not without incidents which showed that all Mexicans didn't trust "The Colossus of the North."

I recall that, as I was leaving Oaxaca, Kirby Smith (son of the great Confederate General) gave me a copy of a handbill that was being distributed as I arrived. It was anti-American, said to have been sponsored by Bolshevists. It charged me with being an emissary of the Octopi of Wall Street, an imperialist, and a murderer of Mexicans at Vera Cruz. During my stay at Oaxaca I was wholly unconscious of its existence. The Governor stopped its distribution as soon as he learned of it. On this trip we visited the famous Monte Alban ruins. We also went to Mitla and saw the Tula tree, so big that twenty-eight persons touching the tips of their fingers can barely make a ring around it. What impressed me most at Oaxaca was that while Díaz and Juárez were both born there, a monument commemorates Juárez, and there is nothing to indicate that it was the birthplace of Díaz.

I was glad to extend my first-hand knowledge of Mexico, in company with my diplomatic colleagues on the "Olive Train." (The names of the pullman cars were truly Mexican—Citlaltepetl and Xinantecatl.) As I wrote home:

"Most of my predecessors have stuck around the capital. I have availed myself of every opportunity to know Mexicans in their habitat. I knew I could not represent the true situation to my government unless I knew the country and its people. You do not know North Carolina by staying in Raleigh, or the United States by staying in Washington. As a matter of fact, capital cities do not usually reflect national sentiment. They are political and in a sense artificial. President Wilson often said that when in doubt about public sentiment in the country, he made it the point to ascertain the public opinion in Washington City, for he then knew that the opposing view represented the people as a whole. It is not so true in this country, for Mexico City is comparatively more representative of sentiment in Mexico than Washington City is of the United States. However, I have often been told since coming here that no program of reform or revolution has originated in the capital city and that its people have been slow to advocate or fight for reforms which have almost always originated in other States, and accepted late or grudgingly by Mexico City."

I kept a diary, giving in detail what we saw of men and things, which enables me in memory to live over again what were halcyon days. The longest of these presidential train trips was the one that took us to the extreme southern end of the republic and to famous Monte Alban and Chichén-Itzá. Of that trip I wrote home:

"I return to Mexico City from the third trip given to Heads of Mission in Mexico by the courtesy of President Cárdenas with memories crowded with knowledge of one of the oldest and most interesting parts of this hemisphere, some portions of which afford evidences of an early civilization preceding and surpassing that possessed by other portions of North America. At every place visited the members of the Diplomatic Corps were received with that hospitality characteristic of the people of Mexico, honored with banquets and balls, including dances and fiestas typical of the section visited.

"Leaving Mexico City Monday morning, March 9, over the *Mexicano,* the party upon arrival at Vera Cruz, embarked on the *Amapala,* an elegant steamer of the Standard Fruit Company. The voyage over the blue waters was a real delight. After a cordial reception by Progreso people, we hurried to Mérida, which was for three days the center of a round of pleasures and festivities. We were introduced into the cultivation and preparation of henequén for the markets of the world, a crop which for generations has brought wealth to its producers. I was told that at one time the average wealth of Mérida exceeded that of any other town of its population in the world, and that it contained one hundred and fifty millionaires, their wealth mainly derived from henequén. I can well believe it, because there exist today more beautiful and dignified homes than are found in other cities of like population. In the early days henequén was to be obtained from no other quarter, and the owners of the lands that produced this necessity could fix their own prices. Though Mérida is still the chief source of supply, it is now grown in a few other countries and the monopoly has gone. Still, Mérida is the henequén metropolis of the world. It is a beautiful city, having an air of dignity and prosperity. One of the most beautiful sights to be seen anywhere was the typical dance, in which the dancers wore the costume which has long been the admiration of all privileged to visit that old city founded in the sixteenth century by Francisco de Montejo, some of whose lineal descendants still live. I was particularly impressed with the excellence of its daily newspapers. The banquet, presided over by Governor Fernando López Cárdenas, afforded the visitors the opportunity to hear the story of Mérida's customs and its development into prosperity, and enabled the Dean of the Corps, Ambassador Manuel Echeverría y Vidaurre, of Guatemala, to express the deep appreciation of the Corps for the entertainment afforded.

"It would take columns to tell of the visit to Chichén-Itzá and Uxmal, the scenes of the early Mayan objects of architectural dignity. As we looked upon the ancient dignity of the structures made many centuries ago, the words of the poet were recalled:

" 'The dense wildwood that hid the royal seat,
The lofty palms that choked the winding street,
Man's hands hath felled, and now in day's fair light
Uxmal's broad ruins burst upon the sight.'

"The latter is yet to be rehabilitated, but the work of the Carnegie Institute and the Mexican Government in uncovering and reconstructing the temple and pyramids at Chichén-Itzá discloses a knowledge of architecture and astronomy and letters that is attracting the attention of archaeologists and scientists all over the world.

"I had heard Dr. Sylvanus Morley, the scholar and archaeologist, tell of the history and mystery of the Mayan architecture and learning, but it seemed like being carried back centuries to stand upon the ancient site and hear Dr. Morley tell the transcendentally interesting story; it was like being transported into another world. And this was particularly true when at night, viewing the heaven studded with stars, he depicted the astronomical knowledge of men who had builded a civilization before the foot of the first white man trod the soil of what is now the United States.

"From Mérida the party travelled to Campeche over the railroad coöperatively operated, to be hospitably received by Governor Eduardo R. Mena Córdoba and entertained with a banquet under beautiful groves, surrounded by orange and cocoanut and banana trees, with rare flowers blooming in profusion. Here the fish afford a living for many, and the company feasted on the most excellent fish. Accompanied by the Governor and his wife, the party embarked on Nos. 26 and 28 of the new Coast Guard ships for Ciudad del Carmen. The Gulf was rocked by angry waves and high winds, but the officers demonstrated their good seamanship by landing the passengers safely after a stormy voyage. Some were seasick. The people of Carmen were anxious for the safety of the passengers, but they were never in worse peril than a wetting and *mal de mer*. Only my wife and I (good sailors) stayed on deck as the surging waters rushed over us, drenching us to the skin. When it was at its height I stood with the Navy captain on the bridge. He was having a hard time to keep the ship on its course.

"About that time the protocol officer, Velos González, white as a sheet, frightened and seasick, came on the bridge and ordered the captain to turn back to Campeche, saying, 'Unless you do we will all be drowned.' I saw that it was as far to Campeche as to Carmen and the going would be as rough. Assuming the prerogative of a Secretary of the Navy, I said, 'The captain of the ship knows what he is doing. Let him alone and he will chart us in safety to our destination. You go below with the Señoras.' He was too sick to question my authority.

"We reached Carmen in safety, but the storm lashed up the waters so that we were marooned there several days. The hospitality of a people, prepared to entertain a large company only one day, was beyond all praise. It was at Carmen we tasted the first frozen cocoanut taken from the rind before it was hardened. The fruit of the gods cannot be so delicious. It was so delicious that I wished I had a giraffe's neck.

"The people gave us a grand banquet when our ship arrived, and Mr. Branson, an Englishman who represents large American corporations owning hundreds of thousands of acres of land on which there is mahogany and other valuable woods, and trees from which chicle is obtained, approached us and said: 'You are to be our guests while you are at Carmen.' He and his wife, a very delightful lady, opened their home to us and we were most comfortable. We had a happy time, but they had expected to entertain us for one day and when time moved on we felt we were imposing on their hospitality. We were told on Thursday evening that on Friday morning we were all to be present at the pier at 8 o'clock and go on board the Coast Guard cutter and be transferred in the Gulf to a Standard Fruit ship to be taken to Vera Cruz. When we arrived at the port, the port officer had received weather bureau reports saying that a norther was blowing on the Gulf and it would be impossible for the party to be transferred at sea and he forbade any ship leaving Carmen. The ship outside, therefore, went on to Vera Cruz and we were marooned there without any information as to when another ship would be sent for us. In this uncertain state of affairs, the French Minister and I and some others of the Corps who felt they must be back in Mexico on Monday, secured an air plane to come to Carmen and take us to Vera Cruz.

"Before leaving the neighborhood, a visit was made by plane to Villa Hermosa, the capital of the State of Tabasco. Welcomed by Governor Aureo L. Calles and the military and civil authorities, the party visited several of the outdoor rural schools, conducted in buildings with thatched roofs and no sides. Adjacent to these open-air schoolrooms were farms cultivated by the school children, who take great pride in the practical study of agriculture. All rural schools apply their knowledge in the cultivation of farm plots near by. Education and temperance were emphasized in this visit. There is no drunkenness and little drinking in Tabasco. It is said to be the only place where intoxicants are taboo by the choice of the people. At the elegant banquet, where the dancing and singing were typical of the State, no intoxicants were served. A large *Frontón* for the use of all the people of Villa Hermosa is nearing completion. Surrounding it are places for playing basket-ball and other sports.

"A side trip by plane was made to Payo Obispo, the seat of the government of Quintano Roo. Governor Rafael E. Melgar received the party, addresses were made, songs were sung by school children in attractive costumes, and a breakfast fit for the gods was served.

"The sections visited were rich in hardwoods, cocoanuts, pineapple, bananas; and the diplomats partook with relish of more tropical fruits than they knew existed. The wealth of the region comes mainly from henequén, hardwoods, chicle, fish, and nearly every tropical fruit known.

"The hospitable welcome everywhere was so cordial as to win the hearts of the recipients. It was to that part of Mexico that Columbus came on one of his latest voyages; it was in Tabasco that Cortés landed and first made the acquaintance of the famous Malinche. It is a country of historical interest beyond compare, of rich and varied natural resources, and peopled by a hospitable population which is concerned with the education of the people and social progress. We found that President Cárdenas is held in high esteem, as was evidenced in the addresses delivered and the expressions of the people in every section visited.

"On our way to Vera Cruz, before the arrival of our plane at Tejería, about twenty miles from Vera Cruz, the Mayor sent his private secretary with a car to meet us there and take us to Vera Cruz, where the President and other chief officers of the *Sindicado* (labor organization) met us and gave us the freedom of the city. They were very courteous. At night, when we were leaving, the military representative and representatives of the Mayor were at the station to say Good-bye. You know in Mexico saying good-bye at the train is a universal function. The officials who came down were dressed in spotless white, and they told us that the Mayor hoped we would honor his city again by a visit; so on the whole I was glad to have the ice broken and know that I was as welcome in Vera Cruz as in other parts of Mexico."

A WREATH ON HIDALGO'S MONUMENT

One of the sacred missions I looked forward to was placing a wreath on the tomb of Hidalgo, the pioneer patriot of Mexico. I had been to the place of *Grito Dolores,* where Hidalgo rang the bell of independence, heard from Acapulco to Vera Cruz. I wrote home about my trip to Chihuahua (March, 1934):

"I went to the plaza, dominated by a high statue of Hidalgo, where I placed a wreath at the base of the statue and made a speech to a large crowd on 'Hidalgo, the pioneer patriot.' The Governor then took me to the prison where Hidalgo was incarcerated after his 1810 fruitless revolution. It is many feet underground. It was then a corner of the old cathedral. The Governor told me that when the Federal Government erected this new structure they built around the Hidalgo prison. It is the foundation at one corner. You go down steps, maybe a score, to an underground prison, with granite walls, with no light or air except that which comes down from the tower. On the walls Hidalgo had, with charcoal, sketched a poem and his patriotic sentiments. Time has almost effaced them. After being captured and incarcerated in this dungeon under the cathedral, Hidalgo was stripped by the church of his priestly office and robes, degraded and excommunicated. That being done, he was tried by a court-martial (Church and State were practically the same then), which found him guilty of treason, and at daybreak he was taken out and shot by a firing squad."

DIPLOMATIC APPRECIATION

Nothing is quite simple. After the last "Diplomatic Junket" over large sections of the republic as the guests of President Cárdenas, the diplomats wished to show their appreciation of the courtesy in some fitting manner. Though I was not then the dean of the Corps, neither the Ambassador of Guatemala, the dean, nor the Ambassador of Brazil went on these trips and that made me dean *pro tem.*

I called a meeting to decide the shape of our thanks. I wrote a letter that seemed correct courtesy. It took two hours to reach a decision on it. Some members of the corps were not keen to commend the good work we saw in the rural and agricultural public schools. They were Roman Catholics who think the State should have exclusive control of education. They did not wish to commend the public schools, though they had expressed their approval of what they had seen and heard. In the end they let me, as acting dean, send the appreciative letter as I had drafted it with recital of what we had seen. After much debate it was decided to have our resolution engraved in silver of appropriate design.

SAN JUAN DE ULÚA NAVY BASE

The first good ships Mexico added to its small navy were built in Italy and it then set about establishing a naval base in Vera Cruz Harbor, utilizing the old Spanish prison of Juan de Ulúa. The cruelties practiced toward political and other prisoners confined in under-water cells, as related, were among the most barbarous practices that disgrace the human race. I visited the old prison with Mexican officers while it was being converted into a Navy supply and repair base, and could well understand that in its lower recesses a man imprisoned might as well say, "Who enters here leaves hope behind." I had heard some gruesome stories about Spanish inhumanity in connection with it from Admiral Fletcher and General Butler during their stay at Vera Cruz in 1914. I was glad to accept the invitation of Navy officers to visit and see the progress in reconverting and reconditioning it to the service of the growing Mexican Navy.

I heard more about it from a Mexican officer who had been incarcerated within its walls. I wrote the story related to me in a letter to my sons (January 11, 1934) as follows:

"At the Marshburn dinner yesterday at San Ángel Inn, General Aguilar said he wished to bring his father (General Leandro Aguilar) to call, seeing his father owed his life to the United States and a ship of the U. S. Navy when I was Secretary of the Navy. They called this morning. The elder General (seventy-eight years old) is as straight as an Indian and looks like a gentleman of the old school. He is an uncle of President Madero, who was murdered by Huerta. He and his son, and two of President Madero's brothers, were incarcerated in the

Vargueno presented by the Embassy and Consular Staffs of the Republic of Mexico to Ambassador and Mrs. Daniels on their leaving Mexico. It is of very old Spanish workmanship, in the style of the royal cabinet maker Vargas of the Golden Age. The central doors open to reveal a small shrine.

Sarape presented to Ambassador Daniels by President Cárdenas who said, "This sarape was woven by an humble Indian of Zacatecas at my request." The Ambassador replied, "I can now sleep under myself in this sarape."

Silver platter presented by the diplomatic Corps of Mexico to Ambassador Daniels, Dean of the Diplomatic Corps, upon his retirement.

San Juan de Ulúa prison at Vera Cruz, to which many Mexicans objectionable to the government were consigned.

"San Juan de Ulúa prison is a part of a fort, the cornerstone of which was laid in 1528. The fort was built on an island which received its name of San Juan de Ulúa from the Spaniards. Until recent times the island was used as a penal settlement. It is said that a twenty-year sentence to the prison there meant death. During the Spanish regime the unfortunates sent there were to be commiserated. Many of the cells were mere holes in the sea wall and were half-flooded at high-tide. Some of the dungeons were so small that a man could not stand in them. When the tide came in the prisoner sat immersed in salt water to his chin. Food was lowered to him through a hole in the upper pavement. Three months of this either killed a man or drove him insane.

"The Mexican Government for many years has not used this island as a penal colony, and has not used the lower dungeons and cells. They continued to use the fort, however, and the prison was also used. The conditions I believe were pretty bad there, even though the dungeons and cells below water were not used.

"This fort of San Juan de Ulúa was the last stronghold of the Spaniards on Mexican soil at the close of the war of independence. On September 15, 1824, the Spanish flag was lowered finally from its towers.

"It was believed that the Aguilars and the Madero brothers were to be shot by Huerta's orders. The young General Aguilar appealed to the Consul at Monterrey (home of the family) and Secretary Bryan sent a wire, by reason of which John Lind, then at Vera Cruz, secured their release from the prison at Vera Cruz and all four were taken to Havana on the *U. S. S. Chester* and thus escaped in safety to the United States.

" 'I owe the last twenty years of my life to the United States Navy,' said the old General, 'and I wished to call and express my grateful appreciation to you and your government.'

"The younger General tells me he is going to the United States in a few days to buy an aeroplane, and expects to use it to accompany General Cárdenas, the candidate of the National Revolutionary party for President, on his trips throughout the country during the next six months.

"General Aguilar told me this story about his father:

"Not long after he had secured safe entry into the United

States, he was in San Antonio. As he was getting aboard a street-car in that city, his leg was badly hurt. While he was in the hospital, an ambulance-chasing lawyer called and asked the General to give him the power of attorney so that he could sue the company and get him $20,000 for his accident. The old General refused to give the power of attorney. The next day an officer of the street-car company called at the hospital to see him. Asked who was responsible for the accident, the General said: 'It was not due to the motorman of your company. I am alone responsible. I refused to sue the company both because it is not liable and because the United States Consul saved my life from Huerta's guns.' Thereupon the street car company gave him a check for $1,000."

Part Fourteen

THE APPROACH OF WAR;
LAST DAYS

XLVI

OUTPOST OF AMERICAN DEFENSE

In BOTH human incidents and international problems the steady steps toward war were clearly perceptible in Mexico City. Like some other places far from the fronts, it was a place which dramatized the dangers. Long before the world war, but as a harbinger of its coming, the Spanish Republican Government in exile had come to Mexico. Agents of Hitler's Fifth Column arrived early, too, and began to spread their poison assiduously. In the Diplomatic Corps, of which I was dean, the antagonisms of nations began to appear as human incidents of arrogance or fear. No formality or protocol could hide the growing bitterness and danger. And long before war, we worked in vigilance and determination in awareness of the war's approach to our hemisphere. As the days went by, we worked under increasing pressure.

The strain upon the American Embassy in the year preceding my resignation was to give every aid in the preparations of our country against the totalitarian threat. We were vigilant to detect any Nazi infiltration across the Rio Grande, to make a complete Black List of concerns aiding the enemy, and to obtain from Mexico the rich variety of war materials needed to strengthen American arms for defense.

At home there was fear that Mexico might be used by Germany and Japan as a base, and early anxiety lest the pro-Nazi sentiment in Mexico, not large but working secretly, might give trouble. There was recollection that in World War I, the Germans had been permitted to erect a powerful wireless station in the outskirts of Mexico City and that then Carranza had been, if not pro-German, at least not pro-American. There was apprehension that, in the event of war, Mexico again might be at least neutral. There was no ground for these apprehensions so far as the officials and the great body of the people were concerned, but, in the early forties, there was a strong Nazi minority ready, if not checked, to lend aid and comfort to the totalitarians.

Daily I was in touch with Mexican officials and found them coöperative in preventing any aid going to Germany and watchful of the Germans in Mexico whose actions aroused suspicions. From the President down, official Mexico was heart and soul against the forces of which Hitler was the head and front. This hostility was intensified because Hitler and Mussolini had ousted the Republican Government in Spain. As a result, Mexican officials believed that a Nazi victory would be a direct threat to all Pan America. As one evidence of its coöperation with the United States, the Mexican government in October, 1940, cancelled an oil concession to the Japanese and rejected an attractive bid of the Japanese for scrap iron.

Mexican authorities worked with officials of our Embassy in the detection of any Nazi sentiment or threat of sabotage, and to obtain the metals and other materials for shipment to the United States to be converted into war weapons. Throughout the whole pre-war period, Mexican Presidents and foreign ministers were as zealous in hostility to Nazi-ism as the officials in our own government at home.

Looking back now, the events on the road to war which I recorded in my Diary take on sharper significance. As early as 1935 I made a note in my Diary about the displeasure of the Italian Minister when the Mexican representative at Geneva had favored sanctions against Italy in its attack on Ethiopia, and Mexicans at home had clearly showed their sympathy for the Ethiopians. I wrote:

"This is not because they think much about the Ethiopians, but they are for the under-dog. They feel that they have suffered from stronger powers and 'a fellow feeling' makes them 'wondrous kind.' Isn't it strange that Mexico feels so deeply against Mussolini, seeing that he was named for Benito Juárez, the patron saint of Mexican revolutionists? The father of Mussolini hated the royal state and the church. Because, in his war against Maximilian, the Indian Juárez was fighting both the imposed Austrian Emperor and the high officials of the Catholic Church, Mussolini's father across the seas gave his son the name of the Indian fighter. And now the Mexican government, controlled by Revolutionists who make Juárez their Washington, are bitter against Benito Mussolini."

Mexican sentiment was even more clearly shown in an official event a year later (November, 1936). In a letter home then I said:

"On Friday afternoon all the members of the Diplomatic Corps were invited to the Chamber of Deputies to a special session of Congress, celebrating Revolutionary Day. It was quite an affair. Every seat was taken and the gallery was crowded and the people were enthusiastic in their patriotism. The high praise given Madero and other Revolutionary chieftains is in line with our Fourth of July praises of Washington and Jefferson. There was a good deal of a stir in the Diplomatic Corps because after inviting all the Corps, the diplomats from Italy, Germany, Guatemala, and El Salvador were told at the Foreign Office that it might be better for them not to attend the celebration at the Chamber of Deputies.

"These four nations had recognized Franco's government and a few days after this recognition assaults were made by demonstrators upon the Guatemalan Embassy and the Salvadorean Legation. Guards were put around the German and Italian Legations, for fear the populace might make an attack upon them. I do not know whether the Foreign Secretary originated the suggestion that these diplomats should not attend. The German Minister told me that he asked the Foreign Minister whether he thought it was best for him to go. He said to me: 'I wanted to go but wished to know how the Foreign Office felt about it.'

"General Hay, the Foreign Minister, advised the German Minister that in view of the deep feeling on the part of the people, he would advise him not to accept the invitation that had been extended. The other diplomats who received the same suggestion shared with the German Minister a good deal of feeling, and the Chilean Ambassador wanted all the Corps to take action and refuse to attend unless protection should be guaranteed for the four members of the Corps whose countries had recognized Franco. However, he never brought this to a head, and nearly all the diplomats except the four mentioned attended."

I had come early into contact with some of the German leaders in Mexico. And long before the war I always had a question in my mind about Baron von Schroeder who lived in a magnificent house in Mexico City and entertained extensively. His wife, a rich American woman—from Colorado, I think—was more outspoken than the Baron in upholding German policies. In November, 1937, I wrote home about them:

"Wednesday night we took dinner at Mr. Newbegin's. Among the other guests were Baron and Baroness von Schroeder. They are not only Germans, but Germans plus, and away from the fatherland they are both intense in their devotion to the German program. At a dinner at their home some time ago she told me that she had read an article in a paper declaring that Germany was responsible for World War I, and that it infuriated her so that she wrote a vigorous article denouncing what she called 'slander upon Germany.' However, after writing it she did not send it, which was the part of wisdom, prompted, I think, by her more practical husband. She told your mother that she was even saving the tinfoil that came off cigars and other things because Germany wanted all of it, and they are sending it to Germany, as are many other Germans all over the world. Later your mother asked someone what the tinfoil was good for and they said to make bullets. The Baron offered me one of his fine saddle horses to use and said that I could have a grand time riding early every morning. I told him that nothing interested me at seven o'clock in the morning except a bed."

URGED ACTION TO AVERT WAR

In the early part of 1938 I was so disturbed over the situation in Europe that from Vera Cruz (March 9) I sent this confidential cable in code to Secretary Hull: "I venture to express the hope that opportunity may offer for the President to tender good offices to avert the war in Europe. If we had acted promptly in 1914 that catastrophe might have been averted or its tragedies ended earlier."

This answer came (March 13): "The President asks me to express his appreciation for your suggestion and the spirit in which it was offered and to say that we are following developments closely and are hopeful that the procedure provided for this situation will obviate any necessity for drastic action."

A few months later (October, 1938) I recorded my own mounting indignation:

"Here, as everywhere in the world, they have been talking about nothing all week except the situation in Europe. I have had my ear glued to the radio more in the last few days than ever before in my life. I hope you heard Hitler's speech; if you did, you have a new conception of hatred, malice, and egoism.

I heard him in the Embassy just as perfectly as if we had been sitting in the stadium where he was singing his song of hate. His words were bad enough, but the contemptuous tone of his speech toward everybody and everything except his own imperialistic law was something I had never imagined I could hear from a man who pretended to be civilized. You could almost feel his gun discharging towards Czechoslovakia when he said, 'Benes is a liar!' There was rage and contempt and passion to the nth degree in his speech, from beginning to end. When he had finished I felt I understood perfectly that the peace of the world in this year depended upon the abject surrender of the so-called democratic nations of Europe to Hitler's dream of empire.

"As we listened, your mother recalled the fact that in 1915 we were in Schenectady and had a talk with the electrical wizard Steinmetz, and as we were talking to him we heard something like the dots you hear in a telegraph office. He said, 'That is radio, and those sounds you hear are from Berlin. We cannot make out what is being said now—but some day we will.' Germany then was trying to bestride the world. We could not hear the Kaiser's voice, but I have an idea that, bad as he was, he could never have spoken with the hatred and malice that were in every intonation of Hitler's voice. I knew then that there was going to be a world war of greatest magnitude unless Chamberlain and Daladier would crawl and say in the voice of suppliants to Hitler: 'Your Majesty, tell us how much subservience you demand. We are your slaves and ready to give it.' I was more than convinced of this when I heard Mussolini's approval of Hitler's demands, and never had any doubt of complete surrender when we heard Chamberlain. I cannot help but feel sorry for him—he was between the devil and the deep blue sea. He either had to compel France to join him in perfect abject and ignominious surrender or witness the wholesale slaughter of men on European battlefields. I have been greatly surprised at the statements in the papers—one of them is saying that Chamberlain ought to be given the Nobel Peace Prize. He ought to be given a halter around his neck and be tied to Hitler's chariot. I may be wrong, but I think Hitler and Mussolini are now in complete control of Europe, and they will take what they want; but they will guarantee to the French and English economic royalists and Tories the continuation of their exploitation of the people in their colonies. Democracy has been slain in the house of her professed friends.

"I say all this, but I must make some qualification: because our own country cannot evade its responsibility. When we permitted Lodge and Jim Reed to keep us out of the League of Nations, we drew into ourselves in a cowardly manner. We set up Czechoslovakia and Poland, and then deserted them and all the democracies, so that they could fall a prey into the hands of men like Hitler and Mussolini."

As everywhere else in the world the situation grew more tense when actual hostilities began in Europe. The tragedy came close to people who knew when Hitler began his great 1940 offensive in the spring. On April 15, I wrote:

"Wednesday night, the tenth, we went to a dinner with the German Minister and Baroness von Collenberg. We had accepted this invitation weeks before and rather wondered why, in view of the situation in Denmark and Norway, the dinner had not been called off, but as acceptances had been received and as the Germans always put up a pretty bold front, I suppose they felt the dinner ought to go on as usual. Not long after I had accepted the invitation, the Belgian Minister called up and said he had been invited and did not want to go unless I had accepted. He then accepted. The Argentine and Brazilian Ambassadors were there, the Belgian and Japanese Ministers, and the other guests were Germans. During the evening a Mexican pianist who had taken lessons in Berlin rendered several selections on the piano which those who understood music were enthusiastic about. The wife of the Belgian Minister kept time to the music with her head and seemed to be enraptured. I wish I had the musical knowledge to get such enjoyment which seemed to take her out of her surroundings. No remark was made about the war except when the Baron said, when offering wine to some one next to him, 'I was lucky to get this wine out of Germany just in time.' The wife of the Belgian Minister told your mother when she called a few days ago, that in proposing a toast to her (the Belgian Minister and his wife are leaving here this week) the Baron said: 'When you get home I hope you will find some handsome young German officers in your country.' She didn't like it very much and was rather bitter about it when she talked to your mother."

Swiftly then the tragedy spread to our friends in the European embassies and legations in Mexico. On June 29, I made an entry in my diary:

"On Saturday I had a call from Mr. Marchlewski, the Polish Minister, who was very much disturbed and told me confidentially that he was quite certain that the Nazi influences here were determined to make trouble and that he believed the first thing they would try to do would be to stir up a bitter feeling between Mexicans and Americans in order to secure the invasion of Mexico by American troops. The method he thought they would employ would be to make an attack on the American Embassy and the American Ambassador, such as were made on Trotsky's residence some weeks ago. Their theory was, he said, that if they did that and wounded or killed the Ambassador, the United States would then make war on Mexico and this would make an open door for the Nazi propaganda. He wanted the Poles and French and other people here other than Germans to form an organization by which they would work together and be ready to thwart any desire on the part of the Nazis to carry out the plan that he was quite certain they had in mind.

"The French Minister called later. He had talked with the Polish Minister but was not so confident that the Nazis contemplated the plan that the Polish Minister outlined. He thought they would not attempt such a move, but thinks there is nothing the Nazi agents would stop at if they could make trouble between the United States and Mexico.

"The same day Mr. Loridan, the Belgian Chargé d'Affaires, called. He is, of course, very much depressed. He really does not know whether he has a government to represent and has not had any news from his people. A day or two later his wife called to see your mother. She said she did not know anything about her parents or their whereabouts. We were both very much distressed at her plight and I obtained the address of her father and mother and wrote the State Department, hoping even against hope that there was some way by which they could be located and this lady's mind set at ease.

"On Saturday I had a call from Señora Palencia, who was the Spanish Minister to Sweden under the Republican Government, and Mr. Villao, a former Cabinet Minister, and Mr. Carner, formerly counsellor of the Spanish Embassy in Paris.

They have not had a word from the Spanish refugees in France since Hitler's victory and they are most desirous that the United States find a way to bring these suffering compatriots out of France. I conveyed their earnest desire to the Washington authorities. One of the most distressing things in the world is these Spanish patriots who sought to have a democratic government and were overthrown, not in a civil conflict as many think, but by Hitler and Mussolini. The greatest blunder of 1939 was that England and France permitted Hitler and Mussolini the use of Spain as a proving ground to give them practice, which they used eventually in fighting France and Belgium."

The fear that Nazi agents in Mexico might engineer an attack on the American Embassy in order to create trouble between the United States and Mexico was not limited to Europeans. Writing home after we had held as usual in 1940 our Fourth of July reception, I said:

"On the morning of the reception, Mr. O'Brien, the *Herald-Tribune* correspondent, came to tell me that he had information that Nazi saboteurs were going to make an attack upon the Embassy that day. It was about like most such information, an expression of what gossipers had feared might take place. I paid no attention to it. However, the Chief of Police of Mexico assigned Captain Pierce, who called at the Embassy at eleven o'clock and said he had been assigned as my aide for the day. He went with me to the Reforma Club and was at the Embassy most of the day. Of course nothing happened. It is a good thing I have no nerves and do not get scared. I have tried to make one rule in life—Never to run into trouble or run away from it.

"At the reception for the Diplomatic Corps nearly all the representatives assigned to this government were present except Baron von Collenberg, the German Minister. It is the first time they have absented themselves on this day. I guess he may have been offended because, under the new regulations as to passports and visas, we had required a member of his staff to present himself in person with photographs before a visa was granted. He was very much perturbed by this. The day before the reception the Norwegian Minister called and asked me to excuse him and his wife from attending the reception because of the situation in Europe. What he really meant was that he did not wish to risk the chance of running into the German Minister."

It is strange now to recall how long under the formalities of protocol the pretenses of regular social intercourse were kept up between nations which were watching each other with increasing enmity. In October, 1940, I wrote:

"Monday night your mother and I went to the Japanese Legation to a dinner. There were about twenty other diplomats and their wives. It was a sort of farewell party of the Minister, Mr. Koshida, who is returning to Japan. He had been called home and said he did not know to what place he would be assigned. A week ago he gave a dinner to the Foreign Minister and others of the Foreign Office and Diplomatic Corps and Monday night he included the balance of the Corps, which embraced all of the Ambassadors accredited here and, of course, the German Minister and his wife and the Italian Minister. The Japanese Minister has a very elegant house which he rents furnished, and your mother was amused that they had a Chinese room, and also a Japanese room.

"After dinner, which was a very elegant affair, they said they wanted to show us some Japanese moving pictures. It turned out to be a picture of the Japanese at war, and a more gruesome picture I have rarely ever seen. You saw no enemy but you saw the Japanese in action, going into battle. In view of the recent actions of Japan in joining the German-Italian axis I thought it was in very bad taste to show us such a picture. This is a sort of boastfulness, trying to show the diplomats here how powerful Japan is in making war. I do not think any of the diplomats enjoyed it with the exception of the German and the Italian. The Japanese Minister told your mother that this was a very remarkable picture and had been shown in many Embassies and Legations and took the second prize at an exhibition in Geneva."

I almost asked him then who won the first prize for photographed barbarism but, as a diplomat, desisted. We were very polite in those days. But increasingly it was the cold, punctilious politeness of men who are aware that a deadly quality is slipping into their relations. And behind the protocol, we worked implacably with no doubts about the intentions of our enemies. Of course, they were at work, too. But I remember now that, when Pearl Harbor came as a tragedy but also somehow as a release, I could count with confidence upon Mexico and the United States as Good Neighbors ready to stand armed together as they had been ready to work together. In World War II our Southern border was not a danger but a strength. We had, as I wrote as war approached, "evident proof that the mutual confidence and collaboration between these two countries has been elevated to a new plane." Good neighbors became comrades in arms. Such friendship can never be allowed to deteriorate in the peace.

RETURN TO PASTE POT AND PEN

My acceptance of a diplomatic post, giving up for nearly nine years the editorship of *The Raleigh* (N.C.) *News and Observer,* was possible because three of my sons had followed in my footsteps and made journalism their life work. My oldest son, Captain Josephus Daniels, Jr., after service overseas in the Marine Corps, became business manager of the paper upon his return from France. My youngest son, Frank Arthur Daniels, after graduation from the University of North Carolina, came on the business side of the paper and later became general manager. My third son, Jonathan Worth Daniels, succeeded me as editor after winning a Guggenheim fellowship that carried a year's stay in Europe. I recall that when Frank W. Buxton, editor of the Boston *Herald,* was a guest at the Embassy, he spoke in high terms of Jonathan's *A Southerner Discovers the South.* Speaking facetiously, I said, "I believe I will suggest to Jonathan to write a book on 'A Southerner Discovers New England,' since that rock-bound section from Narragansett to Passamaquoddy has long been waiting to be discovered." He did that very thing, but neither Buxton nor I thought it as good as when he discovered his own South.

The "chips off the old block," or as I often said of them "the blocks off the old chip," carried on so much better than "The Old Man" that there was no urge to return to the paper. However, after Pearl Harbor, they were called into service and I put on the editorial harness which fits as well as when in 1885 I began my editorial work in the capital of my native State.

XLVII

A NEIGHBOR GOES HOME

H APPY as we were in Mexico, neither my wife nor I was getting younger. I was seventy-one when I undertook the Mission. I celebrated my seventy-fifth birthday at mid-term of my service, and I remember that when I called on President Cárdenas that day, he gave me a big bear-hug *abrazo* of congratulations in his office at the Palace. I had been awakened early by a serenade of a marimba band. There were many callers. Next to home, Mexico seemed the happiest possible place to celebrate such a birthday. I kept a poem which one of my friends of the press, Robert Hammond Murray, wrote and brought to me:

"1862—for J.D.—1937"
"Oh, they raise 'em tough, long-lived
        In Carolina;
The stoutest men contrived
        In Carolina;
They grew slowly, like tree oaken;
By storms and years they can't be broken;
Young Methuselah's a joke in
        Carolina!

"They bring babies up on tar,
        In Carolina;
That makes the kind of folks they are
        In Carolina;
It preserves them from decay,
Keeps the germs of ills away,
They grow stronger every day,
        In Carolina.

"In turpentine their pone they dunk,
        In Carolina;
That gives 'em pep and spunk,
        In Carolina;

So they never do wear out,
Cark of time and toil they flout,
Arm chairs and slippers scout,
    In Carolina.

"At seventy-five a man's a lad,
    In Carolina;
With the steam he's always had,
    In Carolina;
He seldom walks; he runs,
Tosses weights, from pounds to tons,
And a fight he never shuns,
    In Carolina.

"They don't dare curl up and die,
    In Carolina!
Jibe the envious, who decry
    Old Carolina,
They're so full of turp, and tar
They're not allowed past Heaven's bar,
So in hell they're doomed to char,
    From Carolina!

"But the reason they know and tell,
    In Carolina;
Why they linger long and well,
    In Carolina;
In Heaven above the canny kneelers
Take no chances with Tar Heelers,
Especially Democrat New Dealers,
    From Carolina!

"For up there they're on to what they do
    In Carolina,
When party foes they barbecue,
    In Carolina;
There prevails a sneaking notion
That they'd make and pass a motion
To all jobs in Heaven portion
    To Carolina!

"So more power to those bred
    In Carolina;
To J.D. and those he's led
    In Carolina;

A SHIRT-SLEEVE AMBASSADOR GOES HOME.

"GOOD-BYE, BOY!"

From a cartoon by Arias Bernal.

Today he's three score, ten and five,
Long may he wave and thrive,
And to a century, at least, arrive,
    In Carolina!"

The years were crowded and happy, but they passed. It seemed to me that very suddenly in 1941 I was seventy-nine years old. I did not feel it. I laughed at the President's note:

> "Hyde Park, N. Y.
> May 31, 1941
>
> "Dear Chief:
> "I meant to send you a line on your birthday. You are dead right when you say that you feel young and act young. Most certainly you and I have got to celebrate your hundredth birthday together, and I will come to Raleigh for it.
> "Much love to you both
>   "As ever yours,
>   (Signed) "FRANKLIN D. ROOSEVELT."
> "Honorable Josephus Daniels,
> American Embassy,
> Mexico, D.F."

I smiled when I wrote my sons:

> "I gather from the above that the President does not expect me to be Ambassador when I celebrate my 100th birthday, but he gives no hint as to whether he will be retiring by that time, though I guess the fact that his letter is written from Hyde Park shows he expects to be in private life at his old home. At any rate we will be having a big fiesta then."

I smiled but I had already made up my mind to go home. In many ways leaving Mexico seemed as strange as my coming to it had been, when I was remembered by many Mexicans as a sort of symbol of the last armed threat of the Colossus at Vera Cruz. Now, leaving Mexico seemed a breaking of some ties of affection which Mexico had been good enough to show me. In more intimate ways than the formal Good Neighbor policy, my good Mexican neighbors were my closest friends. Next to my own, I never loved any land so well. Indeed, sometimes my children insisted that I put Mexicans and North Carolinians in a category of special affection by themselves. I have a notion that any Good Neighbor doctrine may begin in a declaration but it must grow in the heart.

I am sure Roosevelt felt that way. I remember how deeply stirred I was when he first compressed his foreign policy into one all embracing declaration, saying: "In the field of world policy I would dedicate this nation to the policy of the Good Neighbor—the neighbor who resolutely respects himself and, because he does so, respects the rights of others—the neighbor who respects his obligations and respects the sanctity of his agreements in and with a world of neighbors."

He restated it less formally to me as I was about to begin my service in Mexico.

"Chief," he said, "I have enunciated the doctrine. I will implement it officially in every possible way. But it is yours to incarnate it, to live it among our nearest neighbors who have sometimes doubted our disinterestedness. They will understand and realize our sincerity only, as in the flesh, they see it in your daily walk and conversation as the representative of your country."

I never had any other policy as Ambassador. I think I can say that the only yardstick by which I measured everything we did in connection with every problem which arose was: "Will it promote the Good Neighbor goal?" There have been, as Roosevelt foresaw, suspicions of our purposes. The fair words had to wait for acts and, as Roosevelt had promised, the acts were forthcoming. The last Marines were withdrawn from the last Caribbean republic. The tie of the Platt amendment was removed from Cuba's freedom. Clearly at Buenos Aires and at Montevideo the American policy was written into its acts.

In Mexico I believe I was helpful in the growth of faith. In 1941 it was deep satisfaction to me to see the solidarity in coöperation which the United States and its nearest Latin American neighbor had attained. As war approached, that proximity of neighbors acquired the warm-heartedness and dependability of comrades. There was much to worry about in the world, but none of it included any fears along the Rio Grande. If I was leaving Mexico, I knew that both I and my country had a friend there still. It was time to go home, but leaving Mexico meant both sadness and satisfaction.

Late in that summer of 1941 my doctor son advised that because of the progressive attacks of arthritis from which my wife had suffered she should not continue the strain imposed upon the mistress of the Embassy. He thought the quiet of home life, surrounded by her children and grand-children and friends was essential. She had negatived former suggestions looking to retirement, but now she felt that this filial and professional advice should not be disregarded.

As officials and hosts of friends gathered to say good-bye and shower us with flowers, almost covering my wife with orchids, it was recalled that shortly after my arrival in 1933, as stones were thrown at the Embassy, a gentleman said, "They are throwing stones today, but the time will come when they will be throwing roses." It literally came true, and we both left with lasting love of Mexico and Mexicans in our hearts.

Soon we were established in the North Carolina home of which my wife had been the real architect and whose garden she had planned. I had discussed the necessity of retirement with President Roosevelt, who offered me another diplomatic post which he thought might not impose such a strain on my wife's strength. However, I told him that I felt impelled to lay down public office and hope that in the old surroundings my wife's health would be restored. He said he could not urge a different course, but suggested that before my resignation took effect it would be wise for me to return to Mexico, make final disposition of pending affairs, to pave the way for my successor, say good-bye to friends, and to carry a message of esteem from him to President Camacho.

I did go back for a few days, but my wife could not accompany me. For me it was a very sad, happy time. On November 5 the American Press Correspondents at a luncheon gave expressions of comradeship. They knew that during the time I had held public office, I had regarded myself as Managing Editor of the Navy and in Mexico I thought of my job as Mexican Official Correspondent to the President of the United States and Secretary of State.

The Rotary Club, Lions' Club, Chamber of Commerce, Pan American Club, Alan Seeger American Legion Post, and other organizations with which I had been associated gave expressions of regard and regret at parting. On November 7 the American Colony in force gave a dinner accompanied by expressions of mutual friendship born of close association for nearly nine years. Referring to my devotion to the Good Neighbor policy I told them that far greater than any part I had played in strengthening ties it was theirs in their every-day life to broaden and make them lasting.

At a luncheon given by Foreign Minister Padilla on November 7, to which all members of the Diplomatic Corps were invited, Mr. Padilla spoke of the pleasant association and the regret of his country at the necessity of the ending of official relations, paying a high tribute to my wife in such terms as to evidence the close place she had in all hearts and added:

"Diplomatic life is not exactly characterized by the predominance of sentiment, but upon this occasion the most genuine emotion inspires our words. Ambassador Daniels represented in Mexico the highest virtues of the United States people because truly in few nations of the world is the spirit of justice so keenly felt as among the popular masses of the United States. The Good Neighbor policy could not have had, in these terrible times, a more cordial representative. Ambassador Daniels' work finds its fulfillment in the increasing friendship between Mexico and the United States and in the fraternity and confidence which are daily more evident in our relations."

In my response I paid tribute to the eloquent leadership of Minister Padilla in continental solidarity and told how association with him and the other Mexican officials and my colleagues of the Diplomatic Corps had enriched my life. To my successor as Dean of the Corps, my dear friend Señor José Manuel Carbonell, I referred to us as "twins" because the birthday of the Republic of Cuba and my own State of North Carolina were celebrated on the same day, May Twentieth.

On my last day in Mexico at a home luncheon with President and Señora Camacho we broke bread and exchanged *abrazos* as a token of the personal relations and the ties that bound the two neighbor countries. Responding to the affectionate farewell telegraphic message from Former President Cárdenas, I wired my warm regards adding: "You have made your place in history alongside of Benito Juárez."

One morning all the members of the Embassy Staff and the Consuls from all parts of Mexico gathered in a body at the Embassy. Joseph McGurk, Counsellor of the Embassy, spoke into a microphone which was also connected with my wife's telephone in Raleigh, and voiced the friendship of our associates. George Shaw, chairman of the presentation committee, described so that my wife could almost see it a rare and beautiful old vargueno—a prelate's carved desk—which they gave to us. My wife spoke to all her old friends and it was as if she were in the room again saying good-bye. My secretary, Robert McGregor, told me about the thoughtful plan to bring her to the party by phone. He said:

"The hook-up with Mrs. Daniels in Raleigh was arranged by me in collaboration with the Mexican Telephone Company. I wrote to Mrs. Daniels to ask if she was agreeable to the procedure and giving the date and time, etc.

"We put an amplifier into one of the two phones in the residence reception room. A cord ran from the receiver to the mantel piece and there the amplifier was placed. At the appointed time the call came through and Mrs. Daniels' voice and my own carrying on the conversation were heard by all present. You carried on quite a bit of the conversation yourself and I remember particularly that you asked for a certain brand of sausage to be served for your breakfast on arrival at home.

"I told Mrs. Daniels we were all assembled and that the hook-up was for the purpose of bringing her lovely presence into our midst even though, while absent, she was never far from our thoughts.

"Her voice was so strong and cheerful that we were all on the verge of tears but she had the word for all of us and to me that little bit was the loveliest of many impressions of your good-bye to Mexico."

I had written my formal resignation on October 30, 1941. In it I said:

"Dear Franklin:
"It is with sincere regret that I am impelled by family reasons to tender my resignation as your Ambassador to Mexico to which diplomatic post you did me the honor to appoint me in March 1933. The physicians of my wife advise that her health will not justify her continuance in the responsible though agreeable duties which devolve upon the wife of the Ambassador to Mexico. And no one knows better than you that I cannot carry on without her.

"It gives us both a sense of the deepest regret to sever the delightful relations with friends in the Mexican Government, colleagues in the diplomatic corps of which I am dean, members of our Embassy staff and many Mexican and other friends with whom our associations have been so pleasant that we will ever cherish them. During our stay in Mexico we have been the recipients of the most gracious hospitality.

"When you did me the honor to nominate me to the post I am now relinquishing, I went to Mexico animated by a single purpose: to incarnate your policy of the Good Neighbor. My constant aim has been to truly interpret the friendship of our country to our nearest southern neighbors. I have visited all parts of the republic as a Good Will Ambassador, never asking anything for any of my countrymen except what our country extends to Mexicans sojourning in the United States. I am glad to report to you that from the day of assuming the duties I have found cordial reciprocation of the sentiment of friendship expressed in your inaugural address.

"In laying down the duties, I need not assure you of my appreciation for the opportunity of serving our country in this important post. I know also that I need not tell you of my happiness in having been a part of your administration which has been distinguished by its devotion to the common weal, and which has, in conjunction with the other twenty Pan-American republics, secured continental solidarity. I am happy to tell you that the relations between Mexico and the United States are on the most sincerely friendly basis in their history and that both are firmly united to prevent any infiltration of alien isms or forces on this hemisphere from any quarter.

"In the great tasks that lie ahead, I will be happy with voice and pen and in any other way that opens, to give any aid in carrying out the great policies for which your administration has won world approval.

"Affectionately yours,

(Signed) "JOSEPHUS DANIELS

"Honorable Franklin D. Roosevelt,
   President of the United States,
   The White House,
   Washington, D.C."

His letter of acceptance voiced the old affection we had formed for each other in 1912. He wrote:

"THE WHITE HOUSE
WASHINGTON

October 31, 1941.

"Dear Chief:

"As you know, I have been worried for some time about your wife's health and hoping all the while that it would justify you both staying on in Mexico.

"Nevertheless, it comes to me as a real shock that we have to face the situation and that the country will have to do without the services of its Ambassador to Mexico, who perhaps, more than anyone else, has exemplified the true spirit of the good neighbor in the foreign field.

"That you have succeeded so completely is the testimony that in a position which, as we all know, was difficult when you first assumed it, our relations with our southern neighbor have, largely because of you, become relations of understanding and real friendship.

"I know that you will miss your colleagues and friends in Mexico City and I think you can realize my own feelings in not having my old Chief as an intimate part of the Administration.

"However, what must be, must be. I can only hope that your good wife's health will improve in her own home in Raleigh.

"I think that it is right that you should make a short trip to Mexico City in order to take farewell of all your friends there, and to present my very warm personal regards to President Camacho and to his Secretary of State for Foreign Affairs.

"I hope, therefore, that it will be agreeable if I do not accept your resignation until you have returned from a short visit to Mexico and completed such leave as may be due you.

"With my affectionate regards to you both, I am
"As ever yours
(Signed) "FRANKLIN D. ROOSEVELT.

"Honorable Josephus Daniels,
United States Ambassador to Mexico,
Mexico City, Mexico."

Durable as I am, I had laughed when he wrote me on my seventy-fifth birthday that he was coming to Raleigh to celebrate my hundredth. But with other Americans I felt left and lost when our friendship ended with his death, which came after he had guided the nation into victory. He was the reliance of mankind in its hope to see the peace he had planned shaped and undergirded. Above all others and in all the world he had been the Good Neighbor. And his policy of the neighbor—a warm, well-understood word in the stiff phrases of the diplomats—still remains the hope of the world.

Appendix

HAIL AND FAREWELL

ADDRESS BY JOSEPHUS DANIELS

AMBASSADOR FROM THE UNITED STATES
TO THE MEXICAN GOVERNMENT,
UPON THE PRESENTATION OF THE CREDENTIALS
TO PRESIDENT ABELARD RODRIGUEZ
IN THE NATIONAL PALACE, APRIL 24, 1933

Mr. President:

I am happy to bring to Your Excellency, to all the agencies of the Government of the Republic of Mexico, and to the whole people of Your Excellency's great country a message of the most friendly regard from the President of the United States of America. He charged me to bear to Your Excellency and to your countrymen the assurances that the people of the country over which he presides entertain the most kindly sentiment of neighborliness founded upon common interest and common destiny. To this assurance of his personal esteem, I am commissioned to convey his confidence that in the wise working out of any problems which may confront both Republics, their action will be such as to knit them together in indissoluble ties of friendship.

In this period when mankind everywhere is moving towards a better social system, it is gratifying that as never before the United States of America and the United Mexican States are facing the necessary changes with no slavish adherence to precedent or tradition. They have rather embarked upon new and well-considered experiments with optimism born of courage. Both are animated by faith that the social order now in the making in both countries will guarantee to all men equality, justice, liberty, and the full enjoyment of the fruits of their labor.

Your nearest neighbors to the north have deep admiration for your marked advance in social reform, in public education, in agriculture, in transportation, in communications, and in all measures which promote the well-being of your nationals. The people and officials of my country feel that each Republic has much to learn from the other. It is in this spirit that I have come to Mexico. I trust to be able to interpret to my countrymen the progressive policies you are projecting and achieving, as I bring to Your Excellency the aims and aspirations which dominate the people of the United States. It is my sincere desire to promote the strongest ties of understanding and amity. If I know my supreme ambition, as I enter upon the duties assigned to me, it is to be an Ambassador of Good Will to your country from the country I am privileged for the time being to represent.

Honored to make known formally to you that the President of the United States has appointed me Ambassador Extraordinary and Plenipotentiary of your Government, I hereby present to Your Excellency the letters of recall of my able and distinguished predecessor, The Honorable J. Rueben Clark, Jr., and tender at the same time my letters of credence.

Grateful for the gracious welcome already extended, I look forward with confidence to such associations and conferences as will insure the approach to and the solving of all matters that concern the two Republics in the spirit of mutual understanding which always characterizes Good Neighbors, both zealous to guard their sovereignty and preserve their territorial integrity.

ADDRESS BY ABELARD RODRIGUEZ

PRESIDENT OF THE REPUBLIC OF MEXICO
IN ACCEPTING THE
CREDENTIALS OF THE NEW AMBASSADOR
FROM THE UNITED STATES

"Mr. Ambassador:

It is with real satisfaction that I receive and cherish the very significant words of your speech. You may be certain—and I should like you to convey this to President Roosevelt and to your fellow-citizens—that there exists in Mexico for the United States the same friendly and neighborly sentiment, based on common interests and a common destiny, which you assure me prevails in your country.

I also entertain the same confidence as yourself, that none but indissoluble ties of friendship will be established by the action which the two countries may take in the solution of any problem which may arise.

The recognition, so frankly and courageously expressed, of the fact that humanity is passing through a period in which it is obliged to seek better social system, is of inestimable worth to this country, which was one of the first, in the new social era which is beginning, to decide to take a new course in meeting vital needs and satisfying the demands of collective justice, without feeling bound by precedent or by tradition.

Ever since this social movement began in Mexico, her administrations have sought a better understanding of human problems and a closer relation of all their actions with those problems, thus meeting the greatest social need of these new times and fulfilling a duty to which your President, also, has given expression in exactly that form, and which you are now so aptly confirming.

It is plain that this recognition of the almost universal phenomenon of the abandonment of the traditional social policy, and the movement of humanity towards a better social system—in order to achieve which nations have had and will have to embark on new economic and social experiments with complete resolution and courage—is a guarantee of increasingly intimate relations between our two countries, because it is an unquestionable sign of better understanding, and will be the source of more effective solidarity.

You may rest assured, Mr. Ambassador, that in Mexico you will meet with every facility for the discharge of your high office, and that the same sentiments of friendship and coöperation which you have expressed animate and will continue to animate the people and Government of Mexico in their attitude toward the Government and the great people of the United States.

Enclosure No. 1 to despatch No. 14177 of November 7, 1941, from the American Embassy at Mexico City

Your Excellencies, the Ambassadors and Ministers Plenipotentiary here present, Messrs. Secretaries of State and Chiefs of Department, and gentlemen:

The honor has fallen to me of assembling you at this table to take our leave of the Dean of the Honorable Diplomatic Corps accredited to the Mexican Government, His Excellency Josephus Daniels, the Ambassador of the United States of America.

Diplomatic life is not usually characterized by the predominance of sentiment, but on this particular occasion my words are inspired by deep and genuine feeling.

Ambassador Daniels has earned for himself among us not only the reputation of a great diplomat who has, in the Americas, helped to define and establish the principles of the Good Neighbor. He has gained among us a more emotional appellation; that of a great and sincere friend of Mexico.

A few days ago I said that Mr. Daniels represented in Mexico the very highest virtues of the American people. Indeed, in but a few nations of the earth do the genuine masses of the nation have so keen a sense of real justice as in the United States.

Mr. Daniels, a citizen of a Republic in which the welfare of all has reached hitherto unprecedented heights, came as its Ambassador to Mexico, a nation where a long-standing and iniquitous organization of society had provoked one of the most justifiable revolutions recorded in history. Wealth and high standards of living render both men and nations heedless of the promptings of justice and indifferent to the sacrifices made by others in their endeavor to obtain it. This is one reason why it has been so hard, throughout the long fought out struggle of the Mexican people, for men or peoples dwelling in the midst of prosperity to understand us.

But actual facts show that a great nation must identify itself with the fight for human freedom, wheresoever it be carried on. If it were otherwise ideals would be swamped beneath the rising tide of materialism.

To understand is to meet as brothers. Not everything must be selfishness, self-interest and gain. Peoples that identify themselves with the cause of justice wield in their hands a sword that will, sooner or later, win the day. This is the moral strength of democracies. This is also the moral strength of the Pan American doctrine, in its firm resolution to keep our Republics indissolubly united against all the dangers that menace the independence and liberties of this continent.

Ambassador Daniels, in his anxiety to fulfill his mission of friendship and understanding as thoroughly as possible, always kept in constant touch with Mexican realities, without ever encroaching on our sovereignty.

To distinguish, while the night is yet dark, the first flush of dawn; to perceive, in the midst of confusion, the outlines of human rights recaptured; to observe, in the clouds of dust arising from destruction, how equity takes to itself new shape and form, are faculties requiring a generous spirit. It must be big enough to view man's struggle for liberty with indulgence for errors committed and encouragement for felicitous achievements. History does not give any people credit for attaining greatness by the royal road of infallibility.

Now, those feelings of understanding, of sympathy with Mexico's just cause, have not only served my own country; they have also been of immense value to the people of the United States.

The Policy of the Good Neighbor could not, in these terrible times, have had a more genuine and a more cordial representative. President Roosevelt, in his letter accepting Mr. Daniels' resignation, a masterpiece of straight-forwardness and depth of feeling, has done him justice when he says that he has been the most eminent Ambassador of the United States in America. Why? Because in conduct and thought he has given expression to the doctrine of Pan American brotherhood. His influence, on passing beyond Mexico's frontiers has evidenced, by means of actual facts, that it is possible to govern relations between the peoples by democratic inspiration, and to substitute feelings of mutual respect, friendship and the rule of Law, for the impulses of brute force.

Mexico's example is of incalculable value to our American continental principle. Mr. Daniels has occupied the front rank among the men who have wrought this noble doctrine, as shown by the growing friendship between Mexico and the United States. His work stands out preeminently in the brotherhood and ever increasing confidence felt by our peoples.

I would not be rendering complete homage to Ambassador Daniels if on this occasion, so deeply tinged with emotion and friendship, I failed to associate with it the name of Mrs. Daniels. There are lives that are as a true equation, joined by the hyphen of love and affection. The lives of

Mr. and Mrs. Daniels are of this kind. Mrs. Daniels, a lady possessing most exceptional qualities, Mr. Daniels' exemplary helpmeet, has been and undoubtedly still is one of the purest founts of inspiration in the Ambassador's useful life.

Mr. Ambassador Daniels:

When you, April twenty-fourth, one thousand nine hundred and thirty-three, delivered the letters accrediting you as Ambassador Extraordinary and Plenipotentiary of the United States of America to Mexico, you spoke the following words: "If I know my supreme ambition, as I enter upon the duties assigned to me, it is to be an Ambassador of Good Will to your country."

Now that you are relinquishing the work for which you were so felicitously designated by President Roosevelt, I have the pleasure of saying to you that the hope then expressed has been more than amply fulfilled. You have, in fact, been an Ambassador of Good Will.

When you return to your home at Raleigh, North Carolina, the satisfaction of duty nobly performed will there be associated with the name of Mexico; Mexico that looks upon you as a friend, as President Roosevelt's sincere interpreter, as a champion of the ideal that unites all the nations of the Americas.

All that now remains for me to do as I emphasize the keen regard which both Your Excellency and Mrs. Daniels have succeeded in inspiring in my fellow-countrymen, is to convey to you, a duty with which I have been charged by President Avila Camacho, the expression of the Government of Mexico's esteem. I wish to add that during the time when I, as Secretary of Foreign Affairs, was privileged to meet you officially, I was enabled to appraise at their true value your lofty virtues of loyalty, frankness and intelligence.

I am sure that your colleagues, whose worthy Dean you have been, will also preserve the pleasantest memories of the solicitude with which you always discharged your duties as such. And as I raise my glass to drink to the prosperity of the Nation which you represent, and to the success of Mr. President Roosevelt, I express my best wishes for the health of Mrs. Daniels and for Your Excellency's future happiness.

Enclosure No. 2 to despatch No. 14177 of November 7, 1941, from the American Embassy at Mexico City

Mr. Minister and dear friends, for such I esteem you one and all:—

On the 24th day of April 1933 I presented my credentials as Ambassador from the United States to President Rodriquez, who graciously gave me cordial welcome. A month previous President Roosevelt, in his inaugural address, had voiced his ambition for unity in the Western Hemisphere and had enunciated the Good Neighbor doctrine, a consummation devoutly desired by like spirits in all Pan America. In the succeeding eight and a half years, under the administration of three Presidents of your Republic—Rodriguez, Cárdenas, and Avila Camacho —whose friendship I will always cherish—I have sought, as I walked among you and with you, to incarnate a civil trinity—understanding, brotherhood, and friendship—which have flowered into a blessed continental solidarity.

In presenting my credentials, after conveying the greetings of President Roosevelt to President Rodriquez, I used these words which I recall today, because in both countries there has been marked progress along the lines which were envisioned at that time:

In this period when mankind everywhere is moving towards a better social system, it is gratifying that as never before the United States of America and the United Mexican States are facing the necessary changes with no slavish adherence to precedent or tradition. They have rather embarked upon new and well-considered experiments with optimism born of courage. Both are animated by faith that the social order now in the making in both countries will guarantee to all men equality, justice, liberty, and the full enjoyment of the fruits of their labor.

Your nearest neighbors to the north have deep admiration for your marked advance in social reform, in communications, and in all measures which promote the well-being of your nationals.

My way in the first days of official residence here was made easy for me by the confidence expressed by President Rodriquez, who responding to my official address, stressed Mexican reforms not unlike in spirit those incarnated by President Roosevelt, saying governments must recognize that "humanity is passing through a period in which it is obliged to seek a better social system" and adding:

Ever since this social movement began in Mexico, her administrations have sought a better understanding of human problems and a closer relation of all their actions with those problems, thus meeting the greatest social need of these new times and fulfilling a duty to which your President also, has given expression in exactly that form, and which you are now so aptly confirming.

My path was also smoothed by public assurances of the able Minister of Relaciones Exteriores, Dr. José Manuel Puig Casaurac, who had read my LIFE OF WILSON and knew from it and from his residence in Washington as Ambassador from your country of the sincere sympathy entertained by the Wilson Administration for the objectives of your revolution which brought Madero to the presidency in 1910 and of its abhorence of "the deep damnation of his taking off." He recalled the ringing of assertion of his friendship for Mexico by Woodrow Wilson when his attitude was not understood and appreciated either in Mexico or the United States. In this tragic hour when democracy is imperilled and the sovereignty and inherent independence of nations is scorned, it is well to refresh our memory with Wilson's brave defiance to his countrymen of those who flouted the right of every country to control its own destiny. In those hectic days, Wilson declared:

There is one thing I have got a great enthusiasm about, I might say a reckless enthusiasm, and that is human liberty. I want to say a word about our attitude toward Mexico. I hold it as a fundamental principle that every people has the right to determine its own form of government; and until this recent revolution in Mexico, eighty percent of the people of Mexico never had a 'look in' in determining who should be their governors or what their government should be. Now, I am for the eighty percent. It is none of my business, and it is none of your business, how long they take in determining it. It is none of my business, and it is none of your business, how they go about their business. The country is theirs. The liberty, if they can get it, and God speed them in getting it, is theirs. And so far as my influence goes while I am President nobody shall interfere with them.

Together we look back today upon the high road toward better living conditions, larger opportunities, fairer wages, better housing, possession of land by more men who till the soil, universal education expressed in a material way in the construction of thousands of rural school houses in which youths are trained for usefulness and citizenship, the building of good roads and increase of irrigation projects, the expansion of industry and the encouragement of the investment of capital—all buttressed by the sacred right to think, to speak, to write, to print, to worship. We have not reached the high goal, but like Paul at Appii Forum we thank God and take courage.

I rejoice to have been witness, and to have made what contribution I could, to the growing friendship between Mexico and the United States, a friendship based upon better knowledge through closer association, and the recognition by each of the sovereignty of the other, and a realization of the mutuality of interest and destiny.

I count the years that have followed as among the happiest of a happy and I hope useful life, because I have been privileged to enjoy association in this friendly country with officials and people whose aspirations are kindred to those of my countrymen. They have embraced a period of peace when free nations were seeking to make democracy safe for the world, followed by this tragic era of slaughter on every continent except our own, in which liberties free men hold dear are imperilled. Before the fires of war threatened all mankind, the course of government on both sides of the Rio Grande were marked by the resolve to make economic and political democracy one and inseparable. And we—Mexico, the United States, and the other nineteen republics represented in this capital today—have highly resolved that neither bursting bombs nor the menace of alienisms shall lessen our irrevocable determination.

Under democracy a nation moulds itself according to its needs and desires. The needs are what give substance to a nation's character, while its desires find expression in the longing of the many who look out of darkened windows yearning for light and a fair chance. Life has a curious way of being ruthless with those that stand in the path of progress. There are in every generation those who are termed extremists and radicals because they are unwilling to live in a static world. But as with birth itself—there is travail in creation. The mother is not selfish, she gives of her pain and her labor, that the child of her creation may live. So a nation develops its national character. From among its strong men its great leaders emerge. Hidalgo, Juarez, and Madero in Mexico; Washington, Lincoln and Wilson in the United States, are men whose character has been forged on the anvil of a nation's struggle for emancipation from chains that fetter its progress to the realization that "for justice all seasons summer and every place a temple."

Mexico has its own particular concept of revolution. It has come to regard good government in the light of revolutionary practice. While with others 'revolution' is a stage reached, preached and past, with Mexico it is a continuing and vital condition to successful government that it shall first be 'revolutionary'. Hence progress is its hallmark.

In taking sorrowful leave of a land where Mrs. Daniels and I have been so happy, I can only say that we shall forever treasure Mexico, its people, its ideals, its art, its character, and its noble beauty, as a second home. The essence of one's home is that it is a place where the hearthstone is one of quiet and peaceful understanding, of tolerant and gracious sympathy, of generous warmheartedness. These are the essence of the people of Mexico, and I cannot pay too high a tribute to this people for their possession of these qualities, so characteristic of their history. It is a proud people, and a people whose pride is seen in its gracious courtesy, in its hospitality and warmhearted sympathy. You will undoubtedly recall that I have often claimed to have been welcomed upon my arrival here by Moctezuma—my stay here has been such that the depth of my affection for Mexico is equal to the years since Cuauhtemoc set the standard for deathless love of his country and a prototype of the noblest American youthful hero of the revolutionary days who regretted, as he faced death, that he had only one life to give for his country.

The expressions of cordial friendship by Minister Padilla are engraved on my heart. They will brighten my days as long as memory lasts. I was privileged early to know him when I came to Mexico. I soon fell under the charm of his eloquence and have been enriched in the years by a delightful association which has been very dear to me. Since his accession to the post of Minister of Foreign Affairs I have enjoyed a closer relationship which has ripened into friendship and has sweetened my life in this delightful country. Diplomacy, I have been told, is the conduct of official relations between States with intelligence and tact. Mr. Padilla has brought to this somewhat stilted interpretation of our profession a concept of sympathy, a concept of fellow understand. In all things I have found him frank and sincere, devoted to the weal and sovereignty of his country and to the principles of democracy of which he is a true apostle. As a pioneer advocate of continental solidarity, Mr. Padilla has evidenced readiness to join other Pan American statesmen in undergirding territorial and spiritual integrity of this hemisphere. In the achievement of this high goal of the New World and in his intercourse with the diplomats assigned to Mexico, he has won the admiration and esteem of all the members of the Diplomatic Corps. He has created an atmosphere in official association—and he has by his urbanity and consideration caused every member of the Diplomatic Corps to feel the association was not merely one of official relationship with all the age-old tenets of diplomatic protocol, but also one of genuine and lasting friendship. We have found him *simpatico*—the best word in the language of this country and one which I fain would see incorporated into every language and which I intend to expropriate for my own country.

His colleagues in the Foreign Office, Undersecretary Torres Bodet,

Licenciado Hidalgo, Licenciado Mena, Licenciado Armendariz, Licenciado Enriques, Licenciado Tello, and the many others are worthy assistants to so splendid a leader. For years, also, we have been indebted to the "palomitas", Luz María and María Luisa, in the Office of Ceremonial, who are as pretty as Don Mariano is kind. To all of these, my heart goes out in affectionate thanks for that pleasant association which has made my stay in Mexico so agreeable and happy.

In saying good-bye, necessitated solely by family reasons, I will carry with me the knowledge that I am a very rich man in that you assure me I have garnered your friendship which I will always regard as a priceless possession.

My wife and I feel that we have two homes—one in our own country and one in Mexico. In whatever concerns these neighbor nations you may be sure will be nearest to my heart. I shall be coming back—the lure of Mexico is irresistible—and we shall hope to welcome you to our home in North Carolina. Adios.

Minister Padilla's tribute to my beloved wife touches me more than I can convey in words. For her and myself I can truly say that the affection in which we hold the Minister and his dear wife will ever abide, and the associations will be renewed when we welcome them on the promised visit to our home in North Carolina.

INDEX

INDEX

AARONSOHN, Michael, 469
Adams, C. F., 291
Adams, Mrs. Fred, 167
Adams, John, 291
Adams, John Quincy, 291
Agrarian Commission, 123
Agrarian problems, 199 ff.
Agricultural College at Chapingo, Rivera's frescoes in, 442
Agricultural College of State of Hidalgo, 301-2
Agricultural school, in San Miguel Tenancingo, Ambassador and Mrs. Daniels visit, 48
Agricultural workers, organized, 206
Águila Oil Company, title of declared invalid, 220
Aguilar, General, son of General Leandro Aguilar, 492, 493
Aguilar, Leandro, 492
Aguiles Caderes, Manuel, cartoon, "Welcome, Mr. Daniels," by, 399
Aguirre, Stephen, and Embassy's aid to Calles, 63; accompanies bodies of victims in airplane crash on their return to the U. S. for burial, 316; mentioned, 162, 178, 416
Alan Seeger Post of the American Legion, 344, 511
Alcantara Machado, José de, 323
Alcoholic beverages, and J. D., anecdotes of, 416 ff.
Alemán, Miguel, elected President of Mexico, 44, 92; gives assurance that Mexico and the U. S. are "twins in resistance," 87; J. D. attends inauguration of as Governor of Vera Cruz, 88 ff.; active for election of Ávila Camacho, 90; in New York, presented silk Mexican flag, to J. D., 92; mentioned, 91, 109
Allen, Henry W., editor of The Mexican Times, 339
Allen, Thomas S., 456
Almada, Pedro J., 10-11
Almazán, Juan Andreu, sketch of, 80-81; and Laredo Road opening, 481
Almazán junta at San Antonio, 86
Altitude, in Mexico, anecdote of, 414-16
Álvarez del Vayo, Julio, Ambassador from Spanish Republic to Mexico, 325; sentenced to imprisonment in Belgium, 329
Amaro, Joaquín, 61, 405

Amatlán, oil property, 214
Ambassadors, classified, 284-85; not messenger boys, 287; censoring of speeches of, 288-89
America, quoted on Almazán, 81
American Cemetery, in Mexico City, 344
American Chamber of Commerce in Mexico City, a Good Neighbor, 386
American Colony, in Mexico, 32; described, 379 ff.; gives farewell dinner for Ambassador and Mrs. Daniels, 511
American Embassy, in Mexico City, stoned by opponents of J. D.'s appointment, 9; described, 29 ff.; Southern hospitality at, 32, 33; a mecca, 351 ff.
American hospitals, 386
American School, Mexico City, 129, 137
American Star, first English-language newspaper published on Mexican soil, 404, 405
Anderson, Mr. of Huasteca Petroleum Co., discusses difficulties of oil companies, 219; said oil companies were determined not to raise wages, 223-24; expresses attitude of oil companies as to negotiation with Mexican government, 242
André Laguna, Santiago, 402
Ángel Ceniceros, José, 104
Anti-alcoholic crusade, 140
Araujo, Antonio P., 132, 133, 134
Arias Bernal, cartoon, "Good-bye, Mr. Daniels," by, 399
Armstrong, Jack, worried about Mexican government's plan to develop Mexico's oil resources, 217-19; and former Ambassador Clark, 221 ff.
Arroyo, A., and case of Kluckhohn, 407 ff. passim
Art, in Mexico, 441 ff.
Artists and craftsmen, Mexico a country of, 450
Assheton, J. A., title of oil company of declared invalid, 220
Association of Producers of Petroleum in Mexico, 217
As Thousands Cheer, 459
Atlantic Monthly, The, publishes special oil edition, after expropriation, 257 ff.
Ávila Camacho, Manuel, as President of Mexico, 79 ff.; presidential campaign of, 80 ff.; pledges that Mexico and U. S. will stand together during war, 87; strength-

Ávila Camacho, Manuel, (*Cont.*)
ened public schools, 140; and labor, 206; welcomed Spanish liberals to Mexico, 328; J. D.'s farewell to, 512; mentioned, 44, 77, 91, 111, 349
Ávila Camacho, Señora de, 512
Ávila Camacho, Maximino, at dedication of "Fraternidad" School, 317
Azaña, Manuel, 330, 332
Azcárate, Juan Francisco, pioneer in Mexican aviation, 26

BAGLEY, Worth, 374
Baker, Mrs. Cora W., 469
Baker, Newton D., 469
Baltimore Sun, quoted, 5; quoted on "Joe Daniels," 194-95
Baptists, in Mexico, 171
Barnard, Frank, 404
Barragán, Sr., 163
Bartolomé, Father, statue of in Mexico City, 447
Baruch, Bernard B., and the calling in of gold, 15; tells Wilson's attitude toward taking over Mexico's oil resources in World War I, 211
Basham, H. A., 379
Bassols, Narciso, educational policies of supported by Rodríguez, 47; mentioned, 152
Batista, Fulgencio, defeats Grau San Martín for presidency of Cuba, 323 ff. *passim;* visits Mexico, 326
Battle, Gordon, 415
Battle Monuments, J. D. tours Europe in dedications of, 469 ff.
Bayard, Thomas F., 98, 291
Beery, Wallace, in Mexico, 435-36
Belaúnde Rafael, 104, 105
Bell, A. D., 12
Benedict, Pope, 178
Benson, William S., 178
Berle, Adolf, Assistant Secretary of State, 253
Berryman, Clifford, 456
Beteta, Ramón, on Obregón, 43; brings message from Cárdenas to Roosevelt, 72; member of Cárdenas "Brain Trust," characterized, 107; delivers address at Embassy, 107-8; on U. S. Boycott, 248; and Kluckhohn, 408-9, 411; and J. D., 425; mentioned, 139, 241
Bingham, Robert Worth, appointed Ambassador to Great Britain, 5, 6; condemns Moley in London, 20; mention, 291, 471, 476
Bishop of Vera Cruz, in hiding in Mexico City, 160-61
Black, Hugo, 476
Bloom, Sol, in Mexico, 349
Boal, Pierre, and case of Kluckhohn, 407 ff. *passim;* mentioned, 163, 169, 178, 482
Bonillas, Ignacio, and Carranza, 41
Boone, Mrs. Howard, 469
"Bootlegging" religion, 162

Borah, Senator, wished to investigate religious situation in Mexico, 186
Borbolla, 298
Borglum, Gutzon, 456
Bowers, Claude, Ambassador to Spain, 15, 325; attitude of toward Franco, 328; mentioned, 332
Brauch, Howard, 462
Brest Naval Memorial, 471-72
British Club, 391
British Colony, 390 ff.
British hospitals, 386
British sense of humor, 395 ff.
British Society of Mexico, 390
British Woman's Charities Committee, 394
Brinkley, Dr., radio advertiser of a goatgland operation, 280, 373-74
Broadkirk, Prof., of University of Michigan, 304
Brooklyn Tablet, on Connally, Garner, and McAdoo, 483
Brown, Philip Marshall, 192
Bryan, Mr. Julian, on Russia, 358, 359
Bryan, Ruth, wishes position in State Department, 21 ff.
Bryan, William Jennings, unveiling of statue of in Washington, 453-56; Mexican interest in, 456; mentioned, 98
Bryan Breakfast, in 1940, 464-65
Bryde, Daniel, 456
Buck, Stepney, 403-4
Bullfights, 439-41
Bullitt, William C., on Russia, 358, 359, 475; mentioned, 472
Burke, Father John J., J. D. seeks advice of on church question, 23-24; on religious differences in Mexico, 143; J. D. on death of, 144; and Mexican church problems, 274-75; mentioned, 173
Burleson, Postmaster General, 406
Bursley, Mr. and Mrs. Herbert, 163, 293
Butler, Dr., 171

CABLE, Ben, "tired of being a debt collector," 121
Cabral, Juan J., on Villa, 306-7
Cabrera, Luis, tells of Carranza's death, 41-42
Cain, H. L., 129, 137
Calderón de la Barca, Madame, writer on Mexico, 31
Callahan, Patrick H., 193, 456
Calles, Aureo L., 489
Calles, Plutarco Elías, and J. D., 44 ff.; J. D.'s estimate of, 45-46; attitude of toward F. D. R., 46; and Rodríguez, 47 ff. *passim,* 52 ff.; subject of correspondence between J. D. and Rodríguez, 50-52 *passim;* and Cárdenas 56 ff. *passim;* expulsion from Mexico by Cárdenas, 59 ff.; change in, 56 ff. *passim,* 60-61; quoted, 62; and Puig Casauranc, 103; address of quoted by J. D. in part, 177; and donation of land,

200; and labor, 206, 208; and Mexican oil, 215, 221 ff. *passim;* arrangement of with Morrow as to foreign oil companies, 217 ff. *passim;* and Morrow, 272 ff. *passim;* discusses church problems with Father Burke, 274-75; mentioned, 22, 37, 82, 122, 184

Calvo Clause, Morrow's arrangement with Calles as to foreign oil companies virtually made void, 217; and expropriation, 228; mentioned, 238

Camacho, President. *See* Ávila Camacho.

Canalizo, Antonio G., accompanies J. D. on call upon Mrs. Madero, 93 ff. *passim.*

Canalizo, Mrs., 94

Cantinflas (Mario Moreno), Mexican comedian, 448-49

Cantrell, Professor, of University of Michigan, 304

Carbonell, José Manuel, 512

Cárdenas, Lázaro, as Secretary of War and Marines, asked to order special precautions for Daniels train, 11; and Calles, 56 ff. *passim;* as President of Mexico, 56 ff.; and Six-Year Plan, 57 ff.; relation of to Indians, 57 ff.; quoted on the departure of Calles from Mexico, 65; and New Deal, 67-68; attitude of toward public education, 68, 127; saw eye to eye with Roosevelt, 72; joins Roosevelt to prevent war, 72-73; quoted on approaching war, 74; upon retirement a Mexican Cincinnatus, 77; vigilant to prevent Nazi propaganda, 77; commands Mexican forces for defense during war, 87; and opening of churches in Vera Cruz, 88-89; would not accept gifts from oil companies, 78; backed antialcoholic crusade, 140; J. D. appeals to for Archbishop's funeral, 148-50 *passim;* indignant at police attack on church in Orizaba, 163; approved and aided Townsend group, 168; and dotation of land, 203; and labor, 206, 208; and Mexican oil, 215; in negotiation with foreign oil companies, 225-26; and labor impasse of foreign oil companies, 225; announces expropriation of oil properties, 227; writes U. S. State Department on expropriation, 230; immediately gives J. D. oral assurance that Mexican government will pay for expropriated oil properties, 230, 235; official pledge of as to payment for expropriated oil properties, 236; writes letter to J. D. praising attitude of U. S. government in matter of expropriation, 236-37; efforts of to get settlement, 241; makes address on anniversary of expropriation, 253-54; accused by propagandists of being in league with Nazis, 257; and the Cedillo rebellion, 259-60; and Richberg, 263 ff. *passim;* Quezon's tribute to, 327; welcomed Spanish liberals to Mexico, 328; congratulates Daniels on result of U. S. 1936 presidential election, 384-85; no official censorship under, 404; and Kluckhohn, 110, 411-12, 413; provides special train for diplomats to tour Mexico, 485; held in high esteem by the people, 490; mentioned, 41, 44, 82, 91, 143, 405, 433, 440

Cárdenas, Señora Amalia Solórzano de, led women in support of expropriation, 247-48; Mrs. Garner called on, 482-83

Career diplomats, 283-84, 285; satirized in skit at Embassy, 292-93

Carlota, story of jewels of, 358; on Confederates in Mexico, 339; mentioned, 25

Carmody, Martin H., asked for J. D.'s recall, 177, 183; charge of against J. D., 186

Carranza, Venustiano, account of death of, 41-42; and Mexican oil, 213, 215; mentioned, 82, 96, 106

Carreño, Alberto M., and Archbishop Díaz's funeral, 148 ff. *passim,* 154

Carrillo, Alejandro, organizer of Workers University of Mexico, 206

Casillas, General, 11-12 *passim*

Caso, y Andrade, Alfonso, on jewels of Monte Alban, 298

Castillo Nájera, Francisco, in conference on oil, 73; tells anecdote of Cárdenas, 78; and J. D., 99; signed agreements settling expropriation difficulties, 266, 268; on Kluçkhohn affair, 409; mentioned, 154, 289

Cathedral in Mexico City, the, 353

Catholic church, and Huerta, 40-41; attitude of Rodríguez toward, 49; history of in Mexico, 145; supported expropriation, 247. *See also* Church, Churches

Cedillo, Saturnino, 259

Cedillo rebellion, 259-60

Censorship, in Mexico, 404; twice applied to U. S. journalists, 405 ff.

Cerro Azul, oil property, 214, 215

Cerro Viejo, oil well, 212

Chamber of Commerce, Mexico City, 511

Chamizal borderline quarrel, 23, 116-17

Chancery, the, described, 30; a clearing house, 367 ff.

Chapingo School of Agriculture, visited by J. D., 130 ff.

Chaplin, Charlie, praised Cantinflas, 448

Chapopote, Indian name for oil, 211 ff. *passim*

Chapopote Nuñez, oil well, 212

Charros, the 438

Chateau-Thierry, memorial at, 470

Chávez, Carlos, Mexican musician, 450

Chavez, Dennis, defends J. D., 187-88

Cheadle, Major, 8

Chichén-Itzá, 487-88

Childs, Marquis, quoted on Davis in Mexico City in 1938, 252

Christ Church, 390

Christié, Mrs. Walter, 419

Church, difference in attitude of in Mexico and the U. S., as stated by Cárdenas, 71; attitude of toward secular education, 128-29; after the Revolution, 142 ff.; as subject to laws of each state, 145-46; view of on control of education, 146; state laws controlling, 146-47; pay for property of wanted, 151 ff.; problems of, Morrow secures a *modus vivendi*, 274-75

Churches, opening of in Vera Cruz, 88-89; closed in some states, open in others, 145-46; open in Mexico City, 160

Científicos, mentioned, 48, 105, 239, 381, 441, 435

Claims, extent and first settlement of, 115 ff.; lump-sum settlement of, 117 ff. *passim*

Clapper, Raymond, says "Joe Daniels" mainly responsible for good Mexican-U. S. relations, 261-62

Clark, Reuben, oil company plans to get American Embassy backing by means of, for protest to Mexican government, 221 ff. *passim;* mentioned, 14, 118, 356

Cobb, Miss Beatrice, 466

Cocktails, Ambassador asked to supply recipe for, 372

Colby, Bainbridge, 98

Collier, John, on Cárdenas, 309

Collier's Magazine, 430

Colmery, Harry W., 469, 472

Committee on Religious Rights, investigates religious problems in Mexico, 191-92; report favorable to J. D., 192-93

Communist, Lord Lochiel's definition of, 65-66

Communist party of Mexico, opposes J. D.'s appointment, 10

Comonfort, Ignacio, 44

Cone, Admiral H. I., 16

Confederates, of U. S. Civil War, emigration of to Mexico after war, 338 ff.

Confederation of Mexican Workers, strength of, 206

Connally, Thomas Terry, 482, 483

Connery, Representative, introduces resolution demanding J. D.'s recall, 183-84

Constantine, Miss, in airplane crash in Mexico, 315 ff. *passim*

Constantine, Amada Morán de, and the *Posada* at the Embassy, 436-37; mentioned, 139, 429

Constantine, Arthur, quoted on Archbishop Díaz, 147-48; dean of newspaper correspondents, 398, 437; on J. D.'s first news conference, 399; mentioned, 439

Conway, George, library of, 392

Conway, Mrs. George, anecdote told by, 395

Cook, George W., anecdote of, 418; mentioned, 381-83 *passim*

Cooke, Morris Llewellyn, represented U. S. in oil settlements, 267

Coolidge, Calvin, on Americans abroad, 228; instructed Morrow to "keep us out of war with Mexico," 272

Cortés, Hernando, and Malinche, 302-3; mentioned, 31, 142, and *passim*

Cortés Palace, Rivera's frescoes in, 442

Cortesi, Arnoldo, 398

Cotton, in Mexico, 202

Coughlin, Father, 188

Cowdray, Lord (Pearson, W. D.), and Mexican oil, 212, 391

Cowdray Hospital, named for Viscountess Cowdray, 391

Creel, George, and Huey Long, 280; mentioned, 38

Creighton, Bishop, 155

Crema de Xtabentun, anecdote, 417

Crowell, Benedict, 469

Cruz, Manuel, 303

Cuba, fear of intervention in, 324-25

Cummings, Homer, 458

Curtis, Charles, and Dr. Brinkley, 280, 373-74

Dallas News, 398

Daniell, Raymond, 398

Daniels, Frank, son of J. D., 506

Daniels, Judge Frank A., 24

Daniels, Jonathan, 506

Daniels, Josephus, appointed as Ambassador to Mexico, 3-4; shirt-sleeve diplomat, 4-5; opposition in Mexico to appointment of, 8-9; trip of to Mexico, 10 ff.; before appointment, makes study of transportation problem for F. D. R., 16 ff.; gives Raymond Moley asked-for advice, 18 ff.; and Ruth Bryan, 21 ff.; troubles facing, in Mexico, 22 ff.; presents credentials and is received by President Rodríguez, 25 ff.; address of at presentation of credentials, 26-27 (address quoted in full, 520-21); describes the American Embassy, 29-30; and Calles, 44 ff.; and Rodríguez, 47; misquoted on Calles, 50 ff.; invited to luncheon by Calles, 52 ff.; speech of for Calles luncheon, quoted, 54-55; promoted Calles' safe entry into the U. S., 62 ff.; attends opening of Congress when Cárdenas speaks, 67; speaks in New York at celebration of enactment of Bill of Rights, 86-87; narrow escape of from death in State of Vera Cruz, 90-91; invited by Alemán to be present at his inauguration as President of Mexico, 92; favorably viewed in Mexico as a liberal, 99; and first settlement of claims, 116 ff.; requests information on claims, 118; interest of in Mexican education, 127 ff.; and the funeral of Archbishop Díaz, 148 ff.; advises Methodists to give their property to government, 152; protests against false propaganda that all churches are closed in Mexico, 156; attacked in U. S. as enemy

of the church, 177 ff.; and Archbishop
Martínez, 174; reaction of to campaign
for recall, 179 ff.; shows attack was based
on misinformation, 181-82; and Mexican
labor leaders, 206-7; refused to demand
special legislation for foreign oil companies, 221 ff. *passim;* criticized for not
preventing expropriation, 228; letter to
Hull on expropriation quoted, 238 ff.; defends Cárdenas against propaganda lies,
257; praised as Ambassador by Raymond
Clapper, 261-62; ignores State Department
as to Quezon, 287-88; visits Indian school
near Actópan, 300-1; and Francisco Sarabia, 318 ff.; and Grau San Martín, 323 ff.
passim; and Álvarez del Vayo, 325 ff.
passim; criticises foreign diplomats in
Spain for favoring Franco, 328; on the
Spanish officials of the Republican government in Spain, 330-31; finds in Mexico
descendants of Confederate emigrants to
Mexico, 338 ff.; on Henry Wallace, 349-
50; on William Randolph Hearst's visit,
353-55; and the matter of intoxicants,
356-57; on the instances of censorship of
U. S. journals in Mexico, 405 ff.; elected
member of the *Charro* select organization
of horsemen, 438; wedding anniversary
of, 450; visits U. S. in April, 434, 453 ff.;
visit at White House, 454-55; at F. D.
R.'s press conference, 461-62; attends
birthday dinner at Raleigh, 462-63; makes
speech at Electoral College Banquet, 467-
68; goes to Europe for the dedication of
battle monuments, 469 ff.; trip of to Ireland, 477-79; attends Laredo Road opening, 480 ff.; tours Mexico with other diplomats as guests of President Cárdenas,
485 ff.; birthday poem to, 507 ff.; end of
Ambassadorship in Mexico, 507 ff.; reply
of to Foreign Minister Padilla on occasion
of farewell luncheon, 512 (quoted entire,
525-29); writes resignation to F. D. R.,
513-14; speech of in reply to Foreign
Minister Padilla's address at luncheon
given by the latter, quoted in full, 525-29
Daniels, Mrs. Josephus, says "You can't go
to Mexico," 3 ff.; on trip to Mexico, 12 ff.
passim; present at J. D.'s presentation of
credentials, 25 ff.; quoted on the American Embassy, 29; as hostess of the American Embassy, 32, 33; friendship of with
Mrs. Madero, 95; and the Y.W.C.A.,
166; interest of in Townsend groups, 168;
and Will Rogers, 278; visits Indian school
at Actópan, 300-1; interest of in story of
Malinche, 302-3; and Villa's favorite
song, "Adelita," 306; interest of in Indians, their art, handicraft, and lives,
309-10; and Connie Mack, 364; and Dr.
Ferguson, 388-89; and Fourth of July
breakfasts, 419; and the *Posada* at the
Embassy, 436-37; enjoyed Mexican flow-

ers, 437; wedding anniversary of, 450; at
the White House, 454-55; at review of
Fleet, 457-58; popularity of in Raleigh,
463; Clary kin of in Ireland, 477 ff.; in
leave-taking from Mexico, 510-11; tele-
phone hook-up of Mexican friends with
her home in Raleigh, 513; Foreign Min-
ister Padilla's tribute to, 523-24, 529
Daniels, Josephus, Jr., 472, 506
Daniels, Melvin, cousin of J. D., 389
Daniels, Worth, attends bullfight, 440-41
D'Armond, Jack, 398
Davies, Marian, in Mexico, 353-54
Davis, John W., 415
Davis, William Rhodes, and John L. Lewis,
208, 252; and Mexican expropriation of
oil, 251 ff.
Deegan, Mrs. Elizabeth, 475
DeLacy, William H., 178
Del Monte, Edmundo, 402-3
Democratic National Conventions, 1936 and
1940, 463 ff.
Democrats, cannot enter Heaven, 431
De Valera, Eamon, 477-78
Dewey, John, praises Mexican educational
movement, 127
Díaz, Bernal, quoted by Mrs. Daniels, 31
Díaz, Archbishop Pascual, wanted more
priests, 147; incident concerning, 147-48;
arrested and released, 148; funeral pro-
cession of, 148 ff.; mentioned, 178-79
passim
Díaz, Porfirio, as president of Mexico, 37-
38; turned over patrimony of his country
to foreigners, 213-14; compared with
Juárez, 307-8; anecdote concerning, 420;
started the Palace of Fine Arts, 434-35
Díaz Dufoo, Carlos, 402
Diplomat, definitions of, 282 ff.
Diplomatic caste system, 290-91
Diplomatic Corps, during presidential cam-
paign of Camacho and Almazán, 84-85;
mentioned, 32 and *passim*
Diplomatic notes, the bane of diplomacy,
285-86
Dodd, William E., 291
Doheny, E. L., and Mexican oil, 212, 213,
219; mentioned, 33
Doheny, Mrs. E. L., gave land on which
Chancery was built, 33, 359
Dollar Diplomacy, repudiated by F. D. R.,
228
Domínguez, Carlos, 403
Dooley, Mr. *See* Dunne, Finley Peter
Dotation of land, attitude of Cárdenas to-
ward, 67
Douglas, Charles A., 41, 456
Douglas, Lewis, 17
Doyle, Michael Francis, and banquet of
Electoral College, 467
Drechsler, Armando, painted J. D.'s por-
trait, 111
Duff Cooper, Alfred, 471

Duffy, F. Ryan, 469
Dugan, Father, 174
Duggan, Laurence, 164
Dunne, Finley Peter, on Ambassadors, 283

EATON, Charles A., 469
Echaniz, Guillermo, 403
Echeverría y Vidaurre, Manuel, 487
Economic problems, Cárdenas' views on, 68 ff.
Education, Cárdenas' views on, 68 ff.; in Mexico, 127 ff.; conflict between church and state concerning, 135-36; increase in, 299 ff. *See also* Socialistic education
Education Department, frescoes of Rivera in, 442; frescoes in described, 443
Ehringhaus, J. C. B., 462, 463, 465
Election of 1936, interest of among American Colony, 384 ff.
Electoral College, banquet of, 467-68
Elías, Francisco S., 130-31, 432
Elizondo, Eduardo, 401-2
Embassy. *See* American Embassy
Enríquez, Jorge, presented portrait of Juárez to Ambassador and Mrs. Daniels, 308
Expropriation of oil properties, prelude to, 217 ff.; announced by Cárdenas, 227; the story of, 227 ff.; issues following, 243-44; celebration of anniversary of in Mexico, 253-54; final settlement of, 266 ff.
Excelsior, on J. D.'s visit, 400; on Rivera, 446; mentioned, 402

FABELA ALFARO, Isidro, 72
Fairfield, Rear Admiral, 472
Fall, Albert, and Mexican oil, 223; mentioned, 33
Fange, Ensign, 172
Farley, James A., in appreciation of J. D., 16; and 1940 campaign, 464; mentioned, 460-61
Farragut, Admiral, anecdote concerning, 430
Federal Council of Churches, opposed Borah's resolution, 186-87
Federation of Labor, and Calles, 61
Fenerty, Clare Gerald, attacked J. D., 185
Ferguson, Dr. M. J., and illness of J. D., 388-89
Fiesta Mexicana, 446
Fish, Hamilton, Jr., for J. D.'s recall, 184
Fletcher, Henry P., in Mexico, 359-60
Football, Universtiy of Mexico team visits Embassy, 439
Foote, Captain P. W., 460
Ford, Henry, in Rivera's painting, 443
Foreign Club, Cárdenas closes, 66-67
Foreign oil companies in Mexico, and Morrow-Calles arrangement, 217 ff. *passim;* attitude of toward subsoil-rights doctrine, 217-18; attack against by means of declaring titles illegal, 218 ff.; attempt to get Embassy backing in talks with Mexican government, 220 ff.; refused to raise

wages of oil workers in Mexico, 223; backed Huerta and Albert Fall, 223; labor troubles of, 223 ff.; asked by Cárdenas to negotiate, 230; refuse to negotiate, 241; anecdote on, 422-23. *See also* Expropriation; Petroleum industry
Foster, John W., 291
Fourth Estate, the, 398 ff.
Fourth of July, at the American Embassy, 419 ff., 435-36, 504
Francis, Kay, in Mexico, 435
Francisco Gaxiola, Javier, author of *El Presidente Rodríguez,* 55
Franco, Francisco, Almazán compared to by Bishop Kelly, 81; regime of drove Spanish liberals to Mexico, 327
Franco, Luis G., 140
Franklin, Benjamin, 291
"Fraternidad" School, built in memory of Bronson H. Rumsey and Daniel S. Roosevelt, 317
Friends Service Committee, 111

GANNON, John Mark, 174
García, León, 242
García Tellez, Ignacio, 334
Gardner, O. Max, and Mrs., 351
Garfield, James R., in Mexico, 360-61, 370-71
Garner, Vice President, at Laredo Road opening, 480 *passim*
Garner, Mrs., 482-83
Garrett, Finis J., 469
Garrido Canábal, Tomás, J. D.'s call upon, 184; Roberto Soto's skit on, 447-48; mentioned, 59, 179
German leaders in Mexico, 499-500
Germany, commercial relations of with Mexico, 74; Davis buys Mexican oil for, after expropriation, 252
Gibbons, Cardinal, 178
Gibson, Ernest W., 469
Gibson, Hugh, 471
Giral, José, 333
Glass, Carter, and 1940 campaign, 464
Gluck, Alma, in Mexico City, 351
Goddard, Paulette, in Mexico, 435
Goiran, Madame, 294
Gómez Morín, Manuel, 138, 139
González Roa, Fernando, and J. D.'s appointment as Ambassador to Mexico, 98-99; authority on claims, 120
Good Neighbor policy, just beginning at time of J. D.'s appointment, 6; based on Golden Rule, 23-24; attempts to sabotage, 257; oil men hoped for overthrow of, 260; importance to of settling oil problems, 267; Mexican legend about, 310-11; Indians incarnated, 316 ff.; Wallace an exponent of, 347 ff.; stated by Wallace before the Mexican Congress, 349; Roosevelt's definition of, 510; J. D. on, 514; mentioned, 14, 120, 228

Grady, Henry, 202

Graham, Frank Porter, and Señor Padilla, 112

Grau San Martín, Ramón, 323 ff. *passim;* became President of Cuba, 326

Gray, Ralph D., portrays Mexican life in his film *Fiesta Mexicana,* 446

"Greasers," use of term, 384

Great Britain, attitude of toward expropriation, 244-45. *See also* British

Green, William, vouched for Daniels on labor matters, 206

Gresham, Walter Q., 98

Griffin, James A., 174

"Gringo," use of term, 383-84

Grito, celebration of Sept. 16, 485; mentioned, 441, 447, 449

Gruening, Ernest, defended Daniels, 187

Guadalupe, the Marqués of, 438

Guadalupe, Virgin of, story of, 311-12; mentioned, 31

Gutiérroz Zamona, Perfecto, 100

Guzmán, Señor, 172

HAGOOD, Johnson, 357

Ham-and-Eggs diplomacy, 272, 273

Hamilton, John W., 457

Harding, Mrs. Bertita, author of *The Phantom Crown,* 31, 357

Harding administration, attitude of toward Mexican oil, 215

Hargrove, David, 456

Harris, Ben R., 462

Hartweg, Professor, of University of Michigan, 304

Harvey, George, 283

Hauser, Mr., 156, 158, 172

Havana Conference, 76

Hawks, Stanley, 11-12 *passim*

Hay, Eduardo, on Calles' entry into U. S., 63; and Sumner Welles, 73; as Secretary of Foreign Relations, 105 ff. *passim;* on U. S. entrance into World War II, 106-7; on ability of oil companies to pay increased wages, 223; surprised at tone of Hull's note on expropriation, 235; and British demand for settlement, 245; at dedication of "Fraternidad" School, 317; on disturbance at time of Sarabia's death, 319; at Laredo Road opening, 480; mentioned, 68, 72, 76, 98, 149-50 *passim,* 482

Hay, Señora de, 420

Hayes, Archbishop, 185

Hearst, William Randolph, in Mexico City, 351, 353-54

Hemispheric solidarity, importance of, 74

Herring, Hubert, in defense of J. D., 181

Hertslet, Joachim, 252

Hickey, Thomas, 156

Hidalgo, and the *Grito,* 323, 441, 449-50, 485; statue of in Mexico City, 447; tomb of, 491

Hidalgo y Costilla, Miguel, 31

Higgins, Representative demands J. D.'s recall, 184

Hill, Clayton, 469

Hill, Lister, 469, 476

Hoey, Clyde, 466

Holt, Ivan Lee, 158

Hope, Bob, in Mexico, 435

House, Edward M., attitude of toward Mexico, 360-61; mentioned, 21

Housing project, for Mexican workers, 50

Howe, Louis, and Raymond Moley, 18 ff. *passim;* and Mrs. Roosevelt, 454-55

Hoy, cartoon of J. D. in, 399-400

Huasteca Petroleum Company, 214, 220-21, 223, 423

Huerta, Victoriano, on the landing at Vera Cruz, 24; anecdotes concerning, 38 ff.; and the Catholic Church, 40-41; and the assassination of Madero, 95; contract of with Japan for munitions, 96; supported by oil men, 215; backed by foreign oil companies, 223; mentioned, 44, 81, 82, 93

Hull, Cordell, informs J. D. of appointment as Ambassador to Mexico, 3; wires Embassy in Mexico City concerning J. D., 5-6; as Secretary of State, 19; and J. D., 22; in sympathy with views of Ezequiel Padilla, 87; and lump-sum settlement of claims, 120, 123; against interference in Mexico's religious affairs, 186; opposed to high tariff rates affecting Mexican oil, 220; and Mexican expropriation of oil properties, 228, 231 ff. *passim;* letter of to Mexican Secretary of State, quoted in full, 232 ff.; memorandum of concerning his note, which had been "not received," 237; makes statement on expropriation, 240-41; signed agreements settling expropriation difficulties, 266; signed settlement for U. S. 268; and Álvarez del Vayo, 329-30; mentioned, 462

Humber, Robert Lee, 476

Hurley, Patrick, and oil negotiations, 73; negotiated successfully with Cárdenas for Sinclair Oil Company, 265

ICKES, Harold L., 456

Illiteracy, decrease in, 127; decreased by method of Torres Bodet, 140-41

Indianapolis, 457-58 *passim*

Indians, of Mexico, work of Townsend Linguistic groups among, 75, 167 ff.; "Oldest Americans," 297 ff.; theories as to origin of, 297-98; Indians of New Mexico visit, 303-4; importance of in Mexican life, 308 ff.; crafts of, 309-10; kindness of at time of death of two American aviators, 315 ff.; incarnated Good Neighbor doctrine, 316 ff.

"In Flanders Fields," quoted, 471

International Industrial Relations Conference, 206 ff. *passim*

Islas, Manvilio, who took the lead in rescuing Miss Constantine in airplane crash, 315 ff. *passim;* asked for education for his son, 316-17
Iturbide, Eduardo, 444
Iturbide family, 437

JACKSON, "Stonewall," and the Señorita, 404-5
Jara, General, 89
Jarabe, J. D. essays to dance, 450
Jefferson, Thomas, 180, 181, 184, 291
Jewish refugees, and Mexico, 336-37
Jews, attitude toward in Mexico, 334 ff.
Johnson, Andrew, 48
Johnson, Gerald, on J. D.'s appointment as Ambassador to Mexico, 5
Johnson, Herschel V., Chief of Mexican Division in State Department, and J. D.'s trip to Mexico, 7-8; and exclusion of *Time* from the mails, 406; mentioned, 118 and *passim*
Johnson, Robert Underwood, 291
Joyner, Joe, on results of 1936 election, 384
Juan Casiano oil property, 214
Juárez, Benito, and the church, 23; Mexico's greatest civilian, 104-5; portrait of, 307; statue of in Mexico City, 447; mentioned, 56, 77, 91, 171, 404, 498

KEARNEY, Brigadier General, 469
Kelly, Bishop, writes article supporting Almazán, 81; claims Almazán elected, 85-86; author of *Blood-Stained Altars,* 179
Kennedy, Martin J., 187
King, Rosa, author of *Tempest Over Mexico,* 31
Kirk, Betty, quoted on attempt to stone Embassy during Wallace's visit, 348
Kluckhohn, Frank L., *The Mexican Challenge* by, quoted, 216; correspondent of the *New York Times,* expelled from Mexico, 407 ff.; writes letter to J. D. on his expulsion from Mexico, 410 ff.; book by quoted on his Mexican experience, 412; in Spain and in World War II, 413; mentioned, 398
Knickerbocker, H. R., said oil companies expected Mexican and U. S. 1940 elections to overthrow Good Neighbor policy, 260; did not believe in Good Neighbor policy, 360
Knights of Columbus, leaders of ask for Daniels' recall, 177, 181, 182; demand intervention in Mexico, 188
Knox, Katherine, anecdotes told by, 425-26
Krausse, Vice Consul, 430

LABOR, in Mexico, "gets its Magna Carta," 206 ff.; force for liberalism, 208; demands of not met by foreign oil companies, 223 ff.
Labor, quoted on the Bryan breakfast, 465

La Fleur, M., 117
La Guardia, Mayor, 460
Laguna agrarian development, 201-2
Lainé, Juan, 175
Lamarr, Hedy, in Mexico, 435
Lamb, Dana and June Cleveland, artists, "enchanted vagabonds," 365-66
Lambeth, Walter, 469, 476
Lamont, General, 76
Lamont, Thomas W., 23, 121, 122
Lamour, Dorothy, in Mexico, 435
Lamp, The, published by Standard Oil Company of New Jersey, as propaganda against Mexico, 255 ff. *passim*
Land, dotation of, 47, 200 ff. *passim*
"Land belongs to those who work it," 199 ff., 447
Lander, William P., 398, 411
Lane, Arthur Bliss, Chargé d'Affaires in Mexico City, and J. D.'s appointment as Ambassador, 5-6, 7; on J. D.'s trip to Mexico, 8; welcomed J. D. to Mexico, 13-14; on Rule Number Six, 421-22; mentioned, 14, 33, 118, 444
Lang, H. L., 185
Lansing, Robert, attitude of toward Mexico, 360-61; mentioned, 98, 285
Lanz Duret, Sr., 401-2 *passim*
Laredo Road opening, 480 ff.
Lathrop, Frank, on W. R. Hearst, 354-55
Latin-American solidarity. *See* Pan American solidarity; World War II
Lawson, Commissioner, 27
Lay, Mr., 106, 121, 122
League of Nations, Mexico supporter of Spanish Republican cause in, 328
Lee, Blair, 456
Lee, Clark, 398
Lee, R. E., did not approve of emigration to Mexico, 343
Lend-Lease, British appreciation of, 394
Leñero, Agustín, 76
Lenin, in Rivera's mural for Rockefeller Center, 443, 444
Leo, Pope, 146
León, Luis, in exile signs statement against communism, 64-65; mentioned, 65, 400-1 *passim*
Lerdo y Texada, Miguel, plays at Embassy, 419, 450
Lesher, Mr. and Mrs., 429
Lewis, John L., in Mexico, 207-8
Lewis, Mrs. John L., guest at Embassy, 208
Liberalism, in Mexico, 323 ff.
Limantour, Señora Iturbide de, 444
Lind, John, sent by Wilson to Mexico City, 38; mentioned, 41, 498
Lindbergh, Charles, importance of in U. S.-Mexico relations, 273
"Lindbergh room," at American Embassy, 30
Linguistic Group. *See* Townsend, Cameron
Lions' Club, in Mexico City, 511

Lippmann, Walter, on Morrow, 22
Lochiel, Lord, defines communism, 66
Lockett, Thomas, Commercial Attaché, 368; reported on Mexico's oil wealth, 215-16; and Kluckhohn, 408-9
Long, Huey, and George Creel, 280
López, Alfonso, President-elect of Colombia, 357; visits Mexiço, 326; anecdote of, 416
López Cárdenas, Fernando, 487
Lowell, J. R., 291
Lowry, Mr. and Mrs., 351
Lozano, Ramón, 171
Luce, Henry R., writes J. D. on *Time*'s being barred from the mails in Mexico City, 406
Lump-sum settlement of claims, 117 ff. *passim*
Luncheon that was called off, 52 ff.
Lund, Fin, anecdote by, 428-29

McADOO, Senator, at Laredo Road opening, 483
MacArthur, Douglas, visits Mexico, 326-27
McBryde, Lewis B., 276
McCoy, Gordon H., 348
McGregor, Robert, as Uncle Sam, 293; made arrangements at time of airplane crash, 315 ff. *passim*
McGurk, Joseph, spoke from Mexico to Mrs. Daniels in Raleigh, 512-13
Mack, Connie, in Mexico City, 351, 364
McKean, Rev. Charles R., 143, 172
McKinnon, Miss Sallie Lou, did not try to evade law, 153-54
McKnight, Pohn P., 398
McMahon, Judge, representative of Standard Oil, talks to J. D. of desire for reduced tariff rates, 219
McNab, Alexander J., 22
McNutt, and 1940 campaign, 466-67 *passim*
McRae, John, author of "In Flanders Fields," 471
Macy, R. H., firm, 5
Madero, Francisco I., as President of Mexico, 38; the shrine of, 92 ff.; and oil industry, 213; mentioned, 81, 106, 200
Madero, Señora de, tried to get Ambassador Wilson to save her husband, 38; J. D. calls upon, 93 ff.
Madrazo, Manuel F., quoted on attacks on education, 135-36
Magner, James A., in Mexico, 137-38
Malinche, story of, 302-3; material on in library of George Conway, 329
Maps, of North Carolina, found in Mexico, 389
Marchlewski, Minister, from Poland to Mexico, 503
Marines, Hymn of, 470
Mariscal, Federico E., and Palace of Fine Arts, 434
Mariscal, Ignacio, 436-37

Markey, John D., 469
Marshburn, Colonel, Military Attaché, 68, 136, 357
Martínez, Archbishop, consecration of, 163-64; J. D. calls upon, 164-65; and theological schools, 173-74; and J. D., 174; supported expropriation, 246-47
Martínez Barrios, Diego, Spanish refugee in Mexico, 330
Martínez del Río Pablo, 139
Martínez Zorrilla, Carlos, generous attitude of, 91-92
Martínez Zorrilla, Señora de, 91-92
Marxism, 128
Massip, Ambassador, of Cuba, 323-24
Maury, Matthew Fontaine, as emigrant to Mexico after Civil War, 338 ff. *passim;* quoted on reasons for going to Mexico, 341-42; attitude of toward Maximilian, 343-44; mentioned, 430
Maverick, Maury, in Mexico, 349
Maximilian, and Confederates in Mexico, 339 ff. *passim;* book on period of, by Mrs. Bertita Harding, 357-58; mentioned, 25
Mayan architecture, 487-88
Mayer, William, 336-37
Meadows, Dr., 158
Medinaveytia, General, 61
Melgar, Rafael E., 490
Memorials, of World War I, dedication of, 469 ff.
Mena Córdoba, Eduardo R., 488
Mendoza, Antonio de, brought first printing press to New World, 403
Mendoza, Vicente, 151
Meredith, Mrs. E. T., visits Embassy in Mexico City, 352 ff.
Messersmith, George S. 360
Methodist Church in Mexico, 151 ff.
Mexican Challenge, The, by Frank L. Kluckhohn, 412
Mexican legend, about the Good Neighbor, 310-11
Mexican Life, 403, 404
Mexican Navy, 492
Mexican national emblem, 434
Mexican reaction to expropriation, 246 ff.
Mexican sympathy with liberals, 323 ff., 327 ff.
Mexican Telephone Company, coöperated in hook-up with Mrs. Daniels in Raleigh, 513
Mexican Times, The, Confederate newspaper published in Mexico, contents of, 338 ff.
Mexican-U. S. coöperation during second World War, 74 ff., 87, 497 ff.
Miaja, General, 331
Micahel, Monsignor, 174
Mijares Palencia, José, anecdote by, 426
Miranda, Miguel Darío, 174
Moley, Raymond, and J. D.'s advice, 18 ff.

Monroe Doctrine, "Funeral of," 101; characterized by *The Mexican Times*, 340

Montavon, William F., 144

Montes, Federico, Chief of Police, guarded Embassy during disturbance after Sarabia's death, 319

Montes de Oca, 121, 276

Montfaucon, memorial at, 472

Moore, Assistant Secretary of State, on mules, 290

Moore, Grace, in Mexico, 435, 436

Morán, Tomás, 437

Mordecai, Alfred, on Confederates in Mexico, 340

Morelos, Mexico's greatest soldier, 104

Moreno, A., on claims, 119-20; mentioned, 147

Morgan, J. Pierpont, in Rivera's painting, 443; mentioned, 359

Morgenthau, Henry, 415

Morley, Sylvanus, 488

Morones, Luis, and Calles, 62; in exile signs statement against communism, 64-65; "kidded out of office" by Roberto Soto, 449; mentioned, 63, 65

Morrison, Cameron, 465

Morrison, Ralph, and the Calles luncheon, 53 ff. *passim*

Morrow, Anne, and Lindbergh, 273, 278

Morrow, Dwight Whitney, said to have settled all Mexican problems, 22; and Calles, 45, 57, 121; did not settle religious controversy in Mexico, 78; arrangement of with Calles as to foreign oil companies, 217 ff. *passim*; as Ambassador to Mexico, 271 ff.; and Mexican oil, 221 ff. *passim*, 273-74; induced Calles to annul subsoil rights, 274; obtained a *modus vivendi* of Church and State in Mexico, 274-75; and land question, 275; offends Mexicans by suggesting plans for a fiscal policy, 276 ff.; bronze plaque on Embassy, in memory of, 277; mentioned, 14, 118, 356

Morrow, Mrs. Dwight Whitney, J. D. buys car of, 430; mentioned, 273

Morrow house at Cuernavaca, Rivera frescoes in, 442-43

Mott, John R., 166, 167

Mules, cause diplomatic difficulty, 289-90

Mundelein, Cardinal, rebukes advocates of interference in Mexico, 188

Murray, Robert Hammond, told anecdotes on Huerta, 38 ff.; poem on J. D. by, 507-9; mentioned, 93

Music, in Mexico, 449

Myers, Ben, 398

Nacional, El, 400-1

National Palace, paintings of revolutionary history on walls of, 441 ff.

Navarro, Rafael, arrests Calles and escorts him into U. S., 64

Nazi agents in Mexico, 76, 504

Negrin, Juan, in Mexico to aid Spanish refugees, 329, 333

Neither Blood nor Sand, Cantinflas featured in, 449

Newbegin, Robert, Bostonian, said by Texan to speak broken English, 427; anecdote by, 427; mentioned, 357, 500

New Deal, just beginning at time of J. D.'s appointment, 6, 15 ff. *passim*; compared with Mexican Six-Year Plan, 48 f.; Cárdenas strong for, 67-68

News and Observer, The, 462

News correspondents, in Mexico, 398 ff.

Newton, Ray, of Society of Friends, 111, 204

New York Times, correspondent of not allowed to continue in Mexico, 405; mentioned, 398

Nezapualcoyotl, quoted, 31

Nicholson, Howard, quoted on diplomacy, 283

Nicolson, Harold, quoted on Morrow, 276

Nicolaus, George, "Hitler's top hatchet man in Mexico City," 348

Nida, Eugene A., member of Townsend group, 168-69

Norweb, Harry, 416

Núñez, Ingeniero, 175

Nuttall, Mrs. Zelia, 298

OBREGÓN, Álvaro, and the death of Carranza, 41-42, 43; Mexican attitude toward, 42-43; mentioned, 82, 106

Obregón Memorial, 42

O'Brien, Father, calls on J. D., 160-61, 162

O'Brien, Frank Michael, *Herald-Tribune* correspondent, 504

O'Connor, William P., 469

Oil. See Expropriation; Foreign oil companies in Mexico; Petroleum industry in Mexico

"Olive train," 485 ff. *passim*

O'Malley, Owen St. Clair, British Minister in Mexico, and expropriation, 244-45

Orozco y Jiménez, Francisco, quoted, 146

Ortega, Melchor, in exile signs statement against communism, 64-65

Ortiz Rubio, Pascual, resignation of as President, 43-44; and Calles, 45, 61; and dotation of land, 200; mentioned, 276, 405

Osuna, Andrés, calls on J. D., 156-57

Otomí Indians, example of what education and improved living conditions can do, 299-300

"Oust Daniels," handbill circulated in Mexico City opposing J. D.'s appointment, 9-10

PADEREWSKI, mass for, 166

Padilla, Ezequiel, won world gratitude for efforts for world peace, 79; as lover of freedom, 87; Secretary of Foreign Relations under Camacho, 108 ff.; eloquently supported coöperation with U. S. during the war, 109-10; refused U. S. contribution of money after earthquake disaster, 110-11; gives Ambassador Daniels a "royal gift," a portrait of J. D., painted by Armando Drechsler, 111; makes address in English at the University of North Carolina, 112; address by at farewell luncheon given by him for Ambassador Daniels and members of the Diplomatic Corps, 512; entire speech of quoted, 522-24; mentioned, 98, 140, 436

Page, Thomas Nelson, 291

Page, Walter Hines, 291

Paine, Mrs. Francis Flynn, and the Rivera murals, 444

Palabra, La, 402, 403

Palace of Fine Arts, formally opened, 434 f.; mentioned, 206, 353

Palacio, Lucas de, 429

Palafox Library, 353

Palencia, Señora Isabel D., 503

Palma, General Guillermo, welcomed J. D. to Mexico, 13

Panama Conference, 73

Pan American Club, 511

Pan American Radio Conference, 374

Pan American solidarity, 326. *See also* World War II

Pancho, Señor, painted retable in commemoration of J. D.'s narrow escape from death, 91

Parry, Mr. and Mrs. L. H., and Carolina maps, 389; and story of Scotch blood transfusion, 391-92

Pascoe, Bishop, on church troubles in Mexico, 151, 152-53

Pasquel, Jorge, with Ambassador Daniels in narrow escape from death, 90; and baseball, 439

Pearson, Drew, on John L. Lewis and William Rhodes Davis, 252-53

Pearson, W. D. *See* Cowdray, Lord

Peláez, Manuel, tells anecdote on ten U. S. oil men, 422-23

Peoples, George, 404

Pérez Treviño, Manuel, 57, 60

Pershing, sent by Wilson to Northern Mexico, 38; in European tour to dedicate battle monuments, 469-79 *passim*

Person, Harlow S., on diplomacy, 284

Pétain, Marshal, 472

Petroleum industry, in Mexico, organization of workers in, 206; in World War I, 211; beginnings of, 211-12; rich resources of, 213; Mexico reasserted subsoil rights in its Constitution of 1917, 215; Morrow-Calles arrangement as to foreign oil companies, 217 ff. *passim;* strikes in, 223; expropriation of oil properties, 227 ff.;

agreement as to valuation and payment reached, 266 ff. *See also* Expropriation; Foreign oil companies in Mexico

Phelps Stokes, Miss Olivie Eggleston, 167

Phillips, Howard S., 403, 404

Phillips, William, informed J. D. of attack, 183

Pino Suárez, José María, 94

Pittman, Key, 120-21, 186

Platt Amendment, annulment of, 324

Plunkett, Admiral, 468

Poe, Clarence, 466

Poinsett, Joel R., as Ambassador to Mexico, 119-20; rule of concerning claims, 123; book on secured by Mr. Conway, 392

Poinsettia, story of, 437-38

Pontifical Mass, J. D., attends, 165

Portes Gil, Emilio, sketch of, 43; head of National Revolutionary party, 104; made Secretary of Foreign Relations by Cárdenas, 104; and dotation of land, 200; mentioned, 98

Portes Gil, Señora de, 104

Posada, the, at U. S. Embassy, 436-37

Potrero del Llano, oil well, 212

Power, Tyrone, in Mexico, 435

Prensa, La, 402

Prescott, William H., and his *Conquest of Mexico,* 31; on Malinche, 302

President Lincoln, 460

Prevost, Julio, 171

Price, K. H., 469

Prieto, Spanish War Minister, thought the joking of Cantinflas dangerous, 449

Printing press, first in New World, 403

Pritchard, Jeter C., 475

Propaganda, in U. S. against Mexico, 156, 255 ff., 483-84

Prorok, Count Byron Kuhn de, theories of concerning Indians, 297

Protestants, in Mexico, 142, 171

Public Health Building, Rivera's frescoes in, 442

Public high schools, outdoor celebration of, 139

Puig Casauranc, José Manuel, Minister of Foreign Relations, and J. D.'s appointment as Ambassador to Mexico, 6; persuades Mexican press not to attack J. D.'s appointment, 28; orders special precautions for Daniels' train, 10 ff.; telegraphs J. D. on taking up matter of claims, 23; at J. D.'s presentation of credentials, 25-26 *Passim;* relations of with J. D., 99-100; toast by to America quoted, 100; death of, 103-4; and the settlement of claims, 115 ff. *passim;* letter of to J. D. quoted, 129; and diplomatic notes, 286; fears U. S. intervention in Cuba, 324; and exclusion of *Time* from the mails, 405 ff. *passim;* mentioned, 51, 53, 54, 98, 103, 400, 462

QUEZON, President, of the Philippines, visits Mexico, 287-88; quoted on Cárdenas, 327

Quintanilla, Luis, 121

RADIO RELATIONS, between U. S. and Mexico, disturbed by Dr. Brinkley, 374

Ragon, C. A., 469

Rake-off, practice of, 122-23

Ransom, General M. W., on Porfirio Díaz, 37

Reading, Lord, 272

Ready, Monsignor, 173

Reed, David, 469

Reed, Edward L., writes J. D. of oil companies' intrigues, 220-21

Rees, Sir Richard, worked for Spanish refugees, 328-29

Rees, T. Ilfor, 394-95

Reforma movement, 146

Reid, Whitelaw, 291

Religious problems, Cárdenas' views on, 68 ff. *See also* Catholic Church; Church; Churches

Revolutionary party, leaders of in sympathy with liberal movements, 323 ff. *passim*

Reynolds, Quentin, 430

Reynolds, Robert R. ("Our Bob"), 351, 362-64

Reyes Spíndola, Octavio, on situation in Cuba, 326

Ribbentrop, Joachim von, used Davis in Nazi effort to defeat Roosevelt in 1940, 253

Rice, Stanley B., oil company of taken over by Mexican government because of defective title, 220

Richardson, W. B., 416, 428

Richberg, Donald, as attorney for the oil companies, attempts settlement of oil difficulties, 73, 243; negotiations of with Cárdenas, 253; loses in negotiation with Mexican government for the oil companies, 263 ff.

Rincón Gallardo, Señora de, 437

Rio de Janeiro Conference, Padilla's speech for unity at, 79

Rippy, J. Fred, quoted, 123

Rivera, Diego, paintings by in chapel at Chapingo, 132; defends Jews, 337; paintings by in Palace of Fine Arts, 353; as artist, 441 ff.; and his murals in Rockefeller Center, 443 ff.; Mexican attitude toward, 446

Roberts, Violet M., tells story of the Poinsettia, 437-38

Roças, Abelardo, 294

Roças, Señora de, 294

Rockefeller, John D., plaque in honor of in Mexico City, 277; in Rivera's painting, 443; mentioned, 241, 444

Rockefeller, John D., Jr., 446

Rockefeller, Mrs. John D., Jr., and the Rivera murals in Rockefeller Center, 445 ff. *passim*

Rockefeller, Nelson, and the Rivera murals in Rockefeller Center, 443 ff. *passim*

Rockefeller Center, and the murals of Diego Rivera, 443 ff.

Rodrigo de Llano, Sr., 402

Rodríguez, Abelardo L., thanked by Roosevelt for prompt acceptance of J. D., 8-9; and J. D's trip to Mexico, 13; received J. D. as U. S. Ambassador to Mexico, 25 ff.; address of at J. D.'s presentation of credentials, 27-28, 521 (quoted in full); and Calles, 45, 54; administration of as President of Mexico, 47 ff.; writes Daniels about reported statement on Calles, 50-51; government of suggested lump-sum settlement of claims, 117 ff. *passim;* no official censorship under, 404; withdrew ban on *Time,* 406-7; at opening of Palace of Fine Arts, 434; mentioned, 44, 91, 152, 405

Rodríguez, Señora de, 48, 434

Rogers, Will, importance of in U. S.-Mexico relations, 273; "Twentieth-Century Uncle Sam," in Mexico, 278 ff.; letters of quoted, 279-91; death of, 281; and President Harding, 448

Rogers, Mrs. Will, 281

Romero, Miguel Alonso, brother of Mrs. Madero, 94; tells how Mexico got the best of Japan, 95 ff.

Romero, José, 386-87

Roosevelt, Daniel S., death of in Mexico, and memorial to, 315 ff.

Roosevelt, Franklin D., and the Vera Cruz incident, 3 ff.; on J. D.'s appointment, 6-7; sends message to President Rodríguez concerning J. D.'s appointment, 8-9; and beginnings of New Deal, 15 ff. *passim;* asks J. D. to make a study of transportation problem, 16 ff.; writes note for Calles luncheon, 53, 55; and Cárdenas, 72, 73, 75-76; election of popular in Mexico, 76; defended J. D. when recall demanded, 184; defers visit to Mexico, 188-89; reply of to Carmody quoted, 189-91; and expropriation of oil, 229-30, 242-43, 265, 267; attacked by John L. Lewis in radio address, 252; organized effort of Nazis to defeat in 1940, 253; opposed to intervention in Cuba, 324-25; replies to J. D.'s request for aid in supplying cocktail recipe, 373; attitude of 102-year-old Mexican lady toward, 424; invites Mr. and Mrs. J. D. to join him in reviewing the Fleet, 453-54; accepts statue of Bryan, 456-57; sends birthday greeting, 462; candidacy of in 1940, 464 ff. *passim;* made radio address to 1940 Convention, 466; in World War I, 467-68; and J. D.'s resignation as Ambassador to Mexico,

509, 515; defines Good Neighbor policy, 510; J. D. on death of, 516; mentioned, 45, 138, 256, 380

Roosevelt, Mrs. Franklin D., gives gift to people of Canonitas, 317; hostess to Mr. and Mrs. J. D. at the White House, 454-55; flew to Chicago to address 1940 Convention, 466

Roosevelt, Henry, 457

Roosevelt, Quentin, 473

Roosevelt, Theodore, attitude of toward Latin America, 228; mentioned, 473

Root, Elihu, on Porfirio Díaz, 37-38; and diplomatic dress, 293

Roper, Daniel, 17, 22, 455

Rotary Club, in Mexico City, 511

Rubin de Borbolla, Daniel, on origin of Indians, 297-98

Rublee, George, 121, 122

Ruiz, Archbishop, 275

Ruiz y Flores, Leopoldo, 174

Rule Number Six, Morrow's account of, told by Arthur Bliss Lane, 421-22; mentioned, 400

Rumsey, Bronson H., death of in Mexico, and memorial to, 315 ff.

Rumsey-Roosevelt school, 316-17

Rural schools, 128

Russell, Richard B., 469, 472

Russell Sage Foundation, 206

Russia, differing views on, 358-59; Bullitt's attitude toward, 475

SÁENZ, Aarón, 50

Sage, Russell, 207

Salvation Army, 171-73

Sands, William Franklin, reports on religious conditions in Mexico, 192-93

San Juan de Ulua, fort, 492-93

Santa Monica Convent, 353

Santa Rosa, Mr. and Mrs. D. visit school at, 133-34

Sarabia, Francisco, aviator who made non-stop flight from Vera Cruz to New York in 1939, 318; death of, 318 ff.

Sarabia, Señora de, fine attitude of at time of husband's death, 319

Schacht, Hjalmar, 252

Schacht, Jean, in Mexico, 252

Schleebrugge, Karl Friedrich von, "Hitler's top hatchet man in Mexico City," 348

Schott, Secretary, of the Embassy, 51

Scotch, the, anecdote of, 391-92

Scott, Hugh, and Villa, 306

Scott, Winfield, 404

Seeger, Alan, 344, 511

Senior, Clarence, of Society of Friends, 204

Serrano, Gustavo P., and claims, 123

Serrano Pareja, Sr., 332

Shand, Mr., 106

Shaw, George P., 12

Sheffield, Ambassador, on American Colony, 379; mentioned, 118, 272

Sheppard, Morris, 456

Sheridan, Ann, in Mexico, 435

Sherman, Carl, 192

Shipping Board, studied by J. D., 16-17

Shirt-sleeve Ambassador, defined, 283-84; distinguished list of, 291-92

Silver, importance of U. S. buying of to Mexico, 249; understanding reached as to purchase of, 266

Simpson, Eyler N., quoted on church's wealth in Mexico, 145; quoted on poverty of peons, 199-200

Sinclair Oil Company, makes agreement with Mexican government, 75

Siurob, José, 140

Six-Year Plan, compared with New Deal, 48 f., 59; incarnated in Cárdenas, 57; oil men hoped for overthrow of, 260

Sizoo, Joseph R., 456

Skidmore, Mrs. Edgar, 338

Smith, Al, 22

Smith, "Cotton Ed," 463-64

Smith, F. Hopkinson, 426

Smith, Kirby, an emigrant to Mexico after Civil War, 338

Smith, Kirby, son of Confederate general, 485

Smith, Perry, 469

Smithers, Jim, friend of Calles and his interpreter, 63-64 passim; 221, 272; on Villa, 307; on failure of ratio conference, 375

Socialistic education, 128-29, 134-35, 145-46

Soto, Roberto, "the Will Rogers of Mexico," 447-48; "kidded" Luis Morones out of office, 449

Spanish liberals, in Mexico, 323 ff.

Spanish-Mexican solidarity, high-water mark of, 327

Spanish refugees, seek homes in New World, 327 ff.; fear for associates, 331-32

"Spanish Swindle," an instance of, 369 ff.

Sports, Mexican love of, 438-39

Spratling, maker of famous tin frames, in Taxco, 91

Spratling's place in Taxco, 442

Stacy, Chief Justice W. P., 4

Standard Oil Company, attitude of Harding administrations toward, 215; wishes reduced tariff rates, 219; fears for Doheny titles, 219; would not place a value upon its Mexican properties, 241

Stapleton, Miss Mary E., 162-63

State Department, and Mexican expropriation of oil properties, 231 ff.; tries for three years to induce oil companies to negotiate, 241

Steffens, Lincoln, and Carranza, 41

Stewart, Consul General, 411

Stockdale, Arthur, on Mexican-U. S. relations, 393-94

Straus, Jesse Isidor, appointed Ambassador to France, 5
Streb, B., 462
Stuart, Graham H., 282
Suárez, Eduardo, Finance Minister, on last-minute negotiations between Cárdenas and oil companies, 225-26; and expropriation, 241; on Richberg's plan, 263-64; mentioned, 121
Suárez, Patricío, doorkeeper at Embassy, 30
Subsoil rights, Díaz surrendered to foreign oil exploiters, 212; Mexico reasserts in Constitution of 1917, 215, 218; Cárdenas defends the reassertion of, 253-54
Sullivan, George S., 164
Summer School, 139
Swanson, Claude A., 458-59 passim
Sykes, Octavius, 374

TABOR, John, requested J. D. to take up matter of dotation of British land, 203-4
Tannenbaum, Frank, tells of Otomí Indians, 299-300; author of Revolution in Mexico, 352
Taylor, Myron C., 336
Teapot Dome scandal, 212
Temple, Miss Laura, school of, 153
Thanksgiving Day, at the Embassy, 351-52
Theological schools not allowed, 173
Thompson, William H., 456
Time, excluded from the mail, 405 ff.
Típica band, played at American Embassy, 419, 450
Toledano, Vicente Lombardo, organizer of Workers University of Mexico, 206, 208; on agreement over oil expropriation, 268
Torres Bodet, Jaime, as Minister of Education, 108-9, 140-41; joined Padilla in refusing U. S. contributions at time of earthquake, 111
Townsend, Cameron, work of his Linguistic Groups among Indians, 75, 167 ff.
Treaties ratified, 123-24
Trejo, Dr. Elena, account of, 170-71
Tritschler, Guillermo, 174
Trotsky, Leon, and Diego Rivera, 337

ULFELDER, Sidney, 334
Ultimas Noticias, 318
Underwood, Oscar, Jr., 121
Universal, El, 129, 401-2
University of Mexico, students in enthusiastic over expropriation, 246; sports at, 438-39; mentioned, 138-39

VALLANDIGHAM, C. L., 355
Van Kleeck, Miss Mary, 206 ff. passim
Van Zeeland, Paul, 471
Velásquez, Víctor, 139, 159-60
Veloz González, Vicente, 25, 488, 489
Vera Cruz, Naval expedition to, as affecting J. D.'s appointment as Ambassador to Mexico, 3 ff.; and appointment of J. D. as Ambassador to Mexico, 3 ff.; came to have a meaning of good luck to J. D., 88 ff.; opening of churches in, 88-89
Verdier, Edward, story of Joe González told by, 309-10
Villa, Pancho, stories about, 305 ff.; mentioned, 41, 106

WALKER, Harold P., and Mexican oil, 219, 221
Wallace, Henry, visit of to Mexico, 347 ff.; and 1940 Convention, 464; won nomination for Vice-President, 465-66; mentioned, 435, 456
Warren, Mr. and Mrs. A. M., 293
Washington, George, statue of in Mexico City, 447
"Watchful Waiting," 38
Water disputes, 116-17
Weatherspoon, W. H., 463
Welles, Gideon, 341
Welles, Sumner, on Mexico-U. S. relations, 73; quoted on American capital abroad, 223; mentioned, 462
Weyl, Nathaniel, on international trade, 207
White, Mr. and Mrs. William Allen, in Mexico City, 351, 355-56, 465
Whittier, John Greenleaf, quoted, 390
Willard, Daniel, 16
Williams, Admiral, 416
Wilson, Henry B., 265
Wilson, Henry Lane, dismissed by Wilson as Ambassador to Mexico, 38; would not save Madero's life, 93; believed to be in league with Huerta against Madero, 95; saved Mexican lives, 103
Wilson, Hugh Robert, on American diplomacy, 291
Wilson, John W., in arrangements at time of airplane crash, 315
Wilson, Woodrow, attitude of toward Mexico, 4, 118-19; dismissed H. L. Wilson as Ambassador to Mexico, 38; attitude of toward Huerta, 38 ff.; and Mexican oil, 211; opposed by oil companies, 223; reason for recognition of Carranza by, 360-61
Wilson, Mrs. Woodrow, in Mexico City, 351 ff.
Wilson Advance, 403
Wise, Stephen S., 176, 334, 337
Wolf, Mr., of Pittsburgh, 335
Woman suffrage, 159
Women, give jewels to support expropriation, 247
Woodul, Ned, anecdotes by, 426
Workers University of Mexico, organized by Toledano and Carrillo, 206
World War II, Mexico as outpost of defense in, 497 ff.; approach of as J. D. saw it in Mexico, 500-1
Worth, Dr. David, 4

Wright, Harry, makes moving picture satirizing Democrats and Republicans, 431-32; mentioned, 381, 418
Wyvell, Mr. and Mrs. Manton M., 455, 456

YOUNG, Samuel Sung, 351
Y.M.C.A., in Mexico, 166-67
Y.W.C.A., in Mexico, 166-67
Yount, Mr., of N. C., 364

ZAPATA, Emiliano, 31, 41
Zawadsky, Alfonso, 84
Zetina, Julio, 402
Zevada, Manuel J, acted for Mexico in oil settlements, 267
Zimbalist, in Mexico City, 351
Zimmerman note, and Carranza, 42
Zuch, William Edward, denies in *Christian Century* sensational stories against Mexico, 257